The Mahābhārata

Book 1 *The Book of the Beginning*

The

The University of Chicago Press *Chicago and London*

Mahābhārata

Translated and
Edited by
J. A. B. van Buitenen

1 *The Book of the Beginning*

The University of Chicago Press, Chicago 60637
The University of Chicago Press, Ltd., London

Paperback edition 1980
Printed in the United States of America
97 96 95 94 93 92 9 8 7 6

Library of Congress Catalog Card Number 72-97802
ISBN 0-226-84648-2 (cloth); 0-226-84663-6 (paper)

The relief sculpture on the title page, dating from the second half of the fifth century A.D., depicts Nara and Nārāyaṇa in Viṣṇu temple, Deogarh, U.P., India, courtesy Pramod Chandra

For Corrie, Hansje, and Jenny van Buitenen
To remember our last year in India
when this book was done

महर्षेः सर्वलोकेषु विश्रुतस्यास्य धीमतः ।

प्रवक्ष्यामि मतं कृत्स्नं व्यासस्यामिततेजसः ।।

Mahābhārata 1.55.2

Of Vyāsa the wise great seer.
Whose spirit is boundless,
Whose fame is spread in all three worlds.
I shall proclaim
The thought entire.

Contents

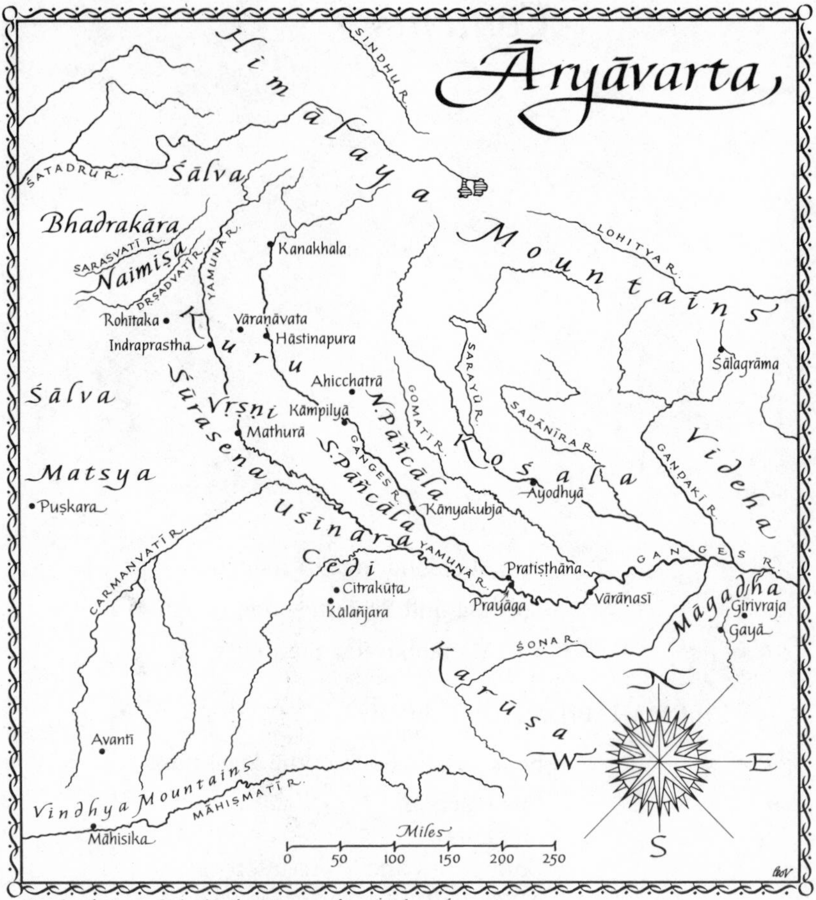

Based on *The Historical Atlas of South Asia*, courtesy of Joseph Schwartzberg, Department of Geography, The University of Minnesota

Preface

The reader will understand that the present work was not undertaken without great apprehension and much deliberation. Rarely has a translation in a modern European language been completed. Nevertheless, the importance of *The Mahābhārata* for our knowledge of Indian civilization and the paucity of knowledge about it in the West persuaded me to go ahead with what was bound to be a very long task. The present volume is the first installment of that task. At the date of this writing, close to two more volumes like the present one are ready in translation, so it is no longer unreasonable to hope that the entire *Mahābhārata* may be available in the not too interminable future.

I am particularly pleased that the work is being published by the University of Chicago Press. It is at this University that the work is being done, and it has been at this University too that my concourse and discourse with colleagues in history, art, anthropology, history of religions, political science, and even demography convinced me that an Indologist owes as much to other disciplines bearing on India as to his own. It was out of this conviction that the decision arose to open up the great epic of India to all of us.

Nevertheless, with all the encouragement I have received from everyone, I could not have gone ahead with the publication had it not been for the substantial subvention it received from a private donor and from a foundation-supported University committee. The donor is George V. Bobrinskoy, Emeritus Professor of Sanskrit at the University of Chicago, warm, ever-helpful, most generous colleague and friend. The committee is the Committee on Southern Asian Studies, which, largely with the aid of the Ford Foundation, has been responsible for the development of Indian studies at this University.

Circumstances could not have conspired more happily to arrange that those to whom I owe so much have earned an even greater claim on my gratitude.

J. A. B. van Buitenen

3 August 1971

The Mahābhārata Introduction

The Central Story

The central story of *The Mahābhārata* takes its matter from the legitimacy of the succession to the kingdom of Kurukṣetra in northern India. This kingdom was the ancestral realm of a clan known by several styles, the most common being that of Bhārata. The last king whose succession was unclouded was Śaṃtanu. He left three sons; the firstborn was Bhīṣma, whom he begot on the river goddess Ganges; Bhīṣma was the legitimate heir. In a second alliance with Satyavatī, the daughter of a fisher tribe chieftain, Śaṃtanu had two younger sons, Citrāngada and Vicitravīrya.

All the complications start with the second alliance. It was no less peculiar than the king's first alliance with a deity: it was a baron's infatuation with a low-class girl. The king tries to disown his amour, but his heir finds out and sells his birthright of succession for his father's privilege to indulge himself. Driving a hard bargain, the girl's father, the chieftain, demands the promise that Bhīṣma will stand aside and allow the girl's sons to inherit; and, as a second promise, that Bhīṣma himself will not have sons that could rival the junior branch. Bhīṣma agrees to both conditions, and is hence known by his name, which means "awe-inspiring."

In the junior line, Citrāngada dies unmarried and without heir. Vicitravīrya, his younger brother, on the other hand, marries two sisters, Ambikā and Ambālikā, yet dies childless. Extinction of a line so precariously begun faces the erstwhile fisher girl, now Queen Satyavatī. But Satyavatī had been a virgin only symbolically when she married old King Śaṃtanu; she had had a son, Kṛṣṇa Dvaipāyana, after a brief encounter with a seer, Parāśara, a passenger on a ferry she plied on the river Yamunā. After Bhīṣma's refusal to oblige his younger brother's wives, Satyavatī calls on this other elder brother by the law of levirate to service them for offspring. By the elder widow, Ambikā, he fathers Dhṛtarāṣṭra, by diminishing rights the heir; by the younger widow, Ambālikā, he fathers Pāṇḍu. He also begets a bastard son of the household, Vidura.

Dhṛtarāṣṭra is born blind, and thus excluded from direct succession. Pāṇḍu becomes king, and, with divine intervention, fathers five sons, the Pāṇḍavas, on a senior wife and a junior one. The eldest of the five is Yudhiṣṭhira, who, to boot, has been born ahead of the senior Dhṛtarāṣṭra's eldest son, Duryodhana. Meanwhile, Pāṇḍu has fallen under a curse, renounces the throne, and retires to the forest, where his children are born and grow up. Dhṛtarāṣṭra, whose name means "he who holds the kingdom," assumes the regency for heirs that by now are hardly identifiable. He agrees that Yudhiṣṭhira continue to have first claim to the realm, but does not commit himself to the cause of Yudhiṣṭhira's issue.

After Pāṇḍu's death, the hermits of the forest to which he had retired bring the princes and the one surviving mother, the senior wife Kuntī, to the Bhārata court at Hāstinapura, their principal fastness. While the Pāṇḍavas's legitimacy is never called into doubt, Duryodhana, eldest son of Regent Dhṛtarāṣṭra, has designs on the throne and attempts to remove his cousins, first by assassination, and, when that fails, by semi-exile to a provincial town. There he plots to burn them in a house fire, but, with their bastard uncle Vidura's help, the Pāṇḍavas discover the plot, leave substitute bodies burned for theirs, and escape with their mother.

After an adventurous period in hiding—they are disguised as young brahmins—they reappear at the court of King Drupada of South Pāñcāla, who is having a tournament for the hand of his daughter Kṛṣṇā Draupadī. Arjuna, the third of the Pāṇḍavas, wins her for them all. They have thus entered into an alliance with the Pāñcālas, who border the Bhāratas down the river Ganges. Inevitably the Hāstinapura Bhāratas take notice: the Pāṇḍava claimants have not only survived, but have also secured a powerful alliance with a neighboring kingdom. To make matters worse, Baladeva and Kṛṣṇa Vāsudeva, champions of a people living to the west on the parallel river Yamunā at the fastness of Mathurā, have entered into an alliance of friendship with the Pāṇḍavas.

A council is held at once in Hāstinapura. Preventive warfare is urged, but great-uncle Bhīṣma upholds the Pāṇḍavas's rights. Yet, Duryodhana, having for so long been in actual possession of the realm that he is king *de facto*, will not be budged. They arrive finally at the only possible compromise short of war, partition of the kingdom. The Pāṇḍavas are offered the uncultivated and forested

Khāṇḍava Tract, southwest of Hāstinapura on the bank of the river Yamunā, where they accept domain as a junior Bhārata branch. Neither party renounces ultimate claim to sovereignty over the entire patrimony.

The Pāṇḍavas found the city of Indraprastha, and they prosper to such an extent that Kṛṣṇa Vāsudeva counsels King Yudhiṣṭhira to celebrate the Royal Consecration, which is to be understood as a ritually legitimized act of independence from Hāstinapura and as a claim to imperial dominion, under which the entire dynasty could again be gathered in. They reduce the present emperor *en titre*, Jarāsaṃdha of Magadha, and subjugate the known world. Yudhiṣṭhira is duly anointed, with the express approval of the Hāstinapura branch. Then, when he seems at the height of majesty, he is challenged by Hāstinapura to a game of dice.

Yudhiṣṭhira cannot ignore this challenge, since it is the concluding ritual of the Consecration ceremony itself.[1] He loses everything to cousin Duryodhana, including the liberty of his sons, his brothers, and himself. In a final act of resignation he stakes his wife Draupadī, and loses. Draupadī, fatefully subjected to unforgettable indignities, raises a dumbfounding issue: was Yudhiṣṭhira at liberty to stake her, when he himself had lost his own liberty: did he still own her when he staked her? The issue is not resolved, and Dhṛtarāṣṭra in fact cancels the game and sends the Pāṇḍavas home with all their possessions. But the game must be played. While they are on their way back, the Pāṇḍavas are intercepted with a final challenge: an all-or-nothing throw: the whole kingdom, or an exile of thirteen years, twelve in the forest and one year incognito. They throw, and Duryodhana defeats Yudhiṣṭhira.

When after thirteen years the Pāṇḍavas reemerge to claim their patrimony, they are rebuffed. War is now unavoidable, and both parties raise armies and forge alliances. Kṛṣṇa Vāsudeva acts as the counselor, and Dhṛṣṭadyumna of Pāñcāla as the general, of the Pāṇḍavas. The war, in which all the world participates, rages for eighteen days and ends with total defeat for the Hāstinapura Bhāratas. Yudhiṣṭhira ritually confirms his dominion with a Horse Sacrifice. Kṛṣṇa Vāsudeva's tribe commits suicide in a drunken brawl; and in the end the Pāṇḍavas and their wife Draupadī go on the last journey to heaven. All the Pāṇḍavas' sons by Draupadī have been slain; the succession goes to Abhimanyu, son of Arjuna, the junior-most Pāṇḍava Kaunteya by his junior wife Subhadrā, from Abhimanyu to

1. The reader will have to take my word for this for the time being; I shall return to this question in my introduction to *The Book of the Assembly Hall.* Meanwhile, he may consult my article, "On the Structure of the Sabhāparvan of *The Mahābhārata*," *Festschrift Gonda*, 1972.

his son Parikṣit, and from Parikṣit to Janamejaya, to whom the entire story is retold.

As is obvious from this outline of the barest skeleton of the central story of the great epic, the plot is extremely complex. The succession rights of the male descendants are a genealogist's nightmare, and, to me at least, there is little doubt that the story was in part *designed* as a riddle. Whatever historical realities may also have been woven into the epic, it is not an accident of dynastic history; however fortuitous its career of expansion, the epic is not an accident of literary history. The grand framework was a *design*.

The Fuzzy Edges

This central story has proliferated to an extreme degree. Of course, the story itself is far from simple; if we compare this warrior epic with the plot of *The Iliad*, the difference is striking. However, it is hard to delineate the perimeter of the "original" narrative.

Since the epic deals primarily with a succession conflict, it must always have demanded a much longer timespan than either *The Iliad* or *The Odyssey*. It had to start with generations of forebears whose interrelations were sufficiently entangled to present the problem of the heirs as a real one. It must also have demanded a clear dénouement: the listener *must* know how the conflict was resolved. On both ends the edges are fuzzy. The complexity necessary at the beginning allowed itself to be extended deeper and deeper into the past. A few examples make this process quite clear.

The early history of the dynasty of the protagonists and antagonists of the epic, which must to some extent have been there originally, is now swollen to the long *Book of the Origins*. Several stages seem discernible. It is likely that the narrative originally began[2] with Śaṃtanu, the birth of his son Bhīṣma from the Ganges, and Śaṃtanu's marriage to Satyavatī. Now, Śaṃtanu was a scion of the dynasty named Bhārata, and this very fact occasioned the inclusion of a story concerning the origins of this dynasty, which was founded by Bharata: so we now find *The Story of Śakuntalā*, who was Bharata's mother. But why stop there? The Bhāratas are also Pauravas, and once one begins to seek origins, the ancient story of Pūru, how he won the kingdom and founded the Paurava dynasty, should be included. And one might as well go all the way and add *The Descent of the First Generations*.[3]

2. I note that C. C. Narasimhan begins his own abbreviated version in *The Mahābhārata* (New York, 1965) at this point.

3. To locate these portions, consult the table of contents of *The Book of the Beginning* (p. 17).

No less fuzzy is the end of the story. It could simply have ended with the total defeat of the opposing party. But does anything end so simply as with a victory? The dead have to be properly mourned, as in *The Book of the Women*;[4] they have to be sped ceremonially on their last journey, as in *The Book of the Funeral Oblation*; the Pāṇḍavas' victory itself must be reaffirmed by a Royal Consecration, and a Horse Sacrifice. And as we go on, the scope and reach of the story become wider and higher. Thus we may, with greater or lesser certainty, identify the central parts of the narrative, and "later" accretions (which may have been hoary to begin with) to the central story. Still, the latter were understood, as I think we should understand them, within the framework of the former.

Besides the uncertain delineation of the central story, we discern a comparable fuzziness of the events and incidents within this story. Patterns have a way of being repeated, detracting from the precision of single incidents here-and-now. This is well illustrated by the patterns of paternity.

One of the striking features of *The Mahābhārata* is the complexity of paternity, demanded indeed by the central succession conflict. This begins with great-grandfather Śaṃtanu, who had an eldest son, Bhīṣma, by the river goddess Ganges. We might expect so eminently qualified an issue to become heir. But no: the father falls in love with a fisher girl, and her canny father insists that *her* issue shall inherit. Bhīṣma gives in, and also promises to sire no children of his own.

Whatever else these rather dramatic developments were intended to convey, they leave us in the grandfather generation with a grandsire patriarchically uncommitted to either party in the later generations, for whom he is now able to act as arbitrator.[5] But this presence of Bhīṣma, surely essential to the epic, seems to have generated a kind of mirror effect: just as Śaṃtanu had a premarital son, so did his wife Satyavatī have one, Kṛṣṇa Dvaipāyana. This provides a neat parallelism:

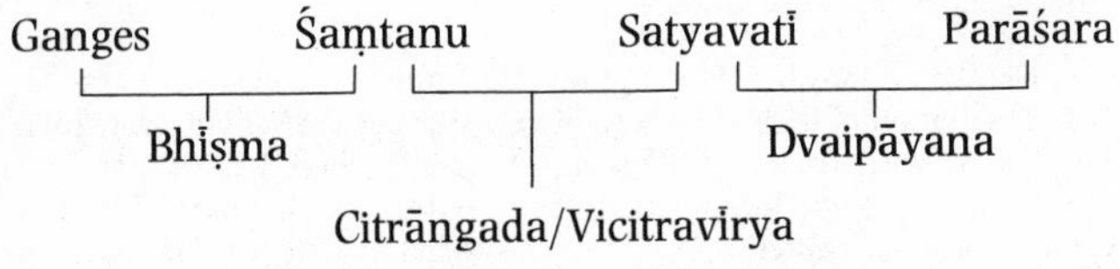

Thus in the grandfather generation there are two older extramarital sons on either parent's side, both unmarried, both

4. To locate this and the following portion, consult the table of contents of *The Mahābhārata*.

5. Not that he much inclines to do so; cf. *The Beginning*, my introduction (p. 16).

deeply involved in the well-being of the dynasty. Bhīṣma provides protection to his two younger half-brothers, and finds Vicitravīrya his two wives; Dvaipāyana sires sons on the widows of Vicitravīrya. The mirror effect also brings out contrasts: Bhīṣma is chaste, a family man, and a baron; Dvaipāyana is virile, ascetic, and a brahmin. Bhīṣma is until his very end a thoroughly visible potentate, whereas Dvaipāyana moves secretly in and out.

The difficulty of having heirs continues to be illustrated. Citrāngada, Śaṃtanu's eldest son by Satyavatī, dies before he can marry. Vicitravīrya, on the other hand, marries two wives, and this prince "of colorful virility"[6] dies of sexual exhaustion without fathering children. It is hard not to sense a certain genealogical playfulness in all this, as though some riddling heralds were designing a family puzzle.

Dvaipāyana's paternity is exclusively physical; the sons he fathers are legally the heirs of Vicitravīrya, beholden to offer their legal father the funerary offerings, and they are heirs to his patrimony. But paternity problems continue to haunt the father generation. Born blind, and therefore useless for the succession, Dhṛtarāṣṭra has no less than a hundred sons, but his younger brother Pāṇḍu, who is king, is under the curse that he will die at the moment of intercourse, and cannot service *his* two wives.

At this point Pāṇḍu's wife Kuntī is like a second Satyavatī. She too had had a premarital son by the Sun God—as a result of a boon she she had received, which allowed her to conjure up any god. This son, Karṇa, the eldest again, plays a mirror effect to the Pāṇḍavas, his juniors. By virtue of the same boon Kuntī now invokes Dharma, the Wind God, Indra, and the Aśvins.

Correlated with the patterns of paternity is the conspicuous pattern of the "disqualified eldest." Śaṃtanu himself was junior to Devāpi,[7] who went to the forest. On the next level both Bhīṣma and Kṛṣṇa Dvaipāyana are eldest sons; so is Citrāngada, who, however, is succeeded by the issue of his own younger brother. On the next level,

6. Or: "of various heroism"; of the latter there is no trace.

7. The notion of their rivalry (which prefigures that of later generations) appears early; cf. Yāska, *Nirukta* 2.20 (-Sarup 2.10–12, whom I cite:) "Devāpi and Śantanu, sons of Ṛṣṭiṣeṇa, were two brothers who belonged to the clan of the Kurus. Śantanu, the younger brother, caused himself to be installed as king. Devāpi retired to practice austerities. From that time the god allowed no rain for twelve years in the kingdom of Śantanu." Whereupon the brahmins blame Śaṃtanu, the latter implores Devāpi, who acts as priest and wins rain. *The Bṛhaddevata* (7.155–8.10) has essentially the same story, but adds the feature that Devāpi disqualifies himself because of a skin disease (*tvagdoṣī* 7.156; *tvagdoṣophatendriyaḥ* 8.5). Both texts comment on *Ṛgveda* 10.98 (supposedly composed by Devāpi), showing how far back these traditions have been taken. The stories also illustrate some constants of the epic tradition: the disqualified eldest, the twelve-year drought in the Kuru kingdom (cf. 1.[11.a]), and the possible leukodermia of Pāṇḍu.

Dhṛtarāṣṭra is disqualified. In the following generation, Karṇa is disqualified. The final paternity irony is that of the Pāṇḍavas themselves. They all share the same wife, by whom each has a son. But these sons die, and eventually the kingdom descends in a junior line, that of Abhimanyu, who was Arjuna's son by his junior wife Subhadrā.

While some of these patterns are clearly demanded by the central story it is hard not to look upon some of these complications as deliberate elaborations, not necessarily demanded by the narrative but easily inspired by it. And, again, they grow so organically out of the main story that it is impossible to amputate them. We have to be satisfied with a fuzzily delineated center, which from the beginning lay open to growth in every direction.

The Second Perimeter

Another matter is the accretion of secondary materials to the central story. Again it is by no means easy to differentiate between them and the principal narrative, because in the course of time the stylistic differences were glossed over. Any line drawn will be subjective up to a point; but one place where the line might be drawn is between man and deity.

There is no reason at all why Bhīṣma should be the son of the river goddess, why Karṇa should be the offspring of the Sun, why the Pāṇḍavas should have been begotten by various deities. Certainly, these heroes are superhuman in the baronial tradition of epics everywhere. Bhīṣma's vow not to sire any children of his own gave him his name: "awe-inspiring." It could have been left at that: a magnanimous self-sacrifice on the part of a son for his father's happiness. There are plenty of other stories where impossible demands are placed on a son in his father's cause. But after the composition of the central epic a newer, and less baronial, imagination could not leave it at that. Such magnanimity as Bhīṣma's was not merely superhuman; it was no less than divine. Bhīṣma ought to be the incarnation of some divinity.

As usual in such pious transformations, the results are less than gratifying; they take away a man's virtue while adding nothing to the God's. It turns out that Bhīṣma is the incarnation of the God Dyaus, who once had insulted the powerful seer Vasiṣṭha by wanting to steal his cow; Dyaus's wife wanted to make some mortal lady happy with it. Since Dyaus had been in the company of a group of Gods called Vasus, all these Gods were similarly cursed to be born as mortals. The unhappy troop came upon the river Ganges, who agreed to give birth to them, then drown them instantly, so that their curse would not last too long—except for the curse of Dyaus, who should live out a full lifetime, and also have no sons. Now why should the goddess Ganges get involved? It so happens that when Gods and saints were in Brahmā's heaven, the Goddess Ganges came in. An indiscreet breeze blew up her skirt. All the Gods modestly looked away, except for the recently sainted King Mahābhiṣa, who watched curiously. Brahmā indignantly cursed him to a new birth. Of course, on earth he reappears as Śaṃtanu. The Ganges, who cherished an intimate memory, demands that he beget children on her, so that she also can do the Vasus a good turn.

Such further elaborations are disappointing because they rob the human actors of much of their motivation. Bhīṣma's noble vow is reduced to the automatic consequence of a curse by a sage, angered over, of all things, a cow. The elaborations are disappointing also because they show little respect for the Gods themselves. The Gods pressed into service to explain human affairs are mostly of a venerable Vedic antiquity, but their mythology is decaying. Dyaus (the word is etymologically related to the Greek Zeus) is a fairly important deity in the *Ṛgveda*; now he is just a member of a roving band of godlings who falls afoul of a human seer.

Once such inept mythification is introduced,[8] persons and events intended thus to be made more significant become less so; the causes that it seeks to elucidate become the murkier. It is not much better with the divine parentage of the Pāṇḍavas. The bastard steward Vidura, uncle to the parties, is the God Dharma himself incarnated. Why? Dharma had once harshly judged a sage for a minor offense, and the sage had thereupon cursed Dharma to be born a mortal. It is the same Dharma, supposedly also alive and well as Vidura,[9] who is first invoked by Kuntī to beget a child for Pāṇḍu. Pāṇḍu, timid against his nature, suggested the choice of Dharma, for if the God of the Law assented to siring a child, no folk could find fault with it. This is extremely silly, for he himself was sired by a father-substitute, on the urging of his grandmother Satyavatī, who was not the type to ask anybody's leave. Besides, Kuntī had already had Karṇa by the Sun before her marriage, and quite unblushingly.

Still, disconcerting as it is, the rather decadent sanctification by mythology of persons standing in no need of saintliness went on, and found its inane perfection in *The Book of the Partial Incarnations*, where every human, bad or good, is the reappearance of demon and God.

8. This puts me in opposition to Georges Dumézil's *Mythe et epopée* 1 (Paris, 1968). Dumézil, in my view unnecessarily, starts from those mythological paternities that I, for the most part, regard as posthumous. I intend to discuss Dumézil's views elsewhere.

9. But I cannot follow the late-lamented Iravati Karve's argument that Vidura could well have been Yudhiṣṭhira's father; see *Yuganta* (Poona, no date), pp. 89 ff.

But all this makes no difference, and is best ignored, as the epic itself does. Arjuna is Indra's son, and Karṇa the Sun God's; so, when the two face each other for the first time at the weapon show, Indra hangs a little rain cloud over Arjuna's head, and the sun shines brightly over Karṇa's. But all this has no influence over their eventual destiny.

Finally, this decaying mythology, with which the reader is so needlessly presented, has a way of subtracting from the meaning of both a newly rising mythology and of a heraldically surviving one. To give an example of the latter: Arjuna and Kṛṣṇa (the "White" and the "Black") are meaningfully said to be the ancient hero pair of Nara and Nārāyaṇa, who, it would appear, are old champions of a rhapsodic tradition drawn into *The Mahābhārata*. But in the mass of other casual identifications this old relation hardly stands out. Again, in an attempt to justify why the Pāṇḍavas should have one common bride, the story is told that the Great God successively punished five Indras[10] for their insolence in proclaiming themselves the king of the Gods; the five Indras were born the Pāṇḍavas, with, of course, one wife. This story, meant to excuse polyandry, by its foolish associations obfuscates the fact that the Great God Śiva had gained ascendancy over the now-languishing Indra.

It would be easy at this point to be traduced into believing that a different mentality has taken over the grand old baronial tradition, and to identify that mentality with that of the brahmins. But it is hard to revive the antibrahminism of Western scholarship of the last century, since all the evidence points to a necessary symbiosis of brahmin and baron; as our text has it, "The baronage is in league with brahmindom, and brahmindom is allied with the baronage."[11] Perhaps we should rather think that the baronial-bardic tradition, out of which the epic grew, was expiring and absorbed into another tradition of wandering reciters of brahmin-type lore. *The Mahābhārata* as a whole is recited by "the Son of the Bard," Ugraśravas, son of Lomaharṣaṇa, both satisfyingly baronial names, "he of the awesome voice" and "he of the hair-raising tales." They are succeeded, reinterpreted, in the end preserved, by such reciters as Lomaśa and Mārkaṇḍeya in *The Book of the Forest*, prototypes of the Paurāṇikas, reciters of Purāṇas, "ancient stories," in which all traditions are mixed.

The Third Perimeter

This perimeter is announced on the first page of *The Mahābhārata*. We are introduced, not to a royal court, where such dynastic struggles as

10. In *The Rgveda* Indra *was* the chief god.
11. *MBh.* 1(7.c) = 1.75.18.

the text relates would appropriately be sung, but to a hermitage, where the hermits press the arriving bard Ugraśravas for interesting tales.

At the more formal opening, in *The Book of Puloman*, the brahmin Śaunaka sits surrounded by priests at a twelve-year Sacrificial Session. He asks the bard to recite to him the entire story of the grand tale of the Bhāratas, which has first been recited by the sage Vaiśaṃpāyana at the Snake Sacrifice of King Janamejaya. The request at first sight looks strange: why should these priests, going about their ritual concerns in a remote forest, be concerned[12] with the warlike doings of generations of kings long since gone? Was it merely because they wished to be entertained? I believe there was more to it. I think their concern was the concern typical of brahmindom: to preserve. For reasons that can never be completely clear the brahmins of the Naimiṣa Forest wished to have a full record of the dynastic epic; and it is in the form it was retold to them that the text has come down to us.

This was hardly the same epic that was recited to Janamejaya; it is doubtful whether that king would have been interested in all the brahminic stories that now have their place in the epic. But it is equally doubtful that the main story, with so much in it that must have been repugnant to the brahmins[13], was seriously changed. Rather it was filled out, at first at points where such filling-out could be considered natural.

An excellent example is provided by Book Three, *The Book of the Forest*. We noted in the main story that after the defeat at the dicing the Pāṇḍavas must depart to the forest for a period of twelve years. Certainly the original epic itself cannot have left it at that; it must have had a substantial text dealing with adventures in the forest. The forest is the domain of demons, which they are sure to have encountered. But the forest is also the domain of those brahmin sages who have retired from the everyday world and are engaged in their contemplations and austerities. And thus, to the encounter with demons is added the meeting with brahmins. *The Book of the Forest* became *The Book of the Forest Teachings* (*āraṇyaka*) and was expanded with a long series of brahminic stories.

Another example is *The Bhagavadgītā*. The brahmins were hardly hearing the story of the epic for the first time; they already knew of the miserable course that the war would take. What could be more appropriate than to add a moment of pause, just as the war is about to begin? A moment of reflection on whether the warriors should

12. Was it because at this approximate time other parties like the Buddhists started hoarding their different kind of records?

13. The prime instance is, of course, Draupadī's polyandrous marriage; yet this is but moderately mitigated by *The Story of the Five Indras* 1.(12a).

really do it? And here then occurs the famous loss of nerve of the heroic Arjuna, who shrinks from the massacre of elders, teachers, and kinsmen.

But, once the gates have been opened to additions, they come in wave after wave. The ultimate examples are the long *Books of the Peace* and the *Instructions*. The wise Bhīṣma, dying on a bed of arrows, interminably expounds on the varieties of dharma in what must be the longest deathbed sermon on record. The last books, too, are doubtless additional, while much of the first book, notably *The Book of Āstīka*, must be later additions.

Thus *The Bhārata* of 24,000 couplets grew to *The Mahābhārata* of 100,000. The original story was in the first phase of complication expanded from within, in the second phase mythologized, in the third phase brahminized. One might even discern a fourth phase, after the epic was first written down, when this collection of manuscripts became, as it were, a library to which new books could be added. Almost any text of "Hindū" inspiration could be included in this expanding library, so that in the end the custodians could rightly boast that "whatever is found here may be found somewhere else, but what is not found here is found nowhere!"[14]

Authorship and Date

From the foregoing it will have become clear that neither a single author nor a single date can be assigned to the great epic. Indian tradition attributes the composition to the same Kṛṣṇa Dvaipāyana who begot Vicitravīrya's children, a kind of immortal brahmin who appears at the Snake Sacrifice of King Janamejaya, his own great-great-great-grandson. But this is more intended as a symbolic authorship, for the same Dvaipāyana is also held to have divided the one Veda into the four Vedas, and compiled the eighteen Purāṇas, as well as the basic text of Vedānta. He is a kind of universal uncle.

The text of *The Mahābhārata* itself gives us some idea how we should picture its authorship. In its present form it is recited by the bard Ugraśravas, who recites after Vaiśaṃpāyana, who was one of the pupils of Kṛṣṇa Dvaipāyana. In other words, we have right here three generations of reciters through whom the text had been transmitted. One cannot expect that this transmission was a literal one, as it has been in the case of the Veda. A reciter's reputation was based on his skill in bringing the old stories to life again. Successive generations would add, embellish, digress; but also understate what might have been emphasized before.

14. *MBh.* 1.56.34.

In a number of typical instances—*The Book of Āstīka* is a good example—the reciter would first give a resumé, a brief summary containing the salient features and little more. Then he would be prevailed upon to give the fuller story with all the detail he could think of. Even then his audience might interrupt him and ask for more information on certain points. All this creates the impression that what would come down from generation to generation were, first, the summaries, and, second, the technique of spinning out a tale to please the listeners. The reciter was thus also a creative poet, within the idiom of his craft.

Also handed down were a number of finished verses[15] that summarized an incident, offered a moral, or in some other way contributed to the narrative. These were not signed, no more than the summaries were. Such a bardic tradition is by its nature anonymous.

That the main story of *The Mahābhārata* was a conscious composition is, to me, undeniable, and one poet, or a small group of them, must have been responsible for it. The original story is now irrecoverable, but it is likely to have been substantially shorter than the shortest recorded summary.[16] It is from this modest beginning, and from a bard whose name has since been forgotten, that *The Mahābhārata* began its incredible career.

When was this old *Bhārata* lay first composed? Certainly after the very early Vedic period, for the area where the conflict is localized lies well east of the Panjāb which is the home of *The Ṛgveda*. On the other hand, knowledge of the countries farther east of the mesopotamia of the rivers Ganges and Yamunā is only sketchy. Whatever one might believe of the historicity of the conflict, a struggle for control over the upper Ganges and the Yamunā was obviously credible to the audience and is likely to have been part of the movement east of the āryans. The eastern countries of Kosala, which in *The Rāmāyaṇa* is the center of the world, and Magadha, where the Buddha preached and where the first Indian "empire" was to rise in the third century B.C., do not play an important rôle in the great epic. On the basis of the meager data, it seems more likely than not that the origins of *The Mahābhārata* fall somewhere in the eighth or ninth century.[17]

Of considerable interest are a few verifiable facts that bear on the history of the text. The first recitation of the full epic is associated

15. For the manner in which these summaries are expanded, cf. 1.13.30ff. with 1.42. For finished verses (here "chronicle verses," *anuvaṃśa*) cf. 1.90.28, corresponding to 1.89.13–14; 1.90.31 = 1.69.29. A close study of the relationship between "summary" and "finished story" is needed to bring out the details of the technique.

16. Viz., in 24.000 *ślokas*, roughly quarter of the present size, *MBL*. 1.1.61.

17. For the archeological evidence cf. below, n. 12, *The Book of the Beginning*: *Introduction* (pp. 10 ff.).

with the reign of King Janamejaya. This king is known as a historical person in the late Vedic literature, where, with his brothers Ugrasena, Bhīmasena, and Śrutasena, he is said to have performed a Horse Sacrifice.[18] In a very late portion of *The Atharvaveda*,[19] Janamejaya's father Parikṣit is known and glorified as one living. In *The Bṛhadāraṇyaka Upaniṣad* (ca. 600 B.C.) his descendants the Pārikṣitas are known as a vanished dynasty: the great teacher Yājñavalkya[20] is asked: "Where have the Pārikṣitas gone. I ask you, Yājñavalkya, where have the Pārikṣitas gone?" The answer is that they have gone where the offerers of a Horse Sacrifice go; and one is once more reminded of the sacrificer Janamejaya, the name of whose grandson is given in the epic as Aśvamedhadatta, "gift of the Horse Sacrifice." All this, while not conclusive, bears out a date not too far removed from the eighth or ninth century B.C.

Not that we have in fact so old a text today. Unlike the Vedas, which have to be preserved letter-perfect, the epic was a popular work whose reciters would inevitably conform to changes in language and style. Not only that, the text has gone through so many reworkings that old and new are inextricably bound together. There is a general agreement that the oldest portions preserved are hardly older than 400 B.C. The oldest testimony of the existence of a *Bhārata* text is barely before this period, in two of the ritual manuals[21] and in the grammar of Pāṇini.[22]

While this *terminus a quo* is reasonable, and generally agreed upon, it is far more difficult to set a date *ante quem*; views on this depend on what one accepts as the "real" *Mahābhārata*. In particular, the didactic portions of what has been called the pseudo-epic were added to very late, perhaps as late as the fourth century A.D.

Such a dating, from 400 B.C. till A.D. 400, is of course absurd from the point of view of a single literary work. It makes sense when we look upon the text not so much as one opus but as a library of opera. Then we can say that 400 B.C. was the founding date of that library, and that A.D. 400 was the approximate date after which no more substantial additions were made to the text.

Fate of the Text in India and Southeast Asia

Its early vicissitudes, the various phases of enrichment it went through, we have discussed earlier. We might now turn to the

18. *Śatapatha Brāhmaṇa* 13.5.4.1
19. *AthV*. 20.127.7–10.
20. *BĀUp*. 16.9.7.
21. Āśvalāyana Gṛhyasūtra 3.4; Śāṅkhāyana Śrautasūtra 15.16.
22. Pāṇini 4.2.56.

influence it has exerted in the culture out of which it had grown.

This influence has been immense. More than any other text in Indian civilization the great epic has been the storehouse of ancient lore. Aeschyles describes his plays as crumbs from Homer's table; with probably more right *The Mahābhārata*[23] itself declares: "From this supreme epic rise the inspirations of the poets. . . . All Lore ranges in the realm of this epic. . . . No story is found that does not rest on this epic. . . . All the best poets live off this epic." This is not to say that *The Mahābhārata* was the only storehouse of the old Lore. During the period of the formation of the great epic, another great work, *The Rāmāyaṇa*, was created whose story has made a profound impression on "Hindū" civilization. But whereas in *The Rāmāyaṇa* it was particularly the main story that exerted its influence, *The Mahābhārata's* strength lay, both, in its principal narrative and in the episodes. This influence extended not only to Sanskrit literature, but also to the literatures in the modern Indo-Aryan languages as well as the Dravidian languages. Nor did it remain confined to the Indian subcontinent; it was felt as far east as Java and Bali.

In Sanskrit literature especially, the theater and the literary form of the *mahākāvya*, or epyllion, drew upon *The Mahābhārata*. Some of the earliest extant plays, by the playwright Bhāsa (A.D. 300?), are based on episodes from the main narrative of the epic. The most famous play of Sanskrit literature, by Kālidāsa (A.D. 500?), was inspired by *The Story of Śakuntalā*. Likewise, the epyllion *Kirāṭārjunīya* by Bhāravi (ca. A.D. 600) takes up the story of the battle of Arjuna with Śiva in the guise of a mountain man, the *Siśupālavadha* of Māgha (ca. A.D. 675) that of *The Slaying of Śiśupāla* in *The Book of the Assembly Hall*. The story was also a favorite of the more esoteric poets of Sanskrit, who delighted in exploiting the wealth of the vocabulary, multiplicity of meanings, and the different ways in which a compound could be broken up, to tell two stories at once with exactly the same words. The *Pāṇḍavīya-rāghavīya* of Kavirāja (ca. 1180) is the most celebrated example: here the narratives of *The Mahābhārata* and *Rāmāyaṇa* are given in identical words.

Perhaps the most popular of all the episodes of the text was *The Story of Nala* in *The Book of the Forest*; there is the *Naiṣadhacarita* by Srīharṣa (1175), the *Nalodaya* by Vāsudeva, the *Nalābhyudaya* by Vāmaṇa Bhaṭṭa, the *Nalavilāsa* by Rāmacandra Sūri, the *Nalacaritra* play by Nīlakaṇṭha Dīkṣita, the *Nalacampū* by Trivikrama Bhaṭṭa, and so on.

Countless are the single references to epic material in the lyric literature. One typical example will suffice:

23. *MBh.* 1.2. past 235.

The cloudy sky grows dark like Dhṛtarāṣṭra's face—
Too prideful, like Duryodhana, the peacock jeers—
The cuckoo, like Yudhiṣṭhira defeated, disappears,
The swans, like Pāṇḍu's sons, have gone and left no trace.[24]
(*Little Clay Cart* 5.5)

Such casual references show how familiar the Indian was with the events and the heroes of the epic, so familiar that they in effect became proverbial.

In other languages than Sanskrit, the continuing influence of *The Mahābhārata* is shown particularly in Old Javanese. During the eleventh century, parts, possibly the whole, of the text were translated into Javanese in the reign of Dharmavaṃśa (ca. 990). The Bhārata epic remained very popular and inspired Javanese counterparts of the Sanskrit epyllion: the *Arjunavivāha* ("Arjuna's Wedding," namely to Subhadrā) the *Bhāratayuddha* ("The Bhārata War"), the *Koravāsrama* ("The Hermitage of the Kauravas," based on Book Fifteen, *The Sojourn in the Hermitage*). Besides, the narrative was adopted in the *wayang* shadow plays that are mostly based on our text, though naturally showing local preferences. The late President Sukarno was called after the Bhārata hero Karṇa.

The epic was translated, or rather adapted, in most of the Indian languages, although it would appear that *The Rāmāyaṇa* was the more popular work. The latter appealed particularly to the devotionalism of the Indian middle ages; to them the sometimes all-too-human heroes of *The Mahābhārata* had less to offer, the less so since the great God of devotionalism, Kṛṣṇa, had in effect been lifted out of the epic and given a romance of his own. Yet the heroine Draupadī became the object of a cult, and she lives on in folk religion.[25]

Indian art equally shows the pervasive influence of the epic. It is sufficient to point to the monumental relief of the so-called Arjuna's penance, based on *The Book of the Mountain Man*, at Mahabalipuram in South India.[26] Nor did this influence remain limited to traditional "Hindū" art; the Persian translation made for the Great Mughal

24. . . . *grows dark*: probably referring to the episode in which he learns of the death of his son Duryodhana. . . . *too prideful*: when he was humiliated by Bhīma, *MBh.* 2.43. . . . *departed*: after the *Gambling Match, MBh.* 2.68. . . . *have gone*: after the fire in the *Lacquer House, MBh.* 1.137ff.—the translation is mine from *Two Plays of Ancient India* (New York, 1968).

25. Kees Bolle of the University of California at Los Angeles is working on a study of that cult.

26. Cf. T. N. Ramachandran, "The Kirāṭarjunīyam in Indian Art," *Journal of the Indian Society for Oriental Art* 18 (1950–51). The original Mahābhārata story is found in 3(31).

Akbar was illustrated by miniatures that are held to be the culmination of Mughal painting.[27]

We have deliberately refrained from mentioning the most famous episode of the text, *The Bhagavadgītā*. This short poem, doubtless formed within the epic, has become the most important single text for "Hindū" religion and has inspired a complete literature of its own. It was commented on numerous times by the great thinkers of Indian philosophy, and became the basic text of the devotionalism of *bhakti*, which has pervaded India since the early middle ages.

In other respects has the text contributed to the history of Indian thought. The twelfth book, *The Book of the Peace*, contains a large number of philosophical chapters that are among the oldest documents for more or less systematic "Hindū" thought. Likewise, the history of Indian law cannot be properly understood without the epic, where the law is the single greatest concern.[28]

Thus there is hardly a province of "Hindū" culture that has not been touched by the story, and stories, of the epic. And it does not appear that its influence is over. In recent years *The Story of Yayāti* was dramatized in Kannada (Kanarese) in a play that is widely considered to be among the best of the modern stage.[29] In intellectual circles Karṇa has become the model for the militantly dispossessed; on the other side of the political spectrum the late President Rajagopalachari, a conservative, wrote a version of *The Mahābhārata*[30] emphasizing the qualities he considered virtues. An endless series of movies have been based on the text; and comic books are appearing that further disseminate its messages.

The Principal Editions

All this influence, it should be pointed out, was not at all exerted through large numbers of widely circulated copies, as, for instance, was that of the Bible after the invention of the printing press; but by a fairly small number of hand-written transcripts, fatefully fragile, that assisted word of mouth. As part of the continuing story of the fate of the text it may be useful to digress slightly on the subject of an Indian book, so that we may gain a clearer understanding of the problems of editing it.

In essence, an Indian book consists of a number of loose leaves held together by two loose boards and tied by a piece of string running

27. *Razm Nāma*, descended in the Mughal family, now held by the Mahārāja of Jaipur. The University of Chicago Library has a later, seventeenth-century manuscript copy that shows in a miniature the committee of scholars (including a European) who worked on it.

28. Cf. P. V. Kane, *The History of Dharmaśāstra* (1930–62), passim.

29. By Girish Karnad, *Yayāti* (ca. 1963).

30. Chakravarti Rajagopalachari, *Mahābhārata* (Bombay, 1953).

through one or two holes in the leaves and the boards. The old writing materials, before the introduction of paper after A.D. 1000, were birchbark in the upper north and palm leaf in the south. Both materials are very perishable in the alternately humid and dry Indian climate and also extremely vulnerable to vermin; for a text to survive it was necessary for it to be transcribed regularly. By way of illustration: the vast bulk of manuscripts that have survived date from the sixteenth century and later.

A manuscript was a person's private property, acquired either with money or by his labor in copying another manuscript. It was his to do with as he pleased. If it pleased him to insert in his loose-leaf book a couple of leaves containing a variant version of one of the stories, he would do so without compunction, just as we do not scruple to write comments on the margins of the books we own. And the loose-leaf arrangement laid it naturally wide open to additions. There is just so much you can scribble on the margins of bound volumes or scrolls, but there is literally no limit to the expandability of a loose-leaf book. It was equally subject to losses; since a book's destiny hung on the thread with which it was tied together, a break in the string could cause the loss of whole chapters.

The ability to copy presupposes literacy. The ability to copy a book in a foreign language, as Sanskrit had become well before the Christian era, also presupposes learning. Most people are literate in one script; if they try to read another, they are functionally illiterate. On the other hand, a man of learning could, with pen in hand, make running corrections where his original was corrupt or otherwise incomprehensible; but he might easily guess wrong. And a scribe barely literate would faithfully copy all the corruptions and probably add a goodly number of his own.

India is, and has been, a land of many different languages and scripts. Sanskrit could be written in any script. Human nature being what it is, a man about to make a new copy of a text would choose as his original a copy written in a script most familiar to him. If none were to be had, his less than perfect literacy in another character would inevitably show. Thus a copy transcribed in one particular script tended to perpetuate itself in that script, with all its additions, omissions, corruptions, and anomalies; and in time there would be a family of copies, with great family resemblance, but distinctly dissimilar from a family in another script.

There would be formed, as we call them, different versions, or recensions. These are the realities that an editor has to recognize if he wishes to establish a reasonably authentic text from the manuscript material before him. In practice he has no other choice but to follow the trail back, from the present to the kind of past that the manuscripts afford to him. All the manuscripts have to be collected; families have to be recognized in the motley assortment; and from the family he has to try to arrive at the founder of the entire pedigree. It is not unlike the task of our present heralds, trying to trace back a family that is confusingly ramified to a clear and undisputed ancestor of some renown. There will be some testimonies on the way, graves, parish records, but it is the collected and collated family accounts that provide most of the evidence to begin with.

It is clear that the tracing of an ancestor gone for more than one thousand five hundred years is by no means an easy task, and early editors of *The Mahābhārata* have confined themselves to editing the recensions of a certain region, or the text as given by a certain commentator.[31] First to be published was the so-called Calcutta edition, which is based on the Bengal recension of the text (completed in 1839). Then came the Bombay edition, largely based on the recension in Devanāgarī script (completed in 1863), and the Kumbhakonam edition (completed in 1910), which incorporates the Southern recension. The last one in this tradition is the edition by P. P. S. Sastri, *The Mahābhārata. The Southern Recension*, completed in 1935.

As expected, there were serious variations between the several traditions. And while they formed a fairly solid basis for scholarly research, and while important work was indeed done, it soon became clear that any definitive study should be based on a definitive text. As early as 1897,[32] the Viennese scholar Moriz Winternitz called on his fellow-Indologists to work toward that end, and in 1899 he submitted to them a proposal to form a "Sanskrit Epic Texts Society," somewhat along the lines of the very successful Pali Text Society, which has been editing a long series of Theravāda Buddhist texts.

Winternitz's proposals met with a good deal of skepticism; his colleagues were doubtful that it would be possible to reconstitute a kind of all-Indian edition. Still, some movement was made, and, with the help of the Berlin, Vienna, and Göttingen academies, Heinrich Lüders prepared a sample fascicle in 1908.[33] After that the collating of some manuscripts continued, but the first World War brought the work to a complete halt; prospects for a satisfactory edition to originate from Europe grew very dim indeed.

In 1918, however, the scholars of an Indian research institution, the Bhandarkar Oriental Research Institute at Poona, decided to

31. Among whom Nīlakaṇṭha (seventeenth century) is the most popular in India.

32. The history is given by V. S. Sukthankar in his *Prolegomena* to the critical edition. Winternitz's paper was read at the International Congress of Orientalists in Paris in 1897; he continued his drive at that congress in Rome, 1899; and again in Hamburg, 1902.

33. An eighteen-page specimen, *Druckprobe einer critischen Ausgabe des Mahābhārata* (Leipzig, 1908).

proceed on their own with a critical edition. Under the direction of several Indian Sanskritists of note, especially V. S. Sukthankar, a pupil of Winternitz's, the colossal task was slowly accomplished, and is now at last completed with the publication of the appendix, the *Harivaṃśa*, in 1970. A large number of manuscripts were collected, collated, and calibrated, and the editors found that great prominence ought to be given to manuscripts originating from distant and conservative Kashmir; and these manuscripts consequently guided the establishment of the readings.

The first fascicles of the edition were received with some reservations on the part of a number of Western scholars, but as the work progressed there has grown a general sense of satisfaction that the text presented by the critical edition from Poona is the best attainable. It must be a matter of great satisfaction to Indian scholarship that Indians in the end successfully completed a work at which their Western colleagues had effectively failed.

The present translation is naturally based on this critical edition; and the meticulous reading that a word-by-word translation demands has borne out, to my own satisfaction, the excellence of the established text. As a matter of course, there have been occasions where I as translator differed with the editor, if only because, with the best will in the world, I was unable to make sense of the adopted reading; but it has been a surprise to me how few such occasions there have been. I have accounted for the variations in the notes.

The Mahābhārata and the West

We said that in the end Western scholarship failed at the task of editing *The Mahābhārata*, a task, if at all, indeed very gingerly undertaken. Nonetheless, some very substantial contributions have been made by European and American scholars, which we shall review briefly.

The earliest explicit notice was given by Charles Wilkins, a merchant employed by the East India Company (1785), in the form of a translation of *The Bhagavadgītā*,[34] of the episode of the Churning of the Ocean[35] in *The Book of Āstīka*, and later of *The Story of Śakuntalā*.[36] But philological investigation into the text began in earnest with the studies of Franz Bopp (1791–1867), principal founder of Indo-European comparative philology, who in 1816 added a text and translation of *The Slaying of Hiḍimba* to his epoch-making

34. Sir Charles Wilkins, *The Bhăgvăt-gēētā, or Dialogue of Krēēshnă and Ărjŏŏn* (London, 1785).
35. Below *MBh.* 1(5).
36. Below *MBh.* 1(7.b); in A. Dalrymple (ed.) *Oriental Repertory*, (1794).

Coniugationssystem der Sanskritsprache, and later (1819) *The Story of Nala* in his *Nalus, carmen sanscriticum e Mahabharato: edidit, latine vertit, et adnotationibus illustravit*—which, incidentally, introduced the pedagogic habit of starting Western students on beginning Sanskrit with the Nala episode—a habit that, I feel moved to say, might well be broken after more than one hundred and fifty years.

In 1846 a more or less systematic study of *The Mahābhārata* as an epic, not as a library of episodes, began in the work of Adolf Holtzmann, Sr.[37] Promptly this study became controversial. Bopp had already declared that the epic text he had in his possession showed portions of varying antiquity, and it was no wonder that in a philological climate in which the Homeric Question flourished the Indian epic too was submitted to drastic study intended to recover the *Urgestalt*. Holtzmann defended the thesis that the present epic story was a reworking of an original in which the sympathy of the authors did not lie with the Pāṇḍavas at all but with their Kaurava opponents; our present text would still show traces of that: the villainy of the Pāṇḍavas as warriors, the deceptions played by Kṛṣṇa, and other such elements. There is a far-off plausibility about the theory, as about a similar one that has been proposed for *The Iliad*: Homer was really on the side of the Trojans, for Hector was a much nicer man than Achilles, and if you count all the dead, more Greeks died than Trojans.

The thesis was accepted by others, Lassen, von Schröder, and more importantly by the elder Holtzmann's nephew, Adolf Holtzmann, Jr., who presented the theory in its final form in 1895 in *Das Mahābhārata und seine Theile*. Other arguments that he adduced, the fact that the older Vedic material is familiar with Bhāratas and Kauravas but wholly ignorant of the Pāṇḍavas, who therefore must have been recent upstarts, lent credibility to his theory (Macdonell and Keith in their *Vedic Index of Names and Subjects* refuse to believe in the historical authenticity of the Bhārata story on that ground). The upstart Pāṇḍavas would treacherously have slaughtered the piously reigning Kurus; the first outrage at this would have been voiced in the older *Bhārata*, but, as the Pāṇḍavas were, and remained, victorious for several generations, the older story was completely reedited in favor of the victors, who presumably commissioned it so.

The theory has now been given up, but Holtzmann's contribution was a substantial one. His wide-ranging and profound erudition and unparalleled knowledge of the epic as a whole still provide a corpus that demands study by anyone seriously working on *The Mahābhārata*. Yet his approach was soon challenged by two very different scholars.

In the same year that saw Holtzmann's *magnum opus*, the scholar Joseph Dahlmann published *Das Mahābhārata als Epos und Rechtsbuch*

37. Adolph Holtzmann, Sr., *Indische Sagen* (3 vols.; Karlsruhe, 1845–47); new edition by Moriz Winternitz (Jena 1920–21).

(1895). Squarely against Holtzmann's reversal theory, which required a painstaking uncovering of layer after layer in the composition of the text, Dahlmann advocated the synthetic view, positing that the text must be viewed as a unity, for it was thus that it was composed; the huge didactic portions are not late and incidental accretions, but form an organic part of the original text, which was intended to have a religious and moralistic message. It is a bit like arguing that *The Iliad*, the Gospels, and the Church fathers form one contemporaneous text.

This theory was received with utter disbelief; for indeed a cursory reading cannot help but reveal that certain portions are far older than others, breathe a completely different spirit, have contrasting syntactic and stylistic devices, while countless contradictions can be pointed out that are incompatible with the notion of a unified work. The great Sanskritist Hermann Oldenberg dismisses the whole theory in one sentence: there is no point in reasoning the unreasonable.[38] One can hardly disagree, but perhaps one virtue of Dahlmann's labors has been overlooked. For at one point of time a number of redactors must have felt that the text as a whole hung together, and made contemporaneous sense; still, history proves that they were wrong in their judgment; for its influence has been through its parts, not the whole.

Meanwhile an American scholar, E. Washburn Hopkins, had been studying *capita selecta* from *The Mahābhārata* in a growing series of articles and books. His was the more pragmatic approach; instead of worrying one theory of reversal to explain the genesis of the text, as Holtzmann had done (for whom Hopkins had great respect, though he thoroughly disagreed with him), or a synthetic theory, to explain that *The Mahābhārata* had undergone no growth to speak of, as Dahlmann had tried (for whom Hopkins had no use at all), he adopted an analytic approach, far more rigorous than Holtzmann's, in order to find out what the text actually has to say about itself. In *The Great Epic of India. Its Character and Origin* (New York, 1901), he analyzes, among others, the differences in the philosophies presented, the varieties of meters used in different portions of the text; and he concludes most persuasively that at one time there was a true epic, around which in several periods a pseudo-epic agglutinated. It is Hopkins's methods and views that have since been largely, if tacitly, accepted by scholarship.

After these fundamental three theories had been voiced, two historicist and one holistic, all of them the products of the nineteenth century, comparatively little work was done by Western scholars on *The Mahābhārata*, and the initiative lay with their Indian colleagues. The history of Western attempts at a critical edition shows the general

38. Hermann Oldenberg, *Das Mahābhārata: seine Entstehung, sein Inhalt, seine Form* (Göttingen, 1922); he mentions no names: "Eine wissenschaftliche Ungeheurlichkeit; so undiskutierbares zu diskutieren wäre verlorene Mühe."

slackening of interest. Few but Winternitz tried to keep the interest alive; he encouraged Sukthankar in his monumental enterprise, on which, he knew, all *Mahābhārata* scholarship really had to wait. Nevertheless, other scholars should be named and honored: the Dane S. Sörensen, without whose utterly reliable *Index to the Names of the Mahābhārata* (1902) any studies of the epic would be difficult in the extreme (it is far more than the title suggests, since it includes detailed summaries of all the major and minor parts). Also Hermann Jacobi, whose *Mahābhārata* (1903), containing summary, index, and concordance, proved very useful before the critical text was published.

There are a number of reasons why comparatively few Western scholars have been drawn to a study of *The Mahābhārata*. The first, surely, is that the text is so dismally intractable. Its sheer size is really forbidding. It was the rare scholar who confidently commanded the whole. Things were simply hard to find in the epic as it then existed. The Roy translation, on which more below, providing no organizational help at all, proved less than useful, for its English was more likely to discourage than inspire. So anyone who really wished to delve into *The Mahābhārata* had to resign himself to five years or so simply to familiarize himself with it, and with far from certain results.

Besides, the historical direction of scholarship in the West was a different one. Most Sanskritists came out of the tradition of classical studies, and approached the literature from that direction. Indo-European philology was thriving, and this more and more perfected tool was used, inevitably, on those texts that were closest to the mystique of Indo-European prehistory that inspirited many, the Vedas. Many others were attracted to the study of Buddhism, which, with its historical dimension, was more intelligible to the Western mind than unhistorical and diffuse "Hindū" traditions. A comparison of the success of the Pali Text Society and the failure of the Indian Epic Texts Society speaks for itself.

Again, *The Mahābhārata* lacked credibility as an epic for many scholars reared on Homer, for whom an epic was either Homeric or no epic at all. *The Mahābhārata* did not stand at the beginning of the culture (that indeed it did they did not discern). It was disorganized, amorphous, overgrown, lacking in true grandeur, fatally brahminized. "Hindū" superstition made everything somehow mythological and not really believable. It was hard to allow that this little war fought around Delhi, a capital seat of the British Empire, was in any way as epochal as that glorious war fought over a coastal city in Asia Minor. The epic was studied mostly in its parts; there was edition after edition of the Nala story for beginners' use, of the Sāvitrī (and of course *The Bhagavadgītā*), and some others. With that those who wished to know the great epic had to be largely content.

New light has been glimmering since World War II; and a new, in a way old, interest in the epic has become visible. The Swedish scholar Stig Wikander published an article[39] in which he argued that the five Pāṇḍava heroes were in fact representatives of the three orders, which, as Georges Dumézil had been arguing for years, were typical of Indo-European religion and society: the sacerdotal-legislative, the martial-kingly, and the popular-fertile. This new idea immediately inspired the erudite Dumézil to a fresh investigation of *The Mahābhārata* and its heroes, the first results of which are being published in his intended multivolume *Mythe et epopée*.[40]

It was, in fact, my own sense of inadequacy in controlling the epic that alerted me to this conspicuous hiatus in Western scholarship. Western erudition about the course of Indian civilization is quite incomplete without a full and conscious absorption into it of the evidence of *The Mahābhārata*. It is an annoying absence, always nagging at the rim of our memory, always somehow to be dealt with, but later—a specter of an obligatory chore, endlessly postponed, for the sylphs of short-term recreations. Nevertheless, I have found the simple experience of it rewarding beyond imagining.

The Translation

As noted, portions of *The Mahābhārata* have been translated in India and Indonesia since the eleventh century, and since 1785 in the West. There is still no satisfactory philological translation of the entire text, although excellent translations exist of some of its parts.

The first complete translation in another language than those of India and Java was commissioned by the Great Mughal, Emperor Akbar (1542–1605). We have an intriguing account of the circumstances that prompted Akbar's commission from his chronicler Badāyūnī or Badāōnī:

> Among the remarkable events of this year [writes Badāōnī (the year being A.H. 1000 or A.D. 1591)] is the translation of *The Mahābhārata*, which is the most famous of the Hindu books. . . . The following considerations disposed the Emperor to the work. When he had *The Shāhnāmah*, and the story of Āmīr Ḥamzah, in seventeen volumes transcribed in fifteen years, and had spent much gold illuminating it, he also heard the story of Abū Muslim, and *The Jāmī'-ul-hikāyat* repeated, and it suddenly came into his mind that most of these books were nothing but poetry and fiction; but that, since they were first

39. Stig Wikander, "Pāṇḍavasagen och Mahābhārata mythiska förutsänniger", in *Religion och Bibel* 6 (1947).

40. Paris (Edition Gallimard), vol. 1: *L'idéologie des trois fonctions dans les épopées des peuples indo-européens* (1968), vol. 2: *Types épiques indo-européens: un héros, un sorcier, un roi* (1971).

related in a lucky hour, and when their star was in the act of passing over the sky, they obtained great fame. But now he ordered those Hindu books, which holy and staid sages had written, and which were all clear and convincing proofs and the pivot on which all their religion, and faith, and holiness turned, to be translated from the Indian into the Persian language, and thought to himself, "Why should I not have them done in my name? For they are by no means trite, but quite fresh, and they will produce all kinds of fruits of felicity both temporal and spiritual, and will be the cause of circumstance and pomp, and will ensure an abundance of children and wealth, as is written in the preface of these books.

Akbar assembled several paṇḍits whom he directed to write an "explanation" (i.e., a synopsis), which for "several nights" he propounded to Nāqib Khān, "so that the Khān might sketch out the gist of it in Persian. On the third night the Emperor sent for me [i.e., Badāōnī] and desired me to translate *The Mahābhārata*, in conjunction with Nāqib Khān."

The consequence was [he continues] that in three or four months I translated two out of eighteen sections, at the puerile absurdities of which the eighteen thousand creations may well be amazed.[41]

No labor of love this for the orthodox Mullā. But in this assignment there may well shine through a glint of imperial humor on the Great Mughal's part, who was once moved to observe,

We thought that so and so [i.e., Badāōnī] was an unworldly individual of Ṣūfī tendencies, but he seems to be such a bigoted lawyer that no sword can sever the jugular vein of his bigotry.[42]

Badāōnī finds occasion for piety, though: "But such is my fate, to be employed on such works. Nevertheless, I console myself with the reflection, that what is predestined must come to pass."

The second set of modern attempts to give a complete translation of *The Mahābhārata* came, and are still coming, from Bengal. One ventures to think, but cannot be certain, that this continual concern finds its source in a Bengali cosmopolitanism that likes to share its heritage with the rest of the world. Thus, one complete translation was published from Calcutta (eleven volumes, 1883–96) under the name of P. C. Roy, but in fact executed by Kesari Mohan Ganguli. This translation was not well received, either in India or the West.[43] Indeed, the English is grating and refractory in the extreme, and does not allow comfortable reading even to one used to Victorian English applied by the Indian provinces to the rendering of Sanskrit classics.

41. 'Abdu-' 1 Qādir bin Māluk Shāh al-Badāōnī, *Muntakhab-ut-Tawārīkh*, vol. 2. *Bibliotheca Indica*, translated by W. H. Lowe, 329 ff.

42. Ib., vol. 3, translated by Sir Wolsely Haig, 413.

43. In India, see, e.g., the newspaper *The Hindu*, Madras, 22 November 1885; in the West, see, e.g., Barth, *Journal Asiatique* 6 (10th series): 367 ff.

The apparatus is minimal to the point of nonexistence, and the reader who tries to wind his way through *The Mahābhārata* finds not even a table of contents to guide him. Still, in spite of the strictures one might level at it, the translation (since reprinted, 1952–62, by the Oriental Publishing Company, 11 D Arpuli Lane, Calcutta 12) was by no means a careless job. The reader who patiently compares it with the vulgate text commented upon by the seventeenth-century scholar Nīlakaṇṭha may protest many renderings, but still recognize that the attempt was a scholarly one. I have of course consulted it often.

Another Bengali scholar, Manmatha N. Dutt, worked on a fresh translation from 1895 till 1905. And at present a Bengali poet and *littérateur*, P. Lal, is publishing regular fascicles or installments of a poetized rendering of the text, which so far seems to have reached *Mahābhārata 3*.

In Europe, two attempts at mastering the mountainous bulk of our epic have been undertaken so far. There is the translation by Hippolyte Fauche in French (Paris, ten volumes, 1863–70), which was disrupted in the Eighth Book by the translator's death. While at times careless, it is far more readable than the Indian translations, not the least enlivened by the author's introductions of each volume to his staunch subscriber-readers whom he exhorts to stay with him. Finally, the Academy of Leningrad is in the process of bringing out a popular translation of the entire epic done or supervised by V. I. Kalyanov. So far have appeared *Mahabharata, Adiparva* (i.e., *MBh.* 1, *The Book of the Beginning*) Moscow-Leningrad: Academii Nauk, 1950; *Mahabharata, Sabhaparva* (i.e., *MBh.* 2, *The Book of the Assembly Hall*) (ib., 1962), and *Mahabharata, Virataparva* (i.e., *MBh.* 4, *The Book of Virāṭa*) (ib., 1967), A notice in the preface to the last volume stated that *The Book of the Forest*, which precedes *Virāṭa*, had at that date been half completed; it has not yet, to my knowledge, appeared.

Although I have no Russian, I was able to go through most of the translation with the help of Professor Emeritus George V. Bobrinskoy, my senior colleague at the University of Chicago. While there are occasional lapses, and the Indian commentators are too religiously followed, the translation is carefully done. It is devoutly to be hoped that Kalyanov and his colleagues will continue and complete their good work.

It is obvious, in view of the both illustrious and checkered history of earlier translations, that mine is being offered with great diffidence. Considering the vast scope of the epic, I am fully aware that I too may have lapsed occasionally and colossally. What I have tried to do is to give as fair and responsive an English translation as is within my ability and thus to open up the vast literature of *The Mahābhārata* to anyone interested in India, in the widest sense, who has neither the skill nor the leisure to go directly to the Sanskrit. It is therefore my purpose to make the text as accessible as I can make it.

In all candor, the great epic is close to unmanageable. As my colleague Murray B. Emeneau once muttered in looking up something in my translation, "In any shape and form *The Mahābhārata* is intractable!" In any case I have since tried to make it a little more tractable by the devices described below under Apparatus. I have worked under the assumption that the Apparatus is as much a part of the translation as the rendering itself, and for some of my colleagues possibly more helpful.

In rendering the Sanskrit I have tried to retain the narrative flow of the original in English, following the lead of the text in embellishing the text here more than there. From the outset the reader must be aware that the translation deviates from the original in two important respects: first, the original is almost entirely in verse, and the translation mostly in prose; second, the original was meant to be listened to, and the translation inevitably intended to be read.

Unlike the Homeric epics, *The Mahābhārata* employs a variety of meters, but by far the commonest used is the *śloka*. This meter presents a very free pattern well suited to narratives. Like all Sanskrit meters, it is divided into two halves, each half containing in its case sixteen syllables, while each half divides into two quarters (*pādas*) of eight syllables each. The first four syllables of each eight are free, the second four parsed. The scheme by and large is like this.

× × × × ⏑ – – ⏓ ′ × × × × ⏑ – ⏑ ⏓ /
× × × × ⏑ – – ⏓ ′ × × × × ⏑ – ⏑ ⏓ //

As in the Classical meters, the variation of short and long syllables provides the scheme. An example of the *śloka* meter is the first verse of the epic:

Nārāyaṇaṃ namaskṛtya Naraṃ caiva narottamam/.
Devīṃ Sarasvatīṃ caiva tato Jayam udīrayet//

This meter renders quite effortlessly into prose, but, in a way, a predictable prose. Normally, the length of a statement runs the length of a *śloka* of 32 syllables. This effect is unavoidably duplicated in the English, so that sentences have a way of being of equal length. While I have tried my best to bring as much variety into sentence length as consistent with both Sanskrit and English, a certain syntactic monotony was hard to avoid.

There are occasions, however, when the texts resorts to more complicated prosody for stylistic reasons. Most frequent among other meters is the *triṣṭubh*, with four quarters of eleven syllables each, usually:

⏓ – ⏑ – – ⏑ ⏑ – ⏑ – ⏑
⏓ – ⏑ – – ⏑ ⏑ – ⏑ – ⏑ /
⏓ – ⏑ – – ⏑ ⏑ – ⏑ – ⏑
⏓ – ⏑ – – ⏑ ⏑ – ⏑ – ⏑ //

For example:

āsāṃ prajānāṃ paripālanena
svaṃ kṣatradharmaṃ paripālayāmi/
prabrūhi vā kiṃ kriyatāṃ dvijendra
śuśrūṣur asmy adya vacas tvadīyam//

I have thought that this prosodic variation ought to show through in the translation. First of all, it is interesting to note what kinds of statements were felt to deserve more than common treatment; but also I have come to believe that at least one, if not several, treatments of *Mahābhārata* matter in *triṣṭubh* have been absorbed into the *śloka* version. There may be an occasion to elaborate on this point elsewhere.[44] In any case, I have indicated this meter oftentimes by resorting to an easy versification in English of four lines with four rises each. While I hope that the interspersed metrical segments are a pleasant variation for the reader, they were in essence inspired by the original.

My second deviation from the text is that while the original was meant to be heard recited, the translation is intended for reading. A narrative that is designed to be listened to has two bodies, the reciter and the listener, and what goes on between the two, mostly the recital. Recitation—in our present experience mostly theatrical pieces—has quite different characteristics from a text meant to be read. For one thing, the pace is far more leisurely. If the reciter is simultaneously improvising his verse—not all that great an achievement once one knows a story well and the metrical patterns are easy—he will need almost automatic breaks of received sentence portions that will fit comfortably into the meter to cast ahead mentally to the more operative part of the narrative. Received sentence portions may be of various kinds: "A had said this, and thereupon B said that"; epithets, or all-purpose adjectival qualifications; vocatives of the person addressed in all his various appellations. A rendering of these in prose inevitably distorts their original function. While they were meant to give the reciter a kind of mental breath to cast his mind forward, and the listener pause to assuage his attention, in a read version they are fortuitous stops, hampering rather than helping comprehension.

44. After writing this I learned that Mary Carroll Smith, a student of Daniel H. H. Ingalls at Harvard University, had been struck by the same idea and is devoting a dissertation to the question, entitled "The Core of the Great Epic of India" (thesis, Harvard, 1972).

Succeeding recited couplets will restate the same subject by name (or by other names he may carry), where the eye-reader is helped by a resuming "he." Verse syntax in Sanskrit is quite free, and an easy-on-the-ear-and-attention adjective qualifying a subject at the beginning may comfortably appear at the end of the couplet. The English translation had no choice but to mass such adjectives together.

Such problems are unavoidable by the very nature of the original and the translation, and should be taken for granted as matters of fact and of course. But there are more subtle pitfalls that bear mentioning. A recited text has a reciter standing there who knows what is going on. While the actual language may not betray it, the reciter knows the tone of it. A wink, a gesture, an irony of enunciation on his part may convey to the listener a specific meaning closed to the reader. Recitals were dramatic performances. The same lines might have been read in a tone heavily sarcastic, or pathetic. What might have been meant to be reservedly romantic may well come out drippingly sentimental. A dispute where opposing views are stated with powerful language might well be a routine exercise in rhetoric: if a less powerful man, the orator may be speaking more bindingly, while the real authority presents his definitive opinion in an understated or unemphatic line.

Here sides have to be taken. Tone, and, most bewildering, humorous tone, depends on the listener's understanding of the speaker's intention. I am quite prepared to accept being shown that on occasion I have mistaken irony for hyperbole, insult for praise, and a no for a yes. Here we are in treacherous quicksand; and if the translator is trapped it is he who is the traitor.

I am not sure what to do about the problem of tone, except to hope that over the years I have developed a bit of an ear. But there is another problem I feel more confident about. Every translator is tempted to give appropriate renderings of a guest term—a word in the original—with a host term, a word in his translation. When either by space or time, or both, the languages and the cultures they give voice to are far apart, there are but few choices: translate the term anyhow, or leave it untranslated—letting it stand in the uncomprehended original form as the name of a name. The latter course is more suitable to a philological translation whose readers already know the scope of the original word. In a more general translation the translator has basically two options: to adjust the Sanskrit guest term to the demands of the English host sentence, bending it thus to another universe of discourse; or to decide on a reasonable approximation, but of course not a perfect equivalent, in the host language, and to go ahead and use the approximation throughout.

I have taken the latter course in a great many instances where I felt that the integrity of the original word and concept should shine through clearly if boldly. This translation has not been made primarily for Sanskritists, to whom the general meaning of a term would be clear enough. The reader who is not a linguist should have a measure of trust in the translation and its consistent use of approximate equivalents. For example, if a social historian wishes to study the range of the word *dharma*—and there is hardly a concept more fundamental to the epic than that of *dharma*—he should be enabled to recognize the original word behind the secondhand at all times.

Choices here are debatable. For *dharma* my choice has been a capitalized "Law," in the hope of evoking other instances like Judaic "Law," not only because "Law" is approximate in its evocative connotations, but also because in practice it allows for syntactic variations: according to Law, by, under, for the sake of, in behalf of, with Law; and law-minded, law-spirited, law-abiding, law-like and even lawly—the last on the analogy of lovely. Obviously, therefore, the word *Law* will occur in odd and unidiomatic contexts. But what is the alternative rendering? One might adapt ancient Indian *Law* to English context and freely dispense such meanings as "order," "justice," "morality," "righteousness," "virtue," "custom," "ritual," and so on. In that case a social historian, or a historian of religion, would lose complete track of the real scope of the concept of *dharma* because of my very helpfulness in providing Christian-European paraphrases.

I am very much aware of the danger that such literalism might result in a quasi-translation. But until we come to the more technically philosophical portions of *The Bhagavadgītā* and *The Mokṣadharma*, it will be confined to a dozen or so terms. Terms for social ranks, *brāhmaṇa*, *kṣatriya*, *vaiśya*, and *śūdra*, have been rendered by the Anglicized "brahmin," and "baron," "commoner," and "serf," respectively. For *kṣatriya* the rendering "baron" was chosen, not only because in its medieval sense it is an acceptable translation, but also because it permits further derivation: "baronage" (*kṣatra*), "baronial" (*kṣatriya*), "baroness" (*kṣatriyā*). Other such renderings are "austerities/asceticism" for *tapas*, "hermit" for *muni*, "seer" for *ṛṣi*. Other words I had to give up on, like *tejas* (usually "splendor"), which in the various speakers' idioms in the *Mahābhārata* shifts widely in context.

There were of course terms that allowed of no translation and were retained in the original Sanskrit, e.g., words from liturgy, like *sadas*, a technical name for a particular area at a sacrifical site, *sadasya*, *brahmán*, *adhvaryu*, names of priests. A different problem was posed by proper names. It was tempting to replace all of the various appellations of a single individual by his most usual one. But the variations do add diversity to the text, and for all I know, a consistent inquiry into the collocation of certain of these appellations may shed light on the provenance of the stories in which they occur.

Apparatus

To facilitate the use of the translation, a number of devices have been employed, the more important ones of them being the divisions of the text into smaller parts.

The traditional division is by Book, Chapter, and Verse. A *Book* here is one of the eighteen *Books* (*parvan*) into which *The Mahābhārata* is primarily divided. A *Chapter (adhyāya)* is a subsection of a Book; a *Verse* (*śloka*) the couplet in such a *Chapter*. This is our basic notation: *MBh.* 1.2.3. refers to the third couplet of the second chapter of the first book.

There is another traditional division that divides the text into one hundred parts, counting many of the component stories. This is a useful division and has been adopted. If we call the *Eighteen Books* the *Major Books*, we may call the *One Hundred Books* the *Minor Books*. The location and sequence of such a Minor Book is indicated by the number of the Major Book in which it occurs, e.g., *MBh.* 1, with the number of the Minor Book in the sequence 1–100 given within parentheses. Thus *MBh.* 1(7) refers to the seventh Minor Book, *The Book of the Origins*, which happens to occur in *Mbh.* 1, *The Book of the Beginning*.

Minor Books can be quite long, and other narratives may be embedded in them. *MBh.* 1(7) has four such narratives; these episodes are indicated by (a), (b), etc., in order of sequence. *MBh.* 1(7.b) refers to *The Story of Śakuntalā*, the second (b) narrative in *The Book of the Origins* (7), in *MBh.* 1, *The Book of the Beginning*. At times the (a) class of episodes contains subsidiary stories, which are indicated by (i), (ii), etc. A glance at the Table of Contents of *The Book of the Beginning* will make the organization immediately clear.

The primary division of *Book*, *Chapter*, and *Verse* is noted in the translation as follows. A major *Book* will have its own title page. The beginning of a *Chapter* is indicated by a line space and the number in the margin. The first, fifth, tenth, fifteenth, etc., verses are indicated in the margin by, 1, 5, 10, 15, etc.

Of additional aid are the *Summaries*. A Major Book is in the translation preceded by its summary, which in that case is simply the table of its component Minor Books. A Minor Book is more fully summarized; but if it contains a subsidiary episode, this is simply noted by its title, and the episode itself summarized immediately preceding it. The *Summaries* show the numbers of the *Chapters* the text contains in the critical edition, with the corresponding number of the *Chapter* in the Bombay edition, and the number of the first *Verse* in the Calcutta edition (which happens not to note chapters). This last device allows the reader to use the translation while having at hand another edition or reading monographs based on this edition. The most precise determination of a passage in the *Summaries* is the parenthesized *Verse* number. The number referred to will be 1, 5, 10, 15, etc.; refinement beyond that seemed unnecessary. If the notation is (5), the incident may occur in any line or all lines of five through nine; if (10), in ten through 14, etc.

Finally the translation is annotated. There are two types of notes, footnotes and more detailed annotations at the end of the translation. The footnotes are no more than simple aids to the reading and serve in particular to identify proper names. For example, Guḍākeśa will be footnoted "= Arjuna" the first few times the name occurs. The final notes present further information on a possible question, elucidate what might be obscure in the body of the text, add philological asides where they are in order, and at times confessions of my own puzzlement.

The style of the notes and what to include in them proved to be a difficult problem: how far should the translator go in his explanations? There are points about which complete essays may be written, which of course was out of the question. On the other hand, repetition threatens continually. How often should the reader be reminded that the Rāma often in the company of Kṛṣṇa is his brother Balarāma, while the Rāma destroying barons is Paraśurāma? A partial answer to the latter question was to provide an alphabetical list of the principal characters in the main story, and genealogical charts. The real problem, of how far to go, could be solved (but not quite) only with a compromise. I have tried to give what I think is a helpful answer or the beginning of one to questions, hoping, but not very confidently, that this may satisfy the reader for the time being. It was obviously impossible to anticipate all the questions; it is also obvious that I myself am incompetent to answer all of them. For some then I will not have gone far enough, for others I will be painfully redundant; still others will find me oddly eclectic. I was greatly helped in composing the notes by a bibliography of over nine hundred titles compiled by my then student, now colleague, Donald Nelson; I should like to acknowledge my debt to him.

In order not to add still more to the markings of the text, the passages commented upon in the annotations are not especially indicated, but key words are repeated in the notes. The locus of the passage is identified by the verse number in the margin under which it occurs. If there are several notes on the same series of verses under that number, they are separated by two asterisks. To save the annoyance of vainly looking up nonexistent notes, I would suggest the reader quickly glance through the notes before reading a chapter.

I have thought it useful to include a concordance of the chapter numbers in the critical edition of the complete *Mahābhārata* with those of the Bombay edition, which is probably the most commonly used edition in the older literature. It was found impractical and unnecessary to extend the concordance to the other major editions, like the Calcutta edition. I have however shown the couplet numbers of the Calcutta edition as well as the chapter numbers of the Bombay edition against the critical edition figure at the beginning of the Summary of each chapter within the *Summaries* preceding each component Minor Book or Story.

An Index, of proper names only, concludes the whole book. For this the Index of the Kalyanov translation has been gratefully consulted.

The Spelling and Pronunciation of Sanskrit Letters and Words

The ancient Indian grammarians of the Sanskrit language have identified forty-eight sounds as worthy of notation, and in the script that was developed over the centuries each character represents that one sound unalterably. Hence there can be no confusion about how a particular word was pronounced, albeit true that different schools of Veda transmission show slight variations in the articulation; yet compared with the haphazard correspondence of Roman notation and English pronunciation, Sanskrit notation is extremely precise.

The sequence of the alphabet again was completely scientific. The order of letters is not the historical jumble of the Roman alphabet, which imitated the sequence of Semitic scripts, but simply the path of the breath through the hollow of the mouth from the throat to the lips, producing the vowels; through the nose, producing these vowels with nasalization; and the same breath with occlusion of the tongue to points in the hollow of the mouth from the throat to the lips, producing the consonants.

The Alphabet

a ā, i ī, u ū, ṛ ṝ, ḷ, e ai, o au
k kh g gh ṅ
c ch j jh ñ
ṭ ṭh ḍ ḍh ṇ
t th d dh n
p ph b bh m
y r l v
ś ṣ s
h
ṃ
ḥ

The Vowels

A vowel may be short or long. Length is indicated in roman transcription by a *macron*, a horizontal line over the vowel; except in the case of the *e* and *ai*, and the *o* and *au*, which are always long. The *ḷ* is only recorded as short.

The *a* is pronounced like the *u* in *but*. The *ā* as *a* in *father*, but with more length. The *i* as in *see*, *ī* as in *machine*. The *u* as *oo* in *pool*, the *ū* as *u* in *pull*, with more length. The *ṛ* is a vocalized *r*, as in *litter*, the *ṝ* the same lengthened, the *ḷ* as the second *l* in *little*. The *e* as in *train*, *ai* as in *aisle*, with strong *a* sound. The *o* as in *know*, *au* as in *house*, with strong *a* sound.

The Consonants

k kh g gh ṅ are velars or gutturals. The *k* is pronounced like *ck* as in *luck*, without aspiration; *kh* as *ck-h* in *blockhead*; *g* as in *go*; always hard; *gh* as *g-h* in *hoghead*; the *ṅ* is a guttural nasal, as the *ng* in *king* (since in the transcription of names this nasal occurs only before k, kh, g, and gh, it is left unmarked there).

c ch j jh ñ are palatals. The *c* is pronounced as *ch* as in *lurch*, unaspirated; *ch* as *ch h* in *pitch hook*; *j* as in *jay*; *jh* the preceding aspirated, a rare sound; *ñ* as *ny* in *canyon*.

ṭ ṭh ḍ ḍh ṇ are retroflexes, pronounced like *t*, etc. with the tip of the tongue touching the hard palate.

t th d dh n are dentals, pronounced like *t*, etc., with the tip of the tongue touching the ridge of the upper teeth. Note that *th* is never as *th* in *thin* or *this*, but as *t h* in *tent hook*.

p ph b bh m are labials, and correspond to the English, with the usual differentiation between aspirated and unaspirated articulations. Note that *ph* is never pronounced as *f*, but as *p h* in *uphill*.

y r l v are semivowels, but for purposes of transcription simply the corresponding consonants. The *y* is pronounced like *y* in *you*; *r* as in *row* but trilled; *l* as in *long*. The *v* is not pronounced as English *v*, but as *w* in *world*. Thus a better transcription of Veda would have been Weda.

ś ṣ s are the sibilants. The *ś* is pronounced as *sh* but with the tongue touching the soft palate; *ṣ* as *sh* with the tongue touching the hard palate; *s* as *ss* in *hiss*.

h is the aspiration, pronounced as the English *h*.

ṃ is a sign for a) a nasal and b) nasalization;

a) before *k*, etc. = *ṅ*; before *c*, etc. = *ñ*; before *ṭ*, etc. = *ṇ*; before *t*, etc. = *n*; before *p*; etc. = *m*.

b) before *y r l v*, *ś ṣ s*, and *h* = *ng*.

The Accentuation of Sanskrit Words

The rule of thumb is that Sanskrit words are accented in English like Greek and Latin words: stress the penultimate vowel, if that is long. Length is indicated either by a long vowel or a short (or long) vowel followed by more than one consonant, e.g., *rāma*, *raṅga*. If the penultimate syllable is short, stress the antepenultimate, whether it is long or short: *Mahābhārata*, *Arjuna* (the antepenultimates are long), and also *Aruṇa* (antepenultimate is short, as in *Herodotus*, *Thucydides*).

The real stumbling blocks in the transcription, which follows international convention, is that of the *c* and the *v*. The *c* is always *ch*, never *k*; the *v* is always *w*, never *v*.

The Mahābhārata Summary

1. The Book of the Beginning (1–225)
2. The Book of the Assembly Hall (1–72)
3. The Book of the Forest (1–298)
4. The Book of Virāṭa (1–67)
5. The Book of the Effort (1–197)
6. The Book of Bhīṣma (1–117)
7. The Book of Droṇa (1–173)
8. The Book of Karṇa (1–69)
9. The Book of Śalya (1–64)
10. The Book of the Sleeping Warriors (1–18)
11. The Book of the Women (1–27)
12. The Book of the Peace (1–353)
13. The Book of the Instructions (1–154)
14. The Book of the Horse Sacrifice (1–96)
15. The Book of the Hermitage (1–47)
16. The Book of the Clubs (1–8)
17. The Book of the Great Journey (1–3)
18. The Book of the Ascent to Heaven (1–5)

The Mahābhārata

Translated

Book 1 *The Book of the Beginning*

Introduction

The first of the eighteen Major Books of *The Mahābhārata* illustrates to perfection all the issues that the text as a whole raises. Parts of it are manifestly components of the main story; others are equally obviously accretions that have no organic relationship to the story whatever; still others are difficult to determine one way or the other.

The book itself takes cognizance of the fact that it may well contain unnecessary episodes: "There are brahmins who learn *The Bhārata* from Manu onward, others again from the tale of *The Book of Āstīka* onward, others again from the tale of Uparicara onward."[1] When we look at the main story, it is reasonably clear that originally it could hardly have begun before 1.90, and all that went before, roughly half the entire book, was added at a later time. In the latter half, too, quite a few additions are evident: the narratives of 1(11), *The Book of Citraratha*, have nothing to do with the story; *The Story of the Five Indras* in 1(12) is a justification of the polyandrous marriage of the five Pāṇḍava brothers; *Arjuna's Sojourn in the Forest*, a clear premonition of the twelve-year exile of the Pāṇḍavas, and therefore presupposing it, can hardly be original; nor is *The Story of the Śārngaka Birds* in 1(19).

Let us discuss these accretions, these exterior portions, first before we turn to the implications for the whole epic of what appears to be the central story of *The Book of the Beginning*. For to call them "exterior" is not to dismiss them; it does not dispense with the task of seeking out why these portions were added.

1. *MBh.* 1.1.50.

Setting the Place

The first two of the Minor Books are precisely what they call themselves: *Lists of Contents* and *Summaries*, obviously composed after *The Mahābhārata* as a whole had been constituted, more or less in its present form. Considerable interest therefore attaches to the counts of verses that are given in the *Summaries*, and they have excited lively discussion.[2] Too lively perhaps, for here, too, the best explanation is the simplest one. Manuscript copying is a business in India even today; and, since the dimensions of the leaves are so variable, the easiest way of computing labor costs was, and is, to count the actual syllables transcribed; and since the bulk of transcribed material is in *ślokas*, the tedious process of counting every syllable was abbreviated by counting them by the number they have in *ślokas*, namely thirty-two, usually called a *grantha*. Give or take a few, the set number of granthas counted was the basic price for the transcription, and it was found expedient to enter the price, so to say, into the body of the text itself, so that it could not be quarreled with. The counts therefore seem to hold little authority, for the manuscript from which they were computed, however honestly, would have been as omissive or permissive as any other.

Far more interesting is the third Minor Book, *Pauṣya*. It is one of the few portions of *The Mahābhārata* that is composed in prose, and its placement right at the beginning is intriguing. The rambling narrative, clearly deriving from some old Vedic brahmin lore, is, in the main, meant to introduce us to King Janamejaya, a descendant of the heroes of the epic. The reference is authentic, for the names of the king's brothers are quoted as they are in the far older *Śatapatha brāhmaṇa*.[3] It is to this king that the brahmin Utanka protests the way he was maltreated by the Snake Takṣaka; he exhorts Janamejaya to avenge him, as well the assassination of Janamejaya's father Parikṣit by the same snake.

In the fourth Minor Book, *The Book of Puloman*, the story seems to start all over again: once more the Bard Ugraśravas arrives in the Naimiṣa Forest and finds the Bhṛgu brahmin Śaunaka who with his colleagues is engaged in a Sacrificial Session that is to take all of twelve years. Once more there is a Vedic reference to this event; the *Pañcaviṃśa brāhmaṇa*[4] reports on such a session in the Naimiṣa Forest, and the report is made credible by the additional mention that it was never completed. I consider it likely that in this initial setting of

2. V. S. Sukthankar, "Epic Questions, II the Parvasaṃgraha Figures," *ABORI* 23; 549 ff.; D. D. Kosambi, "The Parvasaṃgraha of the Mahābhārata," *JAOS* 66 (1946); E. D. Kulkarni, "The Parvasaṃgraha Figures," *JAOS* 66 (1946); M. V. Vaidya, "The Extent of the Mahābhārata," *Festschrift Karmarkar*, pp. 77 ff.

3. *Śatapatha Brāhmaṇa* 13.5.4.1.

4. *Pañcaviṃsa Brāhmaṇa* 25.6.

a twelve-year session the memory of such a grandiose, though abortive, enterprise survives.

There is even more: scholars like Sukthankar and Vaidya[5] have pointed out the significance of the fact that Śaunaka is a member of the Bhṛgu clan, and have argued that our present text shows many traces of "Bhṛgu" influence, not hesitating to speak of the Bhṛguization of the original. However that may be, it is noteworthy that right at the beginning of the text a report is found that the retelling of the Bhārata story was carried out with who knows what collaboration from the brahmins present. The story we are told was the story narrated in priestly surroundings. It was reported by Ugraśravas as he remembered it told by Vaiśaṃpāyana at the Snake Sacrifice of King Janamejaya. What we have is what was told in the Naimiṣa Forest.

Being a Bhṛgu, Śaunaka typically asks for a narrative of the origins of the Bhṛgus, and this includes the curious tale of the sacrificial Fire being cursed to become omnivorous; the charming story of Ruru who sacrifices half his life to revive his bride, who had died of snakebite, and Ruru's consequent hatred of snakes: the ultimate message of *The Book of Pauṣya*. So, in the end, *The Book of Puloman* returns to the theme of Janamejaya, who is said to have held a Snake Sacrifice.

In my view, the inclusion of these stories was at least partly motivated by a desire, first, to set the place of the last recitation of *The Mahābhārata*, and, second, to set the place of the previous recitation at the Snake Sacrifice of Janamejaya from which the Naimiṣa account expressly derived. It is now time to establish the authenticity of the original setting. This is done in *The Book of Āstīka*. Whatever else it does, in the large cadre of the "descent" of the epic the entire long *Book of Āstīka* serves to establish that a Snake Sacrifice was in fact held by King Janamejaya, a descendant of the Pāṇḍava heroes, and this fact is important *only* insofar as at that ritual the Bhārata saga was recited by Vaiśaṃpāyana in the presence of the original author, Kṛṣṇa Dvaipāyana.

Nevertheless, *Āstīka* has become an extremely interesting narrative. It takes the beginnings of Janamejaya's ritual killings of snakes close to the beginning of creation, when two sisters, both mothers of egg-laying races, mother Kadrū of snakes, mother Vinatā of birds, lay a wager on the color of the archetypal horse Uccaiḥśravas, which had appeared on the horizon. This stallion's appearance leads to the story of how it originated, and so to the narrative of the Gods and Anti-Gods, who churned the ocean for the Elixir of Immortality; a by-product of their labor was that Horse of Mighty Sound. Returning to the wager, Kadrū commands the snakes (her sons) to insert

5. V. S. Sukthankar, "The Bhrgus and the Bharāta: a text historical study," *ABORI* 18: 1 ff.

themselves into the tail of the horse, and thus to blacken it (cobras, for that is what the snakes are supposed to be, are considered to be black). The snakes refuse, a terrible curse is put on them, yet they do their mother's bidding; the wager is won, and Vinatā is reduced to slavery. But Vinatā had had a son, the bird Garuḍa, whose hatred for the snakes is proverbial. And so, in the end, *The Book of Āstīka* not only authenticates Janamejaya's sacrifice as the setting of Vaiśaṃpāyana's recitation of the epic; it also reconfirms the evil of the snakes. This pouring on of hatred for the snakes through *Pauṣya, Puloman,* and *Āstīka* is extremely effective in helping us to accept the historical reality of Janamejaya's Snake Sacrifice; and effective it had to be made, for to the ancient Indians, among whom the non-Aryans must be counted, such a sacrifice must have been an abomination.

The Beginning of the Beginning

The place has been set, and the fact of Janamejaya's Snake Sacrifice and its causes have been established. The next Minor Book, *The Descent of the First Generations,* can now open with the question of what kind of stories were told during the ritual: The answer is that "in the pauses between the rites the brahmins told tales that rested on the *Veda*; but Vyāsa told the wondrous epic, the grand *Bhārata.*"[6] This Kṛṣṇa Dvaipāyana Vyāsa visits King Janamejaya at his religious site in the company of his pupils. The king asks him to relate the *Breach* between the cousins. Vyāsa turns to his student Vaiśaṃpāyana, who then begins the recitation.

As so frequently in the epic, the story is preceded by a summary. At Janamejaya's bidding the bard then begins the story in earnest with the tale of King Uparicara, which at one time was one true "beginning" out of several.[7] *Uparicara* merely serves to introduce the miraculous birth of Satyavatī, matriarch of the Kauravas, her encounter with Parāśara, and the subsequent birth of Kṛṣṇa Dvaipāyana. This inspires the narration of more miraculous births, which in turn leads to a wholesale catalogue of miracles, introduced by the tyrannization of Earth by the Asuras, or Anti-Gods. To relieve Earth of her burden, Brahmā asks the Gods to incarnate themselves with a part of their being.

This starts *The Book of the Origins,* which, as a glance at the Table of Contents shows, is quite complex. *The Origins* contains, first of all, the origins of the Gods and Demons and continues with those of the seers, among whom the Bhṛgu dynasty, as usual, predominates.

6. *MBh.* 1.53.32.
7. *MBh.* 1.1.50.

Then follows the *Partial Incarnations* of Gods and Demons, who become kings and princes on earth, many of whom will eventually participate in the Bhārata war.

But who were the Bhāratas? *The Story of Śakuntalā* gives the answer: descendants from the Bharata born by Śakuntalā to King Duḥṣanta, the "ill-tamed one," himself dynastically a Paurava. Considerable interest attaches to the *Śakuntalā*, if only for the freedom of women that it illustrates. This story has been sublimated, and its tone and thrust completely reversed, by Kālidāsa in his famous play *Abhijñānaśakuntala*, which Indian tradition considers the greatest single work of art in the history of Sanskrit literature.

Duḥṣanta, and thus Bharata, was a Paurava; and this occasions a question on the part of King Janamejaya about the origin of the dynasty, which began with Pūru, a son of King Yayāti. No less than two stories can suffice to do justice to this most remarkable personality, Yayāti—*The Story of Yayāti* and *The Latter Days of Yayāti*. The first one takes us back to yet another hoary account of the struggle over the Elixir of Immortality between the Gods and the Asuras. Kaca, an emissary of the Gods, tricks the teacher of the Asuras out of the secret by inspiring the infatuation of his daughter Devayānī, who has complete command of the affections of her father. Spurned by the trickster, she marries King Yayāti, who, in the end, is less faithful than his authoritarian wife confidently expects. Yayāti subjects his sons, by his queen and his concubine, to a severe trial; out of which his youngest son by his concubine, named Pūru (we see that the theme of the "disqualified eldest" is by no means limited to the Kauravas), emerges the victorious heir. *The Story of Yayāti* is almost entirely told in dialogue, so vividly that it can practically be divided into acts; it is easy to see how Sanskrit theater could have developed out of such dramatic bardic dialogues.

All this experience does not exhaust Yayāti's capacity for it; his life continues after his dilatory death, when his arrogance in heaven causes him to return to earth again in *The Latter Days of Yayāti*, in what assuredly is the oldest narrative account of the actual circumstances of transmigration, clearly linked with Upaniṣadic accounts of the theory of transmigration.[8] It has nothing to do, however remotely, with *The Origins*, of which the story forms part; but it is delightful that it has survived as a kind of appendix.

At this point, *The Book of the Origins* begins once more with the dynasty from Pūru down, including the incidents in the life of King Saṃvaraṇa and his bride Tapatī, which brings Vasiṣṭha, a famous Vedic seer, into the history of the dynasty; of him we shall hear more.

8. J. A. B. van Buitenen, "Some Notes on the Uttara-yāyāta," *Festschrift Raghavan*, Adyar Library Bull. 31–32 (1967–68): 617 ff.

And then *The Origins* begins a second time with a prose chronicle that has scarcely more than nodding acquaintance with the previous one. At last *The Origins* setttles down to the narrative of the more directly relevant beginnings of the conflict of *The Mahābhārata* with the narration of the birth of Bhīṣma, from whose fateful self-abnegation the events of the epic follow.

While it is easy, and indeed natural, to be skeptical of the authenticity of many of the beginnings of the true beginning, the fact that they are there carries its own relevance. At an early enough date *The Mahābhārata* was conceived as standing close to the beginning of national history, so that it was only appropriate to include right at *its* beginning all kinds of still earlier matter. Thus *The Mahābhārata* became the central storehouse of Brahminic-Hindū lore; it could only have done so if it were widely considered to be what the editors of the critical edition of the text proudly proclaim it is: "The National Epic of India."

The Beginning

The remaining part of *The Book of the Origins* takes us from the reign of King Śaṃtanu, and his son Bhīṣma's birth, down to the apprentice years of the Pāṇḍavas and Kauravas. The epic tone is very much in evidence in the vicissitudes of Bhīṣma; his vow; and his abduction, on his half-brother's behalf, of the Kāśi princesses Ambā, Ambikā, and Ambālikā. The enemies he makes are no less epic: King Śālva, who had been chosen as bridegroom by Princess Ambā; and Ambā herself who, having been released by Bhīṣma but then rejected by Śālva, will eventually reappear in a tragic story.[9]

When Vicitravīrya, for whom the damsels were abducted, dies childless, Mother Satyavatī seeks to persuade Bhīṣma to beget sons on his widows; Bhīṣma refuses, while upholding the rightness of the injunction itself. Then the matriarch reveals that she had a premarital son, Kṛṣṇa Dvaipāyana; the latter agrees to do the service, and begets the blind Dhṛtarāṣṭra, the (probably leukodermic) Prince Pāṇḍu whose name means "pallid," and the bastard Vidura. During Bhīṣma's regency the kingdom prospers. The regent finds wives for Dhṛtarāṣṭra and Pāṇḍu. Pāṇḍu's senior wife is Kuntī, an aunt of Kṛṣṇa Vāsudeva; she had had a premarital son Karṇa by the sun.

Pāṇḍu goes on an expedition of conquest, and returns laden with booty. For reasons unexplained, Pāṇḍu decides to devote his life to hunting in the forest. With great difficulty a hundred sons are born to Dhṛtarāṣṭra, of whom Duryodhana is the eldest; but Kuntī gave birth to Yudhiṣṭhira before that, also not without difficulty. Pāṇḍu had shot a buck while it was mating with a doe; the buck was a disguised seer,

9. *MBh.* 5.170 ff.

who cursed Pāṇḍu that he would die under similar circumstances. Henceforth Pāṇḍu remains continent, but has Kuntī bear children by various Gods: Yudhiṣṭhira by Dharma, Bhīma by the Wind God, Arjuna by Indra; his other wife Mādrī bears twins by the Aśvins. After his curse Pāṇḍu resigns the kingdom to the regency of Dhṛtarāṣṭra, and becomes a hermit. One day he forgets himself with Mādrī and succumbs. Mādrī follows him into death. Fellow-recluses take the Pāṇḍavas and Kuntī to the Kaurava court at Hāstinapura where they are warmly received and grow up.

Bhīma proves to be a bully, and Duryodhana reacts with assassination attempts in order to win the kingdom. Bhīṣma judges it is time for the boisterous princes to be educated and engages a teacher Kṛpa. Soon another brahmin, Droṇa, appears on the scene, impresses the princes with his marksmanship, and wins a position as a teacher, Arjuna becomes Droṇa's favorite.

The Book of the Fire in the Lacquer House starts off with a trial tournament, in which Droṇa's pupils display their fighting skills. Bhīma is locked in a wrestling battle with Duryodhana, until Droṇa orders them separated; Arjuna dazzles the audience with his brilliance at war games. Suddenly a stranger presents himself, Karṇa, the unknown half-brother, who challenges Arjuna to a duel. When he cannot present proper aristocratic credentials, he is laughed out of court. But Duryodhana quickly bestows a principality on him (with what right is not clear; this episode is quite unbelievable, and "fuzzy"). The duel proceeds and ends undecided. But Karṇa is now the implacable enemy of the Pāṇḍavas and the ally of the Kauravas.

Duryodhana continues his plotting and persuades Dhṛtarāṣṭra to send the Pāṇḍavas into quasi-exile in a provincial town.[10] He lodges them in a house he had built to burn, but this is found out; and the five brothers and their mother make good their escape, disappearing incognito into the forest.

There follows now a succession of tales of adventures in the forest: a demon Hiḍimba is slain by Bhīma, who marries his sister. He sets a brahmin free from the awful obligation to feed himself to the Demon Baka by killing the fiend. Finally they hear that Drupada, king of Pāñcāla, is holding a tournament for the hand of Kṛṣṇā Draupadī, his daughter. Kṛṣṇa Dvaipāyana, their grandfather, appears and advises them to join the tournament. In *The Book of Citraratha* they trespass at night on the playing ground of a Gandharva on the bank of the Ganges. Arjuna bests him, but spares his life. The grateful Gandharva addresses him as Tāpatya—which occasions the story of the ancestress Tapatī, whose marriage to the Kuru Saṃvaraṇa had earlier been mentioned in *The Origins*. Since the seer Vasiṣṭha is involved in the matchmaking, *The Story of Tapatī* leads to *The Story of*

10. Vāraṇāvata, present Barnāwā, Meerut District.

Vasiṣṭha and his battle with Viśvāmitra; this story includes the tale of his irascible grandson Aurva.

The Pāṇḍavas emerge disguised as young brahmins at the court of Drupada in *The Book of Draupadī's Bridegroom Choice.* All kings fail at the feat demanded, but Arjuna succeeds. Draupadī follows him home. Kuntī, their mother, had been superbly unaware that her sons were off tourneying; she was under the impression that they had gone begging. Arjuna, coming home with Draupadī, triumphantly shouts: "Look what we found!" Kuntī, without looking up, replies, "Now you share that together!" And so it befell that the five brothers shared the same wife. Drupada is aghast, but is persuaded by Kṛṣṇa Dvaipāyana that it had been so ordained in *The Story of the Five Indras.* The marriage is celebrated in *The Book of the Wedding.*

The strength and importance of the alliance between Pāṇḍavas and Pāñcālas gives second and third thoughts to the Hāstinapura Kauravas. One party favors preemptive warfare but is overruled by saner minds who want to try partition first. Thus Vidura is sent as envoy, and on their conciliatory return to the capital of the Land of the Kurus, the Pāṇḍavas accept the Khāṇḍava Tract on the river Yamunā, in *The Acquisition of the Kingdom.* They settle down, are lectured by the divine messenger Nārada on the perils of brothers loving the same woman (*Sunda and Upasunda*), and make a compact that anyone interrupting a brother with Draupadī shall forthwith exile himself to the forest. Promptly an occasion presents itself for Arjuna to do so, when he has to go in aid of a brahmin whose cattle has been stolen—the late juncture is obvious. In spite of Yudhiṣṭhira's pleas, Arjuna absents himself at once, has lovely amorous adventures, and ends up abducting Subhadrā, Kṛṣṇa Vāsudeva's sister and a princess of the Vṛṣṇis, in *The Abduction of Subhadrā.* Feeling insulted at first, the wild warriors are talked out of retribution by the wily Kṛṣṇa, who says that the alliance is an honorable one. He and his elder brother Baladeva, and the other Vṛṣṇi potentates, then bring a nuptial present in *The Fetching of the Gift.* After his fellow-tribesmen have departed, Kṛṣṇa Vāsudeva tarries, and, with Arjuna, is summoned to tender the entire Khāṇḍava Forest as food to the Fire God, *The Burning of the Khāṇḍava Forest.* This rather grisly venture is at the end relieved by the narrative of four exceedingly skeptical and precocious little birds, that prefer future danger to present disaster (the *Śārngakas*).

The Land of the Kurus

With all the familiar compass directions lacking in *The Mahābhārata* as a whole—no clear story, no clear date, no clear author, no clear beginning—one might well be excused for despairing at being totally lost, if one is at all attuned to the tangibilities of time and space. Are we in the never-never-land of *The Iliad* before Schliemann discovered layers upon layers of Troy? Assuredly not. Whatever else may be indefinite, the locale is still very much there.

The epic calls it, above all, Kurukṣetra, "Land of the Kurus," with *kṣetra*, "land," having the same intention of providing both a dwelling place *and* a place off which to live. It is the patrimony of the Kaurava dynasty, and has its capital seat in the city of Hāstinapura, in the hills that will gradually mount to the foothills of the Himālayan range. It is located on the upper Ganges River, and thus commands, at least for a stretch, the riverine traffic downstream. Their territory stretches west to the no less important river Yamunā, where they own the Khāṇḍava Tract, an uncultivated expanse of forested land. Their realm sits squarely astride the most obvious route for northwestern immigrants to take to the rice fields of Magadha.

In a way it is "high ground," and strategically important. But rivers do not respect high ground, and leave it immediately; once effective control of a river stretch ends, the southern neighbor is in full command. This complex geography of high ground and escaping rivers seems to dominate the complicated alliances that *The Book of the Beginning* presents.

Of first interest is the Kuru's neighbor down the Ganges, Drupada Yajñasena, king of Pāñcāla. He occurs first in one of those dramatic premonitions that subsequently are filled out as stories of their own. It all seems to start with an anecdote. As boys, Drupada, the later king, and Droṇa, the later teacher of the Kauravas, were schoolmates and friends. Upon his father Pṛṣata's death and his own ascension, Drupada disowns the friendship: "An old friend, who needs him?"—which hurts Droṇa to the quick.[11] So Droṇa is going to show who needs an old friend. After the successful matriculation of his pupils, Droṇa exacts his guru's fee: a guerrilla raid on Drupada's fastness of Ahicchattrā, southeast of Hāstinapura, but off the river now, not in command of it.[12] The raiders capture the town, or at least the person of King Drupada, and Droṇa has his revenge: he takes away the northern half of the kingdom, including Ahicchattrā, but leaves Drupada his seat of Kāmpilya, which controls the Ganges downstream from Hāstinapura.

This raid, if it occurred, would be deserving of a little lay all its own. That is what later scribes felt,[13] but our critical editor reduces

11. *MBh*. 1.122.

12. The easiest source of information on the identity of epic cities is B. B. Lal's book-length article. "Excavation at Hastināpura and other explorations in the Upper Gangā and Sutlej basins 1950–52,.." *Ancient India* 10–11 (1954–55). On Ahicchattrā in particular, A. Ghosh and K. C. Panigrahi "The Pottery of Ahicchattrā,"*Ancient India* 1 (1946).

13. The Vulgate offers an extended version in the dropped chapters, Bombay ed. 1.139–40.

the entire fable to less than twenty stanzas,[14] on excellent testimony. Droṇa, after all, is just an improverished teacher working hard to get a job at Bhīṣma's court,[15] not a prince sitting crowned at Ahicchattrā. It is much like Karṇa's being endowed by Duryodhana with the kingdom of Anga, just to be able to challenge Arjuna to a duel. And it seems like the same mirror effect; since one day Pāñcāla is going to challenge Hāstinapura when the Pāṇḍava-Kaurava battle breaks out, there should be a cause of it in this Book that insistently seeks to provide causes for causes. This Kaurava raid on Ahicchattrā (in which Arjuna as usual shines) does not prevent the Kaurava princes later from actively seeking the hand of Drupada's daughter. (Previous literature, incidentally, knows only of an *alliance* of Kurus and Pāñcālas[16]; as prudent policy on both sides, of high ground and low water, would indeed be sensible to dictate.)

While there can be no doubt that Kuru and Pāñcāla are old acquaintances, however they want to reaffirm their acquaintance for the nonce, the Vṛṣṇis are quite a different matter. They are sitting on the bank of the river Yamunā across the mesopotamia from the city of Kāmpilya. (Kāmpilya, to which the reigning Pāñcāla king Drupada has been reduced by the raid that took Ahicchattrā, lies on the right bank of the Ganges.) The interests of the Vṛṣṇi clan, tribe, or people, follow the river downstream into the land of Cedi, then past the confluence of the Ganges and the Yamunā, into the kingdom of Magadha. Śiśupāla, a Vṛṣṇi kinsman, is a general to the Magadhan king Jarāsaṃdha; he is the ruler of Cedi.[17]

It is worth noting that archeological evidence indicates that Ahicchattrā had been founded on the bank of the Ganges and lasted until the river changed course; and the epic expressly states that Kāmpilya was on the southern bank of the river, where its remains have been excavated. In other words, the capital seat of Pāñcāla was moved with the moving of the river; so Hāstinapura's extension of territorial control to Ahicchattrā was little more than the appropriation of a ghost town. The Pāñcālas moved back to the river that had left them temporarily and established their domain between the Ganges and the Yamunā.

Thus they bordered on the Vṛṣṇis, whose interests, we said, moved southeast down the southern bank of the river Yamunā. Still, they were hardly in a position to ignore the Pāñcāla hegemony across their river to the Ganges. It is not surprising, therefore, that the moment the claimants to the Hāstinapura throne, the Pāṇḍavas, effect a marriage

14. *MBh.* 1.123.
15. Cf. *MBh.* 1.122.
16. See Macdonell-Keith, *Vedic Index,* s.v. "Pañcāla" for references.
17. More on this in *The Book of the Assembly Hall* 2(22) = 2.18–22, *The Slaying of Śiśupāla.*

alliance with Pāñcāla, the two major Vṛṣṇi potentates, Baladeva and Kṛṣṇa, promptly appear on the scene, recognize them[18] (though they were still incognito) in every sense of the word, and follow up the newly struck friendship, consolidated by Arjuna's marriage to a Vṛṣṇi princess, with a lavish wedding gift.[19] The Vṛṣṇis in one sense were securing their left flank, and they lost no time in doing so.

The oval figure beginning at Hāstinapura, continued through Ahicchattrā and Kāmpilya, and reversed through Mathurā of the Vṛṣṇis, must, if it is to return to its source, once more intersect the river Yamunā. It is at this approximate spot that we find Indraprastha, the city founded by the Pāṇḍavas in the Khāṇḍava Tract given them by Hāstinapura after their alliance with Pāñcāla. It is surely Kuru country, but it is Vṛṣṇi riverside, and it is the Vṛṣṇi diplomat Kṛṣṇa who helps them to clear the area and establish themselves. A triangle of alliances has been forced by Kṛṣṇa, from Indraprastha to Mathurā to Kāmpilya, and the security of Mathurā is secured by the marriage bond of Indraprastha with Kāmpilya. In the process Kṛṣṇa has also wound up with the balance of power: if war is to break out, Indraprastha, Mathurā, and Kāmpilya can jointly converge on Hāstinapura; or Indraprastha on Hāstinapura, and Mathurā on Kāmpilya; and so on.

That Kṛṣṇa needed the alliance is made amply clear in *Mahābhārata 2, The Book of the Assembly*. The warriors–clan, tribe, or people—of Mathurā had suffered severe defeat at the hands of another party, the kingdom of Magadha, with the obvious help of Cedi. Since Cedi is declared a traitor, it seems reasonably clear that Śiśupāla of Cedi played a game of his own against his parent stock of Mathurā, but with clear designs on the inheritance of Magadha. The only way to undo this design, it transpires, is by assassinating the designer–which Kṛṣṇa does without a moment's hesitation.[20]

It is hard to tell what layers of historic lore have gone into this whole picture. But it is somewhat hard to ignore the basic outline of the picture. For epic Kurukṣetra, Land of the Kurus, is no Camelot; it is a geopolitical fulcrum. There obviously are pressures from the northwest as there are from the southeast. Archeology tends to support this.[21] The oval delineated by the major cities that find themselves embattled belonged to what appears to have been the same material culture. It has been authoritatively shown that the common denominator of the cities was the pottery, the horse, and the iron they shared. While it is sad to reflect that the identification of ancient cultures must depend on the sherds of the utensils used

18. *MBh.* 1.183.
19. 1(18) = 1.213, *The Fetching of the Gift.*
20. *MBh.* 2.18–22.
21. I refer to Lal's article quoted in n. 12.

for eating, there is no denying the rightness of it. It is clear now that the culture centrally depicted by *The Mahābhārata* used gray painted ware, found from about 1,000 B.C. (the carbon dating does allow variation) in all the major sites. There can be no reasonable doubt about the locations of Hāstinapura, of Indraprastha (Delhi's Purānā Qilā, the Ancient Fort, now pleasantly inhabited by a zoo), and of Mathurā, still on the Yamunā River, and still wholeheartedly, and lucratively, devoted to the worship of its once and always hero, Kṛṣṇa.[22]

Hāstinapura survived, though not as long as Indraprastha, where a continuous, archeologically documented series of levels takes it down even before the Pāṇḍavas; in this capital of the sovereign Republic of India, or rather, Bharat, named after our Bharata. Hāstinapura descended for quite a few generations in the Pāṇḍava family, until a change of the river Ganges—no longer, unsurprisingly, an alien protagonist in our story—washed part of it away and caused the capital to be changed to Kauśāmbī, by King Udayana, a contemporary of Buddha; by the two of whom hang two other stories.[23]

The Book of the Beginning and the Central Story

While much of the *Beginning* must be regarded as extraneous to the story, much again is essential to it. We noted the entanglements of the earlier generations that account for the obscurity of the succession rights of the Pāṇḍava generation. The childhood stories are surely romanticized, yet they set, from the beginning, the tone for the incompatibility of the two sets of cousins. The book as a whole is devoted to that early segment of the epic that is called the *Breach* (*bheda*). It has three principal moments: *The Fire in the Lacquer House*, *The Bridegroom Choice of Draupadī*, and *The Burning of the Khāṇḍava Forest*, two of which are essential to the central story. *The Lacquer House* illustrates the perfidy of Duryodhana, at whose instigation they are sent into semi-exile in the provincial town of Vāraṇāvata, and this dissension to all intents and purposes constitutes the *Breach*. The exile is authorized by Dhṛtarāṣṭra and tacitly allowed by Bhīṣma and the other elders. It is worth remembering that the Pāṇḍavas are still youths when exiled and have to travel in the company of their mother. There is an interesting parallellism between this first exile when the Pāṇḍavas travel with their mother and the second exile to the Forest when they travel with their wife. There is a similar parallel in that both exiles are followed by a period lived incognito.

22. Particularly at Brindavan (Vṛndāvana), the site of Kṛṣṇa's youth.
23. The first one being the Bṛhatkathā, the "Great Romance."

Their retreat to Vāraṇāvata had been preceded by their education that culminated in the weapon show. At this latter event we are first introduced in the flesh to the hero Karṇa, whose challenge of and engagement with Arjuna—it remains inconclusive—forebode a lifelong feud between the two warriors who are unaware that they are the sons of the same mother. Karṇa attaches himself to the Kauravas in a way comparable to the attachment of Kṛṣṇa Vāsudeva to the Pāṇḍavas.

The raid on Ahicchattrā of North Pāñcāla by the Pāṇḍavas and Kauravas by way of their teacher's fee to Droṇa does not organically belong to the central story. On the contrary, it seems contradictory, for at one point King Drupada, allegedly dethroned and driven across the river, will declare that he had always hoped to marry his daughter to the Pāṇḍavas—which seems out of character if he had been defeated at their hands.

The *Books of Hiḍimba, Baka, and Citraratha* are hardly part of the central story; still, they have an appropriateness about them, for they give *us* a sense of time of the duration of the Pāṇḍavas' exile and *them* time to grow from youths to young adults. It is as the latter that they appear at Drupada's court for the second of the three principal moments of *The Book of the Beginning. The Bridegroom Choice of Draupadī.* The alliance—the marriage of the Pāñcāla princess with the Pāṇḍava pretenders—is one of the salient events of the epic; the molestation to which the princess will eventually be subjected by the Kauravas will have its own awesome consequences. Crucial to the story also is the appearance of Kṛṣṇa Vāsudeva and his brother Balarāma, and the alliance of friendship that is instantly contracted by them and the Pāṇḍavas.

The strong ally with whom the Pāṇḍavas are suddenly blessed effects a partial conciliation, which leads to the partition of the kingdom and the gifting of the Khāṇḍava plateau to the princes. In order to found their own kingdom, the Pāṇḍavas need to clear the forest, which is done by fire in the form of the God of Fire. It is debatable how far this account of *The Burning of the Khāṇḍava Forest* belongs to the central story, but surely it is an ancient story, and part of the cycle of the heroes of the epic.

The Characters

We will not expect to find in the epic finely chiseled profiles of the heroes, but roughly hewn personalities who are subject to little change. Oldest of the living is Satyavatī, the daughter of the fishing chief, who became in many ways the progenitrix of the younger generations—by being the mother of both Kṛṣṇa Dvaipāyana and Vicitravīrya; on the widows of the latter the former begets Dhṛtaraṣṭra and Pāṇḍu. Her task in *The Book of the Beginning* is indeed to beget children, and the text repeatedly refers to her "hunger for offspring." Her son Kṛṣṇa Dvaipāyana is hardly visible, appearing mostly as a *deus ex machina* to keep the story moving—not inappropriately so for the man who is supposed to have written the story. Bhīṣma, on the other hand, looms large, a mighty warrior, a fair-minded regent, and in the end a stern patriarch, still the head of the dynasty. But he is impassive, ready with advice, and except for rare occasions not actively interfering with the younger generations. He does not stop his nephew Dhṛtarāṣṭra from sending the Pāṇḍava youths to Vāraṇāvata, although later he confesses to shame when the treachery of the *Lacquer House* has been perpetrated and the brothers are believed to have burned alive.

Dhṛtarāṣṭra, the elder son in the next generation, is a puzzling character, but that is perhaps because it is demanded that we have more sympathy for him than he deserves. He requires an Indian respect because he is the father; just as Bhīṣma demands our awe because he is a grandfather. Also, his blindness may elicit our compassion. Still, he lets himself be used by his son Duryodhana in the cause of his own offspring, not that of Pāṇḍu, although he had recognized the primogeniture of Yudhiṣṭhira. It is hard to believe that Dhṛtarāṣṭra had no inkling at all of Duryodhana's designs on the lives of his cousins, while his brother Vidura immediately guessed them. Dhṛtarāṣṭra is strictly on the Kauravas' side, and allows his "eye of insight" to wink on occasion.

Wholly different is Vidura, whose position in the household is an odd one. He might have had no standing at all, for he is no blood relation of the dynasty. When Ambikā was faced with the prospect of another night with Kṛṣṇa Dvaipāyana, she recoiled and sent, in her own stead, a serving girl. She served him well, and Kṛṣṇa bestowed on her the sole child of that generation without defects. Apparently, two substitutes produce an at least partially real child, for the ensuing Vidura, though a bastard, had good standing in the household. He commanded respect for his judicious intelligence and his advice was frequently sought, if rarely followed. In the family he is the typical benign Indian uncle, younger than the father and avuncularly disposed toward his nephews. In his case, he is partial to the Pāṇḍavas, whom he quietly protects from disaster. He pleads their cause and warns them in veiled language about the assassination plot hatched against them; when the Kauravas must reconcile the Pāṇḍavas after their reemergence, it is Vidura who is dispatched as envoy to the court of King Drupada.

Dhṛtarāṣṭra's sons are vile. It is Duryodhana's undying ambition to possess himself of the throne of Hāstinapura, by any means, but mostly foul. By and large he fulfils this ambition. Surely his character has been blackened even more in the course of time, but equally surely was he cast in the role of the villain from the beginning, treacherous and lawless, dark contrast to Yudhiṣṭhira.

This son of Pāṇḍu by Kuntī has been fathered by the God Law, Dharma, and his function is to represent Law. One of his constant names is King Dharma. He himself considers himself the representative of Law, and identifies with it to such an extent that he can exclaim quite spontaneously: "How can it fail to be the Law, if I do it?"[24] All his actions are dictated by Law, less dramatically so in *The Book of the Beginning* than in the later ones.

If Yudhiṣṭhira is brahminic—the king as the constant upholder of the good Law—his younger brother Bhīma is strictly baronial. He was fathered on Kuntī by the Wind God, and this wind is not a gentle evening breeze but the gales that precede and accompany the exploding monsoon. His favorite weapon is the club; but even more favored are his own arms—and the baron was created from the creator's arms—with which he wrestles his adversaries until he has literally broken their backs. But he has a surprisingly gentle side that is lacking in both his older and younger brothers. Among the five Pāṇḍavas he is the family man, always moving with the family and always protecting it. He seems to have no ambitions for himself, but submits his whole being to the greater good of the family.

In this Bhīma contrasts markedly with Arjuna, whom I myself find the most puzzling of the epic characters. If Bhīma is Dionysian, complete with club, so Arjuna with his favorite bow is Apollonian. Nor is Arjuna much of a family man, whether in *The Book of the Beginning* or later. He has a tendency to go off on his own and have private adventures, and he is a hero in search of glory. He goes into voluntary exile—that is, out adventuring—for twelve months (or years, depending how one reads the text), and behaves more of a pair with Kṛṣṇa than as a junior member of the family. He likes to associate with the Vṛṣṇis, whose Princess Subhadrā he abducts and marries. He forms a warrior pair with Kṛṣṇa to burn down the Khāṇḍava Forest, while his brothers are not even watching. When the whole family pines in the forest, with Draupadī replacing Kuntī, Arjuna journeys to the world of Indra, fights on his way Śiva in the form of a mountain man, and spends a good part of the ten years in Indra's heaven, where he learns to dance.

The women in *The Book of the Beginning* are rather self-effacing,

24. Cf. 1.186.29; 188.13 ff: note that this lawfulness is backed up by the veracity of his mother Kunti.

with the exception of Satyavatī. Kuntī, urged on and on by her husband Pāṇḍu to demand children from the Gods, finally protests, as she also does when her co-wife Mādrī cheats her by having two children at once by the twin gods the Aśvins; and as she vehemently does when she suspects Mādrī of having contributed to Pāṇḍu's death. But for the rest she is mostly silently fulfilling her role of mother, with the notable exception of her fateful demand that the five brothers share together their alms, which happens to be Draupadī.

Draupadī herself hardly seems to say a word in this book, but she shall more than make up for it in the next one, *The Book of the Assembly Hall.*

Contents

1(1) *The Lists of Contents*

1 (B. 1; C. 1). The Bard Ugraśravas arrives at the Naimiṣa Forest where the seers ask him to recite The Mahābhārata. *He agrees and glorifies the text and its author (1–25). The beginning of creation till the rise of the epic lineages (25–45). Contents and origin of the book (45–60). Summary of the book up to the gambling match (65–100). Second summary by Dhṛtarāṣṭra up to the killing by Aśvatthāman of Parikṣit in the womb (100–160). Saṃjaya admonishes the mourning Dhṛtarāṣṭra (160–90). Glorification of* The Mahābhārata *and the reward of reading the present book (190–210).*

The Bard shall intone the song of the Triumph after having bowed to Nara and Nārāyaṇa, supreme among men, and to the Goddess Sarasvatī.

1.1 The Bard Ugraśravas, the son of Lomaharṣaṇa, singer of the ancient Lore, once came to the Naimiṣa Forest where the seers of strict vows were sitting together at the Twelve-year Session of family chieftain Śaunaka. Courteously he bowed; and when the son of the Bard reached the hermitage, all the hermits who lived in the Naimiṣa Forest crowded around him to hear tales of wonder. Hands folded at his forehead, he greeted all the sages; and after his proper hosts had bid him welcome, he inquired how well their austerities were faring.

5 Afterward, when all the hermits had sat down, the son of Lomaharṣaṇa politely took the seat he was shown. And observing that the Bard was sitting at ease and was rested, one of the hermits raised a question to begin their discourse. "From where have you come, son of the Bard, and where have you whiled away your days, lotus-eyed one? Pray tell me at my bidding."

The Bard said:

I was at the Snake Sacrifice of the great-spirited royal seer Janamejaya, son of Parikṣit, where Vaiśaṃpāyana recounted all manner of auspicious tales of events, just as they had happened, in the presence of the king. They were tales that had first been recited by
10 Kṛṣṇa Dvaipāyana. I myself listened to these stories of manifold import that form part of *The Mahābhārata.* And after wandering about many sacred fords and sanctuaries, I journeyed to that holy place called Samantapañcaka, which is sought out by the twiceborn, the country where once was fought the War of the Kurus and Pāṇḍavas, and of all the kings of earth. From there I traveled to you, my lords, wishing to set eye on you; for I think of all your honored persons as of Brahmā himself!

Now that your lordships, lustrous like the sun and the fire, have accomplished the unction at this sacrifice, completed the recitations, and brilliantly performed the fire oblations, now you are sitting at ease. So what may I tell you, ye twiceborn? The edifying stories of ancient Lore that bear upon the Law, the past exploits of the kings of men and the great-spirited sages?

The seers said:

15 Tell us that ancient Lore that was related by the eminent sage Dvaipāyana, which the Gods and brahmin seers honored when they heard it! That divine language of the sublime Histories, in all the varieties of words and books, the sacred Account of the Bhāratas, that language of complex word and meaning, ruled by refinement and reinforced by all sciences, which Vaiśaṃpāyana, at Dvaipāyana's bidding, repeated truthfully to the satisfaction of King Janamejaya at the king's sacrifice. We wish to hear that Grand Collection, now joined to the Collections of the Four Vedas, which Vyāsa the miracle-monger compiled, replete with the Law and dispelling all danger of evil!

The Bard said:

20 I bow to the Primeval Person the Lord, widely invoked and lauded, who is the True, the One-Syllabled Brahman, manifest and unmanifest, everlasting, at once the existent and the nonexistent, Creator of things high and low. I bow to Him who is the Ancient One, supreme, imperishable, blissful and blessing, the most desirable Viṣṇu, faultless and resplendent, who is Kṛṣṇa Hṛṣīkeśa, the preceptor of all creatures,

those that move and those that move not; the God Hari.
I shall speak the entire thought of that great seer and saint who is
venerated in all the world, Vyāsa of limitless brilliance. Poets have
told it before, poets are telling it now, other poets shall tell this
25 history on earth in the future. It is indeed a great storehouse of
knowledge, rooted in the three worlds, which the twiceborn retain in
all its parts and summaries. Fine words adorn it, and usages human
and divine; many meters scan it; it is the delight of the learned.
When all this was without light and unillumined, and on all its
sides covered by darkness, there arose one large Egg, the
inexhaustible seed of all creatures. They say that this was the great
divine cause, in the beginning of the Eon; and that on which it rests
is revealed as the true Light, the everlasting Brahman. Wondrous it
was and beyond imagining, in perfect balance in all its parts, this
unmanifest subtle cause that is that which is and that which is not.
30 From it was born the Grandfather, the Sole Lord Prajāpati, who
is known as Brahmā, as the Preceptor of the Gods, as Sthāṇu, Manu,
Ka, and Parameṣṭhin. From him sprang Dakṣa, son of Pracetas, and
thence the seven sons of Dakṣa, and from them came forth the
twenty-one Lords of Creation. And the Person of immeasurable soul,
the One whom the seers know as the universe; and the Viśve Devas,
and the Ādityas as well as the Vasus and the two Aśvins. Yakṣas,
Sādhyas, Piśācas, Guhyakas, and the Ancestors were born from it,
and the wise and impeccable Seers. So also the many royal seers,
endowed with every virtue. Water, Heaven and Earth, Wind,
35 Atmosphere, and Space, the year, the seasons, the months, the
fortnights, and days and nights in turn, and whatever else, has all
come forth as witnessed by the world. Whatever is found to exist,
moving and unmoving, it is all again thrown together, all this world,
when the destruction of the Eon has struck. Just as with the change of
the season all the various signs of the season appear, so also these
beings at the beginning of each Eon. Thus, without beginning and
without end, rolls the wheel of existence around in this world,
causing origin and destruction, beginningless and endless.
There are thirty-three thousand, thirty-three hundred, and
thirty-three Gods—this is the summing-up of creation.
40 The great Sun is the son of the sky and the soul of the eye, the
Resplendent One who is also Savitar, Ṛcīka, Arka, Āśāvaha, the
Bringer-of-Hope, and Ravi. Of all the sons of the Sun Vivasvant,
the last one was Mahya, who had a son that shone like a God, who is
hence known as Subhrāj—the Well-Shining One. Subhrāj had three
sons of much fame who had abundant offspring, Daśajyoti, Śatajyoti,
and the self-possessed Sahasrajyoti. The great-spirited Daśajyoti had
ten thousand sons, Śatajyoti ten times that number, and Sahasrajyoti

45 again ten times that. From them arose the lineage of the Kurus,
those of the Yadus and of Bharata, the lines of Yayāti and Ikṣvāku and
of the royal seers in general—many dynasties arose and creations of
creatures in their abundant varieties.

All are abodes of being. And there is a triple mystery—Veda, Yoga,
and science—Law, Profit, and Pleasure. The seer saw the manifold
sciences of Law, Profit, and Pleasure, and the rule that emerged for the
conduct of worldly affairs. And the ancient histories with their
commentaries, and the various revelations—*everything has been
entered here*, and this describes this Book.

Having expatiated upon this great erudition, the seer thereupon
made a summary thereof; for the wise wish to retain it for this world,
50 in its parts and in its entirety. There are brahmins who learn *The
Bhārata* from Manu onward, others again from the tale of *The Book of
Āstīka* onward, others again from *The Tale of Uparicara* onward.
Learned men elucidate the complex erudition of this Grand
Collection; there are those who are experienced in explaining it,
others in retaining it.

The son of Satyavatī* composed this holy History after he had
arranged the Eternal Veda by the power of his austerities and
continence. Kṛṣṇa Dvaipāyana, son of Parāśara, the wise brahmin
seer of strict vows, begot at his mother's behest, and that of the sage
Bhīṣma, lawfully and powerfully, the race of the Kurus in the field of
Vicitravīrya. When he had brought forth Dhṛtarāṣṭra, Pāṇḍu, and
55 Vidura, the sage repaired to a hermitage for a life of austerities. After
these sons had been born, grown old, and departed on the last
journey, the great seer revealed *The Bhārata* to the world of men. At
the request of Janamejaya and of thousands of brahmins he taught it
to his pupil Vaiśaṃpāyana, who sat in his presence. It was the latter
who, while seated with the sacrificial priests, recited *The Bhārata*
during the pauses of the sacrifice at their repeated bidding. The
detailed history of the lineage of the Kurus, the law-abiding virtue of
60 Gāndhārī, the wisdom of the Steward, the equanimity of Kuntī—
Dvaipāyana recounted it all precisely. The greatness of Kṛṣṇa Vāsudeva,
the truthfulness of the Pāṇḍavas, the wickedness of the sons of
Dhṛtarāṣṭra—the blessed seer said it all.

First he composed the collection of *The Bhārata* in twenty-four thousand couplets, without the minor narratives; this much the learned call *The Bhārata* proper. The seer then made a summary of them in a hundred and fifty couplets, the *Book of the Lists of Contents*, of the events and their books.

Dvaipāyana first taught it to his son Śuka, and later the master passed it on to other students who were fitted for the task. Nārada

* = Vyāsa.

recited it to the Gods, Asita Devala to the Ancestors, and Śuka to the Gandharvas, Yakṣas, and Rākṣasas.

65 The wrathful Duryodhana is the great tree, Karṇa its crotch,
Śakuni the branches, Duḥśāsana the plentiful blossoms and fruits,
and the witless King Dhṛtarāṣṭra the root.

The law-minded Yudhiṣṭhira is the great tree, Arjuna its crotch, Bhīmasena the branches, Mādrī's two sons* the plentiful blossoms and fruits, and Kṛṣṇa, Brahman, and the brahmins the root.

Pāṇḍu, after having conquered many countries with war and bravery, settled down with his family in a forest, as he was wont to hunt. He came to dire grief by killing a deer when it mated. His and Pṛthā's** sons spent their lives there from birth. Their two mothers conceived, in accordance with a secret Law, from Dharma, the Wind God, Śakra, and the twin Gods the Aśvins.

70 They grew up with hermits and were looked after by their two
mothers in holy and pure forests, and in the hermitages of the great.
Then the hermits conducted them of their own accord to the family of
Dhṛtarāṣṭra, when they were still handsome boys who wore the
hairtuft and studied the *Veda*. "These are the sons of Pāṇḍu," the
sages said, "your sons, brothers, pupils, and friends," and thereupon
they departed. On seeing the sons of Pāṇḍu, who had thus been
entrusted to them, the Kauravas, the learned men, the four classes,
and the townspeople exclaimed loudly with joy. Some said, "They are
not his." Others, "They are his." Others again, "How can they be his,
when Pāṇḍu has been dead long since?" "Welcome in any case!
75 How fortunate that we see Pāṇḍu's offspring. They must be bid
welcome!" Thus voices were heard to say everywhere.

When the tumult subsided, all the regions reverberated, and there
was a noisy outcry of hidden creatures. As the Pāṇḍavas entered,
there was a shower of flowers, delicious fragrances, and the music of
conch shells and drums; it was a great marvel. All the townspeople
were joyful because of their love of them. A loud clamor arose that
touched the sky and increased their fame. The Pāṇḍavas lived there,
studying all the *Vedas* and the various sciences, honored and
80 unthreatened from anywhere. The people were pleased with the
purity of Yudhiṣṭhira, the constancy of Bhīmasena, the bravery of
Arjuna, and the twins' discipline, and with Kuntī's obedience to her
elders. The whole world was content with their heroic virtue.

At an assembly of kings thereupon Arjuna won the maiden Kṛṣṇā*** who chose her own bridegroom, after he had performed a most

* = Nākula and Sahadeva.
** = his first wife.
*** = Draupadī.

difficult feat. Henceforth he was to be honored in the world by all
archers, and in battle too he became no less hard to face than the sun.
Having defeated all kings and all great oligarchies, Arjuna offered the
85 grand offering of the Royal Consecration to the king; and
Yudhiṣṭhira obtained the consecration, which was rich in food and
priestly stipends and adorned with all virtues. Then through the wise
policy of Vāsudeva and the might of Bhīma and Arjuna, he killed
Jarāsaṃdha and the king of Cedi,* who was swollen with pride.
To Duryodhana came valuables from everywhere, precious stones,
gold, gems and cattle, horses, elephants, and treasure. When
Duryodhana saw how the fortune of the Pāṇḍavas throve in this
fashion, a mighty anger arose in him from envy. And on seeing that a
Hall was offered to them, beautifully built by Maya, and the like of a
celestial chariot, he seethed.

90 It was here that he was mocked by Bhīma and stumbled from
nervousness before the very eyes of Kṛṣṇa, like a commoner. And
after enjoying all kinds of delights and all manner of jewels, he told all
to Dhṛtarāṣṭra–wan, yellow, wasted. Thereupon Dhṛtarāṣṭra approved
the gambling match, since he loved his son; and Vāsudeva, hearing
this, waxed greatly angry. Being none too pleased, he encouraged the
quarrels and looked away from the lawless and ghastly events of the
gaming and so forth as they increased. Despite Vidura, Droṇa,
Bhīṣma, and Kṛpa Śāradvata, the baronage killed off one another in a
tumultous battle.

95 When the sons of Pāṇḍu had triumphed, Dhṛtarāṣṭra, hearing the
very ill tidings and knowing the mind of Duryodhana, Karṇa, and
Śakuni, pondered awhile and then spoke to Saṃjaya, "Listen, Saṃjaya,
and pray grudge me nothing—you are learned, wise, alert, and respected
by the wise. I did not intend, nor do I rejoice in, the ruin of the Kurus. I
have no preference between my own sons and the sons of Pāṇḍu. My
sons, bent on revenge, are indignant with me, who am an old man, but
I, eyeless, endure it out of weakness because of my fondness for my son.
I err after my errant son Duryodhana, who lost his mind after he saw
100 the fortunes of that most august Pāṇḍava at the Royal Consecration,
when he was mocked at seeing the assembly hall raised. Resentful,
but himself incapable of vanquishing the Pāṇḍavas in battle, lacking
the energy to obtain great fortunes himself, like one not a baron, he
counseled a crooked gambling match, and the king of Gāndhāra
sided with him. Learn from me, Saṃjaya, whatever I know about it
and even as I know it. For when you have heard these words of mine,
which in truth are informed by my spirit, you will know, son of the
Bard, that I am indeed gifted with the eyesight of insight.

"When I heard that the wondrous bow had been drawn and the

* = Śiśupāla.

target had been hit and dropped to the ground, and Kṛṣṇā had been taken as all the kings looked on—then, Saṃjaya, I lost hope of victory.

"When I heard that in Dvārakā Arjuna had forcibly carried off Subhadrā of the Madhu clan and that both the Vṛṣṇi and the champion had set out for Indraprastha—then, Saṃjaya, I lost hope of victory.

"When I heard that the king of the Gods had rained forth, but was checked by Arjuna with divine arrows, and that thus the Fire had been gratified in the Khāṇḍava Forest—then, Saṃjaya, I lost hope of victory.

105 "When I heard that Yudhiṣṭhira had been defeated by Śakuni Saubala in a game at dice and was divested of his kingdom, yet still was followed by his inscrutable brothers—then, Saṃjaya, I lost hope of victory.

"When I heard that Draupadī, tears in her throat, had been dragged into the assembly, grieving, in a single garment, and she in her period, while her protectors stood by as though she had no one to protect her—then, Saṃjaya, I lost hope of victory.

"When I heard of the manifold feats of the law-minded brothers the Pāṇḍavas, who had departed for the forest and suffered out of love for their eldest—then, Saṃjaya, I lost hope of victory.

"When I heard that Yudhiṣṭhira, the King Dharma, was followed by thousands of Snātaka brahmins when he lived in the forest, and by great-spirited brahmins who lived on alms—then, Saṃjaya, I lost hope of victory.

"When I heard that Arjuna had appeased the God of Gods, who wore the guise of a mountain man, the Three-Eyed God, in a battle, and had obtained the great Paśupati missile—then, Saṃjaya, I lost hope of victory.

110 "When I heard that Arjuna learned from Indra himself of honed, divine missiles when he was taught in heaven, keeping faith with his promise—then, Saṃjaya, I lost hope of victory.

"When I heard that Bhīma and the other Pāṇḍavas had met with Kubera Vaiśravaṇa in that country that is inaccessible to mortals—then, Saṃjaya, I lost hope of victory.

"When I heard that the Kauravas had gone on a cattle expedition and been captured by the Gandharvas, and that they, my own sons so set on Karṇa's plans, had been freed by Arjuna—then, Saṃjaya, I lost hope of victory.

"When I heard, Bard, that Dharma had had an encounter with the king of Dharma in the guise of a Yakṣa and had correctly solved the riddles put to him—then, Saṃjaya, I lost hope of victory.

"When I heard that the very best of my sons had been crushed by Arjuna who was on a single chariot, when the great-spirited warrior lived in Virāṭa's kingdom—then, Saṃjaya, I lost hope of victory.

115 "When I heard that the king of the Matsyas* with great honor bestowed his daughter Uttarā on Arjuna and he accepted her for his son—then, Saṃjaya, I lost hope of victory.

"When I heard that the Yudhiṣṭhira, defeated, penniless, exiled to the forest, expelled from his own family, had mustered seven armies—then, Saṃjaya, I lost hope of victory.

"When I heard that Kṛṣṇa and Arjuna were Nara and Nārāyaṇa, according to Nārada's word, who said, 'In Brahmā's world I am always the witness'—then, Saṃjaya, I lost hope of victory.

"When I heard that Vāsudeva Mādhava had wholeheartedly come out for the Pāṇḍavas, he of whom they say that this earth is one of his footsteps—then, Saṃjaya, I lost hope of victory.

"When I heard that both Karṇa and Duryodhana had set their minds on punishing Keśava and that he had shown himself in his manifold ways—then, Saṃjaya, I lost hope of victory.

120 "When I heard that Pṛthā in her sorrow had been consoled by Keśava when she, alone, stood still in front of his chariot at his departure—then, Saṃjaya, I lost hope of victory.

"When I heard that Vāsudeva had become their councillor and that Śaṃtanu's son Bhīṣma and Bhāradvāja had recited blessings for them—then, Saṃjaya, I lost hope of victory.

"When I heard that Karṇa had said to Bhīṣma, 'I shall not fight if you are fighting,' and deserted his army and strode away—then, Saṃjaya, I lost hope of victory.

"When I heard that Vāsudeva and Arjuna, and also the measureless bow Gāṇḍīva—awesomely powerful triad—had banded together—then, Saṃjaya, I lost hope of victory.

"When I heard that when Arjuna himself had been seized with cowardice and sat down on his chariot stool, Kṛṣṇa showed him all the worlds within his own body—then, Saṃjaya, I lost hope of victory.

125 "When I heard that Bhīṣma, crusher of his enemies, was striking down myriad chariots on the battlefield, but no one of *them* was visibly killed—then Saṃjaya, I lost hope of victory.

"When I heard that Bhīṣma, supreme champion, was struck down by Arjuna, undefeated though he was in many a battle, after Arjuna had stood Śikhaṇḍin in front—then, Saṃjaya, I lost hope of victory.

"When I heard that the aged hero, felled by bright-hued arrow feathers, was lying on a bed of arrows, after massacring the Somakas till few remained—then, Saṃjaya, I lost hope of victory.

"When I heard that at the time that Śaṃtanu's son Bhīṣma was lying there dying, the earth split open to well up water and Arjuna at his bidding slaked Bhīṣma's thirst—then, Saṃjaya, I lost hope of victory.

* = Virāṭa.

"When I heard that Śukra and Sūrya* combined in favor of the Pāṇḍavas's victory, and that beasts of prey constantly roared around us—then, Saṃjaya, I lost hope of victory.

130 "When Droṇa, while displaying all manner of missile trajectories, warrior as he was in battle, yet failed to strike down the superior Pāṇḍavas—then, Saṃjaya, I lost hope of victory.

"When I heard that our great warriors, the Oath-Companions, had lined up to kill Arjuna but were slain by him—then, Saṃjaya, I lost hope of victory.

"When I heard that Subhadrā's heroic son** had secretly and by himself broken through the battle line, which was unbreachable to others and safeguarded by Bhāradvāja with sword drawn—then, Saṃjaya, I lost hope of victory.

"When our great warriors, after surrounding and killing the young Abhimanyu, all rejoiced, while they were no match for his father—then, Saṃjaya, I lost hope of victory.

"When I heard that the men of Dhṛtarāṣṭra, after killing off Abhimanyu, were cheering, mindless with joy, and Arjuna unleashed his fury on Jayadratha Saindhava—then, Saṃjaya, I lost hope of victory.

135 "When I heard that Arjuna had sworn a vow to kill Saindhava and kept his word in the midst of the enemies—then, Saṃjaya, I lost hope of victory.

"When I heard that as Arjuna's horses were exhausted, Vāsudeva*** himself came forth, unyoked them, and watered them till they recovered, and yoked them again—then, Saṃjaya, I lost hope of victory.

"When I heard that, his horses recovered and standing in his chariot pit, Arjuna fended off all warriors with the Gāṇḍīva bow—then, Saṃjaya, I lost hope of victory.

"When I heard that Yuyudhāna Vārṣṇeya had wreaked havoc in Droṇa's army, which, with its elephant forces, was well-nigh unassailable, and then escaped to Kṛṣṇa and the Pārtha—then, Saṃjaya, I lost hope of victory.

"When I heard that Bhīma had attacked Karṇa, but then spared his life and merely abused him with words, and hit the hero on his ear with the tip of his bow—then, Saṃjaya, I lost hope of victory.

140 "When I heard that Droṇa, Kṛpa, Kṛtavarman, Karṇa, Droṇa's son,**** and the heroic king of the Madras allowed Saindhava to be slain—then, Saṃjaya, I lost hope of victory.

* = the planet Venus and the sun.
** = Abhimanyu.
*** = Kṛṣṇa.
**** = Aśvatthāman.

"When I heard that the divine spear, which had been granted by the king of the Gods, had been spirited away by Mādhava to the abominable demon Ghaṭotkaca—then, Saṃjaya, I lost hope of victory.

"When I heard that in the duel between Karṇa and Ghaṭotkaca the Bard's son unleashed his magic spear that was to have killed the left-handed archer—then, Saṃjaya, I lost hope of victory.

"When I heard that teacher Droṇa, alone in the pit of his chariot, was sped to his death and mutilated by Dhṛṣṭadyumna, who outraged the Law—then, Saṃjaya, I lost hope of victory.

145 "When I heard that Mādrī's son Nakula fought a chariot duel with Droṇa's son and that the warring Pāṇḍava held his own amidst the people—then, Saṃjaya, I lost hope of victory.

"When, after Droṇa's death, his son abused the divine missile Nārāyaṇa but failed to achieve the annihilation of the Pāṇḍavas—then, Saṃjaya, I lost hope of victory.

"When I heard that Karṇa, incomparable champion, unvanquished in all his battles, had been killed by Arjuna in that War of the Brethren, unfathomable even to the Gods—then, Saṃjaya, I lost hope of victory.

"When I heard that neither Droṇa's son, nor Kṛpa, nor Duḥśāsana, nor the awesome Kṛtavarman dared assail the lone Yudhiṣṭhira—then, Saṃjaya, I lost hope of victory.

"When I heard, Bard, that the heroic king of the Madras had been slain in a fight with King Dharma, he who always could rival a Kṛṣṇa in war—then, Saṃjaya, I lost hope of victory.

"When I heard that the evil Saubala, powerful wizard, root of the discord and the gambling, had been killed in battle by Sahadeva Pāṇḍava—then, Saṃjaya, I lost hope of victory.

150 "When I heard that Duryodhana, his chariot lost, his pride broken, had waded into a pond and was lying there alone, causing its water to freeze—then, Saṃjaya, I lost hope of victory.

"When I heard that the Pāṇḍavas stood with Kṛṣṇa Vāsudeva at that pond of the Ganges and menaced my rancorous son—then, Saṃjaya, I lost hope of victory.

"When I heard, son, that Duryodhana ran his various tracks in a circle at the battle of the bludgeons, and then was cowardly slain by the wiliness of Kṛṣṇa—then, Saṃjaya, I lost hope of victory.

"When I heard that Droṇa's son and the others had massacred the sleeping Pāñcālas and Draupadī's sons and wrought a loathsome feat of infamy—then, Saṃjaya, I lost hope of victory.

"When I heard that Aśvatthāman, pursued by Bhīmasena, had furiously unleashed his ultimate weapon Aiṣīka, with which he killed an unborn child —then, Saṃjaya, I lost hope of victory.

155 "When I heard that Arjuna had repelled the Brahmā-Head weapon,

which had been blessed with hail, with his own and that Aśvatthāman had given his jewel crest—then, Saṃjaya, I lost hope of victory.

"When I heard that the great weapon had been hurled by Droṇa's son at the womb of the Daughter of Virāṭa,* and that Dvaipāyana and Kṛṣṇa cursed Droṇa's son with curses that were returned—then, Saṃjaya, I lost hope of victory.

"Woe! Mourning befits Gāndhārī bereft of sons and grandsons, mourning befits the wives bereft of their fathers and brothers. The Pāṇḍavas have accomplished their impossible task, they have gained a kingdom that has no rivals.

"Woe! Ten, I hear, have survived the war, three of ours, and seven of the Pāṇḍavas. Eighteen armies perished in that battle, that war of the barons. Now a dullness that is all overspread by darkness seems to permeate me. No sign of sense do I see, Bard, my mind seems to go crazy."

Having so spoken and much lamented, Dhṛtarāṣṭra, tormented, fell in a faint; and upon coming to, he once more spoke to Saṃjaya. "Saṃjaya, as this has befallen I want to give up my life, now, at once—I see not the slightest profit in going on living."

But the wise son of Gavalgana** spoke to the wretched lamenting king these words full of meaning.

"Thou hast heard of many kings, kings of great enterprise and great strength. Thou hast heard talk of them from Dvaipāyana and the wise Nārada. They were born in great lineages of kings that were prosperous with virtues, they knew celestial weaponry, their splendor was a match for Indra's. They conquered earth with Law, they offered up sacrifices of large stipends, acquired fame in this world—and then they succumbed to Time.

"Thou hast heard of the warlike champion Vainya, of Sṛñjaya, greatest of warriors, of Suhotra and Rantideva, Kakṣīvat and Auśija, Bāhlīka, Damana, Śaibya, Saryāti, Ajita, Jita, Viśvāmitra, Amitraghna, Ambarīṣa of great strength, Marutta, Manu, Ikṣvāku, Gaya and Bharata, Daśaratha's son Rāma, Śaśabindu, Bhagīratha, Yayāti of blessed acts, to whom the Gods themselves sacrificed and who has left the marks of sanctuaries and sacrificial poles all over earth with her mines and forests.—These were the two-dozen kings who were once cited by the divine seer Nārada to the king of the Śibis when he mourned his son.

"Other kings than they have gone before, puissant kings, great warriors, great-spirited, prospering with all virtues—Pūru, Kuru, Yadu, Śūra, Viśvagaśva of great endurance, Anenas, Yuvanāśva, Kakutstha, Vikramin, Raghu, Vijitin, Vītihotra, Bhava, Śveta, Bṛhadguru,

* = Uttarā.
** = Saṃjaya.

Uśīnara, Śataratha, Kanka, Duliduha, Druma, Dambhodbhava, Para,
Vena, Sagara, Saṃkṛti, Nimi, Ajeya, Paraśu, Puṇḍra, Śaṃbhu, the
175 faultless Devāvṛdha, Devāhvaya, Supratima, Supratīka, Bṛhadratha,
Mahotsaha, Vinītātman, Nala of the Niṣadhas, Satyavrata, Śāntabhaya,
Sumitra, the lord Subala, Jānujangha, Anaraṇya, Arka, Priyabhṛtya,
Śubhavrata, Balabandhu, Nirāmarda, Ketuśṛnga, Bṛhadbala,
Dhṛṣṭaketu, Bṛhatketu, Dīptaketu, Nirāmaya, Avikṣit, Prabala, Dhūrta,
Kṛtabandhu, Dṛḍheṣudhi, Mahāpurāṇa, Saṃbhāvya, Pratyanga,
Parahan, Śruti—these and many others, numbered by the millions
180 and the count of lotuses, have been heard of. Relinquishing their
most ample pleasures, these wise and powerful kings went to their
end—as did your sons, very great kings who performed supernatural
feats, who had courage, generosity, magnanimity, faith, trow, purity,
sincerity. The ancient great and learned poets have told their tales in
the world—they were abounding in virtues and riches. And yet they
went to their death.

185 "Your sons were wicked and consumed by rancor, greedy, mostly
evil in their ways—you need not mourn them. You have learning,
insight, wisdom; the knowledgeable approve of you! Those whose
minds do follow the scriptures do not fall into confusion, Bhārata!
You know what punishment is and what benevolence, lord of the
people. One should not go too far, so it is said, in protecting one's
sons. It was to be thus, and you must not grieve beyond it. With the
greatest wisdom, who can ward off fate? No one steps beyond the path
the Ordainer has ordained. All this is rooted in Time, to be or not to
be, to be happy or not to be happy.

"Time ripens the creatures. Time rots them. And Time again puts
out the Time that burns down the creatures. Time unfolds all beings
in the world, holy and unholy. Time shrinks them and expands them
190 again. Time walks in all creatures, unaverted, impartial. Whatever
beings there were in the past will be in the future, whatever are busy
now, they are all the creatures of Time—know it, and do not lose
your sense."

The Bard said:

In this book Kṛṣṇa Dvaipāyana has uttered a holy Upaniṣad. They
who learn even a quarter couplet of the holy study of the *Bhārata*,
and have faith in it, will be purified of all their sins. The holy divine
seers and brahmin seers and royal seers, all of auspicious deeds, are
glorified in this book, and so are the Yakṣas and the great Snakes.
And Kṛṣṇa Vāsudeva is glorified here, the sempiternal Blessed Lord—
for He is the true, and the right, and the pure, and the holy. He is the
eternal Brahman, the supreme Surety, the everlasting Light, of whose
divine exploits the wise tell the tales. From Him begins the existent
195 that is not yet, and the nonexistent that becomes. His is the
continuity and the activity. His is birth, death, and rebirth.

That which concerns the soul shall be heard here, and that which consists in the five Elements and the three Properties: the unmanifest cause and its products are sung here, and the One who transcends it—that which the greatest of mystics, yoked and possessed of the vigor of the Yoke of meditation, see lodged in their own selves, as an image in a mirror.

A man of faith, always striving, relying on the Law of the Truth,
who cherishes this chapter is freed from all that is evil. One who is
always a true believer will never despair even in great straits, when
he has heard from the beginning this *Book of the Lists of the Contents*
200 of *The Mahābhārata*. If at either twilight one makes one's prayers with
some from the *List of Contents*, one is instantly freed from any guilt he
may have earned that day or that night. Truth and Elixir inform
The Bhārata—as butter does the curds, the brahmin does two-footed
men; even as the ocean is the best of the lakes, the cow the choicest
of animals—just as all these are the choicest, so is said to be *The
Bhārata*.

He who makes the brahmins at a *śrāddha* listen to a single quarter
of a couplet—imperishable food and drink comes to his ancestors.
With both *Epic* and *Purāṇa* one should support the *Veda*—the *Veda* is
205 afraid of one of little knowledge; me it shall ferry over! A wise man
reaps profit if he has this *Veda* of Kṛṣṇa recited: for without a doubt
even the crime of wilful abortion will be atoned. A pure man who
recites this chapter at every change of the moon has, I think, learned
the entire *Bhārata*. One who listens day after day to this blessed and
ancient chapter in good faith shall obtain a long life, fame, and an
entrance into heaven.

Once the divine seers foregathered, and on one scale they hung the
four *Vedas* in the balance, and on the other scale *The Bhārata*; and
both in size and in weight it was the heavier. Therefore, because of its
size and its weight, it is called *The Mahābhārata*—he who knows this
etymology is freed from all sins.

210 Mortification is not dregs, Vedic study is not dregs, and the nature-
given rules of the *Veda* are not dregs, the vigorous acquisition of wealth
is not dregs—but that is what they become when they are beaten by
the beings.

1(2) *The Summaries of the Books*

2 (B. 2; C. 270). Origin and name of Samantapañcaka (1–10). The composition of an army; summary of the days of battle; praise of the text (10–30). Summary of the text in one hundred Minor Books by a list of their titles (30–70). Summary in narrative form of the text in eighteen Major Books (70–230). Praise of the text and the reward of hearing the present book (235–40).

The seers said:
2.1 This Samantapañcaka you spoke of, son of the Bard, we wish to
hear it described in full as it really is.
The Bard said:
If such is your wish, good brahmins, then pray hear from me, as
I tell my beautiful stories, good people, about the place that has the
name of Samantapañcaka.
During the juncture between the Age of the Trey and the Age of
the Deuce, Rāma,* greatest of swordsmen, urged on by his rancor,
destroyed over and again the baronage of the earth. When he,
lustrous like the fire, had annihilated the entire nobility with his own
might, he made five lakes filled with their blood in Samantapañcaka.
5 In those lakes with their waves of blood he, insensate with rage,
offered up bloody oblations to his ancestors, so we have heard.
Thereupon Ṛcīka and his other ancestors appeared to this bull among
brahmins, and, saying "Have mercy!" restrained him, so that he
desisted. The countryside close to those lakes of blood became
celebrated as the sacred Samantapañcaka. Wise men have said that a
country should be called by the name of the landmark that
distinguishes it.
It was at this same Samantapañcaka that at the juncture of the
Age of the Deuce and the Age of the Nought the war between the
10 armies of the Kurus and the Pāṇḍavas was fought. In that country,
innocent of any flaws of the soil and supremely firm in the Law,
eighteen armies massed together to wage war.
Thus did the name of the country come into existence, ye twiceborn, and that was the lovely and holy country that I spoke of to you.
I have told you now entirely, strictest of sages, how that country
became famed and renowned in the three worlds.
The seers said:
Son of the Bard, you spoke of "armies." We wish to learn exactly
what the strength of an "army" is, in men, chariots, horses, and
elephants. Tell it to us precisely, for you know everything!
The Bard said:
15 Experts declare that the unit of a "file" is made up by five footmen,
three horses, one chariot, and one elephant. Three files form one
"troop head"; three troop heads one "cluster"; three clusters one

* = Paraśu-Rāma.

"troop"; three troops make up one "convoy." Three convoys again
the experts call a "column," three columns a "brigade," and three
brigades a "division." And ten of such divisions constitute, the wise
say, one "army."

The number of chariots in one army, good brahmins, has been
20 calculated by those familiar with arithmetic as 21,870. The strength
in elephants is the same, while the footmen number 109,350 and the
horses 65,610. This is what those who know how to reckon with
figures call an "army," which I have now fully explained to you,
eminent brahmins. And of this figure were the armies of the Kurus
and the Pāṇḍavas, eighteen of them in total, O best of the twiceborn.
25 They assembled in that country, and there they went to their
perdition, by miracle-mongering Time, which made the Kauravas
its tool.

Ten days did Bhīṣma do battle, he who knew weapons extremely
well. For five days Droṇa safeguarded the convoy of the Kurus. Karṇa,
tormentor of enemy forces, fought two days. Śalya lasted half a day,
and so did the battle of the bludgeons that followed. And at the end
of the same day Kṛtavarman Hārdikya, the son of Droṇa, and Kṛpa
Gautama slaughtered the troops of Yudhiṣṭhira, who were sleeping
unsuspectingly.

I shall narrate to you the full story of *The Bhārata* from *The Book of*
30 *Puloman* onward, as it was told at Śaunaka's Session—that story of
complex word and meaning, and of numerous covenants, which is
sought out by men of wisdom as salvation is sought out by its
aspirants. Even as the soul is the chief among matters of knowledge,
and one's life among things that are dear to one, so this epic with its
preeminent matter is the chief among all textbooks. To this supreme
epic has been dedicated a superb spirit and the entire language of
vowel and consonant, Vedic and profane. Now hear of this epic *The*
Bhārata, brimming with wisdom, in all its variety of words and books,
The Summary of the Books.

First comes *The List of the One Hundred Books*, second *The Summary*
of the Books.

(3) *The Book of Pauṣya*
(4) *Puloman*
(5) *Āstīka*
(6) *The Descent of the First Generations*
35 (7) *The Origins*—a wondrous book compiled by the Gods
(8) *The Fire in the Lacquer House*
(9) *The Slaying of Hiḍimba*
(10) *The Slaying of Baka*
(11) *Citraratha*

(12) *The Choice of a Bridegroom*—by the divine Daughter of the Pāñcālas, where victory is gained according to the laws of baronage.
(13) *The Wedding*
(14) *The Arrival of Vidura*
(15) *The Winning of a Kingdom*
(16) *Arjuna's Sojourn in the Forest*
(17) *The Abduction of Subhadrā*
(18) *The Fetching of the Nuptial Gift*
(19) *The Burning of the Khāṇḍava Forest*, where Maya is encountered
(20) *The Assembly Hall*
(21) *The Council*
(22) *The Slaying of Jarāsaṃdha*
40 (23) *The Conquest of the World*
(24) *The Royal Consecration*
(25) *The Taking of the Guest Gift*
(26) *The Slaying of Śiśupāla*
(27) *The Gambling Match*
(28) *The Sequel to the Gambling*
(29) *The Forest Teachings*
(30) *The Slaying of Kirmīra*
(31) *The Battle of Arjuna and the Mountain Man*
(32) *The Journey to the World of Indra*
(33) *The Pilgrimage*—of the wise king of the Kurus
(34) *The Slaying of Jaṭāsura*
(35) *The War of the Yakṣas*
(36) *The Boa*
45 (37) *The Meeting with Mārkaṇḍeya*
(38) *The Dialogue of Draupadī and Satyabhāmā*
(39) *The Cattle Expedition*
(40) *The Deer in the Dream*
(41) *The Measure of Rice*
(42) *The Abduction of Draupadī*—from the forest by Saindhava
(43) *The Theft of the Earrings*
(44) *The Fire Drilling Woods*
(45) *Virāṭa*
(46) *The Slaying of Kīcaka*
(47) *The Cattle Robbery*
(48) *The Wedding of Abhimanyu and the daughter of Virāṭa*
(49) *The Effort*—which is full of marvels
50 (50) *The Coming of Saṃjaya*
(51) *The Sleeplessness*—of Dhṛtarāṣṭra, from worrying
(52) *Sanatsujāta*—which expounds the secret doctrine of the soul
(53) *The Suing for Peace*

(54) *The Coming of Kṛṣṇa*
(55) *The Quarrel* of the great-spirited Karṇa
(56) *The Marching Out*—of the armies of the Kurus and Pāṇḍavas
(57) *The Warriors and the Greater Warriors*
(58) *The Arrival of the Messenger Ulūka*
(59) *The Narrative of Ambā*
(60) *The Wonderful Installation of Bhīṣma*
(61) *The Creation of the Continent of Jambū*
(62) *The Earth*—which describes the Expanse of the Continents
(63) *The Bhagavadgītā*
(64) *The Slaying of Bhīṣma*
(65) *The Installation of Droṇa*
(66) *The Slaughter of the Sworn Warriors*
(67) *The Slaying of Abhimanyu*
(68) *The Promise*
(69) *The Slaying of Jayadratha*
(70) *The Slaying of Ghaṭotkaca*
(71) The hair-raising account of *the Slaying of Droṇa*
(72) *The Casting of the Nārāyaṇa Weapon*
(73) *Karṇa*
(74) *Śalya*
(75) *The Entering of the Lake*
(76) *The Battle of the Bludgeons*
(77) *The River Sarasvatī*—with the virtues of sacred fords and lineages
(78) The grisly *Massacre of the Sleeping Warriors*
(79) The fearful *Aiṣīka Weapon*
(80) *The Offering of the Water*
(81) *The Women*
(82) *The Funeral Oblation*—the funerary rites of the Kurus
(83) *The Royal Consecration*—of the wise King Dharma
(84) *The Subduing of Carvāka*—a Rākṣasa who took the guise of a brahmin
(85) *The Distribution of the Houses*
(86) *The Peace*—in which are related *the Law of the King*
(87) *The Law of Emergencies*, and
(88) *The Law of Salvation*
(89) *The Instructions*
(90) *The Ascent to Heaven*—of the wise Bhīṣma
(91) *The Horse Sacrifice*—a tale that destroys all evil
(92) *The Anugītā*—which teaches matters of the soul
(93) *The Sojourn in the Hermitage*
(94) *The Encounter with the Sons*
(95) *The Arrival of Nārada*
(96) The cruel *Battle of the Clubs*

(97) *The Great Journey*
(98) *The Ascension to Heaven*
(99) *The Appendix of the Genealogy of Hari*, and
(100) The great wondrous *Book of the Future*, among the Appendixes.

70 This full Century of Books, which was recited by the great-spirited
Vyāsa, was later exactly so recounted by Ugraśravas, son of the Bard
Lomaharṣaṇa, in the Naimiṣa Forest, but in Eighteen Books. The
summing up of *The Bhārata* is given there as *The Summary of the Books*.

The *Pauṣya* glorifies the greatness of Utanka. In *Puloman* the
ramifications of the lineage of the Bhṛgus are described, in *Āstīka* the
birth of Garuḍa and all the Snakes, the churning of the milky sea,
and the origin of Uccaiḥśravas. Then the story begins of the great-
spirited Bhāratas as told to the king, the son of Parikṣit, when he was
75 offering with the Session of the Snakes. The various origins of the
kings are related in *The Book of the Origins* as well as those of
Dvaipāyana and other brahmins. The *Partial Incarnations* of the Gods,
the origins of the Daityas, the Dānavas, and the mighty Yakṣas, of the
Nāgas, the Snakes, the Gandharvas and the birds, and all kinds of
other creatures. The birth of the great-spirited Vasus from the Ganges,
Bhagīratha's daughter, in the house of Śaṃtanu, and their ascension
to heaven. The birth of Bhīṣma, from combined particles of their seed,
his renouncing of the kingdom, his firmness in the vow of celibacy,
80 his keeping of his promise, his safeguarding of Citrāngada and, after
Citrāngada's death, of his younger brother Vicitravīrya, and his
enthroning of the latter to the kingdom. The birth of Dharma among
men, as the result of Aṇimāṇḍavya's curse, and the births, caused by
the gift of a boon, of Dhṛtarāṣṭra and Pāṇḍu from Kṛṣṇa Dvaipāyana,
and the origin of the Pāṇḍavas. Follow the plot of Duryodhana and the
journey to Vāraṇāvata, the digging of the tunnel at Vidura's advice,
the encounter of the Pāṇḍavas with Hiḍimba in the ghastly woods, and
the birth of Ghaṭotkaca.

85 The disguised life of the Pāṇḍavas and their sojourn in the
brahmin's house, the death of Baka, and the astonishment of the
townspeople. After defeating Angāraparṇa on the bank of the Ganges,
Arjuna goes with all his brothers to the Pāñcālas. The grand tales of
Tapatī, Vasiṣṭha, and Aurva are told, and the wondrous story of the
five Indras. Drupada's indignation that his daughter Draupadī should
be the common wife of all five, and the superhuman marriage as
ordained by the Gods. Vidura's arrival, the meeting with Kṛṣṇa, the
90 sojourn in the Khāṇḍava Tract, and their rule over half the kingdom.
The manner of intercourse with Draupadī, as at Nārada's behest, where
the story of Sunda and Upasunda is told. Arjuna's exile in the forest,
his encounter on the way with Ulūpī, his pilgrimage to sacred fords,

and the birth of Babhrūvāhana. Arjuna wins the loving Subhadrā in
Dvārakā on the miracle vehicle with Kṛṣṇa's approval. At the arrival
of Devakī's son Kṛṣṇa, the acquisition of the discus and the bow, and
the burning of the Khāṇḍava Forest. The birth of the mighty
Abhimanyu from Subhadrā, the deliverance of Maya from the fire, and
the escape of the snake; and the birth of sons to the great seer
Mandapāla by the Śārngī bird.
95 All this is found in the first long book, *The Book of the Beginning.*
The supreme sage, the august Vyāsa, counts two hundred and
eighteen chapters; and the text as it was seen by the great-spirited
seer numbers seven thousand nine hundred and eighty-four couplets.
The second book is called *The Book of the Assembly Hall,* with many
vicissitudes. The building of the Assembly Hall by the Pāṇḍavas, their
meeting with the Kiṃkaras, the story by the divinely sighted Nārada
about the assembly halls of the Guardians of the World. The
undertaking of the Royal Consecration, the slaying of Jarāsaṃdha,
and the rescue by Kṛṣṇa of the kings imprisoned in Girivraja. The
killing of Śiśupāla at the time of the quarrel about the guest gift at the
100 Royal Consecration. Duryodhana's grievous resentment at seeing the
grandeur at the sacrifice, and Bhīma's mockery of him in the Assembly
Hall, where his rancor is aroused, wherefore he causes a gambling
match at which the crooked Śakuni defeats the son of Dharma,*
Draupadī saves the brothers who are drowning in the sea of gambling
like a lifeboat in the ocean, and Prince Duryodhana, finding them
saved, challenges the Pāṇḍavas to another match.
All this has been named by the sage *The Book of the Assembly Hall,*
seventy-two chapters in number, while two thousand five hundred and
eleven couplets are cited in the book.
105 Thereafter follows the third long book, *The Book of the Forest.* The
wise son of Dharma is followed by the townspeople; the Vṛṣṇis and
Pāñcālas all arrive. The story of the razing of Śaubha, the slaying of
Kirmīra, the wandering of Arjuna of boundless might in quest of
weapons, his battle with the Great God in the guise of a mountain
man, his encounter with the Guardians of the Worlds, and his ascent
to heaven. The grieving Yudhiṣṭhira's meeting with the great seer
Bṛhadaśva, who had cultivated the soul, and his tormented
lamentation over his vice. Here occurs the narrative of Nala, which is
110 greatly illustrative of the Law and excites our compassion, where is
told the fortitude of Damayantī at the onslaught of Nala's vice.
Lomaśa brings to the great-spirited Pāṇḍavas in their forest dwelling
the news of Arjuna's being in heaven. Follow the pilgrimage of the
great-spirited Pāṇḍavas, and the description of the slaying of Jaṭāsura.
Bhīmasena is enjoined by Draupadī to go to Gandhamādana, and he

* = Yudhiṣṭhira.

violates a lotus pond for a *mandāra* flower; he has a great battle with
the Rākṣasas and the mighty Yakṣas led by Maṇimat. The story of
Agastya, where the seer devours Vātāpi and lies with Lopamudrā to
115 beget a son. Thereafter follows the narrative of the vulture and the
pigeon, where Indra, Agni, and Dharma try King Śibi. The geste of
Ṛśyaśṛnga, a celibate from boyhood, and the geste of the puissant
Rāma, son of Jamadagni, where the slaying of Kārtavīrya and the
Haihayas is related. The story of Sukanyā, where the Bhārgava
Cyavana allows the Aśvins to drink the Soma at Śaryāti's sacrifice,
and the sage obtains perpetual youth from them.

Here also occurs the narrative of Jantu, where King Somaka
sacrifices his son in order to gain more sons, and obtains a hundred
120 sons. The story of Aṣṭāvakra, where this seer defeats Bandin in an
argument and regains his father, who had fallen into the ocean. The
left-handed archer Arjuna obtains divine weapons for his eldest
brother and battles with the Nivātakavacas of Hiraṇyapura. Arjuna
rejoins his brothers in Gandhamādana. The cattle expedition, where he
fights a battle with the Gandharvas. Their return to Lake Dvaitavana.
The abduction of Draupadī from the hermitage by Jayadratha, where
Bhīma, who in speed matches the pace of the wind, pursues him. The
encounter with Mārkaṇḍeya and the series of tales that ensues. Kṛṣṇā's*
125 meeting and conversation with Satyā. The story of the measure of
rice, and that of Indradyumna, the stories of Sāvitrī, Auddālaki, and
Vainya, and the very detailed narrative of the Rāmāyaṇa. The theft of
Karṇa's earrings by Indra, and the story of the fire drilling woods,
where Dharma instructs his son, and where the Pāṇḍavas, after
obtaining a boon, depart for the West.

This is the third long book, *The Book of the Forest*, in which the seer
counts two hundred and sixty-nine chapters, and eleven thousand
six hundred and sixty-four couplets.

130 Thereafter comes the long *Book of Virāṭa*. The Pāṇḍavas go to the
city of Virāṭa and, finding a large *śāmī* tree on the burning ground,
hide their weapons in it. They enter the city and dwell there in
disguise. The evil Kīcaka is slain by the Wolf-Belly, and Arjuna defeats
the Kurus in battle at the cattle robbery. The Pāṇḍavas set free Virāṭa's
wealth of cows, and Virāṭa gives Arjuna his daughter Uttarā as a
daughter-in-law, for Abhimanyu Saubhadra, slayer of enemies, to wed.

Herewith I have described the long *Book of Virāṭa*. The great-
spirited seer has counted in this book sixty-seven chapters in full, and
135 now I shall tell you the number of couplets: the great sage counts in
this book two thousand and fifty couplets.

The listener may not know that the fifth book is *The Book of the
Effort*. While the Páṇḍavas are residing in Upaplavya, Duryodhana and

* = Draupadī.

Arjuna both approach Kṛṣṇa Vāsudeva, hoping to ensure victory. They
say, "You must help us in our war," and the sagacious Kṛṣṇa
replies, "Bulls among men, myself as a noncombatant councillor, or
a full army of troops—to whom shall I give which?" The slow-witted,
evil-minded Duryodhana chooses the troops, and Arjuna chooses
140 Kṛṣṇa as a noncombatant councillor. The great king, majestic
Dhṛtarāṣṭra, sends Saṃjaya as an envoy to the Pāṇḍavas to sue for
peace. Hearing that the Pāṇḍavas are led by Kṛṣṇa, Dhṛtarāṣṭra is
sleepless with worry. Vidura speaks many words of sage advice to the
wise king Dhṛtarāṣṭra, and Sanatsujāta recites to the grief-stricken and
anguished king the incomparable doctrine of the soul. On the morrow
Saṃjaya discourses to the overlord in the assembly of princes on the
145 identity of Kṛṣṇa and Arjuna. Kṛṣṇa is seized with compassion, and the
famous man, wishing for peace, himself goes to the City of the
Elephant to sue for peace. Kṛṣṇa, who has the well-being of both
parties at heart, is in his quest for peace rebuffed by Prince
Duryodhana. Realizing the wickedness of the counsels of Karṇa and
Duryodhana, Kṛṣṇa shows the princes his mastery of wizardry.
Karṇa is taken by Kṛṣṇa on his chariot and counseled about
opportunities, but he arrogantly rebuffs him. Follows the marching out
from the city of Hāstinapura of charioteers, horsemen, footmen, and
150 elephants, and the counting of their numbers. The prince sends Ulūka
on a cruel-spoken embassy to the Pāṇḍavas concerning the great war
beginning on the morrow. The count of the warriors and greater
warriors, and the narrative of Ambā.

This is the fifth book in *The Bhārata*, with vicissitudes aplenty,
which is entitled *The Book of the Effort* concerning war and peace. It
counts one hundred and eighty-six chapters, and six thousand, as
many hundreds, and ninety-six couplets according to the great-
spirited and magnanimous Vyāsa, couplets filled with misery.

After that begins *The Book of Bhīṣma*, of varied contents, where
155 Saṃjaya describes the creation of the continent of Jambū. Ten days of
the most cruel warfare occur in it, and Yudhiṣṭhira's army falls prey
to utter despair. The wise Kṛṣṇa Vāsudeva eradicates Arjuna's
faintheartedness, which is caused by confusion, with arguments that
expound salvation. Arjuna, great archer, puts Śikhaṇḍin in front, and
fells Bhīṣma from his chariot, hitting him with honed arrows.

This is described as the sixth large book in *The Bhārata*, with one
hundred and seventeen chapters, and five thousand eight hundred and
eighty-four couplets are counted in this *Book of Bhīṣma*, by Vyāsa,
scholar of the Veda.

160 Then follows the wondrous *Book of Droṇa*, with many happenings.
The Sworn Warriors drive Arjuna off the battlefield. The great King
Bhagadatta, Indra's match in war, is, along with the elephant
Supratīka, chastised by Arjuna. A large number of the world's great

warriors, headed by Jayadratha, kill the brave boy Abhimanyu before
he is fully grown. At the slaying of Abhimanyu, Arjuna, insensate,
kills off seven armies in the battle and completely finishes King
Jayadratha and the remaining Sworn Warriors. In *The Book of Droṇa*
Alambuṣa finds his death, as do Śrutāyus, the mighty Jalasaṃdha,
Saumadatti, Virāṭa, and the warlike Drupada as well as Ghaṭotkaca
165 and many others. When Droṇa himself is felled in the battle,
Aśvatthāman, unforgiving, unleashes the awesome Nārāyaṇa weapon.

This is declared to be the seventh long book in *The Bhārata*. Here
in *The Book of Droṇa* most of the herdsmen of earth meet their death,
the heroes and bulls among men who have been mentioned. There are
one hundred and seventy chapters, while Vyāsa the seer, who sees the
truth, after reflection counts eight thousand nine hundred and nine
couplets.

Thereupon follows *The Book of Karṇa*, filled with great wonders. The
wise king of the Madras* is charged to be a charioteer. The downfall of
170 the citizens of Tripura is described. The abusive discussion of Karṇa
and Śalya at the marching out, and the story of the swan and the
crow, with an insulting moral. The anger that flares up between
Yudhiṣṭhira and Arjuna. The great warrior Karṇa is slain by Arjuna
in a chariot duel.

Students of *The Bhārata* call this the eighth book. Sixty-nine
chapters are numbered in *The Book of Karṇa*, and four thousand nine
hundred couplets.

The next book is the variegated *Book of Śalya*. The king of the
Madras is made general, when the army has lost its principal
champions. The chariot battles that now occur are one by one
described, and the destruction of the chief Kurus is depicted in *The*
175 *Book of Śalya*. The death of Śalya at the hands of the great warrior,
King Dharma, and the tumultuous battle of the bludgeons. The holiness
of the fords of the Sarasvatī River.

This is given as the ninth book, full of wonders and meanings, in
which the experts at numbers count fifty-nine chapters with many
happenings, and a total number of three thousand two hundred and
twenty couplets has been promulgated by the sage of the renowned
Kauravas.

Next I shall mention the pitiful *Book of the Sleeping Warriors*. Three
warriors, Kṛtavarman, Kṛpa, and the son of Droṇa, smeared over with
blood, come in the evening, after the Pāṇḍavas have withdrawn, upon
180 the rancorous Prince Duryodhana whose thighs have been broken. The
warlike son of Droṇa flies in a fierce rage and vows that he will not
shed his armor before he has killed all the Pāñcālas led by
Dhṛṣṭadyumna, as well as the Pāṇḍavas with their retinue. These

* = Śalya.

bulls among men, headed by the son of Drona, thereupon massacre the
Pāñcālas and their relations as they are sleeping peacefully. The five
Pāṇḍavas and the great archer Sātyaki are saved by Kṛṣṇa's vigor;
all the others perish. Draupadī, grief-stricken over her sons and
mourning the deaths of her father and brothers, sits below the five
brothers, resolved to fast unto death. Bhīma, whose might is terrible,
upon hearing Draupadī's vow, furiously rushes after Bhāradvāja, his
185 teacher's son. From fear of Bhīmasena and urged on by fate, the son
of Droṇa unleashes his missile to annihilate the Pāṇḍavas. Kṛṣṇa vows
that this must not be and cancels the other's vow. Phalguna cancels
out the other's missile with his own, and the son of Droṇa,
Dvaipāyana, and others throw curses at one another. After the water
oblations for the funeral of all the kings have been performed follows
the narrative by Pṛthā of how Karṇa was mysteriously born from her.

This is declared to be the tenth book, *The Book of the Sleeping*
190 *Warriors*. Eighteen chapters are recounted in this book by the great-
spirited seer, with a total of eight hundred and seventy couplets, the
books of the *Sleeping Warriors* and of *Aiṣīka* having been combined by
the sage of limitless wisdom.

Thereafter, they recite *The Book of the Women*, source of compassion.
The most pitiful laments of the heroes' wives are described and the
anger and serenity of Gāndhārī and Dhṛtarāṣṭra. They see the warlike
heroes, those who failed to escape their fate, slain in the battle—sons,
brothers, fathers. The wise king, foremost of the upholders of the Law,
has the bodies of the kings cremated according to scripture.

195 This most pitiful long book is stated to be the eleventh. Twenty-
seven chapters are enumerated in it, and seven hundred and seventy-
five couplets are counted. The great-spirited author has composed this
story of *The Bhārata* to bring terror and tears to the hearts of good
people.

Now follows *The Book of the Peace*, the twelfth, which increases
wisdom. The King Dharma, Yudhiṣṭhira, has fallen into a state of
despondency, after having caused the deaths of fathers, brothers, sons,
kin, and relatives. In *The Book of the Peace* the Laws are explained of
the "bed of arrows," which kings who wish to recognize the right
policies should know. Also, the Laws of Emergencies, illustrating both
time and cause, knowing of which a person attains to complete
omniscience. And the Laws of Salvation are explained in all their
multitudinous variety.

This is designated as the twelfth book, which is dear to men of
wisdom. In this book there are three hundred and thirty-nine chapters
200 filled with the fruits of austerities, and they say that the couplets
number fourteen thousand five hundred and twenty-five.

It is followed by the important *Book of the Instructions*. Yudhiṣṭhira,

king of the Kurus, after hearing the definitive truths of the Law from
Bhīṣma, son of the Ganges, regains his composure. The process of
Law and Profit is illustrated in its fullness, and the various rewards of
the different kinds of gifts. Also, the varieties of recipients and the
ultimate rules that govern gifts, the rules governing good conduct, and
the supremacy of truth.

This is the excellent *Book of the Instructions*, which contains a great
many matters. In it is recounted Bhīṣma's attaining to heaven. It is the
thirteenth book, providing decisive knowledge of the Law, and it
205 numbers one hundred and forty-six chapters and six thousand seven
hundred couplets.

Then comes the fourteenth book, *The Book of the Horse Sacrifice*,
where the fine narrative of Saṃvarta and Marutta is found. The
acquisition of gold treasuries, the birth of Parikṣit, the revival by
Kṛṣṇa of Parikṣit when he has been burned by the fire of the missile.
The battle of Arjuna in various places with resentful princes as he
follows the freed horse on its wanderings. Arjuna is shown a risk in
his battle with Babhruvāhana, the son of the puppet Citrāngadā. The
story of the mongoose at the great Horse Sacrifice.

210 This wondrous book is called *The Book of the Horse Sacrifice*. One
hundred and thirty-three chapters are counted and three thousand
three hundred and twenty couplets by the sage who sees the truth.

Then follows the fifteenth book, *The Sojourn in the Hermitage*, in
which King Dhṛtarāṣṭra renounces his kingdom; accompanied by
Gāndhārī, he and Vidura go to a hermitage. Seeing him depart, the
good Pṛthā, always bent on obedience to her elders, leaves her sons'
215 kingdom and follows them. Through the grace of Kṛṣṇa the seer, the
king beholds an incomparable wonder: he sees his slain sons,
grandsons, and the other kings who had gone to the other world but
have now returned. Shedding his grief, he attains with his wife to
supreme fulfillment; Vidura, too, having had recourse to the Law, goes
the good journey, and so does Saṃjaya, the learned and restrained
minister, Gavalgana's son. King Dharma, Yudhiṣṭhira, meets Nārada
and hears from him the great destruction of the Vṛṣṇis.

This is the very marvelous *Book of the Sojourn in the Hermitage*,
which numbers forty-two chapters, and in which the seer of the truth
counts one thousand five hundred and six couplets.

220 Then, you may know, follows the cruel *Book of the Clubs*, where the
bulls among men, who had endured sword blows in battle, now are
squeezed down by the staff of Brahmā on the shore of the ocean:
dissipated by liquor at a drinking bout, on the prompting of fate, they
kill off one another with thunderbolt-like clubs of *eraka* grass. Rāma*

* = Balarāma

and Kṛṣṇa, having wrought total destruction, do not survive all-
destroying, impartial Time, which has now come to them. Arjuna,
bull of men, goes to Dvāravatī and, finding it empty of Vṛṣṇis, falls
225 prey to utter despair and sorrow. After performing the rites for
Vasudeva Śauri, the chief of the Yadus who is his maternal uncle, he
sees the great butchery of the Yadu heroes at their drinking ground.
He then has the funeral rites performed for the bodies of Kṛṣṇa
Vāsudeva, the great-spirited Rāma, and the chiefs of the Vṛṣṇis.
When he takes the children and the aged with him from Dvāravatī,
he witnesses in a disastrous pass the defeat of his bow Gāṇḍīva, the
unfavorableness of all his celestial weapons, the destruction of the
Vṛṣṇi women, and the impermanence of power. The sight makes him
desperate; urged by Vyāsa's advice, he goes to King Dharma and
seeks leave to enter upon total renunciation.

This is the sixteenth book, *The Book of the Clubs*, numbering eight
chapters and three hundred couplets.

230 Then comes the seventeenth book, *The Book of the Great Journey*.
The Pāṇḍavas, bulls among men, abandon their kingdom and,
accompanied by the divine Draupadī, attain to final fulfillment. Three
chapters are recounted in it, and the seer of the truth counts one
hundred and twenty couplets.

Thereafter the divine and supernatural *Book of Heaven*, five chapters
and two hundred couplets long, rich in austerities.

This sums up all the eighteen Books. Among the Appendixes are
mentioned *The Genealogy of Hari* and *The Book of the Future*. Thus the
entire *Bhārata* has been related through this *Summary of the Books*.

Eighteen armies came together, eager to see battle; and their grand,
cruel war lasted for eighteen days.

235 A brahmin who knows the four *Vedas* with their branches and
Upaniṣads, but does not know this epic, has no learning at all. Once
one has heard this story so worthy of being heard no other story will
please him: it will sound harsh as the crow sounds to one after
hearing the cuckoo sing. From this supreme epic rise the inspirations
of the poets, as the configurations of the three worlds rise from the five
elements. Just as the four kingdoms of creatures range in the realm of
space, so, ye twiceborn, all Lore ranges in the realm of this epic.
Even as all the senses rest on the manifold workings of the mind, so
240 all works and virtues rest upon this narrative. No story is found on
earth that does not rest on this epic—nobody endures without living
off its food. Even as servants that strive for preferment live off a
high-born master, so all the best poets live off this epic. If a man
learns *The Bhārata* as it is recited, as it once fell from the lips of
Dvaipāyana, immeasurable, sanctifying, purifying, atoning, and

blessing – what need has he of ablutions in the waters of Puṣkara? When they have first heard this great, incomparably rich epic as it has been laid out in *The Summary of the Books*, it becomes for all men as safe to plunge into as the wide ocean is with the aid of a boat.

1(3) Pauṣya

3 (B. 3; C. 661). The bitch of the Gods, Saramā, curses Janamejaya for a slight to her son (1–5). Janamejaya, to expiate the crime, chooses a priest and conquers Takṣaśilā (10–15). The brahmin Dhaumya Āyoda tests his pupils Uddālaka, Upamanyu, and Veda (15–80). Veda's pupil Utanka goes on a quest for the earrings of the wife of the baron Pauṣya. He is set upon by the Snake Takṣaka and becomes embroiled with the Snakes, whom he lauds (80–175). Utanka exhorts King Janamejaya to sacrifice the Snakes (175–95).

The Bard said:
3.1 Janamejaya the son of Parikṣit attended with his brothers a long
Sacrificial Session in the Field of the Kurus; he had three brothers,
Śrutasena, Ugrasena, and Bhīmasena. As they were sitting at this
session, a dog came by, of Saramā's brood. The dog was beaten up
by Janamejaya's brothers and, howling mightily, ran to his mother.
The mother asked her yelping son, "Why are you crying? Who beat
5 you?" He answered, "Janamejaya's brothers beat me." The mother
said again, "Obviously you did something wrong there that you were
beaten." The dog replied, "I did not do anything wrong! I neither
looked nor licked at the offerings."
Upon hearing this, the dog's mother Saramā, aggrieved over her
son, went to that place of sacrifice where Janamejaya was attending
the long Session with his brothers. Angrily she said to him, "This son
of mine did nothing wrong here! Why was he beaten! As he was
beaten without doing wrong, therefore an unseen danger will befall
you!" On these words of Saramā, the bitch of the Gods, Janamejaya
became quite upset and dejected.
10 When the Session had come to an end, he returned to Hāstinapura
and spent much effort searching for a priest "who," he declared,
"should pacify the evil I have done." One day Parikṣit's son Janamejaya
went hunting and in a lonely neck of his own domain saw a
hermitage. A seer was sitting there, by the name of Śrutaśravas,

and so was his beloved son Somaśravas. Parikṣit's son Janamejaya
approached the seer's son and chose him for his priest. Bowing, he
15 said to the seer, "Sir, your son must be my priest." Replied the seer,
"Worthy Janamejaya, this son was born to me by a Snake woman.
This great ascetic and accomplished student was begotten by the
power of my austerities and grew in the womb of this Snake woman
who had imbibed my seed. He is able to appease any evil deeds you
may have done excepting the evil against the Great God. But he has
sworn one secret vow—if a brahmin solicits any possession from him,
he must surrender it to him. If you will bear with that, take him with
you!" Janamejaya replied to the seer, "Sir, thus shall it be."
Having accepted him as his priest, he returned and said to his
brothers, "I have chosen him as my preceptor. You must carry out
without question whatever he says." And upon his word his brothers
did so. After instructing his brothers he marched on Takṣaśilā and
put that country in his power.
Meanwhile there was a certain seer by the name of Dhaumya
20 Āyoda. He had three students, Upamanyu, Āruṇi,* and Veda. One of
them, Āruṇi, who came from Pāñcāla, he sent off saying, "Go and
repair the breach in the dike." And at his preceptor's behest Āruṇi
of Pāñcāla betook himself there but was unable to close the breach
in the dike. He was disturbed, then saw a way: "Let it be, this is what
I shall do." He entered the breach and when he lay down in it the
water was halted.
Then on one occasion teacher Dhaumya Āyoda questioned the
25 students, "Where has Āruṇi of Pāñcāla gone?" They replied, "Sir, you
yourself have sent him to go and repair the breach in the dike."
Thereupon he said to his students, "Then let us all go where he is."
Having gone there, he cried out to call him. "*Bhoḥ* Āruṇi of Pāñcāla!
Where are you? Come, my calf." Hearing his teacher's word, Āruṇi
at once stood up from the breach in the dike and came up to his teacher.
And he said to him, "Here I am! I was lying down in the breach
to halt the escaping water, which was not to be stopped. As soon as I
heard your voice I came to you at once and opened the same breach
again. I greet you, sir. Give me your orders, sir. What should I do
now?" The teacher said to him, "Since you broke open the breach in
the dike by standing up, you shall be known as Uddālaka, Puller-
30 of-the-Stop!" The teacher granted him a favor: "Since you obeyed my
word, you shall obtain the highest good. All the Vedas will be
manifest to you and all the books of the Law." After these words of
his teacher he departed for the country he chose.
Now this same Dhaumya Āyoda had another student by the name
of Upamanyu. The teacher sent him out: "Upamanyu, my son, herd

* = Uddālaka.

the cows." On his teacher's orders he herded the cows. And after herding the cows by day and returning at nightfall, he stood before his teacher and bowed. The teacher saw that he was fat and said to him, "Upamanyu, my son, how do you feed yourself? You are quite fat." He replied to his teacher, "I feed myself with alms." The teacher rejoined. "You are not to eat the alms without offering them to me."

He promised thus and herded the cows. After herding them and returning he stood before his teacher as before and bowed. Seeing that he was still fat, the teacher said: "Upamanyu, my son, I take all your alms completely from you. What do you eat now?" He replied to his teacher, "I go on a second begging round after offering the alms of the first one to you, sir. That is how I eat." The teacher rejoined, "That is not a proper way to behave to your betters. When you act like that you deprive others of their sustenance. You are a glutton!"

He agreed and herded the cows. And after having herded them and returning to his teacher's house he stood before his teacher and bowed. The teacher saw that he still was fat and again said, "I take all your alms and you do not go on a second begging round. What do you eat?" He replied to his teacher, "I live off the milk of these cows." The teacher rejoined, "It is not proper for you to drink the milk without my permission."

He gave his promise, herded the cows, and upon returning to his teacher's house stood before his guru and bowed. The teacher saw that he was still fat and said to him, "You do not eat alms or go abegging a second time. You do not drink milk. You are fat. What do you eat?" He replied to his teacher, "Sir, I drink the froth that the calves spit out when they drink at their mother's udders." The teacher rejoined, "These virtuous calves spit out generous amounts of froth because they pity you. Therefore when you act like this you deprive the calves of their sustenance. You may not drink the froth!"

He gave his promise and herded the cows and went without food. Having been forbidden, he neither ate the alms nor went begging a second time, he drank no milk nor drank the froth. One day in the forest, starving grievously, he ate the leaves of the *arka* plant. And by eating the acrid, pungent, hot, ripe *arka* leaves, he was smitten in the eye and went blind. He wandered blindly about and fell into a well.

Now, when he failed to return, the teacher said to his students, "I have forbidden Upamanyu everything. Surely he is angry. That is the reason he does not return and stays out too long." Having said this, he went to the forest and cried out to summon Upamanyu. "*Bhoḥ*, Upamanyu! Where are you? Come, my calf!" Hearing his teacher summon him, he replied in a loud voice, "I am here, master, I fell into a well." The teacher answered, "How did you come to fall into a well?" He said, "I ate *arka* leaves and went blind, so I fell into this well." The teacher said, "Sing the praises of the Aśvins. Those divine healers will restore your eyesight."

And upon his word he began to praise the divine Aśvins with verses of the *Ṛgveda.*

60 "First Guides, firstborn, of wondrous luster,
Ye twins will I praise, ye glowing and endless,
Ye Birds Divine, beyond regions and measure,
Who range and alight upon all beings.

"Birds golden, fine-beaked psychopomps,
Munificent Nāsatyas, surely triumphant,
Who on fine looms swiftly weave the light in,
And swiftly weave out that darker sun.

"With the might of the Bird the Aśvins freed
The swallowed Quail, for our good luck;
Rolling well, ye: for to your wizardry bow
They that stole the dawn cows, excellent pair!

"Those three hundred sixty milking cows
Give birth to one calf, and yield milk for it.
Many sheds divide them, but they suckle one:
The Aśvins milk them of the *ukthya gharma.*

"Seven hundred spokes do rest on one nave,
To the wheel rims are stuck another twenty;
But rimless runs this Wheel forever–
Popular Aśvins, magic adorns ye!

65 "One is the Wheel, with its twelve rims,
Six naves, one axle, that bears the Elixir
To which the Gods are all addicted:
Do, Aśvins, dispense it–sit not aside!

"As Indra, at killing the Vṛtra, once won
The Elixir, so have won it the Aśvins:
Triumphant they cleft the mountain, and freed
Those cows with known might, whose prowess was seen.

"At first ye engender all of the ten space points,
Pointing all to the sky, and wheeling above:
Their course do follow the seers in succession,
The Gods, the men that inhabit the earth.

"Ye do display the many-hued colors
That range and alight upon all the beings:
The celestial lights, too, follow in suit,
The Gods, the men that inhabit earth.

"Nāsatyas, Aśvins, it's ye I laud,
And the lotus garland that ye two wear:
O ye Nāsatyas, undead, who make order:
It bears on its way, without help of the Gods!

"Let, youths, it conceive the child through the mouth:
This dead man bears it along the path:
No sooner than born the child eats the mother—
Ye, Aśvins, ye free the cows, so we live!"

Thus praised, the Aśvins drew near. They spoke to him, "We are pleased. This cake is yours. Eat it." He replied, "You never speak lies. But I cannot bear eating the cake without offering it to my teacher." Thereupon the Aśvins told him: "Long ago we bestowed a cake upon your teacher when we were pleased at similar praise from him. And he ate it without offering it to his teacher. You too should act as your teacher did in his time."

At the Aśvins' word, he said again, "I beseech you, O Aśvins! I cannot eat it without offering it to my teacher." The Aśvins said to him: "We are pleased with your devotion to your teacher. Your teacher has teeth of black iron—yours shall be golden! And you shall see again and you shall attain well-being."

Having been thus addressed by the Aśvins, he regained his eyesight. He returned to his teacher, greeted him, and told all. He was much pleased with him and said to him, "You shall attain to good fortune, as the Aśvins have said. And all the Vedas will become manifest to you."

This was the trial of Upamanyu.

Now Dhaumya Āyoda had another student by the name of Veda. Him his teacher instructed, "Veda, my son, stay here. Spend some time obediently in my house. Fortune will befall you."

He gave his promise and lived for a long time in his guru's house, obeying his guru. Like a bullock forever yoked to pull burdensome loads, he endured the miseries of cold and heat, hunger and thirst, and was ever compliant. After a long time his teacher waxed satisfied with him; and because of his teacher's satisfaction he attained to fortune and full knowledge.

Thus was the trial of Veda.

Having been granted leave by his teacher, he returned home from his teacher's lodgings and entered upon the householder's stage of life. Three students came to live with him. He never told his students anything like "Observe this rite, obey your teacher"; since he himself knew the sorrows of lodging at a teacher's house, he did not wish to burden his students with vexations.

85 Then, after some time had elapsed, two barons came to the brahmin
Veda, Janamejaya and Pauṣya, and they elected him as their preceptor.
One day, when the brahmin was about to depart from his house in
order to officiate for a patron, he charged one of his students,
Utanka by name: "Utanka, whenever anything is lacking in our
house, I wish you to make up for it." Leaving him with this charge,
Veda went ajourneying.

Meanwhile, Utanka lived in his guru's house, obediently carrying
out his teacher's charge. And while he lived there the women of his
teacher assembled, summoned him, and said, "Your teacher's wife
has had her period, and the teacher is abroad. See to it that her
90 season be not barren. She is in a bad way now." He said to the
women, "I cannot commit this crime upon some women's word, for
my teacher has not charged me to go so far as crime."

After a while his teacher returned home from his stay abroad. He
heard the entire story from him and was pleased. And he said to him,
"Utanka, my son, what favor can I do for you? For you have shown
me obedience in accordance with the Law. As a result a fondness has
grown between us. I grant you leave to go. You will find complete
success. Now go!" He replied, "What favor can I do for you? For they
say, 'If one raises questions against Law and the other proposes
answers against Law, either one of them will die and become hateful.'
95 Now that you have given me leave to go, I wish to bring you any
guru's gift you want." The teacher answered him, "Utanka, my son,
then bide a while."

One day Utanka said to his teacher, "Sir, give your orders. What
shall I bring you for a guru's gift?" The teacher replied, "Utanka, my
son, so many times do you prod me about what guru's gift to bring!
Go then and visit my wife, and ask her what you should bring. Bring
whatever she demands." When he had heard his teacher speak, he
asked the teacher's wife, "Mistress, the master has given me leave to
go home. I wish to bring a guru's gift that gives pleasure and then go
home acquitted of my debt. Give me your orders, mistress, what shall
100 I bring for a guru's gift?" To these words the teacher's wife replied,
"Go to King Pauṣya. Beg from him the earrings that his lady is
wearing and bring them here. Four days from now there will be a
ceremony, and I wish to receive the brahmins with those earrings on.
Make me that day shine with those earrings! You shall indeed fare
well if you seize your chance."

Utanka, thus instructed by his teacher's wife, set out. And as he
went on his way, he saw an oversized bull and, mounted on it, an
oversized man. The man addressed Utanka: "Utanka, eat the dung of
my bull!" He refused. Once more the man spoke: "Eat it, Utanka, do
not hesitate. Your teacher himself has eaten it in his time."

105 Hereupon Utanka said, "Surely!" and partook of the bull's dung and
urine, then departed for where the Baron Pauṣya sat.

Drawing near, Utanka found him seated. He approached, greeted
him with blessings, and said, "I have come to you as a beggar!" The
other answered his greeting and said. "My reverend sir, I am indeed a
Pauṣya! What can I do?" Utanka said to him, "I have come to beg
from you a pair of earrings to present to my guru as a parting gift–
the earrings your lady is wearing. Please give them." Pauṣya
answered, "Go to the women's quarters and ask the lady."

110 Utanka did as he said and went to the women's quarters, but
did not find the lady. Again he spoke to Pauṣya, "It is not right for you
to treat us with a lie! In truth, your lady is not in the women's
quarters. I do not see her." Pauṣya replied, "Then you must now be in
a state of pollution. Search your memory! The lady cannot be seen by
anyone who is polluted or unclean. Since she is a faithful wife, she is
not visible to an unclean person." Utanka, remembering now, said,
"True, after I had eaten I sipped hurriedly and while I was walking."
Pauṣya rejoined, "That is it then–one should not sip while walking or
115 standing." Utanka agreed and sat down facing the east. He cleaned
his hands, feet, and face properly first, then silently sipped just enough
water to reach his heart, drank three times, wiped twice, and cleansed
the orifices with water. Then he entered the women's quarters and saw
the lady.

And she upon seeing Utanka arose, greeted him, and said, "Be
welcome, reverend sir. Instruct me what I can do." He said to her,
"Please give me the earrings you are wearing–I beg them for a
guru's gift." Pleased with his directness and reflecting that such a
worthy recipient should not be denied, she took off the earrings and
proffered them to him. And she told him, "Takṣaka, the King of the
120 Snakes, wants to have these earrings. Please take care carrying them."
He replied, "My Lady, rest assured. Takṣaka, King of Snakes, cannot
overcome me."

With these words he bade the lady farewell and returned to
Pauṣya. When he found him, he said, "Pauṣya, sir, I am pleased."
Upon which Pauṣya replied, "Sir, at long last we have found a worthy
vessel in your person. Also, you are a guest of parts–I will therefore
perform a *śrāddha*. Stay for a time." Utanka replied, "I have little time
125 left. I wish to have the food offered quickly, such as is at hand." "So
shall it be," said Pauṣya, and fed him with food that was at hand.

Now Utanka observed that the food, which was cold, had a hair in
it, and judging that it was unclean, he said to Pauṣya: "Since you
have offered me unclean food, you shall go blind!" Pauṣya rejoined:
"Since you have spoiled unspoiled food, you shall stay barren!" Pauṣya
then inspected the uncleanliness of the food from close by. Finding further

that the food had been cooked by a woman with disheveled hair, that it was cold, and that it contained a hair, he judged that it was impure and proceeded to pacify Utanka. "Reverend sir, this food, with a hair in it, was cold and offered by mistake. I seek your pardon for this, sir.
130 Let me not go blind!" Utanka replied, "I never speak idly. You shall go blind, but soon you will recover your eyesight. Be it also that I have not been cursed by you." Pauṣya answered, "I cannot take back my curse! Even now my anger has not quieted. And do you not know that 'mild as butter is a brahmin's heart, in his word lies a honed blade—not so the baron: his word is buttered, but his heart is honed'? This being so, I cannot change my curse, for my heart is honed. Leave." Utanka rejoined, "I had to make sure that the food was impure and permitted you to appease me. It was before that that you said, 'As you spoil unspoiled food, therefore you shall stay barren.'
135 Now the food *was* spoiled, so there can be no curse on me. Let us be done now." And, saying this, Utanka departed, taking the earrings.

On his path he saw a naked mendicant approach who by turns was visible and invisible. Putting the earrings on the ground, Utanka went for water. Meanwhile the mendicant hurried by, seized the earrings, and ran off. Utanka rushed upon him and took hold of him. The other doffed his disguise, assumed his true shape as Takṣaka, and entered a chasm that suddenly had opened in the ground. By this way he made off to the realm of the Snakes, which was his dwelling place. Utanka followed him through that same chasm; and upon entering he praised the Snakes with these verses:

"The Snakes, lorded over by Airāvata, shining in
assemblies, are like wind-driven rain clouds with
their lightning.

140 "Well-formed and many-shaped with checkered coils,
they who sprang from Airāvata have shone as the sun
shines in the vault of heaven.

"Many are the pathways of the Snakes on the northern
bank of the Ganges. Who would wish to march without
Airāvata in the army against the sun's rays?

"Twenty thousand and eight hundred and eight Snakes
march as companions when Dhṛtarāṣṭra sets out.

"To those who crawl close to him and to those who
go far beyond I pay obeisance—Airāvata is their
eldest brother.

"Takṣaka do I praise, scion of Kadrū, for the sake
of the earrings, him I praise who has always dwelled in
the Land of the Kurus and the Khāṇḍava Forest.

> "Takṣaka and Aśvasena, two fast friends, dwelled in the land of the Kurus down the river Ikṣumatī.
>
> "To the last-born brother of Takṣaka, famed as Śrutasena, must I also pay homage, the great-spirited one who dwelt in Mahaddyuman, seeking the overlordship of the Snakes."

When in spite of his praise of the Snakes he did not receive the earrings, he saw two women who were weaving a cloth that they had mounted on a loom. And in that loom were woven black and white threads. And he saw a wheel that was being turned around by six boys. And he saw a man who was handsome.

He praised them all with these verses from the Recitation of Spells:

> "Three hundred and sixty spokes are affixed to the nave in this abiding wheel, forever moving in a cycle of twenty-four fortnights, which the six boys keep turning.
>
> "Two young women are weaving this colorful loom, forever turning back and forth their threads, turning them from black ones to white ones, which are for always the past creatures and the present.
>
> "The bearer of the thunderbolt, the guardian of the world, the killer of Vṛtra and slayer of Namuci, the great-spirited one clad in two dark clothes, who severs truth and lie in the world, he who obtained the horse Vaiśvānara, the ancient fruit of the waters, as his mount—to him there shall be obeisance forever, to the master of the universe, lord of the three worlds, stronghold-breaching Indra!"

Thereupon the man said to him, "I am pleased with this your song of praise. What favor can I do for you?" He said to him, "The Snakes shall be in my power!" The man replied, "Blow into this horse's arse." He blew the horse in the arse, whereupon from the blown-up horse smoking flames billowed out from all the orifices. With them he smoked out the world of the Snakes. Frenzied, desperately afraid of the hot power of the fire, Takṣaka seized the earrings, fled at once from his dwelling, and said to Utanka, "Sir, take back these earrings!"

Utanka took them back. When he had done so, he worried: "That ceremony of my teacher's wife is today, and I have strayed far away. How, to be sure, can I give them to her?" Even as he was worrying, the man spoke. "Mount this horse, Utanka. It will take you to your teacher's house in an instant." He consented, mounted the horse, and returned to his teacher's house.

The wife had bathed, and while she sat combing her hair she thought, "Utanka is not coming," and she decided to curse him. Then Utanka entered, greeted her, and handed her the earrings. She said to him, "Utanka, you came to the right place at the right time! Welcome, my boy, I was close to cursing you. Luck has been with you. Achieve success!"

165 Then Utanka saluted his teacher. The teacher replied to him,
"Welcome, Utanka, my son! What kept you so long?" Utanka replied,
"Sir, Takṣaka, the King of the Snakes, hindered my business. He lured
me into the Snake world. And there I saw two women who were
weaving a cloth on a loom. And in that loom there were woven
black threads and white threads. What does it mean? And I saw
there a wheel with twelve spokes—six boys were turning it around.
170 What was the meaning of that? I also saw a man. Who was he? And
an oversized horse—what was that? And as I was on my way, I saw a
bull, and a man was riding it. In a courtly manner he spoke to me,
'Utanka, eat this bull's dung, your teacher has done it too.' On his
saying so, I did take the bull's dung. I wish to be enlightened by you,
sir: what is the significance of this?"

Thus questioned, the teacher replied: "Those two women were the
One-that-Places and the One-that-Disposes. The black and white
threads are night and day. And that wheel with twelve spokes and
the six boys who were turning it, they are the six seasons and the
wheel is the year. That man is the Rain God. The horse is the Fire
God. And that bull you saw on your way, that was Airāvata, the
King of Snakes. The one who rode him was Indra. The dung of that
175 bull that you ate was the Elixir of Immortality. That, to be sure, was
the reason why you did not succumb in the dwelling place of the
Snakes. Indra is my friend. It is by his grace that you have come
back with the earrings. Therefore, my good friend, you must go now.
I give you my leave to depart—you shall attain to good fortune."

Now that his teacher had given him leave to go home, Utanka, enraged, wished to wreak vengeance on Takṣaka and made his way to Hāstinapura.

Reaching Hāstinapura after a short spell, that eminent brahmin
Utanka met with King Janamejaya who himself had earlier arrived
undefeated from Takṣaśilā. He found the monarch entirely surrounded
180 by his councillors. He first, as was proper, pronounced blessings of
victory for him, then addressed him with this speech in accomplished
language:

"While another duty fell due to be duly done by you, most eminent king, you well-nigh childishly satisfied yourself with some other sport, most prominent prince!"

Thus addressed by the brahmin, King Janamejaya himself replied graciously with full respect for the hermit:

> "I guard my own baronial Law
> By guarding these people of mine.
> Tell, brahmin, what should I have done?
> I obediently wait on thy word."

And at this answer of that most excellent king, that most excellent brahmin, choicest of the meritorious, spoke to that king of no mean mettle on what was his own task, and the king's.

185 "Lord over lords of men, it is Takṣaka who did violence to your
father, upon whom you should wreak vengeance, the evil-minded
Snake. Now is the time, I believe, for the feat to be done that is found
in the Rules. Go, sire, and acquit yourself of your debt to your great-
spirited father. For it was because of a bite of this corrupt Takṣaka that
he innocently succumbed to the five elements, he a king, like a tree
struck by lightning. Splashed over by the arrogance of his power, this
pariah among snakes did a crime and bit your father, shepherd of a
lineage of sages among kings, incomparable monarch; he assassinated
190 the king, and he yet, the evil one, turned Kāśyapa back! You, grand
king, must burn this heinous Snake in the blazing offering fire at a
Snake Sacrifice—for this is enjoined upon you. Thus you will avenge
your father, and thus, O king, you shall do me the utmost favor. It was
Takṣaka, O guardian of the earth, who waylaid me evilly, great king,
on my quest for a guru's gift, O prince sans blame."

Upon hearing this the king waxed wroth with Takṣaka; and as the
fire blazes forth with the offered oblation, he blazed forth with the
offering of Utanka's speech. Most aggrieved, the king thereupon
interrogated in Utanka's presence his councillors concerning his
195 father's journey to heaven. Then indeed did the king become flooded
with grief and sorrow, when he learned from Utanka about his
father's fate.

1(4) Puloman

4–12 (B. 4–12; C. 851–1091).
4 (4; 851). Ugraśravas arrives in the Naimiṣa Forest, ready to recite. The seers request him to wait until Śaunaka has finished his rites (1–10).
5 (5; 863). Śaunaka asks Ugraśravas to recite the origins of the Bhṛgu lineage; he complies (1–5). The birth of Cyavana from Pulomā. The Rākṣasa Puloman

sees Bhṛgu's wife Pulomā, who had been promised him first, as the Fire testifies (5–25).
6 (6; 897). Puloman abducts Pulomā; Bhṛgu's son Cyavana is born and destroys Puloman; Pulomā's tears become a river (1–5). Bhṛgu rejoins his wife and upon hearing of the Fire's testimony he curses the Fire that it become omnivorous (5–10).
7 (7; 911). Outraged, the Fire withdraws from all the sacrifices (1–15). At the God's urging Brahmā asks the Fire to accept the curse (15–25). The Fire agrees (25).
8 (8; 939). The story of Ruru. The descent of Ruru and the birth of Pramadvarā (1–10). Ruru loves Pramadvarā and prepares to marry her, but she dies of snakebite (10–20).
9 (9; 964). Ruru cries out in the forest; with divine intervention he agrees to revive Pramadvarā with half of his own life; ever after he kills snakes (1–15). Mistaking a lizard for a snake, he beats it; the lizard protests (15–20).
10 (10; 986). Ruru spares the lizard, which tells of its curse (1–5).
11 (11; 995). The lizard tells the story of its being cursed by a friend, whom it had startled with a straw snake (1–10). It cautions Ruru against killing snakes and reminds him of Janamejaya's Snake Sacrifice and the salvation of the Snakes by Āstīka (10–15).
12 (12; 1014). Relieved of its curse, the lizard vanishes. Ruru demands from his father the story of Āstīka (1–5).

4.1 The Bard Ugraśravas, son of Lomaharṣaṇa, teller of ancient Lore,
came to the sages who had gathered to attend the twelve-year
Sacrificial Session of family chieftain Śaunaka in the Naimiṣa Forest.
The Bard, who had devoted much toil to ancient Lore, folded his hands
at his forehead and said to them, "What shall I tell you?" The sages
said to him, "Later we shall ask you, son of Lomaharṣaṇa, and you
shall relate your repertory of stories, which we shall be eager to hear.
But for the time being the reverend Śaunaka is sitting in his fire hall.
He knows the celestial tales, the tales that are told of the Gods and the
Asuras, and he knows fully the stories of men, Snakes, and
5 Gandharvas. At this feast, son of the Bard Lomaharṣaṇa, the learned
family chieftain has taken the office of the *brahman* priest, capable,
keeping to his vows, filled with wisdom and conversant with both
Scripture and Forest Book. An invariably truthful man, given to

serenity, austere and strict in his vows, he is esteemed by all of us—he must be waited for. When this guru will have taken his most honorable seat, then you shall recite whatever that most excellent brahmin will ask you."

The Bard said:

And so it shall be. When the great-spirited guru has sat down, I shall narrate at his bidding the hallowed tales on all manner of topics.

Thereupon when that bull among brahmins had finished his ritual
entirely and in proper sequence, and had given the gods their due
10 with spells and the ancestors with water, he came in where the
brahmin seers were seated, who themselves were successful and
prompt in their vows, with the son of the Bard sitting first upon the
terrain of sacrifice. And, settling himself among priests and *sadasyas*
who were seated, the family chieftain Śaunaka spoke thus.

Śaunaka said:

5.1 Your father, my boy, long ago learned the entire stock of ancient Lore. Have you perchance, too, son of Lomaharṣaṇa, learned it all? For in that ancient Lore are recounted both celestial tales and the first lineages of the wise—we have heard them before, and long ago it was, from your own father. Now from among all the tales, I would first like to hear the one of the Descent of the Bhṛgus. Tell the tale—we are eager to hear you.

The Bard said:

Whatever was so perfectly committed to memory long ago, O best
of the twiceborn, by such great-spirited brahmins as Vaiśaṃpāyana
5 and his successors, and was recited by them of yore to my father and
again committed to memory by him—all that I myself learned no less
perfectly. Listen then to the story of that lineage honored by the Gods,
and Indra, and Agni, and by the host of the Maruts, O scion of the
Bhṛgus, the lineage of the Bhṛgus.

I shall now recite, great hermit and brahmin, the Descent of the Bhṛgus with all its attendant stories, as it is found in the ancient lore.

Bhṛgu begat a child whom he loved much, a son by the name of Cyavana Bhārgava; and heir to Cyavana again was the law-abiding Pramati. Pramati in turn had a son by his wife Ghṛtācī, named Ruru, and to this Ruru, your own great-grandfather, a son was born by Pramadvarā—Śunaka, perfect in the Veda and abiding by the Law, austere and renowned, learned and most knowledgeable expert on the Brahman, most scrupulous in the Law, a truthful man, controlled and master of his senses.

Śaunaka said:

10 Son of the Bard, I ask you tell me how that great-spirited son of
Bhṛgu chanced to become renowned as "Cyavana."

The Bard said:

Bhṛgu had a wife whom he loved dearly, widely known as Pulomā.
A child that sprang from Bhṛgu's virility was conceived in her. As in
time the fruit took shape in Pulomā's womb, O scion of Bhṛgu, in the
womb of this ever-equable lawful wife of a famous man, her husband
Bhṛgu, foremost of those who carry on the Law, departed for a Royal
Consecration. It was at that time that the Rākṣasa Puloman came to
Bhṛgu's hermitage; and entering the hermitage and spying Bhṛgu's
impeccable wife, he became possessed by love and lost his mind.

15 Now, the lovely Pulomā welcomed that Rākṣasa who had come,
with forest fare like fruits, roots, and such. But upon seeing her,
brahmin, this love-struck Rākṣasa became excited and wanted to
abduct the faultless woman. He saw the ritual fire ablaze in the fire
hall, and the Rākṣasa put this question to the blazing fire: "Tell me, O
Fire, whose wife she is, for I ask you with an oath. Thou art true,
Fire—tell the truth to me who asks thee! This light-colored woman
had first been chosen by me, but her father later married her off to Bhṛgu,
20 who thus broke the troth. If this buxom woman is Bhṛgu's
clandestine wife, say so in truth, and I shall carry her off from the
hermitage. For a fury has been burning my heart that Bhṛgu should
have got the slim-waisted wife that was mine first!"

The Rāksasa, having thus put his spell on the blazing fire of
sacrifice, questioned it doubtingly many a time about Bhṛgu's wife.
"Fire! Forever dost thou dwell within all creatures, as a witness to
25 their good and evil works. Speak, sage, the truth! If she is my
promised wife and was abducted by troth-breaking Bhṛgu, then thou
shall tell me the truth. When I shall have heard thy word, I shall carry
Bhṛgu's wife from his hermitage, in plain sight of thee, Fire—say
sooth!"

The seven-tongued Fire heard the Rākṣasa's words and became
much distressed. "I am no less fearful of speaking untruth than of
Bhṛgu's curse," it whispered.

The Bard said:

6.1 Having heard the Fire speak, the Rākṣasa assumed the guise of a
boar, brahmin, and seized her with the speed of wind and thought.
And the child she bore alive in her womb, O descendant of the Bhṛgus,
angrily fell from his mother's womb and thus became known as
Cyavana. When that Rākṣasa saw the child aborted from his mother's
belly and shining like the sun, he turned into ashes, fell, and let the
woman go. The buxom mother picked up Bhṛgu's son Cyavana
Bhārgava, O brahmin; and, well-nigh fainting with pain, Pulomā ran.

5 Brahmā himself, grandsire of all the worlds, noticed her as she
cried out, eyes filled with tears, Bhṛgu's impeccable wife. And the
venerable grandfather Brahmā comforted the wife. Springing from her

tears, a mighty river welled forth that traced the footsteps of famous
Bhṛgu's wife. And on seeing how the river traced her path, the
venerable grandsire of the world gave it the name Vadhūsāra, the
Run-of-the-Bride, where it flowed to Cyavana's hermitage.
Thus was Cyavana born, the mighty son of Bhṛgu.
Father saw son Cyavana there and his angry wife. And the Bhṛgu
10 wrathfully questioned his wife Pulomā: "Who told that Rākṣasa here
about you that he wanted to abduct you? For that Rākṣasa knew not
for sure that you, sweet-smiling woman, were my wife. Now tell me
who said so, for my fury drives me to curse him forthwith! Who does
not stand in awe of my curse? Who has committed this outrage?"

Pulomā said:

My lord, it was the Fire that betrayed me to that Rākṣasa. It was on the Fire's account that the Rākṣasa took me, screeching like an osprey. And I myself, I was set free by the power of this son of yours—that Rākṣasa let go of me, turned into ashes, and fell dead.

The Bard said:

When he heard this from Pulomā the greatest fury took possession of the Bhṛgu, and in a rage he cursed the Fire, "Thou shalt eat anything!"

The Bard said:

7.1 But the Fire was outraged at the Bhṛgu's curse and said, "What
new rashness hast thou wrought today, brahmin? While I keep
striving for the Law and speak the truth whatever comes? I was
questioned and I spoke the truth—where did I go wrong? For a
witness who is questioned and knowing the facts bears false testimony
will kill his ancestors and progeny to the seventh generation. And he
who knows the truth concerning a matter of duty and knowingly
fails to speak is without doubt tainted by the same crime.
5 "I am no less capable of cursing you, but I must honor the
brahmins. I shall now assert the matter clearly before you, albeit you
know the truth. Now hear it.
"By my wizardry I divide myself into many parts and reside in
many incarnations—in *agnihotras*, in *sattras*, and in other rituals and
ceremonies. Whatever oblation is offered into me according to the
precepts that have been ordained by the Veda, the deities and the
ancestors will be satisfied; by it the Gods and ancestors are gratified;
therefore the Gods are the ancestors and the ancestors are the Gods.
The hosts of deities are water and so are the hosts of ancestors—
new moon and full moon offerings are for the Gods along with the
ancestors—both are worshiped as one, as well as separately on the
10 moon days. As both Gods and ancestors always offer unto me, I am

returned as the very mouth of the Thirty Gods and the ancestors.

"Through this mouth of mine are the ancestors given their offerings on new moon day, and the Gods on full moon day, and do they eat the offered oblation. How then should I, *their* mouth, become omnivorous?"

And this thought led the Fire to withdraw from the brahmins' *agnihotras* and from their large sacrifices and sessions. And being without Fire, and thus deprived of the *OṂs* and *Vaṣaṭs*, devoid of the *svāhās* and *svadhās*, all creatures thereupon became most miserable. Much disturbed, the seers approached the gods and spoke their word. "By losing the Fire the innocent three worlds have lost their rites and lost the way. Lay down what is to be done now so that no time be lost."

Hereupon seers and Gods repaired to Brahmā and gave him to know that Fire had been cursed and had withdrawn from the rites. "Fire, your worship, has been cursed by the Bhṛgu, for no cause whatever. How could he who has been the mouth of the Gods and eater of the prime portions of the sacrifices, the eater of oblations in all the worlds, ever become omnivorous?"

Having listened to their speech, the Maker of the World summoned Fire and addressed him with these gentle words that are immortal and prosper the creatures: "Thou art the maker of all these worlds and thou art their end. Thou art the sustenance of the three worlds and the furtherance of the rites—then act so that the rites do not cease, lord of the worlds! How is it that thou that art the sovereign Fire hast become confounded? When thou art in this world the purifier and present in all creatures? Thou shall not become omnivorous in thine entire body. Only those flames that are for acceptance, O flame-crested Fire, will devour everything. Even as all things that are touched by the rays of the sun are thereby made pure, thus anything that has been burned by thy flames will be rendered pure. Thou, Fire, art the great fiery power that has issued forth from thine own might—now by the virtue of this same fiery power of thine make the seer's curse come true, O lord. Accept the Gods' portions, and thine own, when they are offered into thy mouth."

"Thus it must be," replied the Fire to the Grandsire. He went forth to carry out the command of the God who dwells on high; and Gods and seers in great joy departed from thence as they had come. And the seers prepared all the rites as they had done before. In heaven the Gods rejoiced, and so did the multitudes of creatures on earth; and Fire himself, his guilt wiped out, attained to the greatest happiness.

So goes the ancient story that sprang from the curse that was laid on the Fire, from the destruction of Puloman, and the birth of Cyavana.

The Bard said:

8.1 Now this Cyavana, son of the Bhṛgu, begot on Sukanyā, O brahmin,
a great-spirited son, the mightily radiant Pramati. And Pramati in
turn begot upon Ghṛtācī a son who was named Ruru, and Ruru begot
Śunaka on Pramadvarā. I shall tell you, brahmin, in all their fullness
the feats of this Ruru of radiant might; therefore, listen.

There was of yore a great seer, endowed with the power of
austerities and with wisdom, devoted to the welfare of all creatures, who
5 was famous as Sthūlakeśa. It was in these days, O brahmin seer, that
the King of the Gandharvas, who was known as Viśvāvasu, made the
Apsarā Menakā great with child; and in due time this Menakā,
O scion of Bhṛgu, was delivered of the child close by Sthūlakeśa's
hermitage. She abandoned the child on the bank of a river and went
away.

The powerful great seer Sthūlakeśa found the girl, who resembled
the child of an immortal and fairly flamed with beauty in a deserted
spot on the river bank where she had been abandoned and orphaned.
Upon finding the girl, that excellent brahmin Sthūlakeśa took her on
to himself, and, seized with compassion, this greatest of sages fostered
her. She grew up a shapely woman, radiant in that hermitage of his,
surpassing all temptresses in all the virtues of her beauty. Therefore,
the great seer gave her the name of Pramadvarā.

When Ruru saw Pramadvarā in that hermitage of his, this man of
much virtue and self-control fell duly in love. Bhṛgu's grandson
caused his friends to inform his father, and when Pramati heard of the
matter, he went to the famous Sthūlakeśa. Thereupon the father
married the virginal Pramadvarā to Ruru, staging a wedding at the
onset of the lunar conjunction over which God Bhaga presides.

15 A few days before the wedding was to be celebrated and while the
fair-skinned maiden was playing with her friends, she failed to notice a
sleeping snake, of the breed that goes askew, and stepped on it with
her foot—she was prompted by Time as she was due to die. The
snake, pressed by the decree of Time, sank its venom-smeared fangs
sorely into the body of the careless girl. No sooner was she bitten than
she fell thudding to the ground, lost consciousness, and breathed her
last breath, no longer worth a look, however beautiful her body.
Felled by the poison of the snake, she seemed to have fallen asleep on
the ground, and the slim-waisted girl looked even more fetching. Her
father and the other ascetics saw her motionless abed on the ground,
20 lustrous like a lotus. Overcome with pity, all the eminent brahmins
flocked together—Svastyātreya, Mahājānu, Kuśika, Śankhamekhala,
Bharadvāja, Kaunakutsa, Ārṣṭiṣeṇa, and Gautama—and also Pramati
with his son and the other forest dwellers. Seeing the maiden dead,
killed by the snake's venom, they wept with pity. But Ruru departed
in pain.

The Bard said:
9.1 While the brahmins were sitting there in a circle, Ruru went into
the dense forest and cried out most grievously. Grief-smitten and
lamenting much and pitifully, he spoke out in mourning, brooding on
his beloved Pramadvarā: "She is lying on the ground, the slender girl,
feeding my grief and that of her kinsmen—what greater sorrow is
there? But if it be true that I have given alms and practiced
austerities, and if it be true that I have fully honored my elders, then
5 for that my beloved shall live. As I have kept control of myself from
the day I was born and have been strict in my vows, so Pramadvarā
shall this instant rise up beaming!"

The Envoy of the Gods said:
The words that you speak in your sorrow, Ruru, are in vain. No
more life is meted out, scholar of the Law, to the mortal whose life has
gone. The poor maiden, daughter of a Gandharva and an Apsarā, is
dead now—don't waste your mind on mourning. However, long ago
the great-spirited Gods devised some means of escape from this. If you
wish to carry it out, you shall regain your Pramadvarā.

Ruru said:
What means did the Gods devise? Tell me in truth, celestial! I shall
carry it out just as I hear it. Deign to save me, good sir!

The Envoy of the Gods said:
10 Bestow half your life on the girl, scion of Bhṛgu, and she shall stand
up, Ruru, your bride Pramadvarā.

Ruru said:
I bestow half my life on the girl, excellent celestial. My beloved must
rise up with the body and adornment of love!

The Bard said:
Thereupon the King of the Gandharvas and the Envoy of the Gods,
eminent both, approached the King of the Law and said to him:
"King of the Law, let Ruru's bride—the beautiful maiden who now is
dead—arise with half his life to live, if you so see fit."

The King of the Law said:
If you wish, Envoy of the Gods, Ruru's bride Pramadvarā shall arise
endowed with half the life of Ruru.

The Bard said:
15 No sooner had he spoken than Pramadvarā arose to live with half
the life of Ruru, as though the fair-skinned girl had merely been
asleep. And this indeed shall in the future be seen: the life of the
illustrious Ruru when past his prime was to be shortened by half for
the sake of his wife!

Then, on the appointed day, the couple's fathers joyfully celebrated
the nuptials and rejoiced and wished each other well. Ruru himself,
having got a bride so dearly got, tender as a lotus fiber, swore an oath
to destroy the snakes, and he was wont to keep his vows. Whenever

he saw a snake a dread fury possessed him, and he ever grabbed a club and killed the snake if it was near enough.

20 One day the brahmin Ruru came upon a large forest and there he saw lying a lizard sated of days. He raised his stick like the staff of Time and, enraged, the brahmin struck the lizard. Then the lizard said, "I have done you no wrong today, ascetic! Why then are you seized by a vehement rage, why do you strike me?"

Ruru said:

10.1 My wife, who is as dear to me as my own life, was once bitten by a snake; and upon that I swore an awful oath to myself, reptile, that I would henceforth kill every snake I saw. Therefore I am ready to kill you, you shall be rid of your life!

The lizard said:

Those are other reptiles that bite human beings, brahmin. Do not kill lizards because we resemble snakes! Lizards share the misfortunes of snakes, though we have our own purposes. We share their sorrows, though we have our own joys. You know the Law, therefore deign not to injure lizards.

The Bard said:

5 Hearing this speech of the reptile, Ruru did not kill it, for he was much frightened and thought that the lizard was a seer. And the venerable Ruru now spoke to him as though in appeasement: "If thou so wishest, speak, reptile! Who art thou that art thus disguised?"

The lizard said:

I was once the thousand-footed seer Ruru—and here I am reduced to a reptile by the curse of a brahmin!

Ruru said:

Why did that brahmin curse you in his anger, most eminent of reptiles? And for how long a time shall you wear this guise?

The lizard said:

11.1 Long ago I had a friend, a brahmin whose name was Khagama, a man, my friend, exceedingly sharp in his words and possessed of the power of austerities. Once when I was playing, still a child, I made a snake out of straw and frightened him with it, while he was preoccupied with an *agnihotra*. He fainted. When the ascetic regained consciousness, he fairly burned with rage; and he, always true to his word and strict in his vows, said to me: "As you made a powerless snake in order to frighten me, so by my anger you shall become a powerless reptile."

5 I knew, ascetic, the power of his austerities, and so I was greatly disturbed in my heart; and standing there, nervously prudent, compliant and prostrate, I said to the forest dweller: "Friend," I said, "I made a joke to make you laugh. Please forgive me, brahmin, turn your curse away!" Seeing how sorely my mind was disturbed, he

heaved many deep sighs; very much upset, the ascetic said to me,
"What I have said cannot be undone. However it shall be, so shall
it be. But hear you, strict in your vows, what I shall tell you. And
once you have heard my word, it may lodge in your heart, ascetic.
10 There shall arise a son of Pramati by the name of Ruru, a pure man–
and on seeing him you shall almost at once be relieved of your curse."

And here thou art, the famed Ruru, the pure son of Pramati. As I
have now regained my own nature, I will tell you here and now what
will be of profit to you. Noninjury is the highest Law known to all
breathing creatures; therefore a brahmin gifted with breath shall
nowhere kill any living creatures. A brahmin–so a most important
scripture asserts–is born in this world to be friendly, erudite in the
Vedas and their auxiliaries, and everready to grant safety to all beings,
my friend. Not to inflict hurt, to speak the truth, and to be forgiving
is assuredly for the brahmin a Law even higher than preserving the
Veda.

15 The Law of the baron, however, that does not become you—to
wield the staff, to be dreaded, and to protect the people. That was a
baron's task—hear it from me, Ruru who live by the Law—that
hoary massacre of the Snakes by Janamejaya. And the salvation of the
frightened Snakes was, at his Snake Sacrifice, to come from a brahmin
alone, one that possessed austerity, courage, and strength, who had
command of the Vedas and their auxiliaries–from Āstīka, foremost
among the twice-born, O most excellent brahmin.

Ruru said:

12.1 How did Baron Janamejaya massacre the Snakes, friend, or say,
good brahmin, why were the Snakes massacred? Then again tell me,
why were the Snakes rescued by this Āstīka? Relate it fully; I wish
to hear it.

The seer said:

"Ruru, you shall hear the entire tale of Āstīka from a brahmin who will tell it." And, having spoken, he disappeared.

The Bard said:

Ruru ran all through the forest, seeking to find the seer, and
5 exhausted fell to the ground. Coming to, Ruru went and told his
father; and at his demand his father told him the entire story.

1(5) Āstīka

13–53 (B. 13–59; C. 1020–2197)
13 (13–15; 1020). Śaunaka asks Ugraśravas for the story of Āstīka; the bard complies with the summary story (1–45).

14 (16; 1069). Śaunaka demands a more detailed story. Kadrū and Vinatā are Kaśyapa's two wives. Each gives birth, Kadrū to a hundred snake eggs, Vinatā to two bird eggs (1–10). After five hundred years Vinatā impatiently opens one of her eggs and a half-grown bird is born—Aruṇa, who is Dawn. He curses his mother to five hundred years of slavery, from which the other son will set her free (10–20). Garuḍa is hatched (20).
15 (17; 1094). The sisters Kadrū and Vinatā see the horse Uccaiḥśravas, which was churned from the ocean. Śaunaka asks for the full story of the Churning of the Ocean *(1). The Gods assemble on Mount Meru to deliberate about finding the Elixir; Nārāyaṇa advises the churning of the ocean (5–10).*
16 (18; 1112). With Ananta's help the Gods uproot Mount Mandara and take it to the ocean, which demands a share of the Elixir (1–10). The mountain is placed on the tortoise Akūpāra, to be the churning staff; the Snake Vāsuki is the lead rope; Gods and Asuras churn the ocean; mountain and ocean are both ravaged (10–25). The ocean turns to milk, the milk into butter, but the Gods weary; Nārāyaṇa imparts strength to them (25–30). Successively appear the Sun, the Moon, Liquor, the horse Uccaiḥśravas, and the jewel Kaustubha; they join the Gods. Dhanvantari appears with the Elixir in a gourd. The Asuras steal it, but Viṣṇu, in the form of a bewitching woman, recovers it (30–40).
17 (19; 1158). While the Gods drink the Elixir, the Asura Rāhu drinks of it, but is betrayed by the Sun and Moon. Viṣṇu cuts off his head, which rises to heaven and henceforth swallows Sun and Moon during their eclipses (1–5). Gods and Asuras battle each other, and Nara and Nārāyaṇa join, till the Gods are the victors (5–25). The Gods return Mount Mandara and have the Elixir guarded (25–30).
18 (20; 1189). Kadrū and Vinatā wager on the color of the horse Uccaiḥśravas; Kadrū orders her Snake sons to insert themselves into its tail and thus make it black; they refuse, and she curses them to be burned in a Sacrifice. Brahmā condones the curse, but gives Kaśyapa the power to heal snakebites (1–10).
19 (21; 1205). Kadrū and Vinatā view the ocean, which is described at length (1–15).

20 (23; 1235). Kadrū and Vinatā view the horse, which now has a black tail; Vinatā is enslaved (1). The Story of Garuḍa. *The Bird is born and glorified by the Gods (1–15).*
21 (25; 1279). Vinatā and Garuḍa are to take Kadrū and the Snakes for an outing; the Snakes are heat-struck (1–15). Kadrū praises Indra so that he may send rain (5–15).
22 (26; 1296). Indra brings rain, and the Snakes are revived (1–5).
23 (29; 1340). Garuḍa takes the Snakes to an island (1–5). He questions his mother why she and he should be their servants. She explains, and Garuḍa asks the Snakes how he may be freed. They demand the Elixir (5–10).
24 (28; 1320). Garuḍa sets out; Vinatā tells him to eat the Niṣādas, but to spare the brahmins. He swallows the Niṣādas (1–15).
25 (29; 1340). Garuḍa sets free an accidentally swallowed brahmin and his wife (1–5). He meets his father Kaśyapa, who tells of a huge tortoise and elephant into which two brothers, Vibhāvasu and Supratīka, have been turned, and advises Garuḍa to eat them (5–25). Garuḍa picks them up, each in one claw, and looks for a perch; alighting on a huge banyan tree, he breaks a branch (25–30).
26 (30; 1384). Garuḍa holds on to the branch from which the Vālakhilyas are hanging. Kaśyapa reappears, orders Garuḍa not to drop the seers, and appeases them; they leave the branch (1–15). He advises Garuḍa to drop the branch in the mountains; Garuḍa eats the elephant and tortoise (15–25). Portents appear among the Gods; Bṛhaspati explains that Garuḍa will steal the Soma; the Gods arm themselves (25–45).
27 (31; 1436). The origin of Garuḍa. The tiny Vālakhilyas were once slighted by mighty Indra; in revenge they sacrifice to engender a creature that will eclipse Indra (1–10). Kaśyapa takes over their rite in order to create an Indra of birds; on Vinatā he begets Garuḍa and Aruṇa; Garuḍa becomes king of the birds, Aruṇa the dawn (10–35).
28 (32; 1471). Garuḍa flies up to the Gods, battles and vanquishes them (1–20). He then quenches a holocaust of fire (20–25).

29 (33; 1496). Garuḍa penetrates the rotating wheel of razors that guards the Elixir, defeats the two guardian Snakes, and takes the Elixir (1–10). In the sky he encounters Viṣṇu, who grants him the boon that the bird shall always perch on top of him (10–15). Indra's thunderbolt proves useless on the bird, which sheds one feather to show his might. Indra seeks his friendship (15–20).
30 (34; 1520). Garuḍa praises himself (1–5) and accepts Indra's friendship. He promises neither to drink nor give away the Soma. Indra grants him a boon, that Garuḍa shall feed on the Snakes (5–10). Garuḍa takes the Elixir to the Snakes and places it on kuśa *grass; while the Snakes bathe, Indra recovers it; the Snakes lick the grass until they become forked-tongued (15–20).*
31 (35; 1546). The principal Snakes are enumerated.
32 (36; 1565). The Snake Śeṣa deserts his mother and performs austerities. Brahmā asks the reason (1–5). Śeṣa replies that he wants to separate himself from his brethren. Brahmā gives him a boon: Śeṣa shall carry the earth, and Garuḍa shall become his helper (5–25).
33 (37; 1589). Vāsuki deliberates with the other Snakes on ways to frustrate Kadrū's curse (1–5). Several cruel deceptions are proposed to circumvent Janamejaya's sacrifice, but Vāsuki remains unsatisfied (5–30).
34 (38; 1622). The Snake Elāpatra reports that Brahmā sanctioned Kadrū's curse, but said that an Āstīka, son of Jaratkāru, would end the sacrifice and save the Snakes that had been law-abiding (1–10). This Jaratkāru will have to marry a woman of the same name; Èlāpatra points to Vāsuki's sister Jaratkāru (10–15).
35 (39; 1641). Vāsuki keeps watch over his sister Jaratkāru; at the churning of the ocean he asks Brahmā for confirmation of Elāpatra's report; Brahmā confirms it. Vāsuki puts a watch of Snakes on the seer Jaratkāru (1–10).
36 (40; 1655). The etymology of Jaratkāru. The sage mortifies himself (1–5). The story of Parikṣit: King Parikṣit, out hunting, loses a wounded deer and questions a hermit who happens to be under a vow of silence; when the hermit fails to reply, Parikṣit angrily insults him by hanging a dead snake over his shoulder (5–20). The hermit's irascible son is told of the insult (20–25).
37 (41; 1690). The son demands explanation and is told

of Parikṣit's deed (1–5). Then he curses the king to die of a bite by the Snake Takṣaka (5–10). He goes to his father, who rebukes him for his curse (10–25).

38 (42; 1725). While the son stands by his word, the father admonishes him further (1–10). The hermit sends a messenger to Parikṣit to tell him of his impending fate (10–20). Parikṣit is contrite and takes counsel and precautions (20–30). Kāśyapa arrives to cure the king when he will be bitten; but Takṣaka waylays him (30–35).

39 (43; 1766). Contest of Kāśyapa and Takṣaka. Takṣaka bites a tree, which burns down; Kāśyapa revives it (1–10). Takṣaka bribes Kāśyapa with riches, and the other turns back (10–20). Takṣaka dispatches Snakes in hermit guise to Parikṣit to give him fruit. They do so, and at the appointed time Pariksit challenges a worm in a fruit to bite him. The worm turns into Takṣaka, who bites and kills him (20–30).

40 (44; 1801). Parikṣit is mourned, and his son Janamejaya is installed and married to Vapuṣṭamā (1–10).

41 (45; 1813). Meanwhile, Jaratkāru finds his ancestors hanging headlong in a cave, ready to fall; he asks how he can help (1–10). The ancestors reply: by sending word to Jaratkāru that he should beget children (1–30).

42 (46; 1846). Jaratkāru identifies himself and promises to do so, under three conditions: that the wife bear the same name; that she be offered to him free; and that he need not support her (1–5). He roams the earth in search of such a bride (1–15). The watchful Snakes report him ready, and Vāsuki appears to give his sister away (15–20).

43 (47; 1869). Vāsuki makes his formal offer. Jaratkāru marries the Snake woman, but compacts with her that she must never displease him. She conceives a son (1–10). Soon after, Jaratkāru falls asleep and seems to be about to miss the evening agnihotra*; his wife decides to wake him up (10–20). On awakening he angrily resolves to leave her; she remonstrates, pointing to the purpose of her marriage (20–35). Jaratkāru assures her that there is* (asti) *a child (35).*

44 (48; 1912). She tells Vāsuki that she has been deserted. He asks if she is pregnant, and she repeats her husband's words (1–10). She gives birth to Āstīka, who is taught by Cyavana's son (10–20).

45 (49; 1933). Janamejaya asks about the circumstances of his father's death. Praise of Parikṣit (1–15). He is told of Parikṣit's meeting with the hermit (15–25).
46 (50; 1964). Parikṣit's curse and the hermit's warning (1–15). Takṣaka's bribe of Kāśyapa and his ambush (15–25). Janamejaya demands proof that Kāśyapa was bribed, and his councillors provide it. He swears revenge on Takṣaka (25–40).
47 (51–52; 2015). Janamejaya resolves on the Snake Sacrifice (1–10). The priests begin preparations, but a bard prophesies failure because of a brahmin's intervention. The gates are closed (10–15). The sacrifice begins, and the Snakes start falling into the fire (15–25).
48 (53; 2041). The names of the officiating priests (1–10). Takṣaka seeks refuge with Indra, while the Snakes keep dying (10–20). Vāsuki prays Jaratkāru to summon Āstīka (20–25).
49 (54; 2067). Jaratkāru explains the covenant to her son Āstīka (1–15). Āstīka agrees, and confirms it to Vāsuki; he proceeds to Janamejaya's sacrifice and demands entrance (15–25).
50 (55; 2097). Āstīka praises the sacrifice and the priests (1–15).
51 (56; 2114). Impressed, Janamejaya wishes to give him a boon, but is warned that Takṣaka is still abroad (1–5). Indra is conjured up and made to drop Takṣaka, whom he is carrying (5–10). Āstīka is now granted his boon. He demands that the sacrifice be stopped. Janamejaya offers him riches instead, but Āstīka remains firm (10–20).
52 (57; 2142). The names of the Snakes that were sacrificed.
53 (58;2166). The moment Āstīka's boon was granted he stayed Takṣaka in the sky; the Snake survives (1–5). Āstīka is cheered by all (5–15). The Snakes give him a boon; he asks safety from the Snakes for those who recount his story (15–20).

Śaunaka said:

13.1 Why did King Janamejaya, a tiger among kings, carry on with the full Snake Sacrifice until all Snakes were finished? Tell me that! And why did that excellent brahmin Āstīka, the best of the mumblers of spells, have the Snakes set free from the fire that had blazed forth?

Whose son was that king who offered the Snake Sacrifice? And tell me, whose son was that eminent brahmin?

The Bard said:

Listen to the full story, O best of interlocutors, in which this has been completely promulgated from of old, O brahmin—the great *Tale of Āstīka.*

Śaunaka said:

5 I wish to hear in full detail this spellbinding tale of the ancient
brahmin and seer, the famous Āstīka!

The Bard said:

The priests used to tell this ancient history, which Kṛṣṇa Dvaipāyana once recounted to the sages that dwell in the Naimiṣa Forest. My father Lomaharṣaṇa the Bard, Vyāsa's wise student, was once asked by the brahmins to tell it. Therefore I shall now relate it just as I have heard it from him on your demand, Śaunaka, this *Tale of Āstīka.*

Āstīka's father was a lord who equaled Prajāpati; he was a celibate
of lean diet, Jaratkāru by name, who was always bent on awesome
10 austerities. He was a great seer who never spilled his seed, preeminent
among the Yāyāvara family, well-versed in the Law and relentless in
his vows. And on his wanderings he once saw his own forebears
hanging in a large cave with their feet up and their faces down.

When Jaratkāru saw his forebears, he said to them, "Who are you who are hanging upside down in this cave from a string of grass that is being devoured by a furtive rat that has made his nest in the cave?"

The ancestors said:

We are the Yāyāvaras, seers of strict vows, who now, O brahmin,
15 go down into the earth for lack of progeny. Only one descendant is
left, Jaratkāru, as he is known to us unfortunates; and this man of
little fortune has become an ascetic. In his folly he does not want to
take a wife in order to beget a son, and therefore we are hanging here
in this cave, because our line is extinct, helpless with such a helper,
as though we were criminals. Who are you who like a kinsman
grieves for us, good man? We wish to know, brahmin, who you are
that stand before us, and why you mourn for us who are so deserving
of mourning?

Jaratkāru said:

You are my forebears, my fathers and grandfathers. Say what I must do now. I myself am Jaratkāru!

The ancestors said:

20 Strive, son, with all effort for the continuation of our family, for
your own sake as well as ours—for such is the Law, O lord. For by
neither merits of Law nor high-piled austerities do people in this world
gain the goal that others reach by having sons. Put your efforts into

wedding a wife and your mind on begetting offspring, as we now
instruct you, son of ours! You are our last recourse.

Jaratkāru said:

I have always been resolved that I would not take a wife. But for
your welfare I shall take a wife. I shall—with this condition now
25 solemnly spoken: I shall do it if—and not otherwise—a virgin who is
my namesake is pressed upon me by her relatives as an almsgiving,
then I shall marry her with the proper rites. Who shall give me a wife,
despite my poverty? I shall accept her as an alms if someone proffers
her. Thus far shall I go in taking a wife, and with this provision,
O grandsires, and never shall I do otherwise. And from her a son will
be born to rescue you; and having attained to an eternal estate my
forebears shall rejoice.

The Bard said:

Henceforth this brahmin of strict vows roamed the earth, searching
30 for a wife to set up house, but he did not find her. One day the
brahmin went into a forest and, calling to mind the words of his
forebears and longing for a maiden who was to be given him as an
alms, he softly wept his three words.

Vāsuki proffered his sister as a gift and accepted him, but he did
not accept her, thinking, "She does not bear my name." For this was
the plan of the great-spirited Jaratkāru: "I shall take my namesake
for a bride if she is offered me freely." The wise and powerful ascetic
Jaratkāru said to Vāsuki: "What is your sister's name? Tell me the
truth, Snake!"

Vāsuki said:

She is my younger sister Jaratkāru, Jaratkāru! Accept her as your
wife—I offer you the slim-waisted girl. I have kept her for you until
now—take her, excellent brahmin.

The Bard said:

35 Now, great scholar of the *Veda*, the Snakes had once been cursed
by their mother: "Fire who is driven by Wind shall burn you at
Janamejaya's sacrifice." It was to appease this curse that the princely
Snake gave his sister to the great-spirited seer of good vows. And he
accepted her with the ritual that is found in the Rules. A son was born
to her: the strong-willed Āstīka, great-spirited ascetic and master of
the Vedas and their branches, impartial to all the world, who
dispelled the fears of his father and mother. Then, after a long span of
time, Janamejaya, king of men, descendant of Pāṇḍu, offered up a
grand sacrifice known as the Session of the Snakes, so we hear.
40 As this sacrifice went on for the destruction of the Snakes, the most
glorious Āstīka had the Snakes freed from the curse. He saved the
Snakes, his maternal uncles, and all the other Snakes as well, and
saved his forebears with his offspring and austerities. With manifold

vows and Vedic studies, O brahmin, he acquitted himself of his debts:
the Gods he satisfied with sacrifices of various stipends, the seers with
his scholarship, and his ancestors with progeny. Having taken away
his ancestors' heavy burden, Jaratkāru of strict vows went to heaven
with his fathers. After he had obtained a son as well as unequaled
merit of Law, the hermit Jaratkāru went to heaven after a very long
life span.
45 I have narrated this *Tale of Āstīka* as I have heard it. Pray tell me,
tiger of the Bhṛgus, what else should I recount?

Śaunaka said:
14.1 Son of the Bard, narrate in its full extent the tale of that good sage
Āstīka, for you listen most obediently to our words. You tell your
stories with verve, son, with gentle sounds and charming words. You
speak like your father, boy, we are very much pleased. Your father
was always attentive to our wishes—now pray tell this tale as your
father used to tell it!

The Bard said:
I shall tell *The Tale of Āstīka* as I have heard it told by my father,
and it shall give long life!

5 Long ago, in the Eon of the Gods, O faultless brahmin, there were
two handsome sisters, the daughters of Prajāpati, gifted with beauty
and full of marvels. Both of them, Kadrū and Vinatā, were the wives
of Kaśyapa; and this Kaśyapa their lord, who equaled Lord Prajāpati,
once when he was pleased and happily disposed granted a boon to
each of his lawful wives. When they heard from Kaśyapa that there
would be a sublime outpouring of boons, the two beautiful women
went from happiness to incomparable joy. Kadrū chose a thousand
Snakes for her sons, all to be equal in splendor, and Vinatā chose two
sons who were to exceed Kadrū's sons in strength and to excel them
in brilliance, beauty, and might. Her husband granted her the boon
she desired—one son and a half: "So shall it be," said Kaśyapa to
10 Vinatā. And having obtained the boon just as she had asked, Vinatā
was pleased and satisfied that she would bear two sons of superior
powers; and so was Kadrū to bear a thousand sons of equal splendor.
"Take good care to keep the fruit alive!" said Kaśyapa the great
ascetic to his two wives, who were pleased with their boons; and
thereupon he went to the forest.

After a long time Kadrū gave birth to ten hundred eggs, O lord
among brahmins, and Vinatā laid two eggs. Their happy servants
placed the eggs of both of them in pots that were steaming, and kept
them there for five hundred years. After five centuries Kadrū's sons
were hatched, but no twins were seen to hatch from Vinatā's two
15 eggs. Thereupon the divine Vinatā, impatient for a son, embarrassed

and aggrieved, broke open one of the eggs and beheld her son: the
upper half of his body was fully grown, the other half stunted. The tale
has it that the son was enraged and cursed her: "Since you, mother,
a prey to your greed, have now stunted the growth of my body,
therefore for five hundred years you shall be the slave of the woman
whom you sought to rival. And your other son, mother, will set you
free from your slavery—unless you disembody him too, like me,
mother, by breaking his egg, or deform his future body miserably!
20 You must patiently wait for the time of his birth, if you wish his
strength to be surpassing, wait for more than five hundred years."
And having thus cursed Vinatā, her son flew up into the sky and can
now be seen, O brahmin, as Aruṇa, the red dawn at daybreak.

In due time Garuḍa too was hatched, who was to feed on Snakes; and no sooner was he born than he deserted his mother and flew into the sky, as the king of the birds who, when he hungered, fed on the food that the Creator had ordained for him, O tiger of the Bhṛgus.

The Bard said:
15.1 It was at this time, O ascetic, that the two sisters saw the horse
Uccaiḥśravas approach, that priceless jewel of a stallion that all the
hosts of Gods joyfully cheered when it sprang from the ocean while it
was being churned. It was a sublime horse, greatest of steeds, of
immense strength, splendid, ever-youthful, divine, and marked with all
marks of excellence.

Śaunaka said:

How did the Gods churn for the Elixir, and, tell me, where? And where was that mighty and resplendent prince of horses born?

The Bard said:
5 There is an all-surpassing mountain that blazes like a pile of fire
and casts forth the splendor of the sun with its golden glowing peaks—
Mount Meru! It is the many-splendored ornament of gold that is
cherished by Gods and Gandharvas, immeasurable and unattainable
by those of little merit of Law. Awesome beasts of prey range over it,
divine herbs illumine it, and the great mountain rises aloft to cover
with its heights the vault of heaven. To others inaccessible even in
their imaginings, it abounds in rivers and trees and resounds with the
most beautiful flocks of many-feathered birds.

It was this mountain's bright and many-jeweled peak of almost
boundless height that all the august Gods together ascended where it
10 thrusts up yonder. The celestials, austere and restrained, foregathered
and seated themselves and began deliberating on how they might win
the Elixir.

Among them God Nārāyaṇa* spoke thus to Brahmā, while the Gods sat around pondering and deliberating: "The bucket of the Ocean

* = Viṣṇu.

must be churned by both the Gods and the assemblies of the Asuras. Then the Elixir shall spring forth when the Ocean is being churned. Churn ye the Ocean, O Gods, and ye shall find the Elixir, after ye have obtained all good herbs and all precious stones."

The Bard said:

16.1 Hereupon the Gods went to Mount Mandara, adorned with soaring peaks like towering clouds, most eminent of mountains, which, overgrown with thickets of creepers and echoing with the songs of all manner of birds and bristling with tusky beasts of prey, is the playground of Kiṃnaras, Apsarās, and the Gods alike. Eleven thousand leagues it rises into the sky, and for as many thousands do its foundations stretch into earth. Indeed, the Gods with all their hosts could not uproot it then; and they repaired together to where Viṣṇu and Brahmā were sitting and said to them: "Ye lords, set your minds on our ultimate welfare. Let there be an effort, for the sake of all of us, to uproot Mount Mandara."

"So be it," said Viṣṇu, and so did Brahmā, O Bhārgava. Ananta arose at Brahmā's summons, and the mighty serpent was ordered to the task by Nārāyaṇa. And the powerful Ananta with all his might pulled out the sovereign of mountains, with all its forests and forest game. Then the Gods marched with the mountain to the Ocean, and they said to him: "For the sake of the Elixir we shall churn your water." The Lord of the Rivers replied, "Spare me a portion of it, then I will endure the mighty pounding from the churning of Mount Mandara." Then the Gods and the Asuras spoke to the King of Tortoises Akūpāra: "Pray be thou the foundation for Mount Mandara." The tortoise consented and lent its back to the mountain; and Indra squeezed down the top of the mountain with his tool. Thus the Gods made Mount Mandara the churning staff; and using the Snake Vāsuki as the twirling rope, started to churn the ocean, treasury of the waters.

So for the sake of the Elixir the Asuras and all Dānavas took hold of one end of the King of Snakes, and the Gods stood together at the tail. Ananta stayed with the blessed Nārāyaṇa and kept on raising the Snake's head and hurling it down again. And as Vāsuki was forcefully pulled up and down by the Gods, puffs of fire and smoke belched forth from his mouth. The clouds of smoke became massive clouds with lightning flashes and rained down on the troops of the Gods, who were weakening with the heat and fatigue. From the mountaintop showers of flowers were loosened and garlands were scattered all around on the hosts of Gods and Asuras. Then, as Gods and Asuras churned the ocean with Mount Mandara, a mighty roar rose from it like rumbling thunder in the clouds. All kinds of creatures that inhabit the deep were crushed asunder by the big mountain and

20 by the hundreds went to their perdition in the salty ocean; and the
mountain drove sea animals of all sorts, such as dwell in submarine
abysses, to their destruction. While Mount Mandara was being driven
around, large trees crashed into one another and tumbled down from
the peak with their nestling birds. The friction of the trees started
fire after fire, covering the mountain with flames like a black monsoon
cloud with lightning streaks. The fire drove out the elephants and
lions and burned them, and all creatures of many kinds found their
death. Then Indra the Lord of the Immortals flooded the fire that
25 was raging everywhere with rain pouring from the clouds. The many
juices of herbs and the manifold resins of the trees flowed into the
water of the ocean. And with the milk of these juices that had the
power of the Elixir, and with the exudation of the molten gold, the
Gods attained immortality. The water of the ocean now turned into
milk, and from this milk butter floated up, mingled with the finest
essences.

Then the Gods spoke to Brahmā, Granter of Boons, who had
remained seated: "We are very weary, O Brahmā—still the Elixir has
not appeared—and so are the Daityas and great Snakes. Without the
aid of God Nārāyaṇa, all the Gods and Dānavas are powerless. And
30 this churning of the ocean has been going on for a long time. . . ."
Brahmā then spoke to God Nārāyaṇa: "Give them strength, Viṣṇu.
Thou art in this the last resort."

Viṣṇu said:

I grant strength to all who have bent themselves to this task. Let
all now shake the bucket and turn around Mount Mandara!

The Bard said:

Hearing Nārāyaṇa's words, they waxed strong and all together
they once more stirred mightily the milk of the ocean. And then from
the churning ocean there arose the Sun of a hundred thousand rays,
which seemed to equal it, and the bright cool Moon of the tranquil
light. And Goddess Śrī came forth from the butter, clothed in white
35 robes, and the Goddess Liquor, and the White Horse; and the divine
and lustrous Kaustubha jewel that hangs on Nārāyaṇa's chest,
resplendent in its radiance, rose from the Elixir. Śrī, Liquor, the Moon,
and the Horse swift as thought all followed the path of the Sun to
where the Gods were standing. And now came forth the beautiful
God Dhanvantari who carried a white gourd that held the Elixir.

When they saw this great marvel, a loud outcry for the Elixir
went up from the Dānavas, who screeched "It is mine!" But Lord
Nārāyaṇa employed his bewitching wizardry and assumed the
40 wondrous shape of a woman; then he joined the Dānavas. Their minds
bewitched, they gave that woman the Elixir, both Dānavas and Daityas
did, for their hearts went out to her.

The Bard said:

17.1 Now the Daityas and the Dānavas massed together and, grasping their best shields and striking weapons of all sorts, rushed upon the Gods. The mighty God Viṣṇu held fast to the Elixir; and the Lord, seconded by Nara, took it away from the princes of the Dānavas. And all the hosts of the Gods received the Elixir from Viṣṇu's hands, and, amidst a tumultous confusion, drank of it.

While the Gods were drinking the yearned-for Elixir, a Dānava by the name of Rāhu took the guise of a God and began to drink it too. The Elixir had gone down as far as the Dānava's throat when the Sun and the Moon gave alarm as a kindness to the Gods. The blessed Lord who wields the discus thereupon cut off his diademed head as he started to drink. The Dānava's gigantic head fell rolling on the ground and roared most frighteningly. Ever since there has been a lasting feud between Rāhu's head and the Sun and the Moon; and even today he swallows them both.

The blessed Lord Hari* then threw off that incomparably beautiful body of a woman and with all manner of fearsome weapons made the Dānavas quake. And a battle ensued more gruesome than any before, and huge, between the Gods and the Asuras, close by the ocean shore. Broad-lamed honed halberds struck home by the thousands, and sharply tipped javelins and all kinds of side arms. Cut up by the discus and vomiting much blood, wounded by swords, spears, and clubs, the Asuras fell on the battlefield. Like nuggets of melted gold, heads severed by three-bladed lances rolled ceaselessly in the merciless battle. The grand Asuras, their limbs anointed with their blood, lay felled like mineral-colored mountain peaks. Screams burst forth, by the thousands, everywhere. They cut up one another with their swords, and the sun shone bloodied. The noise of them killing one another with copper-spiked bludgeons, or with their fists if they were close by, seemed to reach up to heaven. "Cut them! Stab them! Rush on, you! Throw them down! Press forward!" such were the horrendous cries that were heard all around.

Thus the terrifying tumult of war was rampant when the Gods Nara and Nārāyaṇa joined the battle. The blessed Lord Viṣṇu, upon seeing the divine bow in Nara's hand, called up with his mind his Dānava-destroying discus. No sooner thought-of than the enemy-burning discus appeared from the sky in a blaze of light matching the sun's, with its razor-sharp circular edge, the discus Sudarśana, terrible, invincible, supreme. And when the fiercely blazing, terror-spreading weapon had come to hand, God Acyuta* with arms like elephant trunks loosed it, and it zigzagged fast as a flash in a blur of

* = Viṣṇu.

light, razing the enemy's strongholds. Effulgent like the Fire of Doomsday, it felled foe after foe, impetuously tearing asunder thousands of Dānavas and Daityas as the hand of the greatest of men let go of it in the battle. Here it was ablaze licking like a fire, there it cut down with a vehemence the forces of the Asuras. Now it was hurled into the sky, then into the ground, and like a ghoul it drank blood in that war.

Undiscouraged, the Asuras hammered blows on the host of Gods
with mountains, and the mighty warriors, their luster fading like
25 shredded clouds, took by the thousands to the sky. Then, like iridescent
clouds, giant wooded mountains with truncated peaks came down
sowing terror and crashed roaring into one another. Earth with its
forests was pounded on all sides by the fall of the big mountains and
began to shake as the battlefield of the warriors, who thundered upon
one another, raged furiously. Now Nara darkened the pathways of the
sky with his gold-tipped arrows, cleaving with feathered shafts the
flying mountain peaks in the horrifying onslaught of the Asura armies.
Pressed by the Gods, the grand Asuras dug into the earth and plunged
into the salty sea, when they heard in the sky the raging Sudarśana
discus that shone like a roaring fire.

And, having won the day, the Gods returned Mount Mandara with
great honor to its own site; and, thundering everywhere along skies
30 and heaven, the clouds went as they had come. The Gods hid the
Elixir securely and gave themselves to the most exultant joy. And the
Slayer of Vala with the other Immortals gave the treasury of the
Elixir to the diademed God for safekeeping.

The Bard said:

18.1 Here I have recounted to you fully how the Elixir was churned and
where that illustrious Horse of matchless might was born.

Now, when Kadrū had seen the Horse, she said to Vinatā: "What color is Uccaiḥśravas, my dear? Judge it this instant!"

Vinatā said:

The regal Horse is white, or do you think otherwise, my pretty? You too tell what color it is, and we lay a wager on't!

Kadrū said:

I think the Horse has a black tail, my sweet-smiling friend. You pout? Come, let us wager—the loser will be the winner's slave!

The Bard said:

5 They made this covenant between themselves that the loser would
be the other's slave and then went back to their house, deciding to
look at the Horse on the morrow. Then Kadrū, intending to corrupt
her one thousand sons, ordered them: "You become like hairs as
black as *kohl* and at once insert yourselves in the Horse's tail, lest I
become a slave."

When the Snakes did not obey her command, she cursed them that
they would be burned in the fire, when the Snake Sacrifice of the
royal seer Janamejaya, the wise scion of Pāṇḍu, was to take place.
The Grandsire himself, however, heard this all-too-cruel curse
pronounced by Kadrū; and, although it went far beyond what fate had
10 ordained, he and all the hosts of the Gods approved her word, for the
good of the creatures, as he saw how many Snakes there were. They
were powerful and mordacious, their poison was virulent; to counter
the virulence of their poison, he bestowed the art of healing poison on
the great-spirited Kaśyapa for the well-being of creation.

The Bard said:
19.1 When night had lit up and day broke and the sun rose, the two
sisters Kadrū and Vinatā, O ascetic, having wagered for slavery, now
impetuously and impatiently made their way to look at the Horse
Uccaiḥśravas nearby. There they beheld the ocean, treasury of the
waters, peopled with monsters that swallow whales and crowded with
crocodiles, thick with myriad creatures of all colors and shapes,
forever forbidding even to the awesome, astir with turtles and sharks.
5 It is the lode of all precious stones as it is also the abode of Varuṇa,
the playground of sea serpents, the sovereign Lord of the Rivers.
There one finds the submarine fire and the dungeon of the Asuras.
Terror of the creatures, ever-restless holder of the waters, resplendent
and divine spring of the Immortals' Elixir, beyond measure and
imagining, most sacred and marvelous, it is also dreadful and
gruesome with the screechings of its denizens and its fearsome
reverberations, aswirl with abysmal maelstroms and a danger to all
beings. Stirring with the winds and the shifting of its tidelines, then
rising up with quakes and turbulence, it seems to dance all about to
the rhythm of its rippling hands, its waves imperviously swelling
10 with the waxing and the waning of the moon. Here was born the
Conch Pāñcajanya; it is the inexhaustible mine of pearls. Muddy were
its waters and turbulent when the blessed Lord Govinda of boundless
might assumed the guise of the Boar and found the Earth at the
bottom of the sea. A hundred years did not suffice for the ascetic Atri
to reach its imperishable, lowermost bed. It is the bed of the
boundlessly powerful Viṣṇu at the beginning of a new Eon, when the
God of the lotus-navel sleeps the sleep of Yoga within the self. Holy, its
shores unexplored, its deeps unmeasured and vast, the Lord of the
Rivers makes his oblations in the blazing flames of the Mare-Head
Fire.
15 The sisters looked at the great ocean to whom come running, day
and night, a thousandfold, the many perennial rivers like rivaling
concubines; they saw it with its depths fearfully awash with whales
and crocodiles, roaring with the dreadful screeching of its animals,

huge, mirroring the sky, the plumbless and endless treasury of the waters. And when they had thus beheld the deep ocean, dense with whale and crocodile and waves, resplendent and mirroring the sky, blazing forth with the flame crests of the submarine fires, they swiftly flew across it.

The Bard said:

20.1 Having crossed the ocean, Kadrū and Vinatā soon—for they moved
nimbly—alighted in front of the Horse. And observing the many black
hairs that were stuck in the Horse's tail, Kadrū submitted the
wretched-faced Vinatā to slavery. Vinatā, who had been defeated in
her wager on the Horse and now faced slavery, was tormented with
grief.

In the meantime Garuḍa when his time had come broke the shell
of his egg and was born in all his might without help from his mother.
5 Ablaze like a kindled mass of fire, of most terrifying aspect, the Bird
grew instantly to his giant size and took to the sky. Upon seeing him
all the Gods took refuge with the bright-shining Bird; and prostrating
themselves they spoke to him of the many hues as he sat perched:
"Fire, deign to grow no more! Would that thou do not seek to burn us.
For this huge mass of thine creeps fierily onward!"

The Fire said:

The case is not as you deem it, Gods and Dānavas. This is the powerful Garuḍa, who is my equal in fieriness.

The Bard said:

At these words of the Fire, the Gods and the hosts of the seers betook themselves to Garuḍa and sang his praise, approaching him closely.

10 "Thou art the seer, thou art illustrious, the God Lord of birds!
Thou art the Lord, of the aspect of fire, thou art our ultimate
redemption,
Rippling with power, kindly, and never cheerless,
Thou art thriving and irresistible.
Of thy heat that never lackest in fame we hear,
All that is future and all that has befallen.
Superbly thou shinest upon all that moves and stands,
Eclipsing the splendor of the sun.
Thou art the finisher of all that is, the lasting and the brief.
Just as the wrathful sun may burn the creatures,
Thus dost thou devour them like the fire of sacrifice.
And terrible at the Dissolution dost thou rise firelike,
Destroying and ending the revolution of the Eon.
To thee, Lord of the birds, do we come for refuge.
To thee, most august One without darkness, roaming the clouds.

Approaching thee, Bird Garuḍa of great strength,
That art the here and the yonder, boon-granting, of invincible valor!"

15 And when he had thus been praised by the Gods and the hosts of
seers, he withdrew his heat.

The Bard said:

21.1 Thereupon that Bird of great power and great strength went to his
mother on the other shore of the ocean—for he could roam at will—
where Vinatā was staying, reduced to slavery by her wager on the
Horse and most sorely tormented with grief. Then one day, when her
son was present, the humbly bowing Vinatā was summoned by
Kadrū, who said to her: "My dear Vinatā, take me to lonely and
lovely Ramaṇīyaka on the ocean bay that is the country of the
5 Snakes." Then the mother of the fair-winged Bird brought the mother
of the Snakes to the Snakes, and so did Garuḍa at his mother's
bidding; Vinatā's son, the Bird, went toward the sun; and the Snakes,
encompassed by the rays of the sun, had fallen in a swoon.

Seeing her sons in such a state, Kadrū gave praise to Śakra*:

"Homage to thee, Lord God of Gods, homage to thee, Slayer of
Vala! Homage to thee, Killer of Namuci, thousand-eyed husband of
Śacī! With thy waters become thou a flood for the sun-stricken
snakes—thou alone, supreme among Immortals, art the ultimate
savior of us. For thou art able to pour forth water aplenty, O Sacker
of Cities, thou art cloud, thou art wind, thou art the fire of lightning
10 in the sky. Thou art the spreader of the massing clouds, thee they
call the dense Cloud itself. Thou art the matchless, dreaded
thunderbolt, thou art the roaring monsoon cloud. Creator of the
worlds art thou and their unvanquished destroyer. For all beings
thou art the light, thou art the brilliant sun, the marvelous Great
Being, and King, and Sovereign of the Gods.

"Thou art Viṣṇu, and the thousand-eyed Indra, and God and last
resort. All Elixir art thou, O God, and the most highly honored Soma.
Thou art the lunar day, and the hour, and the instant, the twinkling
of the eye, the bright fortnight and the dark, the daily sliver of the
moon, and a fraction thereof, and a fraction of that. And year, and
seasons, and months, nights and days.

15 "Thou art the sublime earth with its mountains and forests, and
stainless heaven with its sun, and the sea with its whales and
swallowers of whales, that rolls its billows, hosts its crocodiles, and
stirs with its fish. Forever art thou honored as great Fame itself,
thou joyful Indra, by the great wise seers; and when thou hast been
praised, thou drinkest the Soma at the sacrifice and the oblations that
are spent with *vaṣaṭ* for thy well-being!

* = Indra.

"Priests are ever offering to thee, for the sake of the fruits, and thou of the matchless flood of might art chanted in the Vedic sciences. Because of thee are the lords of the twiceborn given to worship and study the auxiliaries along with all the Vedas!"

The Bard said:

22.1 Upon this praise by Kadrū, the blessed Lord of the bay horses covered all the sky with layers of black clouds. The clouds, asparkle with lightning, poured out their waters, ceaselessly thundering, it seemed, at one another in the sky. It was as if all space was packed up with those marvelous rain-givers that, roaring, poured forth their incessant, incomparable water. The sky seemed to dance with the countless billowing showers and grew noisy with the clap of the thunderheads.

5 And as Indra rained, the Snakes were transported with joy, and Earth was everywhere filled with water.

The Bard said:

23.1 Borne by the fair-winged Bird,* they soon came to the island, which was encompassed by the waters of the ocean and resonant with the songs of birds. It was wooded with rows of groves that glistened with fruit and blossoms; lovely villas were laid out and lotus beds. Colorful lakes with tranquil water adorned it, while whiffs of pure breeze that wafted divine fragrances fanned it with cool air. It was lustrous with sandalwood trees that seemed to perfume space and, stirred by the wind, sent forth a rain of flowers to strew showers of blossoms on the Snakes that dwelled there.

5 It was a holy and lovely island, beloved of Gandharvas and Apsarās, who ever rejoiced in it; and awarble with all kinds of birds, it gave delight to the sons of Kadrū. Scarcely had they come to the woods before they started cavorting joyously, then said to the powerful fair-winged Bird who is the Indra of birds: "Carry us to still another lovely island with plentiful water. For as you fly about, bird, you see many enchanting countries."

The Bird reflected and said to his mother, Vinatā: "Why is it, mother, that I must obey their every word?"

Vinatā said:

I have been made the slave of my ignoble sister, sublime Bird. The Snakes tricked me and cheated me at a bet.

The Bard said:

10 Now when his mother had told him the reason, the Bird suffered with her grief; and he said to the Snakes: "What can I fetch you or

* = Garuḍa.

find you, or what feat can I perform so that I may be freed from being bound to you? Speak the truth, Snakes!" The Snakes answered: "Bring us the Elixir with all your might, then you shall be freed from your slavery!"

The Bard said:

24.1 When he had heard the words of the Snakes, Garuḍa said to his mother, "I am going to fetch the Elixir, but I shall want to find something to eat."

Vinatā said:

On a solitary ocean bay lies the great realm of the Niṣādas. Have your meal of those thousands of Niṣādas and bring the Elixir. But never set your mind on killing a brahmin. Among all creatures the brahmin, like fire, should never be killed. A brahmin angered is a fire, a sun, a poison, a sword. The brahmin is the first eater among all beings, the first among all classes, the father, the teacher.

Garuḍa said:

5 By what blessed signs shall I recognize a brahmin? I ask for the reason—pray tell me, mother.

Vinatā said:

If a man has gone down your throat like a swallowed fishhook and burns like a coal, then, my son, you will know that he is an eminent brahmin!

The Bard said:

And then out of love for her son, for all she knew of his matchless strength, Vinatā pronounced this blessing over him: "The Wind shall protect your wings, the Moon shall protect your back, my son. The Fire shall protect your head, and the Sun shall guard all of you. And I myself shall always pray for your peace and welfare. Go a safe path, my son, for the success of your task."

10 And, having listened to his mother's word, he stretched his wings and flew up to the sky. And the powerful Bird came hungrily upon the Niṣādas like great Time the Finisher. Working the destruction of the Niṣādas, he raised a huge cloud of dust that touched the sky, laying dry the water in the ocean bay and shaking the mountains that surrounded it. Then the king of birds laid his beak on the road of the Niṣādas and waylaid them; and the Niṣādas came rushing out to the beak of the Eater of Snakes. They swarmed into his huge, wide-open beak as frightened birds crowd into the sky—by the thousands they came, bewildered by the clouds of wind-swept dust, like birds in a wood that is strafed by a gale. And the mighty, ever-swooping Bird, scourge of his enemies, hungrily closed his beak, the lord of the fowl that sweep the sky, and crushed that race that feeds on all kinds of fish.

The Bard said:

25.1 Then a brahmin got in his throat with his wife and burned fiercely
like a burning coal. The Bird said to him: "Good brahmin, escape at
once from my open beak. For I must never swallow a brahmin, even if
he is a friend of evil-doers." And to Garuḍa who had thus spoken, the
brahmin replied: "This wife of mine is a Niṣāda woman. Let her
escape with me!"

Garuḍa said:

Take this Niṣāda woman too, and escape at once. Save yourself
before the fire of my belly starts digesting you!

The Bard said:

5 Thereupon the brahmin and his Niṣāda wife escaped from his
mouth; and, after having praised Garuḍa, he went to a country he
chose. When the brahmin and his wife had departed, the King of
Birds stretched his wings and flew into the sky, fast as thought. Then
he saw his father Kaśyapa, and upon his bidding told him: "I have
been sent by the Snakes and am ready to steal the Soma. I shall steal
it this very day, to set mother free from her slavery. Mother told me to
eat up the Niṣādas, but even after I ate them by the thousands, I am
not yet sated. Show me therefore some other food I can eat, my lord,
and grow strong enough to steal the Elixir."

Kaśyapa said:

10 There was once a great seer by the name of Vibhāvasu who was
very quick to anger. He had a younger brother, an ascetic too,
Supratīka. This brother Supratīka, a great sage, did not like it that
their property was held in common and did not cease to advocate that
they divide it between themselves. Then brother Vibhāvasu said to
Supratīka, "There are many who from sheer folly always want to
divide common property; but once they have divided it, they are so
deluded by their possessions that they ignore one another. Enemies
spring up at once, disguised as friends, who, whenever they find
kinsmen that foolishly divide their holdings and then only care about
their own, estrange them even more. And others, thus finding them
estranged in matters of property, bring them down, and so divided
15 kinsmen very soon meet total ruin. This is the reason why the strict
do not approve of the division of property between those kinsmen
who are beholden to the precepts of their teachers and wish each
other well. Supratīka, you are beyond managing! Since you forever
hold out your hand for your own broken-up property, you shall
become an elephant!"

But when he was cursed in this fashion, Supratīka said to Vibhāvasu: "And so shall you become a tortoise that lives in the sea!" Thus upon each other's curse Supratīka and Vibhāvasu became elephant and tortoise, for their thoughts were beclouded by greed.

Ever since they have persisted in their common vice of anger and,
brutes now, pleasure themselves with feuding, prideful of their size
20 and strength. It is here in this lake that the huge beasts pursue their
ancient quarrel. There's one of them coming, this huge handsome
elephant, and at its trumpeting sound emerges the giant tortoise that
lives under water, shaking the entire lake. Seeing it, the elephant curls
his trunk; and tusks, trunk, tail, and feet moving furiously, it falls
upon the tortoise with all its might. The lake aswim with fish breaks
up in billows. The tortoise raises its head and no less mightily rises to
the battle. The elephant stands six leagues tall and is twice as long;
the tortoise is three leagues high and ten around.
25 Now devour you the two of them since they are mad with battle-
fury, each out to vanquish the other, and then swiftly finish the
task you have set for yourself.

The Bard said:

Hearing his father's word, the sky-sweeping Bird came down with
a terrifying swoop and struck the elephant with one claw and the
tortoise with the other. Up flew the Bird, high up in the sky. He made
for the sacred Ford of Alamba and came upon its divine trees; in a
fright, they began to tremble under the wind of the Bird's wings, the
golden-boughed trees of the Gods, lest the Bird should break them.
30 And seeing them quiver with their fruits and shoots that grant wishes,
the wanderer of the skies went on to other trees of incomparable
colors and shapes, giants of the forest that were radiant with gold and
silver fruit and with branches of beryl, washed by the waters of the sea.

A very large banyan tree stood there, grown out surpassing wide,
which addressed that greatest of birds when he swooped down swift as
the mind: "Alight on this big branch of mine that stretches for a
hundred leagues, and eat the elephant and the tortoise." And shaking
to its roots that mountainous tree in which a thousand birds were
nestling, the grand Bird nimbly swept down and alighted—and broke
the thick-leafed branch.

The Bard said:

26.1 No sooner did the mighty Garuḍa touch the branch with his talons
than it snapped and he held on to the broken-off branch. When he had
broken that huge branch and smilingly looked down at it, he noticed
the Vālakhilyas hanging upside down from it. For fear of killing them
the King of the Birds flew up again and with a careful concern for
them took the branch in his beak. Quietly the Bird circled about,
razing the mountains before him, and in this fashion winged over
many countries with his elephant and tortoise. And in his pity for the
Vālakhilyas he found no place to light.
5 Then he flew to that greatest of mountains, imperishable

Gandhamādana, and there he saw his father Kaśyapa standing in self-mortification. And the father saw the divinely colored Bird, filled with glow, might, and strength, swift as mind and wind, huge like a mountain peak, who rose like the upraised staff of Brahmā—beyond imagining and comprehension, terror of all creatures, wielder of the power of wizardry, the upthrusting kindled fire incarnate—unassailable and invincible to Gods, Dānavas, and Rākṣasas, cleaver of mountaintops, drier of the water of the rivers, whirler of the worlds, awesome image of Death.

10 Seeing him come and surmising his intentions, the blessed Kaśyapa said the words: "Son, do not act rashly, lest you incur sudden pain, lest the sunbeam-drinking Vālakhilyas wax angry and burn you!" Thereupon, for his son's sake, Kaśyapa appeased the Vālakhilyas of accomplished austerities, pointing out the purpose of it: "The good of the creatures is served by Garuḍa's enterprise, ye ascetics. He seeks to do a great feat; pray give him your leave!"

At these words of the blessed Kaśyapa the sages left the branch and together they repaired to the holy Mount Himālaya, in search of
15 austerities. When they had departed, Vinatā's son, his beak still distended by the branch, asked his father Kaśyapa, "Sir, where can I let go of this tree limb? Is there a country without brahmins? Tell me, sir." Then Kaśyapa told him of a mountainous place uninhabited by men, with caves that were covered with snowdrifts—an inaccessible fastness that others would fail to penetrate even with their thoughts. Penetrating that large mountainous enclave with his mind, the Bird Tārkṣya* swiftly flew to it with branch, tortoise, and elephant. A long thin leather strap cut from a hundred cowhides would have fallen short of girding the giant branch that the Bird carried in his flight.
20 In no time at all Garuḍa, greater than all that flies, had covered a stretch of a hundred thousand leagues; and after an instant, reaching the mountain his father had described, the Bird let go of that branch that now roared downward.

That king of mountains began to shake under the onslaught of the wind of the Bird's wings and, as its trees collapsed, showered a rain of blossoms. All around, the mountain peaks shattered that adorned the great mountain aglow with gems and gold. And many trees that were hit by that branch shone with golden blossoms like lightning-streaked
25 clouds. The golden radiance of the trees, marrying the minerals of the mountain, glowed up as though mirroring the red rays of the sun. Then the superb Bird Garuḍa lit upon the top of that mountain and fed on the tortoise and the elephant.

Fast as thought, he flew up from the peak, and ominous portents began to appear to the Gods. Indra's beloved thunderbolt blazed

* = Garuḍa.

forth in pain; smoking, fire-trailing meteors came loose from heaven
and shot down. The weapons proper to each of the Vasus, the Rudras,
the Ādityas, the Sādhyas, the Maruts, and of all the other hosts of
30 Gods began attacking one another—this had never happened before,
not even in the war between Gods and Asuras. Winds blew with
hurricane gusts, meteors fell all around, and the cloudless sky rumbled
with thunder. He who is the God of Gods rained a rain of blood; the
Gods's garlands withered, and the lights in the sky went out. Horrible
clouds of shooting stars sent forth dense showers of blood, and
swirling dust obfuscated the lofty diadems of the Gods.

Indra of the hundred sacrifices who, along with the other Gods,
was greatly upset with fear at beholding these ghastly portents,
addressed Bṛhaspati: "Why, reverend Lord, do these great portents
arise? I do not see an enemy who could defy us in battle."

Bṛhaspati said:

35 It is through your own fault, Lord of the Gods, and your own
negligence, you of the hundred sacrifices, that the Vālakhilyas have
armed themselves with the power of their austerities and engendered a
marvelous creature. It is a Bird, son of Kaśyapa the sage and Vinatā,
powerful and of many disguises; and he has now come to steal the
Soma. This Bird, strongest of the strong, has the power to steal the
Soma: I believe anything of him; he'd accomplish the impossible.

The Bard said:

Indra, hearing this, said to the guardians of the Elixir, "A Bird of
great power and strength stands ready to steal the Soma here. I give
you warning so that he will fail to take it by force. For incomparable
is his strength, so Bṛhaspati has told me."

40 On hearing this the Gods were astounded and painstakingly took
stations around the Elixir, and so did the majestic Indra of the
hundred sacrifices. Wisely they wore golden armor, preciously
patterned and encrusted with beryl, and among their multitudes
brandished multitudes of terrible arms, the edges and points honed
razor-sharp, throwing sparks and flames in a cloud of smoke—discuses,
bludgeons, tridents, battle-axes, sharp javelins of all kinds, and
spotless scimitars, arms that fitted their bodies, and ugly looking
45 clubs. And splendid with their resplendent weapons, and sparkling
with divine gems, the hosts of the Gods, pure of heart, stood guard.
Strength and might and glow unequaled, minds bent upon the
guarding of the Elixir, the Gods, razers of the Asura cities, shone with
bodies like kindled fire. Thus the grand battlefield, arrayed with the
ranks of the Gods and thick with hundreds of thousands of clubs,
seemed to surpass the boundaries of heaven and bathed in the
radiant rays of the sun.

Śaunaka said:
27.1 How had the great Indra been at fault, and where had he been
negligent, son of the Bard? And how indeed did Kaśyapa, who was a
brahmin, beget a son who became King of the Birds through the
austerities of the Vālakhilyas? How did he become invincible and
indestructible to any creature? How could the Bird roam at will and
have every power at will? This I would like to know, if it is related in
the ancient Lore.
The Bard said:
5 This is indeed one of the topics in the ancient Lore, what you are
asking me. Listen, O brahmin, as I recount it all in summary.
When Kaśyapa, who was a Prajāpati, offered up a sacrifice
because he desired a son, the seers, the Gods, and the Gandharvas
came to his aid, so it is said. Kaśyapa had charged Indra to fetch the
firewood for the sacrifice, and also the sage Vālakhilyas and all the
other hosts of Gods. Now Indra lifted up a mountainous load of
firewood that matched his strength, and the Lord carried this load
with hardly any effort at all. Then he saw on his way the tiny
Vālakhilyas, no larger than the thick joint of the thumb, who all of
them together were carrying a single leaf—the ascetics, having gone
without food, seemed to have shriveled into their bodies and were so
weak that they came to grief in a cow hoofprint that had filled up
10 with water. The Sacker of Cities, drunk with his strength, burst with
mirth and laughing down at them overtook them quickly and stepped
contemptuously over their heads. This angered them mightily, and in
their rancor they undertook a grand sacrifice that spelled danger for
Indra. The great priestly ascetics poured their libations into the ritual
fire according to the precepts and with a variety of spells with, hear,
this intention: "There shall be another Indra to all the Gods, with
every power at his call, and with every range at his will, who shall
be the terror of Indra," they announced, strict in their vows. "As the
fruit of our austerities there shall now arise a terrible creature, swift
as thought, who shall match Indra a hundredfold in power and
bravery!"
15 Learning this, the King of the Gods, of the hundred sacrifices,
became greatly upset and sought refuge with Kaśyapa, strict in his
vows. Kaśyapa, lord of creation, listened to the King of the Gods and
thereupon went up to the Vālakhilyas and enquired if their sacrifice
was succeeding. "Succeed it shall," replied the truthful sages.
Kaśyapa Prajāpati said to them appeasingly: "This Indra was made
the Indra of the three worlds at the order of Brahmā. And even
though you ascetics are striving for another Indra, pray, good folk,
do not belie the word of Brahmā! But neither should your intention
20 be made a lie by me. Then let there arise an Indra of the birds, of

surpassing strength and mettle. And let grace be shown to the King of the Gods who is begging you."

Thus addressed by Kaśyapa, the ascetic Vālakhilyas paid homage to that supreme hermit Prajāpati; and they said in reply, "This enterprise of all of us is for another Indra; it is also an enterprise that is dear to your heart, as it is meant to beget you a son. Therefore you yourself should take over this rite and its fruit as well. You may dispose in whichever way you deem best."

It was at this very time that the radiant Goddess, Dakṣa's
25 beautiful and famous daughter Vinatā, was wishing for a son. Her
austerities performed, her vows for the birth of a son faithfully
fulfilled, the pure woman lay with her husband. Kaśyapa then said
to her, "This enterprise, O Goddess, shall have the fruit you wish
for. You shall give birth to two heroic sons, overlords of the three
worlds, who will be born from the austerities of the Vālakhilyas and
from my own intention. You shall have two sons of great good
fortune, who will be honored by the world." And again the blessed
Lord Marīci said to her, "Take very good care bearing this most
prosperous fruit. He shall become an Indra to reign alone over the
birds, a heroic Bird; esteemed by all the world, he will have every
power in his grasp."
30 Then Prajāpati, pleased, spoke to the God of the Hundred
Sacrifices*: "Two powerful brothers will be born to you, two birds,
and they will be your helpers. No wrong will come to you from them,
Sacker of Cities. Your anxieties are over, Śakra. Indra you shall
remain, but nevermore hold light these scholars of the Brahman, nor
ever pridefully despise them: their wrath is fierce, their word is
poison." And at these words Indra shed his fears and repaired to
his heaven. Vinatā, her wish fulfilled, was overjoyed. She gave
birth to two sons, Aruṇa and Garuḍa. Of the two, Aruṇa was deformed
35 and became the dawn that brings in the sun. Garuḍa was
consecrated as the Indra of the birds. Now listen to his great exploit, O
scion of the Bhṛgus.

The Bard said:

28.1 Now then, when all this confusion was going on, O best of
brahmins, the King of Birds Garutmat* quickly reached the Gods. On
seeing him to be of surpassing strength, they started to shiver all
around, and even to attack one another with all their weapons.
Viśvakarman stood among them, soul beyond measure, bright as
lightning and fire, that most powerful guardian of the Soma.

* = Indra.

** = Garuḍa.

Instantly a grandiose battle took place; and Viśvakarman, ripped by
the Bird with wings, beak, and talons, was struck down in the fight.
5 With the wind of his wings the Bird blew up a huge dust storm that
darkened the worlds and scattered it over the Gods. Covered with the
dust, the Gods were confounded, and under that tent of dust the
guardians of the Elixir lost sight of him. Thus Garuḍa brought
heaven to total disarray and tore the Gods asunder with strokes of his
wings and beak.

Thereupon the God of the Thousand Eyes* hurriedly ordered the
Wind: "Blow this rain of dust away, Wind, here lies your task!"
And the strong Wind hastened to scatter the dust cloud. When the
darkness had lifted, the Gods pressed in on the Bird and the powerful
10 Bird screeched aloud with the thunder of a monsoon cloud. Hit by
the hosts of the Gods, the King of Birds, destroyer of enemy heroes,
flew up powerfully, terrifying all creatures. Then when he had flown
up and hung in the sky above the Gods, the celestials, armored and
led by Indra, all rained blows on him with their three-bladed spears,
clubs, pikes, bludgeons, and all manner of swords, and with sharp-
edged disks that resembled the sun. On all sides assailed by the
onslaught of these weapons, the King of Birds remained unshaken
and waged a tumultuous battle. Like roaring thunder in the sky, the
majestic son of Vinatā scattered the Gods every which way with his
15 wings and chest. Routed and pressed by Garuḍa, the Gods took to
flight, and those wounded by talons and beak shed much blood.
Sādhyas and Gandharvas fled to the East and, overcome by the Indra
of the birds, the Vasus and Rudras took to the South, the Ādityas to
the West, the two Nāsatyas** to the North, glancing back time and
again at the august Bird with whom they were embattled. He joined
battle with the brave Aśvakranda, with Reṇuka who roams the sky,
with heroic Krathana and Tapana, Ulūka and Śvasana, and the bird
20 Nimeṣa, Praruja and Praliha – Vinatā's son tore them to pieces with
his wings, claws, and pointed beak, like the mighty Bowman*** who
rages on Doomsday. Laid low with their many wounds, the high and
mighty and enterprising fighters looked like bursting clouds raining
showers of blood.

When that grand Bird had rid them all of life, he strode across them
to look for the Elixir. He saw fire everywhere; blazing fiercely, it filled
all the skies with its flames, burning hot and razor-sharp rays, and
evil under the stirrings of the wind. Thereupon Garuḍa, fierce and
great-spirited, took on ninety times ninety mouths, drank up with

* = Indra.
** = Aśvins.
*** = Śiva.

these mouths the water of the rivers, returned with great speed and
25 driving the chariot of his wings, the burner of his enemies sprinkled
the burning fire with the rivers. Then, after putting out the fire, he
took on another tiny body to make his entry.

The Bard said:

29.1 With a golden body that shone like bundled sunbeams, the Bird
entered with a will, like the impact of a river on the sea. He saw, in
front of the Elixir, an iron wheel with a honed edge and sharp blades,
which ran incessantly, bright like fire and sun, the murderous cutting
edge for the robbers of the Elixir, a surpassingly dreadful device that
had been skillfully forged by the Gods. No sooner had the Bird seen a
way through it than he started revolving in time with the wheel and,
contracting his body, flew instantly between the spokes. And behind
5 the wheel he saw two big snakes, shimmering like blazing fires,
tongues darting like lightning, mouths blazing, eyes burning, looks
venomous, no less powerful than gruesome, in a perpetual rage and
fierce, that stood guard over the Elixir, their eyes ever-baleful and
never blinking. Whomever either snake's eyes were to fall upon would
turn to ashes.

The fair-winged Bird at once threw dust in their eyes and when
they no longer could see him chased them all about. Then he strode
across their bodies, the sky-roaming son of Vinatā, cut through them
10 with a will, and rushed to the Soma. The mighty Garuḍa gathered up
the Elixir, shattered the torture wheel, and flew sweepingly upward.
The powerful Bird quickly enveloped the Elixir without drinking it
and, unwearied, attained the luster of the now-darkened sun.

The son of Vinatā now encountered Viṣṇu in the sky. Satisfied with
the even tenor of his course, Nārāyaṇa said to the Bird, "I am the
imperishable boon-granting God." And the wanderer of the sky asked
the boon: "I shall always stay above you!" And again he spoke this
word to Nārāyaṇa: "May I even without the aid of the Elixir never
15 age and never die!" Having received these two boons, Garuḍa spoke
to Viṣṇu: "I grant you a boon too—choose, my lord!" And Kṛṣṇa
chose the mettlesome Garutmat for his mount: the blessed Lord made
a flagpole: "You shall perch above me!"

But as the Bird, enemy of the Gods, flew onward with the Elixir,
Indra smote him forcefully with the thunderbolt. And in the tussle
that ensued Garuḍa, struck by the thunderbolt, greater than all that
flies, said laughing with polished words: "I pay honor to the seer from
whose bone the thunderbolt has sprung, and to the thunderbolt, and
20 to you yourself, God of the Hundred Sacrifices. Here I let go of one
feather, and you will never explore its ends. For the blow of your

thunderbolt did not hurt me at all."

And, seeing the beauty of the feather, all creatures exclaimed, astounded: "He must be the Fair-Winged Bird!" And upon witnessing this marvel, the Sacker of Cities* of the thousand eyes reflected that the Bird was a great being, and he said: "I wish to learn the farthest limit of your incomparable strength; and I want eternal friendship with you, greatest of birds!"

Garuḍa said:

30.1 There shall be friendship between us, God Sacker of Cities, as you
wish. But know that my strength is great and unendurable. Surely,
the strict do not approve of one's praising his own strength and
glorifying his own virtues, God of the Hundred Sacrifices.* But
deeming you my friend and at your bidding, friend, I shall speak; for
5 never should one praise oneself without cause. Wide earth with her
mountains and oceans and forests, and thyself that art suspended here,
and all the worlds together, with all that moves and stands, I can
tirelessly carry with the quill of one feather! Thus know the greatness
of my strength!

The Bard said:

When he had thus spoken, the diademed Lord Indra of the Gods, most illustrious well-wisher of all creatures, said to the hero, O Śaunaka: "Now accept my friendship, eternal and supreme. If you have no need for the Soma, return the Soma to me. For those to whom you may give it will forever best us."

Garuḍa said:

It was with some purpose in mind that I stole this Soma. I shall not give it to anyone to partake of. But, God of the thousand eyes, when I myself shall put it down anywhere, you can take it at once and carry it off, sovereign of the three worlds!"

Indra said:

10 The word that you now have spoken pleases me, O Bird. Take from
me whatever boon you desire!

The Bard said:

Thus addressed, he reflected on the sons of Kadrū; and remembering the deception they had wrought to make a slave of his mother, he replied: "I am the master of all, but still I shall become your supplicant: let the mighty Snakes become my staple, Indra!" "So shall it be," said the Slayer of the Dānavas, then followed him and said behind him: "And I shall carry off the Soma when you have put it down."

Thereupon the fair-winged Bird went quickly near his mother and,

* = Indra.

15 overjoyed, spoke as follows to the Snakes: "I have brought the Elixir! I shall place it for you on *kuśa* grass. Bathe and sanctify yourselves, and then drink of it, O Snakes. And from now onward my mother shall be freed from slavery, for I have done just as you demanded of me." The Snakes replied: "So shall it be," and they went to bathe; and Indra scooped up the Elixir and went to his heaven.

Then, having bathed and repeated their prayers and rites of sanctification, the Snakes returned happily to that spot, looking for the Soma. Finding that it had been stolen and recognizing that they in turn had been deceived, the Snakes began licking the *darbha* grass,
20 as it had been the seat of the Soma. And, because of their licking the sharp grass, the Snakes got their forked tongues; and the *darbha* stalks became purifiers, as they had been in touch with the Soma.

Thereafter the fair-winged Bird most happily roamed in the forest with his mother. Feeding on Snakes, highly honored by the birds, and never lacking in fame, he gladdened the heart of Vinatā.

Whatever man shall ever hear this tale, or shall ever recite it in the assembly of the first of twiceborn, he shall be certain to go to heaven and have his share of merit for his glorification of the great-spirited Lord of the Birds.

Śaunaka said:

31.1 You have related, son of the Bard, the reason why the Snakes were cursed by their mother, why Vinatā was cursed by her son, and how Kadrū and Vinatā were granted boons by their husband. The names have been given of both the Birds that were born from Vinatā, but you have made no mention of the names of the Snakes, son of the Bard.

We wish to hear their names, at least the chief ones.

The Bard said:

The names of the Snakes are very many, ascetic—I shall not mention all of them. But hear from me the chief ones.

5 The firstborn was Śeṣa, and Vāsuki came after him. And Airāvata, Takṣaka, Karkotaka and Dhanaṃjaya, Kālīya, Maṇināga and the Snake Āpūraṇa; Piñjaraka, Elāpatra, Vāmana, Nīla and Anīla, Kalmaṣa and Śabala; Āryaka, Ādika, Śālapotaka, Sumanomukha, Dadhimukha, and Vimalapiṇḍaka. Then Āpta, Koṭanaka, Śanka, Vāliśikha, Niṣṭhyūnaka, Hemaguha, Nahuṣa, and Pingala; Bāhyakarṇa, Hastipāda, Mudgarapiṇḍaka, Kambala and Aśvatara, and Kālīyaka, Vṛtta, Saṃvartaka, and the two Snakes known as Padma; Śankhanaka and Sphaṇḍaka, Kṣemaka, Piṇḍāraka, Karavīra, Puṣpadaṃstra, Elaka, Bilvapāṇḍuka, Mūṣakāda, Śankhaśiras, Pūrṇadaṃstra, and Haridraka, Aparājita, Jyotika and Śrīvaha, Kauravya and Dhṛtarāṣṭra, Puṣkara and Śalyaka, Virajas, Subāhu and the mighty Śālipiṇḍa; Hastibhadra,

15 Piṭharaka, Kumuda, Kumudākṣa, Tittiri and Halika, Karkara and
Akarkara, Mukhara, Koṇavasana, Kuñjara, Kurāra, Prabhākara, and
Kuṇḍodara and Mahodara.

Herewith, O best of the twiceborn, are the chief Snakes enumerated.
Since there are too many names, I shall not mention the others. Their
issue and the offspring of their issue are innumerable, I believe, and I
shall not cite them, great brahmin. The many thousands and millions,
O ascetic, and tens of millions of Snakes are beyond enumerating.

Śaunaka said:

32.1 So the Snakes had become powerful and unassailable, my son. Now
that you have told me of their curse, what did they do thereafter?

The Bard said:

One of them, the famed and blessed Lord Śeṣa, deserted Kadrū and
undertook abundant austerities, feeding on the wind and observing
harsh vows. He went to Mount Gandhamādana, and he devoted
himself to his mortifications in Badarī, Gokarṇa, Puṣkarāraṇya, and on
the slopes of the Himālaya. In all these holy places, fords as well as
sanctuaries, he was bent solely upon his exercises, lived strictly, and
mastered his senses.

5 The Grandfather saw the lord perform his awesome austerities,
wearing the hermit's hair tuft and bark shirt, his skin, flesh, and
muscles dried out. And as the Snake was doing his exercises, holding
on to his vow of truth, the Grandfather spoke to him: "What are you
doing, Śeṣa? Work for the well-being of the creatures! For with these
severe mortifications you mortify creation, O faultless Snake! Tell me,
Śeṣa, what desire has been lodging in your heart?"

Śeṣa said:

All my nest brothers are slow of wit. I cannot endure to live with
them, sir, pray condone me. Like enemies, they do not cease
quarreling with one another. Therefore I devote myself to austerities,
10 so that I am spared their sight. They suffer neither Vinatā nor her son,
and yet, Grandfather, Garuḍa is our brother as well. They bear him
grudge to excess; and so does he, very powerful as he is, ever since he
obtained that boon from the great-spirited Kaśyapa, his father.
I myself shall carry on my mortifications until I shed this carcass. In
no wise shall I consort with my brothers, here or hereafter!

Brahmā said:

Śeṣa, I know the way of life of all your brothers and the great
danger that looms for them because of their mother's crime. But long
before an exception was made in this matter, Snake—you need not
grieve over any one of your brethren. Choose a boon from me, Śeṣa,
15 whatever it is you desire. I wish to grant you a boon, for I am very

pleased with you. It is by good fortune, O best of Snakes, that your mind is set upon the Law: and on the Law it shall be set ever firmer.

Śeṣa said:

This is the boon I desire, God Grandfather. May my mind rejoice in the Law, and in dispassionateness and austerity, my Lord!

Brahmā said:

I am pleased, Śeṣa, with your restraint and dispassion. Let the word that you have spoken be fulfilled at my behest for the well-being of the creatures. This wide earth abounding with mountains and forests, with her oceans and minefields and settlements, which so far has rocked unsteadily, you must now encompass and hold so that she be stable.

Śeṣa said:

20 As hath spoken the boon-granting God Prajāpati, sovereign of earth, sovereign of creatures, sovereign of worlds, so shall I hold earth steady—bestow her upon my head, Prajāpati.

Brahmā said:

Then go underneath the earth, thou best of the Snakes. She herself will open a way for thee. And carrying this earth, O Śeṣa, thou shalt do me a great kindness.

The Bard said:

Śeṣa consented; the firstborn of the first among the Snakes passed through a chasm in the earth and stayed there. He carries Goddess Earth on his head, encompassing all around the felly of the ocean.

Brahmā said:

Thou art Śeṣa, greatest of Snakes, thou art the God of Law, for thou alone lendest support to this earth, encircling her entire with endless coils, not less than I support her, or the Cleaver of Vala.*

The Bard said:

So the majestic Snake Ananta dwells underneath the ground,
25 ubiquitous, holding good Earth up at the bidding of Brahmā. And the
blessed Lord who is the first among the Immortals, the Grandfather,
gave Vinatā's son, the fair-winged Bird, to Ananta as his helper.

The Bard said:

33.1 When the best of the Snakes Vāsuki heard the curse from his mother, he pondered on how it could be averted. He took counsel with all his brothers, Airāvata and all others, who were bent upon their Law.

Vāsuki said:

You know, my innocent brothers, what curse has been pronounced over us. Let us take counsel together and do our best to escape from the curse. There is not a curse that has no cure, but, Snakes, one

* = Indra.

cursed by his mother has no escape. I have heard that we have been cursed before imperishable and immeasurable Truth, and my heart trembles. Surely utter extinction has been pronounced over us, for the imperishable God failed to stop her from cursing us. Therefore we must deliberate together how the health of the Snakes may be preserved, lest time passes us by—for as we deliberate we may see a means of escape, as the Gods once did when the fire was lost and lay hidden in a cave—so that Janamejaya's sacrifice for the destruction of the Snakes come to nought, or be overcome.

The Bard said:

All the sons of Kadrū who had assembled there said, "So be it!" And being wily in counsels and plans, they began to seek agreement. Some Snakes there said: "Let us become grand brahmins and beg Janamejaya to call off the Sacrifice!" But other Snakes who thought themselves clever proposed: "We should all become highly respectable councillors. He will ask our decisive opinion on all matters of ritual task, and we shall express the view that the Sacrifice ought to be stopped.

"Knowing that we are of high reputation, the king, himself a wise man, will ask about the effect of his Sacrifice, and we shall reply that there will be none, pointing out its many dreadful evils, here and hereafter, and showing cause and reason why the Sacrifice should not be held. Or if a guru who is devoted to the king's affairs and knows the precepts that govern a Snake Sacrifice is selected for the ritual, one of us will kill him so that he returns to the ten elements. When the sacrificial priest has died, the Sacrifice will not be held. Whatever other priests are chosen as experts on Snake Sacrifices, we shall bite them all, and it will be done with."

There were, however, other Snakes who abided by the Law, and they counseled: "Yours is a poor plan—brahmin murder is unforgivable. In any disaster ultimate peace is possible only when it is completely rooted in the Law. The ascendancy of lawlessness, as we know, will only destroy the entire world." Other Snakes again said, "Let us become clouds with lightning and all, and put out the kindled fire of Sacrifice with rain showers!" "Or let us steal in by night," said some superior Snakes, "and take away the wrapped offering ladles when no one is looking. That will make short shrift of it. Or the Snakes should bite all the people at the Sacrifice, by the hundred and thousands, so that there will be a panic. Or the Snakes should befoul the prepared food with dung and urine, which will destroy all the eatables." But others said, "Let us become the priests of the Sacrifice, and then obstruct it by demanding our fees!" "Let us overpower the king, so that he does what we want." Others said, "When the king is playing about in the water, we will take him home and tie him up so that the

Sacrifice will not be held." There were other Snakes there, virtuous enough, who said, "We lay hold of him and bite him at once, and it will be over with. Once he is dead the root of all our reverses is cut. This is the final view and consensus of all of us. If you approve, King, let us proceed at once."

Having spoken, they all looked at Vāsuki, King of the Snakes; and
30 after some reflection Vāsuki said to the Snakes, "Your final plan does not seem right to carry out, Snakes. No one of the Snakes's plans looks good to me. What is to be done now that is to your benefit? This worries me greatly. And both right and wrong are mine."

The Bard said:

34.1 Having heard all the Snakes speak their word and Vāsuki say his, Elāpatra made the following speech. "This Sacrifice is inevitable, and no less unavoidable is King Janamejaya Pāṇḍaveya, from whom this great danger now looms for us. If a man in this world, O king, is struck by fate he has only fate to resort to—he has no other recourse. And such is our fated danger now, good Snakes, that we must resort
5 to fate alone. Now listen to my word. When the curse was hurled at us, good Snakes, I was afraid and climbed in Mother's lap. Then I heard the Gods speak. 'Harsh are the great Snakes,' they said, O lord, 'harsh!' while they were sorrowfully drawing near to Grandfather, O illustrious king."

The Gods said:

What woman indeed, Grandfather, would bear the sons she loved and then curse them in this way? Who but harsh Kadrū, and in front of yourself, God of Gods! And you, Grandfather, even approved of her curse and said, "So shall it be!" We wish to know the reason why she was not stopped.

Brahmā said:

There are too many Snakes, they are harsh, terribly brave, and covered with poison. At that time I did not stop her, as I wished the
10 creatures well. It is the eagerly biting Snakes, the mean and evil and virulent ones, that are doomed to die, not the law-abiding Snakes. Now hear by what cause those Snakes will escape from their deadly danger when that time has come. A great seer will arise in the lineage of the Yāyāvaras, who will be famed as Jaratkāru, an ascetic and master of his senses. This Jaratkāru will have a son, an ascetic too, by the name of Āstīka: he will put an end to the sacrifice. And those Snakes will escape who have been true to the Law.

The Gods said:

And on whom will that powerful ascetic and eminent sage Jaratkāru beget this great-spirited son, O God?

Brahmā said:
15 Powerful namesake, first of the twiceborn, will beget on a namesake
virgin a son of great potency, O Gods!

Elāpatra said:

"So must it be," said the Gods to the Grandfather; and having spoken the Gods went away, and so did the God Grandfather. Now here before me, Vāsuki, I see your sister, who bears the name of Jaratkāru. Present her to him as an alms when he comes abegging, so that the danger of the Snakes may be appeased. Give her to the seer of good vows, for thus I have heard shall we escape.

The Bard said:
35.1 When the Snakes had heard this speech of Elāpatra, O most eminent
of the twiceborn, they all applauded happily, "Good! Good!" From
then onward Vāsuki guarded that maiden sister of his, Jaratkāru, and
found great relief. Not too long a time had passed since all the Gods
and Asuras churned Varuṇa's ocean. The Snake Vāsuki, strong among
5 the strong, acted thereat as the twirling rope. When they had finished
their task, the Gods went to the Grandfather along with Vāsuki, and
they said to the Grandfather: "Lord, Vāsuki fears for the curse and
worries greatly. Pray pull out this thorn that sticks in his mind
because of his mother's curse, for he wishes his kinsmen well, O God.
For this King of the Snakes has our welfare at heart and does us
favors. Show him your grace, Lord of the Gods, and appease the fear
of his mind."

Brahmā said:

I myself, O Immortals, was the one who inspired the speech that the Snake Elāpatra at the time recounted to him. Let the King of the Snakes carry out those words for which the time now has come. The evil Snakes are doomed to die, the law-abiding ones are not. The brahmin Jaratkāru has been born and is devoting himself to awesome austerities. When the time comes, Vāsuki must give him his sister Jaratkāru. Such was the word that the Snake Elāptra pronounced at the time. This will spell well-being for the Snakes, O Gods—it will not be otherwise.

The Bard said:

The Lord of the Snakes, upon hearing the Grandfather's words, put many Snakes on a perpetual watch of Jaratkāru: "When Lord Jaratkāru wishes to choose a wife, hasten here and tell me. That will be our salvation."

Śaunaka said:
36.1 This great-spirited seer whom you have called Jaratkāru, son of the
Bard, why was his name Jaratkāru, a name famous on earth? This I

wish to hear. Pray tell me the etymology of *jaratkāru.*

The Bard said:

Jarā, they say, means "destruction," and *kāru* denotes "monstrous." He had a monstrous body, and this body, so it is said, the sage destroyed little by little with severe mortifications. And Vāsuki's sister, O brahmin, was likewise called "Jaratkāru." And upon hearing this, the law-abiding Śaunaka started to laugh, and he complimented Ugraśravas, saying, "That fits!"

The Bard said:

So for a long time this sagacious hermit of strict vows devoted himself to austerities and had no desire for a wife. Holding back his seed, he bent himself to mortification, studied, and lived without fear and fatigue, his own master. And the great-spirited sage roamed the entire world without harboring even in thought any desire for a wife.

Then, upon another time, there was a King Parikṣit, O brahmin, born from the lineage of the Kurus. Like Pāṇḍu himself he was a strong-armed bowman, the greatest on earth, and as given to the hunt as his great-grandfather of yore. This king of the world went about shooting deer, swine, hyena, buffalo, and other kinds of wild beasts. One day he shot a deer with a smooth arrow and, slinging his bow over his back, stepped into dense jungle. Like the Lord Rudra after he had shot the beast of sacrifice in heaven, he pursued it bow in hand, searching everywhere. For no deer he had shot had ever run alive in the forest—this surely was a portent of King Parikṣit's own death, that a deer he had shot should be lost. So this deer lured him deep into the forest, until the king, weary and thirsty, came upon a hermit in the woods. He was sitting in a cow pasture, where he fed himself on the plentiful froth that trickled from the mouths of suckling calves. The king quickly ran to that hermit of strict vows, raised his bow, and, being hungry and tired, put his question to him: "*Bhoḥ* brahmin! I am King Parikṣit, son of Abhimanyu. I shot a deer, and it disappeared. Have you chanced to see it?" But the hermit gave him no answer, for he was under a vow of silence then. The king became angry and picked up a dead snake with the end of his bow, draped it around the hermit's neck, and gazed at him. He still did not say anything to him whether good or bad. The king had spent his anger and was troubled to see the hermit in that state. Thereupon he went to his city, but the seer remained as he was.

This hermit had a young son who was prickly as well as austere, Śṛngin by name, a choleric, unforgiving boy, prone to grand vows. From time to time he diligently worshipped the supreme God, Lord Brahmā, who benefits all creatures; and when he was given leave by Brahmā he went home. A friend of his, Kṛśa, also a hermit's son, was cavorting about and even laughed at him, at this all-too-quickly

enraged and venomous son of the seer, and said as a great joke, O
brahmin: "You are full of power and full of heat, but your father is
carrying a corpse on his shoulder! Don't be too puffed up, Śṛngin!
25 You had better keep quiet when hermit's sons like us, successful and
learned and austere, are passing the time together. What will happen
to your arrogance and your high and mighty speeches when you see
your father carrying a corpse?"

The Bard said:

37.1 When the prickly and ill-tempered Śṛngin heard that his father was carrying a corpse, he was consumed with rage. He looked at Kṛśa and, abandoning all pleasantness of speech, asked, "Why should my father now carry cadavers?"

Kṛśa said:

King Parikṣit was running about hunting today and then hung a dead snake from your father's shoulder, friend.

Śṛngin said:

What had my father done wrong to that evil king? Tell me the truth, Kṛśa! Beware the power of my austerities!

Kṛśa said:

5 This King Parikṣit, son of Abhimanyu, had gone hunting and after shooting a deer with a feathered arrow trod about alone. The king did not find the deer as he roamed in the wilderness, but then he saw your father and asked him about it. The one was weak with hunger, thirst, and fatigue, the other sat still like a tree trunk and said nothing. He asked your father again and again about the lost deer, but since the hermit was under a vow of silence he gave no reply at all. The king flung a snake over his shoulders with the crook of his bow, and so your father is still sitting, Śṛngin, true to his vow. The king himself has departed for his city Hāstinapura.

The Bard said:

10 When the seer's son heard this, he stiffened like a pillar of the sky; his eyes bloodshot with anger and fairly blazing with rage, he was seized with fury. And glaring with heat, prey to the vehemence of his anger, he touched water and cursed the king there and then.

Śṛngin said:

That foul and evil king who has thrown a dead snake on my father's shoulder, aged and feeble though he is, him the great Snake Takṣaka, enraged and virulent with all the fury of his venom, shall hurl into the kingdom of Yama within seven nights from now, at the prompting of my word—that despiser of the brahmins and disgrace of his line of Kurus!

The Bard said:

15 Having thus cursed the king in his anger, Śṛngin went to his

father who was sitting in the cow pasture carrying the dead snake
on his shoulders. When Śṛṅgin saw his father with the corpse of a
snake on his shoulders, he was even more possessed by rage.
Shedding tears of grief, he said to his father, "When I heard how you
had been insulted by that evil King Parikṣit, father, I cursed him in
anger such an awful curse as that lowest of the line of Kurus deserves!
On the seventh day the greatest of Snakes Takṣaka will hurl the evil
man into Yama's ghastly domain."

20 Thereupon the father said to his furious son, "You have done me
no kindness, son. This is not the Law of ascetics. We are living in the
realm of this mighty king and are protected by him in accordance
with the Laws. I do not approve of his crime, yet our like must always
and in every way condone the ruling king, son. The Law that is hurt,
hurts back. Were the king not to protect us, we should be severely
oppressed; we should not be able to live the Law as we desire. It is
because we are protected by kings who *do* see the scriptures, son, that
we reap abundant merit of Law, and they have their share of it.
25 Parikṣit especially has been protecting us, like his great-grandfather
did, as subjects should be protected by a king. He came here today
hungry, tired, and wretched; and that he did what he did was
doubtless because he did not know of my vow. Therefore you have
acted foolishly and rashly, and done him a wrong, for the king in no
wise deserves a curse from us, son."

Śṛṅgin said:

38.1 If I have acted rashly, father, or if I have done a wrong, or
whether it pleases or displeases you, the word I have spoken will not
be belied! It shall never be altered, here I stand and tell you, father.
I do not speak idly even when joking, let alone when cursing!

Śāmīka said:

I know you have awesome power, my boy, and that you are true
to your word. Never before have you spoken a lie, nor shall this curse
be belied. But a father must always speak up to his son, even when
the son is full-grown, so that he becomes a man of virtue and attains
5 to a great name—how much more, then, a child like you. Your
mortifications have prospered you—you lord it now. And the anger
of puissant men of great spirit waxes to excess. I see that you deserve
reproof, you diligent upholder of the Law, as I see that you are my son
and a child, and as I observe your rashness. Go and eat the fruit of the
forest and become serene. Give up your anger, or give up the Law.
For the anger of ascetics kills the merit they have painfully gathered;
and deprived of the merits of Law, their course becomes evil. Serenity
alone works success for ascetics who are also forgiving. This world is
10 of the forgiving, and of the forgiving is heaven. Therefore be the

master of your senses and live a life of forgiveness. With forgiveness you will win the worlds that lie beyond Brahmā's. With the tranquillity that I cherish I shall now do what I still can do, my boy. I shall send word to the king: "My son who is a child of immature judgement has cursed you, O king, when he saw your slight of me, which he could not forbear."

The Bard said:

After these admonitions, the ascetic of good vows, having been seized with compassion, sent a pupil of his, Gauramukha by name, a well-behaved and attentive student, to King Parikṣit, instructing him to inquire about the king's welfare and the progress of his affairs. Gauramukha quickly made his way to the king of Kuru's lineage, and after his arrival had been announced by the gate keepers, he entered the royal palace. The king received the brahmin Gauramukha with honor; and when the brahmin was fully rested he conveyed to the king in the presence of the councillors the entire, terrible message of Śāmīka.

"There is a seer named Śāmīka, O lord among kings, who lives in your domain, a great ascetic, supremely law-abiding, serene, and restrained. He was observing a vow of silence when you, tiger among princes, hung the lifeless carcass of a snake over his shoulders with the crook of your bow. He forgave you this act, but his son forgave it not, and unbeknownst to his father he has now cursed you, Sire. 'In seven nights Takṣaka will be your death,' quoth he; and Śāmīka repeats again and again: 'Protect yourself against it.' But no one can change the curse. He was unable to control his son who is obsessed with his rage; and so, as he has your welfare at heart, he has sent me to you, sire."

The Bard said:

The king, scion of the Kurus, heard the terrible message, and he became contrite at having wronged the seer, and aggrieved. Learning that the great hermit had been under a vow of silence, the king felt even greater remorse, and on comprehending Śāmīka's compassionate disposition he was the sorrier for the wrong he had done him. For the king did not rue the death of which he had now learned, but, as though he were an Immortal, sorrowed only that he had done the deed. Thereupon the king sent Gauramukha back with a message: "May the saint again show his grace to me!"

No sooner had this Gauramukha left than the king, disturbed, took counsel with his councillors. Along with his councillors, and himself knowing the best of counsels, he decided to have a platform built upon a single pillar, which was to be well-guarded. For this protection he set up physicians and curative herbs, and all around he posted brahmins of proven spells. And there he lived, protected on every side, while he, aware of his lawful role, carried on the royal business with his councillors.

When the seventh day had come, the most eminent brahmin
Kāśyapa arrived in order to cure the king, as he possessed that
knowledge. For he had learned that Takṣaka, the first of the Snakes,
was to send the good king to the kingdom of Yama. "When the King
of the Snakes has bitten him, I shall cure him of his fever," so he
reflected, "and I will earn wealth and merit." Takṣaka the Snake saw
Kāśyapa as with a single mind he was on his way. The King of the
Snakes became a very aged brahmin and spoke to Kāśyapa, bull
35 among hermits: "Whither art thou hastening and what task dost thou
seek to accomplish?"

Kāśyapa said:

Today Takṣaka, chief among Snakes, will try to set the victorious King Parikṣit the Kuru afire with his heat. I am hurrying along, good friend, to heal that most august king of the line of the Pāṇḍavas at once of his fever, when he has been bitten by the King of the Snakes, whose heat rivals fire.

Takṣaka said:

I am that Takṣaka, brahmin, and I shall set the king afire. Turn back! You cannot heal whom I have bitten.

Kāśyapa said:

I shall go to the king and cure his fever when you have bitten him, Snake! This I know, for I rely on the power of my knowledge.

Takṣaka said:

39.1 If you are able here and now to cure anything that I have bitten,
then I shall bite this tree and you must revive it, Kāśyapa. Show me
that great magic power you possess. Do your best! I shall now set this
banyan tree afire before your eyes, great brahmin!

Kāśyapa said:

Bite the tree, King of the Snakes, if that pleases you; I shall revive it, Snake, when you have bitten it.

The Bard said:

Upon these words of the great-spirited Kāśyapa, the greatest of the
5 Snakes went to the banyan tree and bit it. Scarcely had the tree been
bitten, illustrious Śaunaka, before it filled up with a virulent fire and
went up in flames. When he had burned the tree, the Snake said to
Kāśyapa: "Now do your best, great brahmin, and bring this mighty
tree back to life!" Whereupon Kāśyapa collected all the ashes of the
tree that had been reduced to cinders by the Snake's heat and said,
"Now behold in this, prince of the forest, the power of my knowledge,
Lord of the Snakes! I shall bring it back to life before your very eyes."

Then the wise and blessed Kāśyapa, strictest of brahmins, proceeded

to revive with his knowledge that tree that now was a pile of ashes.
10 First he grew a sapling, gave it two leaves, then twigs and branches.
When Takṣaka saw that the great-spirited Kāśyapa was bringing the
tree back to life, he said, "Brahmin! It is most marvelous that you,
lord among priests, are able to kill the poison of me and my likes!
What profit are you seeking where you go, ascetic? Whatever results
you hope to gain from that great king, I myself will give them all,
however hard they are to find. The king has been struck by the curse
15 of a brahmin, and his life is awasting. Your miracle-mongering will
have doubtful effects—and then your radiant fame, renowned in the
three worlds, will be obfuscated like a darkened sun!"

Kāśyapa said:

I am going there for riches. You give them to me, Snake, and then I shall return home, most eminent Serpent.

Takṣaka said:

Whatever riches you seek from that king, I shall give you more today. Turn back, great brahmin!

The Bard said:

The good brahmin Kāśyapa heard Takṣaka's word, and being wise as well as puissant, reflected upon the king. Since the powerful Kāśyapa was gifted with second sight, he knew that the life of this king of the Pāṇḍavas's line had to come to an end. Thus the great hermit took from Takṣaka all the wealth he wanted and turned back.

20 When Kāśyapa retraced his steps as they had agreed, Takṣaka
hurried to the City of the Elephant.* And while he traveled he heard
how the lord of the world was carefully protected by magic herbs
that cured poison. He thought to himself, "Then I shall have to
deceive the king with my wizardry . . . what would be the right way?"
Thereupon Takṣaka dispatched several Snakes in the disguise of
ascetics to take fruit, leaves, and water to the king.

Takṣaka said:

Go ye undaunted to the king as though you were engaged in a rite, and make him accept your gift of fruit, leaves, and water.

The Bard said:

25 The Snakes followed the orders that Takṣaka had given them and
brought *darbha* grass, water, and fruit to the king. And that powerful
Indra among kings accepted everything. "Now go," he said to them,
when they had performed their rites. When the Snakes, disguised as
ascetics, had departed, the king of men said to his ministers and
friends: "Now all of you must eat with me of this sweet fruit that
the ascetics have presented!" As the king was about to eat the fruit
with his ministers, O Śaunaka, there appeared a small worm in the

* = Hāstinapura.

fruit he had taken, quite tiny with black eyes, and the color of copper.
30 Picking it up, the grand king said to his ministers, "The sun is setting,
and I have no more danger to fear from poison. Now let the hermit's
word come true—this worm may bite me! It shall be Takṣaka himself,
so that a lie be averted!" The councillors, prompted by Time,
applauded him. And having spoken, the king placed the little worm
on his throat and, doomed to die and robbed of his senses, gave a
quick laugh. He was still laughing when Takṣaka coiled around him—
he had come out of the fruit that the king had been given.

The Bard said:

40.1 When the ministers saw their king entangled in the Snake's coils,
their faces paled and they all wept with utter sorrow. And, hearing
his hissing, the ministers began to flee; grief-stricken, they saw that
wondrous Nāga, the King of Snakes Takṣaka, fly through the sky, a
lotus-colored streak that parted the hair of heaven. Then they saw
that tree house enveloped by flames and ablaze with the fire from the
Snake's poison; and in a panic they deserted it and fled in all directions. The king fell as though smitten by lightning.
5 When the king had been felled by the heat of Takṣaka, the king's
house priest, a pure brahmin, and also the royal councillors, performed
all the rites that concern the world hereafter. Then all the folk that
lived in the town assembled and made his young son their king, whom
the people called Janamejaya, slayer of enemies, hero of the Kurus.
Still a child, he was a great king of noble purpose; and together with
his ministers and priest he reigned over his kingdom, firstborn of the
bulls of the Kurus, as once his heroic great-grandfather had reigned.
Thereupon observing that the king was the funeral pyre of his
enemies, the royal ministers went up to King Suvarṇavarman of the
Kāśis and sued him for his daughter Vapuṣṭamā. This king made
inquiries and married off Vapuṣṭamā to the hero of the Kurus according
to the rites of Law. And when he had obtained his bride, Janamejaya
10 became filled with joy and never set his heart on other women. The
puissant king roved at leisure amidst ponds and blossoming woods
with peace in his mind; and the chief of the barons lived joyfully as
Purūravas after he married Urvaśi. And loveliest of women,
Vapuṣṭamā, having wed a king of the earth as her handsome husband,
loved him with great love at his times of leisure.

The Bard said:

41.1 In the meantime, Jaratkāru the ascetic traversed the entire earth,
bedding down at night wherever he found himself. Potently observing
consecrations that the irresolute find impossible, doing his ablutions at
sacred fords, the hermit wandered everywhere, abstaining from food,

living off the wind, drying out his body day after day.
He saw his own forebears hanging in a cave with their faces down,
hanging on to a single remaining strand of grass; and he saw a rat
5 that lived in the cave gnawing slowly through this string. They were
bereft of food and emaciated and wretched in their cave; and they
suffered and yearned for deliverance. He drew near to the wretched
shades, and, looking wretched, he spoke to them: "Who are you that
are hanging down from a string of grass that grows weaker as its roots
are eaten by a rat that lives in this cave? This rat is slowly gnawing
through the string with its sharp teeth. So little is left of it that it too
will soon snap. Then you will surely fall headlong down into the cave.
Seeing you upside down, fallen into this dire distress, I am seized with
10 grief. How can I help? Ward off your downfall with a quarter of my
austerities, with a third, or even half? Tell me at once! Or rather you
must all save yourselves from this with all of my austerities. I am
willing to do so!"

The Ancestors said:

You are an aged celibate and wish to rescue us here! But, great
brahmin, austerities cannot lead us to safety—austerities have caused
our downfall, great preacher and good friend! We are falling into a
foul hell because our line is extinct, brahmin. For all our hanging here
our memories are failing, so that we do not recognize you who surely
are famous in this world for your virility!
15 Old man, you are a magnanimous man that you care to grieve
over us who in our misery deserve grieving and that you come to us
with your compassion. Listen who we are, brahmin. We are the
Yāyāvaras, seers of strict vows, who have now fallen from heaven,
O lord, because we are wanting in offspring. Our sacred austerities are
lost, for we have no more thread. Yet there is one single thread left to
us still, but it might as well be lost: the one unfortunate son who
remains to us unfortunates in our line is given solely to austerities.
He is known as Jaratkāru, scholar of the Vedas and their branches,
controlled, great-spirited, observing his vows, and of massive mortifications. He is the one who out of greed for more austerities has
20 brought us to this pass. He has no wife, or son, or any kin. And
therefore we are now hanging in this cave, at our wits' end and with
none to protect us. Be you our protector, and if you see him say to
him: "Thy wretched forebears are hanging face down in a cave. Take
a wife as is proper, masterful man, and get children!" This string of
grass from which you see us hanging, that is the string of our family
from which our lineage grows. And the plant fibers that you see here,
they are our threads, eaten away now by Time, good brahmin. And
this half-eaten fiber you see, we are hanging by it—and he, the last of
our line, is practicing austerities! The rat you see is mighty Time

25 itself, brahmin. And bite by bite it is killing off that foolish ascetic
Jaratkāru, who is greedy for more mortifications and a witless fool!
For all his austerities will not save us, good man—our roots have been
cut, we have fallen, and our minds are bruised by Time. See how we
flounder in Hell like sinners! And when we have sunk here with all
our ancient ancestors, he too will be cut down by Time and he shall
travel to Hell. Whether mortification, or sacrifice, or any other great
purification, nothing equals offspring; this is the view of the strict.

When you see him, friend, tell the wretched Jaratkāru what you
have witnessed, and bring him in full our message that he should take
30 unto himself a wife and beget children on her. Tell him this, brahmin,
if you will afford us protection!

The Bard said:

42.1 Hearing all this Jaratkāru became utterly miserable with grief, and
he said to his forebears in a voice blurred by tears of sorrow, "I am
Jaratkāru, your guilty son. Raise your staff over me, for I have done
wrong fecklessly."

The Ancestors said:

Son! How fortunate it is that you have chanced to come to this
place! And why is it, brahmin, that you have taken no wife?

Jaratkāru said:

Because it has always been my purpose in my life, O ancestors, to
contain my seed and carry my body whole to the world hereafter.
5 But now that I see you hanging here like bats, my mind recoils from a
life of celibacy, grandfathers. I shall do as you so dearly wish and
marry, no doubt of that. If ever I find a virgin who is my namesake,
and if she will be held up to me, by her own free will, as a gratuitous
alms, and if I shall not have to support her, then I shall accept her as
my wife. Such a marriage will I contract, if I find one, but I shall not
if it be otherwise—this is my promise, grandfathers!

The Bard said:

And having spoken thus to his forebears, the hermit roamed the
earth and failed to find a wife; for they said, Śaunaka: "He is too
10 old." Once he fell to despairing of fulfilling his ancestors' charge, and
he went into the wilderness and in his misery cried out aloud, "Ye
creatures that are here, ye that move and that stand, and ye that are
hidden, hear ye my word! While I was set on awesome austerities, my
ancestors have charged that I take a wife, for they are much aggrieved.
To do their desire and willing to marry, I now roam all the earth begging
the alms of a virgin, hear ye! Though, poor and wretched, I carry my
ancestors' charge. Ye creatures that I have invoked, whosoever of you
15 has a virgin, give me the virgin, as I am wandering everywhere. If
there is a virgin of my name, and if she is given me as an alms, and if

I need not support her, give me that virgin!"
Thereupon the Snakes that had been watching Jaratkāru took
these tidings to Vāsuki and made him acquainted with them. When
the King of the Snakes had heard this from them, he took his virgin
sister decked with ornaments to the wilderness and went to the hermit.
There he gave the virgin away to the great-spirited sage as an alms,
did Vāsuki, King of the Snakes, O brahmin, but the other did not yet
20 accept her. Reflecting that she might not bear his own name, and
that her support had not been discussed, and still standing a free
man, and being of two minds about taking a wife, he asked the virgin's
name, O scion of Bhṛgu; and he said, "Vāsuki, I will not support her!"

The Bard said:

43.1 Vāsuki then gave the seer Jaratkāru his reply: "Most excellent of
brahmins," he said, "this austere virgin, my own sister, bears your
name, and I myself shall support your wife—accept her! I myself shall
watch over her, ascetic, with all my might."
When the Snake had made the promise that he would support his
sister, Jaratkāru went to the Snake's dwelling. And there this greatest
of Vedic scholars, rich in austerities, great in his vows, and devoted to
the Law, took her hand with the proper rites and spells. Thereupon,
5 glorified by the great seers, he took his bride and entered the luminous
bedroom that the Snake had approved for him. A couch was made up
there, covered with matchless spreads, and there Jaratkāru spent his
nights with his wife. There, too, this very strict man made a covenant
with his wife: "Never do or say aught that displeases me. I shall
abandon thee and my lodgings in thy house if thou ever causest me
displeasure. Mark this word that I have spoken!" The sister of the
King of Snakes thereupon grew surpassing anxious, and cheerlessly
10 she gave her word: "It must be." And so this woman of renown, eager
to please, waited on her melancholy husband with favors rare as a
white crow.
One time, when she was past her month, Vāsuki's sister bathed
and, by the rules of propriety, lay with the great hermit, her husband.
And she conceived a child, bright as fire, endowed with the utmost
heat, of the splendor of the Fire. And just as during the month's bright
fortnight the moon waxes, so did the child in her womb.
Then, not many days later, Jaratkāru the ascetic lay his head in her
lap and fell asleep like a man who is tired. While the princely brahmin
was sleeping, the sun went down to the mountain of its setting; and
as the day drew to its end, O brahmin, she began to worry, Vāsuki's
sister, mindful and afraid that her husband might decrease in the
15 merits of the Law. "What should I better do—awaken my husband, or
let him sleep? For my melancholy husband is devoted to the Law. . . .

How can I fail to wrong him? Either he will grow angry, or he will lose merit as he lives by the Law. Surely the loss of merit must weigh heavier," thus she decided. "If I awaken him, he will of a certainty be angry; but of a certainty he will decrease in the Law, if he transgresses the Twilight."

Having made this decision in her mind, the Snake woman Jaratkāru
spoke to the seer of fiery austerities, as he lay sleeping like smoldering
fire, these gentle words in a sweet whisper: "Awake, your worship,
the sun is setting. Touch the water, sir, and honor the Twilight, as it
20 is your wont to do. The lovely and perilous hour is here when the
agnihotra should be lit. Dusk, my lord, is already creeping upon the
western sky."

At these words the blessed ascetic Jaratkāru said to his wife with
trembling lips: "Snake woman, you have insulted me! I will no
longer live with you. I shall depart as I came! I know in my heart,
woman with the shapely thighs, that the sun does not have the
courage to set at its appointed time while I am asleep! No one likes to
tarry when he has been insulted, let alone me, who practice the Law,
or one like me!"

25 When her husband spoke to her these heart-shaking words, Vāsuki's
daughter Jaratkāru said there in their dwelling, "It was not to slight
you that I awakened you, but lest you should lose merit, brahmin!"
Anger seized the great seer and ascetic Jaratkāru, and, being ready
to desert his wife, he said to the Snake woman, "My tongue has never
spoken a lie! I shall leave, Snake woman, for such was the covenant
we made before between us. My life with you has been happy, good
woman. When I am gone, fair wife, you must tell your brother, timid
one, that the lord has left. And after I have departed, pray do not
grieve for me."

30 The flawless woman then made her reply to her husband, Jaratkāru
to Jaratkāru, filled with grief and worry, her mouth dry and her voice
stammering with sobs; and she raised her hands to her forehead, eyes
awash with tears, but steadying herself though her heart was
shivering: "Pray do not leave me who am innocent—you know the
Law! You who are firm in the Law, do not leave me who am firm in
the Law, and am always willing to please you. The purpose for which
I was given to you, best of brahmins, I have not achieved—what will
Vāsuki say to his foolish sister? My kinsmen are beset by our mother's
curse. They wanted a child from you, good man, but it still does not
35 show. Had I received a child from you my kinsmen would have been
saved! Do not let my lying with you remain barren, brahmin, I
beseech you, as I long to save my kinsmen. After planting in me a
child that is still to show, how, good man, with your greatness of
spirit can you wish to desert an innocent wife?"

Then the hermit, ascetic Jaratkāru, said to his wife what was both right and seemly: "There *is* a child in you, fortunate woman, who shall be a seer bright like the Fire, supreme in the Law, and perfect in the Vedas and their branches!" And, having thus spoken, the law-abiding Jaratkāru, the great seer, left her and once more resolved on awesome austerities.

The Bard said:

44.1 No sooner had her husband gone, O ascetic, than Jaratkāru hurried
to her brother and told him all that had happened. When the eminent
Snake heard these most unkind tidings, he said to his wretched sister,
more wretched himself, "You know, my dear, what had to be done,
what was the purpose that I gave you in marriage: that you were to
have a son for the well-being of the Snakes. He, of course, was to be
the powerful man that would set us free from the Snake Sacrifice: this
5 the Grandfather told me of yore with all the Gods. Are you with child,
fortunate woman, from that strictest of hermits? I do not wish that the
sage's marriage be barren. Surely, it is not proper that I should ask
questions of you about such a matter; but the matter is too grave for
me not to prompt you. I know how quick your all-too-austere husband
is to anger, and I shall not pursue him, for he might one day curse me.
Tell me, dear, all that your husband has wrought and pull out the cruel
thorn that so long has lodged in my heart!"
On his questioning, Jaratkāru gave him her answer and reassured
10 the tormented Vāsuki, King of the Snakes: "I asked the great-spirited
ascetic concerning our offspring, and he answered, 'There *is*,' and then
he went. Even at play I do not recall him ever to have spoken a lie,
why then should he tell one, O king, in a matter of life and death?
'Do not sorrow, Snake woman,' he said, 'about your task. A son shall
be born of you, splendid like the fire and sun.' And with these words,
brother, my husband left for the wilderness of austerities. Therefore the
great anxiety that preys on your mind must depart."
When he heard this, the King of the Snakes Vāsuki was overjoyed,
15 and he accepted his sister's word: "So shall it be!" And the Chief of
the Snakes paid homage to his nest-sister with kindnesses, honors,
gifts, and other suitable homage. The child she was bearing grew in
her womb, lustrous like the sun, as in the sky the moon grows, O best
of the twiceborn, that rises in the light fortnight.

At her time the sister of the Snake gave birth, O brahmin, to a man child that was like a child divine, dispelling the fears of his father and his mother. And in that very dwelling of the King of the Snakes, he grew up and learned the Vedas and their branches from the sage Bhārgava, son of Cyavana. Even as a child, he kept to his vows, rich in spirit, character, and virtue; and in all the worlds his name Āstīka

20 became famous. Since his father before departing for the forest had
said of him, "There *is*," while he was still in his mother's womb, his
name was known as "Āstīka." A child of boundless spirit, he lived
there in Vāsuki's dwelling and was most carefully watched over. Like
the Blessed Lord, the Sovereign of the Gods, the Giver of Gold who
wields the Trident, he grew up to gladden all the Snakes.

Śaunaka said:

45.1 What did King Janamejaya at the time ask his councillors concerning
his father's journey to heaven? Tell me once more in detail.

The Bard said:

Listen, O brahmin, how the king questioned his councillors and how they related to him the end of Parikṣit.

Janamejaya said:

Sirs, you know what manner of life my father led and how the famous king in time met his death. When I have heard from your worships in full detail all that befell my father, I shall have learned only good things, and no evil at all.

The Bard said:

5 At the bidding of the great-spirited king, the wise councillors, who
knew the whole Law, replied to Janamejaya, "Your father was a law-abiding and great-spirited herdsman of his people. Listen how the great-spirited man led his life.

He made the society of the four classes firm in the Law and watched
over them according to the Law as a king versed in Law, who was
like Law incarnate. He guarded Goddess Earth, he was illustrious and
of matchless might—no haters had he, nor did he hate anyone. Like
Prajāpati himself, he was impartial to all creatures; brahmins, barons,
commoners, and serfs all bent themselves happily to their own tasks,
10 O king, well-governed by their king. He fed the widowed and the
orphaned, the maimed and the poor, and to all creatures he showed,
like another moon, a benign countenance. Majestic king was he, his
people fed and content, his promise true, his prowess proven. The
king became Śāradvata's pupil in the science of the bow, and, Janamejaya, your father was friendly to Govinda.* To all the world the famous man was friend.

When the Kurus were near wasted away, his father begot him on
Uttarā, and thus being a direct son of Abhimanyu Saubhadra this
man of strength became known as "Parikṣit." The king was clever in
the laws of princes and the profit of princes; he lacked in no virtue,
he was master of himself as well as his senses, and wise, and cherished
15 by the aged. His understanding was wide; he knew the six vices and

* = Kṛṣṇa.

was the foremost scholar of the science of polity. For sixty years your father herded his people.

Then the end that was set for him overtook him, through a Snake, and beyond avoidance. And after him, you, O best of men, have by Law ascended to this kingdom bequeathed in the line of the Kurus, to reign for a thousand years! Even as a child you were born to it, to be the herdsman of all the creatures.

Janamejaya said:

Never was there king in this lineage who was not a benefactor of his people and a friend. Behold in particular the feats of my grandfathers whose aim was a great life! How did my father, a man like them, meet his end? I wish to hear it, tell me truly how it befell.

The Bard said:

Commanded by their king, the councillors all told what had happened, for they rejoiced in the prince's well-being.

20 "Sire, your father was fond of hunting. Like lordly Pāṇḍu, he was a
marksman in war. He entrusted all matters of the kingdom completely
to us. One day, while roaming the woods, he shot a deer with his
arrow, and when he had shot it he pursued the deer nimbly into the
dense jungle, on foot, his sword girt, with quiver and corded bow
ready. Your father could not find the lost deer in the thicket. Being an
old man of sixty years, he became tired and hungry; then he noticed
a hermit close by in the deep forest. The lord of kings questioned the
hermit, who chanced to be observing a vow of silence, and to all his
25 asking the hermit did not respond at all. Suffering as he did from
hunger and fatigue, the king soon flew in a rage at that peaceable
hermit, who sat still like a tree trunk, observing his silence, for he did
not know that the hermit was under a vow. Seized with anger, your
father insulted him; with the crook of his bow he lifted a dead snake
from the ground and, O best of the Bhāratas, placed it on the shoulder
of the pure-spirited hermit. The sage did not say anything to him,
either good or bad, and remained as he was, not angry, carrying the
Snake on his shoulder."

The councillors said:

46.1 Thereupon, great king, the king, after hanging the snake from that
hermit's shoulder, returned to his own city, weak with hunger.

The seer, however, had a renowned son, who had been born from
a cow, Śṛngin by name, a boy of great heat, prickly prowess, and
extreme rage. This hermit had gone up to Brahmā and made *pūjā* to
him; and when he had been given leave to go and had left, he heard
from a friend that your father had insulted his father, that your father,
Janamejaya, had hung a dead snake on him, and that he was still
carrying it on his shoulder, innocent though he was, O tiger of the
5 Kurus. A most eminent hermit was his father, O king, extreme in his

austerities, master of his senses and pure, and given to miraculous feats. His spirit was luminous with the heat of his mortifications, in all his limbs he was restrained; his way of life was serene, his speech was serene. He was a man of perfect poise, without greed or meanness or envy, an old man who liked to observe the vow of silence. And this man, refuge of all creatures, your father had insulted.

The son of the seer cursed your father in the heat of his rage when he heard it. Though still a child, he surpassed his elders in heat. He immediately touched water, and fairly blazing with heat spoke with a fury about your father: "Him who evilly hung a dead snake on my innocent father, him the furious Snake Takṣaka shall bring down with the heat of his venom seven nights from now. Behold the power of my austerities!" Having spoken he went to where his father was; and when he saw his father he told him of his cursing. The great hermit himself sent word to your father: "You have been cursed by my son. Be prepared, lord of the earth, Takṣaka shall bring you down with the heat of his venom, great king."

When your father heard this cruel message, Janamejaya, he grew frightened of Takṣaka, the Chief of the Snakes, and prepared himself. It was by the seventh day that the brahmin seer Kāśyapa made plans to come to the king. Takṣaka saw Kāśyapa, and the King of the Snakes said to him as he was hurrying along, "Where are you going so hastily? What is it you wish to do?"

Kāśyapa said:

Where the mighty Kuru, King Parikṣit, is sitting, O brahmin. For there he shall be burned, so I hear, by the Snake Takṣaka. I am hastening to him so that I may cure him at once of his fever. No Snake whatever can overcome him if I protect him. Takṣaka said: "Why do you wish to revive him when I have bitten him? Speak freely, I'll give it to you, go back home."

The councillors said:

When the other said, "I am going there in quest of riches," the Snake said to the great-spirited seer, coaxing him, with gentle words, "Whatever wealth you seek from that king, take more from me and return, blameless." At the Snake's words, Kāśyapa, greatest of two-footed men, took riches from Takṣaka, as much as he wanted, and returned.

After the brahmin had turned back, Takṣaka came in disguise to your law-abiding father, a king and chief of kings, while he was sitting on his platform, fully prepared; and he burned him with the fire of his venom. Thereafter you yourself, tiger among men, were consecrated to a victorious reign.

This is the gruesome history that we now have told you entire and complete, as it was seen and heard, good king. Now that you have heard, herdsman of men, how the king was vanquished and the seer

Utanka insulted, you must dispose of the immediate future.

Janamejaya said:

I first wish to hear what was said between the King of the Snakes and Kāśyapa in that forest, which must have been empty of people. By whom was it witnessed and who heard what came to your ears? When I have heard that, I shall set my mind on the destruction of the Snakes.

The councillors said:

Sire, listen to the tale that someone has told us about the encounter
on the road between this prince among brahmins and this Prince of
the Snakes. A certain man had been looking for dead branches to use
as kindling wood for a sacrifice and had climbed up that tall tree.
30 The Snake and brahmin were unaware of him sitting in the tree, and
he was burned to ashes along with the tree itself; the power of the
brahmin brought both him and the tree back to life, good king. Afterward he came here and told his story in the city. What we told you
about the encounter of Takṣaka and the brahmin was precisely as it
happened and was witnessed. Now that you have heard it, you must
provide as it pleases you.

The Bard said:

King Janamejaya had listened to the words of his councillors, and
he was hot with grief and kneaded hand in hand. Eyes streaked like
a lotus, the king kept heaving deep, hot sighs and shed streaming
tears from his eyes. Then the warden of the earth spoke in grief and
35 sorrow, "Now that I have heard your tale, good sirs, concerning my
father's journey to heaven, I have made a decision, which you must
now hear from me. At once, methinks, measures are to be taken
against the evil Takṣaka, since he is the one who hurt my father. For
he alone made the curse of the seer Śṛngin come true, and he burned
the king. If that evil-doer had gone, my father would surely have
lived—and what would the Snake have lost had my father lived?
Lived by the grace of Kāśyapa, and the well-laid plans of his
councillors? It was the Snake's blindness that made him stop that
good brahmin Kāśyapa, who had come to return his life to the
40 unvanquished king. This is the great transgression of the evil Takṣaka:
that he gave riches to the brahmin lest he gave life back to the king!
To please Utanka, and to please greatly myself and all of you, I shall
go and avenge my father!"

The Bard said:

47.1 Thus spoke the illustrious king and, applauded by his councillors, he
undertook the promise of a Snake Sacrifice. The tiger of the Kurus,
King Son of Parikṣit, Overlord of the Earth, summoned his house
priests who were versed in sacrifice, and he made a solemn pronounce-

ment that was to assure success. "Speak, ye sirs, so that I may act against the evil Takṣaka who has slain my father. Know ye a rite by which I can lead the Snake Takṣaka and his kinsmen into the blazing fire? Even as my father was burned by the fire of his venom, so I too now wish to set fire to the guilty Snake."

The priests said:

Sire, there is a great Session that the Gods have devised for you. The Ancient Lore describes it with the name of the Session of the Snakes. No one but you, overlord of men, can be the offerer of this Session, thus declare the masters of the Lore; and we possess this rite.

The Bard said:

Having thus been enlightened, the royal seer willed, O good brahmin, that the Snake Takṣaka enter the blazing mouth of the fire of sacrifice. Thereupon the king spoke to brahmins who were scholars of the spells: "I shall offer up this Session. Collect for me the ingredients!" Upon this, the sacrificial priests measured out the terrain according to the scriptures to prepare the sanctuary of the sacrifice in the prescribed manner since they were all experts in ritual knowledge and most fully resolved. The oblation grounds, which were decked with the greatest opulence and attended by multitudes of brahmins, were laid out well by the priests and further enriched with abundant riches and rice. After measuring the sacrificial terrain, as the precepts demanded it, they consecrated the king for the receiving of the Session of the Snakes.

Now earlier, when the Session of the Snakes was yet to begin, there appeared a great portent that predicted that the sacrifice would be disrupted. As the sacrificial terrain was being laid out, a master builder of much wisdom and well versed in the arts of building spoke up. This Holder of the Cord, who was a bard of the ancient Lore, said: "Seeing the place and time that the measuring was carried out, I say the sacrifice will not be concluded, a brahmin being the cause." Whereupon the king, before the time of his consecration, ordered the steward: "Let no one enter who is unknown to me!"

Thereafter the ritual unrolled according to the rules of a Snake Session. Each of the priests went religiously about his own task. All had donned black robes, and with their eyes red from the smoke, they made the oblations with the proper spells into the fire of sacrifice. They offered up all the Snakes into the mouth of the fire, wreaking terror in the minds of all the serpents. The Snakes began to drop into the blazing flames, writhing and wretched and crying out to one another. They darted and hissed and wildly coiled about with tails and heads as they fell into the radiant fire—white, black, blue, old, and young—screeching terrifying screams, they fell into the high blazing flames, hundreds of thousands and millions and tens of millions of the

25 Snakes died powerless, O best of brahmins, some tiny like mice, others
fat like elephant trunks, or huge and strong like rutting bull elephants,
all sorts of them in vast numbers, manycolored, poisonous, and
loathsome, mordacious and powerful, they fell into the fire, punished
by their mother's curse.

Śaunaka said:
48.1 At this Session of the Snakes of the sage king Janamejaya Pāṇḍaveya
—who were the great seers who acted as his sacrificial priests? Who
were the *sadasyas* at that terrible and fearful sacrifice that brought the
Snakes to utter despair? Pray tell me all the particulars, for they surely
should be remembered as the ritual experts of the Session of the
Snakes, son of the Bard.

The Bard said:
To be sure, I shall tell you now the names of the sages who were
5 the priests and the *sadasyas* of the king at that time. The *hotar* was the
brahmin Caṇḍabhārgava, the celebrated great scholar of the Veda,
who was born in Cyavana's lineage. The aged and wise brahmin
Kautsārya Jaimini was the *udgātar*, Śārngarava the *brahmán*, and
Bodhapingala the *adhvaryu*. Vyāsa was a *sadasya*, in the midst of his
sons and pupils, and so were Uddālaka, Śamaṭhaka, Śvetaketu,
Pañcama, Asita Devala, Nārada, Parvata, Ātreya, Kuṇḍajaṭhara, the
brahmin Kuṭighaṭa, Vātsya, the old Śrutaśravas, always bent to his
studies and austerities, Kahoḍa and Devaśarman, Maudgalya and
10 Śamasaubhara—these and many other brahmins of strict vows were
sadasyas at the Session of Parikṣit's son.

While the priests were making the oblations at the grand ritual of the Session of the Snakes, the loathsome Snakes that terrify the creatures kept falling. The fat and marrow of the Snakes streamed in rivulets, and as they were burning one after another, a loud stench drifted off. The screams of those that were falling and of those still hovering in the sky and of those that were frying in the fire reverberated along the skies.

Takṣaka, King of the Snakes, however, had gone at once to the
palace of the Sacker of Cities, as soon as he had heard that King
15 Janamejaya had undergone the sacrificial consecration. The great
Snake recounted all that had befallen; and confessing the evil he had
done, he sought refuge with Indra in panic. Well-pleased, Indra said
to him, "You are in no danger here at all, Takṣaka, King of the
Snakes, from that Snake Sacrifice. I had already appeased Grandfather
on your behalf. Therefore you are in no danger, and your mind's fever
should depart."

When he had been so reassured, the Snake happily stayed in Indra's house. But as the Snakes kept ceaselessly falling into the fire, Vāsuki

became much grieved and dejected, seeing his family dwindling.
20 A mean despair took possession of Vāsuki, Chief of the Snakes; and
with trembling heart he said to his sister: "My limbs are burning,
good woman. I have lost all sense of direction. I feel as though I am
sinking from utter confusion, my mind seems to rock, my eyes do not
focus at all, my heart feels like bursting, and I am ready to fall
without resisting into the blazing fire. That sacrifice of Parikṣit's son
will be going on until it has killed us all, and clearly I too must make
my journey to the realm of the king of the Fathers. The time has
come now for which I gave you to Jaratkāru, sister. Save us and our
25 kinsmen! Āstīka, will he not stop this sacrifice that keeps going on,
Princess of the Snakes? Grandfather himself has promised me! My
calf, tell your beloved son, whom the old men esteem as most learned
in the Vedas, to save me now and those I support!"

The Bard said:

49.1 Thereupon the Snake woman Jaratkāru summoned her son; and,
following the words of Vāsuki, King of the Snakes, she said to him,
"Son, I was given to your father by my brother for a purpose. The
time has come. Do what must be done!"

Āstīka said:

Why did my uncle give you to my father? Tell me the truth, and
when you have told me I shall do as I must.

The Bard said:

Then undaunted, for she wished her kinsmen well, Jaratkāru,
sister of the King of the Snakes, told him, "Kadrū was the mother of
5 all the Snakes, so it is revealed. And she cursed her children in a rage.
Learn the reason for her curse. 'You have refused in my face to
counterfeit the King of Horses Uccaiḥśravas, sons, while I had wagered
my freedom with Vinatā. Therefore the wind-driven Fire shall burn
you at Janamejaya's sacrifice. You shall return to the five elements
and journey to the world of the dead!' And the God Grandfather of
the worlds himself heard her curse and consented to it, saying, 'So
shall it be.' Vāsuki, however, on hearing Grandfather's word, sought
refuge with the Gods, my son, when the Elixir was churned from the
10 ocean. And the celestials, once they had gained their desire and
obtained the incomparable Elixir, gave my brother the place of honor
and went to the Grandfather. All the Gods sought to appease him
together with Vāsuki, 'Let that curse pass by King Vāsuki! This
Vāsuki, who is the King of the Snakes, is sorrowing for his kinsmen.
Make it so that his mother's curse will pass, O Lord!' "

Brahmā said:

When a Jaratkāru shall take a Jaratkāru for his wife, a brahmin
shall be born who shall set the Snakes free from the curse.

Jaratkāru said:

When the sovereign of the Snakes Vāsuki heard this promise, he
gave me, oh my godlike son, to your great-spirited father, well before
15 the event was to befall; and your father begot you on me. The time
has come now, save us from our danger, save my brother from the
fire! Let it not remain fruitless that I was given to your father—or
think you otherwise?

The Bard said:

And upon hearing his mother's word, Āstīka said, "So must it be."
Then he spoke to the suffering Vāsuki, as though to bring him back
to life, "Vāsuki, mettlesome Chief of the Snakes, I shall free you from
the curse—this I pronounce as truth! Be of tranquil mind, Snake, for
no danger awaits you. I shall strive for your welfare, my friend. Never
20 has my tongue spoken a lie in jest, let alone in earnest! Indeed, I shall
go to that best of kings, Janamejaya, who has now undergone his
consecration; and with the words that spell good fortune I shall
satisfy him, uncle, so that the king's sacrifice be brought to an end.
Place all your trust in me, high-minded Prince of Snakes, and the
confidence you place in me shall never be belied."

Vāsuki said:

Āstīka, I am shivering and my heart is bursting. I no longer have a sense of direction, and I sway under the staff of Brahmā!

Āstīka said:

Be not afraid of anything, good Snake. I shall put an end to the danger that arises for you from the blazing fire. And the dreadful staff of Brahmā that glows like the Fire of Doomsday, I shall destroy it, have no fear!

The Bard said:

25 Then, after having lifted the horrible fever from Vāsuki's mind and
placed it on his own limbs, that excellent brahmin Āstīka departed
with great haste for the sacrifice of Janamejaya that flourished with
all good things, to the rescue of the Princes of the Snakes. Āstīka
went and beheld the splendid terrain of the sacrifice, crowded with
numerous *sadasyas* who were radiant like sun and fire. When the
brahmin wanted to enter, he was stopped by the keepers of the gate;
but to gain his entrance the great brahmin lifted his voice in praise of
the sacrifice.

Āstīka said:

50.1 As Soma's rite, as Varuṇa's rite,
As at Prayāga the rite of Prajāpati,
So is thy sacrifice, son of Parikṣit,
Best of the Bhāratas, hail to our friends!

As Śakra's one hundred sacrifices,
So many are thine and a hundredfold,
So is thy sacrifice, son of Parikṣit,
Best of the Bhāratas, hail to our friends!

As the rite of Yama and Harimedhas,
As the rite of King Rantideva,
So is thy sacrifice, son of Parikṣit,
Best of the Bhāratas, hail to our friends!

As the rite of Gaya and King Śaśabindu,
As the rite of Vaiśravaṇa the King,
So is thy sacrifice, son of Parikṣit,
Best of the Bhāratas, hail to our friends!

5 As the rite of Nṛga and Ajamīḍha,
As the rite of Daśaratha's son,*
So is thy sacrifice, son of Parikṣit,
Best of the Bhāratas, hail to our friends!

As the rite of Yudhiṣṭhira, famous in heaven,
Of the son of a God, Ajamīḍha's scion,
So is thy sacrifice, son of Parikṣit,
Best of the Bhāratas, hail to our friends!

As the rite of Kṛṣṇa,** Satyavatī's son,
When he himself did the priestly duties,
So is thy sacrifice, son of Parikṣit,
Best of the Bhāratas, hail to our friends!

These priests that sit here, their splendor matching
The Sun's and the Fire's, as at Indra's rite,
No knowledge is still hidden from them,
No fee given them will come to nought.

In none of the worlds can a priest be found
Who equals Dvaipāyana, this I know.
His pupils now roam all over this earth,
All expert priests in their proper parts.

10 Great-spirited Fire, the Many-Splendored,
The Widely Radiant, the Golden-Spermed,
All-Eating, South-Crested, whose Trail is Blackened,
Now longs for the offering, to eat it, the God.

Than thee in the world of the living none
Is found a greater herdsman of people.

* = Rāma.
** = Vyāsa.

My mind delights in your fortitude always,
Thou art king, or Yama, the king of the Dead.

As Śakra himself, the Thunderbolt-Wielder,
So art thou in this world the saviour of people,
So do we deem thee, Lord, in this world,
No offerer matches thee at the rite.

A Khaṭvanga, Nābhāga or Dilīpa,
In might the match of Māndhātar, Yayāti,
In splendor the mirror of Sun's splendor,
Thou shinest like Bhīṣma, keeping thy vows.

Like Vālmīki's thy firmness is gentle,
Like Vasiṣṭha's thy wrath is restrained,
Thy kingdom surpasses, methinks, that of Indra,
Thy radiance shines like Nārāyaṇa's.

15 Like Yama thou knowest the sureties of Law,
As Kṛṣṇa every virtue adorns thee,
Abode thou art of fortunes and riches,
The offering ground of the rituals.

Thou matchest Dambhodbhava in thy strength,
Like Rāma* thou masterest arrow and sword,
Thy heat is equal to Aurva's and Trita's,
Thy aspect is dread like Bhagīratha's.

The Bard said:
Thus praised they all sat serene, the king,
The *sadasyas*, the priests, and the offering fire;
And observing the gestures they all displayed,
King Janamejaya began to speak.

Janamejaya said:
51.1 A child he is, but he speaks like the old;
No child do I deem him, but a man of age.
I wish to bestow a boon upon him,
Priests, grant it to me as ye are assembled.

The sadasyas *said:*
A brahmin demands a king's respect,
Even a child, and a wise one more.

* = Paraśu-rāma

All wishes he deserves from thee,
As soon as Takṣaka comes to us!

The Bard said:

The wish-granting king was ready to say
To the brahmin, "Choose a boon," when first
The *hotar* spoke up none too joyfully:
"Not yet has Takṣaka come to our rite!"

Janamejaya said:

Then strive that my rite be brought to its end
And that Takṣaka swiftly come to us,
So strive ye all with all your might,
For he is the one most hated of me!

The priests said:

5 The scriptures reveal to us, and the fire confirms, O king, that Takṣaka is now in Indra's palace beset by fears.

The Bard said:

Lohitākṣa, too, the great-spirited Bard
Well-versed in the Lore, had known it before;
And he spoke at that time at the king's demand:
"It is as the priests say, God among men!

"I have learned the Lore, and I say unto thee
That Indra has granted a boon to him, king:
'Dwell here in hiding where I am near,
And Fire shall never burn thee.' "

At this the anointed king grew wroth
And prodded his *hotar* to work at the rite,
And the *hotar* did offerings and spoke spells,
Till Indra himself thereupon appeared,

In puissance great, on a chariot mounted,
While the praise of the Gods surrounded him,
And trailing a wake of mighty clouds
And crowds of aerial spirits and nymphs.

10 The Snake was tucked in the hem of his robe,
But he found no shelter and was greatly alarmed.
Quoth the king to his priests who knew the spells,
Waxing angry and set on Takṣaka's death:

Janamejaya said:

Priests! If Takṣaka the Snake is in Indra's keeping, then hurl him into the fire with Indra himself!

The priests said:

Takṣaka is coming soon now, O king, and he will be in your power. Already we hear his mighty roar as he hisses from fear!

> The Thunderbolt-Wielder has let him go,
> He falls from his lap; his body limp
> From our spells, he comes writhing in the sky,
> Witless, hissing his harsh sighs.

Thy sacrifice, lord among kings, is working toward its proper end. Now thou mayest grant a boon to the worthy brahmin.

Janamejaya said:

15 Immeasurable one in the guise of a child,
> I grant thee a boon such as may befit thee.
> Now choose what desire is lodged in thy heart,
> The ungrantable even I shall grant thee!

The Bard said:

And the instant that Takṣaka, King of the Snakes, was to fall into the fire of sacrifice, Āstīka spoke this in answer to the king: "If thou givest me a boon, then, Janamejaya, I choose that your Session be stopped and no more Snakes come down." Upon these words, O brahmin, the son of Parikṣit none too joyously said to Āstīka: "Gold, or silver, or cows, or whatever else you have set your mind on, lord, I shall give it to you for a boon. But let my sacrifice not be stopped, O brahmin!"

Āstīka said:

20 Gold, or silver, or cows I do not choose from thee, king. Thy Session must stop, and the race of my mother must be safe!

The Bard said:

The king, son of Parikṣit, again and again eloquently urged Āstīka, "Be blessed, but choose another boon, greatest of brahmins!" And the scion of the Bhṛgus refused to ask for another boon. Thereupon the *sadasyas*, knowing their Veda, all said to the king: "The brahmin must have his boon."

Śaunaka said:

52.1 Those Snakes that fell into the offering fire at the Session of the Snakes, I wish to hear the names of all of them, son of the Bard!

The Bard said:

There were many thousands of them and millions and tens of millions. There were too many of them, great scholar of the Veda, for me to enumerate them all. But hear from me as far as I can remember the names that are given of the Snakes that were offered into the fire of sacrifice. First, hear those of the race of Vāsuki, the

chief ones—blue, red, white, loathsome, huge, and of virulent venom.
5 There were Koṭika, Mānasa, Pūrṇa, Saha, Paila, Halīṣaka, Picchila,
Koṇapa, Cakra, Koṇavega, Prakālana, Hiraṇyavāha, Śaraṇa, Kakṣaka,
Kāladantaka: these were of Vāsuki's line that entered the offering
fire.

Now I shall mention the ones of Takṣaka's lineage, listen.
Pucchandaka, Maṇḍalaka, Piṇḍabhettar, Rabhenaka, Ucchikha,
Surasa, Dranga, Balaheḍa, Virohana, Śilīśalakara, Mūka, Sukumāra,
Pravepana, Mudgara, Śaśaroman, Sumanas, and Vegavāhana. These
were of Takṣaka's line that entered the fire of sacrifice.

10 Pārāvata, Pāriyātra, Pāṇḍara, Hariṇa, Kṛśa, Vihanga, Śarabha,
Moda, Pramoda, and Saṃketāngada are the ones of Airāvata's line
that entered the fire of sacrifice.

Now, good brahmin, hear which Snakes from Kauravya's lineage.
Aiṇḍila, Kuṇḍala, Muṇḍa, Veṇiskandha, Kumāraka, Bāhuka,
Śṛngavega, Dhūrtaka, Pāta, Pātara.

Hear precisely which ones were born in the lineage of
Dhṛtarāṣṭra as I recite them, O brahmin, Snakes that were fast as
wind and virulently poisonous: Śankukarṇa, Pingalaka,
15 Kuṭhāramukha, Mecaka, Pūrṇāngada, Pūrṇamukha, Prahasa,
Śakuni, Hari, Āmāhaṭha, Komaṭhaka, Śvasana, Mānava, Vāta,
Bhairava, Muṇḍavedānga, Piśanga, Udrapāraga, Ṛṣabha, Vegavat,
Piṇḍāraka, Mahāhanu, Raktānga, Sarvasāranga, Samṛddha, Pāṭa,
and Rākṣasa, Varāhaka, Vāraṇaka, Sumitra, Citravedika, Parāśara,
Taruṇaka, Maṇiskandha, and Āruṇi.

Thus I have enumerated, O brahmin, the Snakes of prosperous
renown, but only the chief ones, for there are too many to enumerate
them all. The numbers of their sons and grandsons and further
20 progeny that entered into the flaming fire are beyond count. The
seven-headed, the double-headed, the five-headed, and others still,
with poisons as fierce as the Fire of Doomsday and loathsome of
aspect, were sacrificed by the hundreds of thousands. Gigantic,
powerful, tall as mountaintops, a league long and wide, or two
leagues long, protean, ubiquitous, venomous with a virulent poison
that burned like a blazing fire, they were all burned at the Grand
Session and brought down by the staff of Brahmā.

The Bard said:

53.1 At this point, so we have heard, Āstīka wrought a great miracle.
Just as he was being gratified with boons by the king the son of
Parikṣit, the Snake that had dropped from Indra's hand remained up
in the air. King Janamejaya became concerned when many oblations
were poured into the fire in the ritual fashion, and yet the frightened
Takṣaka did not fall into the flames.

Śaunaka said:

Was it, Bard, because those wise priests failed to remember the canons of spells that Takṣaka did not fall into the fire?

The Bard said:

When the great Snake was shaken from Indra's hand and had lost consciousness, Āstīka said to him three times, "Stay! Stay!" And the Snake stood still in the air with fluttering heart, as a body would stand still in a circle of bulls. Thereupon the king, urged by his *sadasyas*, pronounced his word and said: "Let his wish be done, even as Āstīka has demanded. This sacrifice must be brought to an end, the Snakes shall be safe. Let Āstīka be pleased, and let also the Bard's prediction come true!"

There was a joyous tumult of cheers when Āstīka was granted his boon, and the sacrifice of King Pāṇḍaveya,* son of Parikṣit, was ended. King Janamejaya Bhārata was greatly pleased and gave to the priests and *sadasyas* who had gathered there fees of riches by the hundred and thousands. Also, he gave much wealth to the Bard Lohitākṣa, the builder who had predicted that a brahmin would become the cause that the sacrifice was stopped.

Thereafter, according to the ritual that is found in the Rules, he performed the concluding ablutions. Then the well-pleased king sent Āstīka back to his own house heaped with honors; and the sage himself was pleased, now that his task was done. "You must come back," the king said to him. "You must be a *sadasya* at the grand celebration of my Horse Sacrifice." "So be it," he said; and after doing his matchless feat and satisfying the king, Āstīka joyfully hastened along. Highly pleased, he went to his mother and uncle. He approached them ceremoniously and embraced their feet; then he related to them what had happened.

The Snakes that were gathered there, freed from their fright
And relieved of their cares on hearing his words,
Were indeed most happy with Āstīka now,
And they said to him, "Choose the boon you wish!"

Again and again they said on all sides,
"What kindness can we do for you, sage?
We are pleased and we all are now set free—
What wish may we grant you now, our calf?"

Āstīka said:

The brahmins and other folk in this world
Who, morning and evening, tranquil of mind,
Will recount this epic of Law of mine
Must never need be in fear of you.

* = Janamejaya.

The Bard said:

And serene they spoke to their sister's son:
"Then this shall be true, we shall do the wish
You have wished, for we all are wholly pleased—
We shall do it willingly, sister's son!"

—May he who was born to Jaratkāru by Jaratkāru, the famous Āstīka, true to his word, guard me from the Snakes!
—Whoever shall think upon Asita, Ārtimat, and Sunītha, whether by day or night, shall be in no danger of Snakes.

The Bard said:

After having set free the serpents from the Session of the Snakes, the great law-minded brahmin went in due time to his fate, leaving sons and grandsons behind.

25 Thus I have recited to you truthfully the Epic of Āstīka. And when one has recited, or when one has listened to this Epic of Āstīka, which is most conducive to Law and increasing merit, O brahmin, these illustrious exploits of the sage Āstīka from their very beginning, he shall nowhere encounter any danger from the Snakes.

1(6) *The Descent of the First Generations*

1.53–59 (B. 59–64; C. 2198–2508)
53.27 (59; 2198). Śaunaka wishes to hear the stories that were told in the intervals of Janamejaya's Snake Session. The Bard points out that while the brahmins told Vedic stories, Vyāsa told The Mahābhārata, *which the Bard heard. He agrees to repeat it.*
54 (60; 2208). Brief background on Vyāsa (1–5). Vyāsa comes to Janamejaya's sacrifice, is welcomed by the king, and asked to sing of the feats of the Kurus and Pāṇḍavas, which he had witnessed. Vyāsa orders his pupil Vaiśaṃpāyana to recite (5–20).
55 (61; 2231). Vaiśaṃpāyana promises the story of the Breach, *the* Sojourn in the Forest, *and the* War *(1–5). Summary prehistory of the* Breach, *covering* The Book of the Beginning *(5–35). Mention is made of the* Gambling Match *and* The Book of the Forest *(35–40).*

56 (62; 2283). Janamejaya questions the motivations of the warriors (1–10). The Mahābhārata *is praised (10–30).*
57 (63; 2334). Vasu Uparicara; he conquers Cedi at Indra's behest, retires to a hermitage, but is dissuaded by Indra, who fears his austerities (1–5). Indra praises the Cedi country and presents Vasu with an airborne crystal chariot, the unfading lotus garland Vaijayantī, (or Indra's Garland), and a bamboo pole that is to be planted at New Year's Eve and erected at New Year as Indra's Banner. It is covered with baskets, garlands, and ribbons, and Indra is worshipped in it as Frolic (5–25). Vasu had five sons who each founded dynasties (25–30). Satyavatī's birth. Śuktimatī, the river by Vasu's city, is molested by Mount Kolāhala; Vasu frees her by kicking a gully through the mountain. The river gives birth to twins, whom she presents to the king; he makes the boy his army commander and takes the girl, Girikā, as wife (30–35). Once when Girikā is ready to cohabit, Vasu's ancestors order him to go hunting. In the forest he ejaculates, catches the seed on a leaf, and asks a kite to take it to Girikā. Another kite attacks it, the leaf falls into the Yamunā, and an Apsarā in fish form swallows it and conceives (35–45). In the tenth month she is caught by fishers, opened, and two human children are found; they are presented to Vasu. The boy becomes king of the Matsyas; the girl smelled of fish and is brought up by fishers; her name is Satyavatī (45–55). She plies a ferry on the Yamunā, where Parāśara sees her, falls in love, and possesses her under cover of a fog. Satyavatī demands that her virginity be restored and the fish smell disappear; the same day she gives birth on an island to Kṛṣṇa Dvaipāyana, who is Vyāsa, the author of The Mahābhārata *(55–75). Further miraculous births. Bhīṣma born from the Ganges, Dharma incarnated as Vidura by Aṇīmāṇḍavya's curse. Saṃjaya from Gavalgana, Karṇa from Kuntī by the Sun. Viṣṇu as Kṛṣṇa from Devakī by Vasudeva. The births of Sātyaki, Kṛtavarman, Droṇa, Kṛpa, Aśvatthāman, Dhṛṣṭadyumna, Kṛṣṇā, Śakuni, Gāndhārī, Dhṛtarāṣṭra, Bhīma, Arjuna, Nakula, Sahadeva, Duryodhana and his brothers, Yuyutsu, Abhimanyu, Kṛṣṇā's sons, Ghaṭotkaca and Śikhaṇḍin (75–105).*
58 (64; 2456). After Rāma Jāmadagnya had cleared the

earth of all male barons, the brahmins begot new barons on the surviving baronesses; it became the golden age (1–25). But the Asuras, defeated by the Gods, reincarnate themselves in prideful and oppressive kings (25–35). Tyrannized, Earth seeks mercy from Brahmā, who orders that the Gods incarnate themselves. Indra and Nārāyaṇa compact to this purpose (40–50).
59. The celestials descend, and wreak havoc on the demons (1–5).

Śaunaka said:
53.27 Son of the Bard, you have recited for me the entire great story,
from the generation of Bhṛgu onward. I am very pleased with you, my
son. Now I wish to ask you once more to recite for me: narrate to me
again, scion of the Bard, the Epic composed by Vyāsa. I want to hear
from you the stories that were told to the great-spirited *sadasyas* at
that well-nigh endless Session of the Snakes during the pauses
30 between the rites, the wonderful stories and the matters of which they
treated, O great poet, just as they were told. For you know them all,
son of the Bard.

The Bard said:
In the pauses between the rites the brahmins told tales that rested on the *Veda*. But Vyāsa told the wondrous Epic, the grand *Bhārata.*

Śaunaka said:
Yes, the Epic of *The Mahābhārata* that made the Pāṇḍavas famous, which Kṛṣṇa Dvaipāyana properly recited at Janamejaya's bidding during the pauses of his sacrifice, that holy Epic I wish to hear no less precisely. It sprang from that saintly seer's oceanic mind—tell it to me, you strictest of people, for I wish for more, son of the Bard!

The Bard said:
35 Aye, I shall tell you that sublime grand tale, *The Mahābhārata,* as
Kṛṣṇa Dvaipāyana's mind contrived it, from the very beginning.
Enjoy it, lofty-minded brahmin, as I tell it. I too have great joy
reciting it here.

The Bard said:
54.1 Hearing that Janamejaya had undergone the consecration for the
Session of the Snakes, Kṛṣṇa Dvaipāyana the sage betook himself
there—he whom the maiden Kālī* had born to Parāśara, son of
Śakti, on an island in the river Yamunā—while she remained a
virgin—and who became the grandfather of the Pāṇḍavas.—And
hardly had he been born before he, by his sheer will, forced his body

* = Satyavatī.

into full maturity; whereupon the famous sage mastered the *Vedas* and their branches, along with the histories; and no one was to surpass him in austerities, in the study of the *Veda*, in the observance of vows and fasts, in progeny, or in temper. Greatest of the scholars of the *Veda*, he divided the *One Veda* into four parts. He was a brahmin seer who knew the high and the low, a poet, a man of his word, and of great purity. It was he who begot Dhṛtarāṣṭra, Pāṇḍu, and Vidura, carrying thus on, with great fame and holy renown, the lineage of Śaṃtanu.

Vyāsa, accompanied by students who knew the whole *Veda* and its branches, entered the sacrificial *sadas* of the royal sage Janamejaya and saw King Janamejaya sitting there, surrounded by his many *sadasyas*, as Indra by the Gods, and also by the lords of many countrysides, whose heads had been anointed, and by experienced priests, equals of Brahmā, seated on the spread-out grass of the sacrifice.

Lord Janamejaya, the royal sage, seeing the brahmin sage arriving with his company, rose quickly to meet him with affection and offered him with the *sadasyas's* consent a golden stool, as Indra offers a seat to Bṛhaspati; and when the boon-granting guest had been seated—he who is worshiped by the hosts of Gods and Seers—the king of kings paid homage to him with the rite that is found in scripture. He offered, according to the rules, water to wash his feet, water to rinse his mouth, a guest gift, and a cow to his grandfather Kṛṣṇa, who well deserved them. And Vyāsa, much pleased, accepted this homage from Janamejaya Pāṇḍava, and set the cow free. After the king had thus carefully paid his respects to his great-grandfather and had himself taken a seat below him, he inquired about his health. The blessed lord in turn looked upon him and asked about his welfare, and upon being honored by all the *sadasyas* returned the honor.

Afterward, Janamejaya folded his hands and put a question to the eminent brahmin, who had been accorded the honors of a guest by all the *sadasyas*. "Sir," he said, "you have been a witness to the deeds of the Kurus and the Pāṇḍavas. I want you to tell me about their acts, brahmin. How did that Breach arise between these men of untroubled deeds, and how did that great War come about, which was to be the destruction of the creatures, between all my grandfathers whose minds were smitten by fate? Tell me all, for you, blessed lord, are the one who knows it."

Having heard his question, Kṛṣṇa Dvaipāyana turned to his student Vaiśaṃpāyana sitting at his side and instructed him: "Tell him in full, as you have heard it from me, how of old the Breach occurred between the Kurus and the Pāṇḍavas." Hereupon that bull among brahmins acknowledged his guru's command and narrated the entire Epic to the king, the *sadasyas*, and all the barons around, the Breach of the Kurus and Pāṇḍavas, which spelled the destruction of the kingdom.

Vaiśaṃpāyana said:

55.1 First I bow to my guru with spirit and mind collected, and I honor
all the brahmins and other learned folk.
Of Vyāsa the great seer, whose puissance is boundless and whose
fame is spread in all the three worlds, I shall proclaim the thought
entire. Sire, you are a man worthy of hearing it. And I, having
received the Story of the Bhāratas from my guru, seem to be moved by
a thrill of joy to recite it!
Listen then, sire, how the Breach between Kurus and Pāṇḍavas
arose from the Gambling Match over their kingdom, how their
5 Sojourn in the Forest came about, and how a War ensued that
destroyed the earth. I shall relate it to you at your bidding, bull of the
Bhāratas!
When their father had died and these heroes had left the forest for
their own estates, they soon became knowledgeable in *Vedas* and in
arms. But the Kurus, seeing the Pāṇḍavas so richly endowed with
beauty, prowess, and might, acclaimed by the townsfolk, and wearing
both fortune and fame, grew resentful. The cruel Duryodhana, Karṇa
and Subala's son Śakuni, plotted various ways to oppress and
dispossess them. Dhṛtarāṣṭra's evil son fed poison to Bhīma, but this
10 wolf-bellied champion digested it along with his food. Then again he
fettered the Wolf-Belly when he had fallen asleep in Pramāṇakoṭi,
threw Bhīma into the water of the Ganges, and walked away to the
city. When Kuntī's son woke up, he cut the fetters and stood up
unhurt, the strong-armed Bhīmasena. Again Duryodhana had him
bitten in all his limbs by virulent black cobras while he was asleep,
but the enemy-killer failed to die.
At all these hostile deeds of the Kurus, however, sagacious Vidura
remained on guard, to rescue them or to ward off their danger. Even
as Indra in his heaven forever brings luck to the world of the living,
15 so Vidura too forever brought luck to the Pāṇḍavas. But when with
all such plots, either covert or open, they could not kill the
Pāṇḍavas, who were protected by fate and destiny, they took counsel
with such advisers as Vṛṣa and Duḥśāsana and, having wrested
Dhṛtarāṣṭra's consent, had a house of lacquer built. They forced the
Pāṇḍavas of boundless power to live there and then burned down the
house with fire when they were least suspecting. At Vidura's warning,
however, a trench was dug that miraculously gave them a way of
escape, and they ran free from the danger. Later, in a large and
terrifying forest, Bhīmasena, who when angered had terrible strength,
20 killed a Rākṣasa named Hiḍimba. In full agreement, the heroes went to

the town of Ekacakrā and there these warriors lived with their mother
in the garb of brahmins. There they killed the mighty Baka for a
brahmin's sake and, accompanied by brahmins, repaired to the city of
Pāñcāla.

There they won Draupadī and dwelled for a year; when discovered,
the warriors returned to Hāstinapura. King Dhṛtarāṣṭra and Bhīṣma
told them, "To avert war between you and your brethren, sons, we
have thought of the Khāṇḍava Tract as your dwelling place.
Therefore, shed your resentment and go to live in the Khāṇḍava Tract,
25 which is well settled and has large roads well distributed." Upon
their word they journeyed with all their friends to their new city,
the Khāṇḍava Tract, taking all their treasures along. The sons of
Pṛthā dwelled there for many years and brought other kings under
their sway by the might of their swords. And thus they lived, always
bent solely upon the Law, faithful in their promises, arising with
alertness, forbearing, and punishing their ill-wishers. The powerful
Bhīmasena subjugated the East, the heroic Arjuna the North,
Nakula the West, and Sahadeva, slayer of enemy champions,
vanquished the South.

30 Thus they all conquered this earth entire; and with these five
sunlike brothers and the wide-shining sun, earth now counted six
suns with the Pāṇḍavas, whose power was their truth. Thereupon, at
some occasion, the King Dharma Yudhiṣṭhira had his brother
Dhanaṃjaya depart for the woods; he spent one full year and another
month living in the wilderness. One time he went to Hṛṣīkeśa* in
Dvāravatī, and there the Terrifier won for his lotus-eyed wife
Vāsudeva's* younger sister, the pleasant-spoken Subhadrā. And as
Śacī with the great Indra, as Śrī with Kṛṣṇa, so Subhadrā fondly
35 joined yokes with Arjuna Pāṇḍava. In the Khāṇḍava Forest Kuntī's
son the Terrifier** gave satisfaction to the Fire of Sacrifice, O strictest
of kings, along with Vāsudeva. For no load was too heavy for Arjuna
together with Kṛṣṇa, as none is for Viṣṇu in slaying his foes when
seconded by his resolve. The Fire gave Arjuna the great bow Gāṇḍīva,
two quivers with inexhaustible arrows, and a chariot with a monkey
banner. It was there, too, that the Terrifier set free the great Asura
Maya. He made him a divine Hall, heaped with all waters of gems,
where the slow-witted Duryodhana of most evil designs had a craving.
40 Through Subala's son Śakuni he cheated Yudhiṣṭhira at dice, and
sent him to the woods for a dozen years, and thereafter, in disguise,
for a thirteenth year in a kingdom.

When after thirteen years they asked for their own property back,
they did not receive it, great king, and this started the war. They

* = Kṛṣṇa
** = Arjuna.

wiped out the baronage and killed Prince Duryodhana; the Pāṇḍavas regained their kingdom, now mostly deserted.

Such is the ancient geste of those men of unwearied deeds—the Breach, the Kingdom's Loss, and the Triumph, triumphant king.

Janamejaya said:

56.1 Indeed, you have recounted in summary, O eminent brahmin, the entire Epic of the *Mahābhārata*, the Great Geste of the Kurus. But now, blameless ascetic, a great curiosity has arisen in me to hear the entire story, with its manifold matters, recounted by you in all its detail. Sir, you must repeat it to me again and entire, for I cannot hear enough of the great deeds of the ancient.

Surely, it was no small cause for which the law-abiding Pāṇḍavas
killed those they should never have slain, and could still be extolled by
5 men. Why did those tigers among men, capable and guiltless though
they were, condone the oppressions to which evil men subjected them?
How could the Wolf-Belly, who with his two arms had the mettle of
myriad elephants, hold his fury even when he was set upon, best of
the twiceborn? Why did Kṛṣṇā Draupadī, beset by evil-minded men,
fail—capable as she was—to burn the sons of Dhṛtarāṣṭra with her
evil eye? Why did the two sons of Pṛthā and the two sons of Mādrī
later follow the tiger among men, when those crooks had cheated him
in a dishonest game at dice? How could that best of the upholders of
the Law, the son of Dharma, who knew the Law, endure such extreme
oppression, of which he was undeserving—and how could Arjuna?
10 Arjuna who with Kṛṣṇa as his charioteer sent alone whole large
armies to the world of the dead with his arrows?

Tell it to me all as it happened, ascetic—all that those great warriors wrought in every instance.

Vaiśaṃpāyana said:

Of Vyāsa the great seer, whose puissance is boundless and whose
fame is spread in all three worlds, I shall proclaim the thought entire.
The epic that was here related by Satyavatī's son of boundless heat
has a hundred thousand couplets that bring bliss. A man who knows
it and makes others listen to it, and also folk who listen to it, attain to
15 the realm of Brahmā and become the equals of the Gods. For it is a
supreme means of sanctification equal to the *Vedas*, this ancient Lore,
praised by the seers, the greatest of the stories that are worth hearing.
In it the Law is set forth in its entirety, and so is Profit; and in this
most sacred History lies the spirit of salvation. A man who knows the
Veda of Kṛṣṇa and makes it known to the elevated, the generous, the
faithful, and the right-minded, will attain to Profit. Even a loathsome
man, once he has heard this History, will doubtless shed the evil even
of killing a child in the womb.

This History, which is entitled the *Triumph*, should be heard recited
by one who desires to triumph: that king shall vanquish his enemies
20 and conquer the earth. It is the best sacrament to secure the birth of a
son, and an avenue to welfare, which both a queen and a crown
prince should hear recited many times.

Vyāsa of boundless spirit has here promulgated a holy and supreme
textbook of Law and Profit and Salvation. People are telling it now,
and others shall tell it in the future. Sons become obedient and servants
compliant, the evil done with body, words, or thought vanishes at
once for a man who listens to it. They who listen without demurring
to the great birth of the Bhāratas will have no fear of sickness, let
alone of the next world. Kṛṣṇa Dvaipāyana, in a desire to do good,
composed this to give wealth, fame, long life, merit, and heaven while
he spread in the world the fame of the great-spirited Pāṇḍavas and of
the other barons who were rich in possessions as well as heat. Just
as our lord the ocean and Mount Himālaya are both famous treasuries
of jewels, so, they say, is *The Bhārata*. He who knows it and recites it
here to brahmins on the moon days is washed of his evil, sure of his
his heaven, and welcome to the eternal Brahman. And one who
recites even as little as one quarter couplet to the brahmins at his
30 *śrāddha*, his *śrāddha* will forever and ever go up to his forebears. If a
man in his ignorance chances to do evil in his day, it will vanish as
soon as he has heard the story of *The Mahābhārata*. *The Mahābhārata*,
they say, is the great Birth of the Bhāratas; he who knows this
etymology is rid of all his sins.

Kṛṣṇa Dvaipāyana the sage rose daily for three years and created this marvelous story of *The Mahābhārata*.

Bull among Bhāratas, whatever is here, on Law, on Profit, on Pleasure, and on Salvation, that is found elsewhere. But what is not here is nowhere else.

Vaiśaṃpāyana said:

57.1 There once was a king, an ever law-abiding lord of the earth, Vasu, scion of the Pauravas, also named Uparicara, who was a devoted hunter. At Indra's behest, this king took the pleasant country of the Cedis when it was for the taking. When this king had laid down his sword and gone to live in a hermitage, happy with his austerities, the thunderbolt-brandishing God himself came up to him. Worrying that the king might well aspire to become Indra himself through his austerities, he personally coaxed this herdsman of men away from his austere ways.

Indra said:

5 May never on earth, O lord of this earth, the Law be confused!
Protect it, for the upheld Law holds up all the world. Guard the this-

worldly Law, forever on guard and attentive; if yoked to the Law, you shall win the blessed worlds of eternity. You standing on earth have become the dear friend of me standing in heaven—now possess, overlord of men, a country that is the udder of earth, abounding in cattle and holy, of stable clime, with wealth and rice aplenty, protected by the skies, friend to the Soma, which has all the delectable virtues of earth. It is a country beyond all others, with riches and jewels and all good things—Mother Earth, mother of plenty: live on her in the land of the Cedis, king of the Cedis!

The country people are accustomed to the Law, quite content and upright. No lies are spoken there even in jest, let alone in earnest. Sons are devoted to their elders there: they do not divide off from their fathers. Cows are never yoked to the cart, and even lean cows yield plenty. All the classes always abide by their own Law, in this land of the Cedis, O king that gives them pride—there is nothing concealed to you, whatever there be in these three worlds.

This large celestial crystalline chariot in the sky, which it is the Gods' privilege to enjoy, this airborne chariot will come to you as my gift. Among all mortals you alone shall stand upon a grand and sky-going chariot, and indeed, you will ride there above, like a God come to flesh! And I give you this garland Vaijayantī, woven of lotuses that never fade, which shall sustain you in battle, never hurt by swords. That shall be your mark of distinction here, sovereign of men—grand, rich, unmatched, and renowned as "Indra's Garland!"

Vaiśaṃpāyana said:

Vṛtra's destroyer Indra also gave him a bamboo pole, as an Indra gift, to protect the informed. To pay honor to Indra, the king had it driven into the earth at the end of the year. Ever since, and even today, the most strict of the lords of the land drive in the pole, O king, just as he started it before. The next day the kings made it stand erect, adorned with baskets and garlands and perfumes and ornaments. It is properly swaddled with garlands and ribbons, and the fortune-bringing blessed Lord is worshipped in it in the form of frolic, a form he himself took on out of fondness for the great-spirited Vasu.

The God great Indra, seeing his beautiful God-made worship done, was pleased with Vasu, foremost of kings; and the Lord said, "The men and kings who shall worship my *Maha* and shall have it set up with joy as the king of the Cedis did, they and their countrymen shall have fortune and victory. So shall the country folk be fat and happy!"

Thus, O great king, did the great-spirited Indra Maghavat affectionately honor the great King Vasu. Men who have this Festival of Śakra* always celebrated, with such donations as gifts of land so

* = Indra.

that they become purified, and with the granting of boons and the offering of great sacrifices and this Festival of Indra, are honored by Maghavat, even as Vasu, the king of the Cedis, was. Ruling the Cedis under the Law, King Vasu protected this earth and out of devotion to Indra set up Indra's *Maha*.

Vasu had five heroic sons of boundless might; and the father,
who was a universal monarch, had his sons anointed kings in different
kingdoms. There were the great warrior called Bṛhadratha, who
became king of the Magadhas; Pratyāgraha; Kuśāmba, who was also
30 called Maṇivāhana; Macchilla; and Yadu; all barons invincible. These
sons, O king, of this royal seer of plentiful vigor founded kingdoms and
cities that bore their own names, the five Vāsava kings themselves and
their different everlasting dynasties. When King Vasu sat on his Indra
Platform or rode in the sky in the Crystal Chariot, Gandharvas and
Apsarās came to the great-spirited monarch to pay homage. So his
name became famous as "King Uparicara."

There was a river that flowed by his city, and that river, so one
hears, called Śuktimatī, was once waylaid by an intelligent mountain,
Mount Kolāhala, which had fallen in love with her. But Vasu kicked
Mount Kolāhala with his foot, and the river flowed free through the
gully that he had kicked open. The mountain itself begot twins on the
river, and the river, pleased at having been set free, presented the
35 children to the king. One was a boy. Him the grand royal seer Vasu,
bestower of wealth, made the chief of his army, the scourge of his
enemies. The daughter, whose name was Girikā, the king himself took
for his beloved wife.

One day Vasu's wife Girikā lovingly announced that her season had
come, and she bathed and made herself pure for the conceiving of a
son. That day his pleased ancestors said "Shoot some deer!" to this
strictest of kings who was the wisest of men. Unable to transgress the
mandate of his ancestors, Vasu went hunting, lovingly musing on
Girikā, who was a surpassingly beautiful woman, a Śrī come to flesh.
40 And while he roamed the lovely woods, his seed burst forth. No
sooner had it been spilled than the king caught it with a tree leaf,
thinking, "My seed should not be spilled in vain," and "Nor should
my wife's season remain barren!" Once the eminent king had this
thought, he kept reflecting on it, and he knew that his seed was not
to go to waste, as he pondered that it was the queen's season when
his seed spilled forth. He spoke the formula over his seed, and aware
of the subtleties of Law and Profit, he said to a fast kite that was
perching close by, "Friend, as a kindness to me, take this seed of mine
to my house and give it to Girikā, for today is her season." The kite
took it and flew up with a fast swoop.

45 The bird was rushing onward at the peak of its speed when another
kite saw it coming and went at it as soon as it had spied it, thinking
it was a piece of meat it held. The two birds fought a battle of beaks
up in the sky, and while they were fighting the seed fell into the water
of the river Yamunā. Now there was a fish that lived in the Yamunā,
as a beautiful Apsarā, Adrikā by name, who had been cursed by
Brahmā to become a fish. This Adrikā in her body of a fish quickly
swam close and swallowed Vasu's seed that had fallen from the kite's
claw.

Then one day fishermen caught that fish, O best of the Bhāratas,
when she was in her tenth month. And from her belly they pulled
50 human twins, a boy and a girl. They thought this a great marvel and
told the king: "Sire, these two human children were born in the body
of a fish!" Thereupon King Uparicara took the boy child and he later
became King Matsya, law-abiding and true in his promises. The
Apsarā herself was instantly freed from her curse, as she had before
been told by the Blessed Lord: "When you are in your animal form,
beautiful woman, you will be rid of your curse if you bear two human
children!" When she had born them and had been butchered by the
fisherman, she shed her fish body; and, once more taking on her
celestial form, the beautiful Apsarā went to the sky where the Siddhas,
Seers, and Cāraṇas roam. The girl, the other child of the fish, smelled
like a fish and the king gave her to the fisherman: "She must be
55 yours." This girl was called Satyavatī. She had beauty and character
and every virtue, but because she lived among fishermen the sweet-
smiling girl carried for a while the smell of fish.

Satyavatī, in obedience to her father, plied a ferry on the river
Yamunā, and so Parāśara came to see her when he was traveling
about on a pilgrimage. Scarcely had he seen Vasu's daughter, who
was surpassingly beautiful and desirable even to the Siddhas, before
the sage began making love to the comely daughter of Vasu, this bull
among hermits, bent on his task. She said, "Sir, look, there are holy
men standing on both the river banks. How can we lie with each
other when they are looking at us?" Whereupon the blessed lord
60 created a fog that seemed to cover the entire region with darkness.
When she saw the fog that the great seer had created, the modest and
spirited girl said smilingly, "Sir, you must know that I am a virgin
and in my father's keeping. If I consort with you, blameless lord, I
shall lose my virginity. And when my virginity is lost, how shall I
be able to go home, good brahmin? I could not endure staying at
home, O man of wisdom. Think upon it, my lord, and then do what
needs to be done."

The great seer was pleased with her words, and he said, "When
you have done my pleasure, you will still be a virgin. Choose a boon,

bashful and blushing girl, whatever you wish; for my grace has never
before proved fruitless, sweet-smiling one."
65 When he had thus spoken, she chose as her boon that her body
would always smell deliciously, and the blessed lord granted her her
heart's desire. And much pleased, her wish granted, the girl bejeweled
with all a woman's charms lay with the wonder-working seer. Thus
it was that her name "Gandhavatī" became renowned on earth.
People on earth could smell her fragrance a league away, and hence
her well-known name "Yojanāgandhā."

The blessed lord Parāśara went on to his own dwelling place, and
the happy Satyavatī, having obtained her matchless boon, gave birth
the same day she lay with Parāśara. The mighty Pārāśarya* was
70 born on an island in the river Yamunā. He stood before his mother
and set his mind on asceticism. "When you think of me, I shall appear
to you if any task needs to be done," he said.

Thus Dvaipāyana was born from Satyavatī by Parāśara; and since
he was put down on an island as a child, he became "Dvaipāyana."
Knowing that in each successive Eon the Law is crippled in one foot
and that the life and vigor of the mortals follow the rules of the Eon,
and being desirous of showing his grace to both Brahman and
brahmins, he divided the *Vedas*, and is therefore remembered as
75 Vyāsa. He, great lord, most eminent granter of boons, taught the
Vedas, and the *Mahābhārata* as the fifth *Veda*, to Sumantu, Jaimini,
Paila, and his own son Śuka as well as to Vaiśaṃpāyana. It is they
who in their separate ways made public the Collections of *The Bhārata*.

Likewise Bhīṣma, heir to Śaṃtanu and puissant and famous and
boundlessly radiant, was born by the Ganges from the seed of the Vasus.

A very renowned ancient seer, known as Aṇimāṇḍavya, was
impaled on a stake, though no thief, on suspicion of thievery. He
summoned Dharma, this great seer, and he said of yore, "When I was
a child, I speared a little bird on a stalk of reed. That sin I do
remember, Dharma, but none other. Why have my thousand
austerities not overcome it? The killing of a brahmin is worse than
80 the murder of any other creature. Therefore, because of your sin, you
shall be born in the womb of a serf!" By this curse Dharma himself
was born in the womb of a serf, as a wise, law-observing, sinless body
in the form of Vidura.

Saṃjaya, equal to hermits, was born a *sūta* from Gavalgana. The
warrior Karṇa was begotten on the virginal Kuntī by the Sun, and he
sprang forth with natural armor and his face ashimmer with earrings.
Viṣṇu, whose fame is great, who is worshiped by all the worlds, the
Unmanifest, Akṣara, Brahman, and Cause, to favor all the worlds
became manifest in Devakī by Vasudeva—God without beginning or

* = son of Parāśara, i.e., Kṛṣṇa Dvaipāyana.

end, the Lord Maker of the universe, who is without attributes as well
85 as the imperishable Soul, and Nature, the ultimate Source, the Man,
the Maker of all things, the Yoker of Being, the stable Intransient, the
Unending, Unmoving God, the Swan, the Lord Nārāyaṇa, whom they
call the unaging, sempiternal Place, supreme and everlasting. He is
the ubiquitous Man, Maker, and Grandfather of all creatures; and so
in order to further the growth of the Law, he was born amidst the
Andhaka-Vṛṣṇis.

The two heroes, experts on weapons thrown, and knowledgeable
on all arms, Sātyaki and Kṛtavarman, who were avowed to Nārāyaṇa,
were born from Satyaka and Hṛdika as expert spearmen. The spilled
seed of Bharadvāja, great seer of awesome austerities, grew in a
90 a trough and from it was born Droṇa. From Gautama Śaradvat, from a
stalk of cane, were born twins, the powerful Kṛpa and the mother of
Aśvatthāman; from her Aśvatthāman was born, greatest of spearmen,
by Droṇa. Likewise Dhṛṣṭadyumna, who matched the luster of Fire,
was born from Fire when a sacrifice had been spread, born a powerful
hero, along with his bow, for the destruction of Droṇa. So also was
Kṛṣṇā born from an altar, effulgent, bright, shining wide with beauty,
and having a superb shape.

Then were born Prahlāda's pupil Nagnajit, and Subalā, whose
progeny became the scourge of the Law through the fury of the Gods—
95 Śakuni Saubala, son of the king of Gāndhāra, and Gāndhārī the
mother of Duryodhana, both clever in Profit. From Kṛṣṇa Dvaipāyana
on the field of Vicitravīrya was born the king of men Dhṛtarāṣṭra and
also Pāṇḍu of great strength. From Pāṇḍu there were born five sons,
each the like of a God, by his two wives. Eldest in virtue was
Yudhiṣṭhira. Yudhiṣṭhira was born from Dharma the Law, the Wolf-
Belly from the Wind, and Arjuna, illustrious and greatest of any
wielders of arms, from Indra. From the Aśvins were born the handsome
twins Nakula and Sahadeva, devotedly obedient to their elders.
A hundred sons were born to the wise Dhṛtarāṣṭra, Duryodhana and
the others, and the half-breed Yuyutsu.

100 Arjuna begot Abhimanyu on Subhadrā, sister of Kṛṣṇa Vāsudeva,
as Pāṇḍu's great-spirited grandson. By all five of the Pāṇḍavas Kṛṣṇā
brought forth five boys, endowed with beauty and wise in all the ways
of weaponry—Prativindhya by Yudhiṣṭhira, Sutasoma by the Wolf-
Belly, Śrutakīrti by Arjuna, Śatānīka by Nakula, and mighty Śrutasena
by Sahadeva. Bhīma begot Ghaṭotkaca in the woods on Hiḍimbā.
Śikhaṇḍin was born a girl child, from Drupada, but later became a
man: the Yakṣa Sthūṇa changed her into a man, to do her a favor.

105 At this war of the Kurus many hundreds of thousands of kings
foregathered, eager to fight in the battle. Their names are innumerable
—not in a myriad years could their number be counted. But the chiefs
have been mentioned, by whom hangs this tale.

Janamejaya said:
58.1 Yet, brahmin, you have mentioned some, and others you have not—
I wish to hear precisely the names of those other brilliant kings. For
what purpose were all these godlike warriors born on earth? Pray
tell me, good sir, with precision.

Vaiśaṃpāyana said:
Sire, we have heard that is indeed a mystery to the Gods. But,
after bowing to the Self-Created One, I shall tell you the story.

Rāma, son of Jamadagni, once cleared the earth of all barons
twenty-one times over, and then did his austerities on great Mount
5 Mahendra. When the world had been rid of barons by that scion of
the Bhr̥gus, the baronesses, sire, came to the brahmins craving for
their wombs. Brahmins of strict vows fell with them, at the right
season, tiger among men, not for lust, nor out of season. Those
baronesses got with child by them, by the thousands, and thereupon
they gave birth, O king, to barons that were proven champions, boys
as well as girls, to increase once more the baronage. Thus the
baronage was begotten on the baronesses by austere brahmins, and
it prospered with the Law and a very long life. All four classes were
thereafter headed by the brahmins. Men lay with a woman at her
season, not for lust, nor out of season; and so did the other creatures,
even of the brute creation, couple with their females at the right
season, O bull among Bhāratas.
10 Thenceforth their offspring grew with the Law, living for hundreds
and thousands of years, O herdsmen of the earth, and bent upon the
vows of the Law. Men were wholly free from worries and diseases.
The baronage once more governed mother earth entire with her ocean
borders, O king of the lordly elephant gait, with her mountains,
wilderness, and woods. And while the baronage reigned over this
earth in accordance with the Law, all the classes, headed by the
brahmins, found surpassing joy. Casting off such vices as spring from
lust and anger, the kings of men protected their subjects, using their
staff according to the Law upon those that deserved it. As the baronage
was law-abiding, the God of the thousand eyes and the hundred
sacrifices rained sweet rain at the right time and place, swelling the
15 people. No infant died then, king of men, no one knew a woman
before he was of age.

Thus, bull among Bhāratas, this ocean-girt earth was filled with long-living people. The barons offered up grand sacrifices for which ample stipends were given. The brahmins studied the *Vedas* with their branches and *Upaniṣads*. No brahmins then sold their Brahman for gain, sire, nor did they recite the *Vedas* in the hearing of serfs. The farmers ploughed the earth with bullocks; they did not put cows to

20 the yoke, and they let the lean cows live. Men did not milk cows
whose calves were still suckling, and merchants did not sell their
wares with false weights. People did their lawful chores looking to the
Law and devoted to the Law, tiger among men. All the classes
devoted themselves to their *own* tasks, O king, and thus, tiger among
men, the Law was in no way diminished in that age. The cows and
women gave birth in time, bull among Bhāratas; trees stood in fruit
and bloom in all seasons. And while thus the Eon of the Winning
Throw went on in its perfection, the entire earth became filled with
many creatures.

25 In this so flourishing world of men, bull among Bhāratas and men,
the Asuras were born in the land of the kings. For the Daityas had
often been defeated in battle by the Gods, and having fallen from
their supernal estate, they took birth here on earth. Wanting to be
Gods on earth, the prideful demons were born, O lord, from men and
from all manner of creatures that live on earth, O king, from cows,
horses, asses, camels, and buffalo, from beasts of prey, elephants, and
deer. And when they were born and went on being born, wide earth,
sire, could no longer support herself.

30 Now some of them were born kings, filled with great strength,
sons of Diti and Danu who had now fallen from their world to earth.
Powerful, insolent, bearing many shapes, they swarmed over this
sea-girt earth, crushing their enemies. They oppressed the brahmins,
the barons, the farmers, even the serfs, and other creatures they
oppressed with their power. Sowing fear and slaughtering all the
races of creation, they roamed all over earth, O king, by the hundreds
of thousands, menacing everywhere the great seers in their
hermitages, impious, drunk with power, insensate with drink.

35 When she was thus tyrannized by the grand Asuras, bloated with
power and strength, Earth came to Brahmā as a supplicant. Neither
the wind, nor the elephants, nor the mountains, O king, were able to
support Earth so forcefully overrun by the Dānavas. Therefore, Earth,
sagging under her burden and brutalized with fear, sought refuge with
the God who is the grandfather of all beings. Surrounded by worthy
Gods, brahmins, and seers, she saw the God Brahmā, the eternal
creator of the world, hymned by joyous Gandharvas and Apsarās, who
are the musicians of the Gods; and approaching, she too greeted him.
40 Then, seeking refuge, Earth spoke to him in the presence of all the
Guardians of the Worlds, O Bhārata. But Earth's business had long
before been known to the Self-Created, the Inspiriter of matter, who
dwells on high. For how could he, creator of the universe, fail to
know entirely what is lodged in the minds of the worlds of Gods and
Asuras, O Bhārata?

And to Earth spoke Earth's Lord, source of all creatures, Sovereign, Hail-bringer, Prajāpati: "For what purpose thou hast come to my presence, Earth, to that purpose shall I yoke all those that live in heaven." Having spoken, God Brahmā dismissed her, O king, and then he himself, maker of the creatures, gave orders to all the Gods. "To throw off the burden of Earth," he said, "you must each be born with a part of yourselves on her to halt them." Likewise he summoned the hosts of Gandharvas and Apsarās, and the Lord spoke to them this great word; "Be born among men with parts of yourselves, in the fashion that pleases you."

All the Gods from Indra onward, upon hearing the word of the eldest of the Gods, meaningful, and apt, took it to heart. Impatient to go to earth and be reborn everywhere with portions of themselves, they went to Nārāyaṇa Vaikuṇṭha, slayer of enemies, he who wields the discus and the club, yellow-robed, dark-complexioned, lotus-naveled killer of the foes of the Gods, whose eyes are wide and soft and slanted. For the cleansing of earth Indra spoke to the Supreme Person: "Descend with a part of thyself!" And Hari said, "So shall it be!"

Vaiśampāyana said:

59.1 Indra then made a covenant with Nārāyaṇa that together with the Gods they would descend from heaven to earth with a portion of themselves. Indra himself gave orders to all the celestials, and thereupon he left Nārāyaṇa's dwelling. And so the celestials in succession descended from heaven to earth, for the destruction of the enemies of the Gods and the well-being of all the worlds; thereupon they were born in the lineages of brahmin seers and the dynasties of royal seers, at their own pleasure, O tiger among kings. They slew Dānavas and Rākṣasas and Gandharvas and Snakes, and other man-eating creatures in great numbers. Neither the Dānavas, nor the Rākṣasas, nor the Snakes, O best of the Bhāratas, slew them; for even in their infancy they stood in strength.

1(7) The Origins

59–123 (B. 65–140; C. 2509–5634)
59.7 (65; 2509). Janamejaya desires to hear the origins of Gods, Dānavas, Gandharvas, Apsarās, men, Yakṣas, and Rākṣasas. Vaiśampāyana obliges. The six will-born sons of Brahmā. Dakṣa's thirteen daughters and their progeny

—Aditi: Ādityas; Diti: Daityas; Danu: Dānavas; Siṃhikā: Rāhu, etc.; Anāyus: Asuras; Vinatā: Garuḍa, etc.; Kadrū: the Snakes; Krodhā (Krūrā): cruel races; Muni: Gandharvas; Prāvā: Gandharvas and Apsarās; Kapilā: Elixir, etc.; Kālā; Ariṣṭā (1–50).

60 (66; 2565). Brahmā's six will-born sons; Marīci, Angiras, Atri, Pulastya, Pulaha, and Kratu: their progeny. Sthāṇu's eleven will-born sons: Mṛgavyādha, Śarva, Nirṛti, Aja Ekapād, Ahi Budhnya, Pinākin, Dahana, Īśvara, Kapālin, Sthāṇu, and Bhava (1–5). Brahmā's son Dakṣa has fifty daughters, adopted by Brahmā, who marries off ten to Dharma, twenty-seven to Dyaus, thirteen to Kaśyapa (5–15). Prajāpati and the eight Vasus: offspring. Dharma: three sons. Kaśyapa: Gods and Asuras. Tvaṣṭrī: two Aśvins. Aditi: twelve Ādityas (15–35). The Groups of Gods. Bhṛgu: Śukra: Cyavana: Aurva: Ṛcīka: Jamadagni: Rāma (35–45). Brahmā: Dhātar, Vidhātar, Lakṣmī; Lakṣmī: sky-flying horses. Śukra's daughter Jyeṣṭhā has, by Varuṇa, Vala and Liquor. Nirṛti has by Adharma the Rākṣasas. Tāmrā and Krodhā mother the animal creation (45–60).

61 (B. 67; C. 2637–2798) (7a) The Book of the Partial Incarnations.

62–69 (B. 68–74; C. 2799–3125) (7b) The Story of Śakuntalā.

70–80 (B. 75–85; C. 3126–3534) (7c) The Story of Yayāti.

81–88 (B. 86–93; C. 3535–3690) (7d) The Latter Days of Yayāti.

89 (94; 3691) Genealogy of Pūru to Saṃvaraṇa (1–30). During Saṃvaraṇa's reign disasters befall; under attack by the Pāñcālas he retreats to the Indus (30–35). After eight years he returns with Vasiṣṭha's help (35–40). Genealogy from Saṃvaraṇa to Śaṃtanu (40–55).

90 (96; 3843). The genealogy of the Pāṇḍavas from Dakṣa to Pūru (1–10), Pūru to Matināra (10–25), Bhārata (30) Saṃvaraṇa (40), Śaṃtanu (50); the begetting of Dhṛtarāṣṭra, Pāṇḍu, and Vidura (60); of the five Pāṇḍavas (70); and their offspring down to Janamejaya's grandson (70–95).

91 (97; 3865). Mahābhiṣa Aikṣvākava sees the Ganges naked in heaven and is cursed by Brahmā to be reborn; he chooses Pratīpa as his father (1–5). Gangā meets the

eight Vasus who have been cursed by Vasiṣṭha to become men; they ask her to become their mother by Pratīpa's son Śaṃtanu, and to drown them at birth (5–15). She agrees, provided that one son may live (15–20).
92 (98; 3896). Gangā appears to Pratīpa and sits on his right thigh. He refuses her as wife, but accepts her as future daughter-in-law. Gangā agrees, provided she remain incognita and unquestioned (1–15). Śaṃtanu is born to Pratīpa, and told of the covenant; he becomes king (15). When hunting, Śaṃtanu sees Gangā and marries her; she demands that her conduct never be questioned (25–35). She drowns her first seven sons; at the eighth Śaṃtanu demurs, and Gangā identifies herself and explains about Vasiṣṭha's curse on the Vasus; the child is Bhīṣma.
93 (99; 3920). The story of Āpava Vasiṣṭha. When he lived on the Meru with his sacrificial milch cow, the Vasus and their wives came to play. Dyaus's wife wanted the cow that bestowed life for ten thousand years (1–25). Dyaus and the other Vasus carry off the cow. Vasiṣṭha curses them to become men (25–30). Placated, Vasiṣṭha limits their lives to one year, except Dyaus's, which will be long (35–40). After telling the tale Gangā disappears with her child Devavrata Gāngeya (40–45).
94 (100; 3968). Śaṃtanu's righteous reign (1–20). While hunting, Śaṃtanu sees the Ganges falling dry under the arrow shots of a large boy who disappears; the boy then reappears with Gangā (20–30). She praises him as Śaṃtanu's son and entrusts him to Śaṃtanu. He is anointed Young King (30–40). Again, Śaṃtanu encounters by the Yamunā a fragrant fisher girl who plies a ferry, Satyavatī. Śaṃtanu sues for her with her father, who agrees, provided that her sons will inherit the throne. Śaṃtanu declines and sadly returns to Hāstinapura (40–50). Devavrata learns the reason of his father's melancholy (55–60) and asks for Satyavatī for his father: he foreswears the throne (65–75) and even marriage (80–90). Hence he is known as Bhīṣma. Śaṃtanu gives him the boon that he may die at will (90).
95 (101; 4067). Satyavatī gives birth to Citrāngada and Vicitravīrya; Śaṃtanu dies. Citrāngada, installed, is killed in a three-year-long battle with a Gandharva. Bhīṣma installs Vicitravīrya (1–10).
96 (102; 4081). At the bridegroom choice of the Kāśi

princesses, Ambā, Ambikā, and Ambālikā, Bhīṣma abducts all three (1–10). The other suitors give battle, but are repulsed (10–20). Śālva challenges Bhīṣma to a duel, is defeated, but left with his life (25–40). Bhīṣma gives the princesses to Vicitravīrya to wed (40–45). Ambā demurs, for she had chosen Śālva; Bhīṣma lets her go (45–50). After seven years Vicitravīrya dies of consumption, without heir (50–55).

97 (103; 4146). Satyavatī pleads with Bhīṣma to father children on the widowed princesses (1–10). Mindful of his vow he refuses (10–15), in spite of further pleas (15–25).

98 (104; 4172). Bhīṣma relates how the brahmins begot sons on the baronesses after Paraśurāma's massacre (1–5). Utathya's younger brother Bṛhaspati tries to seduce Utathya's wife Mamatā, who is with child; the child interrupts the cohabitation and is cursed to be born blind as Dīrghatamas (5–15). Dīrghatamas's sons cast him off on a tree log in the Ganges. Afterward he is rescued by King Balin, who enjoins him to father sons on his wives, and sends him his wife Sudeṣṇā (15–20). She is repelled by his age and blindness, and sends him a serf woman, on whom he begets Kakṣīvat and ten other sons. Balin claims the sons but is refused. Dīrghatamas begets Anga on Sudeṣṇā (25–30).

99 (105; 4223). Satyavatī tells Bhīṣma that she had had a premarital child by Parāśara, story of the seduction (1–10). Their issue is Kṛṣṇa Dvaipāyana. Bhīṣma approves that he father heirs for Vicitravīrya (15–20). Kṛṣṇa appears, and Satyavatī implores him to beget children on the princesses. He agrees if they observe a year-long vow (20–35). Satyavatī pleads urgency, Kṛṣṇa agrees but stipulates that the women endure his ugliness (40). Satyavatī prepares Ambikā Kausalyā (40–45).

100 (106; 4274). Ambikā is terrified at Kṛṣṇa's sight and keeps her eyes closed while cohabiting; for that the child, Dhṛtarāṣṭra, will be born blind (1–10). Kṛṣṇa lies with Ambālikā, who pales with terror; Pāṇḍu, the boy, is pale (10–15). Satyavatī asks for a third son, but Ambikā sends a slave woman in her stead; on her Kṛṣṇa fathers Vidura (20–30).

101 (107–08; 4305). Story of Māṇḍavya. This ascetic was taken for a robber, when robbers hid their plunder in his hermitage; he is impaled (1–10). He fails to die;

other seers, in the guise of birds, cannot free him. Informed, the king sets him free, but the stake will not come out (10–20). Māṇḍavya demands explanations from Dharma, who declares that this was the punishment for spearing flies as a child. Māṇḍavya curses Dharma to be born a man: he becomes Vidura (20–25).

102 (109; 4337). The happy state of Kurukṣetra during Bhīṣma's regency (1–10). Dhṛtarāṣṭra, Pāṇḍu, and Vidura grow up (15–20). Pāṇḍu succeeds (20).

103 (110; 4363). At Bhīṣma's instigation Dhṛtarāṣṭra marries Gāndhārī, who has received the boon that she will bear a hundred sons; she lives henceforth blindfolded because of her husband's blindness. Her brother Śakuni brings her to the Kurus (1–15).

104 (111; 4382). Śūra of the Yadus, father of Vasudeva, gives his firstborn child, the girl Pṛthā, to his cousin Kuntibhoja to adopt; she serves the irascible Durvāsas, who gives her a spell by which she can have a son from any God (1–5). She tries it out on the Sun God, by whom she has Karṇa; he is born with armor and earrings. The God restores her virginity. The sūta *Adhiratha adopts the abandoned child and names him Vasuṣeṇa (5–15). He worships the sun and during his worship cannot refuse a brahmin anything. Indra in the guise of a brahmin demands his armor and earrings; he cuts them off. Indra rewards him with a never-failing spear. He is henceforth known as Karṇa Vaikartana (15–20).*

105 (112–13; 4412). Pṛthā chooses Pāṇḍu as her bridegroom choice. Bhīṣma buys Mādrī from the king of the Madras for Pāṇḍu (1–5). Pāṇḍu goes out on conquest and defeats the Daśārṇas, Dārva of Magadha, the Videhas, Kāśis, Suhmas, and Puṇḍras (5–10) and returns with much booty in great triumph (15–25).

106 (114; 4469). The booty is distributed and sacrifices are held (1–5). Pāṇḍu lives in the forest with his wives (5–10). Vidura marries a bastard daughter of King Devaka (10).

107 (115; 4483). Gāndhārī, who had been promised a hundred sons by Kṛṣṇa Dvaipāyana, is pregnant for two years. On hearing that Kuntī has given birth she aborts herself and produces a hard ball of flesh. When she wants to dispose of it, Kṛṣṇa intervenes (1–15). He has the ball sprinkled and it severs into a hundred and one parts that are incubated in separate pots (15–20). Duryodhana is born first, and Dhṛtarāṣṭra suggests he succeed Yudhiṣṭhira, who was born earlier; portents of evil appear. Vidura advises that Duryodhana be abandoned (20–30). Within a month all one hundred sons are born and one daughter. Dhṛtarāṣṭra has a bastard son Yuyutsu (30–35).

108 (117; 4540). The names of the one hundred sons (1–10). They are eventually married; the sole daughter, Duḥśālā, is wedded to Jayadratha of Sindhu (10–15).

109 (118; 4558). Pāṇḍu shoots a mating buck, who proves to be an ascetic; he berates Pāṇḍu, who defends himself (1–15). The ascetic curses him that he will die under the same circumstances, and dies (15–30).

110 (119; 4592). Pāṇḍu laments and resolves on total renunciation, which he describes (1–20). His two wives dissuade him, and he decides to become a forest-dweller; he relinquishes his regalia. Dhṛtarāṣṭra grieves (25–40). Pāṇḍu travels to Mount Gandhamādana (40–45).

111 (120; 4640). The seers there prevent him from going north (1–10). Pāṇḍu laments his childlessness; the seers predict that he will have offspring (15–20). Pāṇḍu proposes to Kuntī that she finds a begetter in his stead, like Śāradaṇḍāyinī (20–35).

112 (121; 4680). Kuntī relates the story of Vyuṣitāśva, a great sacrificer (1–10). He lusts with his wife Bhadrā and dies childless. Bhadrā laments (15–25). Her husband's voice promises that she shall conceive from his corpse (25–30).

113 (122; 4716). Pāṇḍu relates that, of old, women were as free as the animals and Northern Kurus are now (1–5). Uddālaka's son Śvetaketu witnesses how a brahmin wants to take his mother off and lays down the Law that wives must be faithful; adultery amounts to aborticide; so does a wife's refusal to have children at her husband's injunction (5–20). Kalmāṣa's wife conceived by Vasiṣṭha (20). Pāṇḍu urges Kuntī to find a begetter (20–30). She tells him of Durvāsas's spell to call on any God. He orders her to call Dharma (30–40).

114 (123; 4759). Kuntī calls Dharma, who begets Yudhiṣṭhira; he is praised by a celestial voice (1–5). At Pāṇḍu's urging, she calls Vāyu, who begets Bhīma. Once when Bhīma fell off his mother's lap, he shattered a mountain. He is born on the same day as Duryodhana (5–10). Pāṇḍu wishes for a superior son; Kuntī calls on Indra, who begets Arjuna. Praise of the child (15–35). Seers, Gandharvas, Apsarās, the Ādityas, Rudras, Aśvins, Maruts, Viśve Devas, Sādhyas, Snakes, and Garuḍa celebrate (35–60). Pāṇḍu wants more sons, but Kuntī refuses (60–65).

115 (124; 4836). Mādrī complains to Pāṇḍu that she has no sons. Pāṇḍu persuades Kuntī to help Mādrī (1–10). Kuntī tells Mādrī to call a God with her spell; she calls the Aśvins, who beget Nakula and Sahadeva. The children are named. Kuntī refuses to call more Gods for Mādrī (15–20). The children grow up in the Himālaya (25).

116 (125; 4866). In spring Pāṇḍu lusts after Mādrī, and overpowers her and dies (1–10). Mādrī calls Kuntī and is berated (10–20). Kuntī demands that she herself follow Pāṇḍu in death; Mādrī points out the benefit for the children if they are brought up by Kuntī and dies on Pāṇḍu's pyre (20–30).

117 (126; 4897). The seers perform the obsequies and take Kuntī, the children, and the two corpses to Hāstinapura (1–5). Crowds form there, and the Kauravas come out to greet the seers (5–15). The seers identify the Pāṇḍavas and describe Pāṇḍu's death; they vanish (20–30).

118 (127; 4932). The Kauravas administer the last rites for Pāṇḍu and Mādrī and mourn for twelve days (1–30).

119 (128–29; 4964). The śrāddha *for Pāṇḍu (1). Kṛṣṇa Dvaipāyana prophesies a time of troubles and tells Satyavatī to retire to the woods. She takes Pāṇḍu's mother Kausalyā with her, and they die in the forest (5–10). The Pāṇḍavas grow up with Dhṛtarāṣṭra's sons; Bhīma playfully bullies the latter (10–20). In revenge, Duryodhana tries to drown Bhīma in the Ganges, but he escapes (20–35); he tries to poison him, but he survives (35–40). The Pāṇḍavas do not reveal these attempts (40).*

120 (130; 5071). The ascetic Śaradvat is sent by Indra the Apsarā Jalapadī; his seed falls on a reed stalk and splits into two, from which twins are born, a boy and a girl (1–10). Śaṃtanu, out hunting, finds them with arrows and antelope skin; he adopts them and names them Kṛpa and Kṛpī (15). Śaradvat returns and teaches Kṛpa the martial arts; he in turn becomes the teacher of the sons of Dhṛtarāṣṭra, the Pāṇḍavas, the Vṛṣṇis, and others (15–20).

121. The seer Bharadvāja sees the Apsarā Ghṛtācī nude; he catches his seed in a trough; Droṇa is born from that. Bharadvāja teaches him the āgneya *missile (1–5). Drupada, son of King Pṛṣata, is Droṇa's schoolmate. Drupada succeeds to the throne of Pāñcāla. Droṇa weds Kṛpī and begets Aśvatthāman (5–15). He obtains the miracle weapons of Rāma Jāmadagnya at his retirement (15–20).*

122 (131; 5134). Droṇa visits Drupada, who disclaims his friendship (1–5). Insulted, Droṇa goes to Hāstinapura. He lifts a toy of the princes from a dry well with a chain of arrows. Bhīṣma receives him (10–20). Droṇa complains of Drupada's hypocrisy (20–35). Bhīṣma engages him as a teacher. Droṇa demands of his pupils assistance in a secret task; only Arjuna gives his promise (35–45). Droṇa also teaches the Vṛṣṇis and Karṇa (45).

123 (132; 5211). Arjuna, his favorite, is instructed by Droṇa (1–5). The aboriginal Ekalavya comes for instruction, but Droṇa refuses him. He goes into the forest and practices before an image of Droṇa (10). When the princes go hunting with a dog, the dog discovers Ekalavya, who shoots it blindly; he is recognized (15–25). Arjuna complains to Droṇa that he has a better pupil than he; Droṇa goes to find Ekalavya, who honors him as his teacher. Droṇa demands his right thumb as his fee; Ekalavya cuts it off and is no longer as fast an archer (25–35). Arjuna excels over all pupils (40). Droṇa places an artificial bird in a treetop and tests each pupil's concentration in aiming. Arjuna wins (45–65). Arjuna shoots a crocodile that has grasped Droṇa (65–70). Droṇa gives him the Brahmā-Head missile (70–75).

Janamejaya said:

59.7 Of all the hosts of Gods and Dānavas, and Gandharvas and Apsarās, of men and Yakṣas and Rākṣasas, I wish to hear the origins,

complete, from the beginning, and in detail, and also of all other
creatures. For you know everything!

Vaiśaṃpāyana said:

Aye, I shall bow to the Self-Created God and narrate to you
precisely the origin and decline of the worlds of the Gods and the
others.

10 Of Brahmā six sons are known, great seers who were born from
his will, Marīci, Atri, Angiras, Pulastya, Pulaha, and Kratu. Marīci's
son was Kaśyapa, and Kaśyapa begot these creatures. Dakṣa begot
thirteen daughters of great shares, Aditi, Diti, Dānu, Kālā, Anāyus,
Siṃhikā, Muni, Krodhā, Prāvā, Ariṣṭā, Vinata, Kapilā and Kadrū, O
Bhārata, tiger among men. From them sprang an endless progeny of
powerful sons and grandsons. From Aditi were born the twelve
Ādityas, sovereigns of the worlds, whom I shall mention by name,
15 King Bhārata—Dhātar, Mitra, Aryaman, Indra, Varuṇa, Aṃśa, Bhaga,
Vivasvat, Pūṣan; and in the tenth place Savitar, in the eleventh
Tvaṣṭar, and in the twelfth Viṣṇu. The last-born surpasses the other
Ādityas in greatness. Diti had only one son, known as Hiraṇyakaśipu,
but of him five great-spirited sons are known by name: Prahrāda, the
firstborn, followed by Saṃhrāda; Anuhrāda was the third, and after
him Śibi and Bāṣkala. Three sons of Prahrāda are known everywhere,
20 O Bhārata—Virocana, Kumbha, Nikumbha. Virocana had one son,
the majestic Bali, who in turn had a famous son, the great Asura
Bāṇa.

Forty sons are everywhere known of Dānu. The first one was the
renowned king Vipracitti; further one knows of Śambara, Namuci, and
Puloman, of Asiloman, Keśin, and the Dānava Durjaya, of Ayaḥśiras,
Aśvaśiras, Aśvaśanku the mighty, also Gaganamūrdhan, Vegavat,
Ketumat, Svarbhānu, Aśva, Aśvapati, Vṛṣaparvan, Ajaka, Aśvagrīva,
25 Sūkṣma, the powerful Tuhuṇḍa, Isṛpa, Ekacakra, Virūpākṣa, Hara
and Āhara, Nicandra, Nikumbha, Kupatha, Kāpatha, Śarabha, Śalabha,
and the Sun and the Moon. Thus by name are recited the Dānavas of
Dānu's line. The Sun and the Moon of the Gods are different ones.
Also cited as sons of Dānu in his line, great king, are these ten
mettlesome and powerful bulls among Dānavas: Ekākṣa, Mṛtapa, the
champion Pralambha, Naraka, Vātāpi, Śatrutapana, the great Asura
Śaṭha, Gaviṣṭha, Danāyu, and the Dānava Dīrghajihva. Their sons and
grandsons, O Bhārata, are innumerable.
30 Siṃhikā bore a son Rāhu, foe of moon and sun, and Sucandra,
Candrahartar, and Candravimardana. The countless sons and
grandsons of Krūrā were of innate cruelty, an ill-tempered race, cruel
in deeds, crushing their enemies.

Anāyus had four sons, bulls among Asuras—Vikṣara, Bala, Vīra,
and the grand Asura Vṛtra. Kālā's renowned sons were, like Time

itself, destructive, powerful enemy-harassers among the Dānavas
and famous on earth: Vināśana, Krodha, Krodhahantar, Krodhaśatru
as well as others are known as the Kāleyas.
35 The priest of the Asuras was Śukra, the son of a seer, and this
Śukra Uśanas had four known sons, who acted as sacrificial priests
for the Asuras—Tvaṣṭāvara and Atri, and two other masters of spells,
equal to the sun in their heat and furtherers of the world of Brahmā.
This is the origin of the generations, as told in the ancient Lore,
of the puissant Gods and the Asuras; and so have I heard it. To
enumerate completely their progeny, multiplied endlessly, I am not
able, my Lord.
Tārkṣya, Ariṣṭanemi, Garuḍa, Aruṇa, Āruṇi, and Vāruṇi are cited
40 as sons of Vinatā. Śeṣa, Ananta, Vāsuki, Takṣaka the Snake, Kūrma,
and Kulika are cited as sons of Kadrū. Bhīmasena, Ugrasena, Suparṇa,
Varuṇa, Gopati, Dhṛtarāṣṭra, Sūryavarcas, Pattravat, Arkaparṇa,
the renowned Pracyuta, Bhīma, Citraratha, famous and omniscient
ruler, Śāliśiras, and O king, Parjanya in the fourteenth place, Kali in
the fifteenth, and Nārada in the sixteenth, are known as the divine
Gandharvas, sons of Muni.
Now I shall recite to you other creatures, O Bhārata. Prāvā gave
birth to Anavadyā, Anuvāśā, Anūṇaruṇā, Priyā, Anūpā, Subhagā, and
40 Bhāsī, while Siddha, Pūrṇa, Barhi, the famous Pūrṇāyu, Brahmacārin,
Ratiguṇa, Suparṇa, Viśvāvasu, Bhānu, and Sucandra are quoted as
divine Gandharvas, sons of Prāvā. Divine Prāvā of great parts also
bore of old by a divine seer the well-known and holy race of the
Apsarās—Alambuṣā, Miśrakeśī, Vidyutparṇā, Tulānaghā, Aruṇā,
Rakṣitā, as well as the lovely Rambhā, Asitā, Subāhu, Suvratā,
Subhūjā, and Supriyā; Atibāhu, the famed Hāha and Āhuhu, and
50 Tumbura are recalled as the four great Gandharvas. The Elixir, the
brahmins, the cows, Gandharvas, and Apsarās were the progeny of
Kapilā as declared in the ancient Lore.
Thus have I told you the origins of the beings, and quoted their
numbers precisely, and of Gandharvas and Apsarās, Snakes, Birds,
Rudras and Maruts, cows, and illustrious brahmins of holy deeds.
This chapter, so worthy of being heard, should be listened to without
demurring; it will bring the listener a long life, merit, wealth, and the
joy of listening. One who will recite this genealogy with proper
restraint, in the presence of great-spirited Gods and brahmins, will
obtain a plenty of offspring, riches, and fame; and after death a
felicitous journey.

Vaiśaṃpāyana said:
60.1 There are six sons known of Brahmā, great seers, born of his will;
while Sthāṇu had eleven will-born sons—Mṛgavyādha, Śarva, the

famed Nirṛti, Aja Ekapād, Ahi Budhnya, the enemy-burning Pinākin, Dahana, Īśvara and the radiant Kapālin, Sthāṇu, and the blessed Lord Bhava. These are known as the eleven Rudras. Marīci, Angiras, Atri, Pulastya, Pulaha, and Kratu are the six sons of Brahmā, powerful great seers.

Angiras had three sons who are renowned everywhere in the world—Bṛhaspati, Utathya, and Saṃvarta, true to his vows. We hear of many sons of Atri, O overlord of men, all scholars of the Veda, of tranquil spirit, and perfect great seers. From Pulastya sprang the Rākṣasas, the apes, the Kiṃnaras; from Pulaha, the deer, lions, tigers, and Kiṃpurusas. From Kratu sprang sons equal to Kratu, who are the companions of the sun, famed in the three worlds, religiously faithful to their vows.

The venerable seer Dakṣa was born from the right thumb of Brahmā, O herdsman of the world, both son and greatest of fathers. From the left thumb sprang the wife of the great-spirited Dakṣa, and on her the sage begot fifty maidens; all these maidens were perfect in body, with lotuslike eyes. Prajāpati, being deprived of sons, made them his *puppets*. By divine rite, O king, he gave ten to Dharma, twenty-seven to Heaven, and thirteen to Kaśyapa. Listen to me recite the names of the wives of Dharma. Kīrti, Lakṣmī, Dhṛti, Medhā, Puṣṭi, Śraddhā, Kriyā, Buddhi, Lajjā, and Mati are the ten wives of Dharma; they are the doors to Dharma that have been ordained by the Self-Existent. Twenty-seven wives are known in the world to be the Moon's; and these faithful wives of the Moon are appointed to the procession of Time: they are the fairies of the lunar mansions, which regulate the life of the world.

The sage God is the Grandfather. His son is Prajāpati, whose sons are the eight Vasus—I shall name them all. Dhara, Dhruva, Soma, Ahas, the Wind, the Fire, Pratyūṣa, and Prabhāsa are known as the eight Vasus. Dhara was the son of Dhūmrā, and so was Dhruva, who knows the Brahman. The Moon was Manasvinī's son, the Wind Śvasā's. Ahas was Ratā's son, the Fire the son of Śāṇḍilī, while Pratyūṣa and Prabhāsa are known to be the sons of Prabhātā. Dhara again begot Draviṇa and Hutahavyavāha. Dhruva begot our Lord Time, who is the reckoner of the world. Soma's son is Varcas of splendor, who begot, on Manoharā, Śiśira, Prāṇa, and Ramaṇa. Light is the son of Ahas, and so are Śrama, Śānta, and Muni. The son of Fire is the illustrious Kumāra, whose abode is the reed bed, and other sons are Śākha, Viśākha, with Naigameśa as the last born. Since Kumāra was prospered by Kṛttikā, he is also known as Kārttikeya. The wind's wife was Śivā, and she bore a son Purojava and one Avijñātagati, both by the Wind. Pratyūṣa's son we know by the name of seer Devala, who himself had two forbearing and

sagacious sons. Bṛhaspati had a beautiful sister, a student of the
Brahman, perfect in Yoga, who, unattached, roamed the entire world.
She became the wife of Prabhāsa, the eighth of the Vasus, and thus
was born the lordly Viśvakarman, progenitor of the crafts, creator of
the thousands of crafts, and carpenter to the Thirty Gods; greatest of
craftsmen, he created all ornaments and fashioned the divine chariots
of the Gods. On the craft of this great-spirited God do the humans live,
and forever they pay worship to the everlasting Viśvakarman.
30 The blessed Lord Dharma, assuming human form, issued forth by
breaking open the right nipple of Brahmā, bringing happpiness to all
the worlds. Three excellent sons had he, fetching the hearts of all
creatures—Tranquillity, Love, and Joy, who sustain the worlds with
their glory. Love's wife was Lust, Tranquillity's was Attainment, and
Joy's wife Delight, upon whom the worlds are founded.

Kaśyapa was Marīci's son, and from Kaśyapa were born the Gods
and Asuras, O tiger among kings—he is the origin of the worlds.
Tvaṣṭrī, who has the form of a mare, is the wife of Savitar; and this
woman of great parts bore the twin Aśvins in the sky. Aditi had
35 twelve sons, from Indra onward; the last-born is Viṣṇu, on whom the
worlds are founded. These are the thirty-three Gods; I shall now
promulgate to you their relations and groups, with their wings, and
according to family.

The Rudras, Sādhyas, Maruts, and Vasus are each a separate wing.
So, one must know, is the Bhṛgu wing, and the wing of All-the-Gods.
Vinatā's son Garuḍa and the mighty Aruṇa, as well as the blessed
Lord Bṛhaspati, are counted among the Ādityas, while the two Aśvins
and all the herbs and cattle one should know as Guhyakas. Thus,
O king, are the groups of Gods recited in sequence; and when he
recites them, a man is freed from all evils.
40 The blessed Lord Bhṛgu issued forth by breaking open Brahmā's
heart. Bhṛgu begot the wise Śukra, son of a sage, who is a planet;
at the behest of the Self-created God, he circles the world presiding
over rain and drought, fear and relief from fear, for the conduct of
life in the three worlds. A master of Yoga, he became the sagacious
guru of the Daityas as well as the Gods, remaining a celibate of
wisdom and strict vows. And while this son of Bhṛgu was thus
charged by the omnipresent One with the well-being of the creatures,
Bhṛgu begot another flawless son, Cyavana, of the blazing austerities,
wise and inspirited with the Law, who wrathfully fell from his mother's
45 womb to set her free, O Bhārata. Manu's daughter Āruṣī became the
wise Cyavana's wife, and from her was born the greatly famous
Aurva, by splitting open her thigh, a man of great austerities and
heat, even as a child endowed with virtues. His son was Ṛcīka, who
begot Jamadagni. Jamadagni begot four great-spirited sons, the last

being Rāma, not the least endowed with virtues, skilled in all weapons and missiles, willful destroyer of the barons. Aurva had a hundred sons before Jamadagni, who in turn had thousands of sons, a proliferation of Bhṛgus.

Brahmā had two more sons, whose mark remains in this world—Dhātar and Vidhātar, who abide with Manu. Their sister is the beautiful Goddess Lakṣmī, who dwells in the lotus, and her mind-born sons are the horses that fly in the sky. The divine Jyeṣṭhā was born from Śukra, to become Varuṇa's wife; she gave birth to a son Vala, and to Goddess Liquor, delight of the Gods.

From the creatures who, hungry for food, began devouring each other Adharma was born, destroyer of all beings. His wife was Nirṛti, whence the Rākṣasas are known as Nairṛtas. She had three loathsome sons, forever bent on evil deeds, Fear, Panic, and Death, destroyer of the creatures. Divine Tāmrā gave birth to five daughters renowned in the world—Kākī, Śyenī, Bhāsī, Dhṛtarāṣṭrī, and Śukī. Kākī gave birth to the owls, Śyenī to the kites, Bhāsī to the vultures and birds of prey, O king, whereas glowing Dhṛtarāṣṭrī bore all the geese and ducks, as well as the *cakravāka* birds—good luck to thee! Śukī, spirited, endowed with beautiful virtues and favored with all good marks, gave birth to the parrots, O man of Law.

Nine angry women she bore, born from herself, Mṛgī, Mṛgamandā, Hari, Bhadramanā, Mātangī, Śārdūlī, Śvetā, Surabhi, and the perfectly favored and famous Surasā. Mṛgī's offspring are all the deer, O scion of the best of men, Mṛgamandā's the bears, marsh deer, and yaks. Bhadramanā bore the elephant Airāvata as her son—the grand elephant Airāvata, elephant of the Gods, is her son. The yellow monkeys and the nimble forest monkeys are Hari's progeny, and likewise—good luck to thee!—they say that the cow-tailed monkeys are Hari's sons. Śārdūlī gave birth to lions and tigers, lordly Bhārata, as well as the spotted big cats, without a doubt. The elephants are the offspring of Mātangī, O king, while Śvetā produced the quick-footed cardinal elephant called Śveta. Surabhi gave birth to two daughters, O king, Rohiṇī—good luck to thee!—and the famed Gandharvī. From Rohiṇī the cows came forth, from Gandharvī the horses. Surasā bore the Serpents, Kadrū the snakes. Analā produced seven kinds of trees that bear round fruit. Śukī was also Analā's daughter, and Surasā was the daughter of Kadrū. Śyenī was Aruṇa's wife; she gave birth to two mighty and powerful sons, Saṃpāti and the strong Jaṭāyus. Vinatā had two famous sons, Garuḍa and Aruṇa.

Thus, O overlord of men, chief among the wise, have I recited to you completely the origins of all great creatures. Having heard their descent completely, a man becomes freed from evil, attains to omniscience, and finds the foremost journey after death.

1(7.a) The Partial Incarnations

61 (B. 67; C. 2637)
Description continues that of 58. The incarnations of Dānavas, Kāleyas, Krodhavaśas; of Devaka, Bṛhaspati, Mahādeva, the Vasus, the Rudras, Dvāpara, the Maruts; the Gandharva king; Kṛṣṇa Dvaipāyana; Atri; Kali; the Rākṣasas; Dhṛtarāṣṭra and his sons; the Pāṇḍava party that derives from specific Gods, except Śikhaṇḍin, who is the incarnation of a Rākṣasa (1–100).

Janamejaya said:
61.1 Of the great-spirited Gods, Dānavas, Yakṣas, and Rākṣasas, and of
all other beings I wish to hear, O venerable Lord, how they respectively took their origins and accomplished their feats, such as they
befell, when they dwelled among men.
Vaiśaṃpāyana said:
I shall first relate to you, O king of men, which celestials all took
birth among men and which of the Dānavas.
The bull among Dānavas, who was famed as Vipracitti, became a
5 bull among men known as Jarāsaṃdha. Hiraṇyakaśipu, son of Diti,
was born in the world of men as the mighty Śiśupāla, O king.
Saṃhrāda, younger brother of Prahrāda, was born a bull of the
Bāhlīkas, and was known as Śalya. The powerful Anuhrāda, who was
the youngest of the brothers, became King Dhṛṣṭaketu. The son of
Diti, Śibi by name, O king, became king on earth, renowned as Druma.
The most excellent of the Asuras, Bāṣkala, became King Bhagadatta.
Ayaḥśiras, Aśvaśiras, mighty Ayaḥśanku, Gaganamūrdhan, and
Vegavat, these five powerful great Asuras, were born great-spirited
bulls of kings among the Kekayas. The other majestic Asura, Ketumat,
was born King Amitaujas on earth. The illustrious Asura Svarbhānu
became King Ugrasena of dread deeds. The splendid grand Asura Aśva
15 became King Aśoka of great might and prowess. His younger brother
Aśvapati was born King Hārdikya, bull among men. The splendid
grand Asura Vṛṣaparvan became on earth King Dīrghaprajña. His
younger brother Ajaka was born King Malla on earth. The mettlesome
great Asura Aśvagrīva became King Rocamāna on earth. The sagacious
20 and renowned Sūkṣma became King Bṛhanta on earth. That chief
Asura Tuhuṇḍa became King Senābindu. That strongest of the Asuras,

Isṛpa, became on earth King Pāpajit of famous courage. The great Asura Ekacakra became known on earth as Prativindhya. The brilliant warrior Asura Virūpākṣa became King Citravarman on earth. The eminent Dānava Hara, abductor of his enemies, was born that bull among men Suvastu. Mighty Āhara, destroyer of the party of his foes, became renowned on earth as King Bāhlīka. Moon-faced Nicandra, eminent Asura, became the illustrious King Muñjakeśa. Unvanquished and wise Nikumbha was born on earth a great lord of the earth, known as Devādhipa. Surabha, great Asura among the sons of Diti, was born King Paurava among men. The second of the Asuras, Śalabha, became the Bāhlīka King Prahrāda. Candra, best of Diti's sons, equal to the lord of the stars in the world, was born the excellent royal seer Ṛṣika. The eminent Asura Mṛtapa is King Paścimānūpaka, O best of kings. The grand and puissant Asura Gaviṣṭha became known on earth as King Drumasena. The splendid Asura Mayūra became king of the land Viśva. His younger brother Suparṇa was on earth known as King Kālakīrti. The greatest Asura of them all, Candrahartar, became the royal seer Śunaka. The great Asura Candravināśana became the royal seer Jānaki. The bull among Dānavas, Dīrghajihva, O scion of the Kurus, is known on earth as king of the land Kāśirāja. That Seizer, to whom Siṃhī gave birth, scourge of sun and moon, became the king of men known as Krātha. The first of Anāyus's sons, the powerful Vasumitra, became King Vikṣara. His next brother, a great Asura, became known as the king of the Pāmśu realm. The eminent Asura Balavīra became King Pauṇḍramatsyaka. That grand Asura Vṛtra, O king, became King-seer Maṇimat. His younger brother, Krodhahantar the Asura, became a celebrated king on earth, called Daṇḍa. Another, named Krodhavardhana, became the lord of men Daṇḍadhara. The eight sons of Kālaka, O tiger among kings, were born kings with the valor of tigers. The first of these eight Kāleyas became the illustrious King Jayatsena of the Magadhas. The splendid second, equal to Indra, became King Aparājita. The third, O great king, a strong-armed Asura, became on earth the king of the Niṣādas of terrible prowess. The fourth one is known on earth as the strict royal seer Śreṇimat. The fifth and greatest of them, a grand Asura, became Mahaujas, scourge of his enemies. The sixth of them, a wise and great Asura, was on earth the great royal seer Abhīru. From that same group one became King Samudrasena, renowned on ocean-girt earth, who knew the principles of Law and Profit. The eighth of the eight Kāleyas, the slayer of enemies, Bṛhat, became a law-abiding king, devoted to the well-being of all creatures. From the group named Krodhavaśa, warlike kings were born here on earth: Nandika, Karṇaveṣṭa, Siddhārtha, Kīṭika, Suvīra, Subāhu, Mahāvīra, Bāhlīka,

Krodha, Vicitya, Surasa, the illustrious King Nīla, Vīradhāman, and
Bhūmipāla, O scion of the Kurus, are their names. Also Dantavaktra,
Durjaya, Rukmī, and King Janamejaya, a tiger among princes, Āṣāḍha,
Vāyuvega, Bhūritejas, Ekalavya, Sumitra, Vātadhāna, Gomukha,
the Kārūṣaka kings, and Kṣemadhūrti, Śrutāyus, Uddhava, Bṛhatsena,
Kṣema, Ugratīrtha, Kuhara, the king of the Kalingas, and King
60 Matimat, and he famed as Īśvara. This host of kings was born on
earth from the group of Krodhavaśa, in the olden days, O great king,
of great fame and strength.

Devaka, whose splendor matched Indra's, was born on earth as the
chief lord of the Gandharvas. From a part of the greatly famous seer
of the Gods, Bṛhaspati, Droṇa was born, who was the son of
Bharadvāja and issued from no womb. He, O tiger among kings, was
the best of archers and the most proficient with all kinds of missiles,
65 of vast fame and great puissance; thus most eminent Droṇa was born
here among men, man of Indra-like feats, joy of his lineage, whom the
Vedic scholars know as an expert both on the *Veda* and the art of
archery. From portions of Mahādeva, Death, Lust, and Fury, which
merged into one, that warlike and powerful slayer of enemies
Aśvatthāman was born on earth, destroyer of the party of his foes,
the lotus-eyed champion, O overlord of men. The eight Vasus were
born the sons of Śaṃtanu by the Ganges, through the curse of Vasiṣṭha
and the behest of Indra. Their youngest became Bhīṣma, the safeguard
of the Kurus, wise knower of the *Veda*, eloquent, destroyer of his foes,
70 that most omniscient hero who puissantly battled Jamadagni's great-
spirited son Rāma Bhārgava. That most virile brahminic seer Kṛpa,
O king, was born on earth from the group of the Rudras. The warlike
Śakuni, who was a king on earth, was, O king, the reborn Dvāpara,
scourge of his foes. Sātyaki, true to his promises, scion of the tribe of
the Vṛṣṇis, slayer of enemies, was born from the divine group of the
Maruts. Drupada too, best of all swordsmen and a royal seer, was
75 born in the world of men from the same group, and so was
Kṛtavarman, the irresistible prince, O king, best of the bulls among
the barons. From the Maruts was also born the enemy-killing king
and sage Virāṭa, who set the realms of his foes ablaze.

Ariṣṭā's son renowned as Haṃsa, who furthered the line of the
Kurus, was born king of the Gandharvas. He who is famous as
Dhṛtarāṣṭra, a king with long arms, great heat, and the eyesight of
wisdom, was born from Kṛṣṇa Dvaipāyana; by his mother's fault and
the anger of the seer he was born blind. Know that that most fortunate
man Vidura, first of fathers, first of the wise, was born into the world
80 as Atri's son. Prince Duryodhana, evil-spirited, evil-minded disgracer
of the Kurus, was born on earth from a portion of Kali; he was a

creature of discord, hated by all the world; it was he, meanest of men,
who caused the massacre of all the earth, he who fanned the great
feud into a blaze that was to put an end to the beings. All his brothers
were born among men as creatures of the Rākṣasas, one hundred in
all, from Duḥśāsana onward, cruel of deeds, Durmukha, Duḥsaha, and
the others who will not be named here. All these companions of
Duryodhana were creatures of the Rākṣasas, O bull among Bhāratas.

King Yudhiṣṭhira, O king, was a portion of Dharma; Bhīmasena of
85 the Wind; Arjuna of Indra; and Nakula and Sahadeva, matchless in
beauty on earth, enchanting to all the world, were portions of the
Aśvins. The majestic son of Soma, who is known as Suvarcas, became
the son of Arjuna, the vastly famous Abhimanyu. Know, sire, that the
warlike Dhṛṣṭadyumna was a portion of the Fire, and the male-female
Śikhaṇḍin of a Rākṣasa. Draupadī's five sons, O king, best of the
Bhāratas, sprang from the group of All-the-Gods; and Karṇa, that
great warrior, who was born accoutred with a coat of mail, issued as
the matchless particle of the divine Sun.

90 The sempiternal God of Gods Nārāyaṇa descended with a portion
of himself among mankind as the majestic Vāsudeva. Baladeva was
a portion of the powerful Snake Śeṣa, and, O king, the very mighty
Pradyumna was Sanatkumāra. Thus many other particles of celestials,
O king among men, were born in the house of Vasudeva, furthering
his lineage. I have already cited the group of the Apsarās; a part of
them was born on earth at Indra's behest, and they became sixteen
thousand queens, O overlord of men, in this world of men, the wives
95 of Nārāyaṇa. A part of Śrī was born here on earth for the sake of love
as a blameless virgin, from the middle of an altar in the house of
Drupada. She was neither too small nor too tall, and fragrant like the
blue lotus; here eyes were long and lotuslike, her hips well-shaped,
her hair long and black. All the marks of beauty favored her who had
the sheen of a beryl stone; and secretly she stirred the hearts of the
five lordly men. The Goddesses Success and Endurance were the two
mothers of the five, born as Kuntī and Mādrī; and Wisdom became
the daughter of Subala.

Thus is described the Partial Incarnation of Gods, Asuras, Gand-
100 harvas, and Apsarās, as well as the Rākṣasas, those who were born
on earth as kings drunk with war; and the great-spirited scions in the
vast line of the Yadus. This *Book of the Partial Incarnations*, which gives
wealth, fame, sons, and a long life, and which brings victory, should
be heard without demurrer. And once one has heard the Partial
Incarnations of Gods, Gandharvas, and Rākṣasas, he gains knowledge
of origins and ends, and wisdom, and he does not falter in adversities.

1(7.b) Śakuntalā

62–69 (B. 68–74; C. 2799–3125).
62 (68; 2799). Janamejaya asks about the origin of the Kuru dynasty. Vaiśaṃpāyana replies with the story of Duḥṣanta Paurava. Duḥṣanta's ideal reign (1–10).
63 (69; 2814). Duḥṣanta goes hunting; description of the chase (1–25).
64 (70; 2845). In the depths of the forest Duḥṣanta finds still another wood of idyllic aspect, and in it, on the bank of the river Mālinī, a hermitage (1–25). He desires to enter it and visit the hermit Kaṇva Kāśyapa; he leaves his armed escort behind. Description of the hermitage (30–40).
65 (71; 2895). Dismissing his councillors, Duḥṣanta goes on alone, fails to find Kaṇva, and calls for attention; a girl appears (1–5). She does the honors and tells that Kaṇva is momentarily gone; Duḥṣanta admires her and asks about her parentage (5–15). Her answer that she is chaste Kaṇva's daughter puzzles the king (15), and she describes, at second hand, her birth from Viśvāmitra and the Apsarā Menakā: Indra, perturbed by Viśvāmitra's powerful austerities, sends Menakā to seduce him; she recalls to him Viśvāmitra's glories and asks for aid from the wind (15–40).
66 (72; 2937). The wind blows off Menakā's skirt as she is prancing before Viśvāmitra. He lusts after the willing wench, and she conceives on the bank of the Mālinī in the Himālaya (1–5). At the girl's birth her mother deserts her, but the birds protect her; hence her name Śakuntalā. Kaṇva, at his ablutions in the river, finds, adopts, and names her (5–15).
67 (73; 2955). Duḥṣanta, in Kaṇva's absence, tries to seduce Śakuntalā, stressing the propriety of the Gāndharva rite. She demands that her son be his heir (1–15). He agrees, lies with her, and departs (15–20). On Kaṇva's return the sage understands, condones, and blesses her (20–30).
68 (74, which combines 69 as well; 2988). Śakuntalā bears her child for three years; he grows up in the hermitage until he is six, and is nicknamed Sarvadamana because he tames everything. Kaṇva pronounces him

ready to be Young King, and orders the anchorites to take him and Śakuntalā to Duḥṣanta (1–10). Śakuntalā presents her son and herself to Duḥṣanta, and reminds him of his promise. Though remembering fully, he denies knowing her (10–15). Śakuntalā speaks severely on the blessings of having a son and a wife (20–65). She reminds him of her parentage; Duḥṣanta refuses to recognize her (65–80).
69. Śakuntalā scolds Duḥṣanta (1–15), holds him to his promise (20–25), and departs. A celestial voice tells Duḥṣanta that the boy is his son, that he should accept him and name him Bharata (25–30). Now that he has cleared his son of suspicion, Duḥṣanta happily accepts him and he explains the reasons for his behavior to Śakuntalā, whom he honors as his queen (30–40). Bharata becomes a Turner of the Wheel, and from him derive the Bhāratas and their glory (45–50).

Janamejaya said:
62.1 I have heard fully from you, O brahmin, how the Gods, Dānavas,
and Rākṣasas, and also the Gandharvas and Apsarās, descended to
earth with a portion of themselves. Now I wish you to tell me from
the beginning in the presence of these brahmins and seers, O brahmin,
how the dynasty of the Kurus came into being.
Vaiśaṃpāyana said:
A dynast of the Pauravas was a mighty hero called Duḥṣanta,
herdsman of all the earth to her four horizons, O best of the Bhāratas.
This triumphant king enjoyed the earth entire with all four quarters,
5 and also countries that are surrounded by the ocean; and the pleasure
of this scourge of his enemies extended as far as the barbarians and
forest tribes to all lands that are skirted by the pearl-rich ocean and
peopled by the four classes.
There was no miscegenation, no one needed plough or mine the
earth, nobody did evil while this king reigned. All the people were
bent on Law and Profit, cherishing a joy in their own Law, while he,
O tiger among men, lorded the countryside. There was no fear of
theft, my friend, no fear whatever of starvation, nor fear of disease,
while he lorded the countryside. The classes delighted in their own
Laws and lacked all selfishness in their acts of worship. Relying on
him as the guardian of the earth, they met with no danger from
10 anywhere. The rain god rained in time and the crops were ample;
earth abounded with all gems and flowed with wealth. The youthful
king, of miraculous great prowess, hard as a diamond, could have

lifted Mount Mandara and carried it in his arms with its woods and
forest. He was equally accomplished with the bow as with the club,
in swordsmanship, on elephant and horseback. In his might he
matched Viṣṇu, in radiance the sun, in imperturbability the ocean, in
endurance the earth. A well-esteemed ruler he was, with town and
realm serene, who dwelled among a people noted for law-minded
intentions.

Vaiśaṃpāyana said:

63.1 Upon a time this strong-armed king rode out, with ample strength
of men and mounts, to a dense forest, escorted by hundreds of horses
and elephants. He progressed surrounded by hundreds of warriors,
carrying swords and lances, brandishing clubs and maces, wielding
javelins and spears. And as the king went on, the lion roars of his
warriors, the blasts of conches and drums, the thunder of the chariot
rims reinforced by the trumpeting of the grand elephants, the
whinnying of the horses, and the growls and arm-slapping of the men
5 rose to a tumultuous noise. From the balconies of their terraced
palaces the womenfolk gazed upon the hero, who made his own fame,
in all his regal magnificence. And watching their king, equal of Indra,
slayer of foes, warder-off of enemy elephants, they thought of him as
the Thunderbolt-Wielder* himself. "He is a tiger among men, of
wondrous prowess in battle, before the strength of whose arms no
enemy keeps his life!" Such were the words that the women spoke;
and with love they sang his praises and strew rain bursts of flowers on
his head. Everywhere he went the brahmins lauded him; and thus,
10 with the greatest joy, he went out to the forest hunting. Town and
country folk followed him a long way, until the king finally
dismissed them and they returned.

The overlord of earth filled earth and the heavens with the
thunder of his chariot that flew like the Fair-Winged Bird.** And as he
rode, the alert king chanced to see a wood like Indra's paradise,
wooded with *bilva* and *arka* bushes and *khadira* trees, abounding with
kapitthas and *dhavas*, rolling with hills and plateaus, overspread with
boulders, which was empty of water and people for a stretch of many
leagues. And in this wood, which teemed with herds of deer and
beasts of prey that stalk the forest, Duḥṣanta, tiger among men, with
retainers, escort, and mounts wrought havoc, killing game of many
15 kinds. Many families of tigers he laid low as they came within range of
his arrows; he shot them with his shafts. Those that were in the
distance the bull among men shot down with his arrows; others that
came up close he cut down with his sword; and antelopes he brought
down with his spear, the powerful spearman, who also knew all the

* = Indra.
** = Garuḍa.

points of the circular club swing and whose courage was boundless.
He stalked about killing wild game and fowl with javelin, sword, mace,
bludgeon, halberd. And when the wondrously valiant king and his
20 warlike warriors raided the great forest, the big game fled it. The herds
of deer, their flocks dispersed, their leaders killed, cried out for help
everywhere. The river they sought out was dry; and thin with
despair for water, their hearts exhausted with exertion, they dropped
down, unconscious. Overcome by hunger and thirst, they fell
prostrate on the ground, exhausted. There were some that were
eaten raw by starving tiger men; other woodsmen built a fire, lit it,
cut their meat in proper pieces, and ate it. There were mighty
elephants that were wounded by swords and ran mad; turning up
25 their trunks, they panicked and stampeded frantically. Dropping dung
and urine and streaming with blood, the wild tuskers trampled many
men. The forest, darkened by a monsoon of might and a downpour of
arrows, its big game weeded by the king, now seemed overrun by
buffalo.

Vaiśaṃpāyana said:

64.1 Having killed thousands of deer, the king with his plentiful mounts
entered into another wood in search of deer. Supremely strong,
though hungry and thirsty, he penetrated by himself into the depths
of the forest till he came to a vast wilderness that was dotted with
holy hermitages, a joy to the heart and a feast for the eye. He crossed
beyond it and made for still another wood where a cool breeze was
blowing, a wood sprinkled with blossoming trees and most prosperous
grasslands. It was a wide woodland that echoed with the sweet
5 warblings of birds. All around stood trees that threw pleasant shade
and burst with their shoots; their creepers were aswarm with bees,
and a sovereign beauty reigned over it. No tree lacked bloom or
fruit, no tree was thorny, nor was there one undarkened by bees in
that wood. Atwitter with birds, adorned with blossoms, and wooded
with trees that bloomed in all seasons, with surpassing-good
grasslands, it was a most enchanting wood, and the great bowman
entered it. Richly blossoming trees shaken by the wind again and
again let loose a colorful downpour of flowers. Brushing the skies,
alive with the sweet music of birds, the trees stood resplendent in
10 their many-colored robes of blossoms. And among their shoots, which
bent under the burden of bloom, birds and bees sang their gentle
songs.

As he gazed upon the many stretches adorned by an outpouring of
flowers and surrounded by creepers that were twined into pavilions,
adding to his heart's delight, the puissant king became filled with joy.
With its blossoming trees whose branches interlaced, the wood

seemed to shine with as many maypoles. A pleasantly cool and
fragrant breeze that carried the pollen of flowers ran around the
woods and accosted the trees as though to make love to them. Such
was the woodland upon which the king gazed, grown in the embrace
of a river, enchanting, lofty like flagmasts.
15 Looking at the forest with its wildly excited birds, he saw an
idyllic and heart-fetching hermitage, covered with all kinds of trees
and alight with blazing fires. Ascetics and anchorites peopled it and
groups of hermits. Fire halls aplenty were scattered all over, and
carpets of flowers. It seemed to shine forth with its large bays of
water on the bank of the river Mālinī, holy and gladdening stream,
which, O king, bestrewn with flocks of all kinds of fowl, added
loveliness to this wilderness of austerities. And on seeing beasts of
prey and deer peaceably together, the king was filled with the purest
joy.

Thereupon the illustrious warrior drew nigh to the hermitage that
most enchanting everywhere, was the image of the world of the Gods.
20 He saw the river that embraced the hermitage with her holy water
spreading out like the mother of all creatures, her banks swarming
with *cakravāka* birds, her current carrying blossoms and foam—the
habitation of Kiṃnaras that was frequented by monkeys and bears.
The sound of holy Vedic lessons wafted over the river; sandbanks
strung pearls upon her; rutting elephants, tigers, and mighty snakes
visited her.

When he saw the hermitage and the river that enclosed it, the
king set his mind upon entering. And he entered the deep woodland,
with its necklace of the Mālinī of the shining isles and lovely banks;
it appeared like the dwelling place of Nara and Nārāyaṇa, adorned by
25 the Ganges, loud with the shriek of madly dancing peacocks. Having
drawn near to the hermitage that resembled Citraratha's park, the
lord of men, intending to see the great seer and ascetic Kaṇva
Kāśyapa, surpassingly virtuous and of indescribable brilliance, halted
his escort of chariots with footmen at the gate of the wood and said
to his army, "I shall go to see Kāśyapa,* that dispassionate hermit of
rich austerities. Remain here until my return." And upon entering
that wood, like another paradise of Indra, the lord of men shed his
hunger and thirst and became overjoyed. Discarding his regalia and
accompanied only by councillor and priest, he walked to the grand
hermitage to see the seer who had piled up austerities everlasting.
30 He saw the hermitage that mirrored the world of Brahmā, echoing
with the humming of bees and aswarm with all kinds of fowl. He,
tiger among men, heard hymns of the *Ṛgveda* that were being
recited, both wordwise and stepwise, as the rituals were spun out by

* = descendant of Kaśyapa, here = Kaṇva.

the foremost of Bahvṛca brahmins. The hermitage was radiant with
strict priests of boundless spirit who strode their strides, experts on
sacrifices and the branches of the *Veda*. Great scholars of the
Atharvaveda, esteemed by the assembled sacrificers, recited the
Saṃhitā in both wordwise and stepwise modes. Other brahmins, who
spoke with refinement of speech, made the hermitage ring so that it
35 gloriously resembled the worlds of Brahmā. It resounded with priests
who knew sacrifice and sacrament, who were conversant with the
stepwise recitation and phonetics, and accomplished in the knowledge
of the rules of interpretation and the significance of the principles
thereof—past masters of the *Veda*, proficient in the combination and
connection of all kinds of sentences, schooled in a variety of rites,
intent upon Salvation and Law, who had acquired knowledge of the
final truth through argumentation, objection, and conclusion and
were the foremost of practitioners. Everywhere the slayer of enemy
champions saw grand and perfected brahmins, controlled and strict in
their vows, engaged in the muttering of spells and the offering of
oblations. The lord of the earth saw colorful, flower-decked seats that
40 had been carefully set out, and he was amazed. And seeing brahmins
doing *pūjā* to the sanctuaries of the Gods, this most strict king thought
himself attending the worlds of Brahmā. Watching the great and
sacred hermitage, protected by Kāśyapa's austerities and hallowed by
the multitudes of its ascetics, he could not watch enough.

And thus the slayer of foes, with councillor and priest, set foot in Kāśyapa's sanctum, which was everywhere crowded with seers rich in austerities, solitary, most enchanting, holy.

Vaiśaṃpāyana said:

65.1 Thereupon the strong-armed king dismissed his councillors and
went on alone. He did not find the seer of strict vows in the
hermitage. Failing to find the seer and finding the hermitage empty,
he spoke in a loud voice, thundering over the woodland: "Who is
here?" Hearing his cry, a young maiden appeared, like Śrī incarnate,
and came out of that hermitage, wearing the garb of a female hermit.
No sooner had the black-eyed girl seen King Duḥṣanta than she bade
5 him welcome and paid him homage. She honored him with a seat,
with water to wash his feet, and a guest gift, and asked, O king, the
overlord of men about his health and well-being.

After honoring him properly and inquiring about his health, she said with a faint smile, "What can I do?" The king, seeing that she had a flawless body and having been honored properly, replied to the sweet-spoken girl, "I have come to pay my worship to the venerable seer Kaṇva. Where has the reverend gone, my dear? Tell me, my pretty."

Śakuntalā said:

My reverend father has gone out of the hermitage to gather fruit. Wait a while, you will see him return.

Vaiśaṃpāyana said:

The king, having failed to find the seer, looked at the girl who had addressed him and saw that she had beautiful hips, a lustrous appearance, and a charming smile. She was radiant with beauty, with the sheen of austerities and the calm of self-restraint. The king now said to the maiden, as perfect of shape as of age, "Who are you? Whose are you? Why, fair-waisted girl, have you come to this wilderness? Endowed with such perfection of beauty? From where are you, my pretty? For one look at you, lovely, has carried my heart away! I want to know about you, tell me, my pretty."

At these words of the king in the hermitage she laughed and said in a very sweet voice, "I am regarded as the daughter of the venerable Kaṇva, Duḥṣanta, the great-spirited and famous ascetic and equable scholar of the Law."

Duḥṣanta said:

The reverend lord, whom the world worships, has never spilled his seed! The God Law himself might stray from his course, but not this saint of strict vows. How could you have been born his daughter, fair maiden? I have great doubts on this, pray dispel them!

Śakuntalā said:

Then listen, my king, how this story has come to me, and how this once came to be, and how in fact I became the hermit's daughter. One day a seer came here who raised questions about my birth, and hear how the reverend spoke to him, sire.

"Viśvāmitra, as you know," he said, "performed of yore such huge austerities that he bitterly mortified Indra himself, lord of the hosts of Gods. Fearful lest the ascetic, whose puissance had been set ablaze by his austerities, would topple him from his throne, the Sacker of Cities therefore spoke to Menakā. 'Menakā, you are distinguished in the divine talents of the Apsarās. Take my welfare to heart, beautiful woman, and do as I ask you, listen. That great ascetic Viśvāmitra, who possesses the splendor of the sun, has been performing awesome austerities that make my mind tremble. Menakā of the pretty waist, Viśvāmitra is your burden. This unassailable man of honed spirit is engaged in dreadful austerities; and lest he topple me from my throne, go to him and seduce him. Obstruct his asceticism, do me the ultimate favor! Seduce him with your beauty, youth, sweetness, fondling, smiles, and flatteries, my buxom girl, and turn him away from his austerities!'"

Menaka said:

The reverend lord is a man of great heat and always of great

austerity and irascible. And you yourself, sir, know that he is like
that. Should I not fear him of whose heat, austerity, and fury you
yourself stand in fear? Him, who divorced the venerable Vasiṣṭha from
his beloved sons? Who was born a baron and by brute force became a
30 brahmin? Who created an unfordable river of plentiful waters just to
wash himself, a most sacred river that people know as the Kauśikī,
where of yore at a time of disaster the law-abiding royal seer Matanga,
having become a hunter, supported the great-spirited seer's wife, and
later, when the famine was past, the mighty sage returned to the
hermitage and gave the river the name of Pārā—the same river where
he, pleased with Matanga, himself officiated at his sacrifice and you
yourself, from fear, came rushing to drink the Soma? Viśvāmitra, who
angrily created a new galaxy of counter-constellations from Śravaṇā
onward, with a wealth of asterisms over and beyond the old galaxy?
One who wrought such deeds I fear greatly. Inform me, my ubiquitous
lord, how shall I escape being burned by his rage? With his heat he
could burn down the worlds, quake the earth with his feet, knead the
mighty Mount Meru into a ball and spin it around! A man of such
austerity, blazing like a fire, master of his senses—how could a young
woman like me ever touch him? His mouth is a blazing offering fire,
sun and moon are the pupils of his eyes, Time itself is his tongue—
how could one like me touch him, O best of Gods? Him of whose
might even Yama and Soma and the great Seers and all the Sādhyas
and Vālakhilyas stand in awe, one like me should not fear, why?
40 Yet, having been so ordered by you, how can I fail to approach
the seer, O lord of the Gods? But contrive to protect me, king of
celestials, so that under your protection I can do your bidding. But
the wind had better blow open my skirt when I am playing before him,
and Manmatha* must be my helpmate in this enterprise, O God, by
your grace. And let a fragrant breeze blow from the woods at the hour
that I shall be seducing that seer!

"So be it," he said, and when it had thus been disposed, she
repaired to the hermitage of Kauśika.**

Śakuntalā [repeating the words of Kaṇva] said:

66.1 "Indra, at Menakā's words, gave orders to the ever-moving wind,
and Menakā at once departed with the wind. Then Menakā,
callipygous nymph, set timid eyes on Viśvāmitra, who, all his evil
burned off by his austerities, was yet engaged in more in his
hermitage. She greeted him and began to play in front of him. Off with
the wind went her moonlight skirt, the fair-skinned nymph dropped
5 to the ground embracing it, bashfully smiling at the wind. And so that

* = God of Love.
** = Viśvāmitra.

strictest of seers saw Menakā nude, nervously clutching at her skirt, indescribably young and beautiful. And remarking the virtue of her beauty the bull among brahmins fell victim to love and lusted to lie with her. He asked her, and she was blamelessly willing.

"The pair of them whiled away a very long time in the woods, making love when the spirit seized them, and it seemed only a day. And on Menakā the hermit begot Śakuntalā, on a lovely tableland in the Himālayas, by the river Mālinī. Once the baby was born, Menakā abandoned her on the bank of the Mālinī; and, her duty done, she returned rapidly to Indra's assembly.

10 "Birds, seeing the baby lying in the desolate wilderness that was
teeming with lions and tigers, surrounded her protectively on all
sides. Lest beasts of prey, greedy for meat, hurt the little girl in the
forest, the birds stood guard around Menakā's child. Then I chanced to
come to the river to rinse my mouth and saw her lying in the
deserted and lonely woods surrounded by birds. I took her home and
adopted her as my daughter. In the decisions of Law they quote three
kinds of fathers respectively: the one who begets the child's body, the
one who saves its life, and the one who gives it food. And, since she
had been protected by birds in the desolate wilderness, I gave her the
15 name Śakuntalā. Thus, you should know, did Śakuntalā become my
daughter, good friend, and innocently Śakuntalā thinks of me as her
father."

In this manner did Kaṇva describe my birth to the great seer who had questioned him, and thus, overlord of men, should you know me for Kaṇva's daughter. For I think of Kaṇva as my father, never having known my own. So, sire, I have told you exactly as I have heard it.

Duḥṣanta said:

67.1 And very clear is it that you are the daughter of a king, the way you told it, beautiful girl. Be my wife, buxom woman! Tell me, what can I do for you? Today I shall bring you golden necklaces, clothes, earrings wrought of gold, and sparkling gems from many countries, my pretty, and breast plates and hides. Today all my kingdom will be yours; be my wife, my pretty! Come to me, timid and lovely, according to the rite of the Gandharvas, for my girl of the lovely thighs, the Gandharva mode is cited as the best of marriage rites!

Śakuntalā said:

5 My father has gone out of the hermitage to gather fruits, O king. Wait a while. He himself will give me away to you.

Duḥṣanta said:

I want you to love me, flawless girl of the beautiful hips! Here I stand for you, for my heart has gone out to you. Oneself is one's own best friend, oneself is one's only recourse. You yourself can lawfully make the gift of yourself. There are eight forms of marriage known in total as being lawful—*brāhma, daiva, ārṣa, prājāpatya, āsura, gāndharva, rākṣasa,* and lastly *paiśāca.* Manu Svāyaṃbhuva has declared their lawfulness in this order of descent. The first four are recommended for a brahmin, you must know; the first six, innocent girl, are lawful for the baronage, in descending order. The *rākṣasa* mode is set forth for kings, the *āsura* marriage for commoners and serfs. Three of the five are lawful, the other two are held to be unlawful. The *paiśāca* and *āsura* forms are never to be perpetrated. Marriage can be done according to this rite, for such is known to be the course of the Law. *Gāndharva* and *rākṣasa* marriages are lawful for the baronage, have no fear of that—either one or the two mixed may be held, without a doubt. You are in love with me as I am in love with you, fair girl—pray become my wife by the rite of the Gandharvas!

Śakuntalā said:

If this is the course of the Law, and if I am my own mistress, then, chief of the Pauravas, this is my condition in giving myself in marriage, my lord. Give your own true promise to the secret covenant I make between us: the son that may be born from me shall be Young King to succeed you, great king, declare this to me as the truth! If it is to be thus, Duḥṣanta, you may lie with me.

Vaiśaṃpāyana said:

Without hesitation the king replied, "So shall it be! And I shall conduct you to my city, sweet-smiling women, as you deserve. This I declare to you as my truth, my lovely." Having thus spoken, the royal seer took his flawlessly moving bride solemnly by the hand and lay with her. And he comforted her and departed, and said many times, "I shall send an escort for you, with footmen, horses, chariots, and elephants; and with that I shall take you to my castle, sweet-smiling Śakuntalā!"

With such promises, Janamejaya, the king departed, and as he went he worried in his heart about Kāśyapa. "What may the venerable hermit not perpetrate when he hears of it, with all his ascetic power . . ."; and with this worry he entered his own capital.

Kaṇva himself returned to his hermitage a little while after the king's departure, and Śakuntalā was too embarrassed to dare approach her father. But Kaṇva, great ascetic, was gifted with divine knowledge and knew all. Seeing with his divine eyes, the master was pleased and said, "What you, of royal descent, ignoring me, have done, this your intercourse with a man, is not a transgression of the Law. For the *gāndharva* style of marriage is said to be the best for a baron, 'done in secret, without formulas, between a loving man and a loving woman.' Duḥṣanta, the man you went to lovingly, is a good man, Śakuntalā,

great-spirited and law-minded. There shall be born a man of great
spirit in the world—a son, yours, of great strength, a king who shall
sway this entire earth to the corners of the oceans. When he marches
out, the sovereign Wheel of that great-spirited Turner of the Wheel
shall forever roll unimpeded."

30 She washed the feet of the weary hermit, put down his burden, laid
out the fruit he had gathered. And she said to him, "I have chosen this
good man, King Duḥṣanta, for my husband. Please bestow your grace
upon him and his ministers."

Kaṇva said:

I have grace for him, fair Śakuntalā, for *your* sake. Ask a boon from me, for *his* sake, whatever you wish.

Vaiśaṃpāyana said:

This did Śakuntalā, wishing to prosper Duḥṣanta, choose as her boon that the Pauravas would be firm in the Law and never stumble from their kingdom.

Vaiśaṃpāyana said:

68.1 When Duḥṣanta had returned to his seat after making his promises
to Śakuntalā, the woman with the lovely thighs gave birth to a son of
boundless might, after bearing him for a full three years, O Janamejaya,
a son radiant like a blazing fire, enriched with all the virtues of
beauty and generosity, true scion of Duḥṣanta. Kaṇva, best minister
to the sacred, administered solemnly upon him the sacraments of birth,
and others, as he grew in wisdom. He was a large child, with shining
and pointed teeth, solid like a lion, wearing on his palm the sign of
the wheel, and illustrious, large-headed, and strong. The boy, who
5 appeared like the child of a God, grew up rapidly there. When he was
six years old, the child in Kaṇva's hermitage would fetter lions and
tigers, boars, buffaloes, and elephants to the trees around the
hermitage and run about playing and riding and taming them. Hence
the hermits who dwelled in Kaṇva's hermitage gave him a nickname:
"He shall be Sarvadamana, for he tames everything!" So the boy
became known as Sarvadamana, and he was endowed with prowess,
might, and strength.

Watching the boy and his superhuman exploits, the seer told
10 Śakuntalā, "It is time for him to become Young King." Since he
knew how strong he had grown, Kaṇva said to his students, "Today
you must quickly take Śakuntalā here with her son from our
hermitage to her husband—she is blessed with all the marks that
bespeak a good wife. For it is not good for woman to live too long
with their kinsmen; it imperils their reputation, good conduct, and
virtue. Therefore take her without delay!"

"So be it," they said; and the mighty anchorites all started out and

followed Śakuntalā and her son to the City of the Elephant. Taking her
lotus-eyed son, who was like the child of an Immortal, the radiant
woman left the woodland that Duḥṣanta had known. She went with
her son to the king, her son shining with the brilliance of the morning
15 sun, and was recognized and admitted. Śakuntalā paid proper homage
to her king and said, "This is your son, sire. Consecrate him as Young
King! For he is the godlike son you have begotten on me, king. Now
act with him as you promised, greatest of men. Remember the promise
you made long ago when we lay together, man of fortune, in Kaṇva's
hermitage!"

When the king heard these words of hers, he remembered very well,
yet he said, "I do not remember. Whose woman are you, evil ascetic?
I do not recall every having had recourse to you, whether for Law,
Profit, or Love. Go or stay, as you please, or do what you want!"
20 At these words the beautiful and spirited woman was overcome
with shame and, stunned with grief, stood motionless like a tree trunk.
Her eyes turned copper red with indignant fury, her pursed lip began
to tremble, and from the corner of her eyes she looked at the king with
glances that seemed to burn him. Yet, although driven by her fury,
she checked her expression and controlled the heat that had been
accumulated by her austerities. For a moment she stood in thought,
filled with grief and indignation, and looking straight at her husband,
she said angrily, "You know very well, great king! Why do you say
25 without concern that you do not know, lying like a commoner? Your
heart knows the truth of it! Good sir, alas you yourself are the witness
to your truth and your lie—do not despise yourself! He who knows
himself to be one way and pretends it is another way is a thief who
robs his own soul—what evil is beyond him? You think you are alone
with your self, but don't you know the ancient seer who dwells in
your heart? Him who knows your evil deeds? It is before him that you
speak your lie!

"A man who has done wrong thinks, 'Nobody knows me.' But the
Gods know him, and his own inner soul. Sun and Moon, Wind and
Fire, Heaven, Earth, and Water, and his heart and Yama, and Day and
Night, and both the Twilights, and the Law all know the doings of
30 each man. Yama Vaivasvata takes away the evil one has done when
the soul in his heart, witness to his doings, remains content with him.
But when the soul is discontented with the wicked man in whom it
dwells, then Yama takes away the evildoer. A man who despises his
soul and dissembles will find the Gods of no avail and his soul of no
benefit.

"Do not despise me, who have been a faithful wife, because I have
come on my own. You fail to honor me with the guest gift that is due

me, your wife, who have come to you of my own accord! Why do you slight me in your assembly as though I were a commoner? I am surely
35 not baying in a desert—why don't you hear me? Duḥṣanta, if you do not do my word as I am begging you, your head will burst into a hundred pieces! A husband enters his wife and is reborn from her—thus the old poets know this as a wife's wifehood. The offspring that is born to a man who follows the scriptures saves with his lineage the forebears that died before. Svayaṃbhū himself has said that a son is a *putra* because he saves his father from the hell named Put. She is a wife who is handy in the house, she is a wife who bears children, she is a wife whose life is her husband, she is a wife who is true to her
40 lord. The wife is half the man, a wife is better than his best friend, a wife is the root of Law, Profit, and Love, a wife is a friend in a man's extremity. They who have wives have rites, they who have wives have households, they who have wives are happy, they who have wives have luck. Sweet-spoken wives are friends in solitude, fathers in the rites of the Law, mothers in suffering. Even in the wilderness she means respite for the man who is journeying. A man with a wife is a trustworthy man. Therefore a wife is the best course. Only a faithful wife follows even a man who has died and is transmigrating, sharing
45 a common lot in adversities, for he is forever her husband. A wife who has died before stands still and waits for her husband; and a good wife follows after her husband if he has died before. This, sire, is the reason why marriage is sought by man, where a husband finds a wife for now and eternity.

"A son, the wise say, is the man himself born from himself; therefore a man will look upon the mother of his son as his own mother. The son born from his wife is as a man's face in a mirror; and looking at him brings as much joy to a father as finding heaven brings to a saint. Men, burned by the sorrows of their hearts and sickly with disease, rejoice in their wives, as overheated people do in
50 water. No matter how aggravated, a man should say no unkind things to his loving women, for in them he sees contingent his love, his joy, and his merit. Women are forever one's sacred field of birth—are even the seers able to have children without one? A son stumbles and covered with dirt embraces his father—is there joy beyond that?

"And you, why do you reject frowningly a son who of his own accord has come to you and fondly looks at you? Ants carry their own eggs and never break them—you, so wise in the Law, won't keep your
55 son? Neither clothes nor loving women nor water are so good to touch as the infant son you embrace. Of two-footed men the brahmin is best; of four-footed beasts the cow is worthiest; of respected men the guru is the first; and of all things to touch a son is the choicest.

Embrace and touch your handsome son! There is no feeling on earth
lovelier than to feel a son. For three full years I have borne this son,
lord of kings, for him to kill your grief. When I was giving birth to
him a voice came from the sky, saying, O Paurava, 'He shall be the
offerer of a hundred Horse Sacrifices.'

60 "Do not men who had gone to another village take their sons
lovingly on their laps and kiss their heads and feel happy? From the
Vedas themselves, as you too know, the twiceborn recite these verses
at the birth ceremony of their sons, 'From each limb hast thou come
forth, thou art born from my heart, thou art myself with the name of
son, live thou a hundred autumns! For my nourishment lies with thee,
and my eternal lineage—therefore live thou, my son, in all happiness
for a hundred autumns!' He has been born from your limbs, one man
from another: look on my son as your other self, as your reflection
65 seen in a clear pond. Just as the *āhavanīya* fire is carried forward from
the *gārhapatya* hearth, so is he born from you, and you, being one,
have been made two.

"In time past while you were going on a chase and were led off by
a deer, you approached me, a young girl, in my father's hermitage.
Urvaśī, Pūrvacitti, Sahajanyā, Menakā, Viśvācī, and Ghṛtācī are the
six greatest Apsarās. And from among them it was the beautiful
Apsarā Menakā, daughter of Brahmā, who came from heaven to
earth and bore me by Viśvāmitra. The Apsarā Menakā gave birth to
me on a peak of the Himālayas and abandoned me pitilessly and went,
70 as if I were another's child. What evil deeds have I done before in
another life that in my childhood I was abandoned by my kin, and
now by you? Surely when you forsake me I shall go to my hermitage
—but pray do not forsake your own son!"

Duḥṣanta said:

I do not know that this is my son you have born, Śakuntalā.
Women are liars—who will trust your word? Menakā, your mother,
was a merciless slut who cast you off like a faded garland on a peak of
the Himālayas! Viśvāmitra, your merciless father, who, born a baron,
75 reached for brahminhood, was a lecher! Menakā is the first of the
Apsarās, Viśvāmitra the first of the seers—how can you call yourself
their daughter, speaking like a whore? Are you not ashamed to say
such incredible things, especially in my presence? Off with you, evil
ascetic! An ever-awesome seer, an Apsarā like Menakā—are related to
you, a wretch that wears a hermit's garb! Your son is too big, and he
is strong even while still a child; how can he have shot up like a
śāla tree in such a short time? Your own birth is very humble, and you
look like a slut to me. So Menakā happened to give birth to you from
80 sheer lust? Everything you say is obscure to me, ascetic. I do not
know you. Go where you want!

Śakuntalā said:

69.1 King, you see the faults of others that are small, like mustard
seeds, and you look but do not see your own, the size of pumpkins!
Menakā is one of the Thirty Gods, the Thirty come after Menakā! My
birth is higher than yours, Duḥṣanta! You walk on earth, great king,
but I fly the skies. See how we differ, like Mount Meru and a mustard
seed! I can roam to the palaces of great Indra, of Kubera, of Yama, of
Varuṇa; behold my power, king!
5 The lesson I shall teach you is the truth, impeccable prince, to
instruct you, not to spite you, so listen and forbear. As long as an
ugly man does not see his face in a mirror he will think that he is
handsomer than others. But when he sees his ugly face in a mirror, he
knows how inferior he is. A very handsome man never despises
anyone, but the constant babbler becomes a foul-mouthed slanderer. A
fool who hears the gossipers speak good and evil always eats up the
10 evil as a swine eats up dung. An intelligent man who hears the
gossipers speak good and evil always finds the good as the swans find
milk in water. As sorry as a good man who reproaches others, so
happy is an evil man reproaching others. Just as good people find joy in
speaking well of the aged, so the fool finds joy in berating an honest
man. Happily live they who know no evil; happily the fools who look
for it. When the good are belittled by others they call such people
enemies. There is nothing more ludicrous found in the world than
15 that the wicked call the honest wicked. Even a heretic fears a liar like
a virulent poisonous snake; how much more the orthodox! He who
does not accept the son he himself begot as his equal will see the Gods
destroy his fortune and will never find the worlds. For the ancestors
call a son the foundation of family and lineage, the highest of all
merits of Law—therefore one should never abandon a son. Manu cites
six kinds of sons—the one begotten on one's wife; and these five:
obtained as gift, bought, reared, adopted, and begotten on other
women. Sons give men merit of Law and a good name, they foster the
happiness of their fathers' hearts and, once born, save the ancestors
from hell like ferries of the Law.
20 Tiger among kings, do not forsake your son, as you protect
yourself, your word, and your Law, O lord of the earth. Do not stoop
to deceit, lion among kings. The gift of one pond is better than a
hundred wells, one sacrifice is more than a hundred ponds, one son
more than a hundred sacrifices, one truth more than a hundred sons.
A thousand Horse Sacrifices and truth were held in a balance, and
truth outweighed all thousand. Speaking the truth, O king, may or
may not be equaled by learning all *Vedas* and bathing at all sacred
fords. There is no Law higher than truth, nothing excels truth; and no
25 evil is bitterer on earth than a lie. Truth, O king, is the supreme

Brahman, truth is the sovereign covenant. Do not forsake your covenant, king, the truth shall be your alliance.

If you hold with the lie, if you have no faith of your own in me, then I shall go. There is no consorting with one like you. Even without you, Duḥṣanta, my son shall reign over the four-cornered earth crowned by the king of mountains!

Vaiśaṃpāyana said:

Having said all this to the king, Śakuntalā departed. Then, a disembodied voice spoke from the sky to Duḥṣanta, as he sat surrounded by his priests, chaplain, teachers, and councillors, "The mother is the father's water sack—he is the father who begets the son. Support your son, Duḥṣanta; do not reject Śakuntalā. The son who has seed saves from Yama's realm, O God among men. You have planted this child. Śakuntalā has spoken the truth. A wife bears a son by splitting her body in two; therefore, Duḥṣanta, keep Śakuntalā's son, O king. This is ruin: what man alive will forsake a live son born from himself?

"Paurava, keep this great-spirited scion of Duḥṣanta and Śakuntalā; for he is yours to keep, and so is our behest. And as you keep him, he will be known by the name of Bharata."

King Paurava heard the utterance of the celestials and, much delighted, spoke to his chaplain and councillors, "Listen, good sirs, to what the Envoy of the Gods has spoken! I myself knew very well he was my son. But if I had taken him as my son on her word alone, suspicion would have been rife among the people and he would never have been cleared of it."

The king, having thus cleared himself of all suspicions, through the words of the Envoy of the Gods, now happily and joyfully accepted his son, O Bhārata. He kissed him on the head and embraced him lovingly; and he was welcomed to the court by the brahmins and praised by the bards. The king upon touching his son became filled with the greatest joy; and, knowing his duty, he honored his wife according to it. His majesty made up to her and said, "The alliance I made with you was not known to my people; that is the reason why I argued, so that I might clear you, my queen. People would think that I had a bond with you because you are a woman, and that I had chosen this son for the kingdom. That is why I argued. And if you have spoken very harsh words to me in your anger, dear wide-eyed wife, it was out of love, and I forgive you, beautiful woman."

Thus spoke King Duḥṣanta to his beloved queen, and he honored her, O Bhārata, with clothes, food, and drink. Thereupon King Duḥṣanta invested his son by Śakuntalā with the name Bharata and anointed him Young King. And the glorious Wheel of the great-spirited Bharata rolled thundering through the worlds, grand, radiant, divine, unvanquished. He defeated the kings of the earth and made them his vassals; he lived the Law of the strict and attained to sublime fame. He was a king, a Turner of the Wheel, a majestic worldwide monarch. He sacrificed many sacrifices, he was an Indra, lord of the winds. Like Dakṣa, he had Kaṇva officiate at a richly rewarded sacrifice, and, an illustrious king, Bharata offered a Horse Sacrifice that was styled Vast-in-Cows, at which he gave a thousand lotus counts of kine to Kaṇva.

From Bharata springs the Bhārata fame, from him the Bhārata race
50 and those other ancient men who are famed as Bhāratas. In the continuing lineage of Bharata there arose great and puissant kings, the likes of Gods, the likes of Brahmā, whose names are famous beyond measure everywhere. I shall celebrate those among them who were their chiefs, O Bhārata, the fortunate and godlike ones, given to truth and honesty.

1(7.c) *Yayāti*

70–80 (B. 75–85; C. 3126–3534).

70 (75; 3126). Genealogy of Yādavas, Pauravas, and Bhāratas. Pracetas had ten sons, from whom Dakṣa was born. Dakṣa begot a thousand sons on Vīriṇī; he adopts fifty maidens as his daughters and marries ten to Dharma, thirteen to Kaśyapa, twenty-seven to the Moon. Kaśyapa begets, on Dākṣāyaṇī, the Ādityas and Vivasvat. Vivasvat begets Yama, who begets Mārtaṇḍa, who begets Manu; Manu is the progenitor of Man. Manu had ten sons, Vena, etc., as well as Ila, who was both man and woman, and gave birth to Purūravas (1–20). He tyrannizes the brahmins and is cursed. Purūravas lived in the Gandharva heaven with Urvaśī, and brought the three sacrificial fires to earth. By Urvaśī he had six sons, Āyus, etc. Āyus has six by Svārbhanavī, Nahuṣa, etc. Nahuṣa has six by Priyavāsas: Yayāti, etc. (20–25). Yayāti begets on Devayānī two sons, Yadu and Turvaśu; on Śarmiṣṭhā, three, Druhyu, Anu, and Pūru. Pūru agrees to assume Yayāti's old age, and he becomes the dynast (25–45).

71 (76; 3183). Yayāti and Devayānī. In the feud between Gods and Asuras the Gods choose Bṛhaspati Angiras for their priest, the Asuras choose his rival Śukra. Śukra revivifies the slain Asuras, but Angiras does not possess this power (1–5). The Gods ask Bṛhaspati's son Kaca to study with Śukra and to gratify his daughter Devayānī. Śukra accepts him (10–15). For five hundred years he waits on Śukra and Devayānī, then the Asuras find him out, kill him, and feed him to jackals. Devayānī prays to her father to revive him; he does so (20–30). The Asuras kill Kaca again, burn him, and mix his ashes in Śukra's wine. Devayānī once more begs her father (30–40). Śukra discovers that Kaca is inside him; he gives him his revivifying magic, and Kaca arises from his belly, killing him, and promptly revives him (40–50). Śukra curses the wine and wine-drinking brahmins. Kaca stays another five hundred years (50–55).

72 (77; 3256). Devayānī wants Kaca to marry her; he refuses because he was reborn from the same loins as she was (1–15). Devayānī curses him that he will never use his magic successfully. Kaca replies that she will not marry a brahmin. He returns to the Gods (15–20).

73 (78; 3279). Kaca teaches the Gods his magic. Indra blows into confusion the clothes of bathing girls, including Śarmiṣṭhā, daughter of Vṛṣaparvan, king of the Asuras, and Devayānī, daughter of his priest. This occasions a quarrel, and Śarmiṣṭhā throws Devayānī in a dry well. Yayāti, out hunting, finds and questions her (1–15). Devayānī identifies herself and asks Yayāti to pull her out by the right hand; this foreshadows her marriage. While Yayāti goes home, Devayānī stays behind and sends a servant to tell her father all. She demands that Śukra avenge her (15–35).

74 (79; 3319). Śukra counsels forebearance, Devayānī seeks revenge on Śarmiṣṭhā, who had insulted her father.

75 (80; 3332). Śukra threatens to leave Vṛṣaparvan, who pleads with him. Devayānī demands that Śarmiṣṭhā become her slave; he consents (1–15). Śarmiṣṭhā too agrees to serve Devayānī, pledging that she will follow her wherever she might marry (15–25).

76 (81; 3359). Devayānī and Śarmiṣṭhā are at play in the forest and seen by Yayāti. Devayānī identifies herself and Śarmiṣṭhā, then questions Yayāti (1–15). She asks him to marry her, but Yayāti hesitates because he is not a brahmin (15–25). Devayānī makes her father give her to Yayāti; Śukra demands the condition that he never sleep with Śarmiṣṭhā. Yayāti returns with the women to his castle (25–35).

77 (82; 3397). Yayāti settles Devayānī in his castle and Śarmiṣṭhā in a grove. Devayānī gives birth to a son. Śarmiṣṭhā grows into a woman and worries about her fate; she decides to have a child by Yayāti (1–10). Yayāti refuses, in view of Śukra's condition, but Śarmiṣṭhā persuades him; she gives birth to a son (10–25).
78 (83; 3424). Devayānī questions Śarmiṣṭhā about the father; she replies that it was a passing seer, but is not specific (1–5). Yayāti has two sons by Devayānī, Yadu and Turvaśu, three by Śarmiṣṭhā, Druhyu, Anu, and Pūru. One day Devayānī, strolling with Yayāti, sees the three boys who resemble their father. She finds out the truth and scolds Śarmiṣṭhā (5–20). She leaves Yayāti and returns to her father. Śukra curses Yayāti that he will fall victim to old age, then, at the other's urging, so modifies the curse that he can pass his old age off to another. Yayāti decides on one of his sons. Śukra declares that that son shall be king (25–40).
79 (84; 3466). Yayāti tries to pass off his old age, for a period of a thousand years, to each of his sons in succession. They all refuse except Pūru. For this refusal they forfeit kingship. Pūru shall be the dynast (1–30).
80 (85; 3500). After a thousand years of pleasure Yayāti returns Pūru's youth (1–10). When he wants to anoint Pūru the people remonstrate. Yayāti explains that Pūru alone had been obedient to his wishes. The people consent. Yadu fathers the Yādavas, Turvaśu the Yavanas, Druhyu the Bhojas, Anu the Barbarians. From Pūru derive the Pauravas (10–25).

Vaiśaṃpāyana said:
70.1 Now I shall celebrate to you, king sans blame, the lineages of all
the Yādavas and Pauravas as well as the Bhāratas, in the genealogy
of Dakṣa Prajāpati, Manu Vaivasvata, Bhārata, Kuru, Pūru, and
Ajamīḍha, and their holy and grand progress in bliss, which brings
wealth and fame and a long life.

Pracetas had ten virtuous sons, all rising in radiance and splendor
like great seers, who are remembered as the first ancestors. These
mighty beings were of yore burned by the fire of monsoon lightning.
From them was born Dakṣa Prācetasa, and from Dakṣa came forth
these creatures, O tiger among men, for he is the world's Grandsire.
5 The sage Dakṣa Prācetasa lay with Vīriṇī and begot a thousand sons,
strict in their vows, who were equal to himself. It was to these one

thousand sons of Dakṣa in assembly that Nārada expounded salvation
in the form of the incomparable wisdom of Sāṃkhya. Thereupon
Dakṣa, Lord of Creatures, wished to create, O Janamejaya, and he
made fifty daughters his *puppets* for progeny. Ten of them he gave to
Dharma, thirteen to Kaśyapa, and twenty-seven to the Moon, who
have since been charged with conducting Time. Upon the choicest of
his thirteen wives, Dākṣāyanī, Kaśyapa Mārīca begot the heroic
10 Ādityas, Indra, and the others, and also Vivasvat. From Vivasvat was
born a son, the lordly Yama Vaivasvata. Mārtaṇḍa in turn, O king,
was born a son of Yama, while the wise and lordly Manu was born
the son of Mārtaṇḍa. The lineage of Manu became famous as the
lineage of Men, for from this Manu were born the Men—the brahmins,
barons, and the others. Among them arose brahminhood, O king,
which was allied with the baronage; and the brahmin men among
them transmitted the *Veda* with all its branches.

They say that Manu had ten mighty sons, Veṇa, Dhṛṣṇu, Nariṣyat,
Nābhāga, Ikṣvāku, Karūṣa, Śaryāti, Ilā the eight, Pṛṣadhna the ninth
of them, who were devoted to the Law of the baronage, and
15 Nābhāgāriṣṭa the tenth. We hear that Manu had fifty more sons on
earth, but they feuded with one another and perished. Thereafter the
wise Purūravas was born from Ilā, and we hear that she was not
only his mother but also his father.

Famous Purūravas reigned over thirteen islands in the ocean, and,
human himself, was surrounded by nonhuman creatures. This
Purūravas was maddened by his prowess and waged war on the
brahmins; and in spite of their protestations, he carried off their gems.
Whereupon Sanatkumāra came to him from the world of Brahmā,
O king, and showed him the error of his ways; but the other did not
20 accept it. Then the great seers angrily cursed him, and he perished at
once, that avaricious king of men who had lost his senses to the
power of his arrogance. It was the wide-ruling Purūravas who, when
he dwelled in the world of the Gandharvas with Urvaśī, brought to
earth the three fires that are solemnly enjoined for sacrifice.

Six sons were born to this son of Ilā by Urvaśī: Āyus, Dhīmat,
Amāvasu, Dṛḍhāyus, Vanāyus, and Śrutāyus. They recount that Āyus
had six sons by Svarbhānavī—Nahuṣa, Vṛddhaśarman, Raji, Rambha,
Gaya, and Anenas. Nahuṣa was Āyus's son; and wise and mighty in
truth, he ruled a very vast kingdom, O lord of the earth, according
25 to the rule of Law. Ancestors, Gods, seers, priests, Gandharvas, Snakes,
and Rākṣasas—Nahuṣa ruled them all as well as brahmin, baron, and
commoner. He slew the hordes of the Dasyus and taxed the seers to
pay tribute: like cattle, he forced them to carry him on their backs,
the mighty prince; and overpowering the celestials with his heat,
austerity, bravery, and might, he swayed as Indra himself.

Nahuṣa begot six sons on Priyavāsas: Yati, Yayāti, Saṃyāti,

Āyāti, Pañca, and Uddhava. Yayāti, son of Nahuṣa, became an overlord of kings, mighty in truth. He ruled the earth and offered with
30 manifold rites, honoring with the greatest power the ancestors and
the God, who were forever arriving. The invincible Yayāti showed his
favor to all his subjects.

His sons were great bowmen who prospered with all virtues. He
begot them on his two wives, Devayānī and Śarmiṣṭhā, great king.
From Devayānī were born Yadu and Turvaśu; from Śarmiṣṭhā,
Druhyu, Anu, and Pūru. After ruling his subjects with Law for years
without end, O king, Yayāti incurred dreadful old age that destroyed
his beauty. A victim of old age, the king said to his sons, Yadu, Pūru,
35 Turvaśu, Druhyu, and Anu, O Bhārata, "I want to taste the pleasures
of youth and as a young man enjoy myself with young women. Help
me, my sons!" Yadu, his eldest son by Devayānī, said to him, "What
is the task that we and our youth have to accomplish for you?"
Yayāti said to him, "Take over my old age from me, and with your
youth I shall sate my senses. A curse from the hermit Uśanas at a
time when I was sacrificing with long Sessions has made me lose all
sense of pleasure, and I suffer under this loss, sons. One of you must
rule my kingdom with my body, and I myself shall be young again
with a wholly new body and obtain my desires."

40 Yadu and the others refused to take over his old age. Thereupon
his youngest son, Pūru, mighty in truth, said to him, "Sire, find your
youth again and pleasure yourself with a new body. I shall take your
old age and rule over the kingdom as you command." At these words
the royal seer drew upon the power of his austerities and made his
old age go into his great-spirited son. The king regained youth with
Pūru's age, and Pūru reigned over the kingdom with Yayāti's age.
After a thousand years the invincible Yayāti, still unsated of desires,
spoke to his son Pūru: "In you I have my heir, you are the son who
45 is the dynast. And after you it shall be known as Pūru's dynasty!"
Then, O tiger among kings, he anointed Pūru king, and after a long
time succumbed to the Law of Time.

Janamejaya said:

71.1 Our ancestor Yayāti, who was the tenth from Prajāpati, how did he
marry Śukra's daughter Devayānī, who was well-nigh inaccessible?
This I wish to hear in all particulars, and then relate to me in succession the various scions of Pūru's dynasty.

Vaiśaṃpāyana said:

Yayāti was a royal seer who had the majesty of Indra. I shall
recount to you at your bidding, Janamejaya, how of yore both Śukra
and Vṛṣaparvan chose him for their daughters, and how the union
came about of Yayāti Nāhuṣa and Devayānī.

5 Between the Gods and the Asuras there arose a great feud over

the sovereignty of the universe with all its moving and standing creatures. To insure victory, the Gods elected the hermit son of Angiras as their priest for the sacrificial invocation, the others chose Uśanas Kāvya. These two brahmins were at all times bitter rivals. The Gods killed off the Dānavas who had gathered for battle, but Uśanas drew on the power of his knowledge and returned them to life. They stood up again and warred on the Gods. The Asuras in turn cut down the Gods in the thick of the battle, but the wise Bṛhaspati could not revive them; for he did not have that knowledge that the mighty Uśanas possessed, the knowledge of revivification, and so the Gods became utterly desperate.

10 The Gods, affrighted of Uśanas Kāvya, went to Kaca, the eldest son of Bṛhaspati, and said to him, "Love us as we love you and render us your best help. Bring us at once the knowledge that resides with Śukra, that brahmin of boundless power, and you shall share in our shares. You can find the brahmin at Vṛṣaparvan's; there he grants his protection to the Dānavas but refuses it to all others. You are younger in years, and you can propitiate the great-spirited sage, and also his daughter Devayānī, on whom he dotes. You can propitiate him—there is no one else. When you have gratified Devayānī with your conduct, dexterity, and sweetness, with acts and self-control, you are sure to obtain that knowledge."

15 Bṛhaspati's son Kaca consented and, honored by the Gods, he went into the presence of Vṛṣaparvan. He went hurriedly, O king, on this errand of the Gods; and finding Śukra in the city of the Lord of the Asuras, he addressed him: "Sir, accept me, the grandson of Angiras and son of Bṛhaspati himself, who am named Kaca, as your own student. I shall do my most chaste studies with you as my teacher. Approve me, brahmin, for a thousand years."

Śukra said:

Be warmly welcome, Kaca. I shall accept your word. I shall honor you who deserve honor, and Bṛhaspati too shall thus be honored.

Vaiśampāyana said:

20 "So be it," said Kaca, and he took the vow, which Śukra Uśanas son of Kavi himself enjoined upon him. And, accepting the term of the vow as it had been stipulated, he began to propitiate his preceptor and Devayānī, O Bhārata. And, paying constant court, the young man, who was at the height of his youth, sang and danced and made music before Devayānī to her great satisfaction. He made a habit of Devayānī, who herself was a virgin in the bloom of her youth, and delighted her with flowers and fruit and little errands, O Bhārata. Devayānī herself sang along with the brahmin, who kept strictly to his vows, and, when they were alone, frolicked happily about him.

25 Five hundred years passed in this way, while Kaca kept his vow;

then came the Dānavas, who had discovered that he was Kaca. They found him herding cows in the wilderness and alone. Secretly, without compunction, they killed him out of hatred for Bṛhaspati, and also to safeguard the magic knowledge. And after killing him they cut him into pieces the size of sesamum seeds and fed him to the jackals.

The cattle later returned to their habitation, without their cowherd. When Devayānī saw that the cows had come back from the woods without Kaca, she spoke up at once, O Bhārata. "The *agnihotra* has not been offered yet," she said, "and the sun has set, my lord. The cows have come back without their herdsman. Kaca is nowhere to be found, father. Surely Kaca must have been killed, father, or have died! Without him I cannot live, I tell you the truth!"

Śukra said:

30 If he is dead, I shall call him and say, "Come back!" And I will revive him.

Vaiśaṃpāyana said:

He employed his reviving knowledge and called Kaca. And by this magic Kaca reappeared happily as soon as he was called. "I had been killed," he said to the questions of the brahmin's daughter.

Once again, when Devayānī asked him to bring some flowers, Kaca chanced to go into the woods and the Dānavas saw the brahmin. They killed him a second time, burned him, ground the ashes to dust, and then the Asuras fed him to the brahmin in his wine. And once more Devayānī said to her father, "Kaca went out on an errand to pluck flowers; father, he is nowhere to be seen!"

Śukra said:

35 He is Bṛhaspati's son, daughter. If Kaca went out on the journey of the dead and has been killed, even though he owed his life to my magic, what am I to do?

Do not sorrow like this or weep, Devayānī—
Your likes shall not grieve over mortal man.
All the Gods and the world entire
Must bow to the change that impends.

Devayānī said:

His grandfather is the ancient Angiras,
His father ascetic Bṛhaspati—
Son and grandson of a seer,
Should I not mourn over him and weep?

My fellow-student is he, an ascetic,
Always alert and skilled in his deeds;
I shall follow his footsteps joylessly,
For, father, handsome Kaca I love.

Śukra said:

Doubtless the Asuras bear me grudge
If they murder my innocent student.
The Gruesome Ones, as the Dānavas promised,
Seek to rob me of my brahminhood.
But be there an end to this evil now—
A brahmin-murder will even burn Indra!

Vaiśaṃpāyana said:

40 Then, at the urging of Devayānī, the great seer Kāvya once more with vigor called out to Bṛhaspati's son Kaca.

Summoned by magic, afraid for his guru,
He softly spoke inside his belly.
Quoth the seer, "Speak, brahmin! What path
Has brought you to lodge in this belly of mine?"

Kaca said:

By your grace my memory survives:
I remember what has befallen and how.
Nor has my misery come to an end,
That I now must suffer this dismal pain.

The Asuras gave me to you in your wine
After killing and burning and grinding me, Kāvya.
But if you are there, can the Asura's magic
Prevail over a brahmin's wizardry?

Śukra said:

But how can I now do your wish, my daughter?
Kaca's life will murder me!
For but by opening my belly up
Can Kaca inside me appear, Devayānī.

Devayānī said:

45 Two sorrows burn me with heat of fire—
The death of Kaca and your destruction.
At Kaca's death I have no more shelter,
At your destruction I cannot live!

Śukra said:

Bṛhaspati's son, thou hast succeeded,
If Devayānī holds you so dear!
Then receive from me my life-giving magic,
If thou art not Indra in Kaca's guise.

No one can return from my belly and still live, bar one brahmin. Therefore receive thou my magic.

I shall bear thee as a son, and thou
Shalt bring me to life, from my body departed.
Bestow thou the gracious look of the Law,
When thou holdest the magic thy guru bestoweth!

Vaiśaṃpāyana said:

Receiving the magic his guru bestowed
And splitting his belly the brahmin came out,
Did beautiful Kaca, from the brahmin's right side,
As out of the bright weeks the moon rises full.

And seeing him felled, a pile of learning,
Did Kaca restore the dead man to life,
Now that he possessed that magic lore;
And Kaca saluted his guru and spoke,

"The bestower of incomparable order,
The treasury of the fourfold Treasuries,
The worshipful guru is disregarded
On pain of evil and rootless hells."

Vaiśaṃpāyana said:

As the drinking of wine had brought him deceit
And awfullest loss of his consciousness,
And seeing Kaca emerged with his beauty,
Whom he had drunkenly drunk in his wine,

That mighty Kāvya arose with wrath,
And wishing to act for the brahmin's good,
Having risked his life he spoke on his own
This commandment against the drinking of wine:

"Whichever brahmin from this day onward
Will stupidly, foolishly, drink of wine,
Will be reckoned an apostate killer of brahmins,
And will be denounced in this world and the next!

"This rule that I enjoin as the Law ordained
And laid down for the brahmins in all the world,
Strict brahmins obedient to their gurus
And the Gods and the people shall all observe."

And thus having spoken, the mighty seer
Unmeasured treasure of great ascetics,
Then summoned the Dānavas, fate-deluded,
And having summoned spoke this word,

"I tell ye, Dānavas, you are strong,
But Kaca succeeded and lived with me.

Having obtained the great life-giving magic
He, a brahmin, now matches you with his *brahman*!"

Kaca, after living for a thousand years in his guru's house, was thereupon given leave by his guru and made ready to go to the realm of the Thirty Gods.

Vaiśaṃpāyana said:

72.1 When Kaca, his vow accomplished, was dismissed by his guru and
started out for the realm of the Thirty Gods, Devayānī said to him,
"Grandson of Angiras the seer, you are radiant in conduct as in birth,
in knowledge, austerities, and self-control. Just as the celebrated
Angiras the seer is to be honored by my father, so must I honor and
worship in turn your father Bṛhaspati. Knowing this, you must also
know what I now say to you, ascetic—and as I acted while you abided
5 by your vow and observed your restraints. You have achieved your
learning—now love me as I love you. Take my hand with proper
rite and spells!"

Kaca said:

Just as I must honor and worship the blessed lord your father, so,
and even more, should I honor you, flawless maiden, for the great-
spirited Bhārgava holds you dearer than his life. The Law commands
that I always honor you as my guru's daughter, my dear. And just
as I shall ever pay honor to your father Śukra, my guru, so must I
honor you, Devayānī. Please do not speak to me like that.

Devayānī said:

You are only the son of the son of his guru, not my father's son!
10 Then I too must honor and worship you, eminent brahmin! When you
were being killed, time and again, by the Dānavas—remember how
I loved you then and always! You know my utter devotion in friendship and affection—you know the Law; do not forsake me who love
you without guilt.

Kaca said:

You who are so splendid in your vows now enjoin upon me an
injunction that may not be enjoined! Be gracious, my beautiful girl
with the lovely brow; for to me you are a guru above my guru. The
loins of Kāvya in which you have dwelled, radiant woman of the long
eyes and moonlike face, I too have dwelled there. By Law you are my
sister—do not speak to me like that, fair-faced Devayānī! I have lived
here happily, my dear, and I hold no rancor. Bid me farewell, I must
15 go. Bless me on my journey! I never offended the Law in our talks,
and so should you remember me. And, ever alert and attentive, you
must pay homage to my guru.

Devayānī said:

If you scorn me, despite my urging, for Law, Profit, and Love, then your magic knowledge shall never have success, Kaca!

Kaca said:

I scorn you because you are my guru's daughter, not because of
any wrong. My guru has given me leave to go. Curse me, if you must.
I who give voice to the ancient Law of the seers, so that you now
curse me, deserve no curse, either from love or by Law, Devayānī.
And therefore your own desire shall never be fulfilled: no son of a
20 seer shall ever take your hand! What you say that my knowledge
shall prove fruitless—let it be. But for him whom I shall teach it,
it will bear fruit.

Vaiśaṃpāyana said:

After Kaca, best of the brahmins, had thus spoken to Devayānī, he made his way quickly to the realm of the Thirty Gods. And the Gods led by Indra on seeing him arrive paid court to Bṛhaspati and spoke joyfully to Kaca: "The great and wondrous feat you have accomplished for our sakes shall never diminish in fame! You shall share in our shares."

Vaiśaṃpāyana said:

73.1 Upon the arrival of Kaca, who had achieved the magic knowledge,
the celestials took great comfort; and they learned that magic from
Kaca and were satisfied, bull among Bhāratas. They all assembled and
said to the God of the hundred sacrifices, "Now is the time of your
puissance. Slay the enemy, Sacker of Cities!"

"So be it," said Maghavat to these words of the gathered Gods, and
set out. And saw women in the forest. And while the maids were
playing about in the woods, which was like Citraratha's park, Indra
5 changed into a breeze and blew their clothes in confusion. Then the
maids came out of the water and they all took the clothes that lay
nearest at hand. Śarmiṣṭhā took Devayānī's skirt: this daughter of
Vṛṣaparvan did not know that the clothes had been mixed up. Thereupon the two began to quarrel, Devayānī and Śarmiṣṭhā, about that
skirt, great king.

Devayānī said:

Why do you take my skirt, you daughter of a demon, who are my pupil to boot! You lack all courtesy, no good will come of you!

Śarmiṣṭhā said:

Your father stands humbly below my father, whether he is sitting or lying, and he flatters and praises him constantly! You are the daughter of a man who must beg, flatter, and hold up his hand—I am the daughter of the one who gives, and does not receive, the one who is flattered. Unarmed and deserted, you tremble before me who am armed, beggar girl! Find your match, for I do not consider you mine!

Vaiśaṃpāyana said

Devayānī rose to her full height and clung to the skirt; but Śarmiṣṭhā threw her in a well and went to her castle. Śarmiṣṭhā in evil mind thought she was dead; she was so overcome by rage that she did not even look down and went home. Now Yayāti, the son of Nahuṣa, came to that place, looking for deer to hunt; his driver was tired, his horses were tired, and he was thirsty. King Yayāti looked in the well, which was dry, and saw the girl there like a raging flame crest.

When he saw the girl, beautiful like a Goddess, that grand king comforted her with the most coaxing gentleness and asked, "Who are you, with your copper-red nails and dark complexion, and those lovely gems and earrings? Why are you brooding so long and sighing so utterly grievously? And how did you come to fall into this well that is covered with plants and straw? Whose daughter are you, slim-waisted girl? Tell me all!"

Devayānī said:

Śukra's daughter am I, the one who with his magic revives the Daityas that are slain by the Gods. He does not know where I am now. Here is my right hand, king, with copper-red nails. Take it and pull me out, for you seem to me like a man of good family. I know that you are serene and brave and famous—therefore pray pull me out of this well into which I have fallen.

Vaiśaṃpāyana said:

Nahuṣa's son understood that she was a brahmin girl, and he took her by the right hand and pulled her from the hole. And after he had pulled her quickly from the well, King Yayāti said farewell to the buxom girl and went to his own castle.

Devayānī said:

Ghūrṇikā, hurry and tell my father everything! For I refuse henceforth to set foot in Vṛṣaparvan's castle.

Vaiśaṃpāyana said:

Ghūrṇikā hastened to the dwelling of the Asura, and when she saw Kāvya she told him, flustered, "I tell you, O sage, Devayānī has been struck in the woods by Śarmiṣṭhā, the daughter of Vṛṣaparvan, sir!" Hearing that this daughter had been struck by Śarmiṣṭhā, Kāvya hurried out anxiously to look for his daughter. And when he found his daughter Devayānī in the woods, Kāvya took her in his arms and said with sorrow, "It is by their own faults that people reap sorrow and happiness. Methinks you once did some wrong, which has thus been avenged."

Devayānī said:
30 Avenged or not, listen closely to me. Śarmiṣṭhā of Vṛṣaparvan told
the truth, to be sure! What she said was that you are the songster of
the Daityas! That is what Śarmiṣṭhā told me, her eyes bloodshot with
rage, in the harshest and sharpest words, "You are the daughter of a
man who must beg, flatter, and hold up his hand—I am the daughter
of the one who gives, and does not receive, the one who is flattered."
That is what Śarmiṣṭhā again and again said to me, Vṛṣaparvan's
daughter, eyes red with fury, swollen with pride. Father, if I am the
daughter of a man who flatters and holds up his hand, I shall seek her
good graces; so I told my friend.
Śukra said:
35 You are *not* the daughter of a flattering beggar who holds up his
hand, my dear! You are the daughter, Devayānī, of the one who is
praised but does not praise. Vṛṣaparvan himself knows it, and Indra,
and King Yayāti. Inconceivable Brahman beyond compare is my
sovereign strength!

Śukra said:
74.1 The man who always bears with the abuse of others, know,
Devayānī, that he has won all. He who holds his rising anger in
check like a horse, him good people call a driver, not the one who
hangs on the reins. The man who dispels his rising anger with
equanimity, knows, Devayānī, that he has won all. The one who
dispels his rising anger with forgiveness, they compare him with a
5 snake that sloughs off its old skin, the man who contains his anger
and bears abuse. He who is hurt and does not hurt back is surely a
vessel of profit. Between the two, the one who tirelessly, month after
month, offers up his sacrifices for a hundred years, and the one who
does not get angry at anyone, it is the man without anger who is
superior.
The feud that boys or girls fight in their folly no sensible man will
imitate. They do not know what strength is or weakness.
Devayānī said:
I may be a child, but I do know, father, the differences between the
Laws on earth, and I know strength and weakness in meekness and
abuse. Still, no one who strives to be a teacher can condone unpupil-
like behavior in a student! Therefore, it does not please me to live
10 with people who behave so improperly. No sensible person who looks
for the best will live with evil-intentioned people who cast blame on
his conduct or birth. But the honest, who recognize another's conduct
and birth, those are the people to live with, and life with them is called
the best. I can imagine nothing more impossible in all three worlds
than the dreadful foul tongue of Vṛṣaparvan's daughter. It is the

failed man who adores the bright success of his rival!

Vaiśaṃpāyana said:

75.1 Kāvya, that best of the Bhṛgus, wrathfully went up to where
Vṛṣaparvan was sitting, and spoke to him unhesitantly: "The
perpetration of lawlessness does not like a cow yield results instantly,
king. But evil does bear sure fruit, like a heavy meal on the stomach;
if you do not see it ripen on yourself, it will on your sons or grandsons. You had Kaca Āngirasa killed, a brahmin who held with no
evil, who knew the Law and was an obedient student attached to my
household. For your killing of him who deserved no death, and for your
injury to my daughter, I, Vṛṣaparvan, listen to me, shall forsake you
and your kin. I cannot dwell with you any longer in your domain,
5 king. Damnation, do you take me for a liar, Daitya, that you overlook
vice and do not check it?"

Vṛṣaparvan said:

Never have I known lawlessness or lies in you, Bhārgava! There is Law in you and truth. Be gracious to us, sir! If you cast us off and leave, Bhārgava, we shall all drown in the ocean; we would have no other recourse.

Śukra said:

Drown in the ocean or run to the horizons, Asuras! I cannot suffer any unkindness done to my daughter, for I love her. Make your peace with Devayānī, with whom my life is lodged. I am your only safeguard, as Bṛhaspati is Indra's.

Vṛṣaparvan said:

10 Whatever riches can be found with the lords of the Asuras,
Bhārgava, whatever wealth on earth of elephants, horses, and cows,
you own it as you own me!

Śukra said:

Whatever wealth the lords of the Daityas own, grand Asuras, I own it only if you make your peace with Devayānī.

Devayānī said:

If you, father, if you, Bhārgava, say you own all the wealth of the king and the king himself, I won't believe it from you. Let the king say it himself!

Vṛṣaparvan said:

Whatever desire you desire, sweet-smiling Devayānī, I shall give it to you with both hands, however hard it may be to find.

Devayānī said:

I want Śarmiṣṭhā as my slave, with a thousand handmaidens. And after me shall she follow wherever my father will marry me!

Vṛṣaparvan said:

15 Rise, nurse! Get Śarmiṣṭhā at once! Whatever Devayānī wants, she
must do it!

Vaiśaṃpāyana said:

The nurse went there and said to Śarmiṣṭhā, "Rise up, dear child Śarmiṣṭhā, and bring luck to your kinsmen. Our brahmin is ready to desert his students at Devayānī's urging. Whatever desire she desires, you must carry it out now, my innocent."

Śarmiṣṭhā said:

Whatever desire she desires, I shall carry it out now, lest Śukra depart with Devayānī because of me.

Vaiśaṃpāyana said:

In a litter, surrounded by a thousand handmaidens, she departed hastily at her father's behest from her beautiful castle.

Śarmiṣṭhā said:

20 With a thousand maidens I am your slave to serve you. And after
you shall I follow wherever your father marries you.

Devayānī said:

Am I the daughter of a songster who flatters and holds up his hand? How is it that the daughter of the man who is flattered will be my slave?

Śarmiṣṭhā said:

Whatever the way, I want to bring luck to my suffering kinsmen. So I shall follow after you, wherever your father will marry you.

Vaiśaṃpāyana said:

When Vṛṣaparvan's daughter had promised to be her slave, O best of kings, Devayānī said this word to her father: "Now will I enter the castle, father. I am pleased, greatest of the twiceborn. Your knowledge is unfailing, and so is the power of your magic."

25 And at these words of his daughter that greatest of the twiceborn
of much fame happily entered the castle, worshiped by all the
Dānavas.

Vaiśaṃpāyana said:

76.1 A long time later, O best of kings, the beautiful Devayānī went out
to that same wood to play. Accompanied by Śarmiṣṭhā and
Śarmiṣṭhā's one thousand slaves, she reached the same spot and
strolled about as she pleased, exhilarated by the company of all those
friends. They all frolicked about excitedly, drinking mead, chewing all
kinds of edibles, and taking bites of fruit. And again King Yayāti
happened to come to that same place, looking for deer to hunt,
5 drawn with fatigue and searching for water. He saw Devayānī and
Śarmiṣṭhā and those women drinking and lolling, aglitter with
celestial jewels. He saw the sweet-smiling Devayānī of matchless
beauty sitting there in the midst of those lovely women, while
Śarmiṣṭhā waited on her with foot massages and so forth.

Yayāti said:

Two maidens surrounded by two thousand maids. I ask the families and names of both of you.

Devayānī said:

I shall tell you and accept my word, king of men! The guru of the Asuras is Śukra by name, and I am his daughter. And this companion is my slave girl, who goes where I go—Śarmiṣṭhā, daughter of Vṛṣaparvan, king of the Dānavas.

Yayāti said:

10 But how can this beautiful maiden with the lovely brow, daughter of the king of the Asuras, be your companion and slave girl? I am most curious, girl of the lovely brows!

Devayānī said:

Every one, tiger among kings, follows after fate. Take it as ordained by fate, and do not ask all kinds of questions. Your appearance and robes bespeak a king, and the language you speak is the brahmins'. What is your name, and from whence do you hail? Whose son are you? Tell me.

Yayāti said:

During my student years the entire *Veda* came to my ears. I am a king and the son of a king, and renowned as Yayāti.

Devayānī said:

For what purpose have you come to this spot, king? To gather some water lilies, or to hunt for deer?

Yayāti said:

15 To hunt for deer, good woman. And now I have come to find water. You ask many questions; pray let me go.

Devayānī said:

With all my two thousand maids and my slave girl Śarmiṣṭhā, I am your servant. Bless you! Be my friend and husband!

Yayāti said:

Bless you, daughter of Uśanas! I am not worthy of you, radiant girl. For no kings are eligible to your father, Devayānī!

Devayānī said:

The baronage is in league with brahmindom and brahmindom allied with the baronage. You are a seer and the son of a seer, Yayāti—by all means marry me!

Yayāti said:

All four classes have sprung from a single body, beautiful maiden, but their Law varies and their purity varies. The brahmin is the best of all.

Devayānī said:

20 No other but you, Yayāti, has ever sought the rite of my hand. You have taken my hand before, and therefore I choose you. How could a proud woman like me suffer another to touch her hand that you, a seer and the son of a seer, yourself had taken?

Yayāti said:

Harder to fight off than an angry and virulent cobra or a spreading fire—thus is the brahmin known to a man who knows!

Devayānī said:

Why do you say, bull among men, that it is harder to fight off a virulent cobra or a spreading fire than a brahmin?

Yayāti said:

The cobra kills one man, the sword kills one, but an angered
25 brahmin kills capitals and kingdoms! Therefore, I think that it is
harder to fight a brahmin, my bashful maiden. And, therefore, my
dear, I will not marry you if your father does not give you away.

Devayānī said:

Then my father shall give me away, and you shall marry me. I have chosen you, king. The one who asks not, but receives the bride that is given him, has nothing to fear.

Vaiśaṃpāyana said:

Devayānī quickly sent a message to her father; and as soon as he had heard it, the Bhārgava went to see the king. And as soon as Yayāti, lord of the earth, saw Śukra come, he raised his hands to his forehead and bowed and greeted Kāvya the brahmin.

Devayānī said:

This is King Yayāti, father, who took my hand when I had come to grief. Honor to you—give me to him. I choose no other husband on earth.

Śukra said:

30 The daughter I love has chosen you for her husband, O hero. Son
of Nahuṣa, take her as your first queen; I give her to you.

Yayāti said:

Let no great breach of the Law taint me, Bhārgava, because of this miscegenation, brahmin; this boon I beseech of you.

Śukra said:

I free thee from the breach of the Law—choose her freely for your bride. Do not shrink from this marriage; I myself absolve your sin. Marry the slim-waisted Devayānī by the Law, and with her you shall find happiness beyond compare! This young maiden too you should always respect, king, this Śarmiṣṭhā, daughter of Vṛṣaparvan, and never call her to your bed.

Vaiśaṃpāyana said:

35 Upon these words Yayāti circumambulated Śukra; and with the
great-spirited seer's leave he returned happily to his castle.

Vaiśaṃpāyana said:

77.1 Yayāti, upon reaching his castle that resembled the castle of great
Indra, entered the women's quarters and settled Devayānī there. With

Devayānī's permission, he settled Vṛṣaparvan's daughter Śarmiṣṭhā in a house he built close by a grove of *aśoka* trees, where the Asura girl lived with her one thousand handmaidens. And he treated her well, equitably distributing clothes, food, and drink.

Together with Devayānī, the king, the son of Nahuṣa, enjoyed himself for many years like a God in perfect joy. When Devayānī's season came to pass, the beautiful woman conceived for the first time and gave birth to a boy. A thousand years passed, and Vṛṣaparvan's daughter Śarmiṣṭhā grew up to womanhood, saw her season, and began to worry. "My season has come, and I have not chosen a husband. What has happened? What to do? How to act so it will be right? Devayānī, she has born a child, but here I am become a woman and in vain! She chose her husband, and I shall choose him the same way. My mind is made up; the king must give me the fruit of a son. But he is a Law-minded king—will he come now and see me in secret?"

At that time the king happened to come out and, coming closer, found Śarmiṣṭhā by her *aśoka* grove. Seeing him by himself in that secluded spot, happily smiling Śarmiṣṭhā rose to meet him, folded her hands, and said to the king: "Who dares to touch a woman in the houses of Soma, or Indra, Viṣṇu, Yama, or Varuṇa—or yours, Yayāti? You have always known me for my beauty, birth, and manners; therefore, I seek your grace and beg you to grant me my season, king of men!"

Yayāti said:

I know you as the blameless Daitya girl of accomplished conduct, and in your beauty I see not a flaw the size of a needle's point! But Uśanas Kāvya said when I married Devayānī that I was never to call Vṛṣaparvan's daughter to my bed.

Śarmiṣṭhā said:

A lie spoken in jest does not hurt,
Nor a lie to women, or at marriage time,
Or on pain of life, or of all property—
These five lies are said to be no sins.

The one who lies when questioned in a suit—
Him they call a liar, king.
But when a common purpose is at stake
It's then a liar is injured by his lie.

Yayāti said:

The king is the measure of all for his people. If he is proven to have lied, he is lost. Even if I come to the lowest fortune, I cannot afford to break my word.

Śarmiṣṭhā said:

King, these two are held to be closely related, one's own husband and one's friend's. A friend's wedding is one's own, they say; I have chosen you, my friend's husband, for my husband.

Yayāti said:

20 "The beggar is worthy of the gift"; that is the rule I have made my
own. And now you are begging my favor—tell me what I should do.

Śarmiṣṭhā said:

Save me from breaking the Law, king, and teach me the Law. If I have a child by you, I shall practice in this world the purest Law! "There are three who own no property, O king—a wife, a slave, and a son: what they acquire belongs to him who owns them." I am Devayānī's slave, and Bhārgava's daughter is your serf. She and I are equally your dependents, king—pleasure me!

Vaiśaṃpāyana said:

At these words of hers the king saw the truth of them. He paid honor
to Śarmiṣṭhā and taught her the Law. He lay with Śarmiṣṭhā and had
his pleasure of her; and after doing honor to each other they each
25 went the way they had come. And from their intercourse Śarmiṣṭhā of
the lovely brow and beautiful laugh conceived her first child by this
strictest of kings. In time, O king, she gave birth, eyes bright like the
blue lotus, to a boy like the child of a God, eyes bright like the blue
lotus.

Vaiśaṃpāyana said:

78.1 Sweet-smiling Devayānī heard that Śarmiṣṭhā had born a son, O
Bhārata, and began grievously to worry about her. Devayānī went
to Śarmiṣṭhā and said to her, "Now what crime have you done, my
dear with the lovely brow, out of hunger for love?"

Śarmiṣṭhā said:

A law-minded seer came by, who was a master of the *Veda*. He granted me a boon, and I asked him my wish that obeyed the Law. I did not fall to indecent lust, sweet-smiling friend. From that seer I got the child; I tell you the truth.

Devayānī said:

5 It would be well, my bashful friend, if you knew that twiceborn. I
should like to know that twiceborn by name, family, and birth.

Śarmiṣṭhā said:

He blazed like the sun with power and heat! When I saw him I was not capable of interrogating him, sweet-smiling friend.

Devayānī said:

If all this is true, I bear you no grudge, Śarmiṣṭhā—if indeed you got your child from the twiceborn who is the eldest and the best.

Vaiśaṃpāyana said:

So they talked together and laughed gaily at each other.
Bhārgava's daughter* went home, having learned the literal truth.
10 King Yayāti begot two sons on Devayānī, Yadu and Turvaśu, who
were like another Indra and Viṣṇu. And by that same royal seer
Vṛṣaparvan's daughter Śarmiṣṭhā bore three boys, Druhyu, Anu, and
Pūru.

Now one day sweet-smiling Devayānī, accompanied by Yayāti,
went out to a big forest, O king. And there she saw three godlike boys
playing without a care, and surprised she said, "Whose children are
those beautiful boys who look like the sons of a God? In spirit and
body they seem to resemble you." And after questioning the king she
questioned the boys; "What is the name of the clan of your brahmin
15 father, sons? Tell me truthfully. I want to hear it myself." With their
forefinger the boys pointed at our excellent king himself, and also told
that Śarmiṣṭhā was their mother. After they had told this, they all of
them walked up to the king; but the king, with Devayānī there, did
not greet them. In tears the children went back to Śarmiṣṭhā.

Seeing how fondly the children behaved toward the king, the queen guessed at the truth; she spoke with Śarmiṣṭhā: "You are my slave; how did you dare to slight me? You have relapsed to the Law of the Asuras! Have you no fear at all?"

Śarmiṣṭhā said:

I told you the truth when I said it was a seer, sweet-smiling friend.
I have acted according to Law and decency, so why should I fear you?
20 When you chose the king, I did too. For by Law the friend's husband is
one's own, my pretty. I must honor and worship you—the brahmin
wife is the eldest and the best; but greater honor than to you do I owe
to the royal seer. Don't you know that?

Vaiśaṃpāyana said:

When Devayānī heard this, she said: "King, I will not live here any
more! You have done me wrong." Seeing the beautiful woman
suddenly start up with tears in her eyes and quickly depart toward
Kāvya, he painfully and nervously followed in her footsteps, trying to
25 dissuade her. But she did not turn back; her beautiful eyes bloodshot
with anger, she refused to reply to the king. Soon she came to Kāvya
Uśanas's dwelling. As soon as she saw her father she greeted him, and
stood before him. Immediately afterward Yayāti too paid homage to
the Bhārgava.

Devayānī said:

Lawlessness has won over Law, the world is upside down! I have been overreached by Śarmiṣṭhā, the daughter of Vṛṣaparvan! This

* = Devayānī.

King Yayāti has fathered three sons on that ill-fated woman, and only two on me, I tell you, father! This king is reputed to know the Law, scion of the Bhṛgu! He has transgressed the limit, Kāvya, I tell you that!

Śukra said:

30 Great king, since you who know the Law have broken the Law for your pleasure, invincible decrepitude shall ravage you this instant!

Yayāti said:

Sir, she begged me for her season, the daughter of the lord of the Asuras! It was with no other thought that I did what was right. A man chosen by a woman who begs for her season must give in to her, or the scholars of the *Veda* call him on earth an aborticide. A man who refuses to lie by the Law with an available lusting woman who begs him in secret is called an aborticide by the wise. Those were the reasons I weighed, and it was for fear of breaking the Law that I lay with Śarmiṣṭhā.

Śukra said:

35 Should I not have been consulted? You are my dependent, king. Duplicity in matters of Law makes one a thief, Nāhuṣa!

Vaiśaṃpāyana said:

So it befell that Uśanas in anger cursed Yayāti Nāhuṣa. And he lost his previous youth and fell instantly to senility.

Yayāti said:

I am unsated of my youth on Devayānī, scion of the Bhṛgu. Show me grace, brahmin; do not let old age lay hold of me!

Śukra said:

Such things I do not say idly. You have reached old age, king of the earth. But if you wish, you may pass on your old age to another.

Yayāti said:

Share in my kingdom, share in my merit, share in my fame shall the son who will give me his youth; brahmin, consent to that!

Śukra said:

40 You shall pass on your old age, as you wish, son of Nahuṣa, if you call me to your mind. Then you will reap no evil. The son who will give you his youth shall become the king, long-lived, famous, and rich in offspring.

Vaiśaṃpāyana said:

79.1 Stricken with old age, Yayāti repaired to his castle and addressed his eldest and dearest son Yadu: "Son, old age and wrinkles and gray hairs have laid hold of me, because of a curse of Uśanas Kāvya, and I am not yet sated of youth. You, Yadu, must take over my guilt with my old age, and with your own youth I shall slake my senses. When the millennium is full, I shall give your youth back to you, and take over the guilt and old age.

Yadu said:

Gray of head and beard, wretched, loosened by senility, the body wrinkled, ugly, weak, thin, incapable of achieving anything, and set upon by younger men and all the people that live off you? I do not crave old age.

Yayāti said:

You were born from my heart, but will not render your youth to me. Therefore, son, your offspring shall have no share in the kingdom!

Turvaśu, take over my guilt with my old age, and with your youth I shall slake my senses, my son. When the millennium is full, I shall give your youth back to you and take over my own guilt with my old age.

Turvaśu said:

I do not crave old age, father, which destroys all pleasure and joy, finishes strength and beauty, and puts an end to spirit and breath.

Yayāti said:

You were born from my heart but will not render your youth to me. Therefore, Turvaśu, your offspring will face extinction. Fool, you shall rule over people whose customs and laws are corrupt and whose walks of life run counter to decency, the lowest ones who feed on meat. They will lust after the wives of their gurus and couple with beasts; evil barbarians that follow the laws of cattle are they whom you will rule!

Vaiśaṃpāyana said:

Thus Yayāti cursed Turvaśu, the son of his body. Then he spoke to Druhyu, his son by Śarmiṣṭhā: "Druhyu, for a thousand years take over my old age that destroys color and beauty, and give me your own youth. When the millennium is full, I shall return your youth and take back again my guilt and old age."

Druhyu said:

An old man enjoys neither elephant nor chariot nor horse nor woman, and speech fails him. I do not crave such old age.

Yayāti said:

You were born from my heart, but you will not render your youth to me. Therefore your dearest wish shall never be fulfilled. Not a king, you, and your line, will acquire the title of Bhoja in a land where the only crossing is by raft and ferry!

Anu, you must take over my evil and my old age. For one thousand years I will live with your youth.

Anu said:

An old man eats his food like a baby, unclean, drooling, and at any time of the day. And he never offers to the fire in time. Such old age I do not crave.

Yayāti said:

You were born from my heart, but you will not render your youth to me. You have spoken of the ills of old age, therefore you shall inherit them. Your offspring, when they reach youth, will perish on you, Anu, and you yourself shall be equally prone to errors by the fire.

25 Pūru, you are my dear son, and you shall be the best. Old age and wrinkles and gray hairs have laid hold of me, because of the curse of Uśanas Kāvya, and I am not yet sated of youth. Pūru, you must take over my guilt and old age, and for some time to come I shall slake my senses with your youth. When the millennium is full, I shall return your youth to you and take back my own evil and old age.

Vaiśaṃpāyana said:

At these words of his father, Pūru replied immediately, "Sir, I shall do as you say. I shall take on, O king, your guilt and old age. Take my youth from me and enjoy the pleasures you are seeking. Covered with your old age and wearing your aged body, I shall live as you say and give you my youth."

Yayāti said:

30 Pūru, my calf, I am pleased with you, and as I am pleased I shall give you this. Your offspring shall prosper in all their pleasures and rule the kingdom.

Vaiśaṃpāyana said:

80.1 So the eminent King Yayāti, the son of Nahuṣa, joyfully sought his pleasures with the youth of Pūru, as he wished, as he could, as he had leisure, as he liked—pleasures that did not offend the Law and such as befitted him, O lord of kings. He contented the Gods with sacrifices, the ancestors with *śrāddhas*, the oppressed with the favors they wished, the good brahmins with boons, his guests with food and drink, the commoners with protection, the serfs with benevolence, the
5 *dasyus* with repression. Yayāti, winning the affection of his subjects as was proper by the Law, ruled his people like another Indra come to flesh. The king, valiant as a lion, sought his pleasure being young again, without transgressing the Law, and enjoyed great happiness.

Having obtained all good pleasure, the king became sated and wearied; and he remembered the term that was to end after a thousand years. Then when he judged that the millennium was full, after having counted days and hours, being expert in Time, the mighty king spoke to his son Pūru: "I have sought pleasure, as I wished and could and had leisure, with your youth, my son, tamer of
10 enemies. Pūru, I am pleased, I bless you. Now take back your own

youth and likewise take the kingdom, for you are the son who did my pleasure." Whereupon the King Yayāti Nāhuṣa took on his old age and Pūru took on his youth.

Then the king desired to anoint Pūru, his youngest son, king of the land; but the classes, led by the brahmins, said to him, "Why is it that you are giving the kingdom to Pūru and pass over your eldest son Yadu by Devayānī, who is the grandson of Śukra? Yadu is your first-born son, after him comes Turvaśu, then, by Śarmiṣṭhā, there is your son Druhyu, then Anu, and lastly Pūru. Why does the youngest deserve the kingdom over the oldest sons? This we call to your attention. Rule according to the Law!"

Yayāti said:

All ye classes led by the brahmins, listen to my word! The reason that I cannot in any way give the kingdom to the eldest son is that Yadu, the eldest, did not heed my behest. The strict do not deem him a son who is contrary to his father. He is a son who does as his father and mother say and always has their welfare and well-being at heart. He is a son who acts like a son with his father and mother. Yadu has disdained me; and so have Turvaśu, Druhyu, and Anu shown their deep disdain for me. Pūru did my behest. He, the youngest, has earned special honor as my heir, for he bore my old age. Like a true son, Pūru did my pleasure. Besides, Śukra Uśanas Kāvya himself has bestowed this boon that the son who obeyed me would be king and lord of the earth. Thus I implore you that Pūru be consecrated to the kingdom.

The subjects said:

The son of virtue who has his parents' welfare at heart deserves all that is good, be he the youngest, O lord. Pūru did your pleasure, and he deserves the kingdom. With Śukra's bestowing the boon there is nothing left to be said.

Vaiśaṃpāyana said:

At this declaration by the city and country people, who were satisfied, Yayāti Nāhuṣa anointed Pūru, the son of his body, to rule the kingdom. And after he had given the kingdom to Pūru, the king underwent consecration for life in the forest and departed from his city with brahmins and ascetics.

From Yadu sprang the Yādavas; Turvaśu's sons are known as the Yavanas; Druhyu's sons became the Bhojas; Anu's, the tribes of the Barbarians. Pūru's line is the dynasty of the Pauravas in which you yourself have been born, sire, to rule this kingdom sovereign for a thousand years!

1(7.d) The Latter Days of Yayāti

81–88 (B. 86–93; C. 3535–3690)
81 (86; 3535). Summary story. Yayāti anoints Pūru and departs for the forest. He goes to heaven and is cast out, but remains suspended in the sky; eventually he returns with four other kings (1–5). Janamejaya demands the full story (5). Yayāti's mortifications (10–15).
82 (87; 3551). Yayāti is honored by the Gods. Indra questions Yayāti about Pūru; Yayāti praises gentleness of speech (1–10).
83 (88; 3564). Indra asks Yayāti who his peer is in asceticism. Yayāti knows of none; for this pridefulness he must fall. Yayāti asks that he fall among good people (1–5). As he is falling he is seen by Aṣṭaka and questioned (5–10).
84 (89; 3577). Yayāti extols equanimity (1–10). Aṣṭaka asks about Yayāti's late worlds; Yayāti describes them and his fall (10–20).
85 (90; 3600). Asked about his fall, Yayāti discourses on transmigration (1–20). He extols virtue and condemns slander (20–25).
86 (91; 3627). On the four stages of life, particularly of mendicants and forest dwellers (1–5); types of hermits (5–15).
87 (92; 3645). Praise of the mendicant (1). Aṣṭaka prays to Yayāti to ward off his downfall by accepting the gift of his worlds (5–10). Yayāti declines, for a king takes no gifts. Pratardana offers his worlds, and Yayāti declines (10–15).
88 (93; 3664). Vasumanas offers to sell his worlds for a straw stalk; Yayāti declines (1–5). Śibi offers his worlds and is refused. Aṣṭaka announces that the four of them will return to rebirth. Five golden chariots arrive, which take them to heaven (5–15). Śibi outpaces the others because of his erstwhile liberality (15). Yayāti identifies himself as the maternal grandfather of all four (20–25).

Vaiśaṃpāyana said:

81.1 Thus King Yayāti Nāhuṣa anointed his beloved son king and he himself joyously became a hermit and forest dweller. And after living in the forest with the brahmins who had gathered around him, and feeding on fruit and roots, he attained to self-control, so that he went to heaven. He dwelled in heaven joyously and blissfully, but after not too long a time he was again cast out of it by Indra. When he was cast from heaven, he fell down and never reached the surface of the earth
5 but remained suspended in the sky, so have I heard. Later, so goes the tradition, mighty Yayāti again returned to heaven, having joined, they say, in an assembly with King Vasumat, Aṣṭaka, Pratardana and Śibi.

Janamejaya said:

By what deeds did the king again attain to heaven? I wish to hear the entire story, precisely and in full, recounted by you, brahmin, in the midst of these hosts of brahmins and seers. For Yayāti, who was like Indra, was a king of the earth who prospered the dynasty of the Kurus, resplendent like the sun. I wish to hear all of the feats, on heaven as well as on earth, of that great-spirited man whose fame is wide and renown is true.

Vaiśaṃpāyana said:

Then surely I shall recount to you the later history of Yayāti that gives merit in heaven as on earth, and destroys all evil.
10 King Yayāti Nāhuṣa, after anointing his youngest son Pūru to the kingdom, joyously departed for the forest; Yadu and the other sons he had cast to the ends of the earth. The king lived in the forest for a long spell, feeding on fruit and roots and satisfying the Gods and the ancestors, his spirit honed, his anger tamed. He offered into the fires, according to the injunctions for those who have departed for the forest; and the prince did homage to his guests with offerings of forest fare. He lived off gleanings, ate off the remnants of others, and in this wise the king passed a full thousand years. For thirty autumns
15 he lived on water alone, disciplining both mind and tongue; for a year he lived, unwearied, on nothing but air; and for another year he mortified his body between five fires. For six months he stood on one foot, living on the wind. Then, having covered heaven and earth with the fame of his holiness, he went to heaven.

Vaiśaṃpāyana said:

82.1 When this lord of kings dwelled in heaven, in the seat of the Gods, he was honored by the Thirty Gods, the Sādhyas, the Maruts, and the Vasus. The masterful man of merit who had been a king on earth roamed from the world of the Gods to the world of Brahmā and lived in heaven for a long time, so goes the tradition.

One time this best of kings, Yayāti, went to Indra, and as they discoursed, Indra questioned the king.

Indra said:

When Pūru in your body, O king,
Had taken your age and roamed over earth
And you had given him all your realm,
How did you speak to him? Tell me the truth!

Yayāti said:

5 "All this country between the Ganges and the Yamunā is yours. You shall be king in the middle of the earth, your brothers shall rule the outer regions.

"The man without anger surpasses the angry,
The man of forgiveness the unforgiving,
And over the animals man stands first,
And over the ignorant stand the wise.

"When abused, do not abuse. The wrath of a forbearing man burns the abuser and reaps all his good deeds.

"Be never hurtful nor speak cruelly,
Nor extort the last from a lowly man;
Nor speak the wounding, hell-earning words
That in their speaking hurt another man.

"The hurtful, chafing, rough-spoken man
Who drives wounds in others with thorns of speech
Is among men the least blessed with luck
And holds in his mouth the fury of evil.

10 "Be honored by the good in front
And in the back protected by the good.
Forbear always the abuse of the bad—
A noble man will imitate the good.

"Words fly like arrows from the mouth.
And the one they hurt grieves day and night;
The ones that hit where the other hurts
No wise man will loose on another man.

"No greater means of propitiation is found in all three worlds than compassion, friendship for creatures, liberality, and gentle words. Therefore one should always speak kindly and never harshly, pay honor to those who deserve it, give, and never ask."

Indra said:

83.1 After having accomplished, king, all rituals,

You left your house and went to the forest:
Therefore I now, son of Nahuṣa, ask you,
Who matches you in austerities, Yayāti?

Yayāti said:

Neither among Gods nor men, nor Gandharvas nor great seers, do I see anyone who equals me in mortification, Indra!

Indra said:

As you disdain your equals and betters,
And inferiors, knowing not their prowess,
Therefore these worlds shall for you be ending—
Your merit gone, you shall fall today, king!

Yayāti said:

If my disdain for Gods, seers, and Gandharvas
Has brought these worlds to an end for me, Indra,
Then, deprived of the world of the Gods, I hanker,
O king of the Gods, to fall with the honest.

Indra said:

5 Cast out, you shall fall, king, among the honest,
Where you once more will find a foundation;
And, knowing this, you shall never more, Yayāti,
Show your disdain for your equals and betters!

Vaiśaṃpāyana said:

Then having departed the holy heavens,
Which Indra frequents, Yayāti, falling,
Was seen by Aṣṭaka, great royal seer,
And addressed by that lord of the Law of the honest.

"Who are you, youth, who resemble Indra,
Who are blazing like fire with your radiance?
You fall as the sun, the first of the sky folk,
Falls away from the sky where dark clouds are massing!

"And seeing you falling from the sun's pathways,
Aglow like the fire and the sun, without measure,
We all are confused as we vainly wonder
Who this might be who is falling amongst us.

"And seeing you travel the God's own roadway
In splendor alike to Sun, Indra, and Viṣṇu,
We have now all together arisen to meet you,
To discover from you the cause of your downfall.

10 "Nor would we have dared to put the first question
If you had asked us about our persons.

Then now we ask you of enviable beauty:
Of whom are you and why you have come here?

"All fear be gone, and despair and delusion
You must dispel, whose might matches Indra's:
For here you are dwelling among the honest—
Not the Slayer of Vala would dare assail you.

"For the good are the refuge of all good people
That have fallen from bliss, you that equal Indra.
The good assembled are the Lords of Creation,
You have found your seat with the good, your equals.

"Fire is the master at burning, earth the master at sowing, sun the master at lighting, the guest of the good is the master of all."

Yayāti said:
84.1 Yayāti am I who am Nahuṣa's offspring
And father of Pūru! Disdain for all creatures
Has cast me from Gods and seers and Siddhas,
And, my merit diminished, I am sped on my downfall.

As I am older in age than your worships
I was not the first to do the greeting.
For he who is older in knowledge, or penance,
Or by birth, earns homage from the twiceborn.

Aṣṭaka said:
If you say, king, that you being the older
Hence did not greet first—it is also stated
That the man of wisdom is older in years
And that he deserves homage from the twiceborn!

Yayāti said:
They say that evil destroys the rituals
And leads at leisure to evil worlds.
The good will never follow the evil,
So that their soul will speak for their good.

5 The wealth I had was surely abundant;
Much as I strive, I shall not retrieve it.
He who holds out thus for his own profit
And lives that way becomes wise while living.

In the world of the living many creatures
Depend on fate, and their acts are wasted—
Whatever he gets, the sage should not bother;
Soul's wisdom knows that his fate is stronger.

Good luck or ill luck, if man will find it,
It is fate that found it, not his own doing.
So understanding that fate is stronger
One does not get overly happy or upset.

In grief he smarts not, in joy he laughs not;
The sage's way is eternal sameness.
For, understanding that fate is stronger,
He does not get overly happy or upset.

In danger, Aṣṭaka, I never falter,
And no anxiety hurts my mind.
I know that that is sure to befall me
What the Disposer has set for me.

10 Bugs born from sweat, birds, vegetables,
The snakes that crawl, worms, fish in water,
And stones and tree trunks and stalks of straw,
At the end of their lot all return to their source.

I know that sorrow passes and gladness,
So why, Aṣṭaka, should I let it upset me?
The what-to-do-what-nows do not upset me,
I stay alert and avoid all concern.

Aṣṭaka said:

O lord of kings, of the glorious worlds
Thou has enjoyed, of the time and the manner—
Do, sire, inform me, of all these matters:
You speak of the Law as one who knows the country.

Yayāti said:

I was a king here, of all the countries,
And won great worlds that lie beyond them.
I lived in them for a thousand-year spell,
And then I attained to the worlds above them.

The lovely world of much-lauded Indra,
Of a hundred leagues and a thousand gateways,
I dwelled in it for a thousand-year spell,
And then I attained to the world above it.

15 That unaging world divine, I attained it,
Prajāpati's world, and few can reach it.
I dwelled in it for a thousand-year spell,
And then I attained to the world above it.

Of God after God did I conquer the world
And lived in his seat as the fancy took me.

The Thirty Gods have all paid me homage,
And I rivaled those sovereigns' power and glory.

In Nandana I lived in what guise might please me,
For a myriad of centuries.
With Apsarās I played, and contemplated
The most fragrant blossoming, beautiful mountains.

Then time beyond count went vastly by me,
As I enjoyed there all the joys that Gods taste.
The Envoy of Gods of awful aspect
Cried three times "Fall!" with the lengthened accent.

King, this much knowledge had been vouchsafed me,
And then I fell, meritless, from paradise.
I heard the Gods' voices speaking in heaven,
Compassionate and mournful, king of men.

20 "O woe, Yayāti has spent his merit,
He falls whose fame and deeds spelled merit!"
And as I fell I myself addressed them,
"Why not let me fall with the honest?"

They pointed me to your site of ritual
And, seeing it, I approached it quickly.
I smelled the instructive smell of oblations
That wafted with the smoke, and was reassured!

Aṣṭaka said:

85.1 In Nandana you lived in what guise might please you,
For a myriad of centuries.
Why, eminent sage of the Kṛta Yuga,
Did you forsake it and come to earth?

Yayāti said:

As kin and kith and friend in this world
Are abandoned by people when their wealth is gone,
So when merit is gone is a man deserted
Hereafter at once by Indra and the Gods.

Aṣṭaka said:

How does one hereafter spend one's merit?
On this my mind is much bewildered.
Whose place does one reach, by what distinction?
Pray tell, for I deem that you know the country.

Yayāti said:

Cast out, they all fall to the hell-on-earth,

With much lamenting, O king of men.
Their merit gone, they grow plentiful,
Fodder for jackals, kites, and crows.

Therefore, a man should avoid in this world
The evil acts that are condemned.
I have told you all, good king—pray speak,
What more do you wish me to tell you now?

Aṣṭaka said:

When the birds of prey have ripped them asunder,
The white-necked vultures, the kites, the flies—
How do they fare, and become again?
I have never heard of the hell-on-earth!

Yayāti said:

When passed from their bodies, they clearly return
To the earth because of their gaping acts.
They fall into hell, this hell-on-earth—
They do not reckon the eons of years.

They fall to heaven for sixty thousand,
Or eighty thousand, returning years.
Then, the Ogres push them to fall their downfall,
The terrible, tusky Ogres-of-Earth.

Aṣṭaka said:

When for their evil they push them to fall,
The terrible, tusky Ogres-of-Earth,
How do they fare, and become again,
How do the dead become germs again?

Yayāti said:

As a raindrop clinging to fruit or green,
Which enters the sperm that is spilled by a man,
He thereupon enters the woman's flux
And lodges with her as the child of her womb.

They enter the herbs and the trees of the forest,
The waters, the wind, the earth, and the sky,
The four-footed and two-footed creation—
Thus do the dead become germs again.

Aṣṭaka said:

Does the germ then bear another body,
Or does he return with his body of old,
When he comes to enter that human womb?
Declare it to us, for I speak from doubt.

How does he grow his different limbs,
Get hearing and eyesight, consciousness?
Declare it all in truth at our bidding,
For we all deem, friend, that you know the country.

Yayāti said:

The ghost draws into the mother's womb,
At her season, the sperm in the flower's sap.
He functions there with the measures of it,
And in time brings the embryo to full growth.

15 When his limbs have stretched out, the man is born
As the sanctuary where the six senses lie.
With his ears he perceives in his body sound,
And so with his eye has a vision of form.

With his nose he knows smell, and taste with his tongue,
And touch with his skin, and thought with his mind.
Thus, Aṣṭaka, know how the large Ātman
Is fully grown in a creature's body.

Aṣṭaka said:

The man that has died may either be burned,
Or buried in earth, or ground to dust:
He has no being when he has died,
Then how does he later know himself?

Yayāti said:

When he sheds his spirits and gasps his last,
His good and evil acts go before him;
To another womb he follows the ghost,
Having shed his body, he takes another.

To a good womb go those who did good,
To a bad womb go those who did evil.
The evil are born as worms and flies;
Of them, mighty king, I shall not speak.

20 Four-footed, two-footed, or six-footed insects,
Thus do the dead become germs again.
I have told you all, in full detail.
What, lionlike king, have you else to ask?

Aṣṭaka said:

Is there ought that mortal man can do
To find the best worlds, by learning or penance?
At my bidding tell me fully and truly
How to reach in time the blissful worlds.

Yayāti said:

Gift, penance, peacefulness, self-control,
Uprightness, modesty, pity for all—
But stricken by darkness, so say the wise,
A man will always perish from pride.

A man of learning and self-deemed sage
Who with his learning defames another,
The worlds he finds will prove to be ending,
And his Brahman will yield no fruit to him.

Four acts there are that dispel all danger,
Or become dangerous when they're done wrongly:
Austerities, sacrifice, learning, worship,
Or each of them performed with pride.

25 If proudly honored, do not rejoice;
And do not sorrow, if abused.
It's the good who honor the good in the world,
The wicked never obtain a good mind.

See how I give, see how I worship, see how I learn, see how I vow—these they call dangers, and one should always avoid them.

The wise who know the Ancient One,
The Foundation, loved with pride of mind,
Will take on that unequaled, fiery form
And here and hereafter find ultimate peace.

Aṣṭaka said:

86.1 How does a householder act to go to the Gods, how does the mendicant and the student whose task it is to serve his teacher? And the forest dweller who is set on the path of the strict? They hold many views on this nowadays.

Yayāti said:

A successful *brahmacārin* recites his lesson when called upon, need
not be exhorted to work for his guru, rises first, goes to bed last, is
sweet, subdued, even-tempered and alert, and makes a habit of
studying. The householder will be the patron of a sacrifice when he
has a wealth that is lawfully acquired; he will make donations often,
feed his guests, and not take what others have not given him: this
is the ancient householder doctrine. That hermit attains the highest
perfection who, while dwelling in the forest, lives on his own
strength, avoids all guile, gives to others, and never vexes them, and
5 is restrained both in his eating and his actions. The mendicant lives
off no special trade, he is forever homeless, the master of his senses,

divorced from all things; he goes about unsheltered, he travels light
in short journeys and roams the countries by himself. The night in
which the worlds are won and desires and joys are overcome, that
night the sage who is self-restrained must strive to become a forest-
dweller. The forest-dweller who has set free the elements of his own
body brings ten generations before him, ten after him, and himself in
the twenty-first place, to good deeds.

Aṣṭaka said:

How many kinds of hermits are there, and how many ways of
being one? Tell us that; we wish to hear it.

Yayāti said:

He is a hermit who, while living in the forest, turns his back on the
village, and he is one too, who, while living in the village, turns his
back on the forest.

Aṣṭaka said:

10 But how does he turn his back on the village, when he lives in the
woods; or on the woods, when he lives in the village?

Yayāti said:

The forest hermit will use nothing from the village, and thus he
turns his back on the village when he lives in the forest. The hermit
who maintains no fires, no house, no clan, no Vedic school, who does
not want more for a hermit's garb than a loincloth, or more to eat
than to sustain his life—he keeps his back to the forest, while living
15 in the village. The hermit who forsakes his desires, gives up the rites,
masters his senses, and pursues this as his hermit's life, will attain
fulfillment in the world. Who will not respect the one who cleans his
teeth, cuts his nails, always bathes and grooms himself, and though
black of complexion is white in his acts? The one who is emaciated
from his mortifications, wan, shrunk in blood, flesh, and bones,
conquers this world and thereafter the world hereafter, when he is a
hermit, living like a hermit, who has transcended the pairs of
opposites. When a hermit like a cow grazes for his food with his
mouth, his previous world is fit for immortality.

Aṣṭaka said:

87.1 Who of these two will first go to union with the Gods, both running
like sun and moon, O king?

Yayāti said:

Homeless among householders, restrained among the passionate,
the mendicant will go first of the two, even while he lives in the
village, without reaching old age; or if he reaches it, he will suffer
deterioration. If he mortified himself, he will, after his mortifications
are done, do more.

What is hurtful is truthless, they say. If one seeks the Law, without thinking of gain, however penniless and poor, O king, that is uprightness, that is dedication, that is nobility.

Aṣṭaka said:

5 By whom are you sent as envoy, king,
Young, beautiful, garlanded, and resplendent?
From whence have you come and in what country,
O lord of the earth, is your royal seat?

Yayāti said:

From heaven cast to this hell-on-earth,
Have I come to Earth, my merit spent.
And after I have told you I must fall onward,
The brahmins and kings are speeding me.

I chose to fall among the honest:
"The virtuous are all assembled there."
And from Indra I did obtain this boon,
As I was near falling to earth, O king.

Aṣṭaka said:

I ask you, do not fall in your downfall,
If there are any worlds that I own here, king;
Here, up in the sky, or lodged in heaven!
For I deem you know the country of Law.

Yayāti said:

As much wealth of horses and cows is set out
On earth with the beasts of forests and mountains—
So much are your worlds set up in heaven,
This, lionlike lord of kings, you must know.

Aṣṭaka said:

10 I will give them to you; do not fall in your downfall:
Whichever worlds, king, are mine in heaven,
Whether they lie in heaven or the sky,
Scourge of the enemy, travel there fast!

Yayāti said:

My likes, not Brahmins but knowers of *Brahman*,
Do not, best of kings, accept any gifts.
As one always must give to the twiceborn, so
Have I before given, O lord of men.

None but a Brahmin shall ever live begging,
Nor the Brahmin wife of a warlike lord.
If I were to act as I never before did,
What benefit would I seek to find?

Pratardana said:

I ask you, king of enviable beauty,
I Pratardana, have I any worlds,
Whether they lie in heaven or the sky?
For I deem you know the country of Law.

Yayāti said:

O king of men, many are your worlds,
Were each to lodge you for seven days only,
Dripping with honey and mixed with butter,
And blissful, they'd last you without end.

Pratardana said:

15 I will give them to you, do not fall in your downfall.
Whichever my worlds, they must be yours,
Whether they lie in heaven or the sky,
Shed your bewilderment, travel there fast!

Yayāti said:

No king, O king, of equal splendor,
Will crave for possessions given as favors,
Though come to grief by fate's disposal.
No king of wisdom will be despotic.

A king of reason will mind the Law
And walk the path of Law and glory.
The likes of me, law-minded and knowing,
Will decline the meanness that you advise me.

Were I to do what others decline,
What benefit would I seek to find?
To King Yayāti who had thus spoken
Great King Vasumanas spoke this word:

Vasumanas said:

88.1 I, Vasumanas Rauṣidaśvi, ask you
If there is a world known for me in heaven,
Or in the sky, great-spirited king,
For I deem you know the country of Law.

Yayāti said:

Whether in the sky or on earth or horizons
Or wherever the sun shines with its heat,
So many worlds are set up in heaven
And waiting for you without ever ending.

Vasumanas said:

I give them to you, do not fall in your downfall;

Whichever my worlds, they must be yours.
King, buy them from me for a stalk of straw,
If, sage, a gift is repugnant to you.

Yayāti said:

I do not remember any false bargain
Who from childhood feared to take anything wrong.
Were I to do what others decline,
What benefit would I seek to find?

Vasumanas said:

5 Accept these worlds as your own, O king,
As my gift, if you decline to buy them.
I surely shall never go near them, ruler,
Let all these worlds henceforth be yours.

Śibi said:

I, Śibi Auśīnara, now ask you,
If any worlds are coming to me, friend,
Whether they lie in heaven or the sky,
For I deem you know the country of Law.

Yayāti said:

You have never, sage, in word or thought
Refused anyone who solicited you, king.
Hence worlds without end await you in heaven,
Aglow with lightning, glorious, immense!

Śibi said:

Accept these worlds for your own, O king,
As a gift, if you do not want to buy them.
I will not own them that now I have given,
The worlds, where you might go and attend.

Yayāti said:

Just as you are Indra's match in might,
And your worlds, king of men, are without end,
So I have no joy in a world that is gifted,
I do not welcome, Śibi, your gift!

Aṣṭaka said:

10 You have not welcomed the worlds of any one of us, king. But we have made our gift to you and shall now go to hell.

Yayāti said:

As you have given to one who deserves, you are strict in your truthfulness and benevolence. Yet I dare not do what I have never done before.

Aṣṭaka said:

Whose are these five golden chariots we see before us, which stand there shining high, ablaze like flame crests?

Yayāti said:

They shall carry yourselves, these golden chariots, which stand there shining high, ablaze like flame crests!

Aṣṭaka said:

King, you ascend your chariot and stride wide in the sky! We shall come after you whenever our time comes.

Yayāti said:

15 We must now go all together; we have conquered heaven together. See how our path goes beyond the sky to the seat of the Gods!

Vaiśaṃpāyana said:

All these excellent kings ascended the chariots and departed, striding up to heaven along with the sun rays, covering heaven and earth with the merit of their Law.

Aṣṭaka said:

I thought I would be the first to go;
Great-spirited Indra was always my friend.
Why is it Śibi Auśīnara
With such speed alone outpaces our horses?

Yayāti said:

Śibi, Uśīnara's son, has given all the wealth he had found to find the Way of the Gods. Therefore he is the best of us.

Austerities, gifts, and truth, and Law,
Forbearance, modesty, patience, luster,
Were ever Śibi's, that matchless king's,
Who, king, knew no cruelty in his heart;
And because his modesty hampered him,
He now outpaces us on his chariot.

Vaiśaṃpāyana said:

20 Once more did Aṣṭaka put a question
To his Indra-like grandfather, curiously:
"I ask you, king, pray tell me the truth,
Whence are you, whose are you, of whom the son?
What have you wrought no one else shall wreak
In this world, be he a baron or brahmin?"

Yayāti said:

Yayāti am I who am Nahuṣa's offspring,
And of Pūru the father. I owned all the world.
To those who are mine I teach mysteries—
As your grandfather do I now stand revealed.

Of this earth entire I had made a conquest,
Then gave it to brahmins, with, tied on a plateau,
Beautiful, single-hoofed sacrifice horses.
Then the Gods obtained their holy shares.

I gave this earth away to the brahmins,
This earth entire, with its fullness of horses,
And cattle, and gold, and the best of riches—
And the cows counted hundreds of myriads.

In truth, the earth was mine, and heaven,
And the Fire blazed up among humankind.
This word of mine is not spoken idly,
For the strict pay homage to the truth.
All these Gods, these hermits, these worlds
I must honor with truth, for so do I crave.

25 He who tells the tale of us all who have conquered heaven, to the
best of the twiceborn that do not demur, shall share our world with us.

Vaiśaṃpāyana said:

And thus was this most great-spirited king,
Scourge of his enemies, saved by his grandsons.
He crossed beyond earth, he of noblest actions,
And went heavenward, threading earth with his feats.

Janamejaya said:

89.1 My lord, I wish to learn who the kings were that became the
dynasts in the line of Pūru, how many they were and what manner
of men, how mighty they were and puissant. For in this dynasty no
king ever lacked in character or prowess or offspring. Of these kings
of famous feats and wisdom I wish to hear the exploits in their fullness, O man of austerities!

Vaiśaṃpāyana said:

Aye, I shall tell you of what you ask, of the heroic dynasts of Pūru,
whose might matched Indra's.
5 Pūru begot on Pauṣṭi three warrior sons, Pravīra, Īśvara, and
Raudrāśva. Pravīra was the dynast. This king had a son by Śūrasenī,
heroic Manasyu, who became the lotus-eyed herdsman of four-
cornered earth. He had three sons by Sauvīrī—Subhru, Saṃhanana,
and Vāgmin, who were all warlike champions. Raudrāśva had ten
sons by an Apsarā, great archers all, who became warriors and
patrons of sacrifices, rich in offspring and widely renowned, experts
on all sorts of missiles and devoted to the Law—Ṛcepu, Kakṣepu,
mighty Kṛkaṇepu, Sthāṇḍilyepu, Vanepu, warlike Sthalepu, strong
10 Tejepu, and wise Satyepu, whose prowess was like Indra's, Dharmepu,

and lastly Saṃtānepu, puissant like a God. Those sons, by Anādhṛṣṭi,
offered up the Royal Consecration and the Horse Sacrifice, my son.
Ṛcepu had a sage son by the name of Matināra, who, O king,
himself had four sons of boundless might, Taṃsu, Mahat, Atiratha,
and the incomparably lustrous Druhyu. Among them it was the
powerful Taṃsu who carried on the line of the Pauravas; he won
blazing fame and conquered the earth. Taṃsu begot Ilina, who was
a great conqueror and won all the earth. Ilina fathered on Rathantarī
15 five sons, like the five elements, O king: Duḥṣanta, Śūra, Bhīma,
Pravasu, and Vasu.

The oldest of them was Duḥṣanta, who became the king, Janamejaya. And from him was born by Sakuntalā the wise King Bharata.
It is from him that the great fame of the line of the Bhāratas began.
Bharata begot nine sons on his three wives, but the king did not
approve any one of them, for they were not of his stature. Thereupon
Bharata offered up grand sacrifices and received a son from Bharadvāja
by the name of Bhūmanyu, O Bhārata. The scion of the Pauravas
deemed himself Bhūmanyu's father and consecrated him Young King,
20 O best of the Bhāratas. Then the king himself had a little son, Vitatha,
and this Vitatha became a son of Bhūmanyu. By his wife Puṣkariṇī
this Bhūmanyu Ṛcīka had Suhotra, Suhotar, Suhavis, and Suyajus.
The eldest of the princes, Suhotra, inherited the kingdom; he offered
up many Soma Sacrifices such as the Royal Consecration and the
Horse Sacrifice. He had the pleasure of all of ocean-skirted earth filled
with elephants, cattle, and horses, and abounding in multifarious
precious stones. Earth seemed to sink under the many burdens he put
on her, massed with elephants, horses, and chariots and teeming with
25 people. While Suhotra reigned and ruled his subjects with the Law,
earth was dotted with sanctuaries and sacrificial poles by the hundreds
of thousands. People and crops prospered on earth, and earth herself
rejoiced in the company of the Gods.

To this King Suhotra, O Bhārata, three sons were born by Aikṣvākī
—Ajamīḍha, Sumīḍha, Purumīḍha. Ajamīḍha was the chief of
them, and the dynasty was lodged with him. He had three
women on whom he fathered six sons—Dhūminī got Ṛkṣa, Nīlī got
Duḥṣanta and Parameṣṭhin, Keśinī bore Jahnu, Jana, and Rūpina. All
the Pāñcālas spring from Duḥṣanta and Parameṣṭhin, and the Kuśika
30 lineages spring from Jahnu of boundless might, O king. They say that
Ṛkṣa, who was older than Jana and Rūpina, became king, and from
Ṛkṣa was born Saṃvaraṇa, who founded your line, O king.

While Saṃvaraṇa Ārkṣa ruled the earth as king, a very great
disaster overtook his people, so we have heard. The kingdom was
torn asunder by all sorts of plagues and hit by famine, pestilence,
drought, and disease. The forces of their rivals set upon the Bhāratas,

rocking the earth with their hosts of elephants, horsemen, footmen, and chariots. The king of the Pāñcālas marched out against him, devastating the country, and with ten armies defeated him in battle. King Saṃvaraṇa, panic-stricken, took to flight with wife, sons, ministers, and friends. He then settled in the woodlands of the great river Indus, at the edge of its watershed close to the mountains. There the Bhāratas, fallen into distress, dwelled for many years—like a thousand years for those who were settled there.

Then the blessed Lord Vasiṣṭha the seer came to the Bhāratas, and when he came they rose religiously to welcome and greet him. All the Bhāratas brought him the welcoming gift that they handed to the resplendent seer with all honors. Eight years he had lived with them when the king of his own accord chose him. "You must be our priest," he said, "and we shall strive to regain our kingdom." Saying "OṂ!" Vasiṣṭha consented to the Bhāratas. Then, we hear, he consecrated the Paurava as the sovereign of all the baronage, to become the one horn of the entire wide earth. Once more the king sat in the grand city where the Bhāratas had sat before, and once more he made all the princes bring their tribute. Having regained his land, Ajamīḍha's mighty son Saṃvaraṇa offered up many great sacrifices with rich stipends.

Saṃvaraṇa's wife Tapatī Saurī bore him a son Kuru, and seeing that he was law-minded the people chose him for their king. It is his name that made Kurujangala famous, the Land of the Kurus, which the ascetic hallowed with his austerities. We hear of these sons of his, Aśvavat, Abhiṣyat, Citraratha, Muni, and the renowned Janamejaya: these five sons were born by the spirited Vāhinī. Abhiṣyat had Parikṣit, the mighty Śabalāśva, Abhirāja, Virāja, the strong Śālmali, Uccaiḥsravas, Bhadrakāra, and lastly Jitāri. In their line were born seven more sons, Janamejaya and others, puissant and famed for the virtues of their enterprise. All of Parikṣit's sons were knowledgeable in Law and Profit—Kakṣasena, Ugrasena, Citrasena the mighty, Indrasena, Suṣena, and Bhīmasena by name. Janamejaya's mighty sons have become famous on earth—Dhṛtarāṣṭra the firstborn, Pāṇḍu, Bāhlīka, Niṣadha of great heat, and the powerful Jāmbunāda, Kuṇḍodara, Padāti, and Vasāti who was the eighth, all experts on Law and Profit and bent upon the well-being of the creatures.

Dhṛtarāṣṭra thereupon became king, and his sons were Kuṇḍika, Hastin, Vitarka, Krātha and Kuṇḍala, Haviḥsravas, Indrābha, and the unvanquished Sumanyu . . . . Pratīpa had three sons, O bull among the Bhāratas, Devāpi, Śaṃtanu, and the warlike Bāhlīka. Devāpi, urged by a yearning for the merit of Law, became a hermit, and Śaṃtanu inherited the kingdom with the great warrior Bāhlīka.

In the lineage of Bhārata many more mettlesome warriors and
55 great kings were born in the image of Gods and seers; and likewise in
the line of Manu there were many other godlike warriors of like
prowess who made prosperous the dynasty that sprang from Ilā.

Janamejaya said:
90.1 I have now heard from you, O brahmin, the vast origins of our
ancestors, and the noble kings in our lineage have been recounted.
But this account, which I hold dear, has been retold too briefly to
please me. Therefore, tell it to me again with greater detail, the same
divine account from Manu Prajāpati onward. For to whom should
their holy genealogy not bring joy, sublime and increased with the
glorification of the virtues of the Law of the good? Abundant fame
stands firmly rooted in all three worlds, of these men who were gifted
5 with virtues and might and prowess and puissance, character, and
enterprise. I cannot listen enough to this history that has the taste of
the Elixir of Immortality!

Vaiśaṃpāyana said:
Then listen to me recite, just as I have heard it from Dvaipāyana,
your own complete illustrious genealogy.

From Dakṣa, Aditi. From Aditi, Vivasvat. From Vivasvat, Manu.
From Manu, Ilā. From Ilā, Purūravas. From Purūravas, Āyus. From
Āyus, Nahuṣa. From Nahuṣa, Yayāti. Yayāti had two wives. Uśanas's
daughter was Devayānī, Vṛṣaparvan's daughter was Śarmiṣṭhā. On
this there is the chronicle: "Devayānī bore Yadu and Turvaśu,
10 Śarmiṣṭhā Vārṣaparvaṇī bore Druhyu, Anu, and Pūru." From Yadu
among them the Yādavas; from Pūru, the Pauravas.

Pūru's wife was Kausalyā. On her he begot Janamejaya, who
offered up three Horse Sacrifices; and after offering with the Viśvajit
sacrifice, he entered the forest. Janamejaya married Anantā of the
Mādhavas, who bore him Prācinvat, who subjugated the East as far as
the sunrise; hence his name Prācinvat.

Prācinvat married Aśmakī, who bore him Saṃyāti. Saṃyāti married
Dṛṣadvat's daughter Varāngī, who bore him Ahaṃpāti. Ahaṃpāti
married Kṛtavīrya's daughter Bhānumatī, who bore him Sārvabhauma.
15 Sārvabhauma triumphed and carried off Sunandā of the Kaikeyas, who
bore him Jayatsena. Jayatsena married Suśravā of Vidarbha, who bore
him Arācīna. Arācīna married another woman of Vidarbha, Maryādā,
who bore him Mahābhauma. Mahābhauma married Prasenajit's
daughter Suyajñā, who bore him Ayutanāyin, who performed a
myriad Human Sacrifices, hence his name Ayutanāyin.

20 Ayutanāyin married Pṛthuśravas's daughter Bhāsā, who bore him
Akrodhana. Akrodhana married Karaṇḍu of Kalinga, who bore him

Devātithi. Devātithi married Maryādā of Videha, who bore him Ṛca. Ṛca married Sudevā of Anga, on whom he begot a son Ṛkṣa. Ṛkṣa married Takṣaka's daughter Jvālā; on her he fathered a son named Matināra. Matināra held a sacrificial Session of twelve years on the river Sarasvatī.When the Session was finished, Sarasvatī came to him and chose him for her husband; on her he begot a son Taṃsu.

On this there is the chronicle: "Sarasvatī gave birth to a son Taṃsu by Matināra; Taṃsu begot a son Ilina upon Kālindī."

Ilina begot on Rathantarī five sons, the first being Duḥṣanta.
30 Duḥṣanta married Viśvāmitra's daughter Śakuntalā, who bore him Bhārata.

On that there are two verses: "The mother is the father's water sack. He is the father by whom the son is born. Support your son, Duḥṣanta, do not reject Śakuntalā. A son who has seed, O king of men, saves from Yama's realm. You are the planter of this child, Śakuntalā has spoken the truth." Hence his name Bharata.

Bharata married Sarvasena's daughter, Sunandā of the Kāśis, who
35 bore him Bhūmanyu. Bhūmanyu married Vijayā of the Daśārhas, who bore him Suhotra. Suhotra married the Ikṣvāku woman Suvarṇā, who bore him Hastin, who had this city Hāstinapura built; hence its name Hāstinapura.

Hastin married Yaśodharā of Trigarta, who bore him Vikuṇṭhana. Vikuṇṭhana married Sudevā of the Daśārhas, who bore him Ajamīḍha. Ajamīḍha had twenty-four hundred sons, by the Kaikeya woman, the Nāga woman, the Gandhāra woman, Vimalā, and Ṛkṣā. They each became kings and dynasts. Among them Saṃvaraṇa
40 carried the line. Saṃvaraṇa married Vivasvat's daughter Tapatī, who bore him Kuru. Kuru married Śubhāngī of the Daśārhas, who bore him Viḍūratha. Viḍūratha married Saṃpriyā of the Mādhavas, who bore him Arugvat. Arugvat married Amṛtā of Magadha, who bore him Parikṣit. Parikṣit married Bahuda's daughter Suyaśā, who bore
45 him Bhīmasena. Bhīmasena married Sukumārī of the Kaikeyas, who bore him Paryaśravas, whom they call Pratipa. Pratipa married Sunandā of the Śibis; on her he begot Devāpi, Śaṃtanu, and Bāhlīka. Devāpi while still a child entered the forest; Śaṃtanu then became king.

On this there is the chronicle: "Every old man he touched with his hands felt joy and became young again. Therefore they know him as Śaṃtanu." Hence his name Śaṃtanu.
50 Śaṃtanu married the Ganges, daughter of Bhagīratha, who bore him Devavrata, whom they call Bhīṣma. Bhīṣma, to do his father a favor, brought him Satyavatī to marry, the mother, whom they call Gandhakālī. She had had Dvaipāyana as a child by Parāśara while still unmarried. She bore Śaṃtanu two sons, Citrāngada and

Vicitravīrya. Of them, Citrāngada was killed by a Gandharva before reaching manhood. Vicitravīrya then became king. Vicitravīrya married two daughters of the king of the Kāśis by his wife Kausalyā—Ambikā and Ambālikā. Vicitravīrya, however, came to die childless. Satyavatī then began to worry lest the line of Duḥṣanta should become extinct. She thought of the seer Dvaipāyana. He appeared before her, saying, "What can I do?" She said to him, "Your brother Vicitravīrya has died childless. Father proper children for him." "The best," he said and fathered three sons, Dhṛtarāṣṭra, Pāṇḍu, and Vidura. Of them, Dhṛtarāṣṭra the king had a hundred sons by Gāndhārī from a boon of Dvaipāyana. Four of Dhṛtarāṣṭra's sons stood out, Duryodhana, Duḥśāsana, Vikarṇa, and Citrasena. Pāṇḍu had two wives, Kuntī and Mādrī, both gems among women.

Once, Pāṇḍu went hunting and saw a seer covering a doe, coupling with her. As he was jumping the doe, before he had reached the sap of his lust and was sated, Pāṇḍu shot him with an arrow. Wounded by the arrow, he said to Pāṇḍu, "Because you, who follow the Law and know the sap of lust, have shot me before I reached the sap of lust, therefore you too will at once return to the five elements when you are in the same state, before reaching the sap of lust." Pāṇḍu paled and, avoiding the curse, did not lie with his wives. And he said, "I have got this because of my own fickleness, and I hear that one who is childless has no worlds." To Kuntī he said, "Bear children for me." She bore children then, Yudhiṣṭhira by Dharma, Bhīma by the Wind, Arjuna by Śakra. Pleased, Pāṇḍu said to her, "Your cowife is childless. Let proper offspring be fathered on her." "So shall it be," said Kuntī. On Mādrī the Aśvins then fathered Nakula and Sahadeva. Once, seeing Mādrī in her finery, Pāṇḍu felt love, and as soon as he touched her he fell dead. Mādrī climbed up after him when he lay on the pyre. She said to Kuntī, "The lady must look after the twins carefully."

Later the five Pāṇḍavas, accompanied by Kuntī, were taken by hermits to Hāstinapura and handed over to Bhīṣma and Vidura. There they were meant to be burned in the lacquer house, but this failed, because of a warning by Vidura. Then, having meanwhile killed Hiḍimba, they went to Ekacakrā. There, in Ekacakrā, they killed the Rākṣasa Baka and set out for the city of the Pāñcāla. Thereupon they found Draupadī for a wife and returned to their own country in good health.

They begot competent sons. Yudhiṣṭhira had Prativindhya, the Wolf-Belly Sutasoma, Arjuna Śrutakīrta, Nakula Śatānīka, Sahadeva Śrutakarman. Yudhiṣṭhira obtained the daughter of Govāsana of the Śibis, Devikā, at her bridegroom choice; on her he begot a son Yaudheya. Bhīmasena married a woman of the Kāśis, Baladharā, the

85 prize of his prowess; on her he begot a son Sarvaga. Arjuna went to
Dvāravatī and married Kṛṣṇa Vāsudeva's sister, Subhadrā; on her he
begot his son Abhimanyu. Nakula married Kareṇuvatī of the Cedis;
on her he begot a son Niramitra. Sahadeva married Vijayā of the
Madras at her bridegroom choice; on her he begot a son Suhotra. But
before Bhīmasena had fathered a son Ghaṭotkaca on the Rākṣasī
Hiḍimbā. These are the eleven sons of the Pāṇḍavas.
90 Abhimanyu married Virāṭa's daughter Uttarā. By her he had a
stillborn child. Pṛthā* took it in her arms, at the behest of Vāsudeva,
supreme among men, who said, "I shall give life to this six-month
baby." Having revived him, he said of him, "Born in an extinct line,
he shall be called Parikṣit." Parikṣit married Madravatī, who bore
him Janamejaya. To Janamejaya two sons were born by Vapuṣṭamā,
95 Śatānīka and Śanku. Śatānīka had a son by the woman of Videha, by
the name of Aśvamedhadatta.
Thus has the lineage of Pūru and the Pāṇḍavas been described: he
who hears this genealogy of Pūru is freed from all evil.

Vaiśaṃpāyana said:

91.1 There once was a king of the name of Mahābhiṣa, a lord of the
earth who sprang from the dynasty of Ikṣvāku, true in his promises
and of proven prowess. With a thousand Horse Sacrifices and a
hundred Horse Race Festivals he satisfied the lord of the Gods, and so
the king attained to heaven.
One day the Gods waited on Brahmā. The royal seers were there,
and so was King Mahābhiṣa. Then the Ganges, greatest of rivers, came
to pay court to the Grandfather. The wind blew up her skirt, which
5 was white like the light of the moon, and the throngs of the Gods
immediately lowered their faces. But King Mahābhiṣa looked at the
river fearlessly. Mahābhiṣa earned the contempt of the blessed Lord
Brahmā, who said, "You shall be born among the mortals and once
more attain to the worlds."
The king thereupon reflected upon all the kings and ascetics and
then chose the many-splendored Pratīpa for his father. The river
goddess, on seeing the king lose his composure, went away musing
about him in her heart. As she went on her way, she spied the
10 celestial Vasus, crestfallen, their puissance darkened by despair. Seeing
them in such a state, the river goddess asked, "Why are you looking
so lost? Is there no safety for celestials?" The divine Vasus said,
"Great river, we made a small mistake and for that the great-
spirited Vasiṣṭha cursed us vehemently! We foolishly passed by that
strict seer Vasiṣṭha when he was sitting at his twilight rites hidden
from our eyes. He cursed us angrily, 'Be born in a womb!' And what

* = Kuntī.

that scholar of the *Veda* pronounces cannot be undone. Therefore, become you a human woman on earth and bear the Vasus as your
15 sons.We cannot enter a human womb which is not pure." The Ganges consented and said to the Vasus, 'What eminent man among mortals shall be your begetter?"

The Vasus said:

A law-minded king, Śaṃtanu by name, will be born in the world of mortals as the son of Pratīpa. He shall be our begetter.

The Ganges said:

That was in my mind too, flawless Gods, precisely so. I shall do him a kindness and so fulfil your desire.

The Vasus said:

You must throw your sons in the water when they have been born, so that, O Goddess who walk in three worlds, our atonement will not last too long.

The Ganges said:

I shall do so, but let him have one son, so his lying with me for a son will not remain fruitless.

The Vasus said:

20 We shall each of us spare you one-eighth of the sperm, and from that sperm the son that you and he desire shall be born. But he shall beget no offspring among the mortals. Therefore your son will remain sonless, for all his virility.

Vaiśaṃpāyana said:

Thus the Vasus made a covenant with the Ganges, and with happy hearts they hastened on their intended way.

Vaiśaṃpāyana said:

92.1 There was King Pratīpa who was devoted to the well-being of all creatures. For many years he sat on the bank of the river Ganges, muttering his prayers. The Ganges assumed the form of a woman who had all the virtues of beauty and most seducingly she rose from the water like Śrī incarnate. As the royal seer sat astudying, the spirited, divinely beautiful Goddess of the lovely face sat on his right thigh, which was sturdy like a *śāla* trunk. King Pratīpa said to the spirited woman, "What can I do for you, my beautiful? What favor do you wish?"

The woman said:

5 I want you, king, lord of the Kurus—make love to me! For the strict do not countenance the rejection of a woman who is in love.

Pratīpa said:

Beautiful woman, I will not lust after the wives of other men or women who are not of my station. That, you must know, is the vow I have sworn by the Law.

The woman said:

I am not unfavored or forbidden or notorious! I am a beautiful celestial virgin! Love me, king, as I love you.

Pratīpa said:

I refuse the favor you urge from me. Otherwise my breaking of the Law will destroy me—I swore a vow! You embrace me while sitting on my right thigh, beautiful woman, but that is the place to sit for children and daughters-in-law, shy girl. The share of a mistress is on the left, but you have avoided that side. Therefore I cannot pleasure you. Become my daughter-in-law, my lovely; I choose you for my son! For you, my buxom girl, came and took the side of the daughter-in-law.

The woman said:

You know the Law—then so shall it be. I shall be united with your son. But it is for my love of you that I shall love the famous lineage of the Bhāratas. However many kings there are on earth, your dynasty is their refuge. Centuries will expire before I have counted the virtues that are famed of this dynasty—its goodness is peerless!

He must not know of my high birth, and whatever I do your son should never question. Living with your son in this way I shall prosper his pleasure; and for his sons, his merits, and favors he shall attain to heaven.

Vaiśaṃpāyana said:

He consented, O king, and she disappeared in the river. And as he waited for his son to be born, the king kept the promise in mind.

In the meantime, Pratīpa, bull of the barons, and his wife performed acts of austerity to obtain a son, O scion of the Kurus; and though they were old, a son was born to them—Mahābhiṣa. Since he was born the issue of a serene man he was called Śaṃtanu; and remembering the imperishable worlds he had conquered with his own acts, Śaṃtanu, O strictest of the Kurus, became a man of good deeds.

When his son Śaṃtanu had grown to manhood, Pratīpa instructed him: "Once a woman approached me for your sake, Śaṃtanu. If that same beautiful woman comes to you in secret, son, a celestial woman of great loveliness, and she seeks love to bear you sons, you must not question her about who she is or whose she is; and if she does anything, you must not question her, blameless son, but love her as she loves you, at my behest," he said to him.

King Pratīpa, thus having instructed his son Śaṃtanu, anointed him king in his own realm and entered the forest. This new king, wise Śaṃtanu, a famous archer on earth, became an ardent hunter who forever ranged the forest. Once, while laying low deer and buffalo, the strict king followed by himself the course of the river Ganges, which is sought out by Siddhas and Cāraṇas. And there he saw one day a beautiful woman who fairly blazed with loveliness, like Śrī the lotus goddess come to earth. Her body was flawless, her teeth impeccable, and celestial ornaments adorned her. She was alone, wearing a sheer skirt; and she shone like the calyx of a lotus. When he saw her, he shivered, astounded by the perfection of her shape; and this overlord of men could not cease drinking her with his eyes.

And she, as soon as she had spied the splendid king on his wanderings, could not cease watching him wantonly, and love brought fondness to her heart. Then the king spoke to her, coaxing her with a gentle voice: "Art thou a Goddess, or a maiden of the Dānavas or Gandharvas, or perchance an Apsarā? Or art thou a Yakṣī, or a Snake sprite, or a mortal woman, slim-waisted lady? Whoever thou art that appearest like the child of a God, be my wife, my beautiful!"

Hearing the king's soft and sweet and smiling word, she remembered the covenant of the Vasus and approached him innocently. And gladdening with her words the heart of the king, she said to him, "I shall be your obedient queen, O lord of the earth. But if perhaps I do something, whether it pleases or displeases you, O king, I must never be stopped nor harshly spoken to. If you will act thus I shall live with you, sire. But once you stop me or scold me, I shall surely forsake you."

"So shall it be!" he replied, O strictest of Bhāratas; and with this great king she found joy beyond compare. And Śaṃtanu, having found her, enjoyed her as he pleased, restraining himself and bearing in mind that she was not to be questioned. The lord of the land became content with the manner of her behavior, the perfection of her beauty, and with her secret ministrations. And the divinely lovely Goddess herself, Gangā the river who travels her three journeys, in the lustrously human form she had assumed became the obedient wife of a man whose love ripened with his fortunes—Śaṃtanu, lionlike king whose majesty matched Indra's might. With the skills of consummate love that were waited on by gentle words and affections she made the king love her; and he loved as she did. And so immersed was the king in his pleasure, and so carried away by the talents of this superb woman, that he was not aware of how many years, or seasons, or months, were passing by. While the lord of men made love to her as the spirit seized them, he begot on her eight sons who resembled immortals. And each son as soon as he was born she threw into the water; and saying "I do you a favor," she drowned each in the river Ganges. It did not please King Śaṃtanu, but he dared not say a word lest she forsake him.

Then when the eighth son was born, she seemed to be laughing, and the king, who yearned for a son of his own, was grief-stricken and said to her, "Don't kill him! Who are you and whose? Why do

you kill your sons? Do not incur the grave sin of infanticide! Stop,
evil woman!"

The woman said:

Good father, so desirous of sons, I shall not kill your son. But my
sojourn is now worn out, for the covenant has been carried out. I am
the Ganges, daughter of Jahnu, cherished by the hosts of the great
seers! It was to accomplish a purpose of the Gods that I have lived
50 with you. They were the eight Vasus of great fortune and might, these
sons, who had become mortals by a curse of Vasiṣṭha. There is no
begetter like you on earth, and no mortal nurse can be found in this
world the like of me, hence I became a mortal to be their mother.
By fathering the eight Vasus you have won the imperishable worlds.
Such was the covenant of the divine Vasus that they concluded with
me: I was to deliver each from his human birth as soon as he was
born. Thus they were freed from the curse of the great-spirited Āpava.
Let all be well with you—I must go. Protect your son who shall be
55 great in his vows. My temporary sojourn here was in the midst of the
Vasus: know that this son is my issue, Gangādatta, Gift-of-the-Ganges!

Śaṃtanu said:

93.1 Who was this Āpava, and what wrong had the Vasus done that he
cursed them to assume human form? And what has this boy
Gangādatta done that he now must live among the mortals? The
Vasus are sovereigns of all the world; then why were they born among
men? Tell me this, daughter of Jahnu.

Vaiśaṃpāyana said:

At his word the Ganges replied to the king, she the divine daughter
5 of Jahnu to her husband Śaṃtanu, bull among men: "Varuṇa had
once a son, O best of the Bhāratas, the famous hermit named
Vasiṣṭha, who is also called Āpava. He had a holy hermitage on the
slope of the king of mountains, Meru, which was peopled with herds
of deer and flocks of birds and in all seasons abloom with flowers.
There Vasiṣṭha did his mortifications, the great saint, in the forest
where sweet roots and fruit and water were plentiful, best of the
Bhāratas.

"Now there was a daughter of Dakṣa, Surabhi, who was very
proud; and this Goddess, O bull among Bhāratas, gave birth to a cow,
by Kaśyapa, for the good of the world, the great cow of all plenty.
The law-minded Vasiṣṭha obtained this cow as his sacrificial milch cow.
10 And this cow lived in that wilderness of ascetics that was peopled
with hermits and grazed in the lovely and lawly woods without a fear.

"Then upon a time there came to this wood that Gods and divine
seers visited all the divine Vasus headed by Pṛthu. They roamed with
their wives all over the woods and made love in its lovely hills and

groves. The slim-waisted wife of one of the Vasus, O prince who are
Indra's peer, wandered in that woods and saw the cow, the great cow
of all plenty, which belonged to the hermit Vasiṣṭha. She was filled
with amazement by the perfection of its manner and abundance, and
she showed the cow to Dyaus, O lord with the eyes of a bull, this
well-fed, well-yielding, well-tailed and well-faced shining cow that had
15 all virtues and a manner beyond compare. Of such excellence was the
cow that the joy-giving wife of the Vasu showed to the Vasu, O lord
of kings, joy of the Pauravas.

"Thereupon, as soon as he saw that cow, O Indra-like, elephantlike
king, Dyaus said to the Goddess, describing its beauties, 'This lovely
black-eyed cow belongs to Vasiṣṭha, my buxom, black-eyed Goddess,
the seer who owns this lovely woods. A mortal who drinks its sweet
milk, slim-waisted queen, will live ten thousand years without losing
20 his youth.' When the slim-waisted, flawlessly shaped Goddess heard
this, O best of kings, she said to her husband of radiant luster, 'I
have in the world of men a friend who is a princess, Jitāvatī is her
name, a beautiful woman in the bloom of her youth. She is the
daughter of a wise royal seer who is true to his vows, King Uśīnara,
and she is famed in the world of men for her perfect beauty. I want
this cow and its calf for her, blessed husband. Fetch it quickly, you best
of immortals that prosper merit, so that my friend may drink its milk
and be the only one, O giver of pride, among humankind who is free
25 from age and disease. Pray do this for me, blessed and blameless
husband, for no other kindness than this would be kinder to me!'

"Hearing this word of the Goddess, Dyaus, to do her a favor,
carried off that cow with the help of his brothers who were headed
by Pṛthu. Charged by the lotus-eyed Goddess, Dyaus was no longer
able to reckon the awesome austerities of the seer, O king. So the cow
was stolen, but his downfall because of it he failed to weigh. Then
Varuṇa's son returned to his hermitage with fruit that he had
gathered and did not find his cow and its calf in his beautiful forest.
The ascetic started searching for it in the woods, but in spite of all
30 his searching the lofty-minded hermit did not find it. Looking with
his divine eye he saw that the cow had been abducted, and at once he
was in the grip of his anger and cursed the Vasus: 'Because the Vasus
have stolen my well-tailed milch cow, therefore they shall all surely
be born among men!' Thus did the blessed lord curse the Vasus, O bull
among Bhāratas, that most strict hermit Āpava, who was seized by his
fury. And having cursed them the blessed man set his mind on
mortifications.

"It was thus, sire, that the ascetic and brahminic seer of much
might cursed in his wrath the eight divine Vasus. Then the great-
spirited Gods returned to his hermitage and, knowing that they had

35 been cursed, approached the seer. The Vasus tried to pacify him, O
bull among princes, but found no grace from that strictest of seers
Āpava, who was wise in all the Laws, O tiger among men. The law-
minded hermit said, 'You, Dhara, and the other Vasus, are cursed, but
after one year you shall come to the end of your curse. But Dyaus,
for whose sake you have been cursed by me, shall live for a long time
in the world of men by his own doing. It is not to commit a falsehood
that I speak to you in my anger! The great-minded God shall bear no
offspring among men. He shall become a law-abiding mortal, expert
on all weapons, and devoted to his father's well-being; but he shall
forsake the pleasure of women.'

"Having thus spoken to all the Vasus, the great seer went his way.
40 Thereupon they all came to me and implored me that I bestow a boon
on them, as I did, O king: 'Throw us in the water of the Ganges when
each of us is born.' And so exactly have I done, to deliver the cursed
Gods from the world of men. But Dyaus alone, O best of kings, shall
have to live in the world of men for a long time, because of the curse
of the seer."

When the Goddess had finished her tale she disappeared there and
then. And, taking the boy child with her, she went her own way. He
became known under two names, Devavrata and Gāṅgeya, this son of
Śaṃtanu, who surpassed Śaṃtanu in virtues. And Śaṃtanu himself
sorrowfully repaired to his own castle.

45 I shall celebrate the boundless virtue of this Śaṃtanu and the
greatness of this great-spirited king who was the scion of Bharata and
whose illustrious history is styled the *Mahābhārata*.

Vaiśaṃpāyana said:

94.1 This King Śaṃtanu was a sage, honored by Gods, kings, and seers,
and inspirited by the Law. In all the worlds he was famous for being
true to his word. Self-control, generosity, forbearance, resoluteness,
perseverance, and a high majesty were the perennial virtues that were
lodged with the mettlesome Śaṃtanu, a bull among kings. And, thus
endowed with virtue, this king, equally proficient in the Law and in
Profit, was the herdsman of the lineage of Bharata, and of all good
people. His neck was marked like a conch shell, his shoulders were
wide, his power was like a rutting elephant's; and Law for him was
5 established over Pleasure and Profit: such were the virtues that were
lodged with the mettlesome Śaṃtanu, O bull among Bhāratas. There
was no baron like him in the Law. Him, most eminent judge of all the
Laws, who lived by his Law, the princes of the earth consecrated to rule
the realm. And with that herdsman of the Bhāratas all the princes of
earth were freed from sorrow, fear, and worry, and woke every
morning from happy dreams. At that time, since the world was
guarded by princes that were led by Śaṃtanu, brahmindom reigned

supreme by the restraint of all the classes. The baronage served brahmindom, the commoners were devoted to the baronage, and the serfs, humbly loving brahmindom and baronage, served the
10 commoners. Seated in lovely Hāstinapura, the central city of the Kurus, he swayed all earth to her boundaries of oceans.

King was he equal to the king of the Gods, who knew the Law, upright, true to his word. The greatest fortune visited him as he sought Law and generosity and austerity. No passion or hatred did he foster; his aspect was benign as the moon's, in heat he emulated the sun, in speed the force of the wind; in his wrath he matched Death, in forbearance the earth. Neither cattle nor boar, deer nor fowl suffered useless death, king, when Śaṃtanu lorded the earth. The kingdom was ruled by brahmindom and Law, while that fair-spirited Śaṃtanu impartially ruled the creatures without lust or passion.
15 That was the time when rites were performed in worship of Gods, seers, and ancestors, and no unlawful death befell any breathing creature. Of the hapless and the friendless, and of all that were born from beast, the king was the father. While that overlord of kings of kings, that greatest of the Princes of the Kurus ruled, speech was wedded to truth, thought to Law and giving. Three times three foursomes of years did the king take his pleasure of women; then he
20 became a hermit. His son Gāngeya, the Vasu who was now named Devavrata, and of like beauty, like conduct, like behavior, like learning, excelled in all weapons and, among all other princes, was mighty of mettle, mighty in strength, mighty in prowess, and mighty with chariots.

Once when he had shot a deer, King Śaṃtanu followed the Ganges downstream and saw that little water stood in the river. Seeing her so, this bull among men Śaṃtanu began to worry. "Why is it that the queen of rivers does not flow as it did before?" The spirited prince looked for the reason and saw a large boy of perfect body and handsome face who was handling a divine bow like the God Sacker of Cities and stood there stopping the entire Ganges with sharp arrows.
25 And as he saw the river Ganges halted by the arrows where he stood, the king was astounded by the sight of this wondrous, superhuman feat. Śaṃtanu, however wise, did not recognize his own son, whom he had seen only once before when he was hardly born. But the boy, on seeing his father, played an illusion on him with his wizardry; and when he had confused him he disappeared there and then.

When King Śaṃtanu saw that wonder, he suspected it was his son, and he said to the Ganges, "Show him!" Wearing a beautiful form, the Ganges showed him the boy bedecked with ornaments,
30 holding him by the right hand. Śaṃtanu failed to recognize her, adorned with all her finery and clad in a dustless skirt, even though he had known her before.

The Ganges said:

This is the eighth son, king, which you have fathered on me—he is yours, tiger among men, take him to your house. He has learned the *Vedas* with their branches from Vasiṣṭha himself, and he is mighty in battle like Indra, an excellent archer and marksman. The Gods esteem him, and so do the Asuras, always; and what knowledge Uśanas has, that he knows entirely. And likewise the knowledge that Angiras's son possesses, he for whom Gods and Asuras bow alike, that knowledge too lies firmly lodged with him, your strong-armed, great-spirited son, with its branches and off-shoots.
35 Jamadagni's son, Rāma the seer, high-mighty and unassailable—what he knows of weapons is also lodged with him. This is your son, king, a great bowman, expert in Law and Profit, a champion—I give him to you, champion, take him home!

Vaiśaṃpāyana said:

When she had thus permitted him, Śaṃtanu took his son, who shone like the sun, and returned to his castle. And as he went to his castle, which was like the city of the Sacker of Cities, the Paurava deemed himself richly fulfilled in all his desires. He thereupon anointed his son Young King over the Pauravas; and Śaṃtanu's famous son won, with the manner of his life, the affection of the Pauravas, his father,
40 and the kingdom, O bull among Bhāratas. So the boundlessly mighty king of the earth enjoyed himself with his son and passed four years.

One day the king went to a forest along the Yamunā River and smelled an indescribably sweet fragrance. He roamed everywhere to seek out its source and found a girl of the fisher tribe, who was lovely like a Goddess. No sooner had he seen her than he asked the black-eyed girl, "Whose are you and who? What are you doing here, shy maid?" She said, "I am a fisher girl, and by the Law of our kind I ply a ferry at the orders of my father, who is the king of the fishermen. Good luck to you."

45 Seeing how the divinely beautiful maiden had loveliness, sweetness, and fragrance, King Śaṃtanu wanted to possess the fisher girl. He went to her father and sued for her and asked her from her father for himself. The chieftain of the fishers replied to the king, "From the instant she was born I have known that I had to marry my lovely daughter to some suitor. But there was an unspoken desire in my heart—hear it now, king of men. If you seek her from me as your wife by the Law, flawless lord, then make a covenant with me on your word, for you are true to your word. According to our covenant I shall give this girl in marriage to you, sire, for never shall I find another suitor the like of you."

Śaṃtanu said:

50 I shall listen to the boon you ask, fisherman, and make my

decision for it or against. If it can be granted, I shall do so. If not, not at all.

The fisherman said:

The son who will be born from her shall be anointed king and lord of the earth after you, and no other son shall inherit, sire!

Vaiśaṃpāyana said:

Śaṃtanu did not want to grant this boon to the fisherman, burn as he did with the sharp pangs of love, O Bhārata. Then the king returned to Hāstinapura, brooding on the fisher girl and with a grieving heart. One day his son Devavrata came upon the sorrowing Śaṃtanu, who was lost in his thoughts, and he said to his father, "You are secure on every side. All the princes are amenable. Why then are you constantly grieving as though you were in pain, and why are you brooding so that you do not speak a word, king?"

Questioned by his son, Śaṃtanu replied, "Surely I am brooding as you say I am. You are the single son in this vast lineage; my son Bhārata, mortal man is impermanent, and hence I grieve. If something untoward happens to you, Gāngeya, our line will be no more. Doubtless you are dearer to me than a hundred sons, nor do I endeavor without cause to marry another wife. Still, I wish for the survival of our lineage—may good luck befall you! Those wise in the Law say that having one son is having none. The daily *agnihotra*, the three *Vedas*, and sacrifices with ample stipends are altogether not worth a sixteenth of a son. It is with man as it is with all other creatures: having sons—on this I have no doubts, my sagacious son—that is the burden of the eternal *Veda*, among the great books of the Lore. And you are a warlike champion, always unforgiving, always in arms, Bhārata, and you shall not find your death but by the sword, prince sans blame. So here I have fallen to worrying—how shall it be when you have found your peace? Now I have entirely told you the reason why I am unhappy, my son."

Thereupon, having learned this as the entire reason, the wise Devavrata went out with afterthoughts. He at once approached an old councillor who wished his father well, and questioned him about the reason for his father's grief. And upon his questioning, this minister told the first of the Kurus of the boon that had been asked for the girl, O bull among Bhāratas. Then Devavrata went in the company of the old barons to the fisher king and himself sued for the daughter on behalf of his own father.

The fisherman received him; and after honoring him properly, O Bhārata, he said to him when he was seated in the king's assembly, "You are a protector sufficient unto Śaṃtanu, O bull among men—you the son, he best of fathers. How could I argue with your word? For who would not be pained overruling such an alliance of wombs,

as laudable as desirable, were he Indra himself? She is the offspring of
an āryan who is the equal of your people in virtues; from his seed
famous Satyavatī has come forth. Oftentimes, my friend, has he
praised your father to me: among all princes, he said, *he* is worthy of
wedding Satyavatī! Even Asita himself, the divine seer, I once rejected
when that greatest of seers came strongly wooing for Satyavatī.

"But as the father of the girl I must say something, bull of the
Bhāratas. The one objection that I see here is a strong one—rivalry.
75 For he whose rival you are, be he Asura or Gandharva, can never live
securely if you resent him, scourge of your foes! This much fault do I
find, and no other, prince. Know it, and luck be with you in the giving
and taking, scourge of your foes!"

At these words Gāngeya* made his proper reply, while the barons
were listening, for the sake of his father: "Now hear what is in my
mind, and accept it as the truth, most truthful king. The man is not
born, nor will he be born, who dares say the same. I shall do as you
are counseling me. The son who is born from her shall be our king!"

80 Once more the fisherman spoke: "Thou that art ready to do an
impossible feat for the sake of the kingdom, bull of the Bhāratas,
thou art a protector sufficient unto Śaṃtanu, lord of boundless luster,
a master sufficient for the girl, law-minded prince, and a patron for
the marrying! But there is one more thing that needs be done—
listen to me since I must speak in the manner of those who love their
daughters. The promise thou hast made for Satyavatī's sake, in the
midst of these barons, is a promise that fits thyself whose highest
recourse is the Law of the truth. It shall not be broken, strong-armed
prince, no doubt about that. But the sons thou shalt have—here we
have great doubts."

85 Divining the mind of the fisher king, the prince whose highest
recourse was the Law of the truth then made his promise, O king, to
do a kindness to his father.

Devavrata said:

Chief of the fishermen, great king! Hear this word of mine that I
speak for my father's sake while these barons are listening. I have
already renounced the kingdom, king—now here I make my resolve
about my progeny. From this day onward I shall live as a monk. And
though I shall remain sonless, the imperishable worlds in heaven shall
be mine!

Vaiśaṃpāyana said:

When he heard this word of his, the law-minded fisherman
90 shuddered with joy, and he made his reply: "I shall give." In the
sky the Gods and the throngs of the seers and the Apsarās rained
flowers, and they said, "He is Bhīṣma, the Awesome One!" Then on

* = son of the Ganges, i.e., Devavrata or Bhīṣma.

his father's behalf he said to the famous maiden, "Ascend my chariot, mother. We shall go to our house." Bhīṣma then helped the beaming Satyavatī on the chariot and, arriving in Hāstinapura, handed her over to Śaṃtanu. The barons praised his impossible feat, and together and singly they said, "He is Bhīṣma!" And seeing the impossible feat that Bhīṣma had accomplished, his father Śaṃtanu, pleased, bestowed himself this boon on him that death would come to him only at his own bidding.

Vaiśaṃpāyana said:

95.1 After the wedding was held, King Śaṃtanu settled the beautiful
maiden in his own house. Then Satyavatī bore Śaṃtanu an
intelligent and brave son, Citrāngada, who surpassed all men in
bravery. The mighty king fathered on Satyavatī a second son, a great
archer and prince, who was named Vicitravīrya. Before his son had
reached manhood, O bull among Bhāratas, the wise King Śaṃtanu
succumbed to the Law of Time.
5 When Śaṃtanu had gone to heaven, Bhīṣma submitted to the
wishes of Satyavatī and placed Citrāngada, tamer of enemies, on the
throne of the kingdom. Citrāngada smote all the kings with his
bravery, for he deemed no one on earth his equal. And when he had
defeated all champions, men and Asuras alike, the mighty king of the
Gandharvas, who bore the same name Citrāngada, came to him. A
great battle took place in the Land of the Kurus between these two
powerful warriors, the chief of the Gandharvas and the chief of the
10 Kurus, on the bank of the river Hiraṇyavatī; and the fight lasted three
years. In that tumultuous duel, overcast by a rain of swords, the
Gandharva proved the better wizard and killed the heroic king of the
Kurus. And having put an end to Citrāngada, first of the Kurus who
wielded bows and arrows of various makes, the Gandharva strode up
to heaven.

That tiger among men of ample splendor having been slain, Bhīṣma Śāṃtanava performed the rites of the dead, O king, Immediately thereafter the strong-armed prince consecrated Vicitravīrya, still a child before his manhood, to the kingdom of the Kurus. Vicitravīrya submitted to Bhīṣma's word and under his regency ruled the domain of his father and grandfather. Fully knowing the precepts of the Law, the king revered Bhīṣma Śāṃtanava according to the Law, and Bhisma protected him in return.

Vaiśaṃpāyana said:

96.1 When Citrāngada had been killed and his brother was still a child, O prince sans blame, Bhīṣma, submitting to Satyavatī's wishes, governed his kingdom. Then he saw that his sagacious brother had reached manhood, and he set his mind on marrying Vicitravīrya.

Bhīṣma then came to hear that the king of the Kāśis had three daughters, beautiful as Apsarās, who all three were to choose their own husbands. So, with his mother's consent, the great chariot warrior, clad in his armor, set out with a single chariot for the city of
5 Benares. There Śaṃtanu's son saw prosperous princes assemble from all directions, and he saw the maidens themselves. As the bards proclaimed the names of the princes by the thousands, the lordly Bhīṣma himself put in his claim for the maidens, O king. With a thunderous voice Bhīṣma, great swordsman, said to the barons as he lifted the girls on to his chariot, "The wise declare that girls may be given to men of virtue who have been invited. Or they will be decked with ornaments; or a dowry is proffered according to wealth. Others may marry off their daughters for a pair of cows. Others again give them for a negotiated price, while others still force their leave by
10 force. Others lie with a girl that is taken off guard. And other girls find for themselves. Now know that this present marriage is the eighth that the sages recall—the bridegroom choice, which the barons praise and observe. But the students of the Law hold that that bride is the best who is carried off by force. So, princes, I am ready to carry these maidens off by force! Now strive with all your might to defeat me or be defeated: here I stand, princes, resolved on battle!"

After thus challenging the barons and the king of the Kāśis, the mighty Kuru lifted all three girls on his chariot, made his farewell to the barons, and drove swiftly off, abducting the girls. Indignantly, all the princes rose in a body, feeling their muscles and grinding their
15 teeth. As they hastened to shed their jewelry and don their armor, confusion reigned supreme. Like a shower of meteors, Janamejaya, it rained all around with sparkling jewels and coats of mail! In a starburst of cuirasses and gems, the champions, wrathfully and indignantly knitting their brows, faces flushed, dashed to the brightly hued chariots their drivers held ready, the fine steeds yoked, and leaped on them with all their weaponry. Brandishing their arms, they went in pursuit of the Kuru in his single chariot, and a battle began between him and them, he single, they many, a tumultuous and
20 hair-raising battle. They unleashed ten thousand arrows at him at a time, but Bhīṣma cut them all off before they struck home. Then all the princes surrounded him on all sides and rained on him a shower of arrows as clouds pelt a mountain with their rain. He warded off that cloudburst of arrows with shafts of his own and returned the shots of the princes with three arrows at a time. The chariot warrior had a lightness of touch over the other men, and his adversaries began to cheer the way he defended himself in the encounter. And when he had thus defeated them all in the battle, expert on every weapon, the

Bhārata rode with the girls toward the Bhāratas.
25 Then the warlike King Śālva, of boundless spirit, set upon Bhīṣma
Śāṃtanava from behind in the battle, like a bull elephant that, king
of his herd, attacks with his tusks a rival in his rear when he is
mounting an elephant cow in heat. "Stay, lecher, stay!" the king
shouted at Bhīṣma, that strong-armed King Śālva driven by his fury.
Bhīṣma, tiger of a man, crusher of enemy forces, was enraged by his
words, and blazing with anger like a smokeless fire he followed the
Law of the baronage; without a tremor of fear the warrior turned his
chariot toward Śālva.
30 Seeing him turn, all the other princes became spectators at the
encounter of Śālva and Bhīṣma. Like two roaring powerful bulls
before a cow in heat, they turned on each other with all their
strength and might. King Śālva besplashed Bhīṣma Śāṃtanava with
swift arrows by the hundreds and thousands. Seeing that Bhīṣma at
first was being crowded by Śālva, the barons were astonished and
cheered him on with "Bravo, bravo!" They saw how nimbly he
35 moved in combat and happily applauded him with cheers. When he
heard the shouts of the barons, Bhīṣma Śāṃtanava, victor of enemy
cities, became incensed and cried, "Hold your ground!" Angrily he
told his driver, "Drive up to that king, so that I can kill him as
Garuḍa kills a snake!" Then the Kaurava fixed the *vāruṇa* arrow to
his bow and crushed the four horses of King Śālva, while warding off
the king's arrows with his own. Then, tiger among men, Bhīṣma
killed the charioteer and with a single arrow felled his excellent
steeds. After winning the day in the maidens' cause, Bhīṣma
40 Śāṃtanava let off the great king himself with his life. Śālva then
departed for his own city, O bull among Bhāratas, and the other
barons, too, that had come to watch the bridegroom choice left for
their own kingdoms, victor of enemy cities.
Thus Bhīṣma, greatest of swordsmen, won those maidens and
went on to Hāstinapura where King Kaurava* sat. Not long afterward,
crossing forests and rivers and richly wooded hills, the prince who
was the Ganges' son, unhurt after laying low his enemies in battle
and of measureless prowess, conducted the daughters of the king of
the Kāśis; and like daughters-in-law, or younger sisters, or daughters
45 did the law-minded man treat them as he traveled to the Kurus. Then
brother Bhīṣma gave all three accomplished girls, whom he had
abducted by force, to his younger brother Vicitravīrya in marriage.
According to the Law of the strict, the prince, who knew the Law,
having accomplished his superhuman exploit, now made ready for the
wedding of Vicitravīrya, as the resolute man had decided with
Satyavatī.

* = Vicitravīrya.

While Bhīṣma was preparing for the wedding, Ambā, the oldest of
the three daughters of the king of the Kāśis, a strict girl, said to him,
"In my heart I had chosen King Śālva of Saubha to be my husband,
and he had chosen me; and it was also my father's wish. I was to
have elected him at the bridegroom choice. You know the Law: now
that you know this you must do as the Law dictates."

50 At the girl's words, which were spoken in the assembly of the
brahmins, Bhīṣma thought upon this problem that now beset the
marrying rite. Reaching his decision in concert with the brahmins, who
knew all the *Veda*, the law-minded prince gave Ambā, eldest daughter of
the Kāśi king, leave to depart. Then Bhīṣma gave the other two girls,
Ambikā and Ambālikā, in marriage to his younger brother Vicitravīrya
to be his wives, according to the ritual that is found in the Rules. When
he had taken their hands, law-minded Vicitravīrya, who was proud of his
looks and youth, was seized with love. The two princesses too, tall and
dark and with blue-black curling hair, red pointed nails, and buxom
55 breasts and buttocks, felt they had found a husband worthy of them
and adored the handsome Vicitravīrya. Matching the Aśvins in
beauty, with the courage and power of a God, he churned the hearts
of all women. Seven years the king of the land whiled away with his
wives; then Vicitravīrya, still young, fell ill of consumption. Despite the
efforts of his friends assisted by capable physicians, the Kuru, like a
setting sun, went to the realm of Yama. Together with the priest and
all the bulls of the Kurus, Bhīṣma, submitting to Satyavatī's wishes,
had all the rites of the dead solemnly performed for King
Vicitravīrya.

Vaiśaṃpāyana said:

97.1 Satyavatī, wretched and hungrily begging for grandsons,
performed the funeral rites with her daughters-in-law. The proud
lady, looking to the Law and the male and distaff lineages, spoke to
Gāṅgeya.

"The ancestral oblation to the famous Śaṃtanu of the Kurus, who
always abode by the Law, and his fame and his progeny now all rest
with you. Even as heaven is sure when one has done good acts, even
as long life is sure when the truth has been obeyed, so the Law is sure
5 when you are there. You know the Laws, in full and in part, you
know the multifarious traditions, you know the *Veda* in every way. I
see the disposition by the Law, the proper custom of family, and the
procedure in distress as securely lodged with you as with Śukra or
Bṛhaspati.

"Therefore, you are my great comfort; and on you, greatest of
those who uphold the Law, I shall enjoin a task. When you have
heard it, pray carry it out. My mighty son was your brother, and he

was very dear to you. A boy still, he went to heaven, leaving no sons,
bull among men. Your brother's queens, the good daughters of the
king of the Kāśis, both lovely and in the bloom of their youth, are
10 yearning for sons, Bhārata! Beget children on them, so that our line
may continue, beget them at my behest, lord. Pray carry out the Law
that applies here. Be consecrated as king of the realm, rule the
Bhāratas, take a wife by the Law, lest you drown your forebears!"

When he was so being urged by his mother and kinsmen, O
scourge of your foes, the law-minded Bhīṣma gave his lawlike reply.

"Doubtless that is the highest Law that you have quoted to me,
mother. Yet you know the sovereign vow I have sworn concerning
offspring, and you know what befell when your bride price was to be
15 paid. Here I vow my truth, again, Satyavatī—I shall forsake the three
worlds, and the sovereignty of the Gods, or whatever surpasses both,
before I forsake my word! Earth shall forsake its fragrance, water its
taste, light its color, wind its touch, the sun shall forsake its
luminousness and smoke-crested fire its heat, air shall forsake its
sounds and moon the coolness of its rays, Indra shall renounce his
power and the king of the Law the Law, but never shall I resolve to
forsake my word!"

At these words of her son whose puissance was high and
20 abounding, his mother Satyavatī quickly replied to Bhīṣma, "I know
that you stand utterly by your word, you whose strength is your word.
If you wished, you could create a new universe of worlds with your
puissance! I know that it was for my own sake that you gave your
word. But look to the Law of Distress and carry the ancestral yoke.
Act, scourge of your enemies, so that the thread of the lineage and
Law itself will not be lost and your kinsmen may rejoice!"

As she was babbling, hungrily begging for grandsons, and was
speaking astray from the Law, Bhīṣma again said, "Queen, look to the
Laws lest you bring ruin to us all! Breaking his word is not counted
25 among the Laws of the baron! I shall tell you the sempiternal baronial
Law by which the line of Śaṃtanu shall survive on earth. When you
have heard me, you may carry it out with your wise priests who know
of the meaning of the Law of Distress, while reckoning the course of
the world."

Bhīṣma said:

98.1 Jamadagni's son Rāma, incensed at the assassination of his father,
killed in his fury the king of the Haihayas, good lady. He sliced off
Arjuna's* ten hundred arms. And once more taking up his bow and
unleashing his mighty missiles, he burned down the baronage, time
and again, conquering earth with his chariot. Twenty-one times did

* = Arjuna Kārtavīrya.

the great-spirited Bhārgava with his various weaponry empty the earth of barons. But then once more all the baronesses everywhere
5 gave birth to children by brahmins of stern spirits. "The son is his who took the hand," so it is decided in the *Vedas*. The women kept their minds on the Law as they lay with the brahmins, and now in all the world the resurgence of the barons is an obvious fact.

And there was once a wise seer called Utathya, who had a wife named Mamatā, whom he held in great esteem. Utathya had a younger brother of great virility, Bṛhaspati, the priests of the Gods; and he lusted after Mamatā, Mamatā said to her brother-in-law, who was a great arguer, "I am with child by your eldest brother, stop! And right here in my womb this child of Utathya's has learned the *Veda*
10 and its six branches, my lord Bṛhaspati. Now you would spill your seed in vain. And since this is the case, you must stop now!" At this apposite rejoinder the greatly virile Bṛhaspati was unable to control his lusting self, and he lay in love with the woman who loved him not. And as he spilled forth his seed, the child in the womb said, "*Bhoḥ* little uncle, there is no room here for two! You have wasted your seed, and I was here first!"

The blessed seer Bṛhaspati thereupon angrily cursed Utathya's son
15 in the womb, who had insulted him: "Since you at such a time that all creatures cherish spoke up as you did, you shall enter a long darkness." And from this curse of the famed Bṛhaspati the seer Dīrghatamas was born, Bṛhaspati's peer in might.

This famous man fathered sons, Gautama and others, to increase the lineage and family of the seer Utathya. Gautama and the others were ridden by folly and greed; they threw him in the Ganges on a floating tree-log, thinking, "We need not support this man, he is both
20 blind and old," and then the cruel men went home. The seer then drifted downstream, O king, on his raft, and blindly passed through many countries. As he was bathing, a king called Balin, who knew all the Laws, saw him float to him down the river. Law-minded Balin whose strength was his truth caught him, recognized him, and adopted him to give him sons, O bull among men. "My lord, who give honor," he said, "please father on my wives sons who know Law and Profit, to continue my line." The virile seer agreed, whereupon the
25 king sent him his wife Sudeṣṇā. Finding him both blind and old, the queen did not go, but sent the old man her nurse. On her, who was born a serf, the stern and law-minded seer fathered eleven sons, the first being Kakṣīvat. When mighty King Balin saw Kakṣīvat and all the others at their studies, he said, "Those are mine!" "No," said the great seer, "they are mine," and continued: "Kakṣīvat and these others here I have fathered on a serf woman. Your queen Sudeṣṇā found me both blind and old, and disdainfully and foolishly gave me her nurse."

30 Balin then pacified that strictest of seers and once more sent him his
wife Sudeṣṇā. Dīrghatamas felt her limbs, then said to the queen,
"You shall have a son of great power and true to his word." And so
the royal seer Anga was born from Sudeṣṇā.
In this way many other barons adept at the bow were born by
brahmins, barons most proficient in the Law, manly and strong.
Having heard this, mother, you too should do as you want.

Bhīṣma said:
99.1 Listen to me, mother, as I tell you how the continuity of the
dynasty of Bharata can assuredly be prospered. Invite a brahmin of
virtue and let him father children on the fields of Vicitravīrya.
Vaiśaṃpāyana said:
Then Satyavatī with a faltering voice said to Bhīṣma, smiling
shyly, "You have spoken the truth, strong-armed Bhārata. Because I
trust you, and to continue the dynasty, I shall speak now. Nor—for
5 such is our distress now—will you be able to gainsay it. In our
dynasty you are the Law, you are the truth, you are the ultimate
resort. Therefore listen to what I say, and act on it at once.
"My father, who had adopted the Law, law-minded prince, had a
ferry, and I myself at one time went on it when I had just become a
woman. Then that greatest of the upholders of the Law, the great
seer, wise Parāśara, came to my ferry since he wanted to cross the
river Yamunā. While I was ferrying him across the Yamunā, the great
hermit came up to me and, possessed by love, spoke to me many
sweet things with great gentleness. Equally fearful of his curse and of
my father, and showered with boons that are not easily come by, I
10 could not reject him. He overpowered and mastered me with his
virility, right there in the boat, after covering the open spaces with
darkness. Before that time I had had a strong odor of fish—loathsome.
He took it away, the hermit, and gave me a pure fragrance. He also
told me that when I had delivered my child on an island in the river,
I would still be a virgin. So was born the great seer and yogin
Pārāśarya, the son I had as a virgin, who is known as Dvaipāyana—
the blessed lord and seer who, by the power of his austerities, divided
the *Vedas* and hence became in the world Vyāsa the Divider, and, for
his blackness, Kṛṣṇa. He is a man who speaks the truth, an ascetic
15 bent upon serenity, all of whose evil is burned away. He surely, when
enjoined upon by me and by you, prince of immense luster, will
beget beautiful offspring on the fields of your brother. He has said to
me, 'Think of me when a task need be done.' I shall now think of him,
strong-armed Bhīṣma, if you wish. For with your permission, Bhīṣma,
the great ascetic will surely beget children on the fields of
Vicitravīrya."

At the mention of the great seer, Bhīṣma folded his hands and said, "He who has an insight into these three, Law, Profit, and Pleasure, who discerns that Profit leads to Profit, Law to Law, and Pleasure to Pleasure, but each singly to contrary ends, and who after reflection
20 with his mind makes the right decision, he is wise indeed. What you have proposed is both lawful and beneficial to our family. It is the best course, and I approve of it."

When Bhīṣma had given his promise, O scion of the Kurus, the Dark Woman called Kṛṣṇa Dvaipāyana the hermit with her thoughts. The sage was propounding the *Vedas* when he divined his mother's thought, and mysteriously he appeared that very instant, O Kaurava. After paying homage to her son with due formality, she embraced him with her arms and sprinkled him with tears—the fisher woman wept as she saw her son after so long a time. The great seer sprinkled his anguished mother with water and greeted her; then her eldest son
25 Vyāsa said to his mother, "I have come to do what you have in mind. Command me, you who know the facts of the Law, and I will do what pleases you." The house priest thereupon paid homage to the sublime seer and welcomed him solemnly with apposite spells. When he had taken his seat, his mother asked him about his unwavering health; then Satyavatī looked him full in the face and continued at once:

"Sons, O sage, are born the common property of the father and the mother. The mother is no less their owner, to be sure, than the father. Just as you are my firstborn son, ordained by the Ordainer, so,
30 O brahmin seer, Vicitravīrya is my lastborn son. Therefore, just as Bhīṣma is Vicitravīrya's brother on the father's side, so you are his brother on the mother's side, as you agree, son. This son of Śaṃtanu, whose word is his strength, is keeping faith with his word and has no mind either to have children or to rule the kingdom. Now, out of esteem for your brother, for the continuity of the family, at Bhīṣma's word and my own behest, blameless sage, out of compassion for the creatures and for the protection of everyone, you must do what I am proposing without any cruelty of heart. The two wives of your younger brother, who are like daughters of a God, lovely and in the
35 bloom of their youth, are yearning for sons by the Law. Beget children on them—for you are fit for the task, son—that are worthy of our family and of continuing our progeny."

Vyāsa said:

Satyavatī, you know the Law, both the higher and the lower. And since your mind is set on the Law and is beneficent to the living, I shall do what is needed with respect to the Law, and at your behest do what you desire. For this is found to be ancient practice. I shall give to my brother sons the likes of Mitra and Varuṇa. Both the queens must punctiliously submit to a vow, which I shall describe, for the

space of a year, so that they become sanctified. For no woman may lie
with me without carrying out the vow.

Satyavatī said:

40 Rather act so that the queen may get with child at once! In
kingless kingdoms no rain falls, no Gods visit. How, my lord, can a
kingdom be preserved that has no king? Therefore, plant the child;
Bhīṣma will watch it grow.

Vyāsa said:

If I must give a child at once, before the appointed time, then her
highest vow shall be that she bear with my ugliness. If she bears with
my smell, my looks, my garb, and my body, Kausalyā shall
straightway conceive a superior child.

Vaiśaṃpāyana said:

Awaiting the time of cohabitation, the hermit disappeared. The
queen went to meet her daughter-in-law in private and made to her
the lawful and beneficent proposition that was to her profit as well.
45 "Kausalyā, listen to what I shall say to you, which is under Law. The
extinction of the Bhāratas is clearly the fruit of the reversal of my
fortunes. Bhīṣma has seen my anxiety and the distress of his father's
dynasty, and he has given me his view on the measure that should
counter it and prosper the Law. But this measure depends on you; I
know it well, daughter. Rescue the lost dynasty of Bharata! Bear a son,
buxom woman, to resemble the king of the Gods. For he shall carry
the burdensome yoke of the kingdom of our dynasty."

Somehow she persuaded the princess, who abode by the Law, by
appealing to the Law; whereupon she feasted the brahmins, the
divine seers, and the guests.

Vaiśaṃpāyana said:

100.1 When her daughter-in-law had bathed at the time of her season,
Satyavatī made her lie on her bed and said to her softly, "Kausalyā,
you have a brother-in-law who will come into you tonight! Stay
awake and wait for him. He will come in the dead of night." When
she heard what her mother-in-law said, she thought, as she was lying
on her beautiful bed, that it would be Bhīṣma or any other of the bulls
of the Kurus.

Then the faithful seer, who had first been enjoined to service
Ambikā, entered her bed while the lamps were still burning. The
5 queen saw dark Kṛṣṇa's matted orange hair, his fiery eyes, his
reddish beard, and she closed her eyes. He lay with her that night, to
carry out his mother's wish, but the princess of the Kāśis could not
look at him for fright. When he came out, his mother met him and
said to her son, "Shall there be a son in her, a prince of virtue?"
Hearing his mother's question, Vyāsa of superb wisdom, whose

knowledge went beyond his senses, answered, impelled by Fate, "He shall be a man with the vigor of a myriad elephants, a wise and great royal seer, of great fortune, great prowess, and great spirit, and he shall have a hundred powerful sons. But because of his mother's defect of virtue, he shall be blind." Hearing this, mother said to son, "No blind man is worthy to be king of the Kurus, ascetic! Pray grant a second king to the dynasty of Kuru, who shall be the herdsman of the lineage of your kinsmen, the prosperer of the ancestral line." "So be it," promised the great ascetic, and departed. In due time Kausalyā gave birth to a son who was blind.

Once more the queen persuaded her other daughter-in-law, and the blameless Satyā* brought the seer as before. He came to Ambālikā in the same manner. She too saw the seer and, desperate, turned a sickly pale. Seeing that she had paled from distress, Satyavatī's son Vyāsa said to her, "Since you paled when you saw my ugliness, you shall have a son of a sickly pallor, and so his name shall be Pāṇḍu the Pale, woman of the lovely face."

Having spoken, he came out, and seeing him come out, Satyā spoke to her son. He told his mother of the pallor of the child, and again she asked for another son, "So be it," answered the great seer to his mother. When her time came, the queen gave birth to a son, pale but endowed with the marks of excellence and blazing with good fortune; it was of him that the five Pāṇḍavas, the mighty archers, were born.

When the season of the older bride came around again, she ordered her to Vyāsa. But as she thought back on the appearance, and the smell, of the great seer, the woman, lovely as a Goddess, was from sheer fright incapable of doing as the queen told her. The princess of the Kāśis decked a slave woman, as beautiful as an Apsarā, with her own jewelry and sent her to Kṛṣṇa. When the seer came, the woman rose to meet him and greeted him; and with his consent she lay with him and served him with all honor. The seer waxed content with the pleasure of love he found with her, and he spent all night with her as she pleasured him. When he rose, he said to her, "You shall cease to be a slave. There is a child come to your belly, my lovely, an illustrious man-child who shall be mindful of the Law and become the most sagacious man in the world." Thus was born Vidura, son of Kṛṣṇa Dvaipāyana, the immeasurably sage brother of Dhṛtarāṣṭra and Pāṇḍu. He was the God Law himself, who, by a curse of the great-spirited Māṇḍavya, was born as Vidura—sure in the principles of polity, innocent of lust and wrath.

Acquitted of his debt to the Law, he told his mother when they met that the woman was with child; then he vanished. Thus in the field of

* = Satyavatī.

Vicitravīrya were born by Dvaipāyana the sons that were to prosper the dynasty of the Kurus, like children of the Gods.

Janamejaya said:
101.1 What had Law done that he incurred a curse? And by whose
curse, brahmin seer, was he born in a serf's womb?
Vaiśaṃpāyana said:
There was a brahmin known as Māṇḍavya, persevering and
knowledgeable on all the Laws, who abode by truth and austerities.
This great ascetic and yogin was wont to stand below a tree at the
gate of his hermitage with his arms raised high while observing a vow
of silence. He had stood there for a long time in mortification when
Dasyus came fleeing to his hermitage, carrying their plunder, hotly
5 pursued by many guards, O bull among Bhāratas. They hid their
plunder about his hovel, and when the troop came after them, they
lay down there in great fear. Scarcely had they lain down when the
troop of guardsmen pursuing the robbers arrived, and they saw the
seer. They asked the ascetic, who still held his posture, king, "Which
way did the Dasyus go, great brahmin? We shall hurry after them the
same way." But the ascetic gave no reply to these words of the
guardsmen, king, neither good nor evil. Thereupon the king's men
searched the hermitage and found the thieves lying there and their
10 loot. The guardsmen now began to suspect the hermit himself, and
they seized him and brought him with the Dasyus to the king. The
king passed judgment on him with the others: "Let him be killed."
The headsmen, who did not know him, strung him on a stake. After
the guardsmen had hoisted the hermit on the stake, they returned to
the king with the plunder.

The law-minded brahmin seer hung on the stake for a long time,
without food, but even so did not die. He held on to his life and
summoned the seers. These hermits became most mortified over the
great-spirited hermit who was mortifying himself impaled on the
stake, O mortifier of your enemies! They returned in the night in the
15 form of birds from everywhere. After showing their powers, as far as
they were capable, they questioned the great brahmin: "We wish to
learn, brahmin, what evil you have done." Thereupon he said to the
ascetics, tigers among hermits, "On whom shall I place the blame?
For no one but me is guilty."

The king heard that he was a seer and came out with his
councillors and sought to appease the great seer on the stake: "What
evil I have done in my folly and ignorance, great seer, I seek to
appease you of it; pray be not angry with me!" At the king's words
the hermit made peace; and, having appeased him, the king lowered
20 him off the stake. When he had lowered him from the top of the stake

and tried to pull the stake out of him, he could not pull it out, and he cut it off at the end. And so the hermit went about with the stake still inside him, winning with his mortifications worlds mostly out of the reach of others. "Māṇḍavya-of-the-Stake" people called him.

Then the brahmin, who knew the higher meanings, went to the realm of Law; and finding Law seated, the mighty man took him to task: "What evil, if any, had I unwittingly done that such a retribution was wreaked on me? Tell me the truth at once—behold the power of my austerities!"

Law said:

You had stuck blades of grass in the tails of little flies, and this was the punishment you received for that deed, ascetic.

Māṇḍavya-of-the-Stake said:

25 The sin was small and the penalty you dealt me vast. Law, for that you shall be born a man from the womb of a serf! Now I lay down the limit on the fruition of the Law: nothing shall be a sin up to the age of fourteen years; but if they do it beyond that age it shall be counted an offense.

Vaiśaṃpāyana said:

So, because he was cursed by the great-spirited hermit for that offense, Law was born from the womb of a serf in the form of Vidura. He was versed in Law and Profit, innocent of greed and grudge, far-sighted, serene, and devoted to the welfare of the Kurus.

Vaiśaṃpāyana said:

102.1 After the birth of the three princes, the Jungle of the Kurus, the Land of the Kurus, and the Kurus themselves all throve, all three. The crops stood high on the earth, the harvests were plentiful. The Rain God rained in season, the trees bore abundant bloom and fruit, the draught animals were happy, deer and fowl joyous, the garlands were fragrant, the fruit was juicy. The cities were crowded with merchants and craftsmen, the people were brave, educated, strict, and content.
5 There were no Dasyus, no folk who loved crime. In all the regions of the kingdoms the Age of the Winning Throw held sway. Bent upon sacrifice and vow, wont to pursue liberality, ritual, and Law, and coupled in mutual affection, the people were prosperous then. People, innocent of pride and anger, devoid of greed, helped one another prosper. Law reigned supreme. The city, bursting like the ocean, packed with hundreds of mansions, displayed with its gateways, arches, and turrets like massing clouds the splendor of Great Indra's city. In rivers and tree groves, in ponds and pools, on hilltop and in
10 lovely forests the people played happily. At that time the Southern Kurus, rivaling the Northern Kurus, walked with Siddhas, seers, and

Cāraṇas. No one was destitute, no women were widowed. In the lovely countryside the Kurus built wells, rest houses, meeting halls, water tanks, and brahmin cottages.

While Bhīṣma was the protector of the land all around and ruled it by the scriptures, the country was delightful, dotted with hundreds of temples and sacrificial poles, and it grew by taking other kingdoms into its fold. Held by Bhīṣma, the Wheel of the Law rolled on in the kingdom. Town and country folk were all forever feasting, while the great-spirited princes accomplished their tasks. The houses of the chief Kurus and the burghers, O king, were everywhere alive with cries like "Let us give! Come and eat!"

15 Dhṛtarāṣṭra, Pāṇḍu, and the sagacious Vidura were from birth
protected by Bhīṣma like sons of his own. They were sanctified by
sacraments, they observed vows and studies, and became skilled in
track and field, until they reached manhood. Then they were trained
in archery, in horseback riding, in club combat, in sword and shield,
in elephant lore, and the science of policy. They toiled on the epics and
the books of the Lore and the various instructions, O lord, and they
knew the verities of the *Veda* and its branches. Wide-striding Pāṇḍu
20 outmatched all men on the bow, Prince Dhṛtarāṣṭra was strong
beyond any, while no one in all three worlds was Vidura's equal in
his perseverance in the Law and his command of the Laws of the
Kings. And on seeing that the lost line of Śaṃtanu had been rescued,
a saying went the rounds among the people in all kingdoms: "Of
mothers of heroes the daughters of Kāśi, of countries the Jungle of the
Kurus, of law-minded princes Bhīṣma, of cities the Town of the
Elephant!"

Dhṛtarāṣṭra, however, did not succeed to the kingdom because of his blindness; Vidura did not, because he was a half-breed. Pāṇḍu became the king.

Bhīṣma said:

103.1 Our famous dynasty, which is prospering perfectly with virtue, has now attained to sovereignty on earth over all other kings. Our dynasty, protected by the great-spirited kings of old who knew the Law, has never fallen to ruin here; and through me, Satyavatī, and the great-spirited Kṛṣṇa, it has been firmly established upon yourselves, the threads of our line.

In order that this dynasty may wax like the ocean, I, but more
5 especially you, Vidura, must take measures. One hears that there is a
young princess of the Yādavas who is suitable to our family, also a
daughter of Subala, and one of the king of the Madras. They are all of
dynastic lineages, beautiful, and well-protected by their kin; and those

bulls of barons are fit to be allied with us. I myself think that we
should woo the girls for the continuity of our line—or what do you
think, most sagacious Vidura?"

Vidura said:

You are our father, our mother, and our first guru. Therefore,
deliberate and then do yourself what is good for our family.

Vaiśaṃpāyana said:

Then Bhīṣma heard from the brahmins that Gāndhārī, the
daughter of Subala, had propitiated the boon-granting Hara, the
God who took the eyes of Bhaga, and that the beautiful girl, it was
said, had received from him the boon of a hundred sons. When he
10 heard this told as truth, Bhīṣma, grandsire of the Kurus, sent a
messenger to the king of Gāndhāra, O Bhārata. Subala hesitated,
since Dhṛtarāṣṭra was blind, but then, weighing in his mind lineage,
fame, and morals, he betrothed the law-abiding Gāndhārī to
Dhṛtarāṣṭra. Gāndhārī heard that Dhṛtarāṣṭra was blind and that both
her father and her mother wanted to marry her off to him, Bhārata.
Thereupon the beautiful woman took a kerchief, folded it many times,
and, vowing utter fidelity to her husband, blindfolded her eyes, king,
resolved that she would not experience more than her husband could.
The son of the king of Gāndhāra, Śakuni, came to the Kauravas to
15 bring his sister, who was decked with a large fortune. After giving his
sister, with a retinue that befitted her, that hero was properly honored
by Bhīṣma, and thereafter returned to his own city. Gāndhārī of the
lovely hips, O Bhārata, gave satisfaction to all the Kurus with her
demeanor, behavior, and deportment. She contented all with her
conduct and was so completely devoted to her husband that the
faithful wife did not even mention other men in speech.

Vaiśaṃpāyana said:

104.1 The chief of the Yadus was named Śūra, the father of Vasudeva.*
He had a daughter Pṛthā who in beauty was peerless on earth. The
mighty chieftain had at one time promised his firstborn child to his
cousin Kuntibhoja, the son of his father's sister, who himself was
childless. After considering that she was the first-born, he in a spirit of
friendship gave the girl to his great-spirited friend who had insisted on
the favor of the firstborn. In the house of her new father she was
charged with honoring Gods and guests; and so she once came to
serve that awesome and dreadful brahmin of strict vows whose
5 decisions on Law were mysterious, him whom they know as Durvāsas.
This awesome man of honed spirit she satisfied with all her efforts,
and, with a foresight of the Law of Distress that would apply, the
hermit gave her a spell combined with sorcery and said to her:

* = the father of Kṛṣṇa Vāsudeva.

"Whichever God you call up with this spell will favor you with a son."
At these words of the brahmin she grew curious; and, being still a
virgin, she gloriously called up the Sun God. There she saw the Sun
come who makes the worlds thrive; and, stunned, the flawless maiden
10 stared at that great wonder. The burning God whose work it is to
spread light planted a child in her; and by him she gave birth to a
hero, greatest of all swordsmen, clad in armor, the illustrious son of a
God covered with good fortune. This son, who in all the worlds is
celebrated as Karṇa, was born wearing armor and his face was
lighted by earrings. The supreme light restored her virginity to her,
and after his gift the greatest of givers strode up to heaven. To hide her
misconduct and out of fear for her relations, Kuntī then threw the boy,
who bore the marks of greatness, into the river. Adhiratha, Rādhā's
renowned husband who was born a *sūta*, saved the abandoned child,
and he and his wife adopted him as their own son. They gave the
15 child a name: "Since he was born with riches, he shall be Vasuṣena."
As he grew up he became a powerful man ready to fight with any
weapon. He worshipped the sun until his back was burned; and
during the time that the hero, who was true to his word, sat
muttering prayers, there was nothing that the great-spirited man
would refuse to the brahmins. Indra, who prospers the creatures, took
on the guise of a brahmin to go begging, and the splendid God
begged from him his earrings and armor. Mindlessly, he cut the
armor from his body, streaming with blood, and cut off his earrings;
then Karṇa proffered them to Indra with folded hands. Indra was
20 astounded; and he gave him a spear and said, "At whomever of the
Gods, Asuras and men, or Gandharvas, Snakes, and Rākṣasas, you
throw this spear shall be wounded and die."
Before this his name was known as Vasuṣena; but because of his
feat Karṇa became Vaikartana.

Vaiśaṃpāyana said:

105.1 This Pṛthā, Kuntibhoja's daughter, was gifted with beauty and
character; she rejoiced in the Law and was great in her vows. At
the bridegroom choice that her father held for her she found, in the
midst of thousands of barons, the powerful lion-toothed, elephant-
shouldered, bull-eyed Pāṇḍu. The scion of the Pāṇḍus joined yoke
with the daughter of Kuntibhoja with boundless happiness as Indra
has joined yoke with Paulomī.
Thereafter he went with Bhīṣma Devavrata to the capital city of the
Madras, where Mādrī, daughter of the king of the Madras, lived,
5 renowned in all three worlds and famed among all barons for her
beauty, which was unmatched on earth. Bhīṣma bought her for
Pāṇḍu at a high price, then prepared for the wedding of the great-

spirited Pāṇḍu. Seeing the lion-chested, elephant-shouldered, bull-
eyed, and spirited Pāṇḍu, tiger among men, all the people in the
world were astonished. When he had wed her, Pāṇḍu, who was
endowed with both strength and enterprise, decided to conquer the
world and went at his enemies in all their multitudes.

First he went at the criminal Daśārṇas; and the lionlike Pāṇḍu,
bearer of the fame of the Kauravas, vanquished them in battle. Then
Pāṇḍu levied an army, flying many flags, with elephants, horses, and
10 chariots aplenty and teeming with troops of foot soldiers. Dārva, the
ruler of the Magadha kingdom, an evil man who feuded with all the
heroes and kings, was killed in Rājagṛha. Pāṇḍu took possession of his
treasury, draft bullocks, and troops. Then he marched on Mithilā and
defeated the Videhas in battle. Likewise, he carried the fame of the
Kurus to the Kāśis, Suhmas, and Puṇḍras, O bull among Bhāratas,
with the power and the strength of his own arms. The kings of men,
once they had encountered enemy-taming, firelike Pāṇḍu, with the
blazing flames of his flood of arrows and the fire of his javelins, were
burned in the conflagration. The kings and their armies saw their
troops crushed by Pāṇḍu and his army; and, defeated and brought
under his sway, they were reduced to tribute and corvée.

15 All the kings of earth whom he vanquished deemed him the sole
champion on earth, like the Sacker of Cities among the Gods. All the
princes of the land came to him bowing with folded hands, bringing
wealth and gems of many kinds, precious stones, pearls, and coral,
gold as well as silver, the choicest cows, horses, and chariots, and
elephants, donkeys, camels, buffalo, goats, and sheep; and the king,
ruler of Hāstinapura, accepted it all. He took it and with his joyous
columns returned to the City of the Elephant, to bring happiness to his
kingdoms and capital.

20 "The glorious battle cry of lionlike King Śaṃtanu and sagacious
Bharata had been lost, but is now once more raised by Pāṇḍu! They
who had taken the lands of the Kurus and the spoils of the Kurus
have now been made tributary to the Pāṇḍu, the lion of Hāstinapura!"
said the princes and the assembled councillors of the princes, their
hearts full of confidence and thrilled; and so also spoke the folk of city
and countryside. Led by Bhīṣma, they all came out to meet him when
he returned. Before they had gone a long way the people of
Hāstinapura happily saw the earth teeming with captives from many
countries, with many-colored gems that were piled on all sorts of
wagons, with choice elephants, horses, and chariots, cows, camels,
and sheep. The Kauravas following Bhīṣma came upon it all and saw
no end to it.

25 He greeted the feet of his father and swelled the bliss of his mother
Kausalyā; and, where due, he paid his respect to townspeople and

countryfolk as well. Reunited with his son who had successfully returned after crushing the enemy kingdoms, Bhīṣma shed tears of joy. With the festive noise of drums and hundreds of bands, he thrilled the townspeople everywhere as he marched into the City of the Elephant.

Vaiśaṃpāyana said:

106.1 With Dhṛtarāṣṭra's consent, Pāṇḍu offered the booty he had won
with his own arms to Bhīṣma, Satyavatī, and his mother. He also
sent some of his booty to Vidura; and his friends, too, the law-minded
prince satisfied with riches. Then Bhīṣma contented Satyavatī and
famous Kausalyā* with the sparkling gems that Pāṇḍu had won,
Bhārata. Kausalyā, his mother, blissfully embraced the boundlessly
5 lustrous bull among men just as Paulomī embraces Jayanta. Then
Dhṛtarāṣṭra offered up many grand sacrifices, equal to a hundred Horse
Sacrifices, which had bravely been won by that hero; and the priestly
stipends ran to the hundreds of thousands.
Then Pāṇḍu, who had won the luxury of leisure, went to roam the
forest with Kuntī and Mādrī, O bull among Bhāratas. He forsook his
palace and beautiful beds and lived solely in the woods, hunting all the
time. He ranged on the lovely southern slope of Mount Himālaya and
spent the nights on mountain ridges and in huge *śāla* forests.
Dwelling in the forest with Kuntī and Mādrī, he shone like the
10 illustrious elephant of Indra between two elephant cows. The forest
rangers looked on that Bhārata as a God, when he with his two wives
ranged about with sword and bow and arrows and colorful breastplate
—a heroic king who knew all about arms. Unweariedly, the men at
Dhṛtarāṣṭra's orders brought him in the forest tracts whatever he
might want of pleasure and joy.

Now Bhīṣma, son of the Ganges, came to hear that King Devaka had a bastard daughter of perfect beauty and youth. He sued for her, had her brought, and married her to the wise Vidura. Vidura, scion of the Kurus, fathered on her many sons of perfect demeanor who matched him in his virtues.

Vaiśaṃpāyana said:

107.1 Thereupon, Janamejaya, a hundred sons were born to
Dhṛtarāṣṭra by his wife Gāndhārī, and one more by a commoner's
wench. Pāṇḍu had five warlike sons by Kuntī and Mādrī, who were
born from Gods for the continuity of his line.

Janamejaya said:

How, best of brahmins, did Gāndhārī give birth to a hundred sons, and over how long a time? What was their life span? And how did Dhṛtarāṣṭra father a single son on a commoner's wench—and bypass

* = Ambālikā.

Gāndhārī, his law-abiding wife who was of his station and suitable to
5 him? How were Pāṇḍu's five warlike sons born from the Gods, when he had been cursed by that great-spirited seer? Recount all this to me as it occurred, with all particulars, wise ascetic, for I never grow weary of the stories of my kinsmen!

Vaiśaṃpāyana said:

Gāndhārī once comforted Dvaipāyana, when he had arrived exhausted with hunger and fatigue. Vyāsa granted her a boon. She chose a hundred sons that would be of equal station with her husband and herself. After some time she was with child by Dhṛtarāṣṭra. For two years Gāndhārī bore her foetus without giving
10 birth, and misery beset her. Then she heard that Kuntī had born a son, splendid like the morning sun; and when she felt the hardness of her own belly she began to worry. Unbeknownst to Dhṛtarāṣṭra, Gāndhārī, fainting with pain, aborted her belly with hard effort. A mass of flesh came forth, like a dense ball of clotted blood, and she made ready to throw it out after she had borne it in her womb for two years. Dvaipāyana divined it and came swiftly; then that best of the mumblers of spells saw the mass of flesh. He said to Subala's daughter, "What is this you are about to do?" She truthfully told the
15 great seer her mind: "When I heard that Kuntī had born her first son, splendid like the sun, I became so miserable that I aborted my belly. A hundred sons you granted me before, to be sure, and now this mass of flesh is born to me for those hundred sons!"

Vyāsa said:

And so shall it yet be and not otherwise, Gāndhārī! I have never spoken a lie in jest; should I do it in earnest? Have at once a hundred pots set up and filled with *ghee*; and sprinkle this ball with cold water.

Vaiśaṃpāyana said:

When the ball was doused, it fell apart into a hundred pieces, each
20 an embryo the size of a thumb joint; a full one hundred and one duly developed one after another from that ball of flesh as time went by, O lord of the people. He put them in the pots and had them watched in well-guarded places. Then the blessed lord told Gāndhārī after how much time the pots were to be broken open. And after taking measures and leaving instructions, the wise and blessed Lord Vyāsa repaired to the rocky Himālaya to perform austerities.

Prince Duryodhana was born first in the sequence of them, but Prince Yudhiṣṭhira was both by birth and by authority the elder one.
25 As soon as his son was born, Dhṛtarāṣṭra summoned many brahmins as well as Bhīṣma and Vidura, and he declared, "Prince Yudhiṣṭhira is the eldest scion in our line. By his own virtue he shall obtain the kingdom, and we shall not demur. But shall this one then become king after him? Tell me truthfully what must be firmly resolved in this matter."

When he ceased speaking, Bhārata, there was a sudden outcry on
all horizons of gruesome beasts that feed on carrion and of jackals of
unholy howls. Remarking these terrible portents everywhere, the
30 brahmins, and also the wise Vidura, spoke, O king: "Clearly this son of
yours will spell the death of the dynasty! In abandoning him there is
appeasement, great disaster in fostering him! Let ninety-nine sons
remain to you, lord of the land, and with the one you shall secure
both the world and your dynasty. 'For the family, abandon one son;
for the village, abandon a family; for the country, abandon a village;
for the soul, abandon the earth!'" Thus spoke Vidura and all the
great brahmins, but the king did not do it, for he loved his son.
Within a month's time the full one hundred sons were born to
Dhṛtarāṣṭra, O king, and over and above the hundred also a girl.
35 When Gāndhārī was ailing in her swelling belly, a commoner's wench,
who had been brought up there, used to serve the strong-armed
Dhṛtarāṣṭra, it is said. In that year a famous and sagacious son was
born to Dhṛtarāṣṭra by that wench, the bastard Yuyutsu, O king. So
one hundred warlike and heroic sons were born to Dhṛtarāṣṭra, and
one daughter, whose name was Duḥśālā.

Janamejaya said:
108.1 My lord, recount to me the names of these sons of Dhṛtarāṣṭra, in
the order of their birth.
Vaiśaṃpāyana said:
Duryodhana, Yuyutsu, Duḥśāsana, Duḥsaha, Duḥśāla, Jalasaṃdha,
Sama, Saha, Vinda, Anuvinda, Durdharṣa, Subāhu, Duṣpradharṣaṇa,
Durmarṣaṇa, Durmukha, Duṣkarman, Karṇa, Viviṃśati, Vikarṇa,
5 Sulocana, Citra, Upacitra, Citrākṣa, Cārucitra, Śarāsana, Durmada,
Duṣpragāha, Vivitsu, Vikaṭa, Ūrṇanābha, Sunābha, Nanda,
Upanandaka, Senāpati, Suṣeṇa, Kuṇḍodara, Mahodara, Citrabāṇa,
Citravarman, Suvarman, Durvimocana, Ayobāhu, Mahābāhu,
Citrānga, Citrakuṇḍala, Bhīmavega, Bhīmabala, Balākin, Balavardhana,
Ugrāyudha, Bhīmakarman, Kanakāyus, Dṛḍhāyudha, Dṛḍhavarman,
Dṛḍhakṣatra, Somakīrti, Anūdara, Dṛḍhasaṃdha, Jarāsaṃdha,
Satyasaṃdha, Sadaḥsuvāk, Ugraśravas, Aśvasena, Senānī,
10 Duṣparājaya, Aparājita, Paṇḍitaka, Viśālākṣa, Durāvara, Dṛḍhahasta,
Suhasta, Vātavega, Suvarcasa, Ādityaketu, Bahvāśin, Nāgadanta,
Ugrayāyin, Kavacin, Niṣangin, Pāśin, Daṇḍadhara, Dhanurgraha,
Ugra, Bhīmaratha, Vīra, Vīrabāhu, Alolupa, Abhaya, Raudrakarman,
Dṛḍharatha, Anādhṛṣya, Kuṇḍabhedin, Virāvin, Dīrghalocana,
Dīrghabāhu, Mahābāhu, Vyūḍhoru, Kanakadhvaja, Kuṇḍāśin, and
Virajas; and Duḥsālā the girl, who was the hundred-and-first.
Herewith are summed up by name the one hundred sons, O king,
15 and the one daughter, in the order of their birth. They were all
surpassing warriors and champions, all expert in combat, all

conversant with the *Veda* and proficient in the sciences of the kings and the arts of intercourse. All shone with knowledge and good birth. And when the time came, O king, Dhṛtarāṣṭra, after due investigation, married them all to wives of equal station. And when the time came, and with Gāndhārī's consent, the king married Duḥśālā to Jayadratha, the king of Sindhu.

Janamejaya said:

109.1 You have narrated the great and hallowed origin of the sons of Dhṛtarāṣṭra, this superhuman birth of human beings, O great scholar of the Brahman. I have heard from you the names of each of them—now tell me those of the Pāṇḍavas, brahmin. In the *Book of the Partial Incarnations* you have related that all these great-spirited men, whose prowess was like Indra's, themselves were particles of Gods. Therefore, I wish to hear how they were born, they whose feats were more than human. Recount it all, Vaiśaṃpāyana!

Vaiśaṃpāyana said:

5 King Pāṇḍu once saw in the great forest, which is haunted by deer and beasts of prey, a buck, the leader of its herd, mate with its doe. Thereupon Pāṇḍu shot both the doe and the buck with five swift, sharp, beautiful, fletched arrows with golden nocks. The buck was a powerful ascetic, O king, the son of a seer, who had been consorting with his wife in the form of a deer. Still coupled with his doe, he fell instantly to the ground and, his powers waning, cried out in a human voice.

The deer said:

Even men who love evil, though wrapped in lust and anger,
10 though bereft of all reason, stop short of atrocity! Man's mind does
not swallow Fate, it is Fate that swallows the mind. No mind attains to things that Fate forbids. You have been born in an eminent lineage that has always been law-minded; then why are you now so overpowered by lust and greed that your good sense is reeling?

Pāṇḍu said:

The ways of kings with deer is as it is with enemies: they kill them. Do not blame me in your folly, deer! Deer are to be killed without subterfuge and trickery: that is the Law of the kings. Why blame me when you know that? The seer Agastya, when sitting at a Session, went hunting, sprinkling the wild deer in the great forest so that they
were dedicated to all the Gods, according to the Law that is found in
15 the Rules. Why blame us? Through Agastya's sorcery the omentum of
your kind is offered at the sacrifice.

The deer said:

They have never yet let loose their arrows on enemies without considering. The best time to kill them is when they are weak.

Pāṇḍu said:
Whether he is on guard or off guard, when he is exposed they kill
him with might, means, and sharp arrows. Why do you blame me,
deer?
The deer said:
I do not blame you for killing deer, king, because of myself. But
out of kindness you should have waited until I was done mating! For
what man of sense would kill a buck that is mating in the woods, at a
20 time beneficent to all creatures and wanted by all creatures? Needlessly
to frustrate a cherished goal of man was not worthy of you, Kaurava,
who are born into the lineage of the Pauravas and those of seers of
unsullied acts! This most cruel act is decried by all the worlds; it is
ungodly and dishonorable, utterly against the Law. You know the
niceties of the pleasure of women, and you know the points of
Scripture, Law, and Profit—it is unworthy of you who resemble a God
to perpetrate such an ungodly deed! You yourself are beholden to
punish people who commit cruelties and do evil, best of kings, people
who have abandoned the three pursuits of life. What did it profit you,
best of men, to kill me, an innocent? Me, a hermit who lives on roots
and fruit, wearing the guise of a deer, who always dwells in the forest,
25 seeking serenity? Therefore, since you have injured me, you yourself
will fall victim to love: when you are helplessly overcome by love,
your love will unfailingly kill you, who outraged a mating couple! I
am Kiṃdama, a hermit of unequaled austerities. I mated with a doe
because I shy away from humans, and as a deer I live with deer in the
depths of the forest. You will escape the guilt of brahmin-murder,
since you did not know that you killed me in the body of a deer when
I was overcome by love. But for that, fool, you shall find the same
fate. When you are lying with a woman you love, blinded by your
passion, you too in that very same state will depart for the world of the
dead. And the beloved woman with whom you shall lie at the time of
your death will fall under the power of the king of the dead, which for
all creatures is inescapable: she shall follow you out of devotion,
30 greatest of sages. Just as you brought me to grief when I moved in
bliss, so shall grief come to you when you have found bliss!
Vaiśaṃpāyana said:
When he had thus spoken, he, the deer, departed from life in great
pain; and in that instant Pāṇḍu was overwhelmed by grief.

Vaiśaṃpāyana said:
110.1 Bereft by the deer's death as by the death of a kinsman, Pāṇḍu and
his wives were sorrow-stricken and lamented grievously.
Pāṇḍu said:
Even though born in the family of good men, those whose spirits

are unmade and are deluded by the net of lust come, alas! to a bad end and through their own acts. My own father, born from an ever-law-minded man, came to his end, still a child, because—so we have heard—he lived for his pleasure. In the field of that pleasure-loving king, the blessed Kṛṣṇa Dvaipāyana himself, a seer restrained in his
5 speech, begot me. And though of such descent, my lowly spirit now again has become addicted to vice; and, deserted by the Gods, I live only for hunting, perversely and evilly.

I resolve on release, for a strong vice is a shackle. I shall follow the imperishable good way of life of my father. I shall yoke myself to extreme austerities, unfailingly. Alone, each single day under another tree, I shall beg my food and, a shaven hermit, wander upon this earth—covered with dust, sheltering in empty hovels, or bedding at the foot of a tree, renouncing all that is dear and hateful, neither grieving nor rejoicing, equable before praise and abuse, without blessings,
10 without greetings, without choices, without possessions—deriding no one, frowning at nothing, always bending myself with serene face to the welfare of all creatures, never offending any of the four orders of moving and unmoving beings, always equal-minded to all breathing creatures, as though they were my children.

I shall beg my food one time a day of seven families, even if there are no alms to be had when they themselves go hungry; a little every time, whatever food they have, whatever I receive first, I shall never beg more, when the seven are full, whether I received anything or not. If a man hacks off my arm with a hatchet, and another anoints the
15 other arm with sandal, I shall think neither good nor ill of either. I shall do nothing out of a will to live, or a will to die; and neither welcome nor turn away either life or death. All the rites for prosperity that the living can perform, I shall pass them all by, when I come to their instants and dates. At all times I shall forsake all that makes the senses work, renounce the Law, and cleanse all the soil of my soul. Delivered from all evil, escaped from all snakes, I shall seek the Law of the wind, beholden to no one. And, forever living by such a way of life, I shall sustain my body, walking the path of fearlessness.
20 Deprived of my manliness, I shall not lust after the way of the dogs that suit the unmanly and wretched, ever astray from their own Law. He who, honored or dishonored, seeks another way of life with hungry eyes, given to his lust, walks the road of the dogs.

Vaiśaṃpāyana said:

When he had spoken, the sorrowful king looked, sighing, at Kuntī and Mādrī and said to them, "Let Kausalyā be told, and Vidura the Steward, and the king with the kinsmen, the Lady Satyavatī, Bhīṣma, the king's priests, the great-spirited brahmins of

strict vows who drink the Soma, and the city elders who live there as
my pensioners—let all be prayed and told that Pāṇḍu has departed for
the forest!"

25 Hearing this word of their husband whose mind was set on life in
the forest, Kuntī and Mādrī made the same reply: "There are other
stages of life that you can undertake together with us, your wives by
the Law, O bull of the Bhāratas, and still mortify your flesh. And
you surely and without fail shall find heaven too. We shall abjure
all our senses and, devoted to our husband's world and forsaking the
pleasures of love, we too shall undertake severe austerities. If you
desert us, wise king who are the lord of your people, then of a
certainty we shall give up our lives this very day!"

Pāṇḍu said:

If you are resolved on this in accordance with the Law, then I shall
follow the imperishable way of my father as my own. Renouncing the
30 pleasant life of the village and performing great austerities, I shall live
in the forest, clothe myself in bark, and eat of fruit and roots. Both
mornings and evenings I shall make offerings in the fire and do my
ablutions, lean, eating little, wearing hides, and matting my hair. I
shall dry out this body, suffering cold wind and heat, hunger, thirst,
and fatigue, with difficult mortifications, seeking solitude, living on
that which is ripe and green, and contenting Gods and ancestors with
forest-fare, words, and water. The sight of a man who has departed for
35 the woods has never offended family men, let alone the villagers. So,
I shall be looking forward to the harsh and ever-harsher rules of the
precepts of the forest, until my body is finished.

Vaiśaṃpāyana said:

After having spoken to his wives, King Pāṇḍu, Scion of Kuru, took
off his crown, neck chain, earrings, and the two bracelets of his upper
arms and gave them all, with the jewelry and the costly robes of his
women, to the brahmins and said, "Go to the City of the Elephant and
say that Pāṇḍu has departed for the woods. Relinquishing all profit,
pleasure, and comforts, and the supreme joy of love, the Bull of the
Kurus has departed with his wives." When his followers and servants
had heard these various grievous words of the lionlike Bhārata, they
40 raised a terrible wail and shrieked pitiably. Shedding hot tears, they
left the king and hastened to Hāstinapura with his message.

When Dhṛtarāṣṭra, best of men, had heard from them all that had
befallen in the great forest, he mourned over Pāṇḍu. But Prince
Pāṇḍu Kaurava, henceforth living on roots and fruit, went with his
wives to Mount Nāgasabha. He journeyed to Caitraratha, crossed the
Vāriṣeṇā, and passed beyond the Himālaya to Gandhamādana.
Watched over by the Mahābhūtas, Siddhas, and great seers, the king

45 dwelt there in smooth and rough country. He went on to Lake
Indradyumna and beyond Mount Haṃsakūṭa, until the ascetic king
arrived at the Hundred-Peak Mountains.

Vaiśaṃpāyana said:

111.1 There the powerful man, bent upon sublime austerities, became the
apple of the eye of the hosts of Siddhas and Cāraṇas. Obedient,
unselfish, disciplined, and the master of his senses, he soon won the
road to heaven by his own power, O Bhārata. To some he was brother,
to others friend, and other seers watched over him like a son. After a
long time Pāṇḍu reached such pure austerity that he became like a
5 brahmin seer, O bull of the Bharatas. Thereupon, wishing to cross to
the other shore where heaven lies, he started with his wives on his
way north of the Hundred-Peak Mountains.

The ascetics said to him, "Going higher and higher northward up
the mountains, we have witnessed many inaccessible regions on that
mountain range, the playgrounds of Gods, Gandharvas, and Apsarās,
the rough and smooth park lands of Kubera, the sloping banks of great
rivers, and impenetrable mountain caves. There are regions of
perpetual snow, where no tree grows, no deer or birds live, and large
lands and inaccessible passes. No bird could cross them, much less land
animals. Only the wind has gone beyond it, and Siddhas and great
10 seers—how could these two princesses go on that king of mountains
without sinking? They do not deserve the misery. Don't go, bull
among Bhāratas!"

Pāṇḍu said:

For a childless man they say, my lords, there is no door to heaven.
Therefore I who am childless am much troubled, I declare to you. The
sons of man are born on earth with four debts, which are to be paid
to the ancestors, Gods, seers, and men, a hundredfold, a thousandfold.
The man who does not heed them when their time comes is destitute
of worlds, so the scholars of the Law lay down. With sacrifices he
pleases the Gods, with study and austerities the seers, with sons and
15 *śrāddhas* the ancestors, with benevolence men. I am acquitted by Law
of my debts to seers, Gods, and men; but not of my debt to the
ancestors, and therefore I am troubled, ascetics. This is certain, that
when my body perishes, so will the ancestors. It is to beget children
that the best of men are born in this world. Should I have offspring in
my field, just as I myself was begotten by the great-spirited seer in my
father's field?

The ascetics said:

We know that there *is* offspring for you, law-minded king,
godlike, beautiful, flawless offspring—we see it with our divine eye.
Bring about with your own deeds, tiger among men, what Fate has
set out for you. The undistracted man of sense finds unspoiled fruit.

20 The fruit is in sight; make an effort, friend. And when you have
obtained your talented offspring, you will find happiness.

Vaiśaṃpāyana said:

Having heard the hermits' words, Pāṇḍu became much worried,
since he knew that his own acting was prevented by the curse of the
deer. In private he spoke to his wife by the Law, famous Kuntī.

"In a time of distress they prescribe a yoking to engender offspring:
'Offspring indeed is in the worlds a firm foundation informed by the
Law.' It is thus, Kuntī, that the wise know the eternal Law, as it was
from the beginning. Oblations offered, gifts given, austerities done, or
voluntary self-restraints—none of them, it is said, sanctify a childless
25 man in this world. Here I am—I know all this; and then I look
forward, sweet-smiling wife, worrying that without children I shall
never attain the bright worlds. For when I did a cruel deed,
beautiful Kuntī, I lost my virility before I was done, through the
curse of the deer, so that it became frustrated.

"In the eyes of the Law there are these six sons who are of the
blood and heirs, and these six who are neither heirs nor of the blood.
Hear from me who they are, Pṛthā: the son fathered by oneself, the
son presented, the son purchased, the son born by one's widow, the
son born by one's wife before her marriage, and the son born by a
loose woman; the others are the son gifted, the son bartered, the son
by artifice, the son who comes by himself, the son come with
marriage, the son of unknown seed, and the son fathered on a lowly
30 womb. One should try to obtain sons, reckoning from the higher
downward; lower people want, in a time of distress, a son from a
higher man. 'The strict find offspring the first granter of the fruits of
the Law, even if born outside one's own seed,' Pṛthā, quoth Manu
Svāyaṃbhuva. Therefore, lacking myself the power of progeny, I shall
now send *you*. Find yourself a child by my equal or better, glorious
wife!

"Listen, Kuntī, to the story of Śāradaṇḍāyinī, that hero's wife,
whom her elders instructed to bear a child. Ritually pure and bathed,
she stood in the night at a crossroads and with a flower chose an
accomplished brahmin; after making an offering into the fire for the
35 Birth-of-a-Son and finishing the rite, she lived with him. He begot on
her three warlike sons, Durjaya and the others, and so you too,
beautiful wife, must at my injunction at once rise to conceive a son
from a brahmin of superior austerities."

Vaiśaṃpāyana said:

112.1 At these words of Pāṇḍu, O great king, Kuntī replied to that heroic
bull of the Kurus, lord of the earth and of her, "You must not speak
like this to me, you who know the Law—I am your wife by the Law
and devoted to you, my lotus-eyed husband. You yourself, strong-

armed Bhārata hero, will father on me heroic sons according to the
Law. I shall go to heaven with you, tiger among men, and you your-
5 self must come to me for children, scion of Kuru. For not even in my
thoughts shall I go to any man but you. What man on earth is
greater than you?

"Listen first to this tale of Law that I shall tell you from the books of the Lore, large-eyed Pāṇḍu, just as I have heard it.

"There was once, so they say, a king known as Vyuṣitāśva, a son
in the dynasty of Pūru, who was a most law-minded man. When this
great-spirited and law-spirited king performed a sacrifice, Indra and
and the Gods came to him with the great seers. Indra got drunk with
Soma, the brahmins with their fees, at the sacrifice of the great-
10 spirited royal seer Vyuṣitāśva. Thereafter, O king, Vyuṣitāśva shone
wide beyond all other mortals, beyond all creatures, like the sun after
the season of the dew. This greatest of kings defeated, captured, and
drove before him the princes of the east, the north, the middle, and the
south. At the grand celebration of his Horse Sacrifice, the majestic
Vyuṣitāśva with the strength of ten elephants became the Indra of the
kings. The men who know the ancient Lore sing a verse about him:

"'Vyuṣitāśva conquered earth
To her boundaries of seas,
All the classes did he watch
As a father watches his sons.'

"Sacrificer of great sacrifices, he gave riches to the brahmins, and with jewels beyond count he offered up grand rituals. Many times he pressed the Soma and celebrated Soma sacrifices.

15 "He had a wife who was greatly esteemed, Bhadrā Kākṣīvatī, who,
king of men, had beauty without peer on earth. The story goes that
they lusted after each other; and, mad with his lust for her, he
succumbed to consumption. Soon afterwards he went like the sun to
his setting. When the king of men had died, his wife was overcome by
grief. Left without sons, stricken with the greatest grief, Bhadrā
lamented, O tiger among men, so we have heard—listen, overlord of
men.

"'Any woman, great knower of the Law, who, bereft of sons, lives
on without her husband, that wretched woman lives no more!
20 Without her husband, a wife's fortune is dead, bull among barons. I
want to go your way, please take me along! Bereaved of you, I cannot
live for an instant. Show me your grace, king, take me quickly from
here! I shall follow behind you, through the rough and the smooth,
tiger among men, without turning back. Faithful as a shadow, king, I
shall ever do your will, always love to please you. From this day on,
hideous sicknesses that dry up the heart will beset me, now that I am

25 bereft of you, lotus-eyed lord. Surely in previous bodies, my prince, I
must have sundered faithful companions or separated those that were
united! The misery that I have piled up with evil deeds in previous
bodies has now come upon me by my separation from you, O king.
From this day on I shall lie on a bed of *kuśa* grass and, seized by my
sorrow, I shall dwell on the memory of your face. Show yourself to me,
kindly, tiger among men, for I am pursued by grief, lord of men,
miserable, deserted, destitute, wailing!
"So she lamented again and again in many ways, as she held the
30 corpse embraced. Then indeed a hidden voice spoke. 'Rise up,
Bhadrā, and go; I shall give you a boon here. I shall father children on
you, my sweet-smiling wife. On your own bed, on the eighth or
fourteenth day of the moon, when you have bathed after your
season, you shall lie with me.' At these words the divine Bhadrā, who
was avowed to her husband, did as she was told, for she longed for
sons. By that corpse the divine woman gave birth to her sons, the
three Śālvas and the four Madras, O king, best of the Bhāratas. And so
you too, bull of the Bhāratas, will be able, by the lasting yogic power
of your austerities, to beget sons on me with your mind."

Vaiśaṃpāyana said:

113.1 The king replied to his queen with this lofty answer informed by the
Law, as he knew the Law: "Yes, so did Vyuṣitāśva act, beautiful
Kuntī, in the olden days, as you have just told the story, for he was
like unto the Immortals. Now I shall tell you the Law, listen to me,
the ancient Law that the great-spirited, law-minded seers saw.
"In the olden days, so we hear, the women went uncloistered, my
lovely wife of the beautiful eyes; they were their own mistresses who
5 took their pleasure where it pleased them. From childhood on they
were faithless to their husbands, but yet not lawless, for such was the
Law in the olden days. Even today the animal creatures still follow
this hoary Law, without any passion or hatred. This anciently
witnessed Law was honored by the great seers, and it still prevails
among the Northern Kurus, Kuntī of the softly tapering thighs, for
this is the eternal Law that favors women. But in the present world
the present rule was laid down soon after—I shall tell you fully by
whom and why, sweet-smiling wife!
"There was, so we hear, a great seer by the name of Uddālaka, and
10 he had a hermit son who was called Śvetaketu. It was he, so we hear,
who laid down this rule among humankind, in a fit of anger, lotus-
eyed Kuntī—now hear why. Once, in full view of Śvetaketu and his
father, a brahmin took Śvetaketu's mother by the hand and said, 'Let
us go.' At this, the seer's son became indignant and infuriated, when
he saw how his mother, as if by force, was being led away. But his

father, on seeing him angered, said to Śvetaketu, 'Do not be angry,
son. This is the eternal Law. The women of all classes are uncloistered
on earth. Just as the cows do, so do the creatures each in its class.'
15 Śvetaketu, the seer's son, did not condone the Law, and laid down the
present rule for men and women on earth, for humans but not for
other creatures, good lady. Ever since, we hear, this rule has stood.
'From this day on,' he ruled, 'a woman's faithlessness to her husband
shall be a sin equal to aborticide, an evil that shall bring on misery.
Seducing a chaste and constant wife who is avowed to her husband
shall also be a sin on earth. And a wife who is enjoined by her husband
20 to conceive a child and refuses shall incur the same evil.' Thus did
Uddālaka's son Śvetaketu forcibly lay down this rule of the Law in the
olden days, my bashful wife.

"We have also heard that King Kalmāṣapāda Saudāsa enjoined his
wife Madayantī to conceive a child, and she went to the seer Vasiṣṭha.
From him the happy woman obtained a son called Aśmaka, in order to
do, like a good wife, a favor for her husband. Our own birth too is
known to have been from Kṛṣṇa Dvaipāyana, bashful lotus-eyed
Kuntī, so that the dynasty of the Kurus might prosper.

"Therefore, on seeing all these good reasons, you must without
25 blame do my word, which obeys the Law. Princess so strict in your
vows, those who know the Law know this for the Law that at every
season the woman may not avoid her husband. At all other times,
however, the woman may exercise her own choice. This the strict
people expound as the ancient Law. Those who know the Law also
know, princess, that whatever a husband tells his wife, by Law or
against Law, she must do it, especially if one, himself deprived of
the power of progeny, is hungry for sons, as I am, flawless Kuntī,
longing to set eyes on a son. Thus I raise my folded hands, cupped like
lotus petals with red fingers, to my head, to beseech you, my comely.
30 At my injunction, beautiful-tressed wife, pray give birth by a brahmin
of superior austerity to sons that are endowed with virtues. With your
help, broad-hipped Kuntī, I may walk the path of those that have
sons!"

When he had spoken, the buxom woman, who loved to please her
husband, replied to Pāṇḍu, conqueror of enemy cities, "When I was a
child in my father's house, I was charged with honoring the guests;
and there I served that awesome brahmin of strict vows, whose
decisions on the Law are mysterious, whom they know as Durvāsas. I
satisfied this man of honed spirit with all my efforts. He gave me a
boon and told me a canon of spells accompanied by sorcery, and he
35 said to me, 'Whichsoever God you will call up with this spell will
come into your power, loving you or not.' This is what he said to me
in my father's house, O Bhārata. The word given by a brahmin is

true—and the time for it has come now. With your assent, I shall call
up a God, sage king, by means of that spell, so that we, O lord, may
have offspring. Which God shall I call? Tell me, you who know things
best. Know that I am ready to act, if you consent to my plan."

Pāṇḍu said:

This very day you must act, beautiful woman, as it suits the
40 matter. Call Dharma, for he among the Gods partakes of merit. For
Dharma would not join yoke with us if it were not lawful, and people
will now think that this is the Law. And of a certainty this son shall
become the standard of Law for the Kurus; and having been given by
Dharma, his mind will not rejoice in lawlessness. Therefore, sweet-
smiling wife, set the the Law before you and be constant to it and
propitiate with service and sorcery God Dharma.

Vaiśaṃpāyana said:

"So be it," said the lovely woman to her husband's words; she
saluted him and with his consent circumambulated his person.

Vaiśaṃpāyana said:

114.1 When Gāndhārī had been with child for a year, Janamejaya,
Kuntī called imperishable Dharma to conceive a child. The queen at
once brought offerings to Dharma and solemnly muttered the spells
that Durvāsas had given her. She lay with Dharma, who had assumed
a yogic body, and the buxom woman received a son who would be the
greatest of all breathing creatures—it was on the Indra day, of the
bright fortnight, at Abhijit, which is the eighth hour, when the sun
5 stood at noon, on a day of blessing that is greatly honored. In time,
Kuntī gave birth to a son of rich fame; and scarcely was he born
when a disembodied voice spoke: "He shall of a certainty be the
greatest of the upholders of the Law, Pāṇḍu's firstborn son, who shall
be named Yudhiṣṭhira. He shall be a celebrated king, widely renowned
in all three worlds, glorious, lustrous, and moral."

Having obtained a son who would be law-minded, Pāṇḍu again
said to Kuntī, "They declare that the baronage triumphs through
strength: choose a son of triumphant strength!" At her husband's
word she called up the Wind; and by him she bore the strong-armed
10 Bhīma whose prowess was terrifying. And over this most forceful
unbeatable child the voice spoke, O Bhārata: "He is born to be strong
over all that is strong!" A marvel occurred soon after Wolf-Belly was
born, when he fell from his mother's lap and shattered a mountain
with his body. It happened that Kuntī was frightened by a tiger and
suddenly started up, forgetting Wolf-Belly who was sleeping in her lap.
The boy, hard as a diamond, fell upon the mountain, and in his fall
shattered it with his body to a hundred pieces. On seeing the
mountain pulverized, Pāṇḍu marveled much. The same day that

Bhīma was born, O best of the Bhāratas, lord of the earth, Duryodhana was also born.

After the Wolf-belly's birth, Pāṇḍu pondered upon this thought:
15 "How shall I obtain a superior son who will be supreme in the world? For this world rests on both fate and man's own deeds; but fate is received from Destiny conjoined with Time. Now Indra is the king and, so we hear, the best of the Gods; his power and enterprise are boundless, his power and luster endless. I shall obtain from him a powerful son when I have satisfied him with austerities. The son that he will give me shall be my choicest. Therefore I shall mortify myself greatly in acts, thoughts, and words." Thereupon the lustrous Pāṇḍu Kaurava took counsel with the great seers and enjoined on Kuntī a
20 holy, year-long vow. The strong-armed prince himself stood on one foot and with a supreme concentration undertook awesome austerities. Wishing to win over the God who is the sovereign of the Thirty Gods, the law-minded Pāṇḍu turned with the sun.

After a long time Indra responded: "I shall give you a son to be famous in the three worlds, who shall accomplish the goals of the Gods, the brahmins, and his friends. I shall give you a superb son who shall destroy all his enemies." After the great-spirited Indra had thus spoken to the king, the law-minded Kaurava spoke to Kuntī, bearing
25 his words in mind: "A son, great-spirited, wise in policy, sunlike in luster, unassailable, vigorous in action, of the most wondrous aspect—such a son you must now bear, to be the abode of all a baron's glories. We have found grace with the Indra of the Gods: call him, sweet-smiling wife!"

Then the glorious woman called Indra; and the lord of the Gods came and begot Arjuna. And when the child was born, the disembodied voice spoke, resonant with a deep rumble that reverberated along the skies: "In prowess the match of Kārtavīrya, in puissance Śibi's peer, invincible like Indra, he shall broadcast, Kuntī, your glory! Just as Aditi's joy was increased by Viṣṇu, so Arjuna, the
30 like of Viṣṇu, shall increase your joy. He shall bring the Madras under his sway, the Kurus with the Kaikeyas, the Cedis, Kāśis, and Karūṣas, and firmly plant the Fortune of the Kurus. By the prowess of his arms he shall sate the Fire of Sacrifice in the Khāṇḍava Forest with the fat of all creatures. The mighty leader of his people shall vanquish the barons, and with his brothers the hero shall offer up the three sacrifices. Equal to Rāma Jāmadagnya, in puissance the peer of Viṣṇu,
35 greatest of heroes, he shall remain undefeated. All celestial weapons he shall obtain, and, a bull among men, rescue the lost fortune."

Such was the wondrous word that the wind in the sky spoke at the birth of Kuntī's son, and Kuntī heard it from him. So did the ascetics that lived on the Hundred-Peak Mountains hear the word, which was

spoken loudly, and supreme joy seized them. And in the sky there was
a boisterous clamor of Indra and the Gods, the seers and the
celestials, and the clangor of drums. A mighty roar rose up wrapped
in showers of flowers, as the throngs of the Gods assembled and paid
40 honor to Pārtha—and the brood of Kadrū and Vinatā, the
Gandharvas and Apsarās, all the lords of the creatures, and the Seven
Seers—

> Bharadvāja, Kaśyapa, Gautama,
> Viśvāmitra, Jamadagni, Vasiṣṭha,
> And he who rises as the sun goes down
> The blessed Lord Atri came there too—

Marīci, Angiras, Pulastya, Pulaha, Kratu, Dakṣa and Prajāpati,
Gandharvas and Apsarās. Wearing celestial garlands and robes,
adorned with all their finery, the Apsarās sang to the Terrifier and
danced around him. Illustrious Tumbura and the other Gandharvas
began to chant—Bhīmasena, Ugrasena, Ūrṇāyus, Anagha, Gopati,
45 Dhṛtarāṣṭra, Sūryavarcas, Yugapa, Tṛṇapa, Kārṣṇi, Nandin, Citraratha,
Śāliśiras, Parjanya, Kali, Nārada, who is the sixteenth. And Sat and
Bṛhat, Bṛhaka and famous Karāla, Brahmacārin, Bahuguṇa, and
renowned Suparṇa, Viśvāvasu, Bhūmanyu, and Sucandra, who is the
tenth, and celebrated Hāha and Āhuhu sweet of songs. These were the
divine Gandharvas who sang to the bull of men.

The Apsarās, decked with all their finery, likewise danced and
50 sang, joyous, long-eyed damsels—Anūnā, Anavadyā, Priyamukhyā,
Guṇāvarā, Adrikā, Sācī, Miśrakeśī, Alambuṣā, Marīci, Śucikā,
Lakṣaṇā, Kṣemā, Devī, Rambhā, Manoramā, Asitā, Subāhu,
Supriyā, Suvapus, Puṇḍarīkā, Sugandhā, Surathā, Pramāthinī,
Kāmyā, Śāradvatī—they all danced there in throngs—Menakā,
Sahajanyā, Parṇikā, Puñjikasthalā, Kratusthalā, Ghṛtācī, Viśvācī,
Purvacitti, she who is famous as Umlocā, and Pramlocā, these ten
and Urvaśī, the eleventh, all sang, the long-eyed Apsarās. Up in
55 heaven stood the Ādityas—Dhātar, Aryaman, Mitra, Varuṇa, Aṃśa,
Bhaga, Indra, Vivasvat, Pūṣan, Tvaṣṭar, Parjanya, and Viṣṇu, all
aglow with fire, to glorify the greatness of the Pāṇḍava. There stood
the Rudras—Mṛgavyādha, Śarva, Nirṛti of great fame, Aja Ekapād,
Ahi Budhnya, Pinākin scourge of foes, Dahana, Īśvara, Kapālin,
Sthāṇu, and the blessed Lord Bhava, O king of the people. In a
circle stood the Aśvins, the eight Vasus, the vigorous Maruts, and All-
60 the-Gods, and the Sādhyas. Karkoṭaka came, and Śeṣa and the
Snake Vāsuki, Kacchapa, Apakuṇḍa, and the mighty Serpent
Takṣaka, all glowing with heat, of great fury and strength; and all the
many other Snakes were arrayed there, as were Vinatā's sons—
Tarkṣya, Ariṣṭanemi, Garuḍa, Asitadhvaja, Aruṇa, and Āruṇi. When

they saw that great wonder, the good hermits, astounded, reached
even greater exultation over the Pāṇḍavas.
But famous Pāṇḍu, greedy for more sons, sent once more his
65 comely wife. But now Kuntī said to him, "They do not speak of a
fourth son, even in times of distress. After three she is loose, after four
she is a harlot. Here you stand, knowing this Law, which stands to
reason: then why do you transgress it and, as though absentmindedly,
speak to me to give more children?"

Vaiśaṃpāyana said:
115.1 After Kuntī's sons had been born, and Dhṛtarāṣṭra's, the daughter
of the king of the Madras spoke privily to Pāṇḍu: "I am not disturbed,
even though you have not been fair to me, nor because I must always
take second place to Kuntī, flawless lord. Nor has it grieved me, my
king, scion of the Kurus, to learn that Gāndhārī has borne a hundred
sons. But this is my great grievance that Kuntī and I were both
equally deprived of sons, but fate would have it that my husband
5 found progeny from her. If the daughter of Kuntibhoja would bring it
about that I too bear children, it would be a favor to me, and to you
too it would be a blessing. Being her cowife, I am too proud to speak
to Kunti's daughter; but if you are gracious to me, please urge her
yourself."

Pāṇḍu said:
I too have often turned this matter over in my heart, but dared not
speak to you for fear I might well offend you. Now that you know
your mind, I shall act at once. I am sure that if I speak to her she will
do what I say.

Vaiśaṃpāyana said:
Thereupon Pāṇḍu spoke to Kuntī when they were alone. "Grant
10 me," he said "the continuity of my line, and the world your favor! To
insure that neither I nor my forebears shall lack the funeral offerings,
and to please me, my beautiful wife, you must accomplish a most
gracious feat. For the sake of your own glory you must do a difficult
deed—so does Indra, although he has already won sovereignty, still
offer up sacrifices, as he seeks glory. So, too, do brahmins who know
the spells and have performed the most difficult feats of austerity, yet
seek out new teachers, for the sake of glory, radiant Kuntī! Likewise
all royal seers and brahmins rich in austerities, for the sake of glory,
go on to manifold, difficult exploits. You, blameless woman, must carry
Mādrī across as with a ship. By bestowing children on her you shall
earn the highest fame."
15 Kuntī at once spoke to Mādrī: "Think, for this once, of a deity, and
of a certainty you shall have a child by him." Mādrī after much
thought went out to the Aśvins with her heart; and they came and

begot two sons on her, Nakula and Sahadeva, whose beauty was
unmatched on earth. And over the twins the disembodied voice again
spoke: "Endowed with beauty, courage, and virtue beyond all other
men, they shall shine with surpassing luster, with comeliness and
opulence."

Then the seers who lived on the Hundred-Peak Mountains gave
them all names, with love and ritual and benedictions, O king of the
20 people. The eldest they addressed as Yudhiṣṭhira, the middle one as
Bhīmasena, the third as Arjuna—thus they named the three sons of
Kuntī. Then the affectionate brahmins named the two sons of Mādrī—
the elder of the twins Nakula, the other Sahadeva. All these chiefs of
the Kurus were born one year apart.

Pāṇḍu once more proposed to Kuntī on Mādrī's behalf, privily, but
Pṛthā replied, "I said to her, 'For this once,' and she got two! I was
deceived! I fear that she will best me. That is the way of women! I
had not known, the more fool I, that by invoking two Gods the fruit
would be doubled. Therefore you shall no more charge me, that must
be my favor from you!"

25 So five God-given powerful sons were born to Pāṇḍu, glorious
furtherers of the dynasty of Kuru. They bore the marks of greatness,
their aspect was benign as the moon's, their pride like a lion's, great
archers all, who strode wide like the lion—lion-necked lords of men
who grew up with the might of Gods. And as they grew up on the
holy Mount Himālaya they astonished the great seers that had
foregathered there. These five, and the other hundred, all scions of the
dynasty of Kuru, grew up quickly like lotuses in a pond.

Vaiśaṃpāyana said:

116.1 As Pāṇḍu saw his five handsome sons grow up in the great
wilderness on the mountain, protected by the might of his own arms,
his heart rejoiced. Once, in the months of spring, when the woods
stood in full bloom, at the season when all creatures are crazed, the
king used to stroll through the forest with his wives. And as he
gazed upon the wood that was resplendent with *palāśas, tilakas,*
mangoes, *campakas, pāribhadrikas,* and many other trees rich in
blossom and fruit, and with manifold lakes and lotus ponds, love
5 sprang in his heart. In happy spirits he was leisurely wandering about
like an Immortal, when Mādrī followed him, alone, wearing one
pretty piece of clothing. And as he watched the nubile Mādrī in her
sheer skirt, his lust grew like a brush fire. Staring at the lotus-eyed
woman, whose mood matched his, where they were alone, he could
not control his lust, and lust overpowered him. He lay forcefully hold
of his queen in that desolate place, while she writhed and with all
her might tried to stop him. His mind wrapped by lust, he forgot the

curse and forced himself upon Mādrī by the Law of copulation.
10 Casting off all fear of the curse, the Kaurava, love-ridden to his death,
forcibly went into his beloved; and the mind of the lusting man was
crazed by Time itself, which churned his senses, and it was lost with
his wit. Pāṇḍu, the supremely law-minded man, joy of the Kurus,
succumbed to the Law of Time in the embrace of his wife.

Mādrī held the king dead in her arms and she shrieked and shrieked
in horror. Kuntī with her children, and Mādrī's own twins, all came
15 to where the king was lying as he did. Pitiably, Mādrī called out to
Kuntī, O king, "Come here by yourself, leave the children there!" She
kept the children at a distance, and with a violent scream "I am lost!"
came closer. Seeing both Pāṇḍu and Mādrī lying on the ground,
Kuntī, her body wrapped in grief, wailed with misery: "I always
watched the hero, and he always checked himself! How could you
overreach, knowing the hermit's curse as you did? Was it not rather
20 your task to protect the king, Mādrī? You, why did you seduce the
king in this lonely spot? How could he come upon you in secret, he
who always somberly had the curse on his mind, and suddenly find
bliss? Lucky you are, Bactrian woman, and more fortunate than I,
that you were given to see our lord's face happy!"

Mādrī said:

It was I who was seduced! I warded him off again and again, but
I could not keep myself from him, he was bent on proving his fate true!

Kuntī said:

I am the elder wife by the Law, and the greater fruit of the Law is
due to me. That which must be shall be; do not turn me back, Mādrī!
I shall follow my husband here who has succumbed to the dead.
Stand up and let go of him! Look after the children.

Mādrī said:

25 No, *I* shall follow my husband before he has fled, for my desire has
not been sated. Let the elder wife permit it! As he was lying with me,
the best of the Bhāratas was cheated of his love. So how could I
deprive him of his love in Yama's seat? Nor will I go on living,
treating your children the same as mine, noble lady, for evil would
touch me that way! Therefore you, Kuntī, must treat my twins as
your own sons. The king went to his death making love to me—let
this carcass of mine be burned with the king's body that covers mine
30 so well. Do this favor, noble lady! Watch over our children and think
kindly of me—there is nothing else I see that I could charge you with!

Vaiśaṃpāyana said:

Having spoken, the daughter of the king of the Madras, Pāṇḍu's
glorious wife by the Law, hastened after the bull among men on his
funeral pyre.

Vaiśaṃpāyana said:

117.1 The God-like great seers performed the last rites for Pāṇḍu. Then
the ascetics assembled and took counsel. "The great-spirited ascetic
relinquished kingship and kingdom and took refuge with the hermits
here to perform austerities. King Pāṇḍu has left his barely born
children and his wife in trust with your worships here as he went to
heaven." Having thus taken counsel with one another, they, being
bent on the well-being of all creatures, put Pāṇḍu's children before
5 themselves, and generously the seers set their minds on journeying to
the City of the Elephant, to render the Pāṇḍavas to Bhīṣma and
Dhṛtarāṣṭra.

That same moment all the ascetics started out with Pāṇḍu's wife,
his sons, and his body. Kuntī, always used to her comforts before, now
from love for her sons and devotion thought the long road short.
After not too long a time the glorious woman reached the Jungle of
the Kurus and came to the Vardhamāna city gate. When the people
of Hāstinapura heard the tidings that thousands of Cāraṇas and
10 hermits had arrived, they were astonished. No sooner had the sun
risen than the townspeople all followed Dharma out in the company
of their wives to gaze at the ascetics. Throngs of women, throngs of
barons, mounted throngs of wagons, and the brahmins and their
wives came out together. There was a huge mêlée of crowds of
commoners and serfs, but there was no trace of jealousy; they all had
their minds on the Law. Bhīṣma Sāṃtanava, and Somadatta Bāhlīka,
and the sage king himself, with the eyesight of knowledge, and the
Steward Vidura himself, and the Lady Satyavatī, and famous Kausalyā*
15 and Gāndhārī came out, surrounded by the princes; Dhṛtarāṣṭra's
heirs led by Duryodhana came out in their hundred, decked with
manifold ornaments.

All the Kauravas greeted the entire multitude of seers with bowed
heads and sat down below them with their house-priests. Likewise, the
town and country folk greeted and bowed their heads to the ground,
and they all sat below them. Aware that the mass of people had all
around fallen silent, Bhīṣma offered kingship and kingdom to the great
seers. Then the oldest among them, a seer wearing the braid and the
deerskin, arose and knowing the mind of the other seers spoke thus:
20 "The heir of the Kauravas, Pāṇḍu, overlord of men, had renounced
all love and pleasure and departed hence for the Hundred-Peak
Mountains. While he himself lived the life of a celibate, this son was
born to him by divine instrument, Yudhiṣṭhira, who was begotten by
Dharma himself. Likewise, the divine Wind gave this son to the great-
spirited king—Bhīma, by name, strong among the strong. From the

* = Ambālikā, Pāṇḍu's mother.

widely-lauded Indra this son was born to Kuntī, a son whose truth is
his strength – Arjuna whose fame shall prevail over all great bowmen.
And here they stand too, these great archers and Kurus, whom
Mādrī bore by the Aśvins, these tigers among men.
25 "Thus famous Pāṇḍu while he lived in the forest, always abiding
by the Law, has rescued the ancestral lineage. As he watched his sons
being born and growing and learning the Vedic lore, contentment
ever waxed in Pāṇḍu. Never straying from the path of the strict and
having won the gift of sons, Pāṇḍu went to join his forebears, seventeen days ago. When Mādrī saw him lying on his pyre to be offered
into the mouth of the sacrificial fire, she gave up her life and entered
the flames. The faithful wife went with him to her husband's world.
30 Let the remaining rites be done for him and her: here are their two
bodies, and here their excellent sons. Let these scourges of their foes
and their mother be graciously received with the welcoming rites.
And when the obsequies have been done, let famous Pāṇḍu, who
knew all the Laws, the bearer of the dynasty of the Kurus, receive the
ancestral offering."

After they had thus spoken to the assembled Kurus, all the Cāraṇas and seers disappeared that instant before the Kurus's eyes. And upon seeing the multitude of seers and Siddhas vanish like a castle in the sky, they were greatly amazed.

Dhṛtarāṣṭra said:

118.1 Vidura, order all the obsequies for Pāṇḍu, regally, as befits the
lionlike king, and also for Mādrī. Give away cattle and garments and
jewels and manifold riches for Pāṇḍu and Mādrī to whoever asks for
them, and as much as he demands. Bring honor to Mādrī as Kuntī
would. Let her body be well covered so that neither wind nor sun may
set eyes on her. No mourning for the pure Pāṇḍu – praise for the
prince! For five man-children have been born to him like sons of the
Gods!

Vaiśaṃpāyana said:

5 Vidura complied and together with Bhīṣma had the sacraments
administered to Pāṇḍu in a spot that was well walled in. Thereupon
the king's priests quickly fetched burning fire from the city for Pāṇḍu,
fed with butter oblations. Then they laid him on a bier and decked
him with all the best scents and garlands of the season, covering him
on all sides with cloth. When he had thus been adorned with garlands
and costly robes, the councillors, kinsmen, and friends drew near him
and placed the lion among men on a superbly ornamented wagon
that was pulled by men and drove him off, well-covered, alongside
10 Mādrī. They made the wagon strong with a white umbrella and
yak-tail fan, and with the music of all sorts of instruments. Men by the

hundreds took handsful of jewels and on the way proffered them to
the beggers as Pāṇḍu's obsequies. On the Kaurava's* behalf, they
bore bright large white umbrellas and sparkling garments. White-
robed sacrificial priests poured oblations into the fire that preceded his
body, blazing and well-strengthened. Brahmins, barons, commoners,
and serfs followed the king by the thousands, weeping and burning
15 with grief: "Where shall the king our protector go, leaving us
unprotected, casting us off into perpetual sorrow!" Lamenting, all the
Pāṇḍavas and Bhīṣma and Vidura lay down, in a lovely corner of the
woods on the bank of the Ganges where the ground was level and
pure, the bier of the truthful, lionlike Pāṇḍu of unsullied deeds and of
his wife.

Now they scented his body with all perfumes, anointed it with pure
fragrant salves, bathed it with the best oils, and sprinkled it quickly
with water from golden pitchers. They smeared the body with choice
white sandalwood essence and with *tunga* juice that was mixed with
20 aloe. Then they wrapped him in white cotton clothes; and dressed in
these clothes the bull among men, tiger among people, appeared as
though alive, worthy of his priceless bed.

The priests who were charged with the ritual of the dead signaled
their consent; and the *ghee*-covered king and Mādrī, adorned with the
fragrantest sandalwood mixed with *tunga* and *padmaka* and many other
plentiful perfumes, were now set afire. And, seeing their two bodies
afire, Kausalyā fainted and, shrieking, "Ah, my son, my son!" fell hard
to the ground. When the town and country people saw her fall in pain,
25 they all wept aloud, seized with pity, out of love for their king. And
along with the people all other creatures cried out with an anguished
wail, even the brutes. So did Bhīṣma Śāṃtanava weep in great sorrow,
and the wise Vidura, and the Kauravas all around.

Then Bhīṣma, Vidura, and the kings, along with the kinsmen and
all the Kuru women, offered the water. All the subjects took to the
Pāṇḍavas, wan with grief, when they had offered the water and
surrounded them mournfully. And just as the Pāṇḍavas and other
kin bedded down on the ground, so, O king, the brahmins and other
30 townsfolk slept on the ground. For twelve nights the city and Pāṇḍavas
were, to the last child, joyless, saddened, ill.

Vaiśaṃpāyana said:

119.1 Later the Steward, the king, Bhīṣma, and the kinsmen proffered to
Pāṇḍu the *śrāddha*, with a nectarlike cake. They fed the Kurus and the
chief brahmins by the thousands and gave masses of gems and choice
villages to the principal brahmins. The townspeople then took the
Pāṇḍavas, bulls of the Bhāratas, when they were cleansed of pollution,

* = Pāṇḍu.

and returned with them to the City of the Elephant. The folk of country and town kept mourning the bull of the Bhāratas, as though he were their own deceased kinsman.

5 When the *śrāddha* had been completed, Vyāsa looked upon the grieving people and said to his mother Satyavatī, who was blinded by the pains of sorrow, "The times of happiness are past and times of trouble lie ahead. The days grow worse every new tomorrow, earth herself is aging. A dreadful time is at hand, confounded by much witchery, beset by many vices, when all the acts and manners of the Law shall be soiled. Go now, leave it all. Yoke yourself and live in the wilderness of austerities, lest you must witness the ruination of your own dynasty."

"So be it," quoth she, consenting. She entered her daughter-in-law's rooms and said to her, "Ambikā, the misguided policies of your son, so we hear, will destroy the Bhāratas and their followers and
10 their grandsons. I shall take Kausalyā, who is suffering grievously under her son's death, and if you consent we shall go to the forest. Good luck to thee." Ambikā consented, and Satyavatī of the good vows bade Bhīṣma farewell and departed for the forest with both her daughters-in-law. They did awesome austerities, and at last the princesses shed their bodies, O great king, and went the great journey.

The Pāṇḍavas received the sacraments that the *Veda* prescribes and grew up in their father's house, enjoying the pleasures of life. When they played in their father's house with the son of Dhṛtarāṣṭra, the
15 Pāṇḍavas excelled in all the games that children play. In racing, in hitting the target, in stuffing himself, in raising dust, Bhīmasena beat all the boys of Dhṛtarāṣṭra. Boisterously, he grabbed them by the hair above their ears as they were playing, held them by their heads, and set them to fight one another. The Wolf-Belly bullied them all, the one hundred and one powerful boys, alone and with little trouble. The strong Bhīma would grab hold of their feet, topple them mightily in the dust, or pull the yelping children over the ground until their knees and heads and eyeballs were chafed. When he was playing in the water, he would catch ten of the kids in his arms and sit down under the water, letting go of them when they came close to drowning.
20 And when they climbed the trees to pick fruit, Bhīma would kick the tree to make it shake, and all shaken up they would tumble down with the fruit from the tree that shuddered from the kick, and fall down limply. Neither in fights nor speed nor drills did the princes ever get the upper hand when they were competing with Bhīma. So Bhīma became the bane of the sons of Dhṛtarāṣṭra when he competed, not out of malice, but because he was a child.

When he had got to know Bhīma's well-publicized strength, the high and mighty Duryodhana revealed his evil nature. Out of folly and ambition an ugly thought occurred to Duryodhana, who was loath of Law and looking for evil: "This Wolf-Belly, strong among the strong, the middle son of Pāṇḍu by Kuntī, must be brought down by trickery. Then I shall overpower his younger brother, and the eldest one, Yudhiṣṭhira, put him in fetters, and thereafter I shall sway the earth!"

Having made up his mind, the evil Duryodhana kept constantly watching for a chance to get at the spirited Bhīma. For their water games he had large and colorful tents made of cloth set up at Pramāṇakoṭi on the Ganges, Bhārata, just above the water line. When they all had stopped playing they would dress in fresh clothes and put on their ornaments and quietly feast on dishes that were opulent for all tastes. At nightfall the heroic Kuru princes, tired from their games, loved sleeping in their outdoor camp.

And so our powerful Bhīma, always the first at sports but now tired from playing piggyback with the boys that had gone playing in the water, climbed up the bank at Pramāṇakoṭi to find a place for the night, and he fell asleep. He had put on a white cloth and, exhausted and befuddled with drink, slept like a corpse without stirring. Whereupon Duryodhana quietly tied him with fetters made from creepers and rolled him from the bank into the deep, dreadfully rushing river. Bhīma woke up, broke his fetters, and the greatest of fighters rose from the water.

Another time when Bhīma was sleeping, Duryodhana brought crazed, poison-fanged, virulent snakes and made them bite Bhīma in all the weak spots of his body. But the fangs of the cobras, even when sunk in his weak spots, failed to cut through the skin, for the broad-chested boy was too tough. Waking, Bhīma ground all the snakes to death and struck his favorite charioteer with the back of his hand.

Again Duryodhana had poison thrown in Bhīma's food, plant poison freshly collected, of a virulence to make one shudder. Vidura now told the Pāṇḍavas, for he wished them well. The Wolf-Belly ate it and digested it without any aftereffect. Even that virulent poison had no effect on him—Bhīma, who was terribly tough, simply digested it. In this way Duryodhana, Karṇa, and Śakuni Saubala made various attempts to kill the Pāṇḍavas. The sons of Pāṇḍu, tamers of their foes, divined it all, but, following Vidura's advice, did not bring it into the open.

(Then, seeing that the boys at play were getting too malicious, the king entrusted them to Gautama, so that they would be taught by a guru—Gautama Kṛpa, master of the precepts of the *Veda*, who had been born from a reed stalk.)

Janamejaya said:
120.1 Pray tell, great brahmin, what was the origin of Kṛpa and how did
he come to be born from a reed stalk and obtain his weapons?
Vaiśaṃpāyana said:
The great seer Gautama had a son who was called Śaradvat, for,
you know, great king, he was born with arrows. He did not have as
much spirit in the study of the *Veda* as he had in the study of
weaponry, scourge of your foes. Just as the scholars of the Brahmin
acquire the *Vedas* by mortifying themselves, so he mortified himself to
acquire all weapons.
5 This Gautama caused the king of the Gods great anxiety, both
because of his expertness in weaponry and because of his many
austerities. Thus Indra sent out a divine maid named Jālapadī, O
Kaurava: "Stop his austerities!" She went to Śaradvat's pleasant
hermitage, the young girl, and tempted Gautama, who was carrying
his bow and arrows. When Gautama saw the Apsarā in the wilderness, wearing one single cloth, with a figure unparalleled in the world,
he stared with wide-open eyes. Bow and arrows slipped from his
hands and dropped to the ground; and the sight of her started a
10 shudder in his body. Yet, so profound was his wisdom and so opulent
his austerity, that the sage held his ground with superb poise. Still, a
sudden spasm overcame him, sire, that made him spill his seed,
though he did not notice it. The hermit left the hermitage and the
Apsarā, while his seed fell on a reed stalk. As it fell on the reed stalk it
split in two, and from the two halves a pair of twins were born to
Śaradvat Gautama.
King Śaṃtanu happened to go hunting, and one of his escorts
15 found the twins in the wilderness. Seeing bow and arrows about them,
as well as black antelope skins, he judged that they were children of a
brahmin who was also adept at the mysteries of weaponry. He showed
the twins and the arrows to the king, and out of pity the king adopted
them. "They are my children," he said as he went home; and he
reared them and gave them the sacraments, while Gautama, who had
departed, became a master on the bow. "I reared them as my own
children out of pity," the king reflected; and so he gave them the
name of Kṛpa.

Through the power of his austerities Gautama found them where
they were hidden, and he came and told the king their family name
20 and all. He taught Kṛpa the fourfold art of archery and the many
different weapons and all the secret lore in its entirety. Soon he
became a great teacher, and from him all the warlike sons of
Dhṛtarāṣṭra and the powerful Pāṇḍavas learned archery; and so did
the Vṛṣṇis and other barons who came from different countries.

Vaiśaṃpāyana said:

121.1 Looking for excellence and demanding discipline for his grandsons,
Bhīṣma asked about for teachers of recognized prowess who knew
archery, since no man of little wit, authority, and expertise in
weaponry, or of less than divine mettle, could discipline the mighty
Kurus.

Now, once the great seer Bharadvāja was busy in the *havirdhāna*
shed when he saw an Apsarā alighting, Ghṛtācī herself, who had just
bathed. A sudden breeze blew her skirt away, whereupon his seed
5 burst forth, which the seer placed in the trough. Right in that trough
a son was born to the sage, Droṇa by name, and he learned the
Vedas with all their branches. Vigorous Bharadvāja, best of the
upholders of the Law, taught the lordly Agniveśya the *āgneya* missile.
And the hermit, who had been born on the Laud-of-the-Fire day,
transmitted that great *āgneya* weapon to Bharadvāja's son, O best of
the Bhāratas.

Bharadvāja had a friend, a king by the name of Pṛṣata; to him was
born a son called Drupada. The bulllike baron, Drupada Pārṣata,
always used to go to the hermitage, where he played and studied the
10 *Vedas* with Droṇa. When Pṛṣata passed away, Drupada became king,
the strong-armed overlord of the Northern Pāñcālas. Blessed
Bharadvāja too ascended to heaven. At his father's injunction, and
himself wishing for a son, Droṇa found Kṛpī Śāradvatī for his wife.
She, who was a Gautamī, ever intent upon the *agnihotra*, the Law
and self-control, obtained a son by the name of Aśvatthāman. No
sooner was he born than he whinnied like the stallion Uccaiḥśravas;
and on hearing this a hidden, airborne being spoke: "Since his range
when he cried out went out to the horizons like a whinnying horse's,
15 this boy shall therefore be called by the name Aśvatthāman." The
wise Droṇa Bhāradvāja was much pleased with his son; he remained
to live there and became a student of weaponry.

He came to hear that great-spirited Rāma Jāmadagnya, tormentor
of his foes, wanted to give all his wealth away to the brahmins,
O king. Droṇa spoke to Rāma when the other had departed for the
woods, "Know that I am Droṇa, bull among brahmins. I have come
to you desiring wealth."

Rāma said:

Whatever I possessed of gold and riches, I have given it all away
to the brahmins, ascetic. In this wise I have given patient Goddess
Earth, bounded by her seas, with her settlements and garlands of
20 cities, to Kaśyapa. Now I have only this body left, and precious missiles
and all sorts of arms. Choose, Droṇa, what shall I give you? Speak
quickly!

Droṇa said:

Pray give me all your arrows and swords, Bhārgava, with all the secrets concerning their use!

Vaiśaṃpāyana said:

The Bhārgava voiced his assent and gave him the weapons, and all his lore of weaponry with its secrets and vows. The excellent brahmin accepted it all and, thus armed, traveled contentedly to his good friend Drupada.

Vaiśaṃpāyana said:

122.1 When mighty Droṇa Bhāradvāja thereupon reached Drupada
Pārṣata, O king, he said to him, "Recognize me, your friend!"

Drupada said:

Your wit isn't well or too sound, brahmin, if all of a sudden you
call yourself my friend! For no exalted king strikes up friendships
anywhere, fool, with men like you, destitute of wealth and deprived
of fortune! As time ages men, so it wears out their friendships. Sure,
we were friends before, but our friendship was based on what power
5 we had. No friendship is ever found on earth that does not age: lust
distracts it, anger lacerates it. Don't dance attendance on old friendship—strike up a new one. I was friends with you, good brahmin,
because it served my purpose. No pauper is friend to the rich, no fool
to the wise, no coward to the brave. An old friend—who needs him?
It is two men of equal wealth and equal birth who contract friendship
and marriage, not a rich man and a pauper. No man of learning
befriends the unlearned, no chariot warrior a man without one, no
king consorts with one who is not. An old friend—who needs him?

Vaiśaṃpāyana said:

10 Mighty Droṇa Bhāradvāja was flooded by wrath at these words of
Drupada, and he thought for a moment. Then he wisely made up his
mind against the Pāñcālas and wended his way to Hāstinapura, the
city of the chiefs of the Kurus.

At that time the young princes together had gone on an outing
from the City of the Elephant, and the little champions ran happily
about playing at tipcat. The tip-wood fell into a well while they were
playing, and no way occurred to them to retrieve it. Mighty Droṇa,
seeing the princes with their problem, began to laugh, and he
15 addressed them pleasantly, speaking slowly. "Now what! Shame on
the might of the barons, shame on your knowledge of weaponry, if
you, who are born in the line of Bharata, cannot recover your tip-
wood! Here is a handful of reeds that I have hexed with my bow—
now, behold their power that nothing else can match! I shall hit the
tip-wood with one reed, and that reed with another one, and that one

with a third, and that chain of reeds will bring the tip-wood to my
hand." And with wide, surprised eyes the princes saw him pull up the
tip-wood, and they said to the tipcat hitter, "We salute you, brahmin.
No one else knows how to do that! Who are you? How should we
know you? And we, what can we do for you?"

Droṇa said:

30 Then tell Bhīṣma of my appearance and skills. He is very wise and
will know what is fitting.

Vaiśaṃpāyana said:

"All right!" they said, and they all went and told their grandfather
Bhīṣma the brahmin's exact words, and told him of his extraordinary
feat. When Bhīṣma heard this, he recognized the man as Droṇa and
reflected that he would be a fitting teacher. He brought him in himself, honored him highly, and then the greatest of swordsmen
questioned him closely.

Droṇa told him the entire reason for his coming. "Before, I used to
go to the great seer Agniveśya to learn the art of weaponry, for I
25 wanted to grasp the lore of arms. I was a proper student, chaste, well-
disciplined, with my hair braided; and for many years I lived there,
because I wanted to master the lore of arms. Yajñasena, the robust
son of the king of Pāñcāla, studied with me under that teacher,
working hard and zealously. He was my friend, affectionate and eager
to please me, and, alas, I too loved his company—from boyhood on we
studied together, Kaurava. He would come to me, saying and doing
what pleased me, and say to me things that made me like him more,
Bhīṣma, like, 'Droṇa, I am the favorite son of my great-spirited father.
30 When the Pāñcāla anoints me to the kingdom, the kingdom shall be
yours to enjoy. I swear it on the truth, friend! All my pleasures and
riches and comforts will be yours.'

"So he spoke to me then. Later, when I had mastered weaponry,
I went forth in search of wealth. When I heard that he had been
anointed, I thought I had it made and happily traveled to my good
friend in his kingdom. Recalling our friendship and his protestations,
I came to Drupada, my old friend, and said to him, O tiger among
men, 'Recognize me, your friend!' But when I presented myself and
joined him as a friend, Drupada laughed at me as though I were a
35 person of no significance and said, 'Your wit isn't well or too sound,
brahmin, if all of a sudden you call yourself my friend! For no exalted
kings strike up friendships anywhere, fool, with men like you, destitute
of wealth and deprived of fortune. No man of learning befriends the
unlearned, no chariot warrior a man without one, no king consorts
with one who is not. An old friend—who needs him?'

"At Drupadi's words I was flooded with anger, and I wended my way to the Kurus, Bhīṣma, in search of talented pupils."

Bhīṣma and the sons of Pāṇḍu accepted him as a teacher; and,
40 taking all his grandsons and many treasures, he handed them, O king,
solemnly to Droṇa: "Here are your pupils!" In turn, the great archer
accepted the Kauravas as his pupils; and, having accepted them,
Droṇa trustingly said to them when they were alone together and
they sat at his feet, "There is a certain task buried in my heart that I
wish to see done. When you have mastered weaponry you must grant
me it: give me your word, blameless princes!" When they had heard
him, the Kauravas remained silent, O lord of the people; but Arjuna
then gave him his full promise, that scourge of his foes. Thereupon
Droṇa kissed him again and again on the head, embraced him fondly,
and shed tears of joy.

45 Mighty Droṇa then taught the sons of Pāṇḍu all manner of
weapons, human and divine. Other princes also gathered there, bull
of the Bhāratas, and came to the eminent brahmin Droṇa to learn
about weapons, such as the Vṛṣṇis and the Andhakas, and also barons
who hailed from various countries. So did Karṇa Rādheya, the son of
the *sūta*, come to Droṇa the teacher, and the *sūta's* son jealously
competed with the Pārtha. With Duryodhana's backing, he showed
his contempt for the Pāṇḍavas.

Vaiśaṃpāyana said:

123.1 Arjuna, however, did his best to honor his teacher and made the
greatest effort at mastering arms. He became Droṇa's favorite. Droṇa
summoned the cook and told him in secret, "Never give Arjuna anything
to eat when it is dark." Then, one day when Arjuna was eating,
a breeze rose and blew out the lamp by which light he was eating.
Arjuna went on eating, nor did his hand fail to find his mouth, so
accustomed was it to the motions of handling food. Realizing now
what practice could accomplish, the Pāṇḍava started practicing at
5 night. Droṇa heard the twang of his bowstring, Bhārata, and he rose
and came and embraced him, and said, "I shall do anything to see
that no archer on earth shall ever be your equal, I promise you!"

Thereafter Droṇa taught Arjuna the arts of fighting from chariots,
on elephants, horseback, and on the ground. He instructed the
Pāṇḍava in combat with clubs, in swordsmanship, in hand-thrown
weapons like spears, javelins, and lances, and in battles with mixed
weapons. Seeing his skill at them, kings and princes came by the
thousands to master the science of weaponry.

10 So, great king, a certain Ekalavya came, the son of Hiraṇyadhanus,
the chief of the Niṣādas. But Droṇa, who knew the Law, declined to
accept him for archery, out of consideration for the others, reflecting
that he was a son of a Niṣāda. Ekalavya, enemy-burner, touched

Droṇa's feet with his head and went into the forest. There he fashioned a likeness of Droṇa out of clay. This image he treated religiously as his teacher, while he spent all his efforts on archery, observing the proper disciplines. And so great was his faith, and so sublime his discipline, that he acquired a superb deftness at fixing arrow to bowstring, aiming it, and releasing it.

Upon a day Droṇa allowed the Kauravas and Pāṇḍavas leisure, and the warlike princes all went out hunting in their chariots. As it happened, sire, the Pāṇḍavas had one man who followed them with their gear and a dog. While they all roamed about, each bent on his own design, the dog wandered off in the woods, got lost, and came upon the Niṣāda. When the dog smelled that black Niṣāda in the woods, wrapped in black deerskin, his body caked with dirt, it kept about him, barking away. When the cur kept on barking, the Niṣāda, displaying his deft skill, shot almost simultaneously seven arrows into its mouth. Its mouth full of arrows, the dog went back to the Pāṇḍavas, and on seeing the animal the heroes were greatly surprised. As they looked and noticed this supreme feat of fast, blind shooting, they became humble and praised its author in every way. The Pāṇḍavas then went out into the woods to look for the forest-dweller and found him, king, ceaselessly shooting arrows. They did not recognize the man with his wild aspect and questioned him, "Who are you and whose?"

Ekalavya said:

Know me for the son of Hiraṇyadhanus, chieftain of the Niṣādas, and also for a pupil of Droṇa, who toils on mastering archery.

Vaiśaṃpāyana said:

The Pāṇḍavas now in fact recognized him, and when they returned they told Droṇa the whole miraculous story as it had happened. But Arjuna Kaunteya kept thinking of Ekalavya, king; and when he met alone with Droṇa, he said to him affectionately, "Didn't you once embrace me when I was alone and tell me fondly that no pupil of yours would ever excel me? Then how is it that you have another powerful pupil who excels me, who excels all the world—the son of the Niṣāda chief?"

Droṇa thought for a moment, then came to a decision, and, taking the left-handed archer with him, repaired to the Niṣāda. He found Ekalavya, his body caked with dirt, hair braided, dressed in tatters, bow in hand, ceaselessly shooting arrows. When Ekalavya saw Droṇa approaching, he went up to him, embraced his feet, and touched the ground with his head. After honoring Droṇa duly, the Niṣāda-born boy declared himself to be his pupil and stood before him with folded hands. Thereupon, sire, Droṇa said to Ekalavya, "If you are my pupil, then give me at once my fee!" Hearing this, Ekalavya said happily,

35 "What can I offer you, sir? Let my guru command me! For, great scholar of the Brahman, there is nothing I shall withhold from my guru!"

Droṇa replied, "Give me your right thumb!" And hearing Droṇa's harsh command, Ekalavya kept his promise; forever devoted to the truth, with a happy face and unburdened mind, he cut off his thumb without a moment's hesitation and gave it to Droṇa. When thereafter the Niṣāda shot with his fingers, he was no longer as fast as he had been before, O king of men. Arjuna's fever was gone and his heart was happy; and Droṇa's word was proved true: no one bested Arjuna.

40 Of the Kurus who studied with Droṇa, Duryodhana and Bhīma excelled in combat with clubs. Aśvatthāman surpassed all in all the esoteric arts. The twins were masters on the sword hilt, beyond all other men. Yudhiṣṭhira was the best on chariots. But Arjuna was the best on every weapon. The Pāṇḍava, chief of the chiefs of warriors, was renowned on earth as far as the ocean for his insight, application, strength, and enterprise in all weapons. Both in weaponry and devotion to his guru, the mighty Arjuna was distinguished by his excellence, even though the arms drills were the same for all; among all the princes he was the outstanding warrior. The evil-minded sons of Dhṛtarāṣṭra could not stand the superior vigor of Bhīmasena and the expertness of Arjuna, O king of men.

45 When all their studies were completed, Droṇa assembled them all to test their knowledge of weaponry, bull among men. He had craftsmen fashion an artificial bird and attach it to a treetop where it was hardly visible, and proceeded to point out the target to the princes.

Droṇa said:

Hurry, all of you! Quickly take your bows, put your arrow to the string, and take your position aiming at this bird. As soon as I give the word, shoot off its head. I shall order you one after the other, and you do it, boys!

Vaiśaṃpāyana said:

The great Āngirasa first turned to Yudhiṣṭhira. "Lay on the arrow, invincible prince," he said, "and as soon as I have ceased talking let
50 go of it!" Yudhiṣṭhira then first took his loud-sounding bow and at his guru's command stood aiming at the bird. And while the Kuru prince stood there with his bow tensed, Droṇa said to him after a while, "Do you see the bird in the treetop, prince?" "I see it," Yudhiṣṭhira replied to his teacher. After a while Droṇa again said to him, "Now can you see the tree or me, or your brothers?" "Yes," he said to each question, "I see the tree, and yourself, and my brothers,
55 as well as the bird." Then Droṇa said, dissatisfied, "Run off then!" and scolded him: "You won't be able to hit that target." Then the famous teacher questioned Duryodhana and the other sons of Dhṛtarāṣṭra one

after the other in the same way, to put them to the test; and also Bhīma and the other pupils and the foreign kings. They all said that that they could see everything, and were scolded.

Thereupon Droṇa spoke smilingly to Arjuna, "Now you must shoot at the target. Listen. As soon as I give the word you must shoot the arrow. Now first stand there for a little while, son, and keep the bow taut." The left-handed archer stretched the bow until it stood in a circle and kept aiming at the target as his guru had ordered. After a while Droṇa said to him in the same way, "Do you see this bird sitting there? And the tree? And me?" "I see the bird." Arjuna replied, "but I don't see the tree or you." Satisfied, the unvanquished Droṇa again waited a spell, then said to the bulllike warrior of the Pāṇḍavas, "If you see the bird, describe it to me." "I see its head, not its body." At Arjuna's words Droṇa shuddered with pleasure. "Shoot!" he said, and the Pārtha shot without hesitation, cut off the tree-perching bird's head with the honed blade of his arrow, and made the target tumble to the ground.

When Phalguna had succeeded in the task, Droṇa embraced him and deemed Drupada and his party laid low in battle.

A few days later the great Āngirasa went with his pupils to the Ganges to bathe, O bull among Bhāratas. When Droṇa had plunged into the water, a powerful crocodile that lived in the river grabbed him by the shin, prompted by Time. Although he was quite able to save himself, he ordered his pupils, "Kill this crocodile and save me!" hurrying them on. He had not finished speaking before the Terrifier* with a burst of five arrows killed the crocodile under the water, while the others were still coming from everywhere in great confusion. And upon seeing the Pāṇḍava make such quick work of his task, Droṇa deemed him the best of all his students and was mightily pleased. The crocodile, cut to many pieces by the Pārtha's arrows, let go of the shin of the great-spirited Droṇa and returned to the five elements. Droṇa Bhāradvāja then said to the great-spirited warrior, "Receive from me, strong-armed Arjuna, this outstanding invincible weapon that is named Brahmā-Head, along with the instructions of how to release and return it. It should never be used against human beings, for if it is unleashed on one of little luster, it might burn up the world. This weapon, son, is said to be without its match in all three worlds. Therefore you must hold it carefully; and listen to my word: should ever a superhuman foe oppress you, hero, use this weapon to kill him in battle."

The Terrifier gave his promise with folded hands and took that ultimate weapon. And the guru again said to him, "No man in the world shall be your peer as an archer!"

* = Arjuna.

1(8) The Fire in the Lacquer House

124–38 (B. 134–51; C. 5312–5926)
124 (134; 5312). Droṇa proposes a weapon show and prepares the arena with Vidura (1–10). The family and the public assemble and watch the princes perform (10–25). Duryodhana and Bhīma start a wrestling match (30).
125 (135; 5347). When the public becomes partisan, Droṇa has Aśvatthāman stop the match (1–5). Arjuna demonstrates his superior skills (5–25). At the gate the loud slapping of arms is heard (25–30).
126 (136; 5379). Karṇa makes his entrance and announces that he will match all of Arjuna's feats (1–10). He does, and Duryodhana embraces him and offers him his friendship; Arjuna berates him as an intruder. Karṇa challenges Arjuna to a duel (10–20). Indra rains on Arjuna; the sun shines on Karṇa. Family and public take sides. Kṛpa quotes Arjuna's lineage and asks for Karṇa's; he hangs his head (20–30). Duryodhana quickly installs Karṇa as king of Anga (30–35).
127 (137; 5419). Enters Adhiratha, foster father of Karṇa, who embraces him. Bhīma derides Karṇa for his low birth, Duryodhana defends him (1–15). At sundown the affair breaks up (15–20).
128 (138; 5444). Droṇa demands from his pupils his teacher's fee, viz., the capture of King Drupada; they storm his city and capture Drupada (1–5). Droṇa returns the king's earlier insults, but sets him free and lets him have the southern half of the kingdom (5–15). Drupada henceforth harbors a grudge (15).
129 (141; 5635). Duryodhana fears that the Pāṇḍavas and their descendants will supplant the Kauravas; the people are for Yudhiṣṭhira (1–10). He exhorts Dhṛtarāṣṭra to act (10–15).
130 (142; 5673). Dhṛtarāṣṭra demurs, fearing a family revolt (1–5). Duryodhana advises him to remove the Pāṇḍavas to Vāraṇāvata (5–10). Dhṛtarāṣṭra objects that the elders will not tolerate their exile (10–15). Duryodhana doubts it (15–20).
131 (143; 5696). The Kauravas consolidate their

regime. Dhṛtarāṣṭra puts pressure on the Pāṇḍavas to visit Vāraṇāvata (1–10). They take their leave from their elders (15–20).
132 (144; 5715). Duryodhana conspires with Purocana, who is to build a highly combustible house for the Pāṇḍavas in Vāraṇāvata (1–15).
133 (145; 5734). Moving farewells of the Pāṇḍavas. The brahmins protest against the groundless exile (1–10). Yudhiṣṭhira admonishes them, but hopes for their favors (10–15). Vidura, in double talk, warns Yudhiṣṭhira against danger from fire and poison; Yudhiṣṭhira explains his meaning to Kuntī (15–25). They arrive in Vāraṇāvata (30).
134 (146; 5768). Entrance and welcome in Vāraṇāvata; they take temporary lodgings (1–10). Purocana then installs them in the lacquer house; Yudhiṣṭhira discovers its inflammability and tells Bhīma (10–15). Yudhiṣṭhira decides to pretend ignorance and wait for their chance; they will build a deep cellar (15–25).
135 (147; 5798). A sapper, friend of Vidura, arrives, identifies himself, and builds the cellar (1–15). They sleep in it by night; by day they reconnoiter the environs under the pretense of hunting (20).
136 (148; 5819). After a year Kuntī holds a feast; a Niṣāda woman and five sons remain behind, drunk (1–5). Bhīma sets fire to the house (10). The Pāṇḍavas and Kuntī escape from their cellar; Bhīma carries all of them (15).
137 (150; 5856). The townspeople search the ashes and find the remains of Purocana and the six Niṣādas. Dhṛtarāṣṭra is informed (1–10). The latter mourns them, orders funeral urns for the bodies, and performs the obsequies (1–15). Bhīma carries the family (15–20).
138 (51; 5882). Bhīma carries on (1–5). At evening they rest under a banyan, while Bhīma fetches water; he bemoans their fate and keeps watch (5–30).

Vaiśampāyana said:

124.1 Bhārata! When Droṇa saw that the sons of Dhṛtarāṣṭra and the Pāṇḍavas had mastered the weapons, he spoke, sire, to King Dhṛtarāṣṭra, in the presence of Kṛpa, Somadatta, the sagacious Bāhlīka, Bhīṣma, Vyāsa, and Vidura: "Sire, chief of the Kurus, the

princes have finished their studies. With your consent they may now
display the skills that each of them has learned." The great king said
with delighted heart, "Droṇa Bhāradvāja, you have done a great feat,
5 good brahmin! You yourself should give me orders how to stage their
trials, at what time, and in what place, as you think fit. On a day like
this I hopelessly envy people who can see, and who now will see my
little sons triumph with their weapons. Steward, carry out what this
teacher and guru commands, for nothing, I think, could be a greater
pleasure, law-loving Vidura!"

Droṇa excused himself from the king's presence and went outside,
followed by Vidura. Then the sage Bhāradvāja* measured out a
stretch of land that was level, without trees and bushes, gently sloping
to the river. On a day governed by an auspicious star he cast on that
land an offering, which, with its purpose, was announced in the city,
10 O eloquent king! In this theater the craftsmen built a very large stand
for the king, and one for the womenfolk, well laid-out according to the
rules that are found in the scriptures and equipped with all kinds of
weapons, O bull among men. The countryfolk had large and high
platforms erected, and the rich had their palanquins set up.

When the day came, the king and his councillors arrived, preceded
by Bhīṣma and Kṛpa, the first of the teachers, and they entered the
royal stand that, decked with gold leaf, was screened off by pearl-
studded lattice and paved with beryl. Then the great lady Gāndhārī
came out, and Kuntī, O victorious king, and all the king's women with
their maids and retainers; and excitedly they stepped up on their
15 platforms as the wives of the Gods ascend Mount Meru. And the
whole fourfold society of brahmins, barons, and the others came
hurriedly from the town and assembled to watch the weapons trials of
the princes. There was a crowd there like an ocean, rippling in waves
with the music that was played, and the people's curiosity.

Then the teacher himself arrived with his son Aśvatthāman,
dressed in white clothes and wearing a white brahmins' thread,
anointed with white ointments, white-haired, white-bearded; and he
entered the middle of the arena, as the Moon enters with Mars the
sky that is cleared of rain clouds. Mighty Droṇa made an offering such
as suited the day, and had brahmins who knew the spells recite Vedic
20 lines as a blessing. Then, as the sacred sounds that blessed the day
subsided, men entered the arena carrying all kinds of weapons and
gear.

Thereupon, the powerful bulls of the Bharatas descended with their
bows, armor, and belts tightened, the quivers fast. Headed by
Yudhiṣṭhira, the mighty princes from the eldest onward each gave a
superb and marvelous exhibition of weaponry. Some of the spectators

* = Droṇa.

ducked their heads, afraid that the arrows might land on them, while
others boldly kept looking, wonder-struck. They hit the targets with
their arrows, which were marked with the name of each of them, all
kinds of arrows, and nimbly let go while they drove past with horses.
25 And watching that army of princes wield their bows and arrows, the
crowds were astounded, as though they were watching a castle in the
air. Their eyes wide with wonder, the men there wildly cheered them
by the hundreds and thousands: "Bravo! Bravo!" The powerful
princes did their courses with the bow, over and again, on chariot,
elephant, or horseback, and in hand-to-hand combat. Then they
seized hold of their swords and shields and, brandishing their arms,
ran through the courses of swordsmanship all over the terrain. The
spectators watched the deftness, skill, flamboyance, balance, and
firmness of grip of them all as they used their shields and swords.
30 Now Suyodhana and the Wolf-Belly descended, as always in high
spirits, clubs in hand, like two single-peaked mountains. The strong-
armed princes buckled their armor, hell-bent on showing off their
masculine prowess, like two huge rutting bull elephants joining battle
over a cow. They circled each other, sunwise and widdershins, with
their sparkling clubs, like two bulls in rut. Vidura described to
Dhṛtarāṣṭra, and Kuntī to Gāndhārī, all the exploits of the princes.

Vaiśaṃpāyana said:

125.1 When the Kuru prince and Bhīma, strong among the strong, had
taken up their positions in the arena, the crowd split into two factions,
each partial to its own favorite. "Hurray for the champion, the prince
of the Kurus!" they shouted, or "Hurray for Bhīma!" and the wildly
rising cheers of the onlookers echoed widely.
The wise Droṇa Bhāradvāja looked at the arena that was like a
stormy sea, and he said to Aśvatthāman, his beloved son, "Stop those
two champions, highly trained as they are, or else there will be a riot
5 in the arena over Bhīma and Duryodhana!" The son of the guru
halted the two as they raised their bludgeons like two violent seas that
are whipped by the tempest of Doomsday.

Droṇa entered the court of the arena, stopped the music band that raised the din of a thundercloud, and began to speak: "Now watch the Pārtha,* the greatest of armsmen, son of Indra and the match of Indra's younger brother, whom I love more than my own son!" Thereupon the young man, whose happy entrance had been blessed by his teacher, entered with bow and full quiver, with wrist guard and finger guards tied on; and so, wearing a golden cuirass, Phalguna** made his appearance like a rain cloud with a golden sun, iridescent as

* = son of Pṛthā, i.e., Arjuna.
** = Arjuna.

10 the rainbow aglow with lightning, red like twilight. There was a huge
commotion all over the arena, and the musical instruments and the
conches exploded into sound. "There is the magnificent son of
Kuntī!" "There goes the middlemost of the Pāṇḍavas!" "There is the
son of great Indra, the safeguard of the Kurus!" "He is the greatest
of armsmen, he is the greatest of the upholders of the Law, of
morality, the supreme treasury of the wisdom of morals!" And when
Kuntī heard these words beyond compare that the spectators voiced,
her breasts became damp with tears that commingled with milk. His
ears filled with the uproar, Dhṛtarāṣṭra, the best of men, happily
15 turned to Vidura and asked, "Steward, what is that uproarious outcry
like the roaring of a stormy sea that has suddenly risen from the
arena as though to rend the skies?"

Vidura said:

Phalguna Pārtha has descended, great king, the son of Pāṇḍu, wearing his armor; and hence this commotion!

Dhṛtarāṣṭra said:

How lucky am I, and favored am I, and protected am I, sage, by these fires of the Pāṇḍavas that were kindled from the block of Pṛthā!

Vaiśaṃpāyana said:

When the rising theater had somehow calmed down, the Terrifier
began to exhibit the skill with weapons he had learned from his
teacher. With the *āgneya* he created fire, with the *vāruṇa* water, with
the *vāyavya* wind, with the *pārjanya* rain; with the *bhauma* he
20 entered earth, with the *pārvata* he brought forth mountains. With the
disappearing weapon he made it all vanish again. One instant he
stood tall, the next squat, then was up in front on the chariot yoke,
then again in the middle of the chariot, and the next instant had
jumped to the ground. Trained to high excellence, the favorite of his
guru hit and shot through fragile targets, and tiny ones, and hard
ones, with different makes of arrows. While an iron boar was moved
about, he loosed into its snout five continuous arrows as though they
were one single one. The mighty archer buried twenty-one arrows in a
25 cow's hollow horn that was swaying on a rope. And in this and other
fashions he gave an exhibition of his dexterity with the long sword
as well as the bow and the club.

When the tournament was almost over and the crowd had thinned and the music stopped, there came from the area of the gate the sound of arms being slapped, like the crash of a thunderbolt, which betokened greatness and prowess. "Are the mountains rending? Is the earth caving in? Is the sky filling up with clouds that are heavy with rain?" Such, overlord of the earth, were the thoughts of the arena that

instant. All the spectators looked toward the gate.
30 Droṇa, surrounded by the five Pāṇḍava brothers, shone like the
moon in conjunction with the constellation of the Hand. The proud
one hundred brothers, joined by Aśvatthāman, surrounded
Duryodhana, killer of his enemies, who had risen to his feet. And he,
brandishing his club, encircled by the brothers who kept their
weapons ready, stood there like the Sacker of Cities of olden times
surrounded by the hosts of the Gods at the Slaughter of the Dānavas.

Vaiśaṁpāyana said:
126.1 The people, eyes popping with wonder, made way, and Karṇa,
victor of enemy cities, entered the spacious arena like a walking
mountain, wearing his inborn armor and his face lit by his earrings,
with his bow and tied-on sword—Karṇa, scourge of the hosts of his
foes, of the wide fame and wide eyes, who had been born by Pṛthā as a
maiden to the sting-rayed Sun, of whom he was a portion. His power
and might were like the regal lion's or bull's or elephant's, and he was
5 like sun, moon, and fire in brightness, beauty, and luster. Tall he
stood, like a golden palm tree, this youth with the hard body of a lion.
Innumerable were the virtues of this magnificent son of the Sun.

The strong-armed champion glanced about the circle of the stands,
then, with none too great courtesy, bowed to Droṇa and Kṛpa. The
entire crowd was hushed and stared at him, and a shudder went
through the people as they wondered who he was. With a voice
rumbling like a thunderhead, the eloquent brother, son of the Sun,
spoke to his unrecognized brother, son of Pāka's Chastiser: "Pārtha!
Whatever feat you have done, I shall better it before the eyes of all
these people. Don't be too amazed at yourself!"
10 He had not finished speaking, eloquent king, when the people all
about rose like one man, like a pitcher heaved from the well.
Pleasure flooded Duryodhana, O tiger among men, and abasement and
anger pervaded the Terrifier instantly. Droṇa gave his permission, and
the powerful, pugnacious Karṇa accomplished every feat that the
Pārtha had achieved. Whereupon Duryodhana and his brothers
embraced Karṇa; and he joyously said to him, "Welcome, strong-
armed hero! Good fortune has brought you here, you who know how
to humble pride. Take your pleasure of me and the kingdom of the
Kurus!"

Karṇa said:
15 Then enough of everything else! I choose to be friends with you.
And I want a duel with the Pārtha, Bhārata!

Duryodhana said:

Enjoy all pleasures with me, show your friends your favor, and set your foot on the heads of your ill-wishers, scourge of your foes!

Vaiśaṃpāyana said:

But the Pārtha thought himself insulted, and he said to Karṇa, who stood like a mountain in the midst of the crowd of his brethren, "The worlds that are set aside for uninvited intruders, and for uninvited prattlers, those worlds you shall attain, Karṇa, when I have done killing you!"

Karṇa said:

This stage is open to all, so what of you, Phalguna? Barons are
20 those who are the strongest. Law obeys might. Why abuse, which is the whimpering of the weak? Talk with arrows, Bhārata, until before your teacher's own eyes I carry off your head with mine!

Vaiśaṃpāyana said:

Droṇa gave his permission, and the Pārtha, sacker of enemy cities, was embraced by his brothers and rushed to the other to fight. Duryodhana and his brothers clasped Karṇa, and he stood there ready for battle, holding his bow and arrows.

Then the sky became overcast with lightning-streaked, thunderous, rainbow-attended clouds that laughed with lines of cranes. And seeing how Indra of the golden horses fondly looked down upon the
25 stage, the Sun carried off the clouds that came too close. Now the Pāṇḍava could be half seen, hidden by the shadow of the clouds, and Karṇa appeared in a nimbus of bright sunlight. The sons of Dhṛtarāṣṭra stood by Karṇa; and Droṇa Bhāradvāja, Kṛpa, and Bhīṣma stood by the Pārtha.

The arena was divided, the women took their sides; but Kuntibhoja's daughter, who knew the issue, fell in a faint. Vidura, who knew all the Laws, brought the fainting woman back to consciousness by splashing her with water in which sandalwood had been sprinkled. When her breath had returned, she stared at her two sons, clad in their armor; but however much grieved, she did not interefere.

30 As the two champions raised their large bows, Śāradvata said to them, for he was experienced in the conduct of duels and knew all the Laws, "This is the youngest son of Pāṇḍu born from Pṛthā, a scion of Kuru, who will engage in a duel with you, sir. You too must now tell the names of your mother, your father, and your lineage, and of the barons whose scion you are. When he has learned them, the Pārtha shall fight you, or mayhap not."

At his words Karṇa hung his head in shame, and his face faded like a lotus that has been showered by the rains.

Duryodhana said:

Master, in the scriptures it is ruled that there are three ways for one to be a king: to be born one, to become a champion, or to lead an

35 army. If Phalguna refuses to fight with anyone who is not a king, then I shall anoint him to the kingdom in the country of the Angas!

Vaiśaṃpāyana said:

That very instant the warlike Karṇa was consecrated by Vedic brahmins with roasted rice grains, flowers in golden pitchers, and enthroned on a golden stool, to rule the kingdom of Anga; and the mighty hero was endowed with fortune. He received a royal umbrella and a yak-tail fan; and when the wishes for victory had died down, the bulllike king said to King Kaurava, "What can I give that matches this gift of a kingdom? Tell me, tiger among kings, and I shall do it so, my liege!" "I want your eternal friendship!" replied Suyodhana.* And upon his word Karṇa answered, "So shall it be!" Joyously the two embraced and became greatly happy.

Vaiśaṁpāyana said:

127.1 Then, his upper cloth awry, sweating and trembling, Adhiratha entered the stage, swaying on his feet, held up by a stick. When Karṇa saw him, he let go of his bow and moved by his reverence for his father he greeted him with his head, which was still wet with the water of the consecration. Nervously, the chariot driver covered his feet with the end of his *dhoti* and said to Karṇa, who was crowned with success, "Ah, my son!" Trembling with love, he embraced him and kissed his head, and with his tears he once more sprinkled the head that was still damp from the consecration to the Anga kingdom.

5 When Bhīmasena Pāṇḍava saw Adhiratha, he decided that Karṇa
was the *sūta's* son and burst out laughing. "Son of a *sūta*," he said,
"you do not have the right to die in a fight with a Pārtha! You
better stick to the whip that suits your family. You have no right
to enjoy the Anga kingdom, churl, no more than a dog has a right to
eat the cake by the fire at a sacrifice!" At these words a slight tremor
started in Karṇa's lower lip, and he sighed and looked up to the sun in
the sky. But Duryodhana leaped up from amidst his brothers, like a
10 rutting elephant from a lotus pond, and he said to Bhīmasena of
terrible deeds, who stood his ground, "Wolf-Belly, you have no right to
speak such words! Might is the father of barons, and even the least of
barons deserves a fight. The origin of both barons and rivers are
surely obscure. Fire that pervades all creatures springs from water.
The thunderbolt that slew the Dānavas was made from a bone of
Dadhīca. The blessed lord God Guha is a complete mystery: he is said
to be the son of Fire, or the Pleiads, or Rudra, or the Ganges. Men
born from baronesses are known to have become brahmins. Our
teacher was born from a trough, Master Kṛpa from a reed stalk. And
15 the princes all know how you yourselves were born. How could a doe

* = Duryodhana.

give birth to this tiger who resembles the sun, with his earrings and
armor and celestial birthmarks? This lordly man deserves to rule the
world, not just Anga! He deserves it by the power of his arms and by
me who shall obey his orders. Or else, if there be a man who will not
condone my action, let him, on chariot or on foot, bend the bow!"

There was a great uproar in the entire arena, mixed with cheers;
then the sun went down. Duryodhana, holding Karṇa by the hand, his
20 way lighted by the flames of torches, left the arena. The Pāṇḍavas,
Droṇa, Kṛpa, and Bhīṣma, O lord of the people, all went to their own
dwellings. The people departed, some hailing "Arjuna!" others
"Karṇa!" others again "Duryodhana!" And when she had
recognized the king of Anga by his birthmarks as her own son,
Kuntī's hidden pleasure grew with love. Duryodhana's fear of Arjuna
also diminished rapidly when he had found Karṇa, O king of the
earth. That hero himself, who had mastered the labor of weaponry,
flattered Duryodhana with the most coaxing words. And at that time
even Yudhiṣṭhira thought that no archer on earth was Karṇa's equal.

Vaiśaṃpāyana said:

128.1 Then, having assembled all his pupils, Droṇa exhorted them to give
him his teacher's fee, O king. "Capture Drupada, king of Pāñcāla, in a
raid," he said, "and bring him here. That will be my greatest reward.
Good luck to you!" "Yes!" they said and, fully armed, they set out
quickly on their chariots, accompanied by Droṇa, to give him his
teacher's reward. The bulls of the Bhāratas rushed upon the
Pāñcālas, laying them low, and crushed the city of the puissant
Drupada.

5 They captured Drupada Yajñasena in a raid and brought him to
Droṇa with his councillors. His pride was broken, his treasure looted,
his person overpowered; and it was to this Drupada that Droṇa said,
dwelling with his mind on his feud with him, "I laid waste your
kingdom with vehemence, and now I have laid waste your city. And
now that you are alive but in your enemy's power, an old friend,
who needs him?" He laughed out loud, then came to a decision and
said, "Don't be afraid for your life, king. We brahmins are not
vindictive. Since you played with me in the hermitage when we were
boys, my love for you was fostered, bull among barons. Once more,
10 bull among men, I implore your friendship. I shall give you a boon,
king: have half the kingdom! For, to be sure, how could we who are
kings have friends who are not? That, Yajñasena, is why I have
busied myself acquiring your kingdom. You shall be king south of the
Ganges, I north of the river. Recognize me, your friend, Pāñcāla, if you
so choose!"

Drupada said:

'Tis no great wonder, brahmin, with such courageous, great-spirited pupils. Yes, I shall be your friend. I want your friendship forever.'

Vaiśaṃpāyana said:

At these words Droṇa set him free, Bhārata, and he honored him in
a spirit of friendship and returned to him half of his kingdom.
15 Dejected, Drupada inhabited Mākandī on the Ganges with its
countryside and the capital city of Kāmpilya, and the Southern
Pāñcālas, as far down as the river Carmaṇvatī. Drupada, brooding on
his feud with Droṇa, did not find peace; nor did he see how to
vanquish him with baronial power, knowing it and himself to fall
short of brahminic power. Waiting for the birth of a son, the king
bore his grudge, while Droṇa settled down in the country of
Ahicchatrā.

Thus, O king, was the city Ahicchatrā with its countryside conquered in battle by the Pārtha and made over to Droṇa.

Vaiśaṃpāyana said:

129.1 Evil-minded Duryodhana, remarking Bhīmasena's superior vigor and
Arjuna Dhanaṃjaya's mastery of weapons, became tormented.
Karṇa Vaikartana and Śakuni Saubala sought to kill the Pāṇḍavas
with many devices, but those tamers of their enemies discovered them
all, though refraining, at Vidura's advice, from bringing them into the
open.

The citizens observed how Pāṇḍu's sons prospered with virtues,
5 and as they met in squares and at assemblies spoke of them: "The
lord of the people Dhṛtarāṣṭra, who has but the eyesight of wisdom,
did not inherit the kingdom at the time because he was blind—then
how can he be king now? Likewise, Bhīṣma Śāṃtanava, of great vows
and true to his promise, once declined the kingdom and he will never
take it now. Then it is now up to ourselves properly to anoint the
eldest Pāṇḍava, who, young as he is, has the conduct of the old—he is
a truthful man who knows the value of compassion. For he, as he
knows the Laws, will surely honor Bhīṣma Śāṃtanava and
Dhṛtarāṣṭra and his sons, and provide them with various privileges."

Evil-minded Duryodhana heard the citizens, who were loyal to
10 Yudhiṣṭhira, speak such words, and they burned him. The ill-
spirited prince, burning, could not forgive such talk and, consumed
with envy, approached Dhṛtarāṣṭra. Finding his father alone, he paid
homage and, burned by the preferences of the townspeople, he then
spoke as follows: "I hear the townfolk babble in ominous ways,
father. Disregarding yourself and Bhīṣma, they want the Pāṇḍava for

their king. Bhīṣma will agree to that, for he does not want to be king.
But on us the people in the city want to inflict the ultimate pressure.
Pāṇḍu at the time received the kingdom from his father because of his
qualities. You yourself did not receive it, although it fell to you,
15 because of your defect. If the Pāṇḍava now receives the patrimony
from Pāṇḍu, his son will surely inherit it in turn, and so will his son,
and his. We ourselves with our sons shall be excluded from the royal
succession and become of slight regard in the eyes of the world, lord
of the earth! Take measures at once, sire, lest we are reduced to an
eternity of hell and must live off the rice balls of others. If you had
been firmly established in the kingdom, king, we would certainly have
inherited the kingdom, however unwilling the populace!"

Vaiśaṃpāyana said:

130.1 When he heard such words from his son, Dhṛtarāṣṭra pondered
awhile, then spoke to Duryodhana: "Pāṇḍu always abode by the Law
and was a friend to me of many favors—to all his kinsmen he was,
but to me in particular. I never knew him to want anything like food
and such for himself; he would always hand it to me, as he handed
over the kingdom, faithful to his vow. Pāṇḍu's son is, like him,
devoted to the Law, full of virtues, well-known in the world, and much
5 respected by the citizens. How can we cast him out by force from his
father's and grandfather's kingdom, with his allies to boot? Pāṇḍu
always took care of his councillors, took care of his army, took special
care of their sons and grandsons. Pāṇḍu used to treat the Paurava
kinsmen well, son—would they not kill us with our relatives for
Yudhiṣṭhira's sake?

Duryodhana said:

That danger I have just weighed in my mind, father. The subjects,
once they find themselves receiving riches and honors, on the whole
will surely change their loyalties to us. The treasury and its ministers
10 are now under my control, sire. You can remove the Pāṇḍavas
straightaway to the town of Vāraṇāvata with some benign device.
When the kingdom is securely lodged with me, king, Kuntī and her
children can always return.

Dhṛtarāṣṭra said:

Duryodhana, the same stratagem had occurred to me, but the
plan was too evil to reveal. Neither Bhīṣma nor Droṇa nor the
Steward* nor Gautama** will ever approve of our exiling the
Pāṇḍavas. For we and they are equal before the Kauravas, son.
These law-minded and sagacious men will tolerate no inequity.

* = Vidura.
** = Kṛpa.

15 Wouldn't we become fair game to kill for those great-spirited
Kauravas, indeed for the world, son?

Duryodhana said:

Bhīṣma will always be neutral. Droṇa's son is on my side, and
Droṇa will be where his son is, no doubt of that. And Kṛpa
Śāradvata will be on the side the three of them can be on together;
he'll never desert Droṇa and his sister's son. The Steward's fortune is
tied to ours, for all that he secretly sides with the others. Nor would
he by himself be able to hurt us on the Pāṇḍavas's behalf. You can
with all confidence banish the sons of Pāṇḍu and their mother to
20 Vāraṇāvata, even today. No evil will come of it. And, doing so, you
must destroy the dreadful thorn that sticks in my heart, leaving me
sleepless, and the raging fire of my grievance!

Vaiśaṃpāyana said:

131.1 Thereafter Prince Duryodhana and his brothers began gradually
to captivate all the subjects with gifts of riches and honors. Some wily
advisers, on Dhṛtarāṣṭra's prompting, began to spin tales of the
beauties of Vāraṇāvata city: "A great gathering is at hand in
Vāraṇāvata, the loveliest in the world," they said. "It is in honor of
Paśupati. That city, which is enchanting to all men, will be covered
with all manner of treasures!" So they spun tales at Dhṛtarāṣṭra's
5 behest. And as they heard that lovely city of Vāraṇāvata told of, the
sons of Pāṇḍu got a mind to go there, O king. When the king judged
that they had become curious, Ambikā's son said to the Pāṇḍavas,
"These people of mine keep telling me over and again that
Vāraṇāvata is the most beautiful town in the world. If you have a
mind to watch the festival in Vāraṇāvata, son, take your troops and
retainers and enjoy yourselves as Immortals! Give largess of gems to
the brahmins and bards, as much as you want, like splendid Gods.
10 While away some time there, and when you have enjoyed yourselves
to the full, you will happily come back to our Hāstinapura."

Realizing that this was Dhṛtarāṣṭra's own wish and that he
himself had no allies, Yudhiṣṭhira replied that he would go. Then,
softly and unhappily, he told the wise Bhīṣma and the sagacious
Vidura, Droṇa, Bāhlīka and Somadatta Kaurava, Kṛpa and
Aśvatthāman, and the famous Gāndhārī, "Friend, we shall go with
our people and live at Dhṛtarāṣṭra's behest in the lovely town of
Vāraṇāvata, which will be teeming with people. Graciously give us
your blessing, and when we are strengthened by your benedictions no
evil will overcome us."

15 At the Pāṇḍava's words the faces of the Kauravas grew tranquil,
and they sped the Pāṇḍavas: "Luck shall befall you always from all
creatures on your journey. May no evil waylay you from anywhere,

scions of Pāṇḍu!" When their way had been blessed, they performed all the rites for the securing of a kingdom and departed for Vāraṇāvata.

Vaiśaṃpāyana said:

132.1 When the king had thus spoken to the great-spirited Pāṇḍavas,
the evil-spirited Duryodhana was overjoyed. He took his minister
Purocana aside, O bull among Bhāratas, and, clasping his right hand,
said to him, "Mine is the earth with her opulence of treasures,
Purocana! But as she is mine, so is she yours. Take care to protect
her! There is no one in whom I have greater trust as an ally than you.
Therefore we shall have a compact, and I shall consult with you.
5 Keep you counsel, friend, and destroy my rivals.
"Use your cunning and do what I tell you. Dhṛtarāṣṭra has sent the
Pāṇḍavas to Vāraṇāvata; at his command they will enjoy themselves
at the festival there. Take a fast donkey cart and see to it that you
reach Vāraṇāvata today. When you get there, have a big, well-
fenced, and rich house built with four halls, adjacent to the armory.
Have them use hemp and resin and so forth, or whatever combustible
10 materials are available. Make them mix the clay with butter, seed oil,
and plenty of lacquer, and plaster the walls with it. Also put lots of
hemp, cane, *ghee*, wood, and various wooden tools all over the house,
but in such a way that the Pāṇḍavas, even if they inspect it, do not
suspect you, or that other people do not think that you built it as a
firetrap. When the house has been built in that way, induce the
Pāṇḍavas with great honor to lodge there, and also Kuntī, with her
ladies of company. Provide beautiful seats, conveyances, and beds for
15 the Pāṇḍavas there, enough to satisfy my father. Make all possible
arrangements so that they enjoy their stay in Vāraṇāvata without any
suspicion, until our turn comes. When you are sure that they have no
inkling of danger and are in bed without fearing any threat from
anywhere, you must start a fire at the door of the house. When they
have been burned to death, the only thing that the people or their
kinsmen will ever say about the Pāṇḍavas is that they were burned
alive in their own house!"

Purocana promised the Kaurava so; and he departed for Vāraṇāvata on a donkey cart. Purocana went and, obedient to Duryodhana, did everything as the prince had told him.

Vaiśaṃpāyana said:

133.1 The Pāndavas yoked their chariots with excellent horses, fast as the wind, and, when about to step on them, they sorrowfully embraced Bhīṣma's feet, and King Dhṛtarāṣṭra's, and the great-spirited Droṇa's, and of the other old men, and of Vidura and Kṛpa. Having bidden farewell to all the elders of the Kurus, for they were strict in their vows, they embraced their equals; even the children made their good-byes. They took their leave from all their mothers and circumambulated them, and from all the subjects, and finally started for Vāraṇāvata.

The wise Vidura as well as other bulls among the Kurus and the townspeople followed, wan with grief, those tigers among men. There were some fearless brahmins among them who, aggrieved over the fate of Pāṇḍu's sons, said, "Our evil-minded King Dhṛtarāṣṭra is totally covered by darkness! He sees danger, but he does not see the Law. For the Pāṇḍava, whose soul is innocent of sin, will condone no sin, nor will Bhīma, strong among the strong, or Arjuna Dhanaṃjaya —and how could the sagacious twins of Mādrī? Dhṛtarāṣṭra could not bear that the kingdom came to them from their father. How can this Bhīṣma permit all this lawlessness, that the Pāṇḍavas, the bulls of the Bhāratas, are exiled for no cause whatsoever? Pāṇḍu's father Vicitravirya Śāmtanava and Pāṇḍu himself, scion of Kuru, the royal seer, were like fathers to us. And now that tigerlike man has gone to his fate, Dhṛtarāṣṭra does not tolerate the princes, young as they are. Neither can we tolerate him! Let us all give up our houses and leave the capital for the place where Yudhiṣṭhira is going!"

When the citizens were talking in this vein, much aggrieved, Yudhiṣṭhira, the King Dharma, himself wan with grief, spoke most fondly: "The king must be honored like a father, like the greatest guru. We have vowed that we would unhesitatingly do what he tells us. Sirs, you are our friends: honor us with your circumambulation, bid us farewell with your benedictions, and return to your homes. When it befalls that we have a need of you, then you shall benefit us with your favors!" They promised thus, and circumambulated them, bade them farewell with benedictions, and went back to the city.

When the townspeople had gone back, Vidura, who knew all the Laws, spoke to Yudhiṣṭhira in order to alert him; the sage, perspicacious in all of Law and Profit, who knew how to speak in riddles, said to the youth, who understood them, "One who knows will act so that he overcomes his danger. There is a weapon, not made of iron, yet sharp, which carves up the body. Him who knows it this weapon fails to kill, and it is turned against the enemy. The weapon that kills the underwood, and kills the dew, won't burn moles in their big hole—he who knows this and protects himself lives. The blind man does not know the way, the blind man does not find his bearings, the unpersevering man does not gain prosperity. Ponder this and be alert. A man takes this ironless weapon that is given by the untrustworthy, seeks the shelter of the porcupine, and escapes the fire. As he runs, he discovers the trails; by the stars he finds his bearings; and subduing five souls by his own power, he escapes being subdued himself." After being instructed by him thus, while he followed them, Vidura circumambulated the Pāṇḍavas, took his leave, and returned to his house.

25 After Vidura and Bhīṣma and the townspeople had gone back, Kuntī called Ajātaśatru and said, "What did the Steward say in the middle of the crowd? It was as though he didn't say anything at all, but you said, 'Yes,' and we did not understand it. If we are allowed to hear it, and if it is not something bad, I should like to hear your entire conversation."

Yudhiṣṭhira said:

Vidura told me to watch out for poison and fire, and that there should be no path unknown to me. Then he said to me that if I master my senses I shall obtain the earth, and I replied to Vidura that I understood.

Vaiśaṃpāyana said:

30 It was on the eighth day of Phalguna, under the star Rohiṇī, that they started out. And they reached Vāraṇāvata and set eyes on the people of that town.

Vaiśaṃpāyana said:

134.1 All the citizens of Vāraṇāvata, as soon as they heard of the arrival of Pāṇḍu's sons, those best of men, came eagerly and joyously from the city, by the thousands, on all kinds of conveyances, carrying all manner of auspicious gifts as the scriptures dictate. The Vāraṇavātakas approached them and stood reverently in a circle around them, pronouncing blessings for victory. The tiger among men, Yudhiṣṭhira, the King Dharma, appeared, surrounded by the people, as godlike as the thunderbolt-wielding Indra in the midst of the Immortals.

5 Welcomed by the citizens and punctiliously returning the honors,
the guiltless men made their entrance into Vāraṇāvata, which was
decorated for the festival and swarming with people. After entering the
town, the heroes immediately went to the houses of the brahmins,
who were bent on their own duties, to those of the authorities of the
city, and of the chariot owners, O king. In fact, these good men went
even to the houses of the artisans and serfs. The townspeople paid
homage to the Pāṇḍavas, and thereafter the bulls among men
repaired to their lodgings, where Purocana welcomed them. This
Purocana provided them with food and drink, with sparkling beds and
10 beautiful stools. There they and their regal retinue lodged, honored by
Purocana and waited upon by the town's inhabitants.

When they had lodged there for ten nights, Purocana offered them the unholy house that had been named the Holy Hall. The tigerlike

men and their retainers entered the house at Purocana's bidding as
the Guhyakas enter Mount Kailāsa. But Yudhiṣṭhira, who was wise in
all the Laws, inspected the house and, smelling the fat mixed with
butter and lacquer, told Bhīma that it was a firetrap. "It is clear that
the house has been built to burn, friend! Obviously hemp and resin
has been used in building the house, and all the building materials, the
15 straw, the bark, the cane, and so on have been sprinkled with *ghee*. It
surely has been built well by craftsmen who know their trade: the
evil Purocana wants to burn me to death as soon as I feel at ease!
This is the danger that the wise Vidura foresaw and warned me about,
Pṛthā. But now that he has warned us, we know this place for the
unholy house it is, completed by secret masters who are in
Duryodhana's service!"

Bhīma said:

If you think that this house has been built as a firetrap, then we'd better go back to our old lodgings!

Yudhiṣṭhira said:

No, I think that we should stay here, eager and guileless, and
seemingly doomed, while we look about for a sure way to escape
20 from here. For if Purocana finds us showing our misgivings, he will
act quickly and suddenly burn us to death. Purocana would not
shrink from any outrage or lawlessness; the fool is acting on
Duryodhana's orders. The question remains whether grandfather
Bhīṣma will not be furious when we are burned alive and make the
Kauravas equally furious. Well he might be, thinking of the Law, and
so may the other bulls of the Kurus. But if we were to run away from
fear of being burned, Suyodhana, who is greedy for the kingdom,
would have us all assassinated by spies. He has rank, we none, he has
allies, we none, he has a large treasury, we are penniless—no doubt
25 he has ways of having us killed! Therefore we must deceive this
crook and his crooked master Suyodhana and lie low and stay hidden
wherever we go. We shall roam over the country like hunters, so that
we get to know all the trails when we have to take flight. Now we
should at once dig a deep trench and hide it well: the fire will not
burn us there if we hide our breathing. Let us spare no effort to see
that neither Purocana nor the townspeople find us out while we are
living here.

Vaiśaṃpāyana said:

135.1 A skillful sapper, who was a friend of Vidura's, said to the
Pāṇḍavas when they were alone, "I am a highly skilled sapper, and
Vidura has sent me here with orders to help the Pāṇḍavas. What can I
do for you? Vidura told me in secret, 'Have all confidence in the
Pāṇḍavas and bring them your best effort!' So what can I do for you?

5 On the night of the fourteenth of this dark fortnight Purocana will set
fire at the door of this house of yours. I have heard, Pārtha, that
Duryodhana has resolved to burn alive the bulllike Pāṇḍavas with
their mother. And Vidura told you something in mysterious language,
Pāṇḍava, and you told him 'Yes': that is my password."
Said Kuntī's son Yudhiṣṭhira, ever-persevering in truth, "I
recognize you, good man, as a friend of Vidura, pure, trustworthy,
and always fiercely loyal. No password from the sage is necessary. As
he is ours, so are you; we regard you as one of us. And we are yours
10 as we are his; protect us as the sage would. I am sure that Purocana
has built this shelter as a firetrap for me on Duryodhana's orders. The
evil-minded crook has treasure and allies, and he has always been
oppressing us maliciously. Help us with all your might escape from
that fire, for when we are burned to death, Suyodhana will have
reached his goal. There is the crook's well-stocked armory. This large
place has been built flush against its walls. Vidura certainly knew in
advance the unholy crime he had in mind, and he warned us about it.
15 Now the danger the Steward foresaw is upon us: help us escape
without that Purocana being the wiser!"

The sapper promised and went to work. He dug out a trench and made a very deep hole. He made it in the middle of the house, with a not too wide opening at the top hidden with wooden boards that were even with the floor. For fear of Purocana, they concealed the opening carefully, and all that time the unholy plotter lived on their doorstep. They all slept in that hole with their weapons, every night. By day the Pāṇḍavas were out hunting, from forest to forest. They appeared trusting but were distrustful, seemed content but were discontented, and so they dwelled there, deceiving Purocana, and they were most unhappy. None of the inhabitants of the city found them out, besides that excellent sapper, Vidura's friend.

Vaiśaṃpāyana said:

136.1 Purocana, on seeing how happily they had been living there, now
for a whole year, and remarking that they held no suspicions, was
quite cheered; and when Purocana became so cheerful, law-wise
Yudhiṣṭhira Kaunteya said to his brothers, "That crooked Purocana
thinks that we have shed all our suspicions. We have deceived the
cruel man. I think the time has come to escape. We shall set fire to the
armory and burn Purocana to death. We'll put six people here and
escape unobserved."
5 Under the pretext of a donation rite, Kuntī held one night a large
feast for the brahmins, O king, and women came too. The women ate
and drank and made merry as they pleased, until the Mādhava
princess allowed them to go and they went home. A Niṣāda woman

had also happened to come to that feast with her five sons, hungry for food and prompted by Time. She and her sons drank wine until they were drunk and besotted; they lost consciousness and slept like the dead in the house, O king.

While a stiff wind was blowing in the night and all the people were
10 asleep, Bhīma started a fire at the spot where Purocana was lying. The intense heat and roar of the fire soon became evident and awakened the people by droves.

The citizens said:

That evil blackguard had that house built and burned on Duryodhana's orders, to his own perdition! A curse on the perverse mind of Dhṛtarāṣṭra, who made his minister burn to death the young and pure children of Pāṇḍu! But as luck would have it that evil-minded crook has now burned himself alive, when he burned those innocent and trusting good men.

Vaiśaṃpāyana said:

15 So did the Vāraṇāvatakas lament as they stood around the house that night. The Pāṇḍavas themselves and their mother, all much perturbed, crept out through the hole and fled secretly and unobserved. But because of their lack of sleep and their terror, the enemy-killing Pāṇḍavas and their mother could not make haste. Then Bhīmasena, whose speed and power were terrific, took his brothers and his mother and carried them all. He put his mother on his shoulder, the twins on his hips, and the mighty Pārthas under his arms. He shattered the trees with his impact and rended the earth with his feet; and so the puissant Wolf-Belly rushed onward with the vehemence of a tempest.

Vaiśaṃpāyana said:

137.1 When the night had passed, all the people in the town assembled there hurriedly to look for the Pāṇḍavas. After they had extinguished the fire they saw that the house that had burned had been built with lacquer and that Minister Purocana had been killed in the fire. "That must have been the doing of the evil Duryodhana, to make the Pāṇḍavas perish!" shouted the people. "No doubt, with Dhṛtarāṣṭra's conniving, Duryodhana has burned the heirs of Pāṇḍu, for the king
5 did not restrain him! Nor, to be sure, is Bhīṣma Śāṃtanava obeying the Law, nor Droṇa, Vidura, Kṛpa, or the other Kauravas. Let us send word to the ill-spirited Dhṛtarāṣṭra: 'Your grand plan has succeeded, you have burned the Pāṇḍavas to death!'"

Removing the smoldering coals to look for the Pāṇḍavas, they found the innocent Niṣāda woman burned with her five sons. That same sapper, while cleaning the house, covered up the hole completely with debris so that people did not notice it. Thereupon the townfolk sent word to Dhṛtarāṣṭra that the Pāṇḍavas and Minister

10 Purocana had been killed in a fire. When King Dhṛtarāṣṭra heard the
very bad tidings that Pāṇḍu's sons had perished, he lamented most
grievously: "Now is King Pāṇḍu, my precious brother, really dead,
now that his men-children have been burned with their mother! Let
men go quickly to Vāraṇāvata and offer the funeral rites for the
heroes and for the princes of Kunti. Have beautiful large urns made
for their bones and let their friends pay homage to those who have
died there. Whatever good I can do for the Pāṇḍavas and Kuntī, now
that matters have come to this pass, spare no treasure to do it!"
15 When he had thus spoken, Ambikā's son Dhṛtarāṣṭra, surrounded
by the kinsmen, offered the water for the sons of Pāṇḍu. Plunged into
grief, all the Kauravas lamented much, but Vidura grieved little, for
he knew more than they.

The Pāṇḍavas themselves, after escaping from Vāraṇāvata, traveled
hastily onward, turning toward the south. And as they journeyed
southward, they knew their way in the night by the stars, going hard,
O king, until they reached the dense jungle. The Pāṇḍavas were
exhausted and thirsty, and their eyes were blinded by sleep. And
20 again they said to the mighty Bhīmasena, "What could be more
disastrous then being in this dense jungle? We can't make out the
directions and we have no more power to go on. And that crook—we
don't know whether Purocana was in fact burned to death. How are
we going to escape unseen from this danger? Carry us again,
Bhārata, as you did before, and travel onward. For you are the
strongest of us, you alone are like the Wind!" And at Yudhiṣṭhira's
word the powerful Bhīmasena once more carried Kuntī and his
brothers and strode apace.

Vaiśaṃpāyana said:

138.1 And as he strode with fast strides, the speed of his thighs raised up a
wind that stormed as it storms at the onset of the months of Āṣāḍha
and Jyaiṣṭha. He trampled giants of the forests that stood in blossom
and fruit and obliterated the trunks and bushes that grew on the
wayside. Boundlessly powerful, he lurched on, snapping the trees, and
his speed dazed the Pāṇḍavas. Many rivers they crossed, their far
banks distant, with the boats of their arms, and on the way they
5 assumed disguises for fear of Duryodhana. Where the going was rough,
Bhīma carried his delicate, glorious mother alone on his back up
banks and hills.

When evening fell, the bulls of the Bhāratas came to a desolate
wilderness where roots, fruit, and water were scarce, infested with
ferocious birds and beasts of prey. Dusk fell grisly, the birds and beasts
became horrific, and the horizons darkened under unseasonable
storms. Exhaustion, thirst, and growing sleepiness pressed down on

the Kauravas, and they could go no more. Then Bhīma breached another ghastly, desolate patch of desert, and he came upon a beautiful banyan tree that threw ample shade. There the bulllike Bhārata unburdened himself of them all and said, "I am going to look for water. You rest. I hear the sweet whooping of cranes that live in the water; I am sure there must be a large pool of water here."

His eldest brother allowed him to go, Bhārata, and he followed the whooping of the cranes till he found them. Then he drank the water and bathed, bull of the Bhāratas, and brought water back in his shawl, king. He hurried back to his mother the space of two leagues, and when he found her and his brothers asleep on the bare ground, the Wolf-Belly was gripped by grief and wept: "Now they must sleep on the ground when in Vāraṇāvata they could not catch sleep on sumptuous couches! Look! The sister of the Vasudeva who ground the herds of his enemies to dust, the daughter of the king of Kunti, Kuntī favored with all beauties, the daughter-in-law of Vicitravīrya, the wife of the great-spirited Pāṇḍu, she who, shining with the sheen of a lotus calyx, was always couched in terraced palaces, most delicate of great ladies, accustomed to sleep on the costliest beds—look how she, so wonted, now beds on the earth! She bore these sons by Dharma, Indra, and the Wind, and now she lies exhausted on the unaccustomed ground. What more grievous sight can I ever see than the sight of these tigers among men now bedding on the ground? The law-wise king who deserves to sway the three worlds, why must he now lie tired on the ground like a commoner! And he, dark like a rain cloud, who has no peer among men in the world, is lying on the ground like a common man—what could be a sorrier sight! And the twins who resemble the Aśvins in the perfection of their beauty are now, like commoners, asleep on the bare earth. Happily lives in this world, like a solitary tree in a villiage, the man who has no kinsmen that find against him and defile his family. For the tree that stands alone in the village, rich in fruit and foliage, becomes a sanctuary and, having no kin, is adored and much worshiped. They who have many relatives who are champions and grounded in the Law, they live happily in the world and healthily. The sons of friendly kinsmen who are strong and prosperous live while supporting one another like the trees that grow in a forest. But we, we were banished by the evil Dhṛtarāṣṭra and his son, and barely escaped the burning he ordered. We escaped that fire and now have sought shelter with this tree—but which way shall we go, having found trouble beyond compare? Not far from this wood I spy a city. Someone must wake while they are asleep—well, I myself shall stay awake. Later when they wake up rested, they will drink water." And so Bhīma decided and waked through the night.

1(9) The Slaying of Hiḍimba

139–144 (B. 152–55; C. 5927–6102)
139 (152; 5927). A man-eating Rākṣasa, Hiḍimba, smells Kuntī and the Pāṇḍavas and sends his sister Hiḍimbā to fetch them (1–10). She falls in love with Bhīma, who is watching, changes into a lovely maiden, and proposes to him; he refuses her (10–30).
140 (153; 5962). Hiḍimba arrives; Bhīma reassures the woman (1–10). Hiḍimba divines that his sister lusts after Bhīma and threatens to kill her, too (10–20).
141. Bhīma boasts (1–10). Hiḍimba challenges him, and they engage in a wrestling match (10–20).
142 (154; 6007). Hiḍimbā tells the others, who have awakened, of her identity, of her love for Bhīma, and of the present duel (1–10). They watch, and Arjuna teases Bhīma (10–25). Enraged, Bhīma breaks the demon's back. (25–30).
143 (155; 6042). When Bhīma wants to kill Hiḍimbā too, Yudhiṣṭhira intervenes. She asks to marry Bhīma, and Yudhiṣṭhira agrees if she brings him back every night (1–15). They make love all over the world (20–25). She gives birth to a Rākṣasa boy, called Ghaṭotkaca, who becomes a favorite with the Pāṇḍavas; then mother and son leave them. Ghaṭotkaca promises to come whenever he is needed. (25–30).
144 (56; 6084). The Pāṇḍavas travel disguised as ascetics. They meet Vyāsa who confesses his partiality for them and advises them to go to the town of Ekacakrā. He predicts to Kuntī the greatness of the Pāṇḍavas (1–20).

Vaiśaṃpāyana said:

139.1 While they were sleeping there, a Rākṣasa by the name of Hiḍimba
was living in a *śāla* tree not very far from the wood. He was a cruel
Rākṣasa who ate human flesh – powerful and strong, malformed, yellow-
eyed, tusked, and loathsome to the eye. He was hungry and looking for
flesh when he happened to see them. Fingers pointed upward, he
scratched his unkempt hair and shook it, and yawned, big-mouthed, as
his eyes kept returning to them. Then this evil, large-bodied, powerful
5 devourer of human flesh, sniffing the smell of humans, said to his sister,

"Now—and how long has it been?—I have found my favorite food! My tongue is slavering with appetite and licks around my mouth! I'll sink my eight sharp-pointed tusks, impatient after all this time they had nothing to bite, into these bodies and their delicious flesh. I'll get on their human throats, cut the artery, and guzzle the plentiful fresh, warm, foaming blood! Go and find out who they are who are lying in the wood—the powerful smell of humans alone seems to sate me! Kill all those humans and bring them to me. You are in no danger of them since they are sleeping in our domain. We'll cook the flesh of these humans the way we like it and gorge ourselves on it together! Now hurry and do as I tell you!"

The Rākṣasī heard her brother's orders and hurriedly went to the spot where the Pāṇḍavas were lying, bull of the Bhāratas. And as she came there she saw the Pāṇḍavas asleep there with Pṛthā, and the unvanquished Bhīmasena, who was awake. No sooner had she seen Bhīmasena, tall like a *śāla* trunk, matchless on earth for his beauty, than the Rākṣasī fell in love with him. "That swarthy, strong-armed, lion-shouldered, lustrous, conch-necked, lotus-eyed man is the right husband for me! I won't follow my brother's outrageous orders. A wife's love is stronger than a sister's friendship! With them killed my brother's appetite and mine will be sated for less than an hour, but if I don't kill them I'll be pleasured for years without end!"

Capable of changing herself, she took on a beautiful human shape and very softly approached the strong-armed Bhīmasena like a bashful creeper, decked with celestial ornaments; and smilingly she said to him, "Where have you come from and who are you, bull of a man? And who are these godlike men who are sleeping here? And who is this tall, dark, delicate woman to you, my blameless man, who is sleeping so trustingly in this wilderness as though she were at home? Doesn't she know that this desolate jungle is haunted by Rākṣasas and that a wicked Rākṣasa lives here by the name of Hiḍimba? He is my brother, and he sent me from sheer wickedness, for he wants to eat the flesh of all of you, godlike human. But I, when I saw you who are like the offspring of an Immortal, I chose you for my one and only husband; I am telling you the truth! Now that you know this, you who are wise in the Laws, you must do right by me. My body and heart are seized by lust—I love you: love me! I shall save you, my strong-armed man, from the man-eating Rākṣasa; we'll live in the fastness of mountains—be my husband, man without flaws! I can fly in the sky and roam where I want—find pleasure beyond compare anywhere with me!"

Bhīma said:

What man would desert his mother and his elder brother and others who are younger than he, were he to be king. Rākṣasī? What man like me would go lusting and leave these sleeping brothers and his mother as fodder for Rākṣasas?

The Rākṣasī said:

I'll do anything to please you. Wake them all up, I'll gladly save you from the appetite of that man-eating Rākṣasa!

Bhīma said:

30 My mother and brothers are sleeping peacefully in the wilderness,
Rākṣasī. No fear for your ill-spirited brother is going to make me wake
them. For there are no Rākṣasas, timid girl, who can withstand my
might, nor, sweet-eyes, are there men or Gandharvas or Yakṣas who
can. Go or stay here, dear, do as you please, or, slender maid, send
that man-eating brother of yours!

Vaiśaṃpāyana said:

140.1 The lordly Rākṣasa Hiḍimba, noticing that his sister was late
returning, descended from his tree and went down to the Pāṇḍavas,
eyes bloodshot, arms strong, hair standing up, strength ample, girth
and height like a rain cloud's, tusks honed, face aflame. As soon as
Hiḍimbā saw him loom with his deformed appearance, she said
trembling to Bhīma, "There is the evil man-eater coming; he is furious!
You and your brothers do what I tell you. I have the powers of the
5 Rākṣasa, hero, and I can go anywhere. Climb on my hip and I'll take
you through the sky. Wake up your sleeping brothers and mother,
scourge of your enemies, I shall take you all and go through the sky!"

Bhīma said:

Have no fear, broad-hipped woman. No one will harm us as long as
I am here. I shall kill him before your eyes, my pretty. This degraded
Rākṣasa is no match for my strength. Not even all the Rākṣasas
combined could stand my throbbing in battle, timorous girl. Look at
my arms, round as elephant trunks, and these thighs like bludgeons,
10 and this hard chest of mine! Today you shall see my might that is
like Indra's, my lovely of the opulent hips. Don't despise me now,
thinking that I am a mere human!

The Rākṣasī said:

I don't despise you, tiger among men, who have the beauty of a God. But I have seen the havoc this Rākṣasa has wrought on humans!

Vaiśaṃpāyana said:

While Bhīmasena was talking with her in this way, O Bhārata, the furious, man-eating Rākṣasa heard her words. Hiḍimba looked at the human form she was wearing, the crown of her head covered with flowers, her face shining like the full moon, with beautiful eyes, eyebrows, nose, and hair, and delicate nails and skin, decked with all

15 sorts of ornaments and wearing a very sheer robe. And as he saw the
very enticing human form she was wearing, he suspected that she was
lusting after a man and the man-eater became angry. Furious with
his sister, he opened his big eyes wide, chief of the Kurus, and said to
her, "What dimwit comes in my way when I am hungry? Aren't you
afraid of my fury, Hiḍimbā, have you lost your senses? A curse on
you, sluttish man-chaser, who are out to hurt me! You defame all the
ancient lords of the Rākṣasas! These humans for whom you have
perpetrated this outrage on me, I'll slaughter them all this instant
20 along with you!" Bloody-eyed, Hiḍimba fell on Hiḍimbā to kill her,
gnashing his teeth.

Vaiśaṃpāyana said:

141.1 Bhīmasena laughed when he saw the Rākṣasa rage at his sister,
and he said to him, "Why must you wake up these people, Hiḍimba?
They are sleeping so peacefully! Hurry up, attack me, nitwit of a
man-eater! Try your blows on me, don't strike a woman who has
done no wrong, who has been wronged herself! For it is not her own
doing that this young woman lusts after me. She has been forced by
the Bodiless God* who ranges inside the body. She is your sister,
5 nitwit, disgracer of your race! You told her to come, and when she
saw my beauty the bashful girl fell in love. She has not defiled her
family. Where the Bodiless God is to blame, you are not going to kill a
woman with me standing by, ill-spirited Rākṣasa! Fight it out with me,
man-eater, one against the other, and I myself shall speed you today
to the seat of Yama. Today your head is going to be squashed on the
ground till it splits, Rākṣasa, as though it was squashed by the foot of
a robust elephant! Today the vultures and jackals will happily tear
10 your body apart, limb by limb, when I have killed you in battle! In an
instant now I shall free this wilderness from its pest! You have
infested it too long, devouring people. Today your own sister will see
you dragged over the ground, fiend, as a mountainous elephant is
dragged by a lion. When I have killed you, corrupt Rākṣasa, the men
that walk in the wilderness shall walk in the wilderness safe from
oppression!"

Hiḍimba said:

Why all this useless boasting and bragging, human? First do it in
fact, then brag about it! Don't take too long. If you think your feeble
15 self strong, fight with me and you'll find out that I am stronger! Them
I won't hurt yet. Let them sleep happily. You I'll kill now, dimwit,
with your vile tongue! And when I have drunk the blood from your
body, I'll kill them too, and then this disagreeable woman.

* = the God of Love.

Vaiśaṃpāyana said:
After saying this, the man-eater stretched out his arms and
furiously rushed on Bhīmasena, tamer of enemies. But as he stormed
toward him, Bhīma of terrible strength immediately struck down his
arm and laughingly brought him down. When he had brought him
to the ground, Bhīma dragged the writhing demon away from that
20 spot to a distance of eight bows, as a lion drags a small animal. The
furious Rākṣasa, forcibly dragged along by Bhīma, threw his arms
around him and uttered a terrifying cry. Again the powerful Bhīma
dragged him away, so that his yelling would not disturb his brothers,
who were sleeping peacefully. They set upon each other and dragged
each other about with all their might, the Rākṣasa and Bhīma, and
exerted their full strength. They shattered big trees and pulled off
creepers like two crazed sixty-year-old elephants in heat. Their great
noise awakened the bulls among men, and they and their mother saw
Hiḍimbā standing before them.

Vaiśaṃpāyana said:
142.1 On waking, the tiger-like men and Pṛthā beheld with astonishment
the unearthly beauty of Hiḍimbā. Amazed by the perfection of her
loveliness, Kuntī stared at her, then said softly and very kindly in a
gentle voice, "Whose are you who resemble a child of the Gods, and
who are you, beautiful woman? What task has taken you here, and
from where? If you are the Goddess of this wood, or an Apsarā, tell
me all, and also why you are standing here."
Hiḍimbā said:
5 The wood that you see, this vast wilderness dark like a rain cloud,
is the habitation of the Rākṣasa Hiḍimba and myself. Know, radiant
lady, that I am the sister of that lordly Rākṣasa, and my brother has
sent me here because he wants to devour you and your sons. So, at
the orders of that cruel demon, I came here and then saw your
powerful son with the golden skin. The God Manmatha,* who ranges
in the hearts of all beings, pushed me and I fell under your son's spell,
good lady. I have chosen your mighty son for my husband. I tried to
carry him off, but I could not master him. Then the man-eater
10 noticed that I was late returning and came himself to kill all these
sons of yours. Now he has been crushed to the ground by your wily
and great-spirited son whom I love, and dragged away from here.
Look at them now, a human and a Rākṣasa, dragging each other
powerfully through the dust with the roar of the thunder, and fiercely
embattled!
Vaiśaṃpāyana said:
Scarcely had Yudhiṣṭhira heard her words before he leaped up,
and so did Arjuna, Nakula, and the mighty Sahadeva, and they saw

* = the God of Love.

the two grapple and wrestle each other, holding out for victory like
15 two battle-crazed lions. They clinched and dragged each other about,
raising dust until it resembled the billowing smoke of a forest fire.
They looked like hills enveloped by the dust of the earth, rocky
mountains covered with sherds of fog. Seeing how Bhīma was
beleaguered by the Rākṣasa, the Pārtha laughed and said softly to him,
"Have no fear, strong-armed Bhīma, we were asleep, wan with
fatigue, and did not know that you were embattled with a terrible-
looking demon. I am here to help you, Pārtha! I'll fight the Rākṣasa.
Nakula and Sahadeva will guard mother."

Bhīma said:

20 You sit aside and watch! Don't get agitated. I have got him in the
bend of my arms, he won't last much longer.

Arjuna said:

Why take your time killing that evil Rākṣasa, Bhīma? We should go, we can't stay here long, enemy-tamer. Before long the east will redden and morning dawn, at the grisly hour when Rākṣasas become stronger. Hurry, Bhīma, don't play with him. Kill the terrifying ogre before he uses his magic. Use the power of your arms!

Vaiśaṃpāyana said:

At these words of Arjuna, Bhīma tossed up the body of the terrible Rākṣasa and spun it around over a hundred times.

Bhīma said:

25 You have uselessly fed on useless flesh, uselessly aged with your
useless wit! You have earned a useless death, so you won't be useless
anymore!

Arjuna said:

If this Rākṣasa is too much for you, I'll help you. Finish him off quickly! Or rather, I myself will finish him, Wolf-Belly. You are tired and at the end of your tether. So far, so good, but now rest.

Vaiśaṃpāyana said:

When he heard this, Bhīma became very indignant; and crushing
the Rākṣasa to the ground, he strangled him to death like a sacrificial
animal. As he was being slaughtered by Bhīma, he gave a mighty
scream, filling that entire wilderness with the sound, like a kettledrum
30 soaked in water. The powerful son of Pāṇḍu racked the body on his
knee and bent it till the spine broke, to the delight of the Pāṇḍavas.
When they saw Hiḍimba dead, they were wildly excited and
complimented the tigerlike, enemy-taming Bhīmasena. And after they
had paid compliments to the great-spirited Bhīma of terrible strength,
Arjuna again said to the Wolf-Belly, "I believe there is a city not far
from this wood, lord. Let us go quickly, and good luck to you;
Suyodhana must not find us." All these burners of their foes and their
mother agreed, and the tigerlike men departed. Hiḍimbā the Rākṣasī
followed them.

Bhīma said:
143.1 Rākṣasas remember their feuds and resort to bewitching magic.
Hiḍimbā, walk the trail that your brother has blazed!
Yudhiṣṭhira said:
Even in anger, tigerlike Bhīma, never kill a woman! Preserve the
Law, Pāṇḍava, before you preserve your life. You have killed the
mighty Rākṣasa who came intending to kill us. But what could his
sister do to us, even if she were angry?
Vaiśaṃpāyana said:
Hiḍimbā, however, folded her hands and saluted Kuntī and
5 Yudhiṣṭhira Kaunteya, and she said, "My lady, you know how women
on earth suffer from love. And such suffering has now beset me
because of Bhīmasena, good lady. I have born this great sorrow,
waiting for my time; but now my time has come, it shall be for my
happiness. For I have forsaken my friends and my Law and my kin,
and, good lady, chosen your tigerlike son for my man. Am I rejected
in my suit by the man I have chosen and by you, because I speak as
I do? Whether you think me a fool, or your devoted servant, let me
join yoke, great lady, with your son as my husband. I shall take the
10 godlike man and go where I please. I shall later come back here, trust
me, good lady. For whenever you shall think of me, I shall come and
take you all. I shall help these bulls among men cross deserts and
impassable roads, or I swiftly shall carry you on my back wherever
you want to go. All of you, take pity on me and let Bhīma love me.
'Let a man hang to his life in any which way, if he is to escape
disaster; let him hold every means to be right and follow this as his
Law. But he is the most Law-wise man who hangs to his Law in
15 disaster: to the Law-minded man, disaster is the vice of Law. Merit
preserves life, merit is the lifesaver; whatsoever way one follows his
Law, he is not condemned.' "
Yudhiṣṭhira said:
It is as you say, Hiḍimbā, no doubt about it. Abide by the Law, as
you have declared it. When Bhīma has bathed and done the daily
rites and received the marriage thread, he shall love you until the
setting of the sun. Enjoy yourself with him by day as you please,
mind-fast woman, but bring him back here every night.
Vaiśaṃpāyana said:
"So be it," promised Hiḍimbā the Rākṣasī, and she took Bhīma and
20 strode up above. On lovely mountain peaks and the sanctuaries of
Gods, always enchanting and noisy with deer and birds, she took on a
superb body and, decked with precious ornaments and sweetly
beguiling, she made love to the Pāṇḍava. In secret corners of the
woods, on mountain ridges blossoming with trees, by lovely ponds
abloom with lotus and water lily, on river islands and mountain

streams with sandbars of beryl where fords and woods and water were
pure, or on lands in the ocean that were heaped with pearls and gold,
25 in charming villages or stands of tall *śāla* trees, in sacred forests of the
Gods, on mountain cliffs, in the habitations of Guhyakas* and the
retreats of ascetics, and by the waters of Lake Mānasa where there is
fruit and flower in all seasons, there she assumed a superb body and
made love to the Pāṇḍava. And while she loved Bhīma everywhere,
nimble as thought, the Rākṣasī gave birth to a son by the powerful
Bhīmasena. He was a terrifying sight, squint-eyed, large-mouthed,
needle-eared, loathsome-bodied, dark-red-lipped, sharp-tusked, and
powerful, born a great archer of great prowess, great courage, great
arms, great speed, great body, great wizardry, tamer of his foes.
30 Inhuman, though born from a human, of terrible speed and great
strength, he surpassed the Piśācas and other demons as he surpassed
human beings. Although a babe, he would have seemed a fully grown
youth among humans, O lord of the people; and on all weapons the
powerful champion attained a sovereign mastery.

Rākṣasa women give birth the day they conceive; and Rākṣasas
assume any shape they want and appear in many forms. The shiny
child bowed and touched his father's feet and his mother's, that
future bowman, and his parents gave him a name. "He is as shiny as
a pot!" Bhīma said to the mother, and that became his name,
35 Ghaṭotkaca, Shiny-as-a-Pot. This Ghaṭotkaca was devoted to the
Pāṇḍavas, and they always loved him—he became their very life.
Then Hiḍimbā said to Bhīma that the time of their life together had
run out; and she made a compact and went her own way. Ghaṭotkaca
promised his father that he would come to them whenever he was
needed; thereupon that best of Rākṣasas departed for the north. For he
had been created by the great-spirited Maghavat** for power's sake, so
that he might destroy the great-spirited Karṇa, whose prowess was
unmatched.

Vaiśaṃpāyana said:

144.1 The warlike heroes went off, hunting many herds of deer from
forest to forest, and they traveled fast, O king. They set eyes on the
lands of the Matsyas, Trigartas, Pāñcālas, and Kīcakas, and on lovely
woods and lakes. The great-spirited men braided their hair and all
wore bark skirts and deerskins, and so did Kuntī, assuming the guise
of ascetics. At some places the warriors ran and carried their mother;
5 elsewhere they journeyed at leisure and went in the open. They
learned the brahmin *Vedas* and all their branches, as well as the
science of policy. Then the Law-wise men met their grandfather.

* = Yakṣas.
** = Indra.

They greeted the great-spirited Kṛṣṇa Dvaipāyana; and the enemy-burners and their mother stood before him with their hands folded at their foreheads.

Vyāsa said:

Long ago I foresaw in my mind, bulls of the Bhāratas, how the sons of Dhṛtarāṣṭra would abide in lawlessness and banish you. Knowing this, I have now come, for I wish to benefit you greatly. Do not despair in this pass. All this will lead to happiness. All the Kauravas and yourselves are no doubt equal before me; yet relations will have their fondness when their kin is distressed and young. Therefore, I now have a greater love for you, and because of that love I wish to help you. Listen. In this vicinity there is a lovely and healthy town. Live there in disguise and wait for my return.

Vaiśaṃpāyana said:

After he had thus encouraged the enemy-taming Pārthas, he went with them to the town Ekacakrā. And the lord comforted Kuntī: "Live, daughter! Your child Yudhiṣṭhira, the son of Dharma, shall hold sway over all the kings on earth as King Law. The Law-wise prince will conquer the entire earth under Law with the aid of the might of Arjuna and Bhīma, and he shall rule it without a doubt. Your sons and Mādrī's, all these warlike men, shall enjoy themselves happily in their own realm! And after conquering the earth the tigerlike men shall offer up sacrifices, the Royal Consecration, the Horse Sacrifice, and other grand rituals of rich stipends. Your sons shall enjoy their father's and grandfather's kingdom on earth, favoring their friends with riches and happiness."

So speaking, the seer Dvaipāyana conducted them to the house of a brahmin. Then he said to those best of princes, "Wait for me until I come back. As soon as you have learned the proper times and places, you shall find supreme joy." With folded hands they made their promise, O king of men; and the blessed Lord Vyāsa, the masterful seer, went where it pleased him.

1(10) The Slaying of Baka

145–52 (B. 157–64; C. 6103–6315)
145 (157; 6103). In Ekacakrā they live with a brahmin and beg for their living (1–5). Once, Kuntī and Bhīma hear the brahmin lament, and she suggests that out of gratitude they should see to his complaint (5–15). The brahmin laments that he must die and thus cause the death of his wife, daughter, and son (20–40).

146 (158; 6143). His wife admonishes him and offers to die for him to save the future of their children (1–35).
147 (159; 6181). His daughter offers to die, for her father must surrender her one day anyhow (1–15). While all three weep, the baby son offers to kill the man-eating Rākṣasa with a straw he picks up. This cheers them (15–20).
148 (160; 6205). Kuntī enters and asks about their grievance. The brahmin relates that a Rākṣasa, Baka, terrorizes the country; while protecting it from outsiders, he demands as his prize a ration of a cartload of rice, two buffalo, and one human. The people take turns. Avoidance means death for the whole family. The king is powerless (1–10). It is now the brahmin's turn (10–15).
149 (161; 6222). Kuntī offers Bhīma. The brahmin protests, but Kuntī is confident that Bhīma will survive (1–20).
150 (162; 6241). Bhīma gives his promise. Returning home, Yudhiṣṭhira guesses that Bhīma is up to some feat and berates Kuntī (1–10). She reassures him (10–25).
151 (163; 6270). Bhīma takes the ransom to Baka, and stops and starts eating the food. He ignores Baka's protests. Baka hits him, but Bhīma ignores him (1–10). Finally Baka attacks him with a tree. They end up wrestling, and Bhīma breaks the demon's spine (10–20).
152 (164; 6295). At Baka's death the demon's family is friendly to the country. Bhīma leaves the corpse at the town gate (1–5). The town folk come out and, on learning that a brahmin has killed Baka, they institute a brahmin festival (5–15).

Janamejaya said:
145.1 When the warlike sons of Pāṇḍu and Kuntī had gone to Ekacakrā, what did they do thereafter, O best of the twiceborn?
Vaiśampāyana said:
When the warlike sons of Kuntī had gone to Ekacakrā, they
dwelled, for not too long a time, in the house of a brahmin. All of
them went abegging, and on their rounds they saw lovely groves of
all kinds, distant corners of the land, rivers and lakes, O king of the
people. They became a pleasant sight to the townspeople because of
5 their virtues. Every night they handed their alms over to Kuntī. She
divided them into parts, and they each ate their share—the heroes and
their mother ate half, and the powerful Bhīma ate all of the other half

of the alms. And when the great-spirited brothers were living there in
this fashion, sire, a good deal of time went by.

Then, one day, when the bulls of the Bharatas had gone on their
begging rounds, Bhīmasena happened to stay home and keep Pṛthā
company. Suddenly Kuntī heard a great outcry in the house of the
10 brahmin, frightful and resonant with grief. When the queen heard
them all shrieking and wailing, her compassion and goodness did not
allow her to bear with it, O king. As though churned in her heart by
sorrow, the gentle Pṛthā spoke to Bhīma these compassionate words:
"We have been living very happily in this brahmin's house, son, and
we have been well-treated. Dhṛtarāṣṭra's people do not know of us,
and we live in peace. I have often thought whether I could not do
something nice for this brahmin, son, as people do who lodge somewhere happily. One is a man, my dear, to the extent of one's gratitude.
15 If someone does something for you, you should do more in return.
Now some grief has struck this brahmin, that is certain. If we could
lend him our help, it would be a good deed."

Bhīma said:

Let us find out what is troubling him and from where it has come.
When we know, I shall decide what to do, however difficult it may be.

Vaiśaṃpāyana said:

While they were talking, they again heard the sounds of grief
coming from the brahmin and his wife, O king of the people. Kuntī
went hurriedly to the woman quarters of the great-spirited brahmin,
like a cow that sees her calf tied up. And there she found him, with
wife, son, and daughter, his face distorted by grief.

The brahmin said:

20 Accursed is this life in this world, with the substance of a flame,
meaningless, rooted in pain, enslaved to others, and only finding
misfortune! To live is to suffer, life is a fever, and the living have only
the choice between evils! Although a man all alone pursues Law,
Profit, and Pleasure, yet they escape him, and it is counted the worst
of sufferings. Some say that release is supreme, but there never is any.
If one acquires possessions, all hell besets him: the craving for riches
is a great grief—if one has riches, it grows worse. When one loves
25 one's possessions, to lose them is a greater grief. I do not perceive any
enterprise by which I can escape my disasters, unless I take flight
with wife and children to a healthier place.

You know I have urged you before that we should go to a place
that is safe, but you didn't listen, brahmin wife. "I was born here,"
you said, "I grew up here. My father lives here," you said witlessly to
all my entreaties. Now your old father and mother have long since
gone to heaven, your relatives are dead—so what joy was there left
to live here? And now, because you wanted your family about and

didn't listen to me, we stand to lose our own family, to my own great
30 grief! No, for this will be my own death, rather. For I couldn't bear to
sacrifice any one of my family and cruelly go on living myself! You have
helped me in the duties of the Law—always self-effacing, you have been
like a mother to me. You were given me by the Gods as a friend, and you
have always been my mainstay. Father and mother gave you to me
to share my life as a householder: I chose you by the rules and
married you with the proper prayers, a well-born, well-mannered
woman, mother of my children. . . . I cannot sacrifice you, who have
been a good and sinless and ever-faithful wife, in order to save my
own life!

How could I sacrifice my daughter, a child still, before the age and
35 without the outward signs of womanhood? The great-spirited creator
has left her with me in trust for her husband; and from her I and my
ancestors hope for the worlds that the sons of one's daughters open to
one. How could I attempt to forsake this girl, after I fathered her
myself? There are men that hold that a father loves his son more than
his daughter—I do not, I love them both as much, though on the son
rests the worlds and continuity and bliss eternal. How could I attempt
to sacrifice this innocent girl? I shall burn among the dead as though
I had killed myself! Yet it is clear that if I leave them behind, they
won't be able to live. The cruel sacrifice of any one of them is
condemned by the wise. Yet, if I sacrifice myself, they will die without
me. Having fallen into this dread disaster, I do not know how to
40 escape. A-ho, calamity! What course must I now take with my family?
It is better to die with them all; I can live no more!

The brahmin's wife said:

146.1 You must not grieve as though you were a common man! For you
who are educated no time is a time of grief. All men in this world
must inescapably come to their end, and if a thing is inevitable, what
point is there in grieving over it? Wife, son, and daughter are all
wanted by a man for his own sake. Rid yourself of your sorrow with
a good spirit: I myself shall go there. For that is the supreme and
sempiternal task for a woman in this world that she pursue her
5 husband's welfare even at the price of her life. My doing this deed
will bring happiness to you too, and to me it will bring, here and
hereafter, fame everlasting. This is the governing Law that I declare to
you, and both Profit and Law aplenty it will visibly bring to you. The
purpose for which a man takes a wife you have gained by me—a son
and a daughter; you have acquitted me of my obligation.

You are capable of feeding and protecting your two children—I am
capable of neither. You have given me all I could desire and saved me
from adversity. How would your young children be able to survive

10 you, and how would I? How shall I, widowed and left without a
protector, and with two young children, sustain both of them and still
walk the path of the virtuous? When our daughter is wooed by selfish
and arrogant suitors, unworthy of being allied to you, how shall I be
able to save her? Just as the birds snap up a piece of raw meat that is
thrown out on the ground, so all men snap up a woman without a
man. Pursued by evil men and seduced, I shall not be able to remain
on the path that the honest cherish, O best of brahmins. And then,
how shall I manage to keep this daughter of yours, young and
15 without a dowry, to the ancestral ways? How shall I be able to
inculcate in this young boy, fatherless and completely deprived, those
desirable virtues that you could inculcate who have an insight in the
Law? Unworthy men will bully me and seek after your fatherless
daughter as the serfs seek after the sacred sound of the *Veda*. If I
refuse to give her, since she will be strengthened by your virtues, they
may carry her off by force, as crows carry off the oblation from the
sacrifice. And when they see your son grown up so unlike yourself,
and your daughter at the mercy of unworthy men, people will despise
me. I won't know myself with arrogant men, brahmin, and I shall die,
20 no doubt of that. My young children, deprived of me as well as yourself, will doubtless perish, like two little fish when the river dries up.
Without a doubt all three of us will perish this way when we are
deprived of you.

Therefore you must surrender me. It is the supreme grace of women
to go the last journey before their husbands do, and not to remain in
the domain of his sons, O brahmin. I give up for you my son and my
daughter, my relatives and my life! A woman's constant devotion to
the well-being of her husband is a greater accomplishment than rituals,
25 austerities, vows, and all manner of donations. The lawlike deed that
I seek to do, which is praised as the supreme deed, is for the good and
the well-being of yourself as well as the family. Children and riches
and kind friends are wanted in order to ward off the Law of Distress—
and so is the wife, as the strict know. Place the whole family on one
scale and oneself on the other, man of rank, and all of them together
do not equal oneself—such is the judgement of the wise. Do through
me what has to be done. Save yourself; let me go, my lord, and
protect my children. Those wise in the Law declare in the decisions on
the Law that women may not be killed. They say that the Rākṣasas
30 know the Law—perhaps he won't kill me. Men are sure to be killed,
but that women are is open to doubt. Therefore, you who are wise in
the Law must let me depart. I have enjoyed my life, I have found much
happiness, I have followed the law, I have borne dear children by you:
to die will not grieve me.

I have borne children, I have grown old, I have always liked to

please you, and looking at all my blessings I have made my decision.
After you have surrendered me, my lord, you will find another woman,
and then your Law will once more stand firm. It is not against Law
for a man to have many wives, good man, but for a woman it is a
35 very grave breach of the Law to leap over her first husband. Looking
at all this and reflecting that self-sacrifice is condemned, you must save
yourself through me, and save the family and these two children.

Vaiśaṁpāyana said:

At her words the husband embraced her, Bhārata, and he and his
wife wept softly in great sorrow.

Vaiśaṃpāyana said:

147.1 When the daughter heard these words of her parents who were
sorrowing beyond measure, she was overcome by great grief and
spoke to them both.

"Why are you lamenting so grievously, as though you had none to
protect you? Now listen to something from me too, and when you
have heard it, carry it out properly! The Law dictates that you must
give me up *some* time. And since I shall have to be given up anyway,
surrender me now and save everyone through me alone. That is the
reason that people want children, so that they can save you. The time
5 has come now, I am your boat, save yourself with it! A child saves
everywhere—either here in this life he will save from distress, or after
one's death he will save one's soul—that is why the wise call him
putra. Grandfathers always want sons by their daughters; now I
myself shall indeed rescue them by saving my father's life. And this
little brother of mine—when you have gone to that yonder world, he
will surely perish in no time at all. When father has gone to heaven
and my little brother has perished, the offerings to the ancestors will
come to an end, and that will much displease them. I myself, deserted
by father, mother, and brother, will go from bad to worse and surely
10 die, for I am not used to that. But when you are healthy and safe,
mother and my little brother and our line and the offering to the
Fathers will go on as always. 'A son is one's self, a wife one's friend,
a daughter one's cross'—now rid yourself of your cross and join me
with the Law. Without you, father, I'll be a wretched, unprotected
girl, going wherever and whenever, woefully wretched. Either I shall
rescue this family, and having done this difficult feat partake of its
fruit; or you yourself must go and abandon me, good brahmin, and I
15 shall be oppressed. Therefore, consider me too. For my own sake, for
the sake of the Law, and for the sake of your progeny, good father,
you must save yourself and sacrifice me who am to be sacrificed
sooner or later. Don't let the time pass you by in doing the inevitable.
By giving the water, you will do me a favor. What could be more

grievous than that we, after you have gone to heaven, must roam
around like dogs, begging food from strangers? But with you and the
family healthy and safe from this affliction, I shall be very happy while
I live in the eternal world!"

When they heard her manifold laments, father, mother, and
20 daughter, all three, burst into tears. Then, as he heard them all
weeping, their little son said in a mumbling and slurring voice, but
with wide-open eyes, "Don't cry, daddy, don't, mummy, and you
stop it too, sister!" And, laughing, he crawled to each of them. Then
he took a straw from the floor and said happily, "With this I am going
to kill the man-eating Rākṣasa!" In spite of the misery that engulfed
them, when they heard the child babble away, they were all cheered
up. Kuntī, knowing that this was the right moment, came nearer and,
as though raising the dead with the Elixir, spoke to them,

Kuntī said:

148.1 What is the cause of this grief? I want to hear it precisely. When I
have learned it, I shall take it away from you, if it can be taken away.

The brahmin said:

What you say, ascetic, is becoming to the good. But no one can
dispel this grief. Close to this city lives a powerful Rākṣasa named
Baka who lords it over the countryside as well as the town. This
5 evil-spirited man-eater feeds on human flesh and, being a powerful
king of the Asuras and possessing the power of Rākṣasas, always
extends his protection to country, city, and land. Because of him we
are in no danger from the circle of enemies, or from any creatures.
The price he has set is a cartload of rice, two buffalos, and the one
human who takes them there. All the people provide him with his
food, each in his turn; and when after many years a man's turn
comes around, he finds it hard to escape. If people anywhere try to
escape their turn, the Rākṣasa kills them with wife and children and
eats them.

Our king, who sits at Vetrakīyagṛha, has no policy whereby his
10 people might be rid of this plague for good. We surely deserve it,
living as we do in the land of a feeble king, constantly harassed as
long as we have recourse to an incompetent king. Brahmins can be
said to be free to move as they please to anyone's land; they will blow
with their own virtues like freely roaming birds: "First one should find
a king, then a wife, then wealth: by collecting all three one can
maintain his kinsmen and sons." But I have collected the three in the
wrong order, and now that we have fallen into this danger we must
suffer sorely. It has now become our turn, and it will destroy our
15 family. I have to give him one person to eat as his price. I don't have
the means to buy a person anywhere, but no more am I able to feed

him one of my family. I see no way to escape from that Rākṣasa. So I am drowning in the vast ocean of grief from which no rescue seems possible. I shall now go to that Rākṣasa with my entire family, so that vile ogre may eat us all up together!

Kuntī said:

149.1 Do not despair in your plight! I perceive a means of escape from that Rākṣasa. You have only one little son, and one unhappy daughter. To me it is not seemly that you and they and your wife should go there. I have five sons, brahmin; one of them shall go and on your behalf bring the offering to that evil Rākṣasa.

The brahmin said:

I shall not allow it, however I hang to my life, that a brahmin and
5 a guest should lose his life for me! It is not done even among the
lowly women outside the pale of the Law that one should sacrifice
herself and her son for the sake of a brahmin! From my own self I
must learn what is good for me; so it seems to me. Between killing a
brahmin and killing oneself, self-murder seems better to me. Brahmin-
murder is the most heinous sin; there is no atoning for it. Even if done
without the right spirit it is better for me to kill myself.

Still, I do not wish to commit suicide, good lady; but if others do
the killing, no sin devolves on me. But if I intentionally were to
encompass the killing of a brahmin, I'd see no way of atoning for such
10 a vile and cruel deed. Surrendering one who has come to your house
or who has sought refuge, or killing a supplicant, is reckoned the
greatest cruelty. "One should never do a condemned or cruel act"; so
knew our great-spirited forebears, who knew the Law of Distress. It is
better that I myself perish with my wife than that I ever condone the
killing of a brahmin.

Kuntī said:

I too am firmly convinced, brahmin, that brahmins ought to be
safe. Nor would I love any son of mine less, had I a hundred sons. But
that Rākṣasa is not capable of destroying my son: my son is powerful,
15 perfected by spells, and resplendent. He shall bring all that food to the
Rākṣasa and, I am convinced, set himself free. Rākṣasas have been
embattled with that hero before, powerful and gigantic ones, and they
were killed one after the other. However, you should not breathe a
word about it to anyone, brahmin, for people would be eager to learn
the secret and bother my sons with their curiosity. Whomever my son
would teach without his guru's permission would not accomplish a
thing with his knowledge; that is the opinion of the strict.

Vaiśaṃpāyana said:

At these words of Pṛthā, the brahmin and his wife joyfully

welcomed her proposal, which was like the life-restoring Elixir.
20 Thereupon Kuntī and the brahmin together said to the son of the
Wind God: "Do so!" and he said to them: "Yes!"

Vaiśampāyana said:

150.1 "I shall do it," had Bhīma promised, O Bhārata, before all the Pāṇḍavas returned with their alms. Pāṇḍu's son Yudhiṣṭhira guessed it from his appearance; and sitting down by his mother, alone and in private, he questioned her: "What exploit is Bhīma of terrible strength about to undertake? Is there something he wants to do here, and you have consented?"

Kuntī said:

At my own bidding this enemy-burner will do a great feat for the brahmin's sake and to set the town free.

Yudhiṣṭhira said:

5 Now what have you done! It is reckless, harsh, and wrong! The
good surely do not praise the sacrifice of a son! Why do you want to
forsake your own son to save someone else's? By forsaking your son
you have only gone against the course of the world! To *his* arms we
all resort to sleep in peace and to regain the kingdom that the vile
have taken from us. On *his* immeasurable prowess does Duryodhana
reflect and with Śakuni lies sleepless from worry every night. By *his*
bravery we escaped from the lacquer house and from other evils and
10 was Purocana killed. With *his* bravery we now seek mercy and flatter
ourselves that we have defeated Dhṛtarāṣṭra's sons and won all this
treasure-filled earth. What notion came into your head, deliberately
to sacrifice *him*? Have your senses been washed away by your
sorrows, that you are left witless?

Kuntī said:

Yudhiṣṭhira! Do not worry about the Wolf-Belly! And I didn't make
my decision because my mind has gone feeble! Son, we have been
living happily in this brahmin's house, and I want to consider this our
compensation, dear. One is a man to the extent of his gratitude.
Having witnessed Bhīma's great gallantry in the lacquer house, and
15 his killing of Hiḍimba, I have confidence in the Wolf-Belly. The
strength of Bhīma's arms is as great as that of a myriad elephants; by
it he carried all of you, each like an elephant, from Vāraṇāvata. There
has been none, nor shall there be anyone as strong as Wolf-Belly, who
could stand up against the best, against the Thunderbolt-Wielder
himself!

You know, before, when he was barely born, he fell from my lap on a mountain, and his body was so hard that he shattered the rock with his limbs. I was perfectly by my wits, Pāṇḍava, when I recalled Bhīmasena's strength, and that is why I decided to reciprocate to the

brahmin. No greed, no folly, no stupidity decided me; what I had in
20 mind was *Law*, and *that* decided me! Two purposes are going to be
accomplished this way, Yudhiṣṭhira, compensation for our lodging,
and a great deal of Law observed. The baron who renders assistance
to a brahmin in any matter, will, so I have heard, obtain the blessed
worlds. And a baron who sets another baron free from death reaps
ample fame in this world and the next. But the baron who helps out a
commoner in battle will in all worlds surely bask in the love of his
people. And a kingly man who sets free a serf who came and sought
refuge with him will be reborn on earth in a wealthy lineage well
25 treated by kings. That is what the blessed Lord Vyāsa used to say, son
of the Kauravas, and he is thoroughly wise. That is why I want it
done.

Yudhiṣṭhira said:

Mother, it is perfectly right what you have put your mind to do, and have done, out of pity for that poor brahmin. And, surely, our Bhīma will kill that man-eater and come back alive. But let that brahmin be carefully told and restrained, so that the townspeople do not find it out.

Vaiśaṃpāyana said:

151.1 Thereupon, when the night had passed, Bhīmasena took the food
and went where that man-eater lived. As he drew near the wilderness
of that Rākṣasa, the mighty Pāṇḍava called out the ogre's name as he
drove up his fodder. The Rākṣasa heard Bhīmasena's call and in a
great rage came where Bhīma was taking his stand.
He was a big one and he moved fast, as if rending the earth,
knitting his brow with three peaked lines and biting the wall of his
5 teeth. The Rākṣasa saw Bhīmasena eating his food and, widening his
eyes, spoke up angrily: "Who are you, eating *this*! This is my tribute!
And in full sight of me, fool! You want to die!"
Bhīmasena heard him and burst out laughing, Bhārata. He looked
the other way, ignored the Rākṣasa, and went on eating. Then the
man-eater let go of a terrifying yell and with both arms in the air
rushed upon Bhīmasena to kill him. Still, the Wolf-Belly, killer of
enemy heroes, ignored the Rākṣasa and refused to look at him while
10 he kept on eating. Infuriated, the Rākṣasa stood behind Kuntī's son
and struck him on the back with both fists. Though Bhīma was sorely
struck by the powerful fiend, he did not look up at him and went on
eating. In even greater rage, the Rākṣasa now pulled out a tree and
mightily stormed upon Bhīma to thrash him with it.

Bhīma, bull among men, had finally finished eating; he rinsed his mouth with water, and then the powerful man stood cheerfully up to the fight. Bravely, he grabbed the tree, which the angry ogre had

15 thrown at him, with his left hand and laughed aloud, Bhārata. Again,
the strong demon heaved trees of all kinds in the air and threw them
at Bhīma, and Bhīma at him. A huge and grisly tree battle went on
between Baka and the Pāṇḍava, O great king, which destroyed the
forest. Trumpeting his name, Baka ran toward the Pāṇḍava and
grasped hold of his mighty body with both arms. Bhīmasena too
threw his big arms around the Rākṣasa and dragged the writhing,
nimble ogre forcefully about. As he was being dragged by Bhīma and
himself dragged the other, the man-eater was overcome by unnerving
20 weariness. The earth shook with their violent jerks, and they splintered
large-trunked trees. When he saw that the Rākṣasa was fading, O bull
of the Bharatas, the Wolf-Belly squeezed him to the ground and
pounded him with his fists. Then he forcefully pushed his back down
with his knee, grabbed his neck with his right hand and his loincloth
with the left, and broke in two the frightfully screaming Rākṣasa.
Blood gushed from the ogre's mouth, lord of the people, as the
loathsome Baka was broken by Bhīma.

Vaiśaṃpāyana said:

152.1 Alarmed by the noise, the Rākṣasa's household and the servants
burst out of the house, king. Bhīma, greatest of fist fighters, calmed the
frightened crowd who had lost their heads and held them to a
compact: "You shall nevermore do injury to humans here. Those who
do will quickly die the same death!" When they had heard him,
Bhārata, the Rākṣasas said, "So shall it be," and they accepted the
5 compact. Henceforth the Rākṣasas there were friendly, Bhārata,
whenever they were sighted by the townfolk about the city. Bhīma
took the dead man-eater, threw him down at the city gate, and went
away unseen.

After the killing, Bhīma went back to the house of the brahmin and
told the prince all that had happened. The next morning people came
out of the town and saw the corpse of the Rākṣasa on the ground,
moist with blood, towering like a mountain peak, spread-eagled,
horrible. They went into Ekacakrā and spread the news in the city.
10 The townspeople came out by the thousands, O king, and went with
wives, old people, and children to see Baka. Astonished, they all gazed
at the superhuman feat and brought grateful offerings to the deities.
They they started calculating whose turn it had been that day to feed
the ogre, found out it was the brahmin, and then all went to him and
questioned him.

To their many questions that bull among brahmins told them all,
while protecting the Pāṇḍavas: "Some powerful brahmin, perfected in
the spells, saw me and my family weep when I had been ordered to do
15 the feeding. He interrogated me about the previous plight of the city,

then that best of brahmins comforted us and said heroically with a laugh, 'I myself will bring that fiend his meal. Do not fear for me.' He took the food and went to Baka's forest. It must have been he who did this deed for the good of the world."

Thereupon all the astonished and delighted people, brahmins, barons, commoners, and serfs, instituted a Brahmin Feast. The people of the country all flocked to the city to see that great marvel; meanwhile, the Pāṇḍavas went on living in the brahmin's house.

1(11) Citraratha

153–73 (B. 165–83; C. 6316–6924).
153 (165; 6316). A brahmin arrives and tells stories; he is questioned about the Pāñcāla court (1–10).
154 (166; 6328). Summary of the story of Droṇa and Drupada from supra 121–22 and 128, up to Droṇa's installation as king (1–25).
155 (167; 6356). Drupada, plotting revenge on Droṇa, seeks a priest for a rite that must give him a powerful son, able to defeat Droṇa. He pays court to Yāja and Upayāja. The latter refuses (1–10), but points out that Yāja is less pure and might be persuaded (10–20). He is, with a myriad cows (20–30). A sacrifice is instituted, and a grown man arises from the offering fire, Dhṛṣṭadyumna, and a maiden from the altar, Kṛṣṇā (30–45). They are named. Droṇa accepts Dhṛṣṭadyumna as his pupil (45–50).
156 (168; 6410). Kuntī remarks that they are getting bored with Ekacakrā, and suggests they leave for Drupada's city; they do (1–10).
157 (169; 6421). They meet Kṛṣṇa Dvaipāyana, who recounts how a maiden once prayed to Śiva for a husband; she did so five times, and Śiva promised her five husbands in her next life (1–10). She is born as Draupadī and is destined for the Pāṇḍavas (15).
158 (170; 6437). On their journey they reach at night the Somaśravāyana ford on the Ganges and trespass on the territory of the Gandharva Aṅgāraparṇa Citraratha, who threatens them (1–10). Arjuna challenges him (15–25) and defeats him with the āgneya missile; his wife prays for mercy, which Yudhiṣṭhira grants (25–30).

The Gandharva gives up his name (30–35) and bestows on Arjuna the magic of Vision, and on all five Pāṇḍavas a hundred Gandharva horses each (40–50). Arjuna reciprocates with the āgneya *weapon (55).*
159. The Gandharva explains that the Pāṇḍavas were vulnerable because they have neither fires nor a priest; a king without a priest is powerless; he addresses Arjuna as Tāpatya (1–20).
160–163. THE STORY OF TAPATĪ.
164–172. THE STORY OF VASIṢṬHA.
173 (182; 6888). At Arjuna's request, the Gandharva relates why Vasiṣṭha lay with Kalmāṣapāda's wife: when the latter, as a Rākṣasa, roams in the forest, he finds a brahmin couple cohabiting; he captures and devours the man. He is cursed by the wife to the same fate; Vasiṣṭha will beget his heir (1–15). Kalmāṣapāda dies (20).

Janamejaya said:
153.1 What did the tiger-like Pāṇḍavas do later, brahmin, when Baka the
Rākṣasa had been killed?

Vaiśaṃpāyana said:
They went on living there, king, after the killing of Baka, studying the supreme Brahman in the brahmin's house.

A few days later a brahmin of strict vows came to that brahmin's
house to seek lodging. Always avowed to his guests, the wise brahmin
5 welcomed him properly and provided him with lodgings. Thereafter,
all the bulllike Pāṇḍavas as well as Kuntī besieged the brahmin, who
was a great teller of stories. He told them of many countries and
sacred fords, of many kings and their feats, and of many cities. And
among his tales, Janamejaya, the brahmin told of the wondrous
bridegroom choice of Yajñasena's* daughter in the land of the
Pāñcālas, of the birth of Dhṛṣṭadyumna and Śikhaṇḍin's birth, of
Kṛṣṇā's motherless origin at Drupada's great sacrifice. Having heard of
these great marvels that had happened in the world, those bulls
among men asked the great-spirited brahmin to tell them the tale in
10 full detail: "How was Drupada's son Dhṛṣṭadyumna born from the fire,
and how did Kṛṣṇā's miraculous birth come about from the middle of
the altar? How did he learn all the weapons from that great archer
Droṇa, and how did those two good friends break with each other and
for what reason?" So these bulllike men queried the brahmin, O king,
and he told them the entire story of the birth of Draupadī.

* = Drupada.

The brahmin said:

154.1 At the Gate of the Ganges there lived a great seer of great
austerities, the wise Bharadvāja, whose vows were at all times strict.
Once he went to the Ganges to bathe, and there the seer saw the
Apsarā Ghṛtācī, who had come earlier and had just finished bathing.
As she was standing on the river bank, the wind blew her skirt askew;
the seer saw her nude and desired her. His heart cleaving to her, the
seer, who had been a virgin from childhood, spilled forth his seed
5 excitedly, and he placed it in a trough. From it the boy Droṇa was
born to that sage, and he learned all the *Vedas* and their branches.
Bharadvāja had a friend, a king by the name of Pṛṣata, to whom a
son had been born, Drupada. This Drupada went all the time to the
hermitage, and the bulllike baron played and did his studies with
Droṇa. When Pṛṣata died, Drupada became king.

Droṇa heard that Rāma* wanted to give away all his wealth; and when Rāma was starting for the forest, Bharadvāja's son said to him, "Bull among brahmins, know that I am Droṇa who have come here seeking wealth."

Rāma said:

10 Only my body is left to me now. Choose either my body or my
weapons, brahmin.

Droṇa said:

Pray give me all your weapons, sir, and the secret of how to employ and withdraw them.

The brahmin said:

The scion of Bhṛgu agreed and gave them to him. Droṇa took them and was contented. Joyously, he received from Rāma that most highly regarded Brahmā weapon, which is the best that men have. Thereupon the majestic Droṇa approached Drupada, and the tigerlike man said, "Recognize me, your friend!"

Drupada said:

15 No man of learning is a friend to the unlearned, no man with a
chariot to one who has none, no king to a man who is not. An old
friend—who needs him?

The brahmin said:

The sage thereupon made up his mind against the Pāñcālya, and he went to the Elephant City of the chiefs of the Kurus. When he arrived there, Bhīṣma collected his grandsons and all kinds of treasure, and entrusted them as pupils to the wise Droṇa, who had arrived. Wise Droṇa assembled all his pupils and, wishing Drupada ill, he said to them, "For my teacher's fee there is something that is on my mind. When you have mastered weaponry, you shall give it to me; promise me that, blameless boys!"

* = Paraśu-Rāma.

20 When all the Pāṇḍavas had mastered the weapons and had finished the labor of study, Droṇa again spoke of his fee: "In Chattravati* there is a king by the name of Drupada Pārṣata. Take his kingdom away from him and give it to me without delay!" Thereupon the five sons of Pāṇḍu defeated Drupada in battle, and they fettered him with his ministers and showed him to Droṇa.

Drona said:

Once more, O king of men, I seek your friendship. You know, no king can be a friend to a man who is not! Therefore, Yajñasena, I have toiled for your kingdom. You shall be king on the southern bank of the Ganges, and I north of the river.

The brahmin said:

25 That great insult was never to leave the king's mind for an instant. He became dispirited and lean.

The brahmin said:

155.1 Harboring his grudge, King Drupada wandered about many settlements of brahmins, searching for eminent twiceborn who were perfect in rituals. He was seeking to obtain the birth of a son, for, his mind being obsessed with his hurt, he was always thinking, "I have no outstanding children." Of his own sons when they were born he said in despair, "Accursed brood!" And he was much given to sighing as he sought to wreak revenge on Droṇa. But however much that best of kings might labor and worry, no way occurred to him how he might counter with his baronial power the might, discipline, learning, and accomplishments of Droṇa, O Bhārata.

5 As he was roaming the bank of the Ganges toward the Yamunā,
the king came upon a holy settlement of brahmins. There was not a
brahmin there who was not a *snātaka*, nor one unbeholden to vows or
of lowly stature. Drupada found two brahminic seers of strict vow,
both practicing serenity, Yāja and Upayāja, who were yoked to the
study of the *Saṃhitās* and by lineage descendants of Kaśyapa. These
two excellent brahmin seers, who were both able to rescue him, he
plied tirelessly with all manner of gratuities. After he had sounded out
the power and spirit of each of them, he circuitously approached the
younger one, Upayāja, who held to his vows, while seeking his whim
10 with aught he might desire. He vowed obedience to his feet, always
flattered him, gave him anything he wanted; and after having courted
him properly, he said to Upayāja:

"Brahmin, is there a ritual by which I could beget a son for the destruction of Droṇa? If there is, I shall give you a myriad cows for its performance, or whatever else might please your heart, Upayāja, I

* = Ahicchattrā.

shall give it all to you—about that I have no doubts." "Not I," replied the seer.

Drupada continued to court him in order to persuade him. After a year had gone by, that greatest of brahmins Upayāja said to Drupada at an appropriate time in a gentle voice, "My elder brother, while walking in the forest, picked up at a waterfall a fruit that had fallen on the ground, but without investigating the purity of the ground! I saw him commit this uncouth act as I was following him. He made no inquiry whatever before taking that offal! He looked and did not see the impurities that clung to the fruit. If a person does not discriminate about purity in one case, why should he in another case? When he lived in his guru's house and studied the *Saṃhitās*, he always used to eat the leftover alms of others and praised the quality of the food without any scruples. Judging from this, I think that my brother would pursue rewards. Go to him, king, he will act as your priest."

When he had heard Upayāja's words, the king, who was wise in all the Laws, reflected on them with his mind, though he disdained Yāja. Then he paid homage to the seer Yāja, who much deserved it, and said to him, "I shall give you eighty thousand cows: sacrifice for me, lord! Pray bring relief to one who burns with hatred for Droṇa. For he is a very great scholar of the *Veda* and unsurpassed on the Brahmā weapon. Thus it came about that Droṇa defeated me in a quarrel between friends. There is no baron in the world, however outstanding, who is the peer of the wise Droṇa, who has since become the principal teacher of the Kauravas. The swarming arrows of Droṇa carry off the lives of creatures, and his huge six-cubit-long bow has been found matchless. With the vehemence of brahmins, the great-minder archer defeats the vehemence of the barons, no doubt. He has been created for the extinction of the baronage, and he has come upon us like another Rāma Jāmadagnya: the ghastly power of his weapons no man on earth can overcome. Flaunting his brahminic splendor, he burns by the grace of his Brahman, like a fire fed by butter oblations, the baronage in battle—and where brahmindom and baronage are engaged, the splendor of brahminhood wins out. With my baronial power alone I lose; but I have attained to the splendor of brahminhood, now that I have found you, supreme scholar of the Brahman, who outmatch Droṇa! I want to obtain a son, unvanquishable in battle, who shall be the death of Droṇa. Perform the rite for me, Yāja, and I shall give you a myriad cows!"

Yāja consented and began preparations for the sacrifice. He pressed Upayāja, who had no desire for rewards, into service as a tribute to his elder brother. Thus Yāja gave his promise for the destruction of Droṇa. Thereupon the great ascetic Upayāja instructed the king in the sacrificial rite for the obtaining of a son: "The son that you desire, of great prowess and splendor and might, such a son shall be vouchsafed you."

Pronouncing his intention for a son to kill Droṇa, King Drupada accordingly fetched all the necessaries for the successful accomplishment of the rite. At the end of the offering, Yāja summoned the queen: "Stride forward to me, Queen Pṛṣatī! The time for cohabitation has come!"

The queen said:

My face is anointed, brahmin, I wear the holy scents. For the sake of a son am I importuned—stay, brahmin, favorable to me.

Yāja said:

The oblation has been cooked by Yāja, has been enchanted by Upayāja. Why should it not bestow the wish? Stride forward or stay!

The brahmin said:

After having spoken, Yāja offered the well-cooked oblation in the fire; and from the sacrificial fire there arose a youth who resembled a God, of the color of fire and terrifying aspect, wearing a diadem and a splendid shield, armed with sword, bow, and arrow, raising many battle cries. He ascended a superb chariot and went forth on it, and the Pāñcālas excitedly roared their approval. "This fear-averting prince, who shall raise the fame of the Pāñcālas and dispel the king's grievance, has been born for the destruction of Droṇa"; thus spoke a great being invisible in the sky.

Thereupon a young maiden arose from the center of the altar, the well-favored and beautiful Daughter of the Pāñcālas, heart-fetching, with a waist shaped like an altar. She was dark, with eyes like lotus petals, her hair glossy black and curling—a lovely Goddess who had chosen a human form. The fragrance of blue lotuses wafted from her to the distance of a league, the shape she bore was magnificent, and no one was her peer on earth. And over the full-hipped maiden as soon as she was born the disembodied voice spoke: "Superb among women, the Dark Woman* shall lead the baronage to its doom. The fair-waisted maiden shall in time accomplish the purpose of the Gods, and because of her, great danger shall arise for the barons." Hearing this, all the Pāñcālas roared like a pride of lions, and earth was unable to hold them so full of joy.

When Pṛṣatī saw them, she approached Yāja, since she yearned for children: "Let them never know of another mother but me!" "So be it," replied Yāja, who wished to please the king. The brahmin, whose hearts were bursting, gave names to the two. "For his boldness and great audacity and Law, and for his birth from the Light, this man child of Drupada shall be Dhṛṣṭadyumna." Her they called Kṛṣṇā, for she was dark of complexion.

* = Kṛṣṇā.

Thus twin children were born to Drupada at his great sacrifice. Majestic Droṇa took Dhṛṣṭadyumna into his own house and became his weapons teacher. The sage Droṇa knew that ineluctable fate would out, and he acted thus to preserve his own fame.

Vaiśaṃpāyana said:
156.1 When they had heard the story, the Pāṇḍavas seemed to be struck
by spears, and all those warriors became much upset. Thereupon
Kuntī, seeing her sons confused and out of their minds, spoke to
Yudhiṣṭhira, and as always she spoke the truth: "We have enjoyed
ourselves in this lovely town and received many alms, Yudhiṣṭhira.
The beautiful woods and park lands here, we have seen them all,
5 again and again, tamer of foes. Seeing them again will not please us
as much. Nor shall we receive as many alms, scion of Kuru. We
might well go to the Pāñcālas, if you agree. It will be a new sight,
son, and surely lovely. Also, the Pāñcālas are known to be generous
with alms, enemy-wrestler, and Yajñasena himself, so we hear, is
brahminic. To stay overlong in the same place does not seem right to
me. We had better go there, son, if you think so too."
Yudhiṣṭhira said:
Your wish is our task, and it will profit us. But I do not know if my
brothers will want to go.
Vaiśaṃpāyana said:
10 Thereupon Kuntī mentioned departure to Bhīmasena, Arjuna, and
the twins, and they all agreed. Kuntī and her sons bade the brahman
farewell, O king, and they started for the lovely city of the great-
spirited Drupada.

Vaiśaṃpāyana said:
157.1 While the great-spirited Pāṇḍavas were living there in disguise,
Satyavatī's son Vyāsa came to visit them. When they saw him come,
the enemy-burners rose to meet him, prostrated themselves, and
welcomed him, then stood before him with folded hands. After
returning the greetings, the hermit, duly honored by the Pāṇḍavas,
graciously spoke to them in affectionate tones when they were all
seated. "Do you live by the Law and by scripture, enemy-burning
sons? Do you pay sufficient honor to the brahmins who are worthy of
worship?"
5 Then, after a discourse informed by Law and Profit, and manifold
narratives, the blessed seer resumed:
"There once was a young girl who lived in a wilderness of
austerities, the daughter of a great-spirited seer, with a narrow waist,
full hips, and a beautiful brow—a girl favored with all virtues. Because
of previous acts, which she herself had done, she was unfortunate in

love, and the girl, lovely though she was, did not find a husband.
Unhappily, she began mortifications for the sake of obtaining a
husband, and, indeed, with her awesome austerities she satisfied
Śaṃkara. Being satisfied, the blessed Lord said to the ascetic girl,
'Good luck to thee! Choose a husband, and I shall bestow the boon,
10 radiant maiden.' She replied to the Sovereign for her own benefit, 'I
want a husband with all the virtues!' And she said it again and again.
Then the eloquent Sovereign Śaṃkara said to her, 'You shall have
your five husbands, dear girl!' When she replied to the God, 'Give me
just one husband!' Śaṃkara said this final word: 'Five times you told
me to give you a husband, and it shall be as you asked for, when you
have been reborn in another body!'

"That maiden was reborn in the lineage of Drupada as the
blameless Kṛṣṇā Pārṣatī, lovely as a Goddess, and she has been
15 destined for you as your wife. Therefore, mighty men, enter the city of
the Pāñcālas. When you have obtained her, you shall of a certainty
find happiness."

After he had thus spoken to the Pāṇḍavas, the lordly and ascetic grandsire bade Kuntī and her sons farewell and departed.

Vaiśaṃpāyana said:

158.1 With their mother at their head, the enemy-burning bulllike men
set out together, as they had been directed, over smooth roads that led
to the north. Day and night they went, the tigerlike sons of Pāṇḍu,
until they reached the sacred ford Somaśravāyana on the Ganges.
Famous Dhanaṃjaya took the lead, holding up a firebrand to light
and safeguard the way.

Now, at a lonely and deserted spot on the Ganges the jealous king
of the Gandharvas had come to play at water games with his women.
5 He heard the noise the others made as they made their way toward
the river. Seized with that noise, the powerful Gandharva flew into a
powerful rage; and on discerning the warlike Pāṇḍavas and their
mother, he opened the eye of his grim bow and said, "When the
dangerous dusk reddens and the early night falls, the hour, save for
the first eighty instants, has been declared to be assigned to the
Yakṣas, Gandharvas, and Rākṣasas to wander at will, while for the
rest of the time the humans may roam at will. If men at these times
selfishly wander about, we and the Rākṣasas set upon them and
10 punish them like the fools they are. The scholars of the Brahman
condemn all men, be they kings with their armies, who go to the
water in the night. Keep your distance and do not come near me!
How can you fail to recognize me who have come to the waters of the
Ganges? Know that I am the Gandharva Angāraparṇa who trust in
my own strength! I am a proud and jealous king, and Kubera's great

friend. This is my own wood, which is called Angāraparṇa, this beautiful wood by the Ganges and the Bākā, where I have my dwelling. Neither corpses nor horned beasts nor Gods nor humans set foot here—then how do you dare to approach?"

Arjuna said:

15 Fool, who can forbid the approach to the ocean, the Himālaya, and this river, whether by day or by night or at twilight? We have the advantage of strength and we dare you, even if it is the wrong time. For it is the weak who worship you in your cruel hour! The Ganges has issued from the golden-peaked Himālaya; and as she goes to the ocean, she runs her course in seven streams. This holy river Ganges flows through the sky among the Gods as the Ekavaprā, then, O Gandharva, she becomes the Alakanandā, and when she comes to the Ancestors, she becomes the Vaitaraṇī, unfordable by evildoers, as Dvaipāyana has said. This wide and sacred river of the Gods leads up to heaven—how can you forbid her to others? That is not the eternal
20 Law! Why should we, at your behest, not touch the irrepressible and unoppressed holy water of the Ganges as we please?

Vaiśaṃpāyana said:

When Angāraparṇa heard this, he drew his bow in a rage and shot blazing arrows like virulently venomous snakes. But the Pāṇḍava Dhanaṃjaya, nimbly wielding his firebrand and excellent shield, brushed off all the arrows.

Arjuna said:

This intimidation, Gandharva, is of no use with those who know
25 their weapons. And if it is used, it collapses like foam. I understand, Gandharva, that Gandharvas outmatch men, therefore I shall fight you with divine weapons, not with magic. This is the *āgneya* missile that, as they say, Bṛhaspati, son of the teacher of the God of the hundred sacrifices, gave to Bharadvāja. From Bharadvāja it went to Agniveśya, and from Agniveśya to my teacher; and he, Droṇa, strictest of brahmins, gave it to me.

Vaiśaṃpāyana said:

With these words the Pāṇḍava angrily loosed the *āgneya* missile at the Gandharva and burned down his chariot. The mighty Gandharva, deprived of his chariot, tottered and fell face down, stunned by the brilliance of the missile, and Dhanaṃjaya seized him by his chapleted
30 hairlocks and dragged him, unconscious from the impact of the missile, toward his brothers. Then the Gandharva's wife, whose name was Kumbhīnasī, sought mercy with Yudhiṣṭhira and prayed that his life be saved.

The Gandharva woman said:

Save me, great king, and set my husband free! The Gandharvī Kumbhīnasī seeks mercy from you, lord!

Yudhiṣṭhira said:

What hero like you would kill an enemy vanquished in battle and powerless, who has lost his fame and needs protection from women? Let him go, enemy-tamer!

Arjuna said:

All right, then, give him his life! Go, Gandharva, and be untroubled: Yudhiṣṭhira, king of the Kurus, extends to you his safety!

The Gandharva said:

35 Defeated, I surrender my previous name and give up being Angāraparṇa. Neither with might nor with name can I now boast in the assembly of people. It was my fortune that I, who wanted to fight a man at the peak of his youth with the magic of the Gandharvas, found myself a treasure who carried divine weapons! My beautiful colorful chariot has been burned by the fire of the missile, and I who was Citraratha have become Dagdharatha! This magic I possess I once acquired with austerities, and now I shall bestow it on the great-spirited man who gave me my life. For he who spares the life of an enemy, defeated by strength and unconscious, when he pleads for mercy, what beautiful gifts does he not deserve?

40 This is the magic of Vision, which Manu gave to Soma, Soma to Viśvāvasu, and Viśvāvasu to me. When this magic is given by a guru to a coward, it vanishes. I have told you its provenance, now learn from me its power. Whatever one wants to see in all three worlds, that one can see with it, and one can see it in any way one wishes. This magic one can acquire if he stands for six months on the same foot. I myself shall bestow this magic upon you, as I have vowed. It is because of this magical knowledge, prince, that we are superior to men, and, propelled by its power, we are not different from Gods.

45 I shall give to you, to the five brethren, a hundred horses each, of those that are bred by the Gandharvas, O best of men. They are divinely fragrant, mind-fast steeds of the Gods and Gandharvas. However exhausted they are, they never diminish in speed.——A thunderbolt was once fashioned for Indra to overthrow Vṛtra, but it shattered into ten, into a hundred pieces on Vṛtra's head. Ever since, the Gods have worshiped the pieces of the thunderbolt, which they shared among themselves. Whatever is a means to success in the world is known as an embodiment of the thunderbolt. Thus the brahmin is known as the thunderbolt-wielder, the baronage ride their
thunderbolt chariots, the vaiśyas's thunderbolt is their gifts, the lower
50 ones' thunderbolt is their labor. The thunderbolt of the baronage is
their steeds—the steeds are known to be indestructible. Vaḍavā gave
birth to the chariot steed—hence the name *sūta* for those who drive
the horses. Gandharva-bred horses take on any color or speed, they
can be approached for any whim, and they fulfil any desire.

Arjuna said:

If you give your magic or treasure or learning because you are grateful or because your life was in doubt, I do not want them, Gandharva!

The Gandharva said:

An alliance made at encounters is found to give pleasure. I give you my magic because I am pleased at the gift of my life. And from you I shall take that superb *āgneya* weapon: thus our friendship, Terrifier, shall last for a long time, bull of the Bhāratas.

Arjuna said:

55 Then from you I choose the horses in exchange for the weapon. And our alliance shall last forever. Tell me, Gandharva, my friend, how can one escape danger from your race?

Arjuna said:

159.1 Tell me the reason, Gandharva, tamer of your foes, why we were set upon as we were traveling at night, though we are all scholars of the Brahman?

The Gandharva said:

You have no fires, you have no oblations, you have set no priest
before you: therefore, scion of Pāṇḍu, were you set upon by me.
Yakṣas, Rākṣasas, and Gandharvas, Piśācas, Snakes, and men recount
the history of the illustrious dynasty of Kuru. I have heard Nārada
and the other divine seers narrate the virtues of your wise forebears,
5 hero. And as I roamed this entire ocean-clad, treasure-filled earth, I
myself have witnessed the might of your lineage. I know your teacher
in the science of archery, Arjuna, glorious Droṇa Bhāradvāja, who is
famous in all three worlds. I know Dharma, the Wind God, Indra and
the Aśvins, and Pāṇḍu himself, the six progenitors of your line,
tigerlike man, your fathers, supreme among Gods and men. You
brothers are divine-spirited, great-spirited, greatest of all who wield
weapons, champions all and of hallowed vows.

Nevertheless, even though I knew the sublime mind and spirit of
all of you, who have perfected your souls, I *did* set upon you here,
10 Pārtha. No man who relies on the strength of his arms condones it
when he sees himself insulted before a woman's eyes. At night our
power waxes even stronger; and therefore, Kaunteya, anger entered me
and my wife. And now I stand defeated by you in battle, scion of
Tapatī. Hear in what manner I celebrate my defeat.

Chastity is the highest Law, and this Law lies firmly lodged with
you. That is the reason why you defeated me in this fight, Pārtha. But
no lustful baron who fought us at night would ever live, enemy-
15 burner. A king, however, even if lustful, can vanquish all the Stalkers

of the Night in battle, Tāpatya,* if he is led by a priest. Therefore, whatever benefit men may want here, they should yoke their priests to that task, Tāpatya, priests of controlled spirits. All kings should have priests who are devoted to the six-branched *Veda*, pure, veracious, law-spirited, and resolved. Victory is assured to the king, and heaven hereafter, if he has a law-wise, eloquent, moral, and pure priest. To acquire unacquired acquisitions and to safeguard them when acquired, a king should employ a priest who is endowed with all
20 virtues. If he follows his priest's advice, a king may aspire to win all of Meru-crowned, sea-girt earth. Not by prowess alone or high birth, Tāpatya, will a priestless king conquer a country. Therefore, know, thou that furtherest the lineage of Kuru, that a kingdom where the brahmins prevail can long be safeguarded.

Arjuna said:
160.1 You have been calling me "Tāpatya," therefore I want to know what "Tāpatya" exactly means. Who was the woman named Tapatī after whom we are called "Tāpatya," as we are called "Kaunteya" after Kuntī?

1(11.a) Tapatī

160–63 (B. 171–73; C. 6516–6632).
160 (171; 6516). Arjuna asks the Gandharva about the origin of the name Tāpatya. The sun had a lovely daughter Tapatī, whom he was concerned to marry off (1–10). An early Kaurava king, Saṃvaraṇa, worships the sun and is elected her husband (10–20). Out hunting, he sees Tapatī and falls in love (20–30). He addresses her, but she disappears (30–40).
161 (172; 6560). The king swoons, and the maiden reappears. He regains consciousness and proposes a gāndharva *marriage (1–10). She refers him to her father (10–20).*
162 (173; 6584). When she vanishes, he swoons again. His minister finds him and brings him back to consciousness (1–5). The king dismisses his armed escort, worships the sun, and thinks of his priest Vasiṣṭha, who appears before the sun (10–15).
163. Vasiṣṭha pleads for Saṃvaraṇa, and the sun grants

* = scion of Tapatī. i.e., Arjuna.

him Tapatī (1–10). The couple plays for twelve years in the mountains, and in Saṃvaraṇa's kingdom there is a drought for as many years, until Vasiṣṭha entices the king to return to his city. Their son is Kuru (10–20).

Vaiśaṃpāyana said:

At this question of Kuntī's son Dhanaṃjaya, the Gandharva narrated the story that is celebrated in the three worlds.

The Gandharva said:

Yea, I shall tell you this entire fetching story so full of the Law, just as it befell, great bearer of the Law. I shall tell you why I have been calling you Tāpatya, so listen with a single mind.

The One in the Sky Who Suffuses the Vault of Heaven with Benevolent Splendor had an incomparable daughter by the name of Tapatī. This Tapatī, who was born to Vivasvat after Sāvitrī, was endowed with the power of heat and famous in the three worlds. No Goddess, no Asurī, no Yakṣī, no Rākṣasī, no Apsarā nor Gandharvī had beauty as was hers. The body of this virtuous and radiant maiden was well-proportioned and flawless, the eyes deep-black and long, the manners seemly, and the robes beautiful. God Savitar* deemed no one in the three worlds a husband equal to her in beauty, conduct, lineage, and learning, O Bhārata.

When he saw his daughter reach the nubile age and ready for marriage, he found no peace as he worried about her marrying. Now, the son of Ṛkṣa, O Kaunteya, the powerful bull of the Kurus, King Saṃvaraṇa, was wont to worship the Sun with offerings of guest gifts and garlands, with fasts and observances, and with manifold mortifications. Obediently and unselfishly and purely, the scion of the Pauravas worshiped the splendiferous Sun with great devotion as He rose. So it came about that the Sun judged the grateful and law-minded Saṃvaraṇa on earth to be Tapatī's equal in beauty. He then desired to give the maiden in marriage to that sublime King Saṃvaraṇa, O Kaurava, whose descent was glorious. Just as in the sky the fiery-rayed Sun spreads light with splendor, so King Saṃvaraṇa was resplendent on earth. And just as the scholars of the Brahman worship the rising sun, so the brahmins and the lower subjects worshiped Saṃvaraṇa, O Pārtha. The illustrious king outdid the moon in benevolence to his friends and the sun in fierceness to his haters. Thus the Sun himself set his mind on marrying Tapatī to the king of such great virtue and such good conduct, O Kaurava.

Once, it is told, this lustrous king of wide repute on earth went on a chase in park land on a mountain slope. While the king was hunting,

* = the Sun.

his peerless horse, overcome by hunger, thirst, and fatigue, died on
that mountain. His horse dead, the king went on foot, Pārtha, upon
that mountain, and he beheld a long-eyed maiden beyond compare in
the world. He was alone, she was alone, and the tigerlike king,
scourge of his enemies, approached the maiden and stood staring at
25 her with unwavering eye. The king speculated from her beauty that
she might be Śrī, then speculated anew that she was the sun's
brilliance fallen to earth. The mountain plateau on which the black-
eyed girl was standing seemed with its trees and shrubs and lianas to
be bathed in gold. Having seen her, the king despised the beauty of
any other creature and judged that his eyes now had found their
purpose fulfilled. Whatever the king had beheld since the day of his
birth, he deemed that nothing had held beauty similar to hers. Mind
and eye caught with the noose of her perfections, the king did not stir
30 from his place nor was conscious of anything else. Surely the Creator
had made manifest the loveliness of the wide-eyed maiden only after
churning the whole universe with its Gods, Asuras, and men. Thus
King Saṃvaraṇa judged by the perfection of her rich beauty that she
was a girl beyond compare in all the world.

No sooner had the king of noble lineage set eyes on the noble
damsel than he was smitten by the arrows of love and plunged into
worrisome thought. Burning with the fierce fire of love, the confident
king spoke to the diffident glorious girl: "Who are you? Whose are
you? And what has brought you here, maiden of the lovely thighs?
Why do you wander alone in this lonely wilderness, sweet-smiling
35 girl? For you, of such flawless limbs and decked with every ornament,
seem like the jewel that your jewels desire! Neither Goddess nor
Asurī, Yakṣī nor Rākṣasī, do I deem you, nor Snake or Gandharvī or
human. For whatever lovely women I have seen or heard described, I
find none of them to match you, bewitching girl!"

Thus did the herdsman of the earth speak to her, but she
vouchsafed the love-struck king no answer whatever in the lonely
woods. And while the king kept prattling, the long-eyed damsel
40 vanished like lightning in the clouds. Like a man out of his mind, the
lord of men strode about searching for the lotus-eyed maiden,
roaming the wilderness. And when he did not find her, the chief of the
Kauravas lamented much and stood a long while without moving.

The Gandharva said:

161.1 When she had disappeared, the king, downfall of enemy hosts, fell
down on the flat of the earth, stunned by the God of Love. Then, at
the king's fall, the maid of the lovely smile and full wide hips once
more showed herself to the king, and in a gentle voice the beautiful
girl said to the king, the dynast of the Kurus, whose mind was

smitten with love, "Stand up, stand up! May good luck befall you. You, the scourge of your enemies, tiger among kings, ought not to lose your senses, visible to all the world!"

At these sweet words the king looked up and saw the buxom girl standing before him. Thereupon the king, wrapped in the flames of love, said to her of the dark glances, in a voice that slurred its sounds, "Love me, bewitching woman of dark glances, love me who am love-struck as I love you, for my senses desert me. For because of you, wide-eyed girl with the sheen of a lotus calyx, Love is piercing me with his honed arrows and does not cease; I am stung by the poison of love, my lovely and unprotected girl. Maiden of the full, wide hips, of the radiant face, content me! For on you whose voice is like a song of the Kiṃnaras do my senses depend, maid of the charming and flawless limbs, of the moonlike and lotuslike face! Bashful girl, without you I cannot live by my own strength. Therefore, take pity on me, wide-eyed woman, and with your dark glances do not forsake me who love you. For you, my radiant maid, must rescue me with your love. Come to me, lovely, with the marriage rite of the Gandharvas, for of all marriages the *gāndharva* is declared the best."

Tapatī said:

I am not my own mistress, sire, for I am a girl with a father. If you have pleasure in me, ask my father for me. For if I have laid hold of your senses, O king, no less have you taken mine, the instant I saw you. I am not mistress of my body, therefore, good king, I cannot come to you; for women are always dependent. But what girl would not wish for her protector and loving husband a king whose descent is famous in all the worlds? Therefore, now that it has come to this, ask my father the Sun, with prostration, mortification, and observances! If he desires to give me to you, scourge of your enemies, I shall forever be yours, my king. I am Tapatī, the younger sister of Sāvitrī, the daughter of Savitar who is the torch of the world, O bull of the barons.

The Gandharva said:

162.1 After she had thus spoken, the blameless virgin quickly went up to heaven, and the king once more fell to the ground. His minister and escort found him in the vast wilderness, fallen on the ground, as, in its season, the lofty Pole of Indra. When the minister saw that great archer lying on the ground, without his horse, he was as though scorched by fire. He quickly drew near and, flustered by his affection, raised from the ground the king, who had been stunned by Love, as a father raises a son who has fallen—this minister who was old in wisdom, age, fame, and self-control. When he had raised him, the minister lost his apprehension and said to his now standing liege in a

noble and gentle voice, "Have no fear, tiger among men, all shall be
well, prince sans blame!" He judged that the king had been exhausted
with hunger and thirst and that thus he, downfall of his enemies in
battle, had fallen on the ground. He sprinkled very cool water,
fragrant with lotuses, on his head, without touching the royal diadem.
When the powerful king had regained his senses, he dismissed his
entire force, excepting the minister alone.
10 After the large force had departed at the king's orders, the king
again sat down on that mountain plateau. He cleansed himself, and
then, on that great mountain, he folded his hands and raised his arms
and remained in that manner on the ground to propitiate the Sun. In
his thoughts he went out to that strictest of seers, Vasiṣṭha, his house
priest, did King Saṃvaraṇa, slayer of foes. Day and night the king of
the people stayed in the same place, then, on that twelfth day, the
brahmin seer came. When Vasiṣṭha found that the king was in love
with Tapatī—the great seer who had perfected his soul knew it by
15 divine insight—he spoke to the eminent, self-controlled prince, for
being Law-minded he wished to benefit him. As the sovereign of men
looked on, the blessed seer, himself of solar splendor, strode up to
heaven to visit the Sun. With hands folded, the seer approached the
Thousand-Rayed Light and announced himself joyfully: "I am
Vasiṣṭha!" The splendid Vivasvat* said to the grand hermit, "Great
Seer, be welcome! Tell me what you desire."

Vasiṣṭha said:

163.1 Resplendent Sun, I have come on Saṃvaraṇa's behalf to woo your
daughter Tapatī, who is Sāvitrī's younger sister. For Saṃvaraṇa is a
king of vast fame, wise in Law and Profit, and of noble spirit: he is a
fitting husband for your daughter, Traveler of the Sky!

The Gandharva said:

At his words, Savitar, who was resolved that he would give her,
saluted and replied to the brahmin, "Saṃvaraṇa is the first of kings,
you, hermit, the first of seers, Tapatī the best of women—why marry
5 her elsewhere?" Thereupon the Sun himself gave the flawless Tapatī
to the great-spirited Vasiṣṭha on Saṃvaraṇa's behalf. The great seer
Vasiṣṭha accepted the maiden, and when he was dismissed he
returned to the place where the famous bull of the Kurus was sitting.
The love-struck king, with his inner soul gone out to her, saw the
prettily laughing Tapatī, daughter of the God, as she came with
Vasiṣṭha; and his bliss shone supreme. The blessed and pure-
spirited seer Vasiṣṭha had come when the king had completed his
twelve-night observance; and having propitiated with his mortifications
the sovereign, boon-granting God, who is the Lord of the Cows,

* = the Sun.

Saṃvaraṇa obtained his wife by virtue of Vasiṣṭha's splendor.

Then, on that best of mountains, haunt of Gods and Gandharvas, the bulllike man took solemnly the hand of Tapatī. With Vasiṣṭha's consent, the royal seer wished to disport himself with his wife on that mountain, and the king assigned that same minister to the city and realm and the mounts and the troops.

Vasiṣṭha took his leave from the king and departed, while the prince himself frolicked on the mountain like an Immortal. For twelve years he made love with his wife in the woods and the streams of the mountain. In the king's city and realm the thousand-eyed Indra failed to rain anywhere for all twelve years. The famished and joyless people turned into corpses, and the dead crowded the city like the City of the King of the Dead.

When the blessed and law-minded Vasiṣṭha saw the country in such a state, he repaired to that good king and brought the tigerlike prince, who had been away from his city for twelve years, back to the city along with Tapatī. Thereupon the Slayer of the Gods' foes rained forth as before, after the tiger among kings had reentered his capital. City and realm now enjoyed supreme joy, as they prospered with that great king who had prospered his soul. Together with his wife Tapatī, the king, like Indra the Lord of the Winds, performed sacrifices for another twelve years.

Thus the Lady Tapatī, daughter of the Sun, became your ancestress, Pārtha, so that after her you are known as Tāpatya. On Tapatī King Saṃvaraṇa begot Kuru, O greatest of burners, and hence you are a Tāpatya, Arjuna.

1(11.b) Vasiṣṭha

164–72 (B. 174–81; C. 6634–6887).
164 (174; 6634). Praise of Vasiṣṭha whose feud with Viśvāmitra is mentioned (1–10).
165 (175; 6649). Viśvāmitra, king of Kanyakubja, out hunting, visits Vasiṣṭha in his hermitage and sees his cow Nandinī. He wants to buy her with his kingdom, but Vasiṣṭha declines (1–15). Viśvāmitra takes the cow by force, and she remonstrates to Vasiṣṭha (20–30). When Vasiṣṭha orders her to stay, whole races of Barbarians emanate from the cow's body and drive off Viśvāmitra's forces (30–40). Viśvāmitra decides to become a brahmin to attain superior power (40).
166 (176; 6696). King Kalmāṣapāda meets Vasiṣṭha's

son Śakti on a narrow path; when the latter refuses to make way, the king whips him. Śakti curses him to become a man-eater (1–10). Viśvāmitra secretly witnesses the incident and orders the Rākṣasa Kiṃkara to take possession of the king (10–15). The king meets a hungry brahmin who asks for a meat dish; he promises but forgets, then wakes up in the night remembering. Since there is no meat, he tells his cook to send human flesh. The brahmin curses him as Śakti did (20–30). The king feeds on Śakti; Viśvāmitra orders the Rākṣasa on to Vasiṣṭha's other sons. Vasiṣṭha learns that Viṣvāmitra is responsible but forgives him; he sets his mind on killing himself; the elements do not receive him (35–45).
167 (177; 6745). More vain suicide attempts (1–5). He decides he cannot die. He learns from his son Śakti's wife that she is pregnant and he turns away from death (10–15). Kalmāṣapāda is about to attack the woman, who pleads with Vasiṣṭha (15–20).
168. Vasiṣṭha stops Kalmāṣapāda and frees him from his curse (1–10). The king aks Vasiṣṭha to father a child on his wife; he agrees (10). The king returns to Ayodhyā, where he is welcomed. Vasiṣṭha lies with the queen who after twelve years gives birth to Aśmaka (10–25).
169–171. The Story of Aurva.
172 (181; 6865). Vasiṣṭha's grandson Parāśara decides to destroy all Rākṣasas in a sacrifice (1–5). Finally Pulastya dissuades him (10–15). He casts the fire on the northern side of the Himālaya, where it is still visible (15).

Vaiśaṃpāyana said:

164.1 When the bull of the Bhāratas had heard the Gandharva's words, Arjuna shone like the full moon with utter joy. And since his curiosity had been excited by the power of Vasiṣṭha's asceticism, the great archer, best of the Kurus, said to the Gandharva, "I wish to hear about that seer whose name you cited as Vasiṣṭha. Tell me how it was. Who was the blessed seer who was the house-priest of our forebears, O king of the Gandharvas? Tell me of him!"

The Gandharva said:

5 Lust and Wrath, invincible even to the Immortals, were defeated by his austerities and massaged his feet. Harboring a great grudge because of Viśvāmitra's offense, he yet nobly did not annihilate the Kuśikas. While mourning the death of his sons, he did not contemplate

any dreadful deed to destroy Viśvāmitra, although he was powerful
and able to do so. Just as the great ocean does not trespass on its
flood line, he did not trespass on Death by bringing his dead sons
back from Yama's realm. By obtaining this great-spirited man, who
had mastered himself, as their priest, the kings of Ikṣvāku's line
10 obtained this earth. Having acquired the great seer Vasiṣṭha as their
eminent house-priest, these kings, O scion of Kuru, offered with
sacrifices. For this brahmin seer offered up sacrifices for all those great
kings, O best of the Pāṇḍavas, as Bṛhaspati for the Immortals.

Therefore, search for a brahmin whose spirit is directed to the Law,
who knows both *Veda* and Law, a desirable brahmin of virtue, to
serve as your priest. For he who, born a baron, wishes to conquer
the earth must first take a priest, Pārtha, for the prospering of his
kingship. A king aspiring to the conquest of the world must set a
brahmin before him; therefore, let a brahmin of virtue be your priest.

Arjuna said:
165.1 What caused the feud between Vasiṣṭha and Viśvāmitra, who both
lived in holy hermitages? Tell it to us all.

The Gandharva said:
This story of Vasiṣṭha they call purāṇic Lore in all three worlds,
Pārtha. Learn from me how it was.

In Kānyakubja once sat a great king, O bull of the Bhāratas, who
was famed in the world as Gādhi, devoted to the Law of Truth. This
Law-spirited king had a son with plentiful troops and mounts, a
5 crusher of enemies, who was known as Viśvāmitra. He was wont to
hunt with his ministers far out in the wilderness, shooting deer and
boar in the lovely deserts and wastelands. Once, when questing for
deer, he became wan with fatigue and thirst, and he went to
Vasiṣṭha's hermitage, O best of men. Seeing him come, Vasiṣṭha, the
lordly seer, received the great Viśvāmitra with homage. He received
him with water to wash his feet, a guest gift, water to rinse his mouth,
greetings of welcome, and an offering of forest fare, O Bhārata.

The great-spirited Vasiṣṭha had a Cow of Plenty, which yielded
10 anything he wished when he told her to yield. Herbs of village and
woods she yielded, and milk, and incomparable elixir with all six
tastes, like the Elixir of Immortality itself, and various foodstuffs of the
kind that are chewed, or drunk, or licked, or sucked, tasty like elixir,
Arjuna. The king was honored with all he desired in great plenty, and
he and his minister and his escort became greatly content. With
astonishment, he looked at Vasiṣṭha's flawless and lovely cow, which
was named Nandī: she was six measures long, three wide, and five
around, with fine flanks and thighs, prominent frog eyes, good
carriage, fat udder, beautiful tail, pointed ears, handsome horns, and

15 long, thick neck and head. Viśvāmitra saluted the beautiful milch cow of Vasiṣṭha and said contentedly to the hermit, "Make Nandinī over to me for a myriad cows or my kingdom! Rule my kingdom, great hermit!"

Vasiṣṭha said:

I keep Nandinī for offerings to the Gods, my guests, and my ancestors, and for melted butter oblations. I cannot give her away, even for your kingdom, prince sans blame.

Viśvāmitra said:

I am a baron, you are a brahmin with no more means than asceticism and Vedic study. How can there be resistance in brahmins who are serene and have mastered themselves? If you do not give me the cow I want for a myriad of mine, I shall not forsake my own Law but take it away from you by force!

Vasiṣṭha said:

20 You are a king at the head of an army, a baron of mighty arms. Make haste and do what you wish, take no time to reflect!

The Gandharva said:

At these words, O Pārtha, Viśvāmitra took the cow Nandinī, translucent like the moon or a wild goose, forcibly away. And as she was driven up and beaten with thongs and sticks, Vasiṣṭha's beautiful cow Nandinī began to bellow. She came back to him and stood before the blessed Lord, lifting up her head to him; and however sorely she was thrashed, she did not stir from the hermitage.

Vasiṣṭha said:

I hear your cry for help, my dear, as you keep lowing again and again. You are being taken from me by force, Nandī, for I am a forgiving brahmin.

The Gandharva said:

25 Frightened by the force of the troops and the terror of Viśvāmitra, she came closer to Vasiṣṭha.

The cow said:

Why do you overlook it, good master, when I am beaten with sticks and stones by Viśvāmitra's dreadful troops and cry out like an orphan?

The Gandharva said:

While the cow was being attacked in this way, the great hermit, who kept to his vows, was not upset or lost his poise.

Vasiṣṭha said:

A baron's strength is his energy, a brahmin's strength his forbearance. Forbearance possesses me; therefore, go if you wish.

The cow said:

Have you forsaken me, good master, that you speak to me so? If you do not forsake me, brahmin, they will not be able to force me away.

Vasiṣṭha said:
30 I do not forsake you, my lovely, stay if you can. They have tied
your calf with tight fetters and are taking it away by force!
The Gandharva said:
When Vasiṣṭha's cow heard him say "Stay!" she curved her head
and neck upward and her aspect became dreadful. Her eyes red with
anger, and bellowing thunderously, she drove the army of
Viśvāmitra about on all sides. As she was beaten with thongs and
sticks and driven hither and thither, her eyes blazed with rage and her
rage waxed stronger. Her body shone with the fires of fury like the
sun at noon, and she spouted a huge rain of burning embers from her
35 tail. From her arse she created the Pahlavas; the Śabaras and Śakas
from her dung; from her urine she created the Yavanas, as she well-
nigh swooned with rage. From her foam she brought forth the
Puṇḍras, Kirātas, Dramiḍas, Siṃhalas, Barbaras, Daradas, and
Mlecchas. And when she had brought forth these manifold hosts of
Barbarians, clad in their manifold armor and brandishing arms, she
scattered with her furious troops that large army before
Viśvāmitra's eyes. Every single soldier was surrounded by five others;
before Viśvāmitra's very eyes his army was routed with a rain of
rocks, till it was everywhere broken down and intimidated. Yet not a
soldier of Viśvāmitra's was separated from his life by Vasiṣṭha's
40 furious soldiers, O bull of the Bhāratas. Viśvāmitra's army was driven
off to a distance of three leagues, and as it yelled in panic it found no
savior.
On seeing this great miracle that sprang from brahminic power,
Viśvāmitra became loath with his baronhood and said, "A curse on
the power that is baronial power! Brahminic power is *power*. On
weighing weakness and strength, asceticism appears the superior
power!"
He relinquished his prosperous kingdom and his blazing kingly
fortune, he put all his pleasures behind him and set his mind on
austerities. He became perfected by his austerities; and suffusing the
worlds with his splendid might, he burned all the worlds with his
fiery puissance and attained to brahminhood. And the Kauśika drank
the pressed-out Soma with Indra.

The Gandharva said:
166.1 Now there was in the world a king by the name Kalmāṣapāda, O
Pārtha, who was born in the lineage of Ikṣvāku and was unequaled
on earth for his prowess. Once this king left his city to go hunting in
the forest, and the crusher of his foes went about shooting deer and
boar. As the king, now athirst and hungry, was following a narrow
hollow path on his way, he met the great-spirited son of Vasiṣṭha, an
eminent seer, who came face to face with him on the path. Śakti

his name was, the lordly scion of Vasiṣṭha's line, the eldest of great-spirited Vasiṣṭha's one hundred sons. "Get off the path, it is ours!" said the king who was undefeated in battle. Attempting to soothe him, the seer spoke to him in a kindly voice, but he did not give way as he walked the path of the Law. Nor did the king give way, out of pique and anger with the hermit; and when the seer refused to clear the path, that great king in his folly hit the hermit with his whip like a Rākṣasa. Stung by the whip lash, the excellent hermit, Vasiṣṭha's son, was enraged and cursed the good king: "Since you strike an ascetic like a Rākṣasa, you shall from this day be a man-eater, degenerate king! You will roam this earth and feed on human flesh. Now avaunt, worst of kings!" Thus he was cursed by Śakti, whose power was his prowess.

Now, there had been a feud between Viśvāmitra and Vasiṣṭha over their patron, and Viśvāmitra chanced to be following the king. As the two were quarreling, the majestic Viśvāmitra, seer of awesome austerities, came closer. From behind, that great baron recognized the seer as the son of Vasiṣṭha and Vasiṣṭha's equal in might. Viśvāmitra hid himself, O Bhārata, and stealthily drew nearer to seek his own advantage. When thereupon Śakti cursed the good king, the latter sought mercy with Śakti and honored him to placate him. Knowing the king's mind, Viśvāmitra then ordered a Rākṣasa to the king. Because of the brahmin seer's curse and Viśvāmitra's command, the Rākṣasa, whose name was Kiṃkara, took possession of the king. When he knew that the king was possessed by the Rākṣasa, Viṣvāmitra the hermit went away from that place, enemy-tamer.

Thereafter the wise king was sorely tormented by the Rākṣasa inside him, yet was able to save himself. A certain brahmin saw the king as he went off and, being hungry, begged the king for a meal with meat. The royal seer Kalmāṣapāda Mitrasaha said soothingly to the brahmin, "Wait awhile here in this same spot, brahmin. When I have returned home, I shall send you the food you want." After these words he left, and that good brahmin stayed there. But the brahmin's request slipped from the king's mind when he entered his women's quarters and settled for the night.

In the middle of the night the king got up and quickly summoned his cook, for he had remembered his promise to the brahmin; and he said: "Go at once. At such and such a place there is a brahmin waiting for me, looking for food. Bring him a meat dish." The cook could not find meat anywhere and unhappily told the king so. But the king, possessed as he was by the Rākṣasa, said unconcernedly to the cook, "Then feed him human flesh!" And he repeated his instructions. "Then I shall," said the cook and went to the quarters of the headsmen, and with no fear at all quickly took flesh from there. He cooked it properly and mixed it with rice, then made haste and

30 offered it to the hungry brahmin ascetic. That excellent brahmin
recognized the food at once by the power of his vision: "That is
forbidden food!" And with angrily rolling eyes he said, "Inasmuch as
the king has given me forbidden food, therefore he himself shall be
crazed and crave for the same. Feeding on human flesh, as Śakti has
told him, he shall roam the earth, the bane of creatures."

The curse of the king, now twice pronounced over him, waxed
strong, and he became fully possessed by the power of the Rākṣasa and
lost his mind. Soon afterward the good king, his senses battered by the
35 Rākṣasa, saw Śakti and said to him, "Since you have put this
insuperable curse on me, I shall begin feeding on humans, from you
onward!" Having said this, he instantly separated Śakti from his life
and devoured him as a tiger devours its favorite prey. When
Viśvāmitra saw that Śakti had been killed, he ordered the Rākṣasa on
to the other sons of Vasiṣṭha. Furiously he ate the other hundred sons
of the great-spirited Vasiṣṭha as a lion eats small game.

When Vasiṣṭha heard that Viśvāmitra had contrived the death of
his sons, he held his grief in place as the great mountain holds the
40 earth. The great hermit set his mind on killing himself rather than
plotting the extinction of the Kuśikas, this greatest of sages. The
blessed seer liberated himself from the peak of the Meru, and when his
head hit the rock it was like a pile of cotton. When the blessed lord
failed to die from the fall, he lit a fire in the wilderness and entered into
it, O Pāṇḍava. Yet, although it blazed up high, the fire did not burn
him, slayer of enemies—the flames turned cold. Seized with his sorrow,
the great hermit went to the ocean, tied a heavy stone to his neck, and
45 threw himself into the water. The current of the ocean waves placed
the hermit back on the mainland and, dismayed, he returned to his
hermitage.

The Gandharva said:

167.1 Then, finding his hermitage empty of his sons, he departed from it
again, sick with his great sorrow. He saw a river full of new water—
for it was the rainy season—that was washing down a great many
trees of many kinds that grew on its banks, O Pārtha. Then once more
the thought occurred to him, O scion of the Pauravas, "I will drown
myself in this water," for he was possessed by grief. The great hermit
bound his body tight with ropes, and in his great distress he threw
5 himself into the stream of the big river. But the river cut his ropes,
crusher of enemy forces, and washed the unfettered seer to its even
bank. The great seer stood up from its waves freed from his fetters,
and he gave the river the name Vipāśā.

Thereafter he resigned himself to his grief and did not stay in any
one place but went to mountains and rivers and lakes. The seer saw a
stream coming down the Himālaya, full of ferocious crocodiles, and he

plunged into its stream. But this good river thought that the brahmin was like fire and ran off in a hundred directions, whence it is now known as the Śatadru.

10 Finding himself once more on dry land there, he said, "I cannot die," and returned to his hermitage. When he came face to face with his hermitage, he was followed by his daughter-in-law Adṛśyantī; and he heard close behind him the sound of Vedic recitations, adorned with the six branches that are filled with significance.

"Who is the man who is following me?" he said. "But I, Adṛśyantī," his daughter-in-law answered, "the wife of Śakti, my lord, austere and miserable."

Vasiṣṭha said:

Daughter, from what man comes this sound of the recitation of the *Veda* and its six branches, just as I seem to have heard it before from Śakti?

Adṛśyantī said:

The child of your son Śakti has been growing in my womb for twelve years now. The sound is his as he rehearses the *Vedas*, hermit.

The Gandharva said:

15 At her words the seer Vasistha, who partook of the best, became greatly joyous. "There *is* offspring then!" he said, Pārtha, and he turned away from death.

Thereupon he returned, together with his daughter-in-law, O
prince sans blame, and found Kalmāṣapāda sitting in the empty
wilderness. As soon as the king, who was possessed by the awful
Rākṣasa, saw him, he arose in a rage and sought to devour him. But
when Adṛśyantī saw the cruel king in front of them, she said to
Vasiṣṭha in a fearful voice, "There he is, like Death itself with its
awful staff; there is the terrifying Rākṣasa coming with the wood he
20 has grabbed! No one on earth has the power to ward him off, no one
but you, mighty lord, who are the first of all scholars of the *Veda*!
Save me, lord, from that horrible-looking fiend, for surely the
Rākṣasa wishes to devour us!"

Vasiṣṭha said:

168.1 Have no fear, daughter, you have nothing to fear from a Rākṣasa. He is not a Rākṣasa, this man from whom you see danger impend. He is King Kalmāṣapāda the mighty, famous on earth. He dwells in this corner of the woods spreading terror.

The Gandharva said:

The blessed seer Vasiṣṭha glanced at him as he came storming
toward them, and the mighty sage stopped him with *hūṃ!* O
Bhārata. He sprinkled him with water that had been purified with
5 spells and set the good king free from the grisly Rākṣasa. It had been

twelve years since he had been swallowed due to the might of Vasiṣṭha's son, as the sun is swallowed by the Swallower at the time of eclipse. And now that he was free from the Rākṣasa, the king reddened the great forest with his splendor, as the sun reddens the clouds of dawn. He regained his senses and, folding his hands, greeted the good seer Vasiṣṭha; at that time the king said to him, "My lord, I am the son of Sudāsa, your patron, good brahmin. Tell me, what is your desire at this time? What may I do for you?"

Vasiṣṭha said:

It has happened as Time demanded. Go and rule your kingdom. And never despise the brahmins, king of men!

The king said:

I shall nevermore despise the bulllike brahmins, O brahmin. Obeying your behest, I shall worship the twiceborn forever. But I wish to obtain from you a boon by which I can acquit myself of my debt to the dynasty of Ikṣvāku, good brahmin, best of the scholars of the *Veda*! Pray go for me to my beloved queen, who has virtue, beauty, and accomplishments, to beget children for the furtherance of Ikṣvāku's lineage.

The Gandharva said:

"I shall give," promised the good brahmin Vasiṣṭha, who was true to his word, to the great royal archer.

Thereupon the king of men, in the company of Vasiṣṭha, returned, O prince sans blame, to the great city Ayodhyā, which is famous in all the worlds. All the subjects came out to meet him and joyfully welcomed back their king, now free from evil and great of spirit, as the celestials welcome their sovereign. Soon after, the king made his entrance into the city of the meritorious in the company of the great-spirited Vasiṣṭha. The citizens, sire, set eye upon him as upon the sun that rises in the sign of Puṣya. The king, greatest of those that are gifted with fortune, filled Ayodhyā with fortune as the cool-rayed moon fills the skies when it rises in the autumn. And the beautiful city, streets washed and spruced up and adorned with lofty flags, brought gladness to the heart of the monarch. The capital city, teeming with contented and well-fed folk, shone with him as Amarāvatī shines with Indra, O scion of Kuru.

After this king, this Indra among kings, had entered the city, the queen at the king's command strode up to Vasiṣṭha. At her season the great seer Vasiṣṭha, who partook of the best, lay with the queen by divine precept. When a child was conceived in her, the good hermit was bidden farewell by the king and returned to his hermitage.

The queen carried the child for a long time, but did not give birth. Then she split her womb with a stone. It was in the twelfth year, O bull among men, that the royal seer Aśmaka was born, he who settled Potana.

1(11.b.i) Aurva

169–71 (B. 178–80; C. 6792–6864)
169 (178; 6792). Vasiṣṭha's grandson Parāśara learns how his father died and wants to destroy the world (1–10). To dissuade him, Vasiṣṭha tells the story of Aurva. King Kṛtavīrya patronized the Bhṛgus. After his death his impoverished heirs demand the Bhṛgus' wealth. When the barons find they have buried their treasures, they massacre all of them down to the children in the womb (10–15). The women flee; one has hidden her embryo in her thigh. When she is discovered, the child splits open the thigh and blinds the barons with his radiance. The barons plead with the woman (20–25).
170 (179; 6820). The barons plead with the child, who restores their eyesight but decides on the destruction of the world (1–5). He begins to burn the world with the fire of his self-mortification. His ancestors appear and explain that they permitted the massacre of the Bhṛgus because they were tired of living. They demand that he stop the destruction (10–20).
171 (180; 6842). He agrees under protest (1–10). His ancestors tell him to cast the fire in the ocean where it can continue to burn the world. The fire becomes a huge horse that spits fire in the depths of the ocean (10–20).

The Gandharva said:

169.1 Adṛśyantī, who lived in the hermitage, gave birth to a son, the
keeper of Śakti's line and like another Śakti himself, O king. The
blessed Vasiṣṭha, bull among hermits, administered the sacraments of
birth and so forth to his grandson, O best of the Bhāratas. Since the
child in the womb had stopped Vasiṣṭha, who at the time was ready to
die, he was known in the world as Parāśara. From birth onward the
law-minded child thought that Vasiṣṭha was his father and behaved
5 toward him as though he was his father. Once he said "Daddy" to
Vasiṣṭha in Adṛśyantī's hearing, Kaunteya; and when she heard that
sweet word "Daddy," so full of meaning, Adṛśyantī said to him with
tears in her eyes, "Don't say 'Daddy, Daddy, Daddy.' The great hermit
is not your daddy. Your daddy was eaten up by a Rākṣasa in the
depths of the forest, my son. The one you think is your daddy is not
your father, innocent child. The lord is the father of your great-
spirited father."

At her words the good seer was vexed, for he always spoke the
10 truth; and haughtily he decided to destroy the entire world. Now hear with what argument the great ascetic Vasiṣṭha stopped the great-spirited Parāśara in spite of his resolve.

Vasiṣṭha said:

There once lived on earth a king known as Kṛtavīrya, a bull among kings, who was in the world the patron of the Bhṛgus, scholars of the Veda. The lord of the people satisfied the precedence-taking brahmins with plentiful grain and riches at the end of his Soma sacrifice.

When this tiger among kings had gone to heaven, there came a time when his relations were in need of substance; and knowing the affluence of the Bhṛgus, my son, all these barons went to the good
15 Bhārgavas to demand their wealth. Some of the Bhṛgus buried their indestructible wealth in the ground, others gave it away to the brahmins, since they knew they were in danger from the barons. But there were also Bhṛgus who gave them the riches they wanted, son, because they saw other uses for the barons.

Then one day one of the barons, while digging up the earth in the dwelling place of the Bhṛgus, came upon a treasure, and all the bulllike barons gathered there and saw the treasure. Thereafter, from anger and contempt, the great archers shot down all those Bhṛgus with their sharp arrows, even though they sought mercy. They went through the land killing them all, down to the children in the womb. While the Bhṛgus were being massacred in this way, son, their wives
20 took flight in terror to the Himālaya. One of the women, with beautiful thighs, carried her effulgent child down in her thigh, for fear of being discovered, to propagate the line of her husband.

The barons found that brahmin woman, who blazed with her own radiance. Then the child split open her thigh and appeared, blinding the eyes of the barons like the sun at noon; and, robbed of their eyesight, the barons wandered about in the straits of the mountain. Frustrated in their designs and haunted by fear, the bulls of the barons sought refuge with that blameless brahmin woman to regain their eyesight. Out of their minds with pain, the barons, who had lost the light of their eyes and were like fires whose flames have been doused, spoke to the lady: "By my lady's grace, may the barons regain their
25 eyes. All of us who have wrought evil shall desist and depart. Pray show us your grace, you and your son, and save the princes with the gift of eyesight."

The brahmin woman said:

170.1 It is not I who robbed your eyes, nor I who am wroth, but surely it is the Bhārgava born from my thigh who is enraged at you! He, to be sure, took your eyes, son, because the great-spirited child no doubt remembered that you had killed his kinsmen. When you, my

sons, even killed the Bhṛgu's children in the womb, I carried this child
of mine in my thigh, for a hundred years. The entire *Veda* and its six
branches came to the child when I bore him, to be once more of
5 benefit to the dynasty of the Bhṛgus. He certainly wishes to kill you,
out of anger over the slaughter of his fathers, for with his effulgence
he robbed you of your eyesight. Plead with him, with my great son
Aurva, sons. When he has been placated by your protestations, he will
restore your eyes.

Vasiṣṭha said:

At her words all the barons pleaded with her thigh-born son:
"Have mercy!" And he had mercy. It is by this name that the very
strict man is famous in the worlds—"Aurva," because the brahmin
seer was born by splitting the thigh. Having regained their eyesight,
the barons returned; but the Bhārgava hermit himself willed the
downfall of the entire world.

10 The haughty man set his intent mind on the total destruction of the
worlds entire. Wishing to bring honor to the Bhṛgus, this best of the
Bhṛgus swelled with the heat of great self-mortification for the
destruction of all the worlds. He began to burn the worlds with their
Gods, Asuras, and men in order to gladden his grandfathers with his
vast and awesome austerity.

Thereupon, when his ancestors had understood that most strict
Bhṛgu, they all descended from the World of the Fathers and said to
him, "Aurva! We have witnessed the power of your awesome
15 austerity, son. Have mercy for the worlds, withdraw your wrath! It
was not because they were powerless, son, that the Bhṛgus, who had
perfected their souls, ignored the slaughter of them all at the hands of
the murderous barons. When boredom with our protracted lives
assailed us, we ourselves wished our death at the barons' hands.
Therefore, one of us buried the treasure in the dwelling place of the
Bhṛgus and put it there just to anger the barons and start a feud.
What use was treasure to us who wanted heaven, bull among the
twiceborn? When death proved wholly incapable of taking us, we
found that an agreeable means, son. A man who kills himself, son,
does not attain to the bright worlds. It was with this consideration
in mind that we did not kill ourselves by our own hand.

20 "Therefore, it does not please us, son, what you now intend to do.
Restrain your mind from this evil destruction of all the worlds. For
none of the barons or any of the seven worlds offended our might and
mortification, son. Rid yourself of the fury that has risen in you."

Aurva said:

171.1 The promise that I pronounced in my anger, fathers, the promise that I would destroy all the worlds, shall not be belied! For I cannot live a man whose wrath and oath are of no consequence. Unless it is diverted, my anger will burn me as the fire burns the drilling block. The man who will appease the anger that had arisen in him for good cause is unable properly to safeguard the Three Goals. For the punisher of the unlearned is the savior of the learned. Kings who want to conquer heaven employ their fury in a just cause. When I was yet unborn and lodged in my mother's thigh, I heard the outcry of my mothers at the massacre of the Bhṛgus by the barons. When the eradication of the Bhṛgus down to the children in the womb, by those degenerate barons, was condoned by the worlds and the Immortals within them, then anger entered me. And indeed! my mothers with their heavy wombs, and my fathers, found no recourse from their danger in any of the worlds. When no one came to the aid of the wives of the Bhṛgus, my good mother carried me in her thigh. When there is a preventer of crime in the world, no criminal will be found in any world. But if the criminal never meets one who prevents him, then many in the world rise to criminal acts. He who, albeit knowing and capable, does not suppress crime may be a master, but he is tainted by the same act. If kings and sovereigns, even though able to do so, could not be made to save my fathers, thinking that life here was happy enough, then I am wroth with the worlds, and now I am master to them.

Yet, I cannot transgress your word—though the same great danger will lurk for me, when I, however capable, once more ignore the evil of the worlds. And the fire born from my wrath, which wishes to set the worlds afire, will too burn me when I suppress it with my own might. Still I know that you have the well-being of all the worlds at heart, therefore dispose whatever is best for the worlds, and for me, my lords.

The fathers said:

Release into the water the fire that is born from your wrath and wishes to set the worlds afire, and be blessed. For the worlds are founded on the waters. All the essences consist in water, the whole world is made up of water—therefore, release the fire of your fury into the water, good brahmin. If you please, let the fire born of your wrath remain in the ocean, burning the waters, for they declare that the worlds are made of water. Thus, blameless son, your oath will still be true, and the worlds with their Immortals will not be destroyed.

Vasiṣṭha said:

Thereupon, my son, Aurva cast out the wrath-born fire into Varuṇa's domain, and it eats the waters of the ocean. Thus do the scholars of the *Veda* know that it became a huge horse head, which spits fire from its mouth and drinks the waters of the ocean. Therefore, be you too blessed and abstain from the destruction of the worlds, Parāśara, as you know the higher Laws, wisest of men.

1(11.b) Vasiṣṭha (concluded)

The Gandharva said:

172.1 After this discourse of the great-spirited Vasiṣṭha, the brahmin seer
restrained his own wrath from destroying the worlds entire. And the
mighty seer Parāśara Śākteya, greatest of all scholars of the *Veda*,
sacrificed with the Session of the Rākṣasas. When the sacrifice was
spread out, the great hermit burned the Rākṣasas, young and old, in
memory of the killing of his father Śakti. Nor did Vasiṣṭha restrain him
from slaughtering the Rākṣasas, having resolved that he should not
5 break this second oath of his. The great hermit, seated at the Session
of the Three Fires that burned in front of him, was himself a fourth
fire. The luminous sacrifice, into which oblations were offered
according to the Rules, illuminated the skies as the sun does at the
end of the rains. Vasiṣṭha and the other hermits deemed him a second
sun blazing with splendor in heaven.

Thereupon Atri, the noble-minded seer, betook himself to that
Session, supremely difficult of access to others, wishing to put an end
to it. So did Pulastya and Pulaha and Kratu come to the great
ceremony, O slayer of enemies, since they wished the Rākṣasas to live.

10 At the slaughter of those Rākṣasas, O bull of the Bhāratas, Pulastya
spoke these words, Pārtha, to the enemy-tamer Parāśara: "Does nothing
stop you? Do you take pleasure, son, in the massacre of all these
unaware and innocent Rākṣasas? You that are so very virtuous are
perpetrating the most lawless, total extinction of my progeny,
Parāśara, greatest of Soma drinkers! And King Kalmāṣapāda himself
is about to ascend to heaven! The younger brothers of Śakti, the sons
of the great hermit Vasiṣṭha, are all joined with bliss and rejoice in the
company of the Gods. All this was always known to Vasiṣṭha, great
hermit, and so was this annihilation of the wretched Rākṣasas, son.
You have been the instrument in this sacrifice, scion of Vasiṣṭha.
Give up this Session and be blessed. Let this be its completion for you!"

15 When Pulastya, and also the wise Vasiṣṭha, spoke to him in this
fashion, Śakti's son Parāśara put an end to the Session of all the
Rākṣasas. The hermit cast out the fire that had been gathered for the
Session into the vast wasteland on the northern flank of the Himālaya.
And there this fire is still visible at every cycle, as it devours the
Rākṣasas, and the trees, and the rocks.

1(11) Citraratha (concluded)

Arjuna said:

173.1 What was the preferred reason, O guru, who are the greatest of the scholars of the Brahman, that King Kalmāṣapāda summoned his wife and gave her the injunction, and that the great-spirited Vasiṣṭha, who knew the higher Law of the world, lay with a woman forbidden him? Pray tell it all at my bidding.

The Gandharva said:

Dhanaṃjaya, learn from me what you are questioning regarding the unassailable Vasiṣṭha and King Mitrasaha.

I have already recounted to you, best of the Bharatas, how the king
5 was cursed by Vasiṣṭha's son, the great-spirited Śakti. When he fell
under the power of that curse, the puissant king, eyes rolling with fury, departed with his wife from his city, enemy-tamer. With her he went to the desolate wilderness and began to roam there in that haunt of the herds of manifold beasts, teeming with all sorts of creatures. As he, in the grip of his curse, roamed the forest, covered with all kinds of shrubs and lianas, dense with all sizes of trees, and echoing with hideous howls, he once, while he was hungrily hunting for food and utterly weary, saw in a thicket of trees a brahmin and his wife who had come there to co-habit.

Terrified, the pair, still undone, ran away when they saw him; and
10 while they ran, the king forcibly laid hold of the brahmin. When the
brahmin woman saw her husband captured she said, "Hear what I shall say to you, king of the good vows! You have sprung from the race of the sun, you are renowned in the world, you are ever-alert and bent to obedience to your guru: you have succumbed to a curse, unassailable king, pray commit no crime! I got together with my husband as my season had come, and I am still not done with my husband, and I have great need for a child. Have mercy, good king,
let my husband go!" While the woman was shrieking, the king most
15 cruelly devoured her husband, as a tiger eats its favorite prey. The
woman, overcome with rage, shed a tear on the ground, and it blazed up into a fire that set the place aglow. In the pain of her sorrow and grief over her husband's disaster, the brahmin woman, enraged, cursed Kalmāṣapāda, the royal seer: "Because today you fiendishly devoured my glorious and masterful husband before my own eyes, degenerate, before I was done, you shall be stricken by my curse, fool, and when you come to your wife at her season you shall instantly shed your life. The seer Vasiṣṭha whose sons you destroyed shall lie with your wife, and she shall give birth to a son; and that son shall

be the keeper of your line, most foul of kings!" When she had cursed the king, the good Āngirasa woman entered the blazing fire before him.

The lordly Vasiṣṭha saw all this through the great yoga of insight and through the power of his austerities, enemy-burner. When the royal seer after a long time was freed from his curse, he once fell together with Madayantī at the time of her season, but was rebuffed; for being confused by the curse, the king had forgotten his curse. When the good prince heard the queen's word, he remembered the curse and became greatly upset.

It was for that reason that the king ordered Vasiṣṭha to his own wife, best of the Bharatas, being seized with the disease of his curse.

1(12) Draupadī's Bridegroom Choice

174–85 (B. 183–92; C. 6913–7173)
174 (183; 6913). Upon the Gandharva Citraratha's advice, the Pāṇḍavas choose Dhaumya as their priest; he accepts them (1–10). They start for Draupadī's Bridegroom Choice (10).
175 (184; 6925). They fall in with a caravan of brahmins traveling the same way; they predict a grand feast and rich stipends (1–20).
176 (185; 6945). On their way they meet Kṛṣṇa Dvaipāyana, who speeds them on. Disguised as brahmins, they take lodgings with a potter and beg their food (1–5). King Drupada had a hard bow made, in order to search out the Pāṇḍavas; the challenge is to string the bow and hit a target. All barons assemble, including Duryodhana and his brothers; the townspeople gather (5–15). Description of the arena and pavilions (15–25). The Pāṇḍavas sit with the brahmins; after a fire oblation by the priest, Dhṛṣṭadyumna gives the challenge (25–35).
177 (186; 6981). He enumerates to Draupadī the names of the barons (1–20).
178 (187; 7005). The barons parade; the Gods arrive, so do Kṛṣṇa, Rāma, and other Vṛṣṇis. Kṛṣṇa thinks he recognizes the Pāṇḍavas (1–10). All the Pāṇḍavas fall in love with Draupadī. The barons try the feat but fail (10–15).
179 (188; 7034). Arjuna now rises from among the brahmins, some of whom protest out of fear of baronial opprobrium; others defend him (1–10). Arjuna circum-

ambulates the bow, strings it, and hits the target with five arrows. Yudhiṣṭhira and the twins hasten home. Arjuna receives the winner's garland, and Draupadī follows him (10–20).

180 (189; 7061). The barons are restive because of Drupada's insult in giving his daughter to a brahmin (1–10). They advance on the king. Bhīma uproots a tree and, with Arjuna, holds his ground. Kṛṣṇa now recognizes them (10–20).

181 (190; 7085). The barons, led by Karṇa, fall on the two brothers. The mêlée is reduced to duels between Arjuna and Karṇa, Bhīma and Śalya (1–10). Karṇa withdraws because he thinks Arjuna is a brahmin (10–20). Bhīma fells Śalya but spares his life. The barons applaud them and return home. The two Pāṇḍavas return to Kuntī, who has been worrying (20–40).

182 (191; 7131). From outside they cry out to Kuntī, "Look what alms we found!" Not seeing them, she replies, "Now you share that together!" On noticing her mistake she is horrified, but does not want to be made a liar. Yudhiṣṭhira assigns Draupadī to Arjuna, who won her. Arjuna points out that Yudhiṣṭhira, their eldest, must marry first. Meanwhile the love of all five brothers becomes manifest. Yudhiṣṭhira decides that she should be their common wife (1–15).

183. While the Pāṇḍavas reflect on this, Kṛṣṇa and Balarāma arrive, present themselves, and greet Kuntī; they are welcomed (1–5). After good wishes they leave (5).

184 (192; 7156). Dhṛṣṭadyumna, Kṛṣṇā's brother, spies on the Pāṇḍavas; Kuntī instructs Draupadī to divide the alms food (1–5). They lie down to sleep and tell tales of war and weapons. Dhṛṣṭadyumna returns home where Drupada questions him about what kind of man now owns his daughter (5–15).

185 (193; 7174). Dhṛṣṭadyumna describes Arjuna's and Bhīma's battling, Draupadī's reception by Kuntī, and the Pāṇḍavas' tales; he assures her father of their identity (1–10). Joyfully, Drupada sends his priest to convey his happiness and for them to identify themselves (10–20). Yudhiṣṭhira answers evasively, pointing out that their descent does not matter in this case (10–25). A messenger from Drupada arrives (25).

Arjuna said:
174.1 Is there a scholar of the *Veda*, Gandharva, who would be a suitable priest for us? Tell us, for you know everything.
The Gandharva said:
Dhaumya, the younger brother of Devala, is practicing austerities in this forest at the Utkocaka Ford. Elect him, if you wish.
Vaiśaṃpāyana said:
Thereupon Arjuna presented the Gandharva in the proper manner
with the *āgneya* weapon and said to him affectionately, "Keep the
horses for the time being, good Gandharva. I shall take them when we
5 need them. Good luck to you!" The Gandharva and the Pāṇḍavas
bade each other farewell, and they departed from the lovely bank of
the Ganges at their pleasure.
The Pāṇḍavas repaired to the Utkocaka Ford for the hermitage of
Dhaumya and chose him to be their priest, O Bhārata. Dhaumya,
greatest of scholars of the *Veda*, accepted them with water to wash
their feet, fruit and roots to eat, and with priestly offices. The Pāṇḍavas,
upon having put a brahmin ahead of themselves, now had high hopes
of winning wealth, a kingdom, and the bridegroom choice of the
daughter of the Pāñcālas. The bulls of the Bhāratas—with their mother
the sixth in their company—deemed themselves well protected, now
10 that they had been joined with a guru. For the noble-minded guru
knew the facts of the sense of the *Veda*; and the Pārthas became the
ritual patrons of the Law-wise, and all-wise, brahmin. He in turn
judged that the heroes would obtain their kingdom by their own
virtues and thought of them, endowed as they were with spirit,
prowess, strength, and enterprise, as though they were Gods. He
blessed the way for them, and thereupon the princes of men decided
to go together to the bridegroom choice of the princess of the Pāṇcālas.

Vaiśaṃpāyana said:
175.1 The five Pāṇḍava brothers, tigers among men, journeyed to see Draupadī and the divine festival. And as the enemy-burners traveled with their mother, they met vast crowds of brahmins and their escort who were going the same way. The brahmins, O king, said to the Pāṇḍavas who were traveling as brahmin students, "Where are you going and from whence have you come?"
Yudhiṣṭhira said:
Good sirs, who are familiar with the Gods, know that we are brothers. We have come from Ekacakrā and are traveling with our mother.
The brahmins said:
5 Then you should now go to the Pāñcālas, to the seat of Drupada.
There will be a grand bridegroom choice there, with plenty of riches.

We are journeying there ourselves, traveling in one large caravan.
There is going to be a very grand festival, full of wonders. The spirited
maiden with eyes like lotus petals and a flawless body, lovely and
delicate, is the daughter of the great-spirited Yajñasena Drupada, and
she was born from the middle of the altar. She is the sister of the
mighty and majestic Dhṛṣṭadyumna, the foeman of Droṇa, who was
born, wearing armor, sword, bow, and arrows, from the blazing fire
10 and is resplendent like the fire. His sister Draupadī of the flawless
limbs and slender waist, whose blue lotus fragrance wafts as far as a
league, Yajñasena's daughter, is holding her bridegroom choice. We
are going to watch her and the divine grand festival. There'll be kings
coming and the sons of kings, sacrificial patrons who reward their
priests richly, observing the *Veda*, pure, great-spirited, and keeping to
their vows, young and handsome, from all kinds of countries, great
chariot warriors, past masters on weaponry, barons all! All these lords
of men will give away largess of all sorts, chattels and cows and food
15 and delicacies! When we have received it all and watched the bridegroom choice and enjoyed the festival, we shall go on again, wherever
we please. Actors and bards will be coming, and dancers, reciters, and
songsters, and powerful wrestlers from different countries. When you
have seen the wondrous spectacle and eaten and received gifts, great-
spirited youths, you'll come back with us again. Perchance, when
Kṛṣṇā sees you all standing there, handsome like Gods, she may choose
one of you for her bridegroom! And this lustrous, handsome, big-armed
brother of yours might win a lot of treasure in the wrestling matches!

Yudhiṣṭhira said:
20 Aye! We shall all go and watch that superb and divine grand
festival with you, the bridegroom choice of the maiden!

Vaiśaṃpāyana said:
176.1 At the brahmins' words, Janamejaya, the Pāṇḍavas traveled to the
Southern Pāñcālas who were ruled by King Drupada. On their way
they saw the great-spirited and pure-spirited Dvaipāyana, free from all
blemishes, and they paid proper homage to him. He in turn comforted
them and at the end of his discourse gave them leave to go; and they
went on to the seat of Drupada. The warriors traveled slowly and
camped wherever they saw lovely woods and lakes.
5 Then the scions of Kuru, diligent students, pure, kindly, and gentle-
spoken, eventually arrived in the Pāñcāla country. When they had
seen the city and the king's fortress, they made their lodgings in the
house of a potter. Affecting the way of the brahmins, they begged their
food; nowhere did people find out that champions had arrived.

It had always been Yajñasena's wish to give Kṛṣṇā to the diademed
Arjuna, but he did not divulge it. Since he hoped to search out the

Pāṇḍavas, the Pāñcālya had a very hard bow made, well-nigh impossible to bend, O Janamejaya Bhārata. He had a contraption built in the sky, and onto the contraption he had a golden target fixed.

Drupada said:

The man who can string this bow and, when he has strung it, can shoot arrows through the contraption into the mark will have my daughter.

Vaiśaṃpāyana said:

Thus went the challenge that King Drupada caused to be proclaimed everywhere; and when they heard it, all the kings came flocking there, Bhārata. Great-spirited seers arrived to watch the bridegroom choice, and so did the Kauravas, led by Duryodhana and accompanied by Karṇa. Lordly brahmins came from the countries around, and hosts of kings were welcomed by the great-spirited Drupada. With the roar of the windswept ocean, all the townspeople gathered in the City of the Crocodile, and the barons settled down there.

On an even and consecrated stretch of land northeast of the city there stood in all its beauty an arena that was completely surrounded by stands. Around it ran a wall and a moat, and it was embellished with grand gateways. The arena was entirely shaded by a colorful awning. The sounds of hundreds of musical instruments filled it, it was perfumed with costly aloe scents, sprinkled with sandal water, and decorated with festoons of flowers. The arena was girt by a belt of well-enclosed, expertly built, high-rising pavilions that seemed to scratch the sky like the peaks of Kailāsa, wrapped in gilded trellises and sparkling with mosaics of precious stones, with steps that rose gently, and fine seats that were shaded by canopies. Carpets, not of the rustic kind, covered those multitudinous pavilions, and they were superbly scented with aloe and white like geese, casting their fragrance to the distance of a league. A hundred wide doors gave access to them, beautiful seats and couches were placed about, and their elements were wrought with many metals as are the peaks of Mount Himālaya. On the many stories of the pavilions all the kings were seated, rivaling one another with the adornment of their persons. The townspeople and country folk, who had come to content themselves with the spectacle of Kṛṣṇā, sat all about on their own rich platforms and stared at the lordly, lionlike kings who were sitting there, of mighty courage and prowess, perfumed with black aloe—gracious and brahminic princes, the protectors of their realms and beloved of all the world for their hallowed good deeds.

The Pāṇḍavas took their seats with the brahmins and gazed upon the matchless wealth of the king of the Pāñcālas. For many days the audience grew while it was heaped with largess of jewels and entertained by actors and dancers. On the sixteenth day, when there was a

lovely crowd, Draupadī appeared, freshly bathed, in new clothes.
30 Carrying the champion's goblet, which was made of gold and finely wrought, she descended into the arena, O bull of the Bharatas. The priest of the Somakas,* a pure brahmin who was learned in the spells, strewed sacred grass around and made an oblation of butter in the fire in the proper fashion. After having satisfied the fire and the brahmins, and having blessed the day, he stopped the music all around. When silence fell, Dhṛṣṭadyumna strode to the middle of the arena and spoke in a thundering voice these polished and most meaningful words:

"Hear ye, all kings who are gathered here!
Mark bow and target, and mark these arrows.
You must hit the mark with these five arrows
By shooting through this hole in the wheel.

35 "Whoever of lineage, beauty, and might
Accomplishes this most difficult feat,
To him shall go my sister Kṛṣṇā
To be his wife, and I say sooth!"

When Drupada's son had spoken to them,
He thereafter spoke to Draupadī,
And heralded the assembled princes
By name and lineage and by their feats.

Dhṛṣṭadyumna said:

177.1 Duryodhana, Durviṣaha, Durmukha, Duṣpradharṣaṇa, Viviṃśati, Vikarṇa, Saha. Duḥśāsana, Sama, Yuyutsu, Vātavega, Bhīmavegadhara, Ugrāyudha, Balākin, Kanakāyus, Virocana, Sukuṇḍala, Citrasena, Suvarcas, Kanakadhvaja, Nandaka, Bāhuśālin, Kuṇḍaja, Vikaṭa—these and many others of the sons of Dhṛtarāṣṭra, powerful all and champions, have come with Karṇa for you!

5 Famous, great-spirited bulls of the barons have come in their hundreds: Śakuni, Bala, Vṛṣaka, Bṛhadbala, the sons of the king of Gāndhāra have all foregathered here.

Asvatthāman and Bhoja, the two excellent armsmen of great spirit, have assembled in their finery.

Bṛhanta and Maṇimat and the puissant Daṇḍadhāra, Sahadeva, Jayatsena and Meghasaṃdhi of Magadha, Virāṭa with his two sons Śankha and Uttara; and Vārdhakṣemi and Suvarcas and King Senābindu: Abhibhū with his magnificent son Sudāman, and Sumitra, Sukumāra,
10 Vṛka, and Satyadhṛti; Sūryadhvaja, Rocamāna, Nīla, and Citrāyudha; Aṃśumat, Cekitāna, and the mighty Śreṇimat; and majestic Candrasena,

* = Pāñcālas.

son of Samudrasena; Jalasaṃdha, and father and son Sudaṇḍa and Daṇḍa; Pauṇḍraka and Vāsudeva and the heroic Bhagadatta; Kalinga, Tāmralipta, and the ruler of Pattana; the great warrior Śalya, king of the Madras, with his sons, the champion Rukmāngada and Rukmaratha.

There Somadatta the Kaurava and his warrior sons come, the three
15 heroes, Bhūri, Bhūriśravas, and Śala; and Sudakṣiṇa, Kāmboja, and
Dṛdhadhanvan the Kaurava; Bṛhadbala, Suṣena, and Śibi Auśīnara. And Saṃkarṣaṇa and the puissant Vāsudeva, son of Rukminī. Śāmba, Cārudeṣṇa, Sāraṇa, and Gada, Akrūra and Sātyakī, and the mighty Uddhava; Kṛtavarman Hārdikya, and Pṛthu and Vipṛthu; Viḍūratha and Kanka, Samīka and Sāramejaya; the champion Vātapati and Jhillin and Piṇḍāraka, the wide-striding Uśīnara, celebrated Vṛṣṇis all.

Bhagīratha has come, and Bṛhatkṣatra and Jayadratha Saindhava;
20 Bṛhadratha and Bāhlīka and the warlike Śrutāyus; Ulūka and King
Kaitava, and Citrāngada with Śubhāngada. And the imperturbable king of the Vatsas and the ruler of Kosala.

These and many other princes of many countrysides, all these barons renowned on earth have come to sue for you, my dear. These brave men shall shoot at the great target to win you. And you, beautiful princess, will choose the one who hits it.

Vaiśaṃpāyana said:

178.1 The young barons with earrings and ornaments,
Come together to vie one with the other,
Each holding himself the strong master of arms,
Did all foregather there boastfully.

In their beauty and prowess and dynasties,
In their merit of Law and their youthful strength,
They gloried all with the drunk vehemence
Of rutting Himālayan elephants.

They stared at each other in rivalry,
Their bodies bathed in their mind-born love,
And proclaiming "Kṛṣṇā shall be mine!"
They suddenly rose from their regal seats,

The barons who gathered in the arena,
Drupada's daughter seeking to win,
Resembled the hosts of Gods who assembled
For Umā, daughter of Himālaya.

5 Their limbs besieged by the arrows of Love,
Hearts gone to Kṛṣṇā, the kings of men

Went down to the pit for Draupadī's sake,
Made even their old friends there their foes.

Then riding the chariots came the Gods,
Ādityas and Rudras and Vasus and Aśvins,
The Sādhyas all and the Maruts too,
Placing Yama ahead and the Lord of Wealth;

The Daityas and Birds and the mighty Serpents,
Divine seers and Guhyakas and Cāraṇas,
Viśvāvasu, Nārada, Parvata,
The chiefs of Gandharvas and Apṣarās.

The plough-armed Rāma and Keśava,
The chiefs of the Vṛṣṇis and Andhakas,
All cast their glances; the bulls of the Yadus
Were all arrayed under Kṛṣṇa's command.

Observing the five Pāṇḍavas,
Like rutting red-spotted elephants,
All covered with ashes like offering fire,
The Yadu hero began to wonder.

10 To Rāma he mentioned Yudhiṣṭhira
And Bhīma and Jiṣṇu* and the brave twins;
And Rāma leisurely looked at them,
Then glanced at Janārdana gleefully.

The many sons and grandsons of kings,
Their eyes, mind, and mettle to Kṛṣṇā gone,
Stared as she walked, flexing their muscles,
Biting their lips, with copper-red faces.

The wide-armed sons of Pāṇḍu by Pṛthā
And the two heroic and powerful twins,
They all kept looking at Draupadī—
They were all struck by the arrows of Love.

The sky was crowded with seers and Gods,
Gandharvas, Birds, Asuras, Siddhas, and Snakes,
A celestial fragrance pervaded it,
Celestial garlands were scattered about.

The thundering roar of kettledrums sounded
And rendered the sky more crowded still,
Its pathways were clogged with the chariots of Gods,
While they echoed with lutes and flutes and cymbals.

* = Arjuna.

Then the hosts of kings one after another
Strode bravely about for Kṛṣṇā's sake,
But so tough was that bow that with all their strength
They failed to cord that bow with its string.

The nardwood bow would recoil and fling
The wide-striding kings of men in the dust.
And as they lay gesturing on the ground
They looked crestfallen and their spirits broke.

The hardwood bow cried out in pain
And shattered and ground their bracelets and earrings.
Their feelings of love for Kṛṣṇā departed—
The circle of kings was woebegone.

The folk got restive in that assembly
And spoke words of abuse to the kings of men;
Then Jiṣṇu arose, the son of Kuntī,
The hero, to string and to shaft the bow.

Vaiśaṃpāyana said:

179.1 When the kings withdrew from the stringing of the bow, the noble-minded Jiṣṇu stood up in the midst of the brahmins. The great brahmins cried out and waved with their deerskins, when they saw the Pārtha start, radiant like Indra's rainbow. Some were displeased, others quite joyous; and some sagacious brahmins, who lived by their wisdom, said to one another, "If world-famous kings like Karṇa and Śalya and others, strong and past masters of archery, were unable to bend the bow, could this mere brat, inexperienced with weapons and much inferior in vigor, string that bow, brahmins? The brahmins will become the laughingstock among all the kings if he fails in this task, which he was too flighty to consider! If he, from pride or excitement or sheer flightiness toward brahmindom, goes out to string the bow, he'd better be stopped from going so that we are not ridiculed and held lightly, and become hateful to the kings of this world!"

Others said, "The youth is grand enough. He is like the trunk of the king of the elephants! His shoulders, thighs, and arms are solid with muscle, and he stands fast like the Himālaya! That he is up to the task is inferred from his enterprise—his power is full of enterprise, no incompetent man would go off on his own. Besides, there's not a task to be found in any one of the worlds that is impossible to the brahmins among the three orders of beings! Whether weakened by living on water, eating off the wind, or feeding on fruit, the brahmin of rigorous vows proves the stronger by the might of his Brahman. No brahmin should be despised, whether he does right or wrong, whether his incumbent task is pleasant or unpleasant, large or small!"

When they were thus voicing their various opinions, Arjuna took
15 his stand by the bow like an immovable mountain. He walked around the bow, making a solemn circumambulation, and bowed his head down to it. Then the enemy-burner joyfully took it in his hand.

In a twinkling of the eye he strung the bow
And took the arrows that counted five.
He pierced the target and brought it down,
Hit through the hole, and it fell with a might.

In the sky above there was applause,
And great cheering in the crowd below.
The God rained down with celestial flowers
On the head of the Pārtha, killer of foes.

The spectators all around waved with their clothes or moaned, and from the sky fell a rain of flowers. The musicians sounded their hundredfold instruments, and melodious bards and songsters lifted
20 their voices in praise. When Drupada, scourge of his enemies, saw him, he was much pleased and stood ready to succor the Pārtha with his army.

As the uproar came to its mighty head,
Yudhiṣṭhira, first of the bearers of Law,
Went hastily back to his own abode
Along with the twins, supreme among men.

On beholding the target hit and on seeing
Pṛthā's son in the image of Indra,
Kṛṣṇā took a festoon of white flowers
And went smilingly up to Arjuna.

Having won in the lists, he took the woman
Whilst the twiceborn brahmins paid him homage.
And the miracle-monger strode from the pit,
And after him followed she, his wife.

Vaiśaṃpāyana said:

180.1 When the king was ready to give the maiden to the great-spirited brahmin, a great anger arose in the barons and they looked at one another. "Here we are assembled," they said, "and he passes us by as though we were straw! He wants to give Draupadī, finest of women, to a brahmin! Let us kill this ill-spirited man who despises us. For he does not deserve our esteem, nor the courtesies of age, for his virtues. Let us kill this churl who hates kings, along with his sons! First he invited and honored all the kings and feasted them properly, and then

5 he condemns them! How is it possible that in this assembly of kings, like a congregation of Gods, he cannot find a single prince who is his equal? Brahmins have no title to the choosing; the scriptures are clear: 'The bridegroom choice is for the barons.' Or else, if this girl wants no part of any one of us, let us throw her in the fire and go back to our kingdoms, kings! But let this brahmin escape with his life, even if he has insulted great kings, either from folly or greed. For our kingdoms, lives, riches, sons, and grandsons, and whatever treasure we possess,
10 are meant for the brahmin. Still, let us watch against contempt and protect our own Law, so that other bridegroom choices do not turn out like this one!"

The tigerlike kings excitedly advanced with clubs in hand on Drupada, brandishing their weapons to finish him off. And seeing them fall upon him in anger with their bows and arrows, Drupada was frightened and sought shelter with the brahmins. But the two enemy-taming sons of Pāṇḍu went to meet the princes, who advanced ferociously like rutting elephants.

Raising their weapons, the kings of the land,
Their fingers gauntleted, indignantly
Fell upon lords Arjuna and Bhīmasena,
To kill the sons of the king of the Kurus.

15 Then Bhīma of wondrous feats of strength,
Of puissance great and of thunderbolt might,
Uprooted, sole champion, a tree with his hands,
And tore off the leaves like an elephant.

This tree he took, that churner of foes,
As the King of the Dead takes his dreadful staff,
And the Pārtha of long, broad arms stood next
To Arjuna Pārtha, bull among men.

Upon seeing the feats of the superhuman
Jiṣṇu and Bhīma, the wonder-monger
Dāmodara* turned to his plough-armed brother
Of awesome deeds, and he spoke his word:

"That man who strides like a rutting bull,
Who bent the big bow that stands four ell,
That man is Arjuna, doubt it not,
If I'm Vāsudeva, Saṃkarṣaṇa!**

"And the one who pulled out the tree with his strength
And now has turned to counter the kings,

* = Kṛṣṇa Vāsudeva.
** = Bala-Rāma.

Is the Wolf-Belly, for no mortal on earth
Is here and now capable of such a feat.

20 "And the one with the eyes like lotus petals,
Slender and modest, with a lion's walk,
Fair-skinned, with an aquiline, shining nose,
Who earlier left must have been King Dharma.

"And those two youths, like two Gods Kārttikeya,
Must have been, methinks, the sons of the Aśvins;
For I heard that Pāṇḍu's sons and Pṛthā
Escaped from that fire in the lacquer house."

The plough-armed Rāma, fair like a cloud,
Was convinced, and he said to his younger brother,
"I am pleased that good fortune set Pṛthā free,
Our father's sister, and the chiefs of the Kurus."

Vaiśaṃpāyana said:

181.1 The bulllike brahmin shook their deerskins and begging bowls and
said to Drupada, "Have no fear, we shall battle the enemy!" Arjuna
laughed and said to the brahmins, "You stand aside and be
spectators! I myself shall sprinkle our angry barons with hundreds of
straight-pointed arrows and ward them off as poisonous snakes are
warded off with spells." With these words the warrior took the bow he
had received as dowry and, with his brother Bhīma, stood fast like an
5 immovable mountain. Thereupon they both fell upon the wrathfully
risen barons, who were led by Karṇa, as two elephants fall upon their
rivals. The murderous kings said harshly, "Even a brahmin is fair
game to kill in battle if he is willing to fight!"
Vaikartana Karṇa went mightily at Arjuna, eager for a fight, as an
elephant goes at a rival over an elephant cow. Śalya, the mighty king
of the Madras, went at Bhīmasena, while Duryodhana and the others
attacked the brahmins—but they fought them gently and without
much effort. As Vaikartana Karṇa stormed toward him, the sagacious
Arjuna stretched his mighty bow and shot him with three arrows.
10 The impact of the fierce-honed arrows stunned Rādheya,* and he
approached more carefully. Their motions blurred by their speed, the
two victorious warriors fought fiercely, each bent on vanquishing the
other. "Look how I countered that one!" "Now watch the power of
my arms!" So they taunted each other in the language of heroes.
When Vaikartana Karṇa found that the power of Arjuna's arms was
unmatched on earth, he fought him furiously. He warded off the fast
arrows of Arjuna and shouted aloud, while the warriors cheered him
on.

* = son of Rādhā, viz., Karna.

Karna said:

15 You please me, eminent brahmin, with the might of your arms in
combat, with your undismayed persistence and your discipline with
the weapons. Are you the Art of Archery in person, or are you
Rāma,* good brahmin? Or bay-horsed Indra, or indomitable Viṣṇu
himself who, disguised as a brahmin, has resorted to the might of his
arms in self-protection, that you fight me so hard? For no man can
withstand me in battle when I am angry, no one but Indra and the
diademed Pāṇḍava!

Vaiśaṃpāyana said:

To these words of his Phalguna replied, "No, Karṇa, I am not the
Art of Archery, nor majestic Rāma. I am a brahmin, the greatest of
20 warriors, the finest of all who wield weapons! At my guru's instance
I have become adept at the Brahmā weapon and Indra's weapon. And
here I stand to defeat you in battle. Stand your ground, hero!"

Upon these words Karṇa Rādheya withdrew from the duel, for the
great warrior held brahminic power to be invincible. In the same
arena Śalya and the Wolf-Belly went to war, both mighty and equally
crazed with rivalry and strength. They called out to each other like
two huge elephants in rut, and beat each other with fists and knees.
For a while they dragged each other about on the battlefield, then
that most powerful Bhīma lifted Śalya up with his arms and hurled
him down on the ground—the brahmins burst out laughing.
25 Thereupon the bulllike Bhīma wrought this miracle that he, strength
pitted against strength, forbore to kill Śalya when he had fallen to the
ground.

With Śalya brought down by Bhīmasena, and Karṇa frightened
away, all the kings, affrighted themselves, surrounded the Wolf-Belly.
And they all said, "Cheers for these bulls of the brahmins! Let us find
out where they were born and where they live. For who can battle
with Rādhā's son Karṇa, save for Rāma and Droṇa and Kṛpa
Śāradvata and Kṛṣṇa, son of Devakī, and the enemy-burning
30 Phalguna? And who can fight back against Duryodhana and Śalya,
that most mighty king of the Madras, save for heroic Baladeva, and
Wolf-Belly the Pāṇḍava? Let us break off this battle that the brahmins
have joined and find out who they are. Then we shall fight them
again."

> Upon seeing the feat of Bhīma, Kṛṣṇa
> Surmised that the two were Kuntī's sons;
> And he gently restrained all these kings of the land:
> 'The maiden was won according to Law."

Thereupon the battle-wise kings turned away from the battle, and

* = Paraśu-Rāma.

all the good princes went wonderingly back to their land. 'The arena
has become dominated by the brahmins, the brahmins have chosen
the Daughter of the Pāñcālas!" they muttered as they went forth who
35 had gathered there. Crowded by the brahmins in *ruru* deerskins,
Bhīmasena and Dhanaṃjaya* found their going hard. When they had
freed themselves from the press of the people, and while their enemies
quizzically stared at them, the two champions followed by Kṛṣṇā
shone radiantly.
Their mother had been worrying much that they might have come
to grief, when the time of begging was past and her sons did not
return. Could the sons of Dhṛtarāṣṭra have recognized the bulls of the
Kurus and killed them? Or had they been killed by most loathsome
Rākṣasas, gifted with magic, who continued their feud? But still,
could even the great-spirited Vyāsa's prediction be belied? In this
40 fashion did Pṛtha worry, filled with love for her sons. Then, far into
the afternoon, Jiṣṇu, like the sun surrounded by clouds, entered with
the brahmins, preceded by the Brahman.

Vaiśaṃpāyana said:

182.1 The two Pārthas went in the potter's shop,
And the powerful men found Pṛthā home,
And the lords of men, in the highest spirits,
Spoke to Kuntī of Draupadī, "Look what we found!"

She was inside the house without seeing her sons
And she merely said, "Now you share that together!"
Later on did Kuntī set eyes on the girl
And cried out, "Woe! O what have I said!"

Afraid to prove lawless and much ashamed
—While Draupadī was exceedingly trustful—
She took the girl by the hand and went in
And spoke this word to Yudhiṣṭhira:

"This girl, the child of King Drupada
Was presented to me by your younger brothers,
And I said, son, as I am wonted to do,
But carelessly, 'Now you share that together!'

5 "Now tell me, bull of the Kurus, how
This word of mine is not made a lie,
Or how the girl of the king of Pāñcāla
Incurs not an Unlaw such as never has been!"

And the king sat pondering there for a while,
That most august King Yudhiṣṭhira,

* = Arjuna.

Then the Kaurava hero comforted Kuntī
And spoke this word to Dhanaṃjaya:

"It was you who won Draupadī, Pāṇḍava,
And *you* shall make the princess content!
Let the fire be lit and an offering made,
And you take her hand by the proper rite!"

Arjuna said:

Do not make me, king, share in lawlessness:
This is *not* the Law that the others accept.
You yourself should be the first to wed,
Then strong-armed Bhīma of wondrous feats,

I next and Nakula after me,
And Sahadeva the last of us all.
The Wolf-Belly, I, and the twins, O prince,
All hold that the girl should go to you!

10 What now in this pass had better be done,
Think upon it and do what brings Law and honor,
And will also please the king of Pāñcāla—
Instruct us, we all are in your command!

Vaiśaṃpāyana said:

They all stared at the glorious Kṛṣṇa who stood there, and sat
looking at one another, holding her in their hearts. And as all these
boundlessly lustrous men gazed at Draupadī, their love became
evident, churning their senses. For the winsome beauty of the
Pāñcāla princess, created by the Creator himself, surpassed all other
women and beguiled all creatures. Kuntī's son Yudhiṣṭhira knew their
manifest feelings; and remembering the entire declaration of
15 Dvaipāyana, O bull among men, the king spoke to his brothers, lest a
breach among them occurred: "The lovely Draupadī shall be the wife
of all of us!"

Vaiśaṃpāyana said:

183.1 The sons of Pāṇḍu then all sat there
And pondered the word of the eldest of them;
And they all sat there and mused with their minds
On its meaning, those boundlessly lustrous men.

Then the chief of the Vṛṣṇis,* who had surmised
That they were the chiefs of the Kurus, came
To the potter's house with Baladeva,**
Where the champions of men had taken their seats.

* = Kṛṣṇa Vāsudeva.
** = Bala-Rāma.

Then Kṛṣṇa and Rohiṇī's son beheld
Ajātaśatru* of the long, broad arms,
Who was sitting there; and below him sat
In a circle the others, resplendent like fires.

Said Vāsudeva upon approaching
To Kuntī's son, best bearer of Law,
"I am Kṛṣṇa," and touched with his hands the feet
Of King Yudhiṣṭhira Ājamīḍha.

So did, after Kṛṣṇa, Rohiṇī's son,**
And the Kurus happily welcomed them.
Then the chiefs of the Yadus, great Bhārata,
Took the feet of their father's sister.

The chief of the Kurus Ajātaśatru
Asked Kṛṣṇa's health, then he queried him:
"How did you find us out, Vāsudeva
While we were living here in disguise?"

Replied Vāsudeva with a laugh.
"Fire, even when hidden, will out, good king!
Who, barring the Pāṇḍavas, of all men
Could be found to display such bravery?

"It was by good fortune that all of you
Escaped from that fire, ye enemy-scourges!
Good fortune that evil Duryodhana
And his councillors failed in their design!

"Good luck to you! May, hid in your cave,
You prosper like fire that is set ablaze!
Now, lest one of the kings may find you out,
The two of us must repair to our camp."

Dismissed by the Pāṇḍava, always-lustrous
Kṛṣṇa and brother departed thence quickly.

Vaiśaṃpāyana said:

184.1 Dhṛṣṭadyumna Pāñcālya had followed the two scions of Kuru when they went to the potter's dwelling. He made his men hide themselves, and he himself sat unobserved near the house of the potter.

In the evening Bhīma, churner of foes,
And Jiṣṇu as well as the powerful twins,
Having done their begging with happy hearts,
Handed Yudhiṣṭhira what they'd received.

* = Yudhiṣṭhira.
** = Bala-Rāma.

Upon that time the sweet-spoken Kuntī
Addressed this word to Drupada's daughter:
"My dear, you take first and offer it up
To the God; and then give the brahmin an alms,

"Give some to the people who want for it,
To those who are lying about this house,
Then divide the remainder into two portions,
One for the four, and for me, and yourself,

"Give the other half to our Bhīma, dear,
Whose bulk matches that of a rutting bull,
That swarthy young man of the solid body;
For he, our champion, always eats much!"

And that king's daughter quite cheerfully,
Not misdoubting these virtuous words of Kuntī,
Religiously did as she was told,
And all of them then partook of the food.

Sahadeva, Mādrī's son, now quickly
Spread out on the ground a *kuśa* grass bed.
Each spread on top of that his own deerskin
And thus all the heroes slept on the earth.

Toward the region blest by Agastya
The excellent Kurus laid their heads.
By the side of their heads did Kuntī lie,
And Kṛṣṇā lay athwart at their feet.

So she lay on the floor with the sons of Pāṇḍu,
As though rendered a foot pillow on the grass;
And no grievance arose in her for that,
Nor did she despise the bulls of the Kurus.

The champions now began to spin tales,
Most wondrous tales that bore upon war,
And celestial arms, and elephants, chariots,
And swords and clubs and battle-axes.

The son of the king of Pāñcāla heard
The stories that they were telling each other,
And all his men had occasion to see
How Kṛṣṇā was humbly lying there.

Then Prince Dhṛṣṭadyumna, to recount it all,
What took place in the night and what tales were spun,
To recount it all to King Drupada,
Made a hasty departure for the king.

The great-spirited king of Pāñcāla, dejected,
For failing to find the Pāṇḍavas.
Now put his question to Dhṛṣṭadyumna:
"Where has she gone, who has taken Kṛṣṇā?

15 "Is she owned by a serf, of lowly birth,
Or a commoner who pays taxes to me?
Has perchance a foot been set on my head?
Has the garland been cast on the burning ground?

"Or a man of distinguished baronial line?
Or perhaps a brahmin of higher rank?
Or has perchance a left foot humbled
My head, O son, by defiling Kṛṣṇā?

"Or may I confidently sacrifice
For having allied with the bulllike Pārtha?
Tell me in truth, what powerful man
Has won today this daughter of mine?

"Can it be that Vicitravīrya's scions,
The sons of Pāṇḍu, are still alive,
And the youngest Pārtha perchance today
Took up the bow and brought down the target?"

Vaiśaṃpāyana said:

185.1 Upon these words of his father, the prince
Dhṛṣṭadyumna, the pride of the Somakas,
Recounted with joy to his father the king
What had happened, and *who* had taken Kṛṣṇā.

"That youth with the handsome long red eyes,
In black deerskin clad, of form divine,
Who corded that ultimate bow with its string
And brought the target down to the earth,

"Left unconcernedly with all speed,
Surrounded and lauded by eminent brahmins;
And he strode as Indra upon the Daityas
Attended by all hosts of Gods and seers.

"And Kṛṣṇā took hold of his trailing deerskin,
And joyously followed, cow after elephant,
While the lords of men became indignant,
Waxed wroth, and together fell on him.

5 "Thereon one other amidst the princes
Uprooted a full-grown tree from the earth,

And drove those rivers of kings to flight
As wrathful Death drives the breathing creatures.

"While the kings were watching, O lord of men,
Those two great men took Kṛṣṇā and went,
Resplendent together like moon and sun,
To a potter's workshop outside the city.

"And there, like a flame of fire, a woman
Was sitting, methinks the mother of them,
In the midst of three firelike heroes of men,
Who sat around her as so many fires.

"The two then greeted the woman's feet
And spoke to Kṛṣṇā to greet her too.
They stood there and handed Kṛṣṇā over,
And then the great men went out abegging.

" 'Twas Kṛṣṇā who took from them the alms,
And offered it up and fed the brahmin,
Then portioned the food out to the old woman,
And those five heroes, and ate herself.

10 "They all went to sleep there, O king, together,
And Kṛṣṇā lay at their feet like a pillow.
Their bed was spread upon the bare earth
With fine antelope skins and *darbha* grass.

"With the thunderous rumble of Doomsday clouds
They began to spin tales, most wondrous tales,
And they were not tales as peasants and serfs spin,
Nor did those heroes tell brahmin tales.

"They are bulls of the barons without misdoubting,
For the tales that they told were of *war*, O king.
Our hope indeed is clearly fulfilled now—
We hear that the Pārthas escaped from the fire!

"The manner in which the bow was strung
And the mark brought down by the warrior's might,
And the way in which they talked to each other,
It is sure they're the Pārthas living in hiding!"

Now joy took hold of King Drupada,
And he sent at once his family priest:
"Go tell them, We know you! Are you perchance
The great-spirited princes, the sons of Pāṇḍu?"

15 The family priest took the word of the king,
And went and gave voice to his praise of them.
And knowing of order he gave in right order
The message entire of the king to them:

"The lord of the earth desires to know you
As worthy of boons, does King Pāñcāla.
For seeing the one who shot the target,
He sees no end to his happiness.

"Now declare the descent of the line of your kinsmen
And set your feet on the heads of your foes!
And gladden with joy this heart of mine,
Of the king of Pāñcāla and all his men!

"For King Pāṇḍu was to King Drupada
A friend of much love who became like himself.
It has been his wish, 'Let this daughter of mine
Be the daughter-in-law of the Kaurava!'

"Forever was lodged in King Drupada's heart
This wish, O heroes of flawless limbs,
'Let Arjuna, he of the long, broad arms,
Find and marry my daughter according to Law!'"

20 When the priest had spoken his word in this fashion,
The prince looked up at the courteous envoy.
He gave orders to Bhīma who was beside him,
"Let water be offered to him and the guest gift.

"The priest of King Drupada is worth honor,
And highest honor be paid to him!"
This Bhīma did, O lord of men,
And the other agreed to accept the homage.

When the family priest was sitting at ease,
Yudhiṣṭhira spoke to the brahmin thus:
"The Pāñcāla king has bestowed his daughter
As his own Law found and his wish desired.

"King Drupada set a price for her,
And this hero has won her accordingly;
No dispute can arise as to his class,
His living, his lineage, or family.

"She has been bestowed by the fact of the bow
Being corded, the fact of the mark being hit.

And thus the great-spirited man has won
This Kṛṣṇā amidst the hosts of the kings.

25 "As this is the case, the Somaka king
Ought neither to regret nor to feel dismay.——
Yet the very desire of King Drupada
Has happily come to be true for the king.

"For methinks this maid of the king of men
Was unattainable, brahmin, by rights.
For no one of failing strength could have joined
That bow to the bowstring in such a way,
Nor one of low birth or unskilled with arms
Could have brought the target down as it was.

"Therefore on this day the king of Pāñcāla
Ought to have no regrets in the cause of his child.
And no man on earth can alter the fact
That he overcame and brought down the mark!"

And while Yudhiṣṭhira thus held forth,
Another and second man came from the side
Of the king of Pāñcālas, making great haste,
To announce on the spot that the feast was prepared.

1(13) *The Wedding*

186–91 (B. 194–99; C. 7203–1365)
186 (194; 7203). The messenger invites the bridegroom's party to the wedding. The Pāṇḍavas, Kuntī, and Draupadī go to the king's palace. Drupada has laid out a variety of articles pertaining to different trades and classes (1–5). Kuntī and Draupadī withdraw to the women's quarters. The Pāṇḍavas take baronial seats and eat baronial food; afterward, they pass up the exhibited articles for the weapons (5–15).
187 (195; 7218). Drupada asks Yudhiṣṭhira to identify himself, and he does so, to the king's joy (1–10). Drupada curses Dhṛtarāṣṭra and promises to restore the Pāṇḍavas. Meanwhile, he invites them to stay (10–15). Then he announces Draupadī's marriage to Arjuna. Yudhiṣṭhira declares that she will be their common wife (15–20). Drupada protests, and Yudhiṣṭhira remonstrates (20–30). Drupada counsels a delay for deliberation. Vyāsa arrives (30).

188 (196; 7252). Vyāsa is welcomed and questioned about the propriety of the marriage; he asks for their own views (1–5). Drupada is against, Dhṛṣṭadyumna undecided (5–10), Yudhiṣṭhira and Kuntī are in favor. Vyāsa agrees. He retires with Drupada to the inner chambers (10–20).
189 (197; 7275). The Story of the Five Indras.
190 (198; 7329). Drupada now acquiesces in the marriage. Vyāsa tells Yudhiṣṭhira to wed Draupadī. The crowds gather. Dhaumya performs the rite for Yudhiṣṭhira and the others, each a day apart; every day Draupadī becomes a virgin again (1–10). Draupadī's dowry (15).
191 (199; 7347). Kuntī blesses Draupadī (1–10). Kṛṣṇā Vāsudeva sends wedding gifts (10–15).

186.1 "For the bridegroom's party King Drupada
Has prepared a feast for the wedding rite.
Your devotions done, you must come with Kṛṣṇā
To Drupada's palace; do not delay!

"Here are chariots, worthy of kings, that are yoked
With fine horses and decked with lotuses golden.
Do mount them, ye all, and come the distance
To the palace grounds of the king of Pāñcāla!"

Vaiśampāyana said:
Thereupon the bulls of the Kurus departed,
And started the priest ahead of themselves.
They rode on those spacious chariots thither,
And Kuntī and Kṛṣṇā rode one together.

When hearing, O king, from his family priest
The words that King Dharma had used to him,
King Drupada, to discover the Kurus,
Now gathered together all manner of things.

5 There were fruit and artfully woven garlands,
And hides and shields as well as stools,
And cattle, O king, and skeins of ropes,
And other gear of the peasantry.

And whatever tools are employed in the trades
Were all and completely provided for,
And articles too that are used in games—
The king had them all collected there.

Magnificent chariot horses and armor,
Large swords and chariots brilliantly painted,
And bows of the choicest and shafts of the best,
And lances and spears that were inlaid with gold.

So javelins, catapults, battle axes,
And all variegated weapon gear,
And likewise couches and seats were there
Of all kinds and of excellent craftsmanship.

Kuntī took the good Kṛṣṇā in charge
And went into Drupada's women quarters.
And the women there, not at all uneager,
Paid court to the wife of the Kaurava king.

10 And casting their glance on the heroes of men
With the eyes of big bulls, and their cloaks of deerskin,
That hid their left shoulders, their lion's stride,
Their long arms that curved like the coils of great snakes,

The king and the councillors all of the king
And the sons of the king and the kinsmen too
And all the retainers together, O king,
Were plunged on the spot in exceeding joy.

The heroes themselves, with nary a thought,
Sought out the best thrones with separate footstools.
The eminent men sat according to age,
Without surprise at the splendor of them.

All manner of food that was worthy of kings
In dishes and bowls of silver and gold
Were brought up by servants and serving wenches
And cooks who were clad in fine clean clothes.

And having eaten, the heroes of men,
And relaxing with utter confidence,
Then passed by the riches that were laid out:
The warriors went for the weapon gear.

The which observing, Drupada's son,
And the king with all his chief councillors,
Approached and paid court with great happiness
To the Pāṇḍavas, sons and grandsons of kings.

Vaiśaṃpāyana said:

187.1 The splendid Pāñcālya then addressed Prince Yudhiṣṭhira in the manner employed with brahmins. In cheerful spirits he questioned the resplendent son of Kuntī: "How should we know you, as barons or brahmins? Or peasants of quality? Or men born from the wombs of serfs? Or as Siddhas that roam all the horizons and, employing their wizardry, have arrived from heaven to look for Kṛṣṇā? Tell us the truth, sir, for we are in great uncertainty on this! When our doubts have ended, shall our hearts be content? Shall our share of fate prove propitious, enemy-burner? Speak the truth with all your heart. Among kings, truthfulness shines forth over sacrifice and gifts, and thus no lie must be spoken. After hearing your word, enemy-tamer of the aspect of an Immortal, I shall surely inaugurate the wedding accordingly."

Yudhiṣṭhira said:

Do not be downhearted, sire; be joyous, Pāñcālya! For the wish you have cherished has doubtless come true. For we are barons, sire, the sons of the great-spirited Pāṇḍu! Know me for the eldest Kaunteya. These are Bhīmasena and Arjuna, by whom your daughter was won in the assembly of kings. The twins are waiting there with Kṛṣṇā. Banish all grief from your heart: we are barons, bull among kings! Like a lotus bed, your daughter has gone from one pond to another! This is the truth that I proclaim to you, great king, for you are our guru and highest recourse.

Vaiśaṃpāyana said:

King Drupada's eyes were dimmed with joy, and at first he could not answer Yudhiṣṭhira properly. Then the scourge of his enemies gained control over his bliss, and the king made a befitting answer to Yudhiṣṭhira. The law-minded Drupada enquired of him how they had escaped that time, and the Pāṇḍava told him everything from the beginning. When the king heard the tale from Kuntī's son, he reviled the Lord Dhṛtarāṣṭra. Drupada reassured Kuntī's son Yudhiṣṭhira, and eloquently promised to restore him to the kingdom. Thereupon Kuntī and Kṛṣṇā, Bhīmasena and Arjuna, and the twins were invited by the king into the large palace; and there they stayed, honored by Yajñasena, O king.

Later the king and his sons said to the brothers who had taken new courage, "Today the scion of Kuru should take her hand in ritual fashion. On this auspicious day the strong-armed Arjuna should make the occasion!" Upon this, King Yudhiṣṭhira the son of Law said to him, "Then I too must take my wife, lord of the people!"

Drupada said:

Then you should rather take my daughter's hand by the rite, or assign Kṛṣṇā to whomever you wish, hero!

Yudhiṣṭhira said:

Draupadī shall be the common queen of us all, sire, for this has my mother said, lord of the people. I am still unmarried and so is Bhīmasena Pāṇḍava. She was won by the Pārtha, your daughter—

and she is a treasure. We have a covenant that we share together every treasure, king! We do not want to give up our covenant now, good king. By Law, Kṛṣṇā will be the common queen of all of us. She shall take the hand of each of us, one after another, before the fire.

Drupada said:

It is laid down that one man may have many queens, scion of Kuru, but *never* that one woman may have many men! Law-minded and pure as you are, you may not perpetrate such a breach of the Law that runs counter to *Veda* and world, Kaunteya! Whence such a design in you?

Yudhiṣṭhira said:

The Law is subtle, great king, and we do not know its course. We follow one after the other the path that was traveled by the Ancient. My voice does not tell a lie, nor does my mind dwell on lawlessness! Thus has our mother spoken, and this is my own desire. This is certain Law, O king; obey it unhesitantly. Let there be no misdoubting of it whatever by you, my prince!

Drupada said:

You yourself, Kaunteya, and Kuntī and my son Dhṛṣṭadyumna must deliberate what is to be done now. On the morrow we shall act.

Vaiśaṃpāyana said:

So they all assembled and deliberated, O Bhārata. Then Dvaipāyana chanced to arrive.

Vaiśaṃpāyana said:

188.1 All the Pāṇḍavas and the glorious Dhṛṣṭadyumna, as soon as they saw him, rose to meet the great-spirited Kṛṣṇa and welcomed him. He returned their greetings and inquired about their health. At last the great-minded seer sat down on a sparkling golden seat. With boundlessly lustrous Kṛṣṇa's leave, they all, those greatest of men, sat down on their precious thrones. After a while Drupada Pārṣata began to speak in a gentle voice and questioned the great-spirited sage anent Draupadī, O lord of the people. "How can one woman be the wife of many men," he said, "and yet the Law be not broken? Declare it all to us, good sir, how this can be."

Vyāsa said:

On this Law, which is mocked and runs counter to *Veda* and the world, I wish to hear the view of each of you.

Drupada said:

In my view, it is a breach of the Law, contrary to *Veda* and the world, for one wife of many men is not found, good brahmin. Nor has this Law been practiced by the Ancient of great spirits. This Law of polyandry is not the eternal Law to be obeyed. Hence, I cannot resolve to put it into practice; for to me all of it appears to be riddled with doubts on the lawfulness thereof.

Dhṛṣṭadyumna said:

10 But then, how can an elder brother have congress with the wife of his younger brother, brahmin, bull of the twiceborn, and still be strict in his virtue, ascetic? Surely, the Law is too subtle for us to know its course entirely! The likes of us cannot decide whether it is Law or a breach of Law, brahmin; hence, I come to no decision at all on whether Kṛṣṇā should be the consort of the five.

Yudhiṣṭhira said:

My voice does not tell a lie, nor does my mind dwell on lawlessness! As my thoughts favor it, it cannot be a breach of Law at all! We hear in the ancient Lore that a Gautamī by the name of Jaṭilā lay with the Seven Seers, O greatest of all the upholders of Law. They also say, most law-wise sage, that the word of a guru is Law, and of all gurus the mother is the first. And she has said the word: "Share as you share the alms." Hence, greatest of brahmins, I hold it is Law.

Kuntī said:

It is as the law-obeying Yudhiṣṭhira says. My fear of lies is severe. How shall I escape the Lie?

Vyāsa said:

You shall escape the lie, my dear. It is the eternal Law. But I shall not divulge it all to all of you; the Pāñcāla must hear it from me by himself, how this Law came to be ordained and whence it eternally came. There is no doubt that it *is* the Law, as Yudhiṣṭhira has said.

Vaiśaṃpāyana said:

The blessed lord Vyāsa Dvaipāyana rose and took the king by the hand and entered the king's chambers. The Pāṇḍavas, Kuntī, and Dhṛṣṭadyumna Pārṣata remained cheerlessly behind and waited for both to return. Thereupon Dvaipāyana related to the great-spirited king how the Law came to be that these many men would have one wife.

1(13.a) The Five Indras

189 (B. 197; C. 7275–7328)

189 (197; 7275). Vyāsa recounts that the Gods and Yama once attended a Sacrificial Session; Yama being preoccupied, no more men died. The Gods demur to Brahmā, who reassures them (1–5). The Gods see a golden lotus float down the river. Indra investigates and sees a woman weeping in the stream (5–10). She leads him to a handsome youth playing dice on the Himālaya. Indra identifies himself as the king of the Gods, but the other pays no attention. When Indra grows indignant, the other immobilizes him with a glance. The alien God orders the woman to bring Indra closer and at her touch he collapses. The God orders Indra to roll away a mountain; in the cave Indra sees four other Indras, previously incarcerated for similar insolence. The Bowman sends all five Indras to earth to be reborn. The Indras ask to be begotten by Dharma, the Wind, Indra, and the Aśvins (10–25). The Bowman grants this and seeks Nārāyaṇa's agreement, which is given. The latter plucks a white and a black hair from his head. The hairs are inserted in Rohiṇi's and Devakī's wombs; they give birth to the light Balarāma and the dark Kṛṣṇa (25–30). Vyāsa explains that the five Indras are the Pāṇḍavas, Draupadī is Lakṣmī; they were destined for each other. He gives Drupada the vision that enables him to see them in their real shapes, and recounts how Śiva granted a hermit girl five husbands (30–45).

Vyāsa said:

189.1 In the olden days the Gods sat at a Session in the Naimiṣa Forest, O king. Yama Vaivasvata held the office of the butcher priest.

Then Yama, when consecrated, O king,
No longer killed any one of the creatures;
And thus the creatures grew numerous,
Being freed from death and the onslaught of Time.

Then Śakra, Kubera, and Varuṇa,
The Sādhyas, the Rudras, the Vasus, and Aśvins
Repaired to Prajāpati, guide of the world—
These Gods, and still others, foregathered there.

And, assembled, they spoke to the sovereign teacher:
"Our fear is severe from this waxing of men.
And atremble with fear, and our joys to pursue,
We have all come seeking shelter with you."

Brahmā said:

5 Why should you stand in fear of man, when you all are immortal? Let there never be fear in you from mortals.

The Gods said:

Since the mortals have become immortal, there is no difference anymore. And, upset by this equality, we have come here to seek difference!

Brahmā said:

The Session keeps Yama occupied,
And that is the reason that men do not die.
When he's done with the rite with his single mind,
The time of death will return for them.

Vaivasvata's body will strengthen thereby,
And employed with the vigor of you yourselves,
It will spell their end at the time of death–
And might it will mean over humankind!

Vyāsa said:

After hearing this word of the firstborn God,
The Gods went where Gods were sacrificing.
As they mightily sat there together assembled
They saw a lotus float down the Ganges.

And when they saw it, they were surprised.
And Indra went up there, the champion of them.
He saw a woman, splendid like fire,
Where the Ganges springs sempiternally.

The woman was crying and, looking for water,
Had plunged in the Ganges and stood in the river.
The drops of her tears fell down in the water
And each became a lotus of gold.

Observing that wonder, the Thunderbolt-wielder
Came closer and questioned the woman there:
"Who are you and what is the cause of your weeping?
Pray tell me the truth if it pleases you."

The woman said:

Indeed, you shall know who I am, O Śakra,
And why I am weeping in my misfortune.
Come, king, I shall go and lead the way,
You yourself shall see wherefore I weep.

Vyāsa said:

He followed her while she led the way,
And he saw nearby a handsome youth,
On a lion-throne seated, young women about him,
Playing at dice on a Himālayan peak.

Quoth Indra: "I am the king of the Gods
And all the world is under my sway!
I am the lord!" said he in anger
As he saw the other absorbed in the game.

The God looked up at the angry Śakra
And laughed at Indra and gently watched him.
And under his gaze the king of the Gods
Grew stiff in his body and stood like a tree trunk.

When he had then become bored with the game,
He said to the Goddess, who was still weeping,
"Now bring him a little closer to me;
We shall see that his pride will no more seize him."

And Śakra, no sooner than touched by the woman,
Felt his limbs go limp and he fell on the ground.
Said the blessed Lord of awesome splendor,
"Now never, Śakra, do this again!

"Roll away this mighty king of the mountains,
For your might and strength are immeasurable.
And when you have done so, enter its center:
There are others like you that are light like the sun."

20 Away he rolled the top of the mountain
And saw four others who matched his splendor;
And seeing this he was much upset:
"Shall I perchance become like them?"

Said the Mountain God to the Thunderbolt-wielder
While he widened his eyes to show his wrath,
"You, much-offered Indra, enter the cave,
For you have in your folly insulted me!"

At these words of the Lord the king of the Gods
Was shaken with shudders because of the curse,
And his limbs went limp, like a fig tree leaf
That is stirred by a breeze on a mountain peak.

Hands humbly folded and face bent down,
And shivering at the God's sudden speech,
He said to the Dread One of many forms,
"Blessed lord, pray see an escape today!"

The God of the Dread Bow laughed and said,
"They who act like this find here no escape.
These ones too shall once more become.
Therefore, enter this cave and lie down in it.

25 "There shall be an escape for you all, no doubt.
You shall all enter a human womb,
Having wrought great feats of violence there
And sped many others to their deaths,

"You shall go again to the world of Indra,
The precious world you had won with your acts,
All this that I say shall be carried out,
And much else of varied significance."

The previous Indras said:

We shall go from the Gods to the world of men
Where release is declared to be hard to obtain.
But Gods must beget us upon our mother,
God Dharma, the Wind God, God Indra, the Aśvins.

Vyāsa said:

Having heard this word, the Thunderbolt-wielder
Once more addressed the greatest of Gods:
"With my seed I shall father a man for that task,
Who shall be their fifth and be born my son."

The blessed Lord of the Dreadful Bow
Good-naturedly granted the wish they asked
And ordained that a woman, beloved of the world,
Śrī herself, should be their wife among men.

30 Together with them the God then repaired
To the measureless God Nārāyaṇa.
He too ordained that it should be so,
And so it befell all were born on earth.

God Hari had plucked two hairs of his head;
One hair was white, the other was black.
These hairs then went into the Yadu women,
Into Rohiṇī and Devakī.
The one of them became Baladeva,
The other, the black one, Keśava.

Those Indra forms that of yore were cloistered
Inside that cave of the lofty mountain,
Have been born here the powerful Pāṇḍavas;
The Left-Handed Archer is Indra's part.

It is thus that the Pāṇḍavas came to be
Who before had been Indras, O king of the land;
And of old was Lakṣmī ordained for them
As their wife and became divine Draupadī.

For how could a woman arise from the earth
At the end of the rite save by God's intercession?
She whose beauty shines like the moon and sun
And whose fragrance blows as far as a league?

35 O king of men, as a favor to thee
I shall give you one more most wonderful boon:
The eyesight of Gods. See the sons of Kuntī
Endowed with their former celestial bodies!

Vaiśaṃpāyana said:

Then Vyāsa of the most liberal works
And brahmin pure bestowed on the king
By his power of mortification the Eye;
And he saw them all in their previous forms.

He beheld the youths divine with golden
Garlands and diadems, each like an Indra,
With the color of sun and fire, adorned
With jewels, broad-chested, and five ell tall.

In celestial dustless goldcloth robes,
Exceeding resplendent with choicest of garlands
Like Three-Eyed Gods, or celestial Vasus,
Or like Ādityas endowed with all graces;
And when he had seen the previous Indras
King Drupada was pleased and surprised.

With the magic divine that has no measure
The king saw the maid, who was Śrī embodied,
The excellent maiden, now prosperous,
Who matched them in beauty, splendor, and fame.

40 Upon beholding this miracle great,
He clasped the feet of Satyavatī's son:
"For you, great seer, this is no wonder!"
Quoth the king to him in a tranquil spirit.

Vyāsa said:

In a wilderness of austerities there once lived a daughter of a great-
spirited seer. Beautiful though she was, she found no husband. Now,
they say, with awesome austerities she satisfied Śaṃkara,* and being
pleased the Lord of his own accord said to the maiden, "Choose a
boon!" At his words the maiden said to the Lord of Gods, the boon-
granting Śaṃkara, "I wish a husband who has all virtues," and said
it again and again. The benevolent Lord of Gods gave her the boon:
"You shall have five excellent husbands!" said Śaṃkara. She
45 propitiated the God and again said: "I deserve one husband from you,
endowed with virtues!" Thereupon the God of Gods, who was in
benign spirits, spoke these hallowed words: "Five times you have said
to me, 'Give me a husband,' and so shall it be, my dear—good luck

* = Śiva.

shall befall you—when you have gone to another body, it shall be as you have said."

So, Drupada, this daughter was born to you, beautiful as a Goddess. Kṛṣṇā Pārṣatī has been ordained to be the wife of the five and remain blameless. Celestial Śrī, after having done her dread mortifications, arose at the grand sacrifice and became your daughter.

The effulgent Goddess sought by the Gods,
Sole wife to the five by the acts she performed,
The Creator created as wife to the Gods,
And hearing this, Drupada, act as you wish.

1(13) The Wedding (concluded)

Drupada said:

190.1 'Twas because I had not heard your word
That I strove, great seer, to act as I did.
What has been ordained cannot be undone.
And this indeed is the ordinance set.

The knot of fate cannot be untied.
There is nothing on earth ordained by one's acts.
The arrangements made for the sake of one wooer
Are the ordinance set for the sake of many.

Since Kṛṣṇā had said in the days of yore
"May the blessed Lord give me many a husband,"
He pronounced his boon in the way she asked.
The God surely knows the best of it.

As Śaṃkara has ordained it so,
Whether lawful or lawless, I bear no guilt.
Let them take her hand in the ritual way,
As they please, for to them is Kṛṣṇā ordained!

Vaiśaṃpāyana said:

5 The blessed lord then said to King Dharma,
"Today is a day of good augury.
The moon today is conjoined with Puṣya.
Take Kṛṣṇā's hand the first of all."

King Yajñasena thereon and his son
Set out much wealth for the bridegroom's party,
And had Kṛṣṇā his daughter brought in to him;
She had bathed, and was decked with gems abounding.

And all his friends and his kin came there,
And the ministers gathered and councillors,
To watch the wedding in confident spirit,
And so did the brahmins and notable townfolk.

His palace adorned with crowds of beggars,
The festive grounds thick with lotuses,
And, brilliant with piles of precious gems,
Shone like heaven sparkling with bright stars.

The young sons of the king of the Kauravas,
Adorned with earrings and ornaments,
And robed in fine clothes and scented with sandal,
Performed their ablutions and hallowing rites.

They entered with Dhaumya in proper pomp,
Their family priest with the luster of fire,
All entered by age the assembly room,
As bulls the cow pen, with joyous mien.

The *Veda*-wise Dhaumya then built a fire;
Having lit it, he offered with apposite spells;
Likewise with spells he brought forward and joined
Yudhiṣṭhira now together with Kṛṣṇā.

The *Veda*-wise priest then made them both walk,
Hands joined, the deasil around the fire.
Then the priest took leave of Yudhiṣṭhira,
Resplendent in war, and left the king's house.

One after the other, a day apart,
The warrior sons of the king of men,
The beautiful scions of Kuru's line,
Took each the hand of the choicest of brides.

And this great wonder the seer declared,
A wonder surpassing the power of man,
That the beautiful bride of majestic might
Each day became a virgin again.

When the wedding was done, King Drupada
Gave the warriors plentiful bounty of gifts,
A hundred of chariots, wrought with gold,
That were yoked with four horses with bridles of gold.

A hundred of elephants, lotus-marked,
Like a hundred mountains with golden peaks,
And a hundred handmaids in beautiful youth
Who were preciously garlanded, robed, and bedecked.

In the presence of Fire the Somaka king
Gave riches to each by the myriad,
Like robes and costly ornaments
And other great bounty befitting his might.

When the wedding was done and the Pāṇḍavas
Had received their Śrī with fullness of treasure,
They disported themselves like the equals of Indra
In the king of Pāñcāla's capital seat.

Vaiśaṃpāyana said:

191.1 When Drupada had entered into an alliance with the Pāṇḍavas,
he lost all fear, even of Gods. Great-spirited Drupada's ladies came to
Kuntī, mentioned their names, and touched her feet with their heads.
Kṛṣṇā, too, dressed in her linen gown, with the marriage thread tied,
made obeisance to her mother-in-law and stood bowed with folded
hands. Lovingly, Pṛthā bestowed her blessing on Draupadī, who was
gifted with beauties and the marks of good fortune, and accomplished
in manners and deportment.
5 "As Indrāṇī is to the bay-horsed God," said she, "as Svāhā to the
sacred Fire, as Rohiṇī to the Moon, as Damayantī to Nala, as Bhadrā
to Vaiśravaṇa, as Arundhatī to Vasiṣṭha, and as Lakṣmī to
Nārāyaṇa, so be thou to thy husbands! Bear live children, bear man-
children, and be, my dear, joined with much happiness, favored with
love, and gifted with joy! Be thou the Wife at their sacrifices, strict
in thy vows, and may the years forever go by thee in the solemn
homage of guests that come, of holy men, of children, of the old, and
of your elders. Be thou anointed Queen, after thy law-loving King,
10 in the cities and kingdoms, before all in the Jungle of the Kurus. When
the might of thy powerful husbands has conquered this entire earth,
make of her a present to the brahmins at a great Horse Sacrifice.
What precious treasures the earth may hold, O treasure of virtue,
obtain them in happiness for a hundred autums. As I bless thee now,
bride, in thy linen raiment, so shall I bless thee again when thou hast
virtuously born a son."
Hari,* upon the Pāṇḍavas's taking a wife, sent them golden jewelry
that was brilliantly set with pearls and beryls. The Mādhava also sent
costly clothes from different countries, blankets, furs, and gems, good
15 to touch and fine, and all kinds of good bedding and stools, and
hundreds of vessels that sparkled with beryls and diamonds. Kṛṣṇa
presented them with serving wenches from different countries by the
thousands, all pretty and young and handy, and handsomely
ornamented; well-trained, tame elephants, and beautifully caparisoned,
thoroughbred horses, and finely controlled chariots that were decked

* = Kṛṣṇa Vāsudeva.

with sparkling gold cloth. And Madhusūdana,* whose spirit is measureless, sent them unworked gold bullion by the millionworth. Yudhiṣṭhira, the King Dharma, accepted it all with the greatest pleasure, for he wished Govinda* well.

1(14) The Coming of Vidura

192–97 (B. 200–206; C. 7366–7544).
192 (200; 7366). News spreads to the baronage that the Pāṇḍavas and Kuntī are alive; they are surprised and pleased (1–5). The Dhārtarāṣṭras return home in low spirits and in fear of the Pāṇḍavas and their new allies (5–15). Vidura delights in the news and tells Dhṛtarāṣṭra that Draupadī has been won. The king, at first understanding that Duryodhana was the winner, recovers and praises the Pāṇḍavas. Vidura agrees with this praise, (15–25). Duryodhana and Karṇa protest against his sentiments (25).
193 (201; 7396). Dhṛtarāṣṭra now takes his son's side, apologizing for favoring Vidura, and asks for his and Karṇa's views. Duryodhana offers many alternative plans to estrange Drupada, Draupadī, and the Pāṇḍavas (1–15).
194 (202; 7416). Repudiating Duryodhana, Karṇa points out that the Pāṇḍavas cannot be alienated (1–10). He counsels that they war at once before they have struck root among their allies, and before Kṛṣṇa arrives. He advocates war power (10–20). Dhṛtarāṣṭra lauds Karṇa, but waits for more advice (20–25).
195 (203; 7441). Bhīṣma declares that the Pāṇḍavas have as much right to the kingdom as the Dhārtaraṣṭras and advises that they partition the kingdom (1–5). He admonishes Duryodhana (5) and confesses his own discomfiture at earlier attempts to unseat the Pāṇḍavas (5–15).
196 (204; 7460). Droṇa agrees with Bhīṣma and speaks for conciliating the Pāṇḍavas and for their return (1–10). Duḥśāsana should receive them with all honors (10). Karṇa protests acidulously; he quotes the parable of the fainéant *king whose minister tried to divest him of his kingship, but unsuccessfully: if kingship is ordained, it cannot be taken away (10–25). Droṇa takes exception to*

* = Kṛṣṇa Vāsudeva.

Karṇa's tone and predicts the doom of the Bhāratas (25).
197 (205; 7488). Vidura upholds the impartiality of Bhīṣma and Droṇa (1–10). Speaking to Dhṛtarāṣṭra, he stresses the latter's responsibility to the Pāṇḍavas as well. Besides, the Pāṇḍavas are invincible and allied with Drupada (10–25). The evil trio of Duryodhana, Karṇa, and Śakuni must fail in the end (25).
198 (206; 2718). Dhṛtarāṣṭra agrees that the Pāṇḍavas are his responsibility (1–5) and sends Vidura to bring them back. Vidura arrives at Drupada's, is courteously received by the king, the Pāṇḍavas, and Kṛṣṇa and presents gifts to the Pāṇḍavas (5–10). He pleads with Drupada that the Pāṇḍavas depart with him (15–25).

Vaiśaṃpāyana said:
192.1 Trusted runners brought tidings to the kings that the beautiful
Draupadī had been bestowed as wife upon the Pāṇḍavas; that the
great-spirited man who had strung the bow and hit the mark was
Arjuna, the greatest of victors and mighty bowman; and that the
strong man who had lifted up Śalya, the king of Madra, and spun him
around, and who had angrily threatened the men in the fight with a
tree, while he, great-spirited, had shown no fear, had been Bhīma of
the terrible touch, the downfall of the armies of his enemies.
5 When they heard that the sons of King Pāṇḍu and Kuntī had been
disguised as brahmins, the kings of men were greatly surprised, for
before they had heard that Kuntī and her sons had been burned alive.
"They have been *reborn*!" Thus all the kings thought of them, and
they cursed Bhīṣma and Dhṛtarāṣṭra Kaurava for that most cruel deed
that Purocana had perpetrated. And when the bridegroom choice was
over, all those kings went out the way they had come, in the
knowledge that the Pāṇḍavas had been chosen.
Prince Duryodhana too returned with his brothers in low spirits,
10 and with Aśvatthāman his maternal uncle,* Karṇa, and Kṛpa, when
he saw that Arjuna of the white stallions had been chosen by
Draupadī. Shamefaced, Duḥṣāsana whispered to him, "If he had not
been a brahmin, he'd never have found Draupadī. For no one knew
him rightfully for Dhanaṃjaya, prince. Fate, methinks, reigns supreme,
and man's efforts are fruitless. A curse on our manly effort, brother, if
the Pāṇḍavas are alive!" So they talked and blamed Purocana, till they
entered Hāstinapura, sad and downhearted. They trembled and all
their enterprise vanished when they found that the august Pārthas

* = Śakuni

15 had escaped the fire and were allied with Drupada, and when they thought of Dhṛṣṭadyumna and Śikhaṇḍin, and the other sons of Drupada, who were all experienced warriors.

But when Vidura heard that Draupadī had chosen the Pāṇḍavas
and that the sons of Dhṛtarāṣṭra had come back shamed and their
pride broken, the Steward, O lord of the people, said in high spirits and
with great wonder to Dhṛtarāṣṭra, "The Kurus prosper with good
fortune!" King Dhṛtarāṣṭra Vaicitravīrya, on hearing this from Vidura,
was overjoyed, O Bhārata, and exclaimed, "Good fortune indeed,
indeed!" For in his ignorance the king of men, who had merely the
eyesight of knowledge, thought that his eldest son Duryodhana had
20 been chosen by the daughter of Drupada. He ordered a great many
ornaments made for Draupadī and sent word to his son Duryodhana,
"Let Kṛṣṇā be brought in!" Later Vidura told him that the Pāṇḍavas
had been chosen, that all the heroes were in good health and had
been honored by Drupada, and that they had many other allies now,
who had armies.

Dhṛtarāṣṭra said:

Pāṇḍu's sons are to me as they were to Pāṇḍu, and even more. And that my joy has grown greater, Vidura, is methinks because the heroes are in good health and the Pāṇḍavas have allies. For what king, deprived of fortune and questing for power, would not seek the alliance of Drupada and his kinsmen, Steward?

Vaiśaṃpāyana said:

When the king talked in this vein, Vidura replied, "May this view of
25 yours last for a hundred years, sire!" Then Duryodhana and Karṇa
Rādheya came up to Dhṛtarāṣṭra and said to him, "We cannot speak
with you in the presence of Vidura, sire. We shall speak in private.
What is this you now wish to do? Do you take the success of your
rivals for your own, father? You praise them in Vidura's presence,
greatest of men! You do one thing when another needs doing, prince
sans blame, for now, father, we must constantly work to break their
strength. This is the time for us to take counsel on what we should do,
so that they won't swallow us up, with our sons, relations, and
armies!"

Dhṛtarāṣṭra said:

193.1 I myself have the same worries as you have. I do not want to reveal my attitude to Vidura. Therefore, I especially praise their virtues, so that Vidura does not find out my intentions by as much as a gesture. Now tell me, Suyodhana, how you think the matter lies, and you too, Rādheya, must tell me your view of it.

Duryodhana said:

Let us at once employ able and dexterous brahmins who have our

5 confidence to alienate the sons of Kuntī and the sons of Mādrī. Or we
might tempt King Drupada, his sons, and all his ministers with huge
piles of riches so that they will desert King Yudhiṣṭhira, the son of
Kuntī. Or we should persuade them to settle down there and describe
to them in all detail how disadvantageous it would be for them to live
here, so that the Pāṇḍavas will decide on staying there and be
separate from us. Or some clever and crafty men should try to
alienate their affection for one another. Or we should set Kṛṣṇā up
against them, an easy matter since they are too many; or we might
10 first alienate the Pāṇḍavas from her, and then her herself. Or else,
let some men who are clever at tricks arrange the death of Bhīmasena
from an ambush, for he is the strongest of all, and when he is dead
they will lose their enterprise and power and no longer covet the
kingdom, for he is their only resort. Arjuna is invincible in battle as
long as the Wolf-Belly covers his back; without him Phalguna is not
worth a fourth of Karṇa in a fight. Realizing their own great
weakness without Bhīmasena and knowing our strength, they will
feebly perish. If the Pārthas come here and submit to our commands,
15 then we can confidently proceed to eradicate them, king. Or we can
seduce them with pretty harlots, one after the other, so that Kṛṣṇā
gets disgusted. Or we might send Karṇa to bring them here and have
them killed by trusted dacoits in an attack on the way here.
Whichever of these stratagems you think faultless, put it at once into
practice before it is too late. As long as that bulllike king Drupada has
not fully become confident, they can be got at, but not later. This is my
view, father, which is to suppress them. What do you think, Rādheya,
am I right or not?

Karṇa said:

194.1 Duryodhana, I do not think you entirely have your wits about you.
The Pāṇḍavas cannot be overcome with trickery, scion of Kuru. For
in the past you have played subtle tricks on them to suppress them,
hero, and you failed. They were living right here, close to you, prince,
mere brats who had not grown their wings yet, and yet they would
not be held down. Now they all have their wings, they are staying
5 abroad, they have matured: I do not think they can be handled at all
with your trickery. Nor can they be yoked with vices, for they are
protected by Fate. They are suspicious and they want their ancestral
kingdom. They cannot be alienated from one another: men who are in
love with the same wife are not split. Nor could we alienate Kṛṣṇā
from them: she chose them when they were down, let alone now that
they are prospering. Women think it a desirable virtue to have more
than one husband, and Kṛṣṇā has managed; she wouldn't be
alienated so easily! King Drupada is an honorable man; he does not

want riches and surely would not desert the Kaunteyas were we to
10 give kingdoms away. Likewise, his son is an honest man and attached
to the Pāṇḍavas. Therefore, I do not think that any stratagem will
succeed with them at all.

But this much we can do, bull among men. As long as the
Pāṇḍavas have not yet struck roots, lord of the people, they can be
cut down. Favor war! As long as our party is large and the Pāñcāla's
slight, we should cut them down without any delay. As long as their
mounts are not plentiful or their allies numerous, Duryodhana
15 Gāndhāri, you must war on them quickly. War on them quickly
before the Pāñcāla king and his powerful sons decide to act. War on
them before the Vārṣṇeya* arrives, bringing his column of Yādavas, to
restore the Pāṇḍavas to the kingdom. Treasures, any kind of pleasure,
yes, his kingdom itself, anything Kṛṣṇa will sacrifice for the Pāṇḍavas'
sake, king of the land. With his war might did the great-spirited
Bharata conquer the earth. With his war might did the Chastiser of
Pāka** conquer the three worlds. It is war might that they praise in a
baron, lord of the people, and warring power is the Law of champions,
bull among kings! We must rout Drupada at once with a large,
20 fourfold army and bring the Pāṇḍavas here. No conciliation, no
bribery, no alienation can succeed in overcoming the Pāṇḍavas,
therefore kill them with war power. And after you have vanquished
them with war power you may enjoy the entire earth. I do see no
other way of doing it, sire.

Vaiśaṃpāyana said:

After he had listened to Karṇa Rādheya's discourse, majestic
Dhṛtarāṣṭra gave voice to his approbation and said: "That speech on
war might is worthy of you, a sagacious and weapon-wise son of a
charioteer! But let Bhīṣma, Droṇa, Vidura, and you two once more
25 plot the course that should bring us advantage." Thereupon the
glorious King Dhṛtarāṣṭra summoned all these councillors and took
counsel with them.

Bhīṣma said:

195.1 I shall never condone war with the sons of Pāṇḍu. Pāṇḍu was as
dear to me as Dhṛtarāṣṭra is, let there be no mistake. And I hold the
sons of Kuntī as high as the sons of Gāndhārī! I must watch over them
as you must, Dhṛtarāṣṭra. And as they are to me and the king, so they
should be to Duryodhana, and to all other Kauravas as well, Bhārata!

As this is the case, I shall want no war.
We must treat with the heroes and give them land:
They are chiefs of the Kurus, and this is the realm
That their forebears swayed and their father held.

* = Kṛṣṇa Vāsudeva.
** = Indra.

5 Just as you look on the kingdom as your ancestral patrimony, so
do the Pāṇḍavas. If the unfortunate Pāṇḍavas do not get the kingdom,
why should you have it, or anyone of the Bhāratas? Or if you, bull of
the Bharatas, have come by the kingdom lawfully, I think that they
have an earlier claim on it. Let us peacefully give half the kingdom to
them, for this, tiger among men, is best for all concerned. If it is done
otherwise, it will be of no avail to us, and all the infamy will fall upon
10 yourself, no doubt of it. Protect your reputation, for a good reputation
is your ultimate strength! The life of a man who has lost his
reputation is barren, they say. As long as a man's reputation survives,
Kaurava Gāndhāri, so long does he live; but he who has lost his good
name is lost. Obey this Law, which befits the lineage of the Kurus, and
act in accordance with your own ancestors, strong-armed prince. It is
by good fortune that the heroes live, good fortune that Pṛthā lives,
good fortune that the evil Purocana died frustrated in his designs!
From that time onward, after I had heard what had happened to
Kuntī, I was unable to look any living creature in the face,
15 Duryodhana. And the people do not blame Purocana as they blame
you, tiger among men! Their survival absolves you from guilt—the
sight of the Pāṇḍavas was devoutly to be wished, great prince. Even
the Thunderbolt-Wielder himself cannot take their patrimony away
while these heroes live, scion of Kuru! For they all stand by the Law,
they are all of one mind, and they have been disinherited against the
Law, especially as they hold equal title to the kingdom. If you desire to
follow the Law, if you desire to please me, and if you desire security,
give them half of the kingdom!

Droṇa said:
196.1 We have heard it said that the friends of Dhṛtarāṣṭra who have been
brought together for counseling should speak according to Law,
propriety, and honor. I am of like mind with the great-spirited
Bhīṣma, friend: the Pāṇḍavas should be given their share; that is the
eternal Law. Send at once some pleasant-spoken man to Drupada, O
Bhārata, with plentiful riches destined for the Pāṇḍavas. Let him go
and take abundant obligating gifts, and let him speak of the great
5 growth of fortune that arises from the alliance. He should say, sire,
that you and Duryodhana are greatly pleased, and repeat it over and
again, Bhārata, before Drupada and Dhṛṣṭadyumna. Let him dwell on
the suitableness and agreeableness of the alliance, while again and
again flattering the sons of Kuntī and the sons of Mādrī. At your
behest, lord of kings, let him present Draupadī with many sparkling
golden ornaments, and likewise all the sons of Drupada, bull of the
Bhāratas, all the Pāṇḍavas and Kuntī, whatever gifts are proper.
When Drupada and the Pāṇḍavas have been conciliated, he should
10 immediately propose that they return. And after the heroes have

taken their leave, let a splendid army go out and have Duḥśāsana and Vikarṇa escort them into the city. Thereafter, O best of kings, they shall, with the consent of the subjects, take their ancestral place, while you yourself should always honor them. This, I believe with Bhīṣma, O Bhārata, is the proper treatment for them as well as your sons, great king!

Karṇa said:

Both of them have been incessantly showered with largess and honors in all they did—what could be more astounding than that now they counsel against your advantage? How can a man with a malicious mind and concealing his true intent speak and make the honest approve of his words as the best advice? In times of trouble
15 friends are neither for better nor for worse. Everything waits on Fate, whether it is happiness or misery! Any man, wise or foolish, young or old, with friends or without friends, finds anything anywhere.

We hear that there once was a king in Rājagṛha who was known as Ambūvīca, the king of the barons of Magadha. That king lacked all ability, the most he could do was breathe air, and in all his affairs he depended on his minister. That minister, Mahākarṇi, became the sole master, and when he was sure he had gained power,
20 he began to despise the king. The fool took for himself all the privileges of the king, his women, his jewels and treasures, and all his powers as he saw fit. But his greed only grew from gaining what he coveted, and when he had taken all, he wanted to take the kingdom. The king lacked all ability, the most he could do was breathe air, and yet, so we hear, with all his enterprise the minister could not take his kingdom away from him. What then was his kingship, surely, if not ordained? If your kingdom has been ordained, lord of the people, it will stay with you for certain, before the eyes of all the world. And if it has been fated otherwise, you may strive all
25 you wish, but you won't have it. Knowing this, weigh the honesty and dishonesty of your councillors and scrutinize the advice of the evil as well as the good.

Droṇa said:

We know with what malice you speak and why! You are evil and broadcast your wickedness to us to get at the Pāṇḍavas. But what I say, Karṇa, is of the highest advantage and benefit to the Kurus. If you think it is wicked, then you tell what our highest advantage is! If my excellent advice is perverted, the Kurus will perish before long, that is what I think!

Vidura said:

197.1 Sire, your relations should give you their best advice, no doubt, but words do not stay with those who do not want to listen. Bhīṣma

Sāṃtanava, the first of the Kurus, has spoken to your advantage, king, but you have not accepted his advice. Droṇa likewise spoke variously to your benefit, but Karṇa Rādheya does not believe so. But when I think on it, I do not see anyone friendlier to you, or more
5 sagacious, then these two lionlike men. Both are old in age, wisdom, and learning, and both are unprejudiced in regard to either you, lord of kings, or the Pāṇḍavas. Surely, King Bhārata, in neither Law nor veracity are they inferior to Rāma Dāśarathi or Gaya! Never before have they given any bad advice or have they been found to do you any injury. Why then should these tigers among men, whose faith is their strength, not counsel what is best for you, who yourself are innocent? These good and sage men will never on earth speak crookedly in your cause, king of men. This is my basic sense, scion of
10 Kuru; and two as Law-minded as they are will not speak to one side or the other for personal gain.

Indeed, they have your best advantage at heart, Bhārata. Just as Duryodhana and the others are your sons, king, so the Pāṇḍavas are your sons, no doubt of that. If your councillors unwisely were to give advice that is inimical to the Pāṇḍavas, they would not keep your advantage in view. Or if you have greater favor in your heart for your own sons, they certainly do not help you by revealing your inner feelings.

These two great-spirited and illustrious personages have not spoken
15 unopenly; still, your decision does not go that way. What these bulls among men are saying, that the Pāṇḍavas cannot be overcome, that is true, tiger among men—and therefore good luck to you. For how can the magnificent Pāṇḍava, the left-handed archer, the burner of his enemies, be defeated in battle, king, were it by Indra himself? Great, strong-armed Bhīmasena, whose strength is like that of a myriad elephants, could he be defeated in war, even by the Immortals? Likewise the twins, deedy in battle, like sons of Yama, how can they be overpowered in a fight by anyone who wishes to live? And how could the eldest Pāṇḍava lose in war, he in whom are perseverance, compassion, forbearance, fidelity, and courage forever? Who have
20 they left to conquer who have Rāma on their side, Janārdana as their councillor, Sātyaki as their supporter? They who have Drupada as their father-in-law, and his sons, the heroic brothers led by Dhṛṣṭadyumna, as their brothers-in-law? Knowing that they cannot be overcome and that they are heirs by prior Law, you must act properly to them!

The vile infamy that besmears you because of Purocana's crime you must wipe clean by showing your favor to them now, king! The great King Drupada has been feuding with us in the past: his alliance
25 will strengthen our party, king. The Dāśārhas are mighty and

numerous, lord of the people; they will stand by Kṛṣṇa, and victory will stand by Kṛṣṇa. What man is so cursed by Fate that he would undertake with war what can be accomplished by conciliation? The people of town and countryside have heard that the Pārthas are alive and are mightily eager to see them. Give them the pleasure, sire! Duryodhana, Karṇa, and Śakuni Saubala are lawless and witless fools! Do not follow their advice! Long ago I told you, virtuous king, that this land and its subject will perish through Duryodhana's fault!

Dhṛtarāṣṭra said:
198.1 The wise Bhīṣma Śāṃtanava and the blessed seer Droṇa have
spoken to my greatest advantage, and so have you, truly! Just as the
heroic and warlike Kaunteyas are the sons of Pāṇḍu, even so they are,
by the Law, my sons too, no doubt of that. And just as this kingdom
has been ordained for my sons, even so it has been for Pāṇḍu's sons,
no doubt of that. Steward, go and bring them here with their mother
5 and the divine Kṛṣṇā, and treat them with honor, Bhārata! By good
fortune do the Pārthas live, by good fortune is Pṛthā alive, by good
fortune do we all prosper, by good fortune has Purocana been silenced,
by good fortune has this great sorrow been taken from me, illustrious
Vidura!

Vaiśaṃpāyana said:
Thereupon Vidura at Dhṛtarāṣṭra's behest went forth to Yajñasena
and the Pāṇḍavas, O Bhārata. Having gone there, the law-minded
man, who was wise in all the sciences, waited properly and
ceremonially on Drupada, O king. He in turn received Vidura
according to the Law, and courteously they exchanged inquiries
10 regarding each other's health. He saw the Pāṇḍavas there, and
Vāsudeva, O Bhārata, and he embraced them lovingly and asked about
their health. One after the other, they paid homage to the most
sagacious Vidura, and he, O king, at Dhṛtarāṣṭra's word, asked the
Pāṇḍavas again and again with loving concern about their well-being.
And he gave the manifold riches and treasures that the Kauravas had
presented to the Pāṇḍavas, and to Kuntī, Draupadī, and Drupada's
sons.

Then the most sagacious Vidura courteously addressed the courtly
Drupada in the presence of the Pāṇḍavas and Keśava.
15 "Sire," quoth he, "with your sons and ministers listen to my word!
Dhṛtarāṣṭra, his son, his ministers, and his kinsmen inquire with great
pleasure and persistence after the health of you all, sire! He is
profoundly pleased with your alliance, O lord of men. The wise
Bhīṣma Śāṃtanava and all the Kauravas likewise ask tidings of your
health. The great archer Droṇa Bhāradvāja, your dear friend,
embraces you and hopes you are well. Dhṛtarāṣṭra, having now
entered into an alliance with you, Pāñcālya, deems himself successful

20 in his aims, and so do all the Kauravas. Not the acquisition of your kingdom would have given them greater pleasure than obtaining your alliance, Yajñasena.

"Knowing this, your Majesty must let the Pāṇḍavas depart. For the Kurus are most impatient to see the heirs of Pāṇḍu. The bulls of men have been abroad for a long time, and they as well as Pṛthā will be eager to see the city. All the first ladies of the Kurus, and the city, and the country, are waiting to see Kṛṣṇā Pāñcālī! Your Majesty must at once give orders for their going with their wife, and for my
25 returning. When you have given the great-spirited Pāṇḍavas leave, sire, I shall send fast runners to Dhṛtarāṣṭra, and the Kaunteyas and Kuntī will depart with Kṛṣṇā."

1(15) The Acquisition of the Kingdom

199 (B. 207; C. 7545–95).
199 (207; 7545). Drupada agrees with Vidura, as does Kṛṣṇa (1–5). The Pāṇḍavas return to Hāstinapura. They are welcomed joyously by the populace (5–20). Dhṛtarāṣṭra offers them the Khāṇḍava Tract, which is half the kingdom, in settlement. They accept. Journey to, and foundation of, Indraprastha, with Vyāsa officiating (20–25). Description of the city, its prosperity and beauty (25–45). Kṛṣṇa returns to Dvāravatī (45).

Drupada said:

199.1 It is indeed as you have now said to me, sagacious Vidura. I too find very great joy in the alliance we have concluded, my lord! It is proper that the great-spirited brothers now go home, but so far it had not been proper for me to say so in my own voice. When the heroic Yudhiṣṭhira, the son of Kuntī, agrees, and Bhīmasena and Arjuna and the bulllike twins agree, and the law-minded Rāma and Kṛṣṇa agree, then the Pāṇḍavas should go; for these two tigerlike men have their welfare greatly at heart.

Yudhiṣṭhira said:

5 Sire, we and our followers are all dependents of you. We shall do what you tell us for our good!

Vaiśaṃpāyana said:

Thereupon Vāsudeva said, "To me it appears that they should go, if King Drupada, who knows all the Laws, agrees."

Drupada said:

My view is decidedly in agreement with the thoughts of the

masterful and strong-armed hero of the Daśārhas,* which indeed fit the occasion. For now the lordly Pāṇḍavas are as dear to Vāsudeva as they are to myself, let no one doubt it! Not even Yudhiṣṭhira Kaunteya, who is the son of Dharma, ponders the well-being of the brothers as the tigerlike Keśava* ponders it!

Vaiśaṃpāyana said:

Then the great-spirited Drupada gave them leave to go; and the Pāṇḍavas, Kṛṣṇa, and the wise Vidura took Kṛṣṇā Draupadī and the glorious Kuntī and journeyed in leisurely fashion to the City of the Elephant in easy stages. Dhṛtarāṣṭra Kaurava, on hearing that the heroes were coming, sent the Kauravas to receive the Pāṇḍus, sent Vikarṇa the archer and Citrasena, the supreme bowman Droṇa, and Kṛpa Gautama. In their midst the warlike heroes radiantly made their slow entry into the city of Hāstinapura. The city where the tigerlike men dispelled all grief and sorrow well-nigh burst with curiosity. Their well-wishers raised their friendly voices in all tones, and the Pāṇḍavas listened to their words, which touched their hearts: "The Law-minded tiger among men has come back, he who protected us with the Law as though we were his own heirs. Today it is as though the great King Pāṇḍu who loved the woods has come back from the woods, and surely to look after our welfare! Can there be any greater pleasure in store for us, now that our heroic lords, sons of Kuntī, have returned? If we have given, if we have sacrificed, if we have practiced austerities, it is for that that the Pāṇḍavas shall stay in the city a hundred autumns!"

They greeted the feet of Dhṛtarāṣṭra, Bhīṣma, and others who deserved it, and after asking the health of the entire city, they entered Dhṛtarāṣṭra's house at his behest. When the powerful, great-spirited men were rested, they were summoned by King Dhṛtarāṣṭra and Bhīṣma.

Dhṛtarāṣṭra said:

Son of Kuntī, harken to my word with your brothers. Lest there be strife again, you must go to the Khāṇḍava Tract. No one can oppress you when you are living there under the Pārtha's protection, like the Thirty Gods under that of the Thunderbolt-Wielder. Go to the Khāṇḍava Tract and take half the kingdom!

Vaiśaṃpāyana said:

They all accepted the king's proposal and bowed. Thereafter the bulllike men departed for the frightful forest; and, taking half the kingdom, they entered the Khāṇḍava Tract. After the undefeated Pāṇḍavas, led by Kṛṣṇa, had gone there, they built a beautiful city like a new heaven. Led by Dvaipāyana, the heroes performed the rite of

* = Kṛṣṇa.

appeasement on an auspicious and holy stretch of land and had the fort measured out. It was made strong by moats that were like oceans and surrounded by a wall that covered the sky, white like clouds, or like a mountain of snow. That grand city shone as Bhogavatī shines with its Snakes, and it was protected by dread-looking, double-hung gates like two-winged Garuḍas, with gate towers that towered like packed clouds, like so many Mount Mandaras. It was covered with spears and javelins of many kinds, surpassing-sharp and smoothly turned, as though with double-tongued Snakes. Guarded by warriors, it was splendid with spiraling turrets and resplendent with sharp pikes and hundred-killers and movable trellises.

The fortress sported massive iron wheels and a well-laid plan of streets that avoided collisions with Fate; and it shone wide with beautiful white buildings of many kinds. Thus Indraprastha shone wide in the image of heaven, grown big like a mass of packed clouds that are encircled by lightning. In this lovely and beautiful place stood the splendid seat of the Kaurava, filled with treasure, which was like the seat of the God of Riches. There did the brahmins come, the wisest scholars of the *Vedas*, O king, who knew all the tongues, and they approved of settling there. From all regions the merchants came to that country to seek their fortune, and artisans of all crafts came to live there. Lovely gardens surrounded the city, with mango trees, *āmrātakas, nīpas, aśokas, campakas, puṃnāgas, nāgapuṣpas, lakucas,* breadfruit, *śālas*, palms, *kadambas, bakulas*, and jasmine, trees charming and blossoming and bending under the burden of fruit, full-grown *āmalakas, lodhras*, flowering *ankolas*, rose apples, *pāṭalas, kubjakas and atimuktakas, karavīras* and *pārijātas*, and many other kinds of trees, always in flower and fruit, swarming with birds of all kinds, echoing with the calls of frenzied peacocks and always joyous cuckoos. There were houses white like mirrors, and all kinds of pavilions made of lianas; and lovely painted houses, and pleasure hillocks, and many ponds filled with pure water; and most charming lakes redolent with the fragrance of lotuses and waterlilies, colorful with wild geese and ducks by droves, and *cakravāka* birds, and lovely, tree-shaded lotus ponds of all shapes, and broad and big tanks of great beauty.

As they dwelled in their great realm, which was peopled with honest folk, the joy of the Pāṇḍavas, great king, grew eternally; and thus the Pāṇḍavas, when Bhīṣma and the king had displayed the Law, became inhabitants of the Khāṇḍava Tract. With the five great Indra-like archers, that grand city shone as Bhogavatī with its Snakes. After having settled them, the heroic Keśava departed with Rāma to Dvāravatī, O king, with the Pāṇḍavas' consent.

1(16) Arjuna's Sojourn in the Forest

200–210 (B. 208–18; C. 7596–7905).
200 (208; 7596). Yudhiṣṭhira reigns happily in Indraprastha (1–5). Nārada arrives, is welcomed and joined by Draupadī; he blesses her, and she leaves (10–15). Nārada warns the brothers against strife over her, and illustrates the danger by the story of Sunda and Upasunda (15). Yudhiṣṭhira demands the story (15–20).
210–4. THE STORY OF SUNDA AND UPASUNDA.
205 (213; 7743). The Pāṇḍavas' happy life with Draupadī (1–5). A brahmin is robbed of his cows and shouts for help, berating the Pāṇḍavas. Arjuna hears him (5–10) and, looking for weapons, sees Yudhiṣṭhira with Draupadī; yet he decides that the brahmin comes first; he recovers the brahmin's cows (10–20). Presenting himself to Yudhiṣṭhira, he insists on going into exile in the forest, in expiation of his breach of privacy (20–30).
206 (214; 7776). Followed and lauded by brahmins and hermits, Arjuna travels to the Gate of the Ganges (1–10). While he bathes in the Ganges, he is abducted by Ulūpī and performs the fire rites (10–15). Ulūpī confesses her love and persuades him to lie with her (15–30). He returns to dry land in the morning (30).
207 (215; 7812). Arjuna visits places of pilgrimage; the brahmins leave him when he comes to Kalinga (1–10). He travels to Maṇalūra, where he sees the king's daughter Citrāngadā; he wants her. The king complies, provided the issue becomes the dynast (10–20). Arjuna stays for three months (20).
208 (216; 7839). Journeying south, he finds five deserted fords and questions the hermits why they are deserted (1–5). They recount that they are inhabited by five crocodiles. Arjuna goes to bathe in the Subhadrā ford, subdues an attacking crocodile, which turns into a beautiful Apsarā. (5–10). She explains that she and four other Apsarās tried to seduce a hermit, who cursed them to become crocodiles for a century (10–20).
209 (217; 7861). The Apsarās ask for a reprieve, and the brahmin hedges about the meaning of "century"; they shall be free when a superior man pulls them out (1–10). Nārada arrives and says that Arjuna will rescue them

(10–15). Arjuna now complies and saves the others too (15–20). He returns to Maṇalūra and sees his son Babhrūvāhana (20).

Janamejaya said:
200.1 Ascetic, when they had thus obtained a kingdom in Indraprastha,
what did the great-spirited Pāṇḍavas do thereafter, they who are all
my ancient forebears? And how did Draupadī, their lawful wife, see to
their wishes? Or how did these five lordly kings of men, in consorting
with their common wife Kṛṣṇā, fail to split in strife? I wish to hear it
all in detail, ascetic, how they behaved to one another wedded to
Kṛṣṇā.
Vaiśaṃpāyana said:
5 When Dhṛtarāṣṭra had dismissed the Pāṇḍavas with Kṛṣṇā, and the
enemy-burners had obtained their kingdom, the tigerlike men
enjoyed themselves. On obtaining the kingdom, the lustrous and
truthful Yudhiṣṭhira reigned over the country with his brothers
according to the Law. Their enemies defeated, and ever-devoted to
truth and Law, the sagacious scions of Pāṇḍu lived there in happiness
sublime. The bulls among men sat on costly royal thrones and fulfilled
all the offices for their citizens.
Then, while all the great-spirited brothers were sitting together,
10 the divine seer Nārada chanced to come. Yudhiṣṭhira gave him his
own splendid throne, and the wise prince himself presented the divine
seer with the guest gift in proper fashion and conveyed the state of
the kingdom. The seer accepted his homage and, being pleased,
prospered them with his blessings. Then he said, "Be seated," and
when King Yudhiṣṭhira with his permission had sat down, he sent
word to Kṛṣṇā that the blessed lord had arrived. Immediately,
Draupadī purified herself with care and went where Nārada was
sitting with the Pāṇḍavas. The law-obeying daughter of Drupada
greeted the seer's feet and stood with folded hands, properly covered.
15 The Law-minded, true-spoken, good seer Nārada pronounced various
blessings over the princess, then he told the blameless woman to go.
When she had left and they were alone, the blessed seer addressed all
the Pāṇḍavas headed by Yudhiṣṭhira.
"The glorious daughter of the Pāñcālas is the common lawful wife
of all of you. You must lay down a rule, lest there be strife over her.
"There were once two Asura brothers, famous in the three worlds,
Sunda and Upasunda, who were always together. No one could kill
them save they themselves. They shared their kingdom, shared their
house, shared bed, seat, and board, and killed each other over
20 Tilottamā. Therefore, preserve the friendship you feel for one another

and act lest there be strife between you, Yudhiṣṭhira!"

Yudhiṣṭhira said:

Whose sons were these Asuras, Sunda and Upasunda, great hermits, and how did their breach occur and did they kill each other? And whose daughter was the celestial Apsarā Tilottamā, by whose love they were crazed and killed each other? We wish to hear it all, ascetic, in full detail, for we are most curious.

1(16.a) *Sunda and Upasunda*

201–4 (B. 209–12; C. 7619–7742)

201 (209; 7619). Sunda and Upasunda, inseparable Asura brothers, can only be killed by each other; they are sons of Nikumbha, a descendant of Hiraṇyakaśipu. They perform severe austerities (1–9), until the Vindhya mountains, where they live, begin to smoke. The Gods wizardry to distract them is of no avail (10–15). Brahmā plies them with a boon; they ask for great powers and immortality, but are denied immortality; they are granted immunity from everyone but each other (15–20). Returning to their fellow Asuras, they make merry (25–30).

202 (210; 7652). The pair decides to conquer the universe, and they drive the Gods to the World of Brahmā, defeat the rest of the world (1–5), and proceed to extirpate the brahmins and barons, so that no Vedism is practiced. (10–15). They go berserk and stop the world's business (15–25).

203 (211; 7679). The seers plead with Brahmā (1–5). Brahmā summons Viśvakarman and orders him to make a perfect harlot (5–10). He takes all the jewels of the world and creates Tilottamā (15). Brahmā orders her to seduce and estrange Sunda and Upasunda. She gives her promise and circumambulates Brahmā; as she does so, all the Gods turn to watch her except Sthāṇu, who instead grows four faces, and Indra, who sprouts a thousand eyes; only Brahmā does not look (15–30).

204 (212; 7711). Sunda and Upasunda make merry (1–5). Tilottamā appears before them; they fall in love and each demands her for himself (5–15). They start fighting and kill each other; the other Daityas flee (15–20). Pleased, Brahmā appears and allows her the run of the world of the Ādityas (20–25). Drawing the moral, the Pāṇḍavas make a compact; if any one of them sees a brother with Draupadī he must retire to the forest for twelve months (25–30).

Nārada said:

201.1 Then hear from me the ancient story with all its particulars just as
it happened, Yudhiṣṭhira Pārtha, you and your brothers. Long ago
there was in the lineage of the great Asura Hiraṇyakaśipu a mighty
and puissant lord of the Daityas by the name of Nikumbha. Two sons
of great prowess and terrible strength were born to him. They always
ate together, never went without each other, sought to please each
other, always spoke kindly to each other, behaved and conducted
themselves in the same way, and they were as one made into two.
5 When they grew older, these powerful demons, whose resolution
in all matters was identical, adopted the identical decision to conquer
the universe. They underwent a consecration, went to the Vindhya
mountains, and practiced awesome austerities. After a long time they
acquired the power of mortification. Wan with hunger and thirst,
wearing the hair braid and bark clothes, their body completely covered
with filth, they lived on the wind. They offered pieces of their flesh
into the fire, stood on the tips of their toes, kept their arms raised in
the air, never blinked their eyes, and kept up their vows for a long
time. Heated up for so long by the power of their mortifications, the
10 Vindhya began to belch smoke—it was most miraculous. Seeing their
awesome austerities, the Gods became afraid and tried to obstruct
them, so that their austerities might be undone. They tempted them
with gems and women, time and again, but the two of mighty vows
did not break their vow. Then the Gods conjured up illusions before
the great-spirited pair: their sisters, mother, wives, and kinsmen were
tremblingly set upon by a Rākṣasa brandishing a pike, while their
ornaments and hair came loose and their clothes fell aside. All the
15 woman ran to them and shrieked "Save us!" Still the two of mighty
vows did not break their vow. When neither of them was shocked or
grieved, the women and the demon all vanished again.

Then the Grandfather went in person to the great Asuras, and the Grandsire of all the worlds plied them with a boon. When the two brothers, Sunda and Upasunda, steadfast in their power, saw the God Grandfather, they stood with folded hands, and they both said to the lordly God, "If the Grandfather is pleased with these our austerities, then may we be wise in magic, wise with weapons, strong, and able to change our forms. May we both become Immortal, if the Lord has grace for us!"

The Grandfather said:

20 Excepting immortality, all that you ask shall befall you. Choose
some other disposition of death that is like the Immortals. Inasmuch
as you have raised this great power of austerities for the sake of a
purpose, therefore no immortality is ordained for you. You have
undertaken it for the conquest of the universe, and for that reason,
lords of the Daityas, I cannot do your wish!

Sunda and Upasunda said:

Then let us be in no danger from any creature, moving or standing,
anyone whatsoever in the three worlds, but the two of us, Grandfather.

The Grandfather said:

This wish I can grant you just as you have asked for it. Precisely so
shall be the disposition of your deaths.

Nārada said:

25 Then the Grandfather, by giving them this boon, turned the pair
away from self-mortification and went back to the world of Brahmā.
And having obtained all their boons and having become invulnerable
to the world, the two lordly Daityas went to their own habitation.
When their kinsmen saw the great Asuras recipients of boons and
successful in their desires, they were all greatly happy with them.
They gave up their braids and wore diadems and very costly ornaments
and spotless robes. Out of season they celebrated the Kaumudī Festival
with all its revelry, and the two lordly Daityas and their kinsfolk
30 enjoyed themselves superbly. In house after house cries went up, "Eat,
feast, make love, sing, drink, treat!" And with great drinking bouts
and the loud clapping of hands the whole city of the Daityas became
delirious with joy. As the protean Daityas played at all their many
games the years went by as though they were a day.

Nārada said:

202.1 When the festival had run its course, the two, desirous to conquer
the universe, took counsel and ordered their army. Their kinsmen, the
elders of the Daityas, and the councillors bade them farewell, and after
performing the traveling rites they set out by night under the stars of
Māgha and journeyed with a large force of Daityas carrying clubs and
three-bladed spears, wielding pikes and hammers, all following the
same Law. Cāraṇas sang their praises with blessings and litanies that
5 wished them victory, and the two marched joyously onward. The two
Daityas, who could move as they pleased, flew up to the sky and,
war-crazed, entered the abode of the Gods. Knowing that they were
coming and that the lord had granted their boon, the Gods deserted
heaven and went to the World of Brahmā. The pair conquered the
World of Indra, the hosts of Yakṣas and Rākṣasas, and with rigorous
prowess overthrew even the creatures that roam the skies. The great

Asuras defeated the Snakes that live inside the earth, the denizens of the ocean, all the tribes of Barbarians.

Thereupon that pair of dread command, undertaking to conquer all of earth, summoned their soldiers and spoke these very harsh
10 words: "The royal seers and the brahmins feed the might, strength, and glory of the Gods with their great sacrifices and oblations. All these prosperous enemies of the Asuras we must attack and annihilate totally!" Having thus given all of them their orders on the eastern shore of the ocean, the two went in all directions with cruel determination. Whosoever sacrificed and whatsoever brahmins officiated at his sacrifices, the powerful pair slew them all ferociously where they found them. In the hermitages of seers who had perfected their souls the soldiers of the two took their *agnihotras* and fearlessly
15 threw them away. The curses sent forth by angered, great-spirited ascetics were of no avail on the pair who pridefully gloried in the boon they had received. Of no more avail were the curses than arrows loosed on a rock; and the brahmins abandoned their life rules and fled in all directions. All advanced ascetics on earth, self-controlled and given to serenity, for fear of them took flight as snakes take flight before Garuḍa, with their hermitages routed, their jars and ladles broken and scattered about. Empty was all the world, as though struck by Time.

When the royal seers and the seers went in hiding, the great Asuras both made the same decision and changed their shapes, bent upon slaughter. They became rutting elephants with oozing temples, and they drove those that were lying in inaccessible regions to the
20 realm of Yama. They became lions and tigers and invisible, and with all kinds of wiles they cruelly slew the seers where they found them. Treasure-filled Earth saw sacrifice and *Veda*-study halt, kings and brahmins perish, festivals and rituals lapse, buying and selling cease, the worship of the Gods stop, and, while she cried out in fear, she was deprived of rites and marriages. And with her ploughing and cattle-tending ended, her cities and hermitages razed, Earth, bestrewn with
25 bones and skeletons, became a loathsome sight. The world, where the ancestral offerings had come to an end and no sacrificial calls and hallowing rites were heard, now became of fearful and ugly aspect. Moon and sun, planets, stars, constellations, and all that dwell in the heavens became despondent on watching the works of Sunda and Upasunda. And having thus cruelly conquered all the countries, the two Daityas, without a rival left, made Kurukṣetra their dwelling place.

Nārada said:

203.1 All the divine seers, the Siddhas, the supreme seers, upon witnessing the huge massacre, were grievously hurt. They, who had mastered their anger, their selves, and their senses, went out of compassion to the dwelling of the Grandfather of all the world. They found the Grandfather seated with the Gods, entirely surrounded by Siddhas and brahmin seers. The God who is the Great God was there, and Fire, with Wind, Sun and Moon, and Law, and the God-who-Stands-on-High. There were the Vaikhānasas, the Vālakhilyas, the Forest-Dwellers, the Beam-Drinkers, the Unborn Ones, the Undistracted, the Fire-Wombs, and other ascetics. And all the seers were waiting on the Grandfather.

All the great seers approached in force and recited all the doings of Sunda and Upasunda, what they had done, how they had done it, and in what order—they told it all to the Grandfather. Placing the matter before the Grandfather, the hosts of Gods and supreme seers animadverted him. When the Grandfather had heard the words of all of them, he pondered awhile, deciding what must be done. Then, ordaining the death of the pair, he summoned Viśvakarman. When he saw Viśvakarman, the Grandfather, great ascetic, ordered: "Create a beautiful woman who can be bidden!" Bowing before the Grandfather and welcoming his words, he created after careful reflection a divine woman. First he gathered from everywhere with great care whatever is beautiful in all three worlds, whether standing or moving, and placed these gems, which numbered by the millions, into her body. He created her out of the gatherings of gems with a celestial loveliness. And she, so diligently created by Viśvakarman, was in all three worlds unrivaled by any woman. There was not the tiniest bit of her body that was not perfectly lovely or failed to hold the eye of the beholder. She, like a Śrī embodied, desirable and beautiful, carried off the glances and the hearts of all beings. Since she had been created bit by bit from gems, the Grandfather gave her the name of Tilottamā.

The Grandfather said:

Go to the Asuras Sunda and Upasunda, Tilottamā, and seduce them, my dear, with your biddable beauty. Act to such purpose that as soon as they see you a quarrel arises between the two over you and your perfect body.

Nārada said:

She made her promise, bowed to the Grandfather, and made a circumambulation of the Gods. The Lord the Great God was sitting in the South facing the East, the Gods sat in the North, the seers sat in all the directions. But when she was making her circumambulation Indra and the blessed Lord Sthāṇu alone preserved their composure. But so great was the desire of the latter to watch her as she was going by his side that another face with curving lashes sprang up on the South of him. When she passed his back, a face came out in the West, and on her passing his other side, a face came out on the North. With great Indra, too, big red eyes popped out of his sides, back and front, all over, till they counted a thousand. Thus the Great God Sthāṇu became of yore four-faced, and the Slayer of Vala thousand-eyed. The hosts of Gods and the seers all turned their faces in the direction where Tilottamā was going. The glances of all the great-spirited Gods, except the God Grandfather, fell plentifully on Tilottamā's body; all the Gods and supreme seers thought that her perfect beauty had already done its work. When Tilottamā had gone, the Prosperer of the World dismissed all the Gods and the throngs of seers.

Nārada said:

204.1 So, after conquering the earth, the two Daityas, without rivals or
worries and with the entire universe safe to themselves, were acquitted
of their task. They took all the gems of Gods, Gandharvas, Yakṣas,
Snakes, kings, and Rākṣasas and were supremely contented. As there
were no more adversaries left in the world, they fell idle, disported
themselves like Immortals, and gave themselves to pleasure with
women, garlands, perfumes, food, delicacies, drink, in great quantity,
5 variety, and agreeableness. They played like Immortals, in their serail,
in forest and garden, on mountains and in parks, and in any place
they fancied.

Then one day they went to play on a rock plateau on the ridge of
the Vindhya amidst *śāla* trees with flowering crowns. All manner of
things that gave pleasure were fetched there, and the two joyously
reclined with their women on beautiful seats. Later, the women waited
on them with music and dance and attended on them with songs of
praise to please them. It was then that Tilottamā appeared, plucking
flowers in the woods, in a suggestive dress of one red piece of cloth.
10 Plucking *karṇikāras* that grew on river banks, she drew slowly near
the spot where the two grand Asuras were sitting. They had been
drinking choice liquors, and as soon as they saw the fine-buttocked
woman with their drink-bloodied eyes they were smitten. Both leaped
from their seats, went to where she was standing, and, crazed with
love, propositioned her. Sunda took the fair-browed Tilottamā by the
right hand, and Upasunda by the left. Maddened by the boon they
had received, by the strength of their chests, by their riches and gems,
15 by the liquor they had drunk, maddened by all these madnesses, they
knitted their brows at each other and, possessed by crazed lust, began
to speak to each other. "She is my wife," said Sunda, "and your guru!"
"She is mine," quoth Upasunda, "and your sister-in-law!" Rage
seized them: "She is not yours, she is mine!" And for her they grasped
their horrible clubs. When they had grasped their horrible clubs, they
hit each other, shouting "Me first, me first!"—blinded by their love
for her. Clobbered by the clubs, the terrible pair fell to the ground,

their bodies smeared with blood, like two suns falling from heaven.
20 The women and the band of Daityas ran off and, shuddering with
despair and fright, all went to the underground world.

Thereupon the pure-spirited Grandfather came there, with the Gods and great seers, to congratulate Tilottamā. When plied with a boon by Brahmā, she chose his pleasure; then the Grandfather, pleased, said to her, "You shall have the run of the worlds that are roamed by the Ādityas, radiant maiden. And because of your luster no one will bear to look upon you for long!" Having granted her this boon, the Grandfather of all the world put Indra in charge of the universe, and then the lord went to the world of Brahmā.

25 Thus did that pair who were always together, always of the same mind in all matters, kill each other in fury over Tilottamā. Therefore, my affection moves me to tell you all, good Bhāratas, act lest you all be split because of Draupadī—and good luck to you—if you wish to do me a kindness.

Vaiśaṃpāyana said:

When the great seer Nārada had thus spoken to the great-spirited brothers, they all together made a covenant with one another, O king, in the presence of the boundlessly august divine seer Nārada: "If one of us sets eye on the other when he is sitting with Draupadī, he must live in the forest like a hermit for twelve months." After the law-abiding Pāṇḍavas had made this covenant, the great hermit Nārada, pleased, went forth where he listed.

30 So they made a compact from the start, at the urging of Nārada, and none of them were ever split ever since, O Bhārata.

1(16) Arjuna's Sojourn in the Forest (continued)

Vaiśaṃpāyana said:

205.1 After they had made a covenant in this fashion, the Pāṇḍavas lived there, subjugating other kings with the majesty of their arms. Kṛṣṇā saw to the wishes of all the five boundlessly august lionlike men. As they were with her, so was she supremely happy with her five heroic husbands, as is the river Sarasvatī with her elephants. While the great-spirited Pāṇḍavas lived by the Law, all the Kurus prospered, sinless and happy.

5 A long time had passed when, O excellent king, thieves stole the cows of a certain brahmin. The brahmin was mindless with anger when his wealth was stolen, and he went to the Khāṇḍava Tract and

berated the Pāṇḍavas: "Mean, cruel, witless thieves are making off with my wealth of cattle from this very domain of yours, by force! Run after them, Pāṇḍavas! Crows are carrying off the offspring of the absent-minded brahmin, a lowly jackal rubs the empty hole of the tiger! When thieves steal a brahmin's property, Law and Profit are plundered! Take up your arms, I am crying for help!"

Dhanaṃjaya Pāṇḍava was in the vicinity of the brahmin who was crying for help, and he heard his words. Immediately the strong-armed champion said, "Have no fear!" Now, the room where the great-spirited Pāṇḍavas kept their weapons was occupied by King Dharma Yudhiṣṭhira, who was with Kṛṣṇā. The Pāṇḍava was no more able to enter than to go away, and the unhappy brahmin kept on urging him on with his tongue. Amid his lamentations, Arjuna thought wretchedly, "The wealth of this poor brahmin is being carried off, and it is certain that his tears must be dried. The king will suffer a great breach of Law by negligence, if I do not protect this man who is weeping at the gate. If I fail to protect, the impiety of us all with regard to protection will be established in the world, and we shall suffer a breach of Law. If I go without taking my leave from King Ajātaśatru,* I shall surely injure him. If I enter at the king's, I must live in the forest. Either a great breach of Law, or death in the forest! But Law wins out, even over the death of one's body."

Having thus resolved, Dhanaṃjaya entered at the king's, took his leave, O king of the people, and after taking a bow said happily to the brahmin, "Come quickly, brahmin. We must catch up with those rascal robbers before they get too far, so that I can turn back your property to you from their hands!" The strong-armed hero, with bow and armor and flagged chariot, pursued and shattered the robbers with his arrows and recovered the brahmin's property. After returning the cows to the brahmin and drinking his praise, the heroic Pāṇḍava, the enemy-burning, left-handed archer, went back to the city. He greeted all his elders, who welcomed him back, then said to King Dharma, "Assign me my vow. I have violated the covenant by looking at you. I shall go and live in the forest, for that was the compact we made." Having been addressed with these unkind words, the King Dharma exclaimed unhappily, in a dolorous voice, "Why?" Then brother Yudhiṣṭhira addressed his undefeated brother Guḍākeśa**: "If I am the authority, listen to my word, prince sans blame. The injury you did me by entering, hero, I forgive entirely and I bear you no grudge. It is no offense if a younger brother enters at his elder's; it breaks the rule if the eldest enters at his younger brother's. Stop, strong-armed Arjuna, and do as I say. You have not breached the Law and I have not taken offense."

* = Yudhiṣṭhira.
** = Arjuna.

Arjuna said:
I have also heard you say not to follow the Law with pretenses.
I shall not waver from my truth, I am armed with my truth!"
Vaiśaṃpāyana said:
30 With the king's consent, he was consecrated for the hermit's life
and went forth to live in the forest for twelve months.

Vaiśaṃpāyana said:
206.1 When the strong-armed creator of the fame of the Kauravas went
forth, great-spirited brahmins, great scholars of the *Veda*, followed
him; and those who knew the *Vedas* and their branches, those who
pondered upon the supreme Soul, and pure devotees of the blessed
Lord, and bards, and reciters of the Lore, storytellers as well, O king,
and hermits who dwell in the forest, and brahmins who gave sweet
voice to celestial tales. Surrounded by them and other companions
with their polished stories, the scion of Pāṇḍu went forth, like Indra
5 surrounded by the Maruts. The bull of the Bharatas set eye on lovely
and colorful woods and lakes, O Bhārata, and on holy fords. When he
reached the Gate of the Ganges, the lord made his dwelling there.
Now hear from me, Janamejaya, the wonder that he wrought, this
chariot-riding chief of the Pāṇḍus whose spirit was pure.
When the Kaunteya and the brahmins had settled there, the priests
offered up many *agnihotras*. And as the fires were awakened and made
to blaze up and offered into, and as offerings of flowers were made on
10 either bank of the river by the rigorous, consecrated, great-spirited
sages who walked the path of the strict, the Gate of the Ganges
became surpassingly beautiful, O king. Now, while his settlement was
busy in this wise, the son of Pāṇḍu and Kuntī descended into the
Ganges to bathe. And having bathed and offered to his grandfathers,
he was about to emerge from the water to perform the fire rites when
the strong-armed man was pulled under the water by the daughter of
the king of the Snakes, Ulūpī, who could travel where she pleased.
Then the Pāṇḍava saw a high-piled fire in the most honored palace of
15 the Snake Kauravya. Kuntī's son Dhanaṃjaya did the rites with that
fire; and the sacrificial fire, as he offered into it unhesitantly, became
gratified with him. After accomplishing the fire rites, the Pāṇḍava said
laughingly to the princess of the Snakes, "What moved you to act so
rashly, my timid and beaming girl? Which is this lovely land, and
who are you, and whose daughter?"
Ulūpī said:
There is a Snake sprung from the lineage of Airāvata, Kauravya by
name, and I am his daughter, O Pārtha, Ulūpī of the Snakes. I saw
you descend into the river to bathe, and I was driven out of my mind
20 by Love. Make me happy today, scion of Kuru, I am churned by the

Bodiless God* for your sake! Make this matchless maiden happy today, in secret, by the gift of yourself!

Arjuna said:

King Dharma has ordered me for twelve months to a hermit's life, my dear. I am not my own master. Still, I want to please you, denizen of the waters! Never before have I ever spoken a lie. How can I act so that I do not belie myself, yet do your pleasure and still not violate my Law, Snake girl?

Ulūpī said:

I know, Pāṇḍava, how you are roaming the earth and how your
25 guru has ordered you to a hermit's life. When you were all living with
the daughter of Drupada, you made a covenant that anyone of you
who would foolishly enter should have to live in the forest as a hermit
for twelve months. But this exile of any one of you would be because
of Draupadī, and be a matter of Law in *her* case only. In my case the
Law is not offended. You are beholden to rescue the oppressed, broad-
eyed Arjuna: rescuing me will not breach your Law. Or if there might
even be a slight transgression of the Law, that would still give merit
to you, as you would render me my life! Love me who love you,
Pārtha: that is the view of the strict, my lord. If you will not do so,
30 rest assured I shall die. Observe the highest Law of all by giving life;
I have now come to you for refuge, strong-armed master of men!
You have always protected the destitute and unprotected, Pāṇḍava.
I am praying to you out of love, therefore do my desire. You must
fulfil me by giving yourself!

Vaiśaṃpāyana said:

At these words of the daughter of the king of the Snakes, Arjuna did as she desired, looking to the Law as his cause. And having spent the night in the palace of the Snake, the majestic hero arose with the rising sun from Kauravya's dwelling.

Vaiśaṃpāyana said:

207.1 The son of the Thunderbolt-Wielder told it all to the brahmins,
O Bhārata, and thereupon went forth to the slope of the Himālaya.
Kuntī's son reached the Banyan Tree of Agastya and the Mountain of
Vasiṣṭha, and he made his ablutions on the Peak of Bhṛgu. The chief
of the Kurus made donations of thousands of cows at the fords and
sanctuaries, and gave dwellings to the brahmins. The eminent man
bathed at the Ford of the Drop of Gold and beheld the great mountain
5 and holy sanctuaries. Then the best of men descended with the
brahmins, and the bull of the Bharatas went on, for he wished to
reach the region of the East. Many a ford did he see in succession,
and the lovely river Utpalinī by the Naimiṣa Forest, the rivers Nandā

* = the God of Love.

and Upanandā, and the glorious Kauśikī, the great river Gayā as well
as the Ganges. Thus seeing all the fords and hermitages, and
hallowing himself with the sight, he gave wealth to the brahmins. In
the lands of Anga, Vanga, and Kalinga he visited all the fords and
sanctuaries found there, and having visited them in the proper fashion
10 he gave away largess. At the gates of the kingdom of Kalinga the
brahmins who had followed him took their leave from the Pāṇḍava
and returned. With their consent, however, Dhanaṃjaya Kaunteya
the champion went on with very few companions as far as the ocean.

Traversing the land of the Kalingas and visiting its spots and
sanctuaries, all lawlike and lovely, the lord went on to cast his gaze
on Mount Mahendra adorned by ascetics; and traveling along the
ocean coast he slowly journeyed to Maṇalūra. There he went to all
the sacred fords and holy sanctuaries, and thereafter the strong-armed
warrior went to visit the law-minded king of Maṇalūra, Citravāhana.
15 This king had a beautiful daughter by the name of Citrāngadā whom
he saw in the city where she chanced to stroll.

When he saw the buxom daughter of Citravāhana, he desired her;
and he went to the king and made known his purpose. Conciliatingly
the king replied, "There once was a king by the name of Prabhaṃkara
in this dynasty. Being sonless and longing for progeny, he practiced
supreme austerities. By his awesome austerities and prostrations, Lord
Śaṃkara, the Great God who is the Consort of Umā, became satisfied.
The blessed Lord granted him that there would be a single child in the
dynasty every generation, and hence there has ever since been a
20 single child in our line. All my forebears had sons, but to me this girl
was born, who surely shall continue the line. My fancy is that she is
my son, and I have styled her my *puppet* according to the provisions,
bull of the Bhāratas. So let her bring forth a son, who shall be the
dynast: this son I demand as my price for her. By this covenant you
must take her, Pāṇḍava."

He gave his promise and took the girl; and he lived with her in that
city for three months.

Vaiśaṃpāyana said:

208.1 Thereafter the bull of the Bharatas went to the fords on the southern
ocean, very sacred all and ornamented with ascetics. These ascetics,
however, avoided five sacred spots there, although in the past they
had been cultivated by ascetics. They were the Ford of Agastya, that
of Subhadra, the very purifying one of Puloman, the serene Ford of
Karaṃdhama, which bore fruit like a Horse Sacrifice, and the Ford of
Bharadvāja, which was a great appeaser of evil.
5 The Pāṇḍava seeing these fords deserted and avoided by the law-
spirited hermits questioned the ascetics with folded hands: "Why do
the scholars of the Brahman avoid these fords?"

The ascetics said:
Five crocodiles are living in them, and they drag away the ascetics.
Therefore, these fords are to be avoided, O scion of Kuru.
Vaiśaṃpāyana said:
Having heard this from them, the strong-armed and good man,
although the ascetics sought to restrain him, went to visit these fords.
He came to the excellent ford of the great seer Subhadra, and with
alacrity the enemy-burning champion dived into it to take a bath. At
once a large crocodile that lived in the water seized hold of the tiger-
10 like Dhanaṃjaya in the water. The strong-armed, powerful Arjuna lay
hold of the splashing water beast and stood powerfully up from the
water. And no sooner had the glorious Arjuna pulled out the
crocodile than it turned into a beautiful woman decked with all the
ornaments, fairly blazing with beauty, O king, celestial and delightful.
Beholding this great miracle, Dhanaṃjaya said to the woman, greatly
pleased, "Who are you, my lovely, and how did you become a
crocodile? And why have you been doing all these wicked things?"
The woman said:
I am an Apsarā, warrior, who used to roam in the woods of the
15 Gods, I am Vargā, the favorite of the Lord of Riches. I had four friends,
all pretty and all capable of going anywhere. Together with them I
once went to the palace of the World Guardian, and on our way we
all saw a brahmin of strict vows, a handsome man who was doing his
studies all by himself in solitude. The forest, my prince, was illumined
by the light of his austerities, and like a sun he set the whole region
alight. When we saw such wondrous power of austerity as was his,
we all alighted in that spot to disrupt his mortifications. I, and
Saurabheyī, and Samīcī, Budbudā, and Latā all went to the brahmin
at the same time, Bhārata. We sang and laughed and tempted the
brahmin, but he gave us not a thought, O hero. The splendid man
20 did not waver as he stood in his stainless austerity, but in anger the
brahmin cursed us, bull of the barons: "You will become crocodiles
and live in the water for a hundred years!"

Vargā said:
209.1 We were all very disturbed, best of the Bhāratas, and sought refuge
with that undefeated brahmin ascetic. "Our beauty, our youth, and
the God of Love have made us conceited, and so we committed an
offense: pray forgive us, brahmin! It spelled our death most sufficiently
that we should come here to seduce you, an ascetic of strict vows.
But those who ponder the Law hold that women may not be killed,
therefore by the Law you, who know the Law, must not injure us!
5 The brahmin is called the friend of all creatures: so may this beautiful
saying of the wise prove true! The correct render help to those who
seek their mercy; we seek your mercy, so pray forgive us!"

Vaiśaṃpāyana said:
At these words the law-minded brahmin, author of holy deeds,
resplendent like sun and moon, had grace for them, O hero.
The brahmin said:
"Hundred" and "thousand" and "always" all bespeak infinity, but
my "hundred" is a finite number and does not betoken infinity. When
you have become crocodiles and grasp people in the water, a certain
superior man shall pull you out, and you shall all regain your own
10 bodies. Never before have I spoken a lie, even while laughing. Henceforth all these fords shall be known everywhere as the Fords of the
Women, and they shall be sacred and purifying to the wise.
Vargā said:
We bade the brahmin farewell and circumambulated his person;
and, quite wretchedly, we came hither from that place, thinking,
"When indeed, and how soon, before we all shall meet with that man
who will restore our bodies to us again?" While we were worrying we
15 saw after an instant the lordly divine seer Nārada, O Bhārata. On
seeing him, we were all cheered and greeted the boundlessly lustrous
divine seer and stood before him with dejected faces. He asked us the
root of our trouble, and we told him; and when he had heard it as it
had befallen, he said: "In the marshes of the southern ocean there are
five sacred watering places, holy and lovely. Go there without delay.
The tigerlike Pāṇḍava Dhanaṃjaya will soon arrive there, and the
pure-spirited man shall doubtless set you free from your trouble."
When we had heard his word, we all came hither, hero, and 'tis
20 the truth, today you have set me free, prince sans blame! But my four
friends are still in the water. Do a good deed, hero, and set them free!
Vaiśaṃpāyana said:
Thereupon the best of the Pāṇḍavas happily and mightily delivered
them all from that curse. The Apsarās rose from the water and
assumed their own bodies and thereafter looked as they had before,
sire. After having sanctified the watering places and dismissed the
women, the lord returned to the city of Maṇalūra to see Citrāṅgadā
again. On her he had begotten King Babhrūvāhana, and having seen
the child, O king, the Pāṇḍava went to Gokarṇa.

Vaiśaṃpāyana said:
210.1 The boundlessly puissant hero visited one after the other all the
sacred fords in the western regions. He went successively to all the
fords and sanctuaries that are found on the western ocean and so
reached Prabhāsa. Madhusūdana* heard word that the undefeated
Terrifier had come to the country of Prabhāsa on his tour of the

* = Kṛṣṇa.

sacred places. Unbeknownst to Arjuna, Madhusūdana the Mādhava went to meet him; and it was in Prabhāsa that Kṛṣṇa and the Pāṇḍava saw each other again. They embraced each other and asked about each other's health and sat down in the forest, the good friends who were the seers Nara and Nārāyaṇa.

Then Vāsudeva queried Arjuna about his doings: "Why are you touring the sacred fords, Pāṇḍava?" Thereupon Arjuna told him all that had happened, and, hearing it, the lordly chief of the Vṛṣṇis approved. Kṛṣṇa and the Pāṇḍava amused themselves in Prabhāsa as they pleased, then went up to Mount Raivataka for a stay. At Kṛṣṇa's behest, men had beautified the mountain and fetched foodstuffs. Arjuna Pāṇḍava accepted and enjoyed it all, and he and Vāsudeva watched actors and dancers. The illustrious Pāṇḍava applauded them all and dismissed them, and himself went to his well-made celestial bed. He told the Sātvata of the sacred fords to which he had been, O Bhārata, and of the mountains, rivers, and forests. And while he was talking, Janamejaya, prince sans blame, sleep carried Arjuna off on his celestial bed, to be awakened again by the sweet sound of song and lute and of praises and blessings. When he had done the necessities, Kṛṣṇa greeted him, and they rode off to Dvārakā on a chariot wrought of gold. Dvārakā was decorated down to the huts in honor of the son of Kuntī, Janamejaya. The inhabitants of the city, eager to see him, hurried out to the royal road by the hundreds and thousands. There was a great commingling of Bhojas, Vṛṣṇis, and Andhakas as their women, by the hundreds and thousands, looked on. Honored by the sons of the Bhojas, Vṛṣṇis, and Andhakas, he greeted those who deserved greetings and was welcomed by all. The boys greeted the hero with great respect everywhere, and his contemporaries embraced him again and again. For many nights he stayed with Kṛṣṇa in Kṛṣṇa's lovely house that was filled with gems and pleasurable things.

1(17) The Abduction of Subhadrā

211–12 (B. 219–20; C. 7906–62)
211 (219; 7906). A festival is held on Mount Raivataka, attended by all the Vṛṣṇis (1–10). Kṛṣṇa and Arjuna stroll about, and the latter sees Kṛṣṇa's sister Subhadrā. He falls in love, as Kṛṣṇa notices (10–15). Arjuna asks Kṛṣṇa how he might marry her; he suggests abduction; Yudhiṣṭhira consents to this (15–25).

212 (220; 7931). With Kṛṣṇa's collusion, Arjuna sets out on his chariot to Mount Raivataka where Subhadrā is doing her devotions and carries her off to Indraprastha (1–5). Her escort gives the alarm; the war drum is sounded, and the tribes gather and are up in arms (5–15). Drunken Baladeva, however, wants Janārdana's advice (20–30).

Vaiśaṃpāyana said:

211.1 A few days later the Vṛṣṇis and Andhakas held a grand festival on
that same Mount Raivataka. The heroes made gifts to thousands of
brahmins, those Bhojas and Vṛṣṇis and Andhakas at the feast of the
mountain. The region of the mountain was embellished all around
with terraces that sparkled with gems and with candelabras. Music-
makers sounded their instruments, dancers danced, and the songsters
5 sang their songs. The august youths of the Vṛṣṇis, sporting their
ornaments, strutted about with their mounts and colorful golden
bracelets. The townspeople had come out by the hundreds and
thousands, accompanied by their wives and retainers, on foot or on all
kinds of vehicles. The lordly Plough-Bearer* walked drunkenly about
with Revatī, followed by musicians, Bhārata. Ugrasena was there, the
majestic king of the Vṛṣṇis, with his one thousand wives, and was
serenaded by the bands. Raukmiṇeya** and Sāmba, both drunk,
always war-crazed, were wearing divine garlands and raiments, and
10 amused themselves like Immortals. Akrūra, Sāraṇa, Gada, Bhānu,
Viḍūratha, Niśaṭha, Cārudeṣṇa, Pṛthu, Vipṛthu, Satyaka and Sātyaki,
Bhangakāra and Sahacāra, Kṛtavarman, Hārdikya, and others not
mentioned, all of them, surrounded by their women and each with his
musicians, shed luster on the festival upon Mount Raivataka.
While the magnificent confusion progressed, Vāsudeva and the
Pārtha strolled about together; and as they were striding about, they
saw, in the midst of her friends, Bhadrā,*** Vāsudeva's beautiful sister.
15 No sooner did he see her than Arjuna fell in love, and Kṛṣṇa noticed
that the Pārtha was absorbed with her. The lotus-eyed hero said,
laughing, "Can it be that the heart of a forest-dweller is turned topsy-
turvy by Love? She is my and Sāraṇa's immediate sister. If your mind
is set on her, I myself shall speak to father."

Arjuna said:

The daughter of Vasudeva, the sister of Kṛṣṇa, and perfect of beauty—whom would she not bewilder? Surely I must have done all

* = Bala-Rāma.

** = son of Rukminī, viz., Pradyumna.

*** = Subhadrā.

good things, if the Daughter of the Vṛṣṇis, your sister, is to be my
20 consort! Tell me, Janārdana, what is the way to obtain her? I shall
do it, if any man can!

Vāsudeva said:

The baron's marriage is the bridegroom choice, bull of men. But
that is dubious, Pārtha, since one's own sentiments have no influence
on the outcome. Forcible abduction is also approved as a ground of
marriage for barons who are champions, as the Law-wise know.
Abduct my beautiful sister by force, for who would know her designs
at a bridegroom choice?

Vaiśaṃpāyana said:

Thereupon Arjuna and Kṛṣṇa, having thus resolved on their course
25 of action, sent off fast runners, O king, to tell all to King Dharma at
Indraprastha. And soon as he heard the message, the strong-armed
Pāṇḍava assented.

Vaiśaṃpāyana said:

212.1 When Yudhiṣṭhira had agreed and consented, Dhanaṃjaya learned
that the girl had gone to Mount Raivataka, Janamejaya; and with
Vāsudeva's consent, having discussed his course of action and knowing
Kṛṣṇa's mind, the bull of the Bharatas started out on a carefully built,
golden-membered chariot, yoked with Sainya and Sugrīva and hung
with a circlet of little bells. It was equipped with all the weapons,
thundered like a rain cloud, shone like the blazing fire—the bane of
5 his enemies. Girt, armored, sworded, wrist and finger guards tied on,
he set out at once on the pretext of a chase, O Bhārata.

Subhadrā, now, paid her homage to Mount Raivata, king of
mountains, as well as its deities, and had the brahmins pronounce
blessings; then she circumambulated the mountain and started out for
Dvārakā. Arjuna rushed at her and forcefully lifted her on his chariot.
As soon as the tigerlike man had taken the sweet-smiling girl he
drove on to his own city in his chariot, which seemed to ride on air.
However, when her armed escort saw Subhadrā abducted, they all ran
10 shouting to Dvārakā city. When they came to the courthouse named
Sudharmā, they related all the Pārtha's gallantry to the magistrate.
The magistrate thereupon sounded the war drum, a drum of mighty
sound, which was inlaid with gold. Shocked by the sound, the Bhojas,
Vṛṣṇis, and Andhakas raced together, throwing away what they were
eating or drinking.

Then the tigerlike warriors of the Vṛṣṇis and Andhakas, in their
hundreds, took, as the fires take their altars, their lion thrones, which
were wrought with gold, covered with precious cushions, sparkling
15 with gems and coral, resplendent like blazing fires. In this gathering of
them, sitting like the Gods, the magistrate and his retinue told of the

feat that Jiṣṇu had accomplished. Upon their hearing of it, the heroes
of the Vṛṣṇis, the whites of their eyes reddened by their drinking,
pridefully crowded together, unforgiving of the Pārtha: "Yoke the
chariots at once, get the spears, and the best bows and big cuirasses!"
Some cried out to their charioteers to yoke the chariots, others fetched
their golden-harnessed horses themselves. While the chariots and
cuirasses and pennants were being brought, there was a vast
hurly-burly amidst the shouting of the champions.
20 At this time, garlanded with wild flowers, sodden, tall as the
Kailāsa peak, clad in a dark cloak, and splashed with drunkenness,
Baladeva* spoke: "What are you doing, fools, when Janārdana keeps
silent? Getting angry without knowing his mind and strutting
pointlessly? Let the sagacious Kṛṣna first tell his own plans, then you
must do without hesitation what he wants done."

Hearing this good advice from the plough-armed Baladeva, they
said, "Good! Good!" And all fell silent; and on the wise Baladeva's
equable words they all resumed their seats in the middle of the hall.
25 Then the Lord of Desires* spoke to the enemy-burning Vāsudeva:
"Why are you sitting here, and why do you look on without speaking,
Janārdana! It was because of you that we all welcomed the Pārtha,
Acyuta! That witless befouler of his family was not worth our
homage! For what man anywhere would break the dish that he had
eaten off, if he deemed himself well-born? And who would act so
recklessly, when he came as a supplicant wishing alliance and
honoring past favors? He has shown his contempt for us, and his
disregard of Keśava, by forcibly abducting Subhadrā, who will be his
30 death! How can I forgive that he has trodden on my head, Govinda?
Can a snake that is stepped upon? Today I alone shall rid the earth of
the Kauravas, for I cannot forbear Arjuna's crime!" And all the
Bhojas, Vṛṣṇis, and Andhakas applauded the thundering man who
sounded like rain cloud and kettledrum.

1(18) *The Fetching of the Gift*

213 (B. 221; C. 7963–8049).
213 (22; 7363). Kṛṣṇa defends Arjuna's action and commends the alliance (1–10). The Vṛṣṇis acquiesce, and Arjuna weds Subhadrā. Arjuna spends the rest of his exile in Puṣkara and returns to the Khāṇḍava Tract (10). Draupadī is jealous of Subhadrā; but Subhadrā, humbly dressed and behaved, wins her over (10–20). Kṛṣṇa and

* = Bala-Rāma.

the Vṛṣṇis arrive bringing the nuptial gift and are welcomed by Yudhiṣṭhira (20–35). Description of the gift: chariots, cows, mares, mules, serving women, gold, elephants (40–50). The Vṛṣṇis disport themselves (50–55). Subhadrā gives birth to Abhimanyu, who is taught by Arjuna (55–70). Draupadī has five sons, each one a year apart (70–80).

Vaiśaṃpāyana said:
213.1 When all the Vṛṣṇis went on to repeat his words, Vāsudeva made
his speech, consonant with Law and Profit: "Guḍākeśa has showered
no contumely on our line, but doubtless has shown us superior honor!
The Pārtha knows that you Sātvatas are not greedy for riches, and he
also judged that he could not win at a bridegroom choice. Who would
approve of giving the girl away, as though she were cattle? And what
5 man on earth would barter his offspring? I believe that Arjuna saw all
these difficulties, and hence abducted the girl lawfully. The alliance is
a proper one. Subhadrā is famous, and an equally famous Pārtha took
her by force. Who would not want Arjuna, the son of the daughter of
Kuntibhoja, born in the lineage of Bharata and the great-spirited
Śaṃtanu? Nor do I see one who could vanquish the Pārtha with
gallantry, my worthy, in any of the worlds with their Indras and
10 Rudras. That kind of chariot and my own horses! The Pārtha is a
nimble archer; who would match him? Rather run after Dhanaṃjaya
and cheerfully make him return with the politest diplomacy! This is
my final opinion. If the Pārtha were to return to his own city after
defeating us gallantly, our fame would be lost instantly. But there is
no defeat in diplomacy!"
After they had heard Vāsudeva's discourse, sire, they acted
accordingly; and Arjuna returned and held his wedding there. He
dwelled there for the last nights of his year, and the lord spent the
remaining time in the Puṣkaras; but when the twelve-month year was
full, he entered the Khāṇḍava Tract.
Thoughtful of the courtesies, he greeted the king; and after greeting
15 the brahmins, the Pārtha came to Draupadī. Her love moved
Draupadī to reply to the scion of Kuru: "Go where that Sātvata
woman is, Kaunteya! It is the first knot that comes loose first on a
load, however well tied!" While Kṛṣṇā thus complained in many ways,
Dhanaṃjaya tried to soothe her and again and again sought her
pardon. Hurriedly, Arjuna had Subhadrā, who was wearing a red silk
skirt, change into a cow maid's dress. The glorious woman, a hero's
wife, looked even more beautiful in it. When she came to the main
house, the glorious Bhadrā of the wide copper-red eyes greeted
Pṛthā, and then, her face shining like the full moon, hastened to

20 greet Draupadī: "I am Bhadrā, your serving maid!" she said. Kṛṣṇā
rose to meet the sister of the Mādhava, embraced her, and said kindly,
"Let your *husband* at least have no rival!" Cheered by this, Bhadrā
replied, "May it be so!" The warlike Pāṇḍavas were delighted, and
Kuntī was most pleased, Janamejaya.
When the lotus-eyed Keśava learned that Arjuna, the best of the
Pāṇḍavas, who had left for Indraprastha, had reached his city, the
pure-spirited hero went there with Rāma and warlike and notable
champions of the Vṛṣṇis and Andhakas. Enemy-burner Śauri also
came, surrounded by his brothers, sons, and warriors by the hundreds
25 and protected by a large host. The glorious and wise Akrūra came, he
of the princely gifts, the enemy-taming commander of the Vṛṣṇi
heroes; splendid Anādhṛṣṭi, and famous Uddhava, the sagacious pupil
of Bṛhaspati himself; Satyaka and Sātyaki and Kṛtavarman the
Sātvata, Pradyumna, Sāmba, Niśaṭha, Śanku, gallant Cārudeṣṇa,
Jhillin and Vipṛthu, strong-armed Sāraṇa, and Gada, the first of the
wise. They and many other Vṛṣṇis, Bhojas, and Andhakas all came to
the Khāṇḍava Tract, bringing a vast nuptial gift.
30 King Yudhiṣṭhira, when he heard that Kṛṣṇa Mādhava had arrived,
sent the twins to receive him. They received the opulent circle of the
Vṛṣṇis, and the party entered the Khāṇḍava Tract, which was
decorated with flags and pennants. The roads were swept and
sprinkled, flowers were scattered about in profusion, and the cool
essence of sandal and other propitious perfumes made the city
redolent. Everywhere very fragrant aloe was being burned, and the
town was thronged with freshly bathed people and flamboyant with
merchants.
Strong-armed Keśava arrived with Rāma; the great man was
35 surrounded by Vṛṣṇis, Andhakas, and great Bhojas. Honored by
thousands of brahmins and townfolk, he entered the king's palace,
which was like the house of the Sacker of Cities. Yudhiṣṭhira met
ceremonially with Rāma and kissed Keśava on the head and clasped
him with his arm. Kṛṣṇa greeted the pleased king with all courtesy,
and also the tigerlike Bhīmasena. Yudhiṣṭhira the King Dharma
received the chiefs of the Vṛṣṇis and Andhakas with proper honors, as
it befitted—some he honored as elders, others as contemporaries, still
others with affection even as he was greeted by some of them.
40 Thereupon famous Vāsudeva gave sublime wealth as a gift to the
bridegroom's party and as a dowry from her kinsmen to Subhadrā. A
thousand golden-membered chariots hung with circlets of little bells,
yoked with four horses, and driven by dextrous charioteers did the
illustrious Kṛṣṇa give, and ten thousand cows from the Mathurā
countryside, fine milkers all and propitiously colored. Janārdana also
gave a thousand golden-harnessed and splendid mares of the color of
moonbeams as a token of friendship; and twice five hundred tame and

wind-fast mules, both black-maned and white; and a thousand
youthful, fair, and well-complexioned women adept at hairdressing
45 and massaging, healthy and well-clad, wearing necklaces of a hundred
gold pieces, all skillful serving wenches. Ten man-loads of the finest
fire-colored gold, both worked and unworked, did the lotus-eyed
Janārdana of Daśārha present. The violence-loving hero gave a
thousand choice elephants in rut, flowing with ichor in three ways,
towering like mountain peaks, never turning in battle, hung with
finely crafted and loud collar bells, caparisoned in gold, and saddled
with *howdahs*: all this the plough-bearing Rāma gave the Pārtha by
way of prostration, for he was pleased and thought highly of the
50 alliance. This huge flood of treasures and gems, frothy with clothes
and blankets, awhale with huge elephants, over which the duckweed
of pennants floated, became a great river debouching in the ocean of
the Pāṇḍus and filling it up, to the chagrin of their enemies!

Yudhiṣṭhira the King Dharma accepted it all, and paid homage to
the warriors of the Vṛṣṇis and Andhakas. The chiefs of the Kurus,
Vṛṣṇis, and Andhakas who had foregathered there disported
themselves as men of good deeds in the abode of the Immortals. Kurus
and Vṛṣṇis amused themselves as they saw fit and were pleased, with
55 great drinking bouts and loud clapping of hands. After the puissant
men had feasted for many days, they returned to Dvārakā city,
honored by the Kurus. Led by Rāma, the warriors of the Vṛṣṇis and
Andhakas went their way, with the sparkling gems that the chiefs of
the Kurus had given them. But the great-spirited Vāsudeva stayed
there with Arjuna in the lovely city of Indraprastha and strolled with
the Pārtha on the bank of the river Yamunā.

Subhadrā, Keśava's dear sister, gave birth to Abhimanyu
Saubhadra as Paulomī* did to the effulgent Jayanta. He was a
long-armed, mettlesome, bull-eyed, enemy-taming bull of a man, the
60 hero Abhimanyu whom Subhadrā bore. He was fearless and wrathful,
and hence they called Arjuna's enemy-taming, bulllike son by the
name Abhimanyu. The superior warrior was begotten on the
Sātvata woman by Dhanaṃjaya, as fire is begotten at a sacrifice upon
the womb of the *śamī* block that is drilled. At his birth the
strong-armed Yudhiṣṭhira, son of Kuntī, gave ten thousand cows to the
brahmins and as many coins. From childhood on he was Vāsudeva's
favorite, and like the moon to his fathers and all his subjects. From
his birth onward Kṛṣṇa celebrated the sacred rites for him, and the
65 child grew as the moon in the bright fortnight. The enemy-tamer
learned from the *Veda*-wise Arjuna the entire four-membered, tenfold
Science of Archery, both human and divine. The powerful child
learned the niceties of the sciences of weaponry, of deftness in

* = Indra's wife.

handling missiles, and of all actions. Arjuna made him his equal in
learning and application, and the sight of his son by Subhadrā
brought contentment to Dhanaṃjaya. Like Indra, the Terrifier saw a
son all muscle, marked with all good lines, unassailable, with the
shoulders of a bull and the wide mouth of a snake, a great archer with
70 the pride of a lion and the power of a mad elephant, the voice of a
thundercloud and a kettledrum, the face of the full moon, the match
of Kṛṣṇa in bravery, might, beauty, and shape.

The well-favored Draupadī, too, obtained five sons from her five
husbands, heroic and bright, like five mountains: Prativindhya by
Yudhiṣṭhira, Sutasoma by the Wolf-Belly, Śrutakarman by Arjuna,
Śatānīka by Nakula, Śrutasena by Sahadeva—five great and heroic
warriors she bore, as Aditi bore the Ādityas. The brahmins told
Yudhiṣṭhira according to the scriptures of Prativindhya that he would
75 be a Prativindhya in the knowledge of his enemies' weapons. By
Bhīmasena she bore the great archer Sutasoma, who shone like sun
and moon, after a thousand Somas had been pressed. "Since this son
was born to you by the Diademed Arjuna when he returned after
accomplishing great feats, he shall be Śrutakarman." Nakula
Kaurava, scion of Kuru, called his son, who increased his fame, after
the royal seer Śatānīka. Then Kṛṣṇā bore a son by Sahadeva under
the asterism of Vahnidaivata, and therefore they know him as
Śrutasena.

Draupadī's famous sons were born one after the other, a year apart,
O lord of kings, and they were devoted to one another's well-being.
80 Dhaumya performed for them the sacraments of birth, tonsure, and
initiation in the regular order according to the rules, O best of the
Bharatas. After these boys of well-conducted vows had finished their
Veda studies, they learned all weaponry, human and divine, from
Arjuna. And as they were followed by their broad-chested, powerful
sons, like children of Gods, O tiger among kings, the Pāṇḍavas found
joy.

1(19) The Burning of the Khāṇḍava Forest

214–25 (B. 222–34; C. 8050–8479).
214 (222; 8050). The happy state of Indraprastha (1–10). Arjuna suggests to Kṛṣṇa an outing on the river Yamunā; they enjoy themselves with their women (15–25). Arjuna and Kṛṣṇa meet a fiery-looking brahmin (25–30).

215 (224; 8157). The brahmin demands food of them; they agree to fetch it (1–5). He identifies himself as the Fire God; he wants to devour the Khāṇḍava Forest; but because Indra's friend Takṣaka lives there, this God protects it with rain (5–10). Arjuna asks for superior weapons (1–15).
216 (225; 8174). The Fire summons Varuṇa, whom he instructs to give Arjuna a bow, quivers, and a chariot, and Kṛṣṇa a discus (1). Varuṇa does so; description of chariot and weapons (5–25). Arjuna declares himself ready, and the Fire begins to burn the forest (25–30).
217 (226; 8211). The conflagration (1–10). The Gods inform Indra, who starts to pour rain (15–20).
218 (227; 8233). Arjuna drives off the rain (1). Aśvasena, the son of the absent Takṣaka, tries to escape; to save him, his mother swallows him; he escapes and is cursed (1–10). Arjuna fights rain and wind, birds and celestials (10–25), Kṛṣṇa fights the demons (25). The principal Gods arm themselves but are warded off by the two heroes (25–45). Indra drops a mountain, which is shattered by Arjuna (45).
219. They continue the massacre, and the Gods withdraw (1–10). A voice tells Indra that they are the invincible Nara and Nārāyaṇa; he retires (10–15). As the Fire rages on, the pair shoot down any creature that flees (20–30). The Asura Maya emerges and is granted safe conduct by Arjuna (35). Six survive: Aśvasena, Maya, and four Śārngaka birds (5).
220–25. The Story of the Śārngakas
225 (234; 8461). The Fire is sated. Indra appears and offers them a boon. Arjuna asks for Indra's weapons, which he promises (5–10). Kṛṣṇa asks eternal friendship with Arjuna, and it is granted (10). The Fire dismisses Arjuna, Kṛṣṇa, and Maya (15).

Vaiśaṃpāyana said:

214.1 While they were living in Indraprastha, at the orders of King Dhṛtarāṣṭra and Bhīṣma Śāṃtanava, they vanquished other kings. All the people, relying on King Dharma, lived happily like souls that rely on their own bodies that are favored with auspicious marks and deeds. The bull of the Bharatas cultivated Law, Profit, and Pleasure alike, like a family man honoring three kinsmen alike to himself. To Law, Profit and Pleasure, now incarnated on earth in equal proportions, the king
5 himself appeared as the fourth. In this overlord of men the *Vedas*

found a superb student, the great sacrifices a performer, the four classes a pure guardian. Luck had found her place, wisdom its apex, all Law its kinsman with this lord of the earth. With his four brethren the king shone forth the more splendidly, like a grand ritual executed with the four *Vedas*. Dhaumya and the other brahmins surrounded and worshiped him, just as the chief Immortals, equals of Bṛhaspati, worship Prajāpati. In their great love the eyes as well as the hearts of the people delighted as much in King Dharma as in the immaculate full orb of the moon. He was sole king, no doubt, and his subjects rejoiced in that, but no less did he endear himself with his deeds. Not a word improper, untrue, mendacious, or displeasing welled forth from the mouth of the gentle-spoken, wise Pārtha. And this most resplendent chief of the Bhāratas delighted in doing what was best for all the world and for himself. Thus, then, happy and cured of their fever, did all the Pāṇḍavas live there, frightening the rulers of the earth with their splendor.

A few days had passed when the Terrifier said to Kṛṣṇa, "The hot days are here, Kṛṣṇa, let us go to the river Yamunā. Let us play there with our friends, Madhusūdana, and return here in the evening, if you like, Janārdana."

Vāsudeva said:

I too, son of mother Kuntī, have a desire to play in the water amidst our friends, as long as it pleases us, son of Pṛthā.

Vaiśaṃpāyana said:

After consulting, and with the consent of, King Dharma, the Pārtha and Govinda went out amidst their friends. Upon reaching their beautiful playground, wooded with all sorts of trees and dotted with manifold houses like the estate of the Sacker of Cities,* where flavorful and costly foods and delicacies and liquors were laid out as well as all manner of garlands that were worthy of the Pārtha and Vārṣneya, they entered the place that was filled with sparkling gems of many waters, and all people began playing to their heart's delight, O Bhārata. Some of the women played in the woods, others in the water, still others in the cabins, whatever spots pleased Kṛṣṇa and the Pārtha. At the height of intoxication, Draupadī and Subhadrā distributed priceless clothes and ornaments to the women. Some danced rapturously, others shouted, some of the women laughed, and others drank the choice liquor. There were some who started weeping, some started fighting, while others whispered secrets to one another. And that most prosperous wood was everywhere filled with the lovely sounds of flutes, *viṇās*, and drums.

While this went on, the scions of Kuru and Daśārha retired to a pleasant spot close by, and having gone there the two great-spirited Kṛṣṇas, conquerors of enemy cities, seated themselves on precious

* = Indra.

stools. The Pārtha and Mādhava recounted many stories of past feats
and loves, and enjoyed themselves. As they were happily sitting there,
like the two Horsemen on the vault of heaven, Vāsudeva and
30 Dhanaṃjaya were approached by a brahmin. Tall like a huge *śāla*
tree, fair like molten gold, orange-colored, with a reddish beard, of
well-proportioned limbs, radiant like the morning sun, black-garbed,
hair braided, eyes like lotus leaves, and fairly blazing with glory, the
red man drew near, and the two Kṛṣṇas, Arjuna and Vāsudeva,
quickly stood up to the splendid brahmin.

Vaiśaṃpāyana said:
215.1 He said to Arjuna and Vāsudeva Sātvata, "The two champions of
the world are standing close to the Khāṇḍava Forest! I am a voracious
brahmin, I always eat boundlessly. I beg you, Vārṣneya and Pārtha,
for once give me enough to eat!"

Upon his words Kṛṣṇa and Pāndava said to him, "What kind of
food would sate you? We will fetch it for you!" Hereupon the
venerable brahmin said to the two heroes, who had asked him what
5 food to prepare for him, "I don't eat food! Know that I am the Fire.
Therefore fetch me the food that suits me! Indra always protects this
Khāṇḍava Forest from conflagration, and as long as the great-spirited
God protects it, I cannot burn it. His friend lives there with his people,
the Snake Takṣaka, and for his sake the Thunderbolt-Wielder protects
it from burning. As it happens, many other creatures are thus
protected. However much I wish to burn it, I fail because of Śakra's
might. As soon as he sees me ablaze, he starts raining with the floods
of the clouds, so that I cannot burn this wood, much as I would love
10 to. But now that I have met with the two of you, my helpers and
experts on arms, I shall burn the Khāṇḍava! This forest is the food I
have chosen. You are fully familiar with weapons: you shall stop any
and all creatures and clouds on all sides!"

At this speech the Terrifier replied to the Fire, who wished to burn
the Khāṇḍava Forest in spite of the God of the Hundred Sacrifices, "I
have many superb and divine weapons with which I can even fight
many thunderbolt-wielders. But, my good lord, I do not have a bow
commensurate with the strength of my arms, which can withstand
15 my power and speed in battle. And I need an inexhaustible supply of
arrows when I shoot fast. My chariot cannot hold all the arrows that
I want. Divine horses I want, white and fast as the wind, and a
chariot that thunders like a cloud and shines bright like the sun!
Likewise, Kṛṣṇa Mādhava has no weapon equal to his strength with
which he could kill the Snakes and Piśācas in battle. Sire, pray tell us
the means to succeed in this task, so that I can stop Indra from
raining on the great forest. What prowess can do, that we shall do,
Fire, but pray give us the tools for it, lord!"

Vaiśaṃpāyana said:
216.1 At these words the venerable, smoke-crested Fire thought of
Varuṇa, the World Guardian, for he wanted to see him, that divine
son of Aditi who lives in the water and lords over it. Knowing the
thought, Varuṇa appeared before the Fire, and the smoke-crested God
paid homage to him and said to the lord of the waters, the fourth
World Guardian, protector and great lord, "Hand over at once that
bow that King Soma once gave, and the two quivers, and also the
chariot with the sign of the monkey. For the Pārtha shall accomplish
a very great task with the bow Gāṇḍīva. And let the discus be
presented to Vāsudeva on my behalf."
5 "I will give them," replied Varuṇa to the Fire. Thereupon he gave
him the miraculous, powerful gem of a bow that would increase his
fame and renown, unassailable by any weapon, wreaking havoc on all
weapons, great lord of all arms that menaced the enemy forces, by
itself the equal of a hundred thousand, enhancer of the realm,
colorfully shining with manifold hues, smooth and unscratched,
which for eternities had been worshiped by Gods, Dānavas, and
Gandharvas. Also he gave the two great and inexhaustible quivers and
the divine, horse-yoked chariot that bore the monkey banner, drawn
by silver Gandharva horses that were harnessed in gold, resembling
white clouds and in speed like the wind or the mind. The chariot was
laden with all the war gear; and it was invincible to Gods and
10 Dānavas, resplendent, thunderous, enchanting to all creatures. The
Prajāpati Viśvakarman, the lord of the worlds, had created it out of the
power of his self-mortifications. Its form was indiscernible, like that of
the sun. King Soma had mounted it, and the Lord had gone on to
vanquish the Dānavas—huge it was, like an elephant or cloud, and
blazing with beauty. On this greatest of chariots was fastened a
shining flagpole, like Indra's rainbow, wrought out of gold, superb and
magnificent. On top of it perched beautifully a divine monkey, marked
with the signs of lion and tiger, which seemed to roar out. On the
banner there were large creatures of many races whose roars made
the hosts of foemen swoon.
15 The Pārtha circumambulated the matchless chariot, which was
adorned with various pennants, bowed to the deities, then, girt,
armored, sworded, with finger and wrist guards tied on, he mounted
the war car as a man of good deeds mounts a celestial chariot. And
when he took hold of Gāṇḍīva, the great and divine bow that Brahmā
had once created, Arjuna grew happy. The powerful hero made
obeisance to the Fire and, applying his strength, strung the bow with
its string. The minds shuddered of those who heard the twanging
20 when the strong Pāṇḍava corded his bow. Having obtained his
chariot, the bow, and the two inexhaustible quivers, the Kaunteya

grew vigorous and joyous for the task that now had become feasible.
Thereupon the Fire gave Kṛṣṇa a discus with a thunderbolt in the
center, a fiery weapon that he loved, and he too became full of vigor.
Quoth the Fire, "With this discus, Madhusūdana, thou shalt doubtless
triumph in battle even over those who are not human. With these
thou shalt always exceed men in war, and even Gods, Rākṣasas,
Piśācas, Daityas, and Snakes, without misdoubting, in the eradication
of great enemies. Whenever thou hast hurled it in battle at thy foes, O
Mādhava, and hast slain them with it unobstructed, it shall return to
25 thy hand!" Varuṇa also gave Hari a club that roared like a
thunderbolt, the dreadful killer of the Daityas, which was named
Kaumodakī.

Then Kṛṣṇa and the Pāṇḍava spoke joyously to the Fire: "Now that we are armed and mounted, and fly our banners, we are eager to fight with all the Gods and Asuras, let alone with a single Indra who is willing to go to battle for the Snake!"

Arjuna said:

When the powerful Vārṣṇeya lets go of the discus in battle, there is
not a thing in the three worlds that Janārdana could not conquer.
And with my bow Gāṇḍiva and the two inexhaustible quivers I too
am equal to the task of conquering the worlds in a war, O Fire.
30 Now blaze up as you please and encircle this forest with a huge
conflagration, O lord—we are equal to the task!

Vaiśaṃpāyana said:

At these words of Arjuna and the Dāśārha, the lord took on his fiery form and began to burn the forest. Surrounding it on all sides with his Seven Flames, the Fire angrily burned the Khāṇḍava, as though to exhibit the end of the Eon. When he encircled and invaded that forest, bull of the Bharatas, burning down all the creatures with the thunderous roar of the monsoon cloud, the burning forest took on the shape of Mount Meru, king of mountains, that sparkles with gold.

Vaiśaṃpāyana said:

217.1 Standing on their chariots at both ends of the forest, the two
tigerlike men started a vast massacre of the creatures on every side.
Indeed, whenever the heroes saw live creatures escaping, such as lived
in the Khāṇḍava, they chased them down. They saw no hole to
escape, because of the vigorous speed of the chariots—both the grand
chariots and their warriors seemed to be strung together. As the
Khāṇḍava was burning, the creatures in their thousands leaped up in
5 all ten directions, screeching their terrifying screams. Many were
burning in one spot, others were scorched—they were shattered and
scattered mindlessly, their eyes abursting. Some embraced their sons,
others their fathers and mothers, unable to abandon them, and thus

went to their perdition. Still others jumped up by the thousands, faces
distorted, and darting hither and thither fell into the Fire. All over, the
souls were seen writhing on the ground, with burning wings, eyes,
and paws, until they perished. As all watery places came to a boil,
10 Bhārata, the turtles and fish were found dead by the thousands. With
their burning bodies the creatures in that forest appeared like living
torches until they breathed their last. When they jumped out, the
Pārtha cut them to pieces with his arrows and, laughing, threw them
back into the blazing Fire. Their bodies covered with arrows and
screeching fiercely, they leaped upward nimbly and fell back into the
Fire. The noise of the forest animals, as they were hit by the arrows
and left to burn, was like the ocean's when it was being churned. The
huge flames of the happy Fire jumped up to the sky and caused the
15 greatest consternation among the Gods. All the great-spirited denizens
of heaven went and sought refuge with the Thousand-Eyed King of
the Gods, the Sacker of Cities.

The Gods said:

Why are all these people being burned by the Fire? Has perchance
the end of the worlds arrived, lord of the Immortals?

Vaiśaṃpāyana said:

When he heard this from them, the Slayer of Vṛtra peered down
himself; then the bay-horsed God set out to rescue the Khāṇḍava.
With a mighty mass of many-formed clouds the Thunderbolt-Wielder
spread over the sky and the Lord of the Gods began to rain. Casting
forth hundreds of thousands of rain shafts, thick as axles, the
Thousand-Eyed God rained upon the Fire that raged over the
20 Khāṇḍava. But before they met their target, the rain shafts were
evaporated by the heat of the Fire, and not a one found its mark.
Thereupon the Slayer of Namuci waxed greatly angry with the Fire
and once more started raining, sending forth much water. Embattled
by flames and rain shafts, billowing with smoke and lightning,
echoing with the roar of thunder, the forest became grisly.

Vaiśaṃpāyana said:

218.1 The Pāṇḍava the Terrifier, showing off his splendid weapons,
stopped Indra as he rained down water with a shower of arrows. And
he covered the entire Khāṇḍava on every side with his arrows, when
he had driven Indra's rain from the forest. Not a single creature could
escape from there anymore, when the left-handed archer blanketed it
with his sky-going reeds.

However, Takṣaka, the mighty king of the Snakes, was not there in
the burning forest: at that time he was in the Field of the Kurus.
5 But Aśvasena was there, Takṣaka's powerful son, and he made

vigorous attempts to escape from the Fire. Crowded by Kaunteya's arrows, he could not get out. His mother, herself a daughter of the Snakes, tried to save him by swallowing him up. First she swallowed his head, then, while she was swallowing his tail, the Snake woman, greedy for her son, stretched upward. When she moved, the Pāṇḍava shot off her head with a sharp, wide-bladed arrow, and the lord of the Gods saw her. The Thunderbolt-Wielder tried to rescue Aśvasena and dazed the Pāṇḍava with wind gusts and rain shafts, and in that instant Aśvasena got free. On seeing his terrifying power of illusion, and having been deceived by the Snake, he cut the sky-going Snakes in two or three pieces, O Bhārata. Wrathfully, the Terrifier cursed the Snake—and so did the Fire and Vāsudeva: "Thou shalt never find shelter!"

Then Jiṣṇu covered the sky with his honed shafts and, remembering the deception that had been played on him, began furiously to war on the Thousand-Eyed God. The King of the Gods, beholding the rage of Phalguna, unleashed his own blazing missile, which streaked across the entire sky. Thereupon the Wind God, who dwells in the sky, thunderously shaking all the oceans, generated towering clouds that sent forth shafts of water. To counter him, Arjuna, who knew his defenses, cast a spell on his great *vāyavya* missile. With it he drained the power and might of the thunderbolts and clouds of Indra; and the clouds dried up, and the lightning flashes died. In an instant the foulness and darkness of the sky was appeased, the virtue of its wind was pleasant and cool, the orb of its sun restored to normality. Delighted at the lack of opposition, the Fire in its many metamorphoses went on burning, incomparably ablaze, filling up the world with its noise.

Seeing that that forest fire was protected by the two Kṛṣṇas, the birds from the fair-winged Garuḍa onward pridefully flew up to the sky. Garuḍas, eager to strike the two warriors with their wings, beaks, and claws, which were as hard as thunderbolts, flew flocking from the sky to Kṛṣṇa and Pāṇḍava. Likewise, nests of Snakes came out close to the Pāṇḍava, spewing with burning mouths their ghastly venom. No sooner did he see the raging, airborne beasts than the Pārtha cut them up with his arrows. Powerlessly, they fell into the fire to part with their bodies.

Thereupon the Gods and the Gandharvas, Yakṣas, Rākṣasas, and Snakes rose aloud with unrivaled noise, eager to fight, arms ready with iron maces, discuses, rocks, and fire-carrying missiles, out to kill Kṛṣṇa and the Pṛthā, their majestic powers obfuscated by their fury. When they attacked and let loose a rain of weapons, the Terrifier churned their topmost limbs with his well-honed arrows.

Most mighty Kṛṣṇa, slayer of enemies, wrought a vast massacre with his discus among the hordes of Daityas and Dānavas. Other august demons, sliced by the arrows and propelled by the impact of the discus, came finally to rest, as waves that reach the tideline. Then, enraged, Śakra, lord of the Thirty Gods, mounted his white elephant and stormed upon both of them. Grasping his lightning, he hurled his missile thunderbolt with force, and the slayer of demons announced to the Gods that the two were killed. Then, seeing the great bolt held ready by the Indra of the Gods, the Gods all grasped their own weapons—King Yama his Staff of Death, the God of Wealth his Palanquin, Varuṇa his Noose, Śiva his Trident. The Aśvins held their phosphorescent Herbs, Dhātar his Bow, Jaya his Pestle. The powerful Tvaṣṭar angrily grabbed hold of a Mountain, Aṃśa of a Spear, God Death of a Hatchet. Aryaman grasped his dreadful Mace and strode about, Mitra his honed-edged Discus and stood about. Pūṣan and Bhaga and Savitar wrathfully took their bows and swords and rushed upon Kṛṣṇa and the Pārtha. The Rudras, Vasus, and mighty Maruts, the All-the-Gods, and the Sādhyas, ablaze with their own glory, these and many other Gods, ready to kill Kṛṣṇa and the Pārtha, advanced with their various weapons.

In that grand battle miraculous portents were witnessed that equaled those at the end of the Eon and prophesied the extermination of the creatures, O Bhārata. When the two Acyutas saw raging Indra accompanied by the Gods, they stood facing battle, tough, their bows ready; and as they saw the Gods advance from every quarter, they furiously checked them with their thunderboltlike arrows. Again and again, their will to war was crushed; and when they were scattered about, the Gods fearfully abandoned the battle and sought refuge with Indra. The hermits who dwell in heaven beheld the Gods held in check by Arjuna and the Mādhava and were amazed. Śakra, too, upon witnessing the constant prowess of the two in battle, was greatly pleased and once more engaged them in fighting. The Punisher of Pāka cast forth a mighty rain of rocks, to probe once more the heroism of the left-handed archer; but impatiently Arjuna countered them with his arrows. The King of the Gods of the Hundred Sacrifices, seeing his deed defeated, again increased his shower. Still the son of Pāka's Punisher brought the shower of rocks to nought with his nimble arrows, mocking his father. Indra then uprooted with his bare hands one tall peak of Mount Mandara and threw it with its trees at Pāṇḍu's son to finish him. Thereupon Arjuna with his fast, straight-flying, tip-burning arrows split the mountain peak into a thousand chips. The crumbling of that mountain was like heaven crumbling with sun, moon, and planets. And the big mountain, falling precipitately on the forest, killed off even more of the creatures that lived in the Khāṇḍava.

Vaiśaṃpāyana said:

219.1 The Khāṇḍava creatures, Dānavas, Rākṣasas, Snakes, hyenas, bears
and other forest beasts, rutting elephants, tigers, full-maned lions, deer
and buffalo, and hundreds of birds, were frightened by the falling
mountain, and, much perturbed, they and other races of beings
crawled away. They saw the conflagration raging and the two Kṛṣṇas
with their weapons ready; and the roaring sound of the upheaval
brought them to terror. Janārdana let loose his discus, which shone
with its own light, and the humble creatures as well as the Dānavas
and the Stalkers of the Night were cut down by the hundreds, and
5 they all fell instantly into the Fire. Rent by Kṛṣṇa's discus, the
Rākṣasas were seen besmirched with fat and blood like clouds at
twilight. The Vārṣṇeya went about like Time, killing off Piśācas, birds,
Snakes, animals by the thousands, O Bhārata. And whenever that
discus of enemy-slaying Kṛṣṇa was thrown, it came back to his hand
after killing numbers of creatures. As he was thus killing all beings,
Bhārata, the aspect of him, soul of all beings, became most dreadful.
No one of the Gods and the Dānavas, who had foregathered
everywhere, was the vanquisher in battle of Kṛṣṇa and Pāṇḍava.
10 When the Gods were unable with all their might to save the burning
forest from them, or to douse it, they turned away their faces. The God
of the Hundred Sacrifices, seeing how the hosts of the Gods turned
away, continued to be pleased and praised Kṛṣṇa and the Pāṇḍava.

When the Gods retreated, a disembodied voice spoke to Indra with
a mighty and deep rumble: "Your friend, the great Snake Takṣaka, is
not here, for at the time of the burning of the Khāṇḍava he went to
the Field of the Kurus. You cannot defeat Vāsudeva and Arjuna when
15 they stand fast in war, Śakra, listen to my word! They are the two
divinities Nara and Nārāyaṇa, who are renowned in heaven. You
yourself know well of their power and bravery. Unassailable,
invincible in battle, these two ancient great seers cannot be
vanquished in any world. They are most worshipful to all the Gods,
and to Asuras, Yakṣas, Rākṣasas and Gandharvas, men, Kiṃnaras,
and Snakes. Therefore, pray depart from here with the Gods, O
Vāsava, and watch this destruction of the Khāṇḍava Forest, which has
been ordained."

Hearing this voice and knowing that it spoke the truth, the Lord of
the Immortals shed wrath and indignation, and he departed for
20 heaven. The celestials saw the great-spirited Indra depart and they
hurried after him, sire. And when they saw the king of the Gods leave
with the Gods, Vāsudeva and Arjuna, the heroes, roared a lion's roar.

When Indra had gone, O king, Kṛṣṇa and the Pāṇḍava rejoiced and
fearlessly continued to burn the forest. Having vanquished the Gods,
as the wind vanquishes the clouds, he dispatched with his hard-hitting
arrows the creatures of the Khāṇḍava. Not a creature could get away

from there but was cut down by the arrow shots of the left-handed
25 archer. Even great beings were unable to gaze upon faultlessly
shooting Arjuna in battle, how much less to wage war on him! He
pierced one with a hundred arrows or a hundred with one, and
lifeless they fell into the Fire, as though struck down by Time itself.
They found no shelter behind banks, in rough terrain, or in the
sanctuaries of ancestors and Gods—the heat grew. The thousands of
herds of creatures cried out wretchedly, elephants screamed, and deer
and birds, and their sound frightened the denizens of the Ganges and
the ocean. No one would look at the strong-armed Arjuna or the
30 mighty Kṛṣṇa, let alone fight them. Some who came by narrow paths
collapsed there; and Hari slew the Rākṣasas, Dānavas, and Nāgas
with his discus. Their heads and bodies sundered by the impact of the
discus, the giants fell dead into the mouth of the blazing fire. Sped
along by the floods of flesh and blood and floods of fat, the Fire
stretched up into the sky, smokeless. Eyes blazing, tongues blazing, the
big, wide-open maw blazing, the upright hair blazing, drinking up the
fat of the living with orange eyes, the sacrificial Fire feasted on the
elixir that Kṛṣṇa and Arjuna had fetched, and became happy, sated,
supremely blissful.
35 Then the Slayer of Madhu saw an Asura by the name of Maya
suddenly dart forth from Takṣaka's dwelling. The Fire God, whose
charioteer is the Wind, became embodied as a hermit with matted
hair and, roaring like a thunder cloud, sought him out to burn him,
while Vāsudeva stood his ground, raising his discus to kill him. Seeing
the discus raised, and the Fire eager to burn, Maya, O Bhārata, cried
out, "Help, Arjuna!" Hearing his frightened voice, Dhanaṃjaya
replied, "Have no fear!" as though to fill Maya with new life, O
Bhārata. When the Pārtha had granted Maya, who was Namuci's
brother, safe-conduct, the Dāśārha lost his desire to kill him and the
40 Fire did not burn him. While the forest was burning, the Fire did not
burn six—Aśvasena, Maya, and the four Śārngaka birds.

1(19.a) The Śārngakas

220–25 (B. 228–33; C. 8285–463)
220 (228; 8285). The ascetic Mandapāla fails to have his reward hereafter. The celestials explain this is because he had left no sons. (1–10). Mandapāla decides to become a bird, to have a nest of young rapidly. He begets four eggs on the bird Jaritā, but runs off with Lapitā (15–20). When the Fire comes, Mandapāla

praises the God (20–25). The Fire promises to spare his sons (30).
221 (223; 8331). Jaritā hatches the eggs. Her lament on seeing the Fire: the fledglings cannot escape. The sons advise her to leave them and flee (1–10). Jaritā tells them to hide in a rat hole; they refuse for fear of the rat (15–20).
222 (23; 8386). Jaritā assures them that the rat was caught by a kite; the sons cannot be sure and refuse to be persuaded (1–15). Jaritā finally flies away (15).
223 (231; 8386). The four sons praise the Fire God and pray for mercy (1–15). The Fire spares them and gives them a boon; they ask to be rid of cats (20–25).
224 (232; 8404). Mandapāla worries and laments before Lapitā, who grows jealous (1–15). Jaritā returns to her safe sons. Mandapāla arrives, is ignored and rebuffed (20–25). He protests and is finally welcomed (25–30).
225 (233; 8429). Mandapāla explains that the Fire had promised to spare them. They leave the country (1).

Janamejaya said:
220.1 Why, brahmin, did the Fire fail to burn the Śārngakas, while the
forest was in such a blaze? Tell me at once! You have sung to us,
brahmin, the reason why Aśvasena was not burned, and Maya the
Dānava; but not why the Śārngakas were saved. The survival of the
Śārngakas is a great marvel, brahmin. Sing to me why, at that
slaughter of the Fire's they did not perish.
Vaiśaṃpāyana said:
I shall tell you the entire true story, Bhārata, why at that pass the
Fire failed to burn the Śārngakas.
5 There was a great seer of strict vows, foremost of those wise in the
Law, a learned ascetic renowned as Mandapāla. He followed the path
of the seers, who held up their seed, king, studying the *Veda*, devoted
to the Law, austere and master of his senses. He went to the farthest
shore of asceticism, and after he had abandoned his body, O Bhārata,
he attained to the world of the ancestors. Yet he failed to find the
fruits of his acts there. Finding his worlds without reward, although he
had won them with his asceticism, he questioned the celestials who
sat around the King of the Law. "Why," he asked, "are these worlds
that I won with my austerities closed to me? Where did I fail that this
10 should be the result of my acts? I shall perform the deeds but for
which the reward of my austerities is closed to me. Tell me, celestials!"

The Gods said:

Listen, brahmin, to what acts men are born indebted: to rites, to the study of the *Veda*, and to offspring, misdoubt it not. One acquits oneself of all these with sacrifice, austerity, and sons. You are an ascetic and a sacrificer, but you have no offspring; these worlds are closed to you because of this matter of offspring. Beget, and you shall enjoy the worlds of eternity. A son saves his father from the hell called *Put*, hermit. Therefore, best of brahmins, strive for the continuity of children!

Vaiśaṃpāyana said:

Hearing the words of the celestials, Mandapāla worried: "Now where do I get children, many of them, and fast?" As he worried it occurred to him that birds had many young. So he became a Śārngaka bird and coupled with a female named Jaritā. On her he begot four sons who were wise in the *Veda*, deserted them on the spot, and ran after Lapitā—the hermit deserted his tiny sons, who were still in their eggs, and their mother in the forest.

When this lordly man had gone to Lapitā, O Bhārata, Jaritā, who was greatly disturbed on account of her love for her children, worried much. Because of her love, wretched Jaritā could not desert in the Khāṇḍava her little seer sons still in their eggs, deserted as they were by their father, however little they deserved it, king. Anxious with love, she supported them in her own way when they had been hatched. Later, Mandapāla the seer saw the Fire arrive to burn the Khāṇḍava while he was running around in the forest with Lapitā. Knowing Fire's design and aware that his own sons were little, the brahmin seer voiced praise of the august Fire God, Guardian of the World, out of fear and in order to protect his sons.

Mandapāla said:

Thou, Fire, art the mouth of all the Gods, thou art the carrier of the oblation! Thou dwellest hidden in all creatures, O Purifier! The wise call thee one and yet call thee triple; rendering thee eightfold, they render thee the carrier of the sacrifice. The great seers declare that thou hast created all this, for without thee this entire world would vanish instantly, O Fire! It is after having bowed to thee that the brahmins go the sempiternal course they have won by their deeds, with their wives and their sons. They say that thou art the clouds in the East that cling to the sky with their lightning. The flames that come forth from thee burn all the creatures.

Splendiferous Fire, thine is the creation of the universe! Thou hast ordained the rite and all that exists, moving and unmoving, thou hast ordained the waters of yore, on thee rests the entire world! On thee rest firmly the oblation to the Gods and the oblation to the ancestors, as they should. Thou, Fire, art the flame, thou art Dhātar, thou art

Bṛhaspati. Thou art the Aśvins and both Yamas, Mitra art thou,
Soma, and the Wind!

Vaiśaṃpāyana said:

30 At this praise from Mandapāla the Fire was pleased with the
boundlessly brilliant hermit, O king. And, kindly, he said to him,
"What favor can I do for you?" Mandapāla folded his hands and said
to the Fire, "Spare my sons, when you are burning the Khāṇḍava
Forest!" The venerable Fire promised this, then at that time struck
flame into the Khāṇḍava, as he wished to burn it.

Vaiśaṃpāyana said:

221.1 When the Fire was raging, the Śārngakas, aggrieved, aghast, and
most upset, found no escape. Listening to her tiny sons, their wretched
mother Jaritā, already consumed by grief, began to lament, O king of
men.

"Here the dreadful Fire is coming, burning the underbrush, setting
the universe aglow, and terrifyingly he increases my miseries. And
these children of little wit pull at me—still without feathers or feet, yet
the final recourse of our ancestors. Here is the Fire coming, terrifying,
5 licking the trees. My sons are powerless and cannot escape, nor can I
escape elsewhere if I take my sons. And I cannot desert them! My
heart is torn—whom of my sons must I leave, whom shall I take and
escape? What am I to do? What do you think, my sons? However
much I ponder your escape, I find none. I shall cover you with my
body and die with you. 'On Jaritāri is this family founded, for he is the
eldest. Sarisṛkva will beget offspring, increasing the lineage of the
ancestors. Stambamitra will practice austerities, and Droṇa will
become an eminent student of the Brahman.'——It was with these
words that your father deserted you cruelly that time. Whom can I
10 take and flee? On whom must the final disaster descend?" Thus,
confused concerning what she should do that would be right, she did
not perceive with her thought how her sons might find escape from
the Fire.

When she had spoken in this fashion, the four Śārngakas replied to
their mother, "Cast off your love, and fly away where there is no fire.
For when we have perished, you shall have other sons. But when you
have died, the continuance of our line will be cut. Reflect on these two
outcomes and do what is best for our family—the ultimate moment
has arrived for you to do so, mother. Don't be misled by your love for
us your sons into destroying the family; for this deed of our father,
who wishes for his worlds, must not be fruitless."

Jaritā said:

15 There is a rat hole in the ground close to this tree. Hurry and go
into it at once; you will be out of danger from the Fire there. I shall

cover the opening with dust, sons: so, I think, we can counter the burning Fire. When the Fire is over, I shall come back to remove the dust pile. Or do you agree to this means of escape from the Fire?

The Śārngakas said:

We are plain flesh, without our feathers. The carnivorous rat will destroy us. With this danger before us we shall not be able to stay there. How can the Fire fail to burn us, or the rat to devour us? How can father do other than fail, how will our mother survive? The birds will either find death from the Fire, or from the rat in the hole.
20 Considering both outcomes, to burn is better than to be eaten. If we are eaten by the rat in his hole, our death will be contemptible. But the relinquishment of the body to the Fire is ordained by the learned.

Jaritā said:

222.1 The rat came out of its hole, and a kite caught the little creature with its claws and carried if off. You have nothing to be afraid of!

The Śārngakas said:

We don't know at all that a kite took the rat; there are sure to be others in the hole, and we certainly are afraid of them. It is doubtful whether the Fire will reach here – the wind is clearly turning – while there is no doubt at all, mother, that the creatures in that hole will kill us. A doubtful death wins out over a doubtless one, mother. Now take to the sky as you should. You will find other beautiful sons.

Jaritā said:

5 I *myself* saw the mighty kite approach the hole, strut around, and fly away from the hole with that rat. I flew quickly after the kite as it went off, pronouncing blessings upon it for having taken away the rat from the hole: "Thou king of kites that fliest away with our hateful enemy, mayest thou in thy heaven be without foes and golden!" When the hungry bird had done eating it, I was dismissed and came back home. Go into the hole, sons, go with all confidence. There is nothing for you to fear. I have seen the kite carry off the rat, without a doubt!

The Śārngakas said:

10 But *we* don't know that the rat has been carried off, mother! And without that certainty we shall not be able to go into that hole.

Jaritā said:

But *I* know full well that the kite took it! Therefore, there is nothing to fear. Do as I say!

The *Śārngakas said:*

You would not dispel our great fears out of hypocrisy. When a person's faculties are deranged, his acts are not aforethought. We have done you no favors, you do not know us at all. Who are you,

so virtuous that you support us under much anxiety, and who are we to you? You are young and beautiful and capable of finding your
15 husband. Follow your husband, and you shall obtain beautiful sons. We shall enter the Fire and attain to blessed worlds; or, perchance, the Fire will not burn us, and you shall come back to us again.

Vaiśaṃpāyana said:

At these words the Śārnga bird left her sons in the Khāṇḍava and flew quickly to a place that was safe and devoid of the Fire. Thereupon the blazing Fire with his prickly flames arrived where the Śārngakas had stayed, the little sons of Mandapāla. Seeing the Fire ablaze with his own glow, Jaritāri spoke this word, so that the Fire could hear it

Jaritāri said:

223.1 The wise man stays awake before he faces times of troubles. When trouble arrives, he suffers not at all. The witless fool who does not wake against trouble to come is pained when it comes and understands nothing.

Sarisṛkva said:

You are imperturbable and sensible. Our lives themselves are in trouble now. Among the many, indeed, only one is brave and wise.

Stambamitra said:

The eldest is the savior, to be sure. The eldest saves from trouble. If the eldest does not know, what can the younger do?

Droṇa said:

5 The Fire God of the Golden Seed hurries blazing to our dwelling place. Eagerly licking with his Seven Tongues, the lean Fire crawls upon us!

Vaiśaṃpāyana said:

At these words of his brother, Jaritāri folded his hands at his forehead, and listen, sire, how he praised the Fire.

Jaritāri said:

Thou art the soul of the Wind, a purifier, and the body of the herbs. Water is thy source, Light, and thou art the source of water. Upward and downward they go, and sideways they spread, thy flames, O most powerful One, like the rays of the sun!

Sarisṛkva said:

> Our mother ignores us, and we know no father.
> Cloud-crested Fire, our wings have not grown.
> We have no savior but thee, O Fire,
> Hence pray protect us that art the sole hero!

10 With they benevolent aspect and thy seven flames, protect thou that art lauded us that seek shelter!

It is thou alone that heatest, O Fire,
No heater but thee among the cloud cows, God!
Grant us, young seers, protection today,
Pass by us, thou that carriest oblations!

Stambamitra said:

Thou alone art the all, Fire. On thee rests the entire world. Thou sustainest the creatures, thou bearest all that exists. Thou art the Fire, the carrier of the oblation, thou alone art the supreme oblation. The wise bring offerings to thee, manifold and simple.

Thou createst the threefold world, O Fire,
And when the time comes, cookest them ablaze.
Of all that exists thou art the source,
And become again its place of rest.

15 Hidden within, O lord of the world, thou cookest the food that the living have eaten, always growing—on thee rests everything!

Droṇa said:

On becoming the sun with thy rays, Jātavedas,
Thou takest the waters of earth and her juices,
Thou takest them all and sends them forth
With thy rain at the time of creation, O Light!

From thee, Light, spring the herbs into their verdure again, from thee are born the lotus ponds, the flood, and the ocean. This seat, O thou of the prickly rays, is the refuge of Varuṇa: be thou our benevolent protector, do not destroy us today. Yellow-eyed, red-throated Fire of the Black Trail, pass us by, set us free like the dwelling places of the ocean.

Vaiśaṃpāyana said:

20 When he had thus been praised by Droṇa of unsullied deeds, the Fire spoke to Droṇa, being persuaded by his promise to Mandapāla: "You are the seer Droṇa. What you have uttered is Brahman. I shall do your desire, and you shall be in no danger. For before, Mandapāla mentioned all of you to me: 'May you spare my little sons, when you burn the forest,' he said. That word of his and what you have just spoken are both of great weight to me. Therefore, tell me what I can do for you. I am greatly pleased, my lord brahmin, with your praise—hail be to you!"

Droṇa said:

These cats, O Light, aggravate us constantly. Now put them between your teeth, Fire, with all their kin!

Vaiśaṃpāyana said:

25 The Fire did so, after dismissing the Śārngakas; and blazing up he burned the Khāṇḍava Forest, Janamejaya.

Vaiśampāyana said:

224.1 Mandapāla, meanwhile, O scion of Kuru, kept worrying about his
sons; although he had spoken to the Fire, he was nonetheless
anxious. In his anxiety over his sons, he said to Lapitā, "Why, my
little sons are incapable of escape, Lapitā! When the Fire spreads and
the wind begins to blow hard, my sons will be unable to make their
escape. Why, their poor mother is unable to save them; she must be
5 anguished when she sees no way of saving her sons! Why, suffering
for my sons, still incapable of either running or flying, she must be
screeching and fluttering about! How is my son Jaritāri, how my
Sarisṛkva, how are Stambamitra and Droṇa, and how my poor wife?"

When the seer Mandapāla went on lamenting in this way in the
forest, Lapitā replied to him jealously, O Bhārata, "You do not care
at all for your sons! You yourself said they were seers of splendor and
power, and had nothing to fear from the Fire. Also, before my very
eyes you commended them to the Fire, and the great-spirited God
10 gave you his promise. The World Guardian won't ever tell a lie! And
they are eloquent speakers—no, your concern is not for them. You
are suffering because you worry about my rival! Surely, you do not
love me as you once loved her. It is not right for one who has two
causes to be loveless to his friends and when he himself is suffering to
be able to ignore them! Go to your Jaritā, for whom you are
suffering so! I shall wander alone, as a woman with a bad man!"

Mandapāla said:

I am not wandering in the world for the reasons you imagine. It
is for the sake of offspring that I roam here, and my offspring have
15 come to grief. He who abandons the things he has and hangs on to
future things is a fool, and the world despises him. Do as you wish.
For this blazing fire is licking the trees and brings a hateful, malign
sorrow to my heart.

Vaiśampāyana said:

When the Fire had passed by that spot, Jaritā hurriedly returned,
eager for her sons. And while she was screeching pitifully, she found
all her sons healthy in the forest, and spared by the Fire. They were
the most incredible sight. Again and again, she embraced each of her
sons and wept.

20 Then suddenly Mandapāla himself arrived there, Bhārata, and
none of his sons welcomed him. Though he chattered at each of them
time and again, and at Jaritā, they spoke not a word to the seer, good
or bad.

Mandapāla said:

Who of you is my eldest son, who the second? Who is the middle
one, and who of you the youngest? Why don't you answer me, who
am speaking from grief? I left you to the Fire, but I found no peace.

Jaritā said:

25 What does your eldest son matter to you, or the second one? What does the middlemost matter, or this poor youngest? You left me completely destitute and went your way. Go back to your Lapitā, young, sweet-smiling Lapitā!

Mandapāla said:

Apart from another man, nothing in the world is so fatal to women as rivalry with another wife! For even the faithful and good Arundhatī, famous in all the worlds, distrusted Vasiṣṭha, the eminent seer. He was always completely pure-hearted and devoted to her happiness and well-being, yet she despised that hermit among the Seven Seers. Because of this contempt she is now a tiny star like a red ember overlaid by smoke, not very lovely, sometimes visible
30 sometimes not, which appears like a bad omen. You yourself obtained me to beget offspring, and giving up the man you wanted, now that it has come to this pass, you become like her. Never should a man put his trust in a woman, thinking she is his wife; for a wife who has sons does not look to her duty.

Vaiśaṃpāyana said:

Thereupon all his sons waited on him properly; and he began to reassure his children, O king.

Mandapāla said:

225.1 I had commended you to the Fire, so that he might spare you; and he promised to me he would do so. Thus, knowing the Fire's promise, your mother's piety in the Law, and your own great power, I did not come sooner. You had no need to worry about your death, sons. Even the Fire knew you were seers, and the Brahman is known to you.

Vaiśaṃpāyana said:

Having thus reassured his sons, Mandapāla took them and his wife, O Bhārata, left that country, and went to another one.

1(19) The Burning of the Khāṇḍava Forest (concluded)

5 The blessed Lord of the prickly rays blazingly burned down the Khāṇḍava Forest with the aid of the two Kṛṣṇas, bringing terror to the world. Having drunk up rivers of fat and marrow, the Fire became completely sated and appeared before Arjuna.

Thereupon the blessed Lord of the Gods descended from the sky, surrounded by the host of the Maruts, and he spoke as follows to the

Pārtha and Mādhava: "You have accomplished a feat that even the Immortals find difficult. I am pleased: choose boons, even such as are hard to obtain and beyond human power!"

The Pārtha chose from Śakra all manner of weapons, and Śakra set for him the time when he would take possession of them. "When the blessed Lord the Great God shall find grace with you, I shall give you all your weapons, Pāṇḍava. I myself shall know the time, scion of Kuru, and I shall give them to you for your great self-mortification. You shall receive all the fire and wind missiles, and all my own weapons, Dhanaṃjaya."

Vāsudeva asked for eternal friendship with the Pārtha, and the Lord of the Gods gave him his wish joyfully. After giving them their boons, the master of the Maruts, pleased, took leave of the Fire and went with the Gods to heaven. The Fire, having burned down the forest with its animals and birds for five days and one, was satiated and came to rest. Having eaten flesh and drunk fat and blood, supreme joy seized him and he spoke to the pair, O lord of the people: "You, tigerlike men, have sated me to fullness of pleasure. I dismiss you now, heroes. Go where you please!" Arjuna, Vāsudeva, and Maya the Dānava took leave of the great-spirited Fire; and all three wandered about, O bull of the Bharatas, and sat down together on the lovely river bank.

Notes

Abbreviations of Sources Quoted in Annotations

Agarwala, 1939	V. S. Agarwala, "Śiṃśumāraśiraḥ," *Journal of the Indian Society of Oriental Art* (Calcutta, 1939).
Agarwala, 1940	V. S. Agarwala, "vāraṇau ṣaṣṭihāyanau," *Annals of the Bhandarkar Oriental Institute 21* (Poona, 1940).
Bailey, 1967	H. W. Bailey, "Vedic Garutmant-," *Festschrift V. Raghavan, Adyar Library Bulletin* 31–32 (Adyar, 1967–68).
Brown, 1972	W. Norman Brown, "Duty as Truth in the Veda," *Festschrift Gonda* (Leiden, 1972).
Caland, 1893	W. Caland, *Altindischer Ahnenkult* (Leiden, 1893).
Caland, 1931	W. Caland (trans.), *The Pañcaviṃśa Brāhmaṇa* (Calcutta, 1931).
Caland-Henry, 1906	W. Caland and V. Ḥenry, *L'agniṣṭoma* (2 vols., Paris, 1906–7).
Charpentier, 1920	Jarl Charpentier, *Die Suparṇasage* (Upssala, 1920).
D.	Devabodha, *Jñānadīpikā*, Mahābhāratatātparyaṭīkā, ed. by R. N. Dandekar (Poona Bhandarkar Oriental Research Institute, 1961).
Dumézil, 1971	George Dumézil, *Mythe et Epopée* (Paris, 1971).

Dumont, 1939	P.-E. Dumont, *L'agnihotra* (Baltimore, 1939).
Emeneau, 1953	Murray B. Emeneau, "The composite bow in India," *Proceedings American Philosophical Society*, 97 (1953): 77–87.
Gonda, 1954a	J. Gonda, *Aspects of Early Viṣṇuism* (Utrecht, 1954).
Gonda, 1954b	J. Gonda, "Reflections on the Ārṣa and Āsura forms of marriage," *Festschrift Sarup*, (Hoshiarpur 1954).
Gonda, 1966	J. Gonda, *Loka: World and heaven in the Veda* (Amsterdam Academy, 1966).
Hacker, 1959	Paul Hacker, *Prahlāda: Werden und Wandlungen einer Idealgestalt* (Mainz Academy, Wiesbaden, 1959–60).
Hopkins, 1915	E. Washburn Hopkins, *Epic Mythology* (Strassburg, 1915).
Jacobi, 1903	Herman Jacobi, *Mahābhārata*. Inhaltsangabe, Index und Concordanz der Calcuttaer und Bombayer Ausgaben (Bonn, 1903).
Kane, 1946	P. V. Kane, *History of Dharmaśāstra* 3 (Poona, 1946).
Kirfel, 1920	Willibald Kirfel, *Das Purāṇa des Weltgebäudes* (Bonn, 1920).
Knipe, 1967	David Knipe, "The Heroic Theft," *History of Religions* (Chicago, 1967).
Macdonell, 1897	A. A. Macdonell, *Vedische Mythologie* (Strassburg, 1897).
Macdonell, 1904	A. A. Macdonell, *The Bṛhaddevatā, attributed to Śaunaka* (2 vols.; Cambridge, Mass., 1904).
M-K, Macdonell-Keith, 1912	A. A. Macdonell and A. B. Keith, *Vedic Index of Names and Subjects* (2 vols.; London, 1912).
Meyer, 1937	J. J. Meyer, *Trilogie altindischer Mächte und Feste der Vegetation* (Zürich-Leipzig, 1937).
N.	Nīlakaṇṭha, *Bhāratabhāvadīpa*, with Mahābhārata text (Poona, *śaka* 1850 = A.D. 1928).
Oldenberg, 1886	Herman Oldenberg, *The Gṛhyasūtras* (*Sacred Books of the East*) (Oxford, 1886).

Renou, 1939	Louis Renou, "L'hymne aux Aśvin de l'Ādiparvan," *Festschrift F. W. Thomas* (Bombay, 1939).
Sieg, 1902	Emil Sieg, *Die Sagenstoffe des Ṛgveda und die indische Itihāsatradition* (Stuttgart, 1902).
Sukthankar, 1937	V. S. Sukthankar, "The Bhṛgus and the Bhārata," *Annals of the Bhandarkar Oriental Institute* 18 (Poona, 1937).
Sukthankar, 1939	V. S. Sukthankar, "Epic Questions (I): Does Indra assume the Form of a Swan?" *Bulletin of the Deccan College Research Institute* 1 (Poona, 1939).
van Buitenen, 1964	J. A. B. van Buitenen, "The Large Atman," *History of Religions* 4 (Chicago, 1964).
van Buitenen, 1968	J. A. B. van Buitenen, *The Pravargya* (Poona, 1968).
van Buitenen, 1959	J. A. B. van Buitenen, "Akṣara," *Journal of the American Oriental Society* 79 (1959).
Weber, 1850	Albrecht Weber, *Indische Studien* 1 (Berlin, 1850).

1(1) The Lists of Contents

1.0. *Triumph* (*jaya*): appears to be the old description, if not title, of that part of the *MBh.* cycle that deals with the battle and final victory. In 1.54.15 and 20 it is contrasted with the *Breach* (*bheda*) between the two parties. Here the word stands for the *MBh.* generally. ***Nara and Nārāyaṇa*, "Man and Scion of Man" (though Nārāyaṇa is also given another etymology, this one seems the primary one), and an old and fairly obscure pair of heroes or Gods who, as a pair, are on the decline in the *MBh.* They seem to be succeeded by Arjuna and Kṛṣṇa, with whom they are identified; Nārāyaṇa merges with Viṣṇu. Nara, also named Kirīṭin ("the diademed God"), has affinities with Indra, so that the pair might reflect the late Vedic pair Indra and Viṣṇu. ***Sarasvatī*: originally the name of a river, became associated with learning, probably because of the sacrifices held on its banks. As a Goddess she is the patroness of learning.

1.1 *Bard* (*sūta*): was first the hero's charioteer, hence witness of his feats, eventually panegyrist and reciter of family lore. It is also the name of a caste, issue of mixed brahmin and baron parents. ***Ugraśravas* ("*of awesome sound*"): he in effect recites the entire *Mahābhārata*, after Vaiśaṃpāyana (1.54.20). ***Lomaharṣaṇa* ("*the hair raiser*"): appears in the *MBh.* only as Ugraśravas's father; he is later associated with the transmission of the Purāṇas. ***Lore, Book of the Lore*: will consistently translate *purāṇa*, "story of old times," which is hard to distinguish from *itihāsa*, "the way it was." Earlier texts couple the two as a joint erudition, often regarded as a fifth *Veda*. Later a technical distinction is made between *itihāsa* (viz. *MBh.*) and *purāṇa* (the *Eighteen Purāṇas*). ***Forest*: is the conventional translation of *vana* and synonyms. It is any tract of land that is not under cultivation, but not necessarily heavily wooded. ***Seer*: will consistently translate *ṛṣi*. Originally describing a poet of Vedic hymns, in the epic it is loosely applied to any brahmin with pretense of learning. "Seers" as a group often refers to a vague group of supernatural beings. The term is further extended to any person with learning: thus there are *devarṣis*, "divine seers," and *rājarṣis*, "royal seers," which describe barons and kings interested in Vedic learning, but may be used as an honorific of any baron; *rājarṣi* in turn generated *brahmarṣi*, "a brahmin seer." A special use is the "Seven Seers," great Vedic seers now visible as the stars of the Lesser Bear. **"*Vow*" or "*life-rule*" will consistently translate *vrata*, a self-chosen life-rule involving various abstinences, usually vowed for a particular term; it cannot be broken except to the detriment of a person's "truth." Since especially the brahmin way of life involves *vratas* of various kinds, the description "of strict vows" can be applied to almost any brahmin. ***The Twelve-Year Session* of the brahmins of the Naimiṣa Forest appears as a historical event in the previous literature (e.g., *Pañcaviṃśa Brāhmaṇa* 26.6.4); it was adjourned after nine years (ib. 5) and the remainder bequeathed to posterity. "Session" is the technical term of a ritual based on the Soma sacrifice, which lasts for more than twelve days. ***Family Chieftain* (*kulapati*) describes the leader of the participating priests in a Session who are all Sacrificers (*yajamānas*). ***Hermitage* will consistently translate *āśrama* as a locality (in contrast to *āśrama* "stage of life"). It is a place in the "forest," i.e., outside the villages, where one retires due to age or for purposes of study. Life in a hermitage is a brahmin idyll. ***Hands folded* (*añjali*), the solemn mode of greeting: the hands, slightly curved to form a scoop, are held high at the forehead or above, to receive either largess or a command, which is then "placed upon the head" as a sign of compliance; the gesture was probably accompanied by a sideways shaking of the head to put the command firmly into place as of one placing a load on his head. This motion survives as a universal Indian sign of consent, while the *añjali* may survive in the greeting with pressed palms at the forehead. ***Austerities*; ascetism, mortification, will consistently translate *tapas*, which is both the act and the powerful rewards of self-mortification. Its literal meaning is "[power of] heat," any undue exertion, emotion, or pain being felt as "heat." While it surely has connections with the heat of priests at fire sacrifices, the term comes to describe any specific act of self-deprivation aimed at an increase in spiritual power. It is quite often represented as sexual abstinence (thus powerful ascetics can be made to lose their power by seduction), but may proceed to extreme forms of self-torture. The power thus acquired makes the ascetics a kind of new Gods on earth, rivaling and surpassing the Gods, and divinely unpredictable. While in Buddhism and Jainism such self-mortification is directed toward release from transmigration, this is distinctly understated in *MBh*. The ascetics are bent on their own purposes, but motivation is oddly lacking.

5. *The seat he was shown*: etiquette demanded that the guest be instantly seated, the place of his seat depending on rank. Great punctilio toward superiors demanded that the host rise and meet the guest to greet him. ***Hermit*: normally translates *muni*, often indistinguishable from "ascetic." He will live in a hermitage and often observe a vow of silence. ***Lotus-eyed* is not only an epithet of beauty but also descriptive of purity, since no mud will stick to a lotus leaf, though the flower grows from it. ***Snake sacrifice*: lit. "session"; for details, below, 1.47 ff. ***Vaiśaṃpāyana* was a pupil of Kṛṣṇa Dvaipāyana and recited *MBh*. as known to Ugraśravas. He is known in the late Vedic literature as a teacher. On Dvaipāyana see below (1.57).

10. *Ford*: a ford (*tīrtha*) is primarily a place of pilgrimage at, and in, a sacred perennial river, secondarily any place of pilgrimage. ***Sanctuary* (*āyatana*) refers mostly to the site of divine worship, often involving images. ***Samantapañcaka*: more details in 1.2.1 ff. ***Twiceborn*: those Indians who belonged to the first three of the four classes into which society was ideally divided (brahmin, *brāhmaṇa*; baron, *kṣatriya*, *rājanya*; commoner, *viś*, *vaiśya*; and serf, *śūdra*), underwent in boyhood a second birth with their initiation; in practice, "twiceborn" refers particularly to brahmins. ***Brahmā* as a personal male God appears principally as the president of the assembled Gods and Creator, with little mythology attached to him.—Since it is necessary to distinguish between the various derivatives of the base *brahman*, the following spellings have been adopted: *Brahmā* (masculine) for the God Brahmā; *Brahman*, or *brahman* (neuter), "power inherent in ritual utterance and act; Vedic erudition; underlying source of existence; supreme being";

brahmin, "member of a social class"; *brahmán* (masculine), name of a priest; *Brāhmaṇa*, name of a class of Vedic texts. ***Unction* (*abhiṣeka*) has strictly speaking no place at a "Session"; however, it was the most important phase of the Royal Consecration (*rājasūya*), no doubt the most public Vedic ritual, and hence extended as characteristic of all higher ritual. ***Law* will consistently translate *dharma*, also in derivatives. It is not an ideal rendering, but there is no better single one. I forego a definition since the concept is in the process of definition and redefinition in the epic, and its scope can only become clear from the epic as a whole. ***Great-spirited* will consistently translate *mahātman*, an epithet so freely bestowed on Gods and men that it carries little more than honorific meaning; recently revived with more meaning: Mahatma Gandhi.

15. *Vyāsa*, lit. the "Divider," another name of Kṛṣṇa Dvaipāyana, because he is supposed to have divided the one *Veda* ("erudition") into four: *Ṛgveda*, *Yajurveda*, *Sāmaveda*, and *Atharvaveda*. Kṛṣṇa's *Mahābhārata* is at times described as Kṛṣṇa's *Veda* (*kārṣṇa veda*); this Kṛṣṇa should not be confused with Kṛṣṇa Vāsudeva, one of the principal heroes. ***Collection*: the conventional rendering of *Saṃhitā*. Every *Veda* divides into at least four parts: the *Collection*, viz., of the verses or lines proper to the *Veda*; the *Brāhmaṇa*, prose expositions on the liturgy; the *Āraṇyaka* ("forest-book"), prose expositions of uncommon or esoteric rituals and doctrines; the *Upaniṣad*, prose, later also versified, expositions of more or less secret and recondite doctrines concerning the nature of ritual, world, and man.

20. *I bow, etc.*: these are introductory auspicious lines (*mangala*) of a somewhat philosophic cast, into which not too great doctrinal significance must be read; many of the phrases are clichés.

20. *Hṛṣīkeśa*: (probably) "with upstanding hair," epithet of Kṛṣṇa Vāsudeva.

30. *Prajāpati*: "lord of creatures." ***Seven sons of Dakṣa*: D. gives Krodha, Tapas, Dama, Vikrānta, Angiras, Kardama, and Aśva. ***Twenty-one lords of creation* (*prajāpatis*): D. gives Brahmā, Sthāṇu, Manu, Dakṣa, Bhṛgu, Dharma, Tapas, Dama, Marīci, Angiras, Atri, Pulastya, Pulaha, Kratu, Vasiṣṭha, Parameṣṭhin, Vivasvat, Soma, Kardama, Śukra, and Vikrānta. ***Viśve Devās . . . Aśvins*: principal Gods. ***Yakṣas . . . Seers*: semidivine beings.

40. *Soul of the eye*: the eye in the microcosm corresponds to the sun.

45. *All are abodes . . .*: I am not sure of this translation.

50. *Begot at his mother's behest*: below, 1.99 ff.

55. *Gāndhārī*: wife of Dhṛtarāṣṭra. ***Steward*: Vidura. ***Kuntī*: wife of Pāṇḍu.

60. *Nārada*: a divine seer. ***Asita Devala*: an ancient priest. ***Ancestors*: the spirits of the dead, who have their own heaven. ***Gandharvas*: heavenly musicians and sometimes horsemen. ***Yakṣas*: chthonic creatures, guardians of wealth. ***Rākṣasas*: earthbound demons.

65. *The wrathful Duryodhana*: eldest son of Dhṛtarāṣṭra. ***Karṇa*: his ally. ***Śakuni*: his maternal uncle. *Duḥśāsana*: his evil brother. ***Pāṇḍu*: below, 1.106–9. ***Their mothers conceived*: 1.113–15.

70. *The hermits conducted*: 1.117.

75. *"How can they be his?"*—This theme is not further developed.

80. *Arjuna won Kṛṣṇā*: 1.176 ff.

85. *The Royal Consecration*: 2.30 ff. ***Jarāsaṃdha*: 2.28 ff. ***The Caidya*: sc. Śiśupāla, king of Cedi; 2.37 ff. ***To Duryodhana came*: only insofar as he was the treasurer at the Royal Consecration: 2.32.

90. *He was mocked*: 2.46. ***Dhṛtarāṣṭra approved*: 2.51. ***Vāsudeva waxed greatly angry*: not developed, unless reference is to Book 3.14.

95. *Knowing the minds*: but all three had already perished. ***Saṃjaya*: his charioteer and reporter.

100. *The king of Gāndhāra*: Śakuni. ***When I heard*: in this independent text, running into 155, a summary is given of *The Mahābhārata* up to *The Book of the Women*. ***The bow had been drawn*: 1.179. ***Carried off Subhadrā*: 1.211 ff. ***Khāṇḍava Forest*: 1.214 ff.

105. *A game at dice*: 2.43–72. ***Draupadī*: 2.60 ff. ***The manifold feats*: 3. ***Snātaka brahmins*: brahmins who have completed their Vedic training and taken the concluding bath (*snāta*); reference is to 3.2 ff. ***A mountain man*: 3.13 ff.

110. *Learned from Indra*: 3.43 ff. ***Kubera*: 3.146 ff. ***Cattle expedition*: 3.225 ff. ***Dharma in the guise of a Yakṣa*: 3.299. ***Crushed by Arjuna*: 4.24 ff.

115. *Bestowed his daughter Uttarā*: 4.65 ff. ***Had mustered armies* 5.1 ff. ***Nara and Nārāyaṇa*, cf. 5.49, where Bhīṣma, not Nārada, is speaking. ***Wholeheartedly come out*: 4.73 ff. ***Punishing Kṛṣṇa*: 5.86.

120. *Consoled by Keśava*: 5.88. ***Vāsudeva . . . their councillor*: 5.122 ff. ***Karṇa said to Bhīṣma*: 5.165. ***Arjuna seized with cowardice*: *Bhagavadgītā*, 6.23 ff.

125. *Bhīṣma striking down chariots*: 6.41 ff. ***Bhīṣma struck down*: 6.115. ***The earth split open*: not developed. ***Śukra and Sūrya*: not developed.

130. *Droṇa*: 7.5 ff. ***The Oath-Companions*: 7.15 ff. ***Subhadrā's son*: 7.35. ***Killing Abhimanyu*: 7.48. ***Mindless with joy*: ib. ***Arjuna's fury*: 7.50.

135. *Arjuna's vow*: 7.51. ***Arjuna's horses were exhausted*: seems to be parallel to 7.122 where, however, Sātyaki is deprived of his own chariot and rides Kṛṣṇa's. ***Yuyudhāna*: 7.122. ***Bhīma attacked Karṇa*: cf. 7.123.

140. *The divine spear*: 7.154. ***Droṇa was sped to his death*: 7.165.

145. *A chariot duel*: not developed. ***The divine missile Nārāyaṇa*: 7.165 ff. ***Karṇa killed*: 8.63 ff. ***The lone Yudhiṣṭhira*: cf. 8.69. ***The king of the Madras had been slain*: 9.15–16. ***Saubala killed by Sahadeva*: cf. 8.69 f., 9.1.

150. *Waded into a pond*: 9.28. ***Battle of the bludgeons*: 9.65. ***Massacred the sleeping*: 10.1–9. ***Aiṣikī*: 1.10–13.

155. *The jewel crest*: 1.15. ***At the womb*: 10.15. ***Mourning befits*: 11.1 ff. ***Three of ours*: Kṛpa, Kṛtavarman, Aśvatthāman. ***Seven*: the five Pāṇḍavas, Kṛṣṇa, and Sātyaki.

165. *Vainya, etc.*: ancient kings, among whom Rantideva, Viśvāmitra, Gaya, Bharata, Bhagīratha, and Yayāti have epic identity.

170. *Two dozen kings*: reference is probably to the Story of the Sixteen Kings, an episode narrated by Nārada in *MBh.* (Bombay) 7.55–71 (dropped by cr. ed.), and (cr. ed.) 12.29; common names between them are Vainya, Suhotra, Rantideva, Śaibya (= Śibi), Ambarīṣa, Marutta, Gaya, Bharata, Rāma, Śaśabindu, Bhagīratha, and Yayāti; cf. also the list *Maitrāyaṇīya Upaniṣad* 1.4.

175. *The count of lotuses*: a very high number; lotuses multiply very quickly.

185. *Fate* (*daivam*): lit., "what comes from the Gods." ***Ordainer* (*vidhātṛ*): the divine agency that enjoins the conditions of life. ***Time* is particularly viewed in its destructive aspect and as fatal destiny. ***Time puts out Time*: the final destruction is succeeded by a new Eon.

190. *Upaniṣad*: here a "book of (esoteric) instruction."

195. *That which consists*: i.e., material nature. ***Elements*: ether/space, wind, fire, water, and earth. ***Properties*: *sattva*, "serenity," *rajas*, "dynamism," and *tamas*, "inertia." ***Yoke* (*yoga*); a strenuous undertaking to a spiritual end.

200. *Śrāddha*: offering to the Ancestors, at which brahmins are fed. ***Of one of little knowledge*: *alpaśrutāt*.

205. *Because of its size* (*mahat*) *and weight* (*bhāra*): pseudoetymology of *Mahābhārata*.

210. *Dregs*: *kalka*; D. *asāra* or *pāpa*; I take the verse as a demurrer to the possible impiety of the suggestion that *MBh.* outweighs the *Vedas*. ***Beings* (*bhāva*): D. takes it as *aśraddhā*, "lack of faith."

1(2) The Summaries of the Books

2.1. *Age of the Trey*: there are four successive ages of increasing deterioration, named after the throws of the dice: the Winning Throw (*kṛta-yuga*), the Trey (*tretā-yuga*), the Deuce (*dvāpara-yuga*), and the Nought or Discord (*kali-yuga*), which is the present one.

***Rāma*: Paraśu-Rāma, a brahmin warrior who annihilated twenty-one successive generations of barons (their women survived and every time bore a new generation; cf. 1.98); later an incarnation of Viṣṇu.

5. *Samantapañcaka*: lit., "the five border regions."

30. *Told at Śaunaka's session*: but he is yet to do it; below, 1.4–5; 13–14.

80. *Plot*: *mantra.*

90. *The birth of Abhimanyu*: misplaced, since it should come before the *Khāṇḍava Forest.*

110. *Mandara*: the coral tree (Erythrina Indica).

185. *Narrative by Pṛthā*: but this occurs later in the *Women,* 11.27.

195. *"Bed of arrows"*: on which Bhīṣma, who promulgated this and the next Book, is dying.

205. *The puppet Citrāngadā*: below, 1.207.

235. *Four kingdoms of creatures*: those born alive, from an egg, from a plant, and from sweat (insects).

240. *Puṣkara*: a famous ford in Rajasthan, present Pokkhar.

1(3) Pauṣya

(3). Exceptionally, most of this Book is written in prose, with topical verse interspersed. After the preliminary matter of the previous two books, it is introductory, since it is intended simply to set the stage for the Snake Sacrifice of Janamejaya, at which *The Mahābhārata* will be told.

The structure is loose and associative. The divine bitch Saramā curses Janamejaya, but no more is heard of the curse after Janamejaya engages a priest to redress the ill done. There follows the stories of Dhaumya Āyoda and his three pupils, only tenuously connected with the main narrative, which brings the third pupil's pupil, Utanka, in contact with both Pauṣya and Janamejaya: from the former's wife he obtains ladies' earrings as a teacher's fee—obstructed by the Snake Takṣaka—to the latter he recalls the assassination by the same Snake of his father Parikṣit. This admonition will find its prehistory, actual circumstances, and fateful consequences in 1(5) *The Book of Āstīka.*

The trials of Dhaumya's students were clearly popular brahmin stories; the book is otherwise diverse: a presence of Snakes, largely forgotten in the rest of the epic; the curious quasi-Vedic hymn to the Aśvins; the hymn to the Snakes; the squabble over pollution between Pauṣya and Utanka; and the curious apparitions of the bull-mounted Indra and the year-weaving women and boys, with incidentally the reduction of Takṣaśilā by Janamejaya.

1. *Janamejaya, son of Parikṣit,* is known to the later *Brāhmaṇa* literature (700 B.C.?) as a king who offered the Horse Sacrifice; his brothers too are known by name (cf. M-K). For Session see above 1.1.1. ***Saramā* is the celestial dog and messenger of the God Indra.

5. *Unseen,* i.e., from an unknown source; the story of this curse is not further developed. In earlier literature Janamejaya is likewise under the threat of some evil, which he expiates with a Horse Sacrifice.

10. *Hāstinapura,* founded by a Kaurava Hastin 1.90.35, = City of the Elephant.

15. The *Snakes* are a mythical race of semidivine serpentine beings who mostly dwell in the nether world; they are able to assume any form.

15. *Takṣaśilā,* or Taxila, a city on the Vitastā (a tributary of the Indus), which commanded the road into India.

20. *Pāñcāla,* the area immediately south of Kurukṣetra. ***Dike,* apparently such as used in wet cultivation.

25. *Bhoḥ,* a familiar form of address, lit., "sir." ***Uddālaka Āruṇi* (= son of Aruna), of the clan Gautama, is a famous teacher in the earlier literature, esp. the *Chāndogya Upaniṣad*; he originated the famous doctrine "Thou art That" (*tat tvam asi*) (chap. 6).

35. It was general practice that students who lived with their teacher subsisted on begged food.

50. *arka* (Calotropis Gigantea) is a bush widely spread in northern India; it has some medicinal properties; that it may cause blindness is further unknown.

55. The *Aśvins* are divine physicians and helpers, to whom a number of Ṛgvedic hymns are dedicated. They are twins. After the Vedic period their importance wanes, which makes their active appearance here a rarity.

60. On the hymn, cf. Renou (1939) with further literature. While not authentic in its present form, it has many Vedic echoes. Its contents are dictated by Upamanyu's circumstances: he has gone blind, has fallen into a well, and feels in danger of his life. Hence he first praises the Aśvins (60), points out their power to bring light after darkness (61, 67, 68), to extricate prisoners (62, 66), and to assist at the regeneration of the Year, which produces a new one, and hence to help him being reborn. ***Psychopomps*: *sāṃparāya* is the passage from this world to the afterworld; the adjective built on it seems to mean something like "psychopomp," as Upamanyu seeks deliverance. Renou, o.c., "qui sauve au moment critique." ***That darker sun*: there is a notion that the sun has a dark side that shines by night (cf. Sieg, 1902); the image here is particularly apposite, since Upamanyu is praying for a return of his eyesight. ***Dawn cows*: refers again to the restoration of light and sight. ***360 cows*: the days of the year, which produces the one calf, viz., the next year. ***Many sheds*, viz., fortnights, months, and seasons. ***One calf*: the new year. ***Ukthya*, epithet of the Aśvins (*ṚV*. 8, 9, 21), transferred to the *gharma*, which is exclusively the Aśvins'. ***Gharma*, the hot milk offering to the Aśvins, cf. van Buitenen (1968). ***Spokes*: a total of 720, i.e., the days and nights in the year. ***Rimless*: it being not a real wheel; these are typical riddling verses.

65. *Twelve*: the twelve months and six seasons resp. ***Vṛtra*, the dragon that keeps the monsoon from breaking. It is Indra's central feat that he kills Vṛtra and sets the rains free; this feat is here ascribed to the Aśvins. ***Known might*; I read *dṛṣṭamahnā prathitā* (instr.) *balasya* "with the famous, witnessed might of prowess." Renou unclear; the text is surely corrupt. ***Ten space points*: four cardinal points, four intermediate ones, zenith and nadir. ***Many-hued colors*: once more the image of the Aśvins' opening up the world to Upamanyu's lost sight. ***I laud*: *āmahe?* Cf. Helmer Smith, quoted Renou o. c. ***It bears*, i.e., it gives birth; the subject is the Year, which, as it goes along (*prapadena*), gives birth to the next.

70. *Conceive*: the notion is that the next year is conceived at the mouth, i.e., head or beginning, of the present year, and is borne for a period of a year, as the old year goes along (*prapadena*). Relevant are passages like *Bṛhad-Āraṇyaka Upaniṣad* 1.2.1 ff., esp. 4. Simultaneously the Year expires in a year ("this dead man"), so that it can be said that the new year kills off the old, which produced it (*BĀUp*. 1.2.4–5).

75. *Black iron*: i.e., he is a miserly man.

80. *A bullock yoked*: Vedic teachers were notoriously severe. ***Householder*, the second of the 4 *āśramas* or stages of life: *Veda* study (*brahmacarya*), householding (*gārhasthya*), forest retirement (*vānaprastha*), and renunciation (*saṃnyāsa*).

85. *Pausya*: this worthy, who loaned his name to this Book, is further unknown. ***Utanka*: critical edition has Uttanka, of which Sukthankar has second thoughts *Addenda ad* 1.3.86. ***Her period*: it is a couple's express duty to cohabit after the menses. Utanka has been ordered to substitute for his teacher, but adultery with a teacher's wife (*gurutalpa*) was one of the great sins, close to incest, since the teacher replaces the father.

95. *Guru's gift*: the fee for his teaching; the study period is considered a rite that, like others, is only completed when the priest's stipend (*dakṣiṇā*) has been given.

100. *An oversized bull*: a later variant of the story of Utanka below, 14.54.12 ff.

105. *A Pauṣya*: in this context the name (from rt. *puṣ*, "nourish," or the asterism Puṣya) seems to signify "benefactor."

110. *Sipped*: for the purpose of rinsing the mouth that is required after every meal.

120. *Śrāddha*: a ceremony in memory of deceased ancestors, at which brahmins should be fed.

135. *Went for water*: the sight of the mendicant was polluting, hence Utanka seeks to purify himself. ***Airāvata*, patronymic of Dhṛtarāṣṭra, a snake demon in *AV*. 8.10.29, where Takṣaka is also mentioned.

140. *The sun's rays*: the snakes hate summer and are revived by the rains. ***Kadrū*: her full story below, 1.14 ff.

170. *One-that-Places*: resp. Dhātā and Vidhātā, creator and dispenser, masculines in *-tar*, which here surprisingly seem to be taken for feminine *ā*-stems.

175. *Reaching Hāstinapura*: at this point the śloka form of the narrative is resumed.

185. *Corrupt Takṣaka*: the full story appears below, 1.36.5 ff. ***Kaśyapa*: below, 1.39. ***His councillors*: the narrative of Janamejaya's interrogation of his councillors about his father's death is resumed below, 1.45.

1(4) Puloman

4.1. *Family chieftain* (*kulapati*): the technical name for the priest who presides over a Session (*sattra*). ***Śaunaka* (scion of Śunaka) is a fairly common clan name (cf. M-K) and hard to identify; perhaps he is the same authority to whom the Bṛhaddevatā refers (Macdonell 1904, I, xxiii). Here he is a brahmin of the Bhṛgu clan.

5. *Brahmán*: name of the chief of the priests of the Atharvaveda at the great rituals; a Śaunaka is indeed known as the eponym of one of the recensions of that *Veda*.

10. *Sadasya*: technically, the name of a particular priest, but used here generally for an officiant seated in the *sadas* part of the sacrificial terrain.

5.5 *Agni*: the God of fire. ***Maruts*: the Wind Gods. ***Bhṛgu*, mythical sage, eponym of a brahmin clan. ***Cyavana*, a famous Bhārgava (= descendant of Bhṛgu), credited with extending the Soma draught to the lowlier Aśvins, who had rejuvenated him (below, 3.122 ff.). ***Ghṛtācī*, specifically the name of an Apsarā.

10. *Royal Consecration*: lit., "unction" (*abhiṣeka*), which is the main event of that ceremony. ***Rākṣasa*, name of a class of demons that live in the forest and threaten man and his rites.

15. *Oath* is approximate: it is an appeal to total veracity, which the Fire, being "true" or veracious, cannot ignore. ***Broke the troth*: the argument is that, while Pulomā was contractually made over to the Rākṣasa, Bhṛgu broke the contract by abducting her. ***It whispered*: thus, by declaring that the truth would bring on Bhṛgu's curse, the Fire confirms the truth.

6.1. *Cyavana* thus derived from rt. *cyu* "to fall," as the "fallen one."

7.1. It seems clear that the Fire's protest at becoming omnivorous repudiates a use of fire for certain purposes. One remembers that the Iranian cousins of the Vedic Āryans could not use the equally sacred fire, e.g., to cremate their dead, lest its purity be impaired. The story points to some such innovation in the use of fire, ascribed as are other novelties in the fire cult to the innovative Bhṛgus.

5. *Agnihotra*: a twice-daily milk offering placed in the fire at dawn and dusk, described by Dumont (1939). ***The Gods and ancestors*: the speculations presume that of the fortnightly sacrifices of full and new moon (*darśapūrṇamāsa*, described by Hillebrandt, 1889), the former are dedicated to the Gods, the latter to the manes: clearly the monthly occurrence of the ancestral *śrāddha* has been inserted here, as has the water offered to the deceased. The point is that the sacred Gods and ancestors receive their unpolluted oblations through the same fire: these oblations are now imperiled by pollution if the Fire becomes omnivorous.

10. *OṂs* and *Vaṣaṭs*: the syllable *OṂ* ("yea") introduces the recitations, the cry *vaṣaṭ* (pronounced *vauṣáṭ*) concludes the offering verses. **The cry *svāhā* accompanies the oblation; the *svadhā* is a libation to the ancestors.

20. *Acceptance*: i.e., fires that are already at hand, not especially lighted for the purpose; I am not sure of this.

8.10. *His father*, who would then sue for the girl on his son's behalf. ***Bhaga*, an ancient sky God, is the regent of the lunar zodiac sign Former Phālgunī, stars δ, ζ Leonis. Early Indian time reckoning went by a lunar zodiac of asterisms (*nakṣatras*, "lunar mansions"), 28 in number, in which the moon rises on the days of its cycle.

15. *Time* has the associations of fate and death.

9.1. *If it be true*: calling on the trueness of one's past correct behavior evokes, on the part of eminent personages, a magic power that can accomplish miracles (Brown, 1972).
5. *The Envoy*: his sudden appearance is dramatic, but not unheard of (e.g., 1.84.18.). In shorter announcements his place is taken by a "disembodied voice," or, in longer episodes, by the divine messenger Nārada.
15. *In the future*: but the matter is not taken up further; hence, D. conjectures: "In the Book of the Future" (*bhaviṣyatpurāṇe*).

20. *Lizard*: *ḍuṇḍubha*, "a kind of legless lizard" (PW), obviously a snakelike but not dangerous reptile; the translation is merely approximate.

11.1. *Khagama*: the name is of interest, meaning "bird": certain birds, particularly geese, mythically the Garuḍa (below, 1.30), harbor an undying hatred of snakes.
5. *Cannot be undone*: propelled by the speaker's power of veracity a curse, once spoken, cannot be canceled, only mitigated by its author.

12.5. *His father*, of course, also being a seer.

1(5) Āstika

13.10. *Yāyāvara*: "much given to traveling".
30. *His three words*: below, 1.42.15.
40. *He satisfied*: a man is born with three debts, to Gods, seers, and ancestors, which he repays with rites, Vedic study, and offspring.

14.5. *Prajāpati*: Dakṣa, a demiurge. ***Kaśyapa*: a demiurge. ***Outpouring of boons*: in other words, that he would give them a boon.

15.1. *Elixir* will translate *amṛta*, "ambrosia," the drink of Immortality.
5. *Meru*: the cosmic mountain in the center of the world (cf. Kirfel, 1920). ***Divine herbs*: phosphorescent plants.
10. *Asuras*: in the epic, Anti-Gods perpetually engaged with the Gods (*devas*) in a losing struggle.

16.1. *Mandara*: a mythical mountain particularly celebrated in the context of the churning of the ocean, identified with a peak in Bhāgalpar. ***Kiṃnaras*, semidivine, horse-headed celestials, musicians, and familiars of Kubera, the God of Riches. ***Apsarās* (I adopt this occasionally found spelling throughout to avoid the cumbersome *Apsarases*): originally female spirits of water and trees, they become heavenly nymphs frequently sent down by Indra to seduce ascetics; cf. 1.65; etc.
5. *Ananta*, or Śeṣa: the cosmic snake that supports the earth; for its story, see below, 1.32. It is considered to be an attendant of Viṣṇu-Nārāyaṇa. ***Akūpāra*: little else is known to the epic of this tortoise, which has been related to the tortoise incarnation of Viṣṇu (Gonda, 1954a). D. takes the word in the sense of "ocean." ***His tool*: i.e., the thunderbolt. ***Vāsuki* is the king of the Snakes (*nāgas*). ***Raising the Snake's head*: in other words, there are two movements: the horizontal turning of the stick by Gods and Asuras, and the vertical pounding by Ananta.
25. *With the milk*: the vegetable juices and the melting gold ore of the mountain turn the water of the ocean into milk.
30. *Śrī* or Lakṣmī is the Goddess of beauty and fortune and the consort of Viṣṇu. ***Liquor*: a fermented beer or hemp brew.
35. *Where the Gods were*: i.e., they chose the side of the Gods against the Asuras. ***Dhanvantari*, physician of the Gods, for the Elixir is, so to say, a medicine. ***Bewitching*, Skt. *mohinī*, which later becomes Viṣṇu's name in this female form.

17.5. *Ever since*: the head had become immortal and survives as a planet demon that periodically still swallows sun and moon, causing their eclipses.

15. *Copper-spiked*: the text has *pīta*, "yellow," which I take to refer to copper.

30. *The diademed God* (*kirīṭin*): Nara, also Indra.

19.5 *The submarine fire*: the fire of Aurva's anger, which was submerged in the ocean; see below, 1.169 ff.

10. *Pāñcajanya*: the conch of Kṛṣṇa. ***The guise of the Boar*: when the demon Hiraṇyākṣa had plunged the earth in the sea, Viṣṇu took the form of a boar and dug it up with his snout. ***Atri*: a seer of Ṛgvedic times, one of the "seven seers," the stars of Ursus Minor. The present incident is further unknown. ***Bed*: at the beginning of the Eon (*yuga*), Viṣṇu-Nārāyaṇa sleeps on the Snake Ananta floating on the primeval waters, in a state of meditation fastened on the self (*adhyātmayoganidrā*); Yoga here has the meaning of a meditative trance. From his navel sprouts a lotus, out of which the demiurge Brahmā arises. ***Mare-Head Fire*: the above submarine fire.

20.1. *The many black hairs*: sic! There is a flagrant contradiction, which is insoluble: on the one hand the fact is embedded in the narrative that Vinatā lost the bet because of the treachery of the Snakes and the consequent enmity of Garuḍa; on the other hand it is a fact that Kadrū cursed the Snakes, so that they will be massacred in Janamejaya's Snake Session for not wanting to obey her orders and change the horse's tail. The Snakes must have had second thoughts after the curse, but this is nowhere indicated. It has occasioned an explanatory interpolation in the Vulgate. ***Garuḍa*, in origin no doubt a bird representative of the sun, becomes in the classical pantheon the mount (*vāhana*) of Viṣṇu. On Garuḍa and the Soma theft cf. Charpentier, 1920; Sieg, 1902, 1926; Knipe, 1967.

21.5. *Swoon*: Snakes become languid and go into hiding during the hot months. ***Śakra* (Indra) being the God of the monsoon.

10. *The lunar day* = a thirtieth of a full lunation, or 27–28 solar days: Indra, as patron of the monsoon, is here identified with the year and its divisions, since the word for rain also stands for "year" (*varṣa*).

15. *Soma*: the inebriating juice of a plant of uncertain origin was pressed at a sacrifice and offered to Indra with the call *Vaṣaṭ*! The sacrifice described by Caland-Henry, 1906. ***Auxiliaries* (elsewhere also rendered "branches") are the supporting studies of phonetics, meter, grammar, etymology, astronomy, and ritual procedure.

24.1. *Niṣādas* ("the settled people") refers to the pre-Āryan autochthones.

25.1. *Friend of evil-doers*: implied is that the brahmin has lowered himself by serving aboriginals.

10. *An elephant*, which characteristically holds out its trunk (in Skt. synonymous with "hand") for gifts, while a tortoise as typically withdraws its limbs.

26.1. *Vālakhilyas*, thumb-sized ascetics of vile temper who derive their name from a series of apocryphal hymns after *ṚV*. 8.48. Their upside-down posture may be inspired by the observation of bats.

5. *Gandhamādana* ("of inebriating fragrance"), a mythical mountain beyond the Himālayas.

27.20. *Dakṣa*, a Prajāpati (demiurge) and son of Brahmā.

28.1. *Viśvakarman* is the Vulcan of the Vedic Gods; his presence here is not explained: possibly he had fashioned the contraption protecting the Elixir.

20. *Bowman* (*śarva*), i.e., Śiva, who wields the bow Pināka; cf. Bailey, 1968.

29.5. *Soma*: note how the Elixir is now identified with the Soma. The relation between the *amṛta* and Soma deserves further inquiry.

10. *Above you*: in Viṣṇu temples there is commonly found a tall pillar upon which perches Garuḍa.

15. *The seer*, i.e., Dadhyak (*dadhyañc*) or Dadhīca, already known to the *ṚV*.

20. *Fair-Winged Bird*: Suparṇa, another name of Garuḍa.

30.15. *Kuśa,* or *darbha* grass (Poa cynosuroides), which has long, sharp stalks, was used to cover the ground, and as strainers, etc., at the sacrifice.

31. While some of the names seem to be true proper names (e.g., Śeṣa, Elāpatra, Vāsuki, Takṣaka), others describe appearance (e.g., *sumanomukha,* "flower-mouthed," *bāhyakarṇa* "with protruding ears"), or habits (e.g., *mūṣakāda,* "mouse-eater," *koṇavāsana* "corner-dweller").

32.1. *Badarī,* place of pilgrimage on the upper Ganges in the Himālayas, present-day Badrinath. ***Gokarṇa,* place of pilgrimage on the southwest coast of India off Mangalore. ***Puṣkarāraṇya,* Forest of Puṣkara, a place of pilgrimage, present-day Pokkhar, five miles from Ajmere, Rajasthan. ***Ford*: *tīrtha,* the common name for any place of pilgrimage, but most involve water—rivers, tanks, lakes, ponds—hence the name. "Ford" will translate *tīrtha* throughout.

33.5. *Truth*: here = Brahmā who witnessed the curse, above, 1.18.5. ***Hidden in a cave*: N. opines that the fire was concealed in its Cause (i.e., higher element), viz., the wind, and seems to think the intention is the God's creation of fire from wind; I have no reference.

35.1. *Varuṇa,* a God of considerable importance in Vedic times is in the epic reduced to the God of the Ocean.

36.5. *Śaunaka started to laugh*: I do not see how this etymology can inspire merriment, unless it is meant to gloss over some more pertinent one, like "aging organ"; but *kāru* is attested only in the sense of "poet."

5. *King Parikṣit* is found praised as a living and gracious king in *AthV.* 20.122.7–10; he is no doubt historical, as is Janamejaya himself.

10. *Beast of sacrifice*: when Śiva-Rudra had not been accorded a share in the sacrifice, he pierced with his arrow the sacrifice, which had taken on bodily form.
***Dead snake*: any corpse is greatly polluting.

20. *Śṛngin*: "horned"; it is stated below (1.46.1) that he was born from a cow.

37.10. *Kuru* is the eponym of a people, the Kurus, or Kuru-Pāñcālas, who are of considerable importance in the Brāhmaṇa period (cf. M-K). In the epic they are a branch of the Pauravas; the Pāñcālas are still a separate people, though there will be a matrimonial alliance (below, 1.170 ff.).

25. *Great-grandfather,* i.e., King Pāṇḍu.

38.30. *He possessed that knowledge,* cf. above, 1.18.10, where Brahmā bestows on Kaśyapa the power of curing snakebite. This Kāśyapa (note spelling) must be a descendant.

39.10. *First he grew a sapling*: one cannot help wondering whether this episode might not be the source of the rumored fakir trick of growing a tree!

30. *A lie be averted*: his intention is that the worm symbolically represent Takṣaka and bite him, so that Śṛngin's curse is not belied.

40.5. *Great-grandfather*: lit., Arjuna, but here more probably Pāṇḍu. ***Kāśis*: name of a people settled about present-day Benares, which is still called Kāśī.

10. *Purūravas,* an ancient king, was wed by the Apsarā Urvaśī and lived happily with her until he broke his covenant with her and she saw him nude. The story, known since *ṚV.* 10.95, was made into the famous play *Vikramorvaśīya* by Kālidāsa.

41.10. *An aged celibate.* Sukthankar's reading *ṛddha* in 41.12 and 15 does not really make sense; I prefer the well-supported *vṛddha* "old," which fits the context much better.

42.5. *If ever I find*: the well-known motif of the three impossible conditions, which are yet miraculously met: a common name, a free gift without bride price, and maintenance by her own family.

10. *Ye that are hidden,* viz., snakes, upon which he thus calls specifically.

43.1. *Took her hand*: the ritual taking of the bride's hand is an important part of the marriage ceremony.

10. *Decrease in the merits of the Law*: it was his dharma to perform the *agnihotra* at dusk.

44.20. *Āstīka*: somewhat fancifully derived from *asti*, "there is."

45.10. "*Parikṣit*," here improbably derived from *pari-kṣi*, "to waste away." *AthV*. 20.122.8 etymologizes *paricchinna*, "circumscribing." More likely the name means "dwelling all around," i.e., "holding wide sovereignty."

15. *Grandfathers*: no doubt the Pāṇḍavas.

46.1. *Pūjā*: worship of an icon with unguents, flowers, fruits, etc. It is clear that here, as above, in 1.36.20, we should think of an *icon* of Brahmā. 25. *Utanka*, cf. above, 1.3.135 ff.

47.1. *His house priest*: but the use of the plural in the next line makes it likely we should adopt the reading *purohitaṃ . . . sartvijam*: "the house priest and the sacrificial priests." Every baronial household had its family priest for rituals as well as consultations.

5. *Session of the Snakes* (*sarpasattra*): such a rite was indeed known to the Pañcaviṃśa Brāhmaṇa (640–42); the difference is that there the Snakes themselves are the sacrificers. In any case Caland (1931) was right in pointing to that Sarpasattra as a model for the epic's. Additional evidence is that the *PVBr*. 25.15.3 painstakingly enumerates the officiating priests, as does *MBh*. (1.48); Caland points out that this list is a unique document in Vedic literature; and in that list figures a Janamejaya. Is it possible that at one time there was indeed held an anti-Snake Sacrifice, of which Brāhmaṇa and epic preserve variant records? ***We possess this rite*: this implies that there was an arcane ritual, by no means widely practiced. ***The royal seer willed*: in other words, he embarked upon the *saṃkalpa*, the ritual pronouncement of his intention to sacrifice.

10. *They consecrated the king*: reference is to the *dīkṣā*, "consecration of the sacrificer," at the beginning of a rite, continuing until the final bath. ***Holder of the Cord* (*sūtradhara*): ropes were used in measuring distances for construction purposes. ***Bard of the ancient Lore*: the combination of the two professions may surprise, but obviously builders had their own oral tradition of which portents of failure were an important part.

48.1. *Sadasyas*: cocelebrants.

5. *Hotar*: chief of the *ṚV*. priests. ***Udgātar*: chief of the *SV*. priests. ***Adhvaryu*: chief of the *YV*. priests. ***Vyāsa*, etc.: well-known among these are Vyāsa, our Vedic author; Uddālaka, a Sāmaveda brahmin, cf. above, 1.3.20; his own son Śvetaketu; Asita Devala, an ancient priest; and Nārada and Parvata, two divine seers.

15. *Well-pleased Indra*: his friendly connection with Takṣaka is puzzling; it recurs in the Khāṇḍava episode below, 1.214 ff. Probably we should hark back to 1.21 and the delight that the Snakes take in the rains, whose God is Indra.

20. *Vāsuki*: the king of the Snakes.

50.1. *Prayāga*, at the confluence of Ganges and Yamunā was, and is, a particularly famous ford, and was styled the "Altar of Brahmā." ***Rantideva*, a celebrated sacrificer.

5. *Ajamīḍha*, an ancestor of the Kurus. ***Daśaratha's son*: Rāma of the *Rāmāyaṇa*. ***Kṛṣṇa*, *sc*. Dvaipāyana, *alias* Vyāsa.

10. *Khaṭvanga*, etc.: ancient kings. ***Vālmīki*: sage and author of the *Rāmāyaṇa*. ***Vasiṣṭha*, cf. below, 1.164 ff.

15. *Kṛṣṇa*, probably Vāsudeva. ***Dambhodbhava*, a mighty but prideful sovereign who was bested by the seer Nara (5.94).

53.20. *May he*: these two lines are clearly charms against snakes.

1(6) The Descent of the First Generations

54.1. *Whom the maiden Kālī*: below, 1.57.55.

5. *He divided the One Veda*: hence his epithet Vyāsa, "the Divider." ***Sadas*: "sitting area," that part of the sacrificial terrain particularly reserved for Ṛgvedic and Sāmavedic priests. ***Spread-out grass*: the terrain was normally covered with straw of *kuśa* or *darbha* grass.

10. *He offered*: this is the rite of *satkriyā*, the hospitable reception of a guest, cf. Manu, 3.77 ff.

15–20. *That Breach*: this indicates an ancient division of the lay of the Bhāratas: Breach (*bheda*), War (*yuddha*), Triumph (*jaya*).

55.1. This recognizes the following episodes: *Dicing* and *Breach* (= Sabhāparvan, *MBh.* 2), the *Sojourn in the Forest* (= Āraṇyakaparvan, *MBh.* 3), and *War* (= Bhīṣmaparvan, etc., *MBh.* 6 ff.).

5. *When the father had died*: full story below, 1.109 ff. ***Cruel Duryodhana*: 1.119.15 ff.

15. *House of lacquer*: 1.(8) = 1.124–38. ***Hiḍimba*: 1(9) = 1.139–44.

20. *Baka*: 1(10) = 1.145–52. ***They won Draupadī*: 1(12) = 1.174–89. ***Khāṇḍava Forest*: 1(15) = 1.199.

25. *Subjugated the East*, etc.: the present *MBh.* version places this episode later in 2(13) = 2.23–29.

30. *Had his brother Dhanaṃjaya depart*: 1(16) = 1.200–210; this summary gives what in my opinion is the original duration of Arjuna's exile: twelve plus one months, a clear foreshadowing of the twelve plus one years of the brother's exile. The cr. ed. gives consistently years for months; cf. my notes on 1(16). ***Won the pleasant-spoken Subhadrā*: 1(17) = 1.211–12.

35. *In the Khāṇḍava Forest*: 1(19) = 1.214–25. ***A divine Hall*: 2(20) = 2.1–11.

40. *He cheated Yudhiṣṭhira*: 2(27) and (28) = 2.

43–72. ***The woods*: *MBh.* 3, Āraṇyakaparvan. ***In a kingdom*: *MBh.* 4, Virāṭaparvan.—Note that in the above summary the following Minor Books of *MBh.* *1* and *2* are missing: 1(11): *Citraratha* (= 1.153–73); 1(13)–(14): the *Wedding*, and the *Coming of Vidura* (= 1.190–98); 1(18): the *Fetching of the Gift* (= 1.213); and Books 2(20)–(26).

56.1. *Those they should never have slain*: precisely the issue over which Arjuna protests; *BhG.* 1.37. ***Condone the oppressions*: sc. the assassination attempts, Draupadī's molestation, and the exiles. ***Hold his fury*: cf. 2.61; 3.13.55 ff.; 3.34; 3.36–37.

15. *The Veda of Kṛṣṇa*, sc. Kṛṣṇa Dvaipāyana, *alias* Vyāsa.

20. *Textbook* (*śāstra*): *MBh.* is considered an authority on Law (*dharma*), which indeed is one of its main themes; Profit (*artha*), esp. the King's Profit, or practical politics, for there are many discussions of correct policy; and Salvation (*mokṣa*), esp. for such texts as *BhG.* and *Mokṣadharma* (in *MBh.* 12).

30. *The great Birth of the Bhāratas*: implied is that *MBh.* has produced both the Bhāratas and their fame. ***Rose daily for three years*: possibly a reference to the duration of the original compilation? ***What is not here is nowhere else*: the famous line that from the outset points up the encyclopedic intentions of the text.

57.1. This story of Vasu Uparicara is one of the recognized starting points of *MBh.*, cf. above, 1.1.50. ***Uparicara*: lit., "moving aloft." ***Cedis*: the countryside immediately south of the rivers Yamunā and Carmaṇvatī. ***Worrying*: this motif of Indra's concern with the power of ascetics will recur repeatedly; implied is a fear of a rival form of religion.

5. *Worlds*: though the plural is unidiomatic in English, the notion of "one's worlds to win" is so typical that it deserves to be retained in translation; on the idea complex see Gonda (1966). ***Of stable clime*, i.e., with dependable monsoon.

10. *They do not divide*: i.e., they continue to live in the joint family, with the property held together. ***Chariot*: this chariot will have an interesting afterlife: it will descend from Vasu to Bṛhadratha of Magadha, to Jarāsaṃdha, and eventually be conquered by Kṛṣṇa Vāsudeva; below, 2.22.10 ff.

15. *A bamboo pole*: *Indramaha* or *-dhvaja*, a kind of maypole erected and decorated to celebrate the beginning of the year (cf. Meyer, 1937).

20. *The form of frolic* (*hāsyarupa*): cf. the discussion of Suthankar (1939); the frolic is the festivity surrounding the event, which can be approximated to the Spring Festival. ***Maha*: "festival," cf. *makha*. ***Maghavat*: "bounteous," Indra being the God of the monsoon.

25. *Gifts of land*: no doubt to brahmins, though this practice is late. ***Yadu* is more commonly known as the eldest son of Yayāti (below, 1.79), who also had five sons; clearly Vasu should be considered a First King, like Yayāti. (Dumézil, 1971).

30. *Śuktimatī*: lit., "shell-rich," name of a stream in Cedi, but esp. of the capital of Cedi.

35. *Girikā*, lit., "little mountain." ***"Shoot some deer"*: the reason for this demand is not clear: for purposes of offering? Otherwise the motif of "the mishap on the deer hunt" is well-known; cf. the stories of Parikṣit (1.36.10 ff), Pāṇḍu (1.109), Duḥṣanta (1.64), etc.

45. *Adrikā*: again, "little mountain."

50. *King Matsya* (lit., "fish"), no doubt eponymous from the Matsya country SW of the Yamunā and NW of the Carmaṇvatī. ***Blessed Lord*: *bhagavat*, a honorific of gurus, here of Brahmā. ***Siddhas, Seers, and Cāraṇas*: a cliché for semidivine denizens of the atmosphere. ***The king gave her to the fisherman*, i.e., the king of a probably aboriginal fishing tribe that worked the river Yamunā; there are any number of adoptions and substitutions in the epic of supposedly well-born but abandoned children; surely a device to legitimize their later high connections in spite of low origins. Thus this Satyavatī (also called Kālī and Kṛṣṇā, "the black one"), obviously a fishing and ferrying wench for the taking, is circuitously legitimized as a king's daughter.

55. *Holy men standing*: pilgrims who had come to the sacred river to bathe.

65. *Gandhavatī*, "fragrant." ***Yojanāgandha*, "whose fragrance reaches a *yojanā's* distance," about nine miles. ***Pārāśarya*: son of Parāśara. ***Born on an island*: numerous are stories of foundlings recovered from or by a river; this reference to Dvaipāyana, "son of an island," seems simply to indicate that he had been a foundling.

80. *Saṃjaya*: *sūta* (charioteer-bard) to Dhṛtarāṣṭra. ***Karṇa*: the full story below, 1.104. ***Akṣara*: either "[mystic] Syllable" or "intransient": van Buitenen, 1959. ***Without attributes*: without human limitations. ***Nature* (*pradhāna*): as source of creation. ***Wild goose*: symbol of the Supreme, being equally at home in the three worlds of earth, water, and sky.

85. *Puruṣa*: God as the primeval Person. ***Andhaka-Vṛṣṇis*: a tribe descended from Yadu (hence Yādavas) whose original seat was Mathurā on the Yamunā River. Also called *Bhojas*. ***Droṇa*: below, 1.121. ***Gautama Śaradvat*: below, 1.120.

90. *Dhṛṣṭadyumna, Kṛṣṇā*: below, 1.155.

95. *Śakuni*: maternal uncle and evil guide of Duryodhana, eldest of the Kauravas. ***The mother*: Gāndhārī. ***On the field*: below, 1.99–100. ***Yudhiṣṭhira*, etc.: below, 1.114–15. ***A hundred sons*: below, 1.107.

100. *Abhimanyu*: below, 1.213. ***Five boys*: ib. ***Ghaṭotkaca*: below, 1.143. ***Śikhaṇḍin*: below, 5.189.

58.1. *Self-created*: Brahmā. ***Cleared the earth*: a cliché; see Sukthankar (1937). ***Mahendra*: a mountain range, often identified with the northern part of the Eastern Ghats in Orissa.

5. *Season*: usually immediately after the menses; for a definition, Manu 3.45 ff.

10. *Thousands of years*: in the first of the four Eons, the Kṛta-yuga, lifespans of a thousand years are regular; cf. 1.71. ***Staff*; power of punishment.

15. *Knew a woman*: there was no child marriage? ***Brahman*: Vedic learning.

20. *Eon of the Winning Throw*: the Kṛta Yuga or Golden Age.

30. *Diti and Danu*: mothers of the Anti-Gods, the Daityas and Dānavas.

35. *The elephants*: viz., those of the cardinal points that with the mountains hold the earth in place; the wind appears to have a similar function, cf. the *pravaha* wind, *Sūryasiddhāntikā* 2.3; cf. also *Maitrāyaṇīya Upaniṣad* 1.4.

45. *Vaikuntha*; a name of Viṣṇu, later esp. of his heaven. ***Yellow-robed*: i.e., in the light of the sun. ***Dark-complexioned*: i.e., Kṛṣṇā. ***Lotus-naveled* (*padmanābha*): in origin probably: "of the lotus-like navel" is later interpreted literally as "having a lotus grown out of his navel," with Brahmā enthroned in it.

1(7) The Origins

59.7. The cr. ed. begins this Book after 1.61, treating 59–61 as part of the *Descent of the First Generations*. The older editions start it at 1.59.1. In view of the fact that in 1.59.7 Janamejaya asks the general question (which normally introduces a new stage), and that his question specifically asks for the origins (*saṃbhava*), I begin the *Origins* here.

10. *Born from his will*: usually translated "mind-born"; the idea is that he willed them into existence without benefit of mothers. ***Dakṣa*: here = Kąśyapa. ***Aditi*, etc.: Hopkins (1915).

15. *Hiraṇyakaśipu*, a demon particularly antagonistic to Viṣṇu. ***Prahrāda* (the older spelling): Prahlāda; for his history see Hacker (1959).

20. *Bali*: known as a great king, bested by Viṣṇu in the Dwarf incarnation.

25. *Vātāpi*: cf. below, the *Story of Agastya*, 3.94–108.

30. *Rāhu*: above, 1.17.5. ***Vṛtra*: the rain-choking dragon killed by Indra.

35. *Śukra*: below, 1.70 ff. ***Tārkṣya*, etc.: of these are especially known Garuḍa (= Tārkṣya) and Aruṇa; above, 1.14.

40. *Śeṣa*: Ananta, the cosmic snake; above, 1.32. ***Vāsuki*: above, 1.33 ff. ***Takṣaka*: above, 1.3; ***Arkaparṇa*: = Angāraparna, below, 1.153? ***Citraratha*: below, 1.153 ff. ***Parjanya*: the God of rain. ***Kali*: the dice demon. ***Nārada*, more generally known as a "divine seer."

60.1. *Mṛgavyādha*, "deer or game hunter"; *Śarva*, "bowman"; *Nirṛti*, "breaker of pacts' "; *Aja Ekapād*, "one-footed goat"; *Ahi Budhnya*, "snake of the depths"; *Pinākin*, "wielder of the Pināka bow"; *Dahana*, "burner"; *Īśvara*, "lord"; *Sthāṇu*, "post"; *Bhava*, "well-being" (? a euphemism); on the Rudras cf. Macdonell (1897).

5. *Bṛhaspati*: priest of the Gods; *Utathya*, cf. below, 1.98. ***From Kratu*: viz., the Vālakhilyas; above, 1.26 f.

10. "*Puppets*" (*putrikā*): daughters whose sons are considered the immediate sons of the daughters' father: Kane (1966). ***Dharma*: the personified Law; hence his wife's names correspond to consequences of dharmic conduct: *Kīrti*, "fame"; *Lakṣmī*, "good fortune"; *Dhṛti*, "equanimity"; *Medhā*, "wisdom"; *Puṣṭi*, "prosperity"; *Śraddhā*, "faith"; *Kriyā*, "rite"; *Buddhi*, "insight"; *Lajjā*, "modesty"; *Mati*, "opinion."

15. *Lunar mansions*: the asterisms of the lunar zodiac. ***Vasus*: Vedic light Gods (Macdonell, 1897).

20. *Śrama*, "ascetic toil"; *Śānta*, "serene;"; *Muni*, "hermit." ***Kumāra*, later the God of War, born from Śiva's *tejas* (fire/seed), which was deposited in the fire; the child emerged from a reed bed. ***Kṛttikā*: the Pleiades.

30. *Tvaṣṭrī*: a feminine of Tvaṣṭar, name of Viśvakarman. ***Mare*: because Savitar (= Sun) takes on the form of a solar horse.

35. *Wings* (*pakṣa*): parties. ***Bhṛgu*: they do not really fit here, being a brahmin clan. ***All-the-Gods* (*viśve devāḥ*): Macdonell (1897). ***Aruṇa* "dawn." ***Guhyakas*: more usually = Yakṣas.

40. *Planet*: i.e., Venus. ***Śukra*: guru of the Daityas; cf. 1.71 ff; but by no means a celibate, since he had a daughter Devayānī, ib. ***Cyavana*: above, 1.6. ***Aurva*: below, 1.69 ff.

45. *Ṛcīka, Jamadagni*: below, 3.115 ff. ***Rāma*: Paraśu-Rāma. ***Dhātar and Vidhātar*: Creator and Ordainer.

50. *Horses that fly in the sky*: Gandharvas? ***Adharma*: Lawlessness.

55. *Cakravāka*: the bird Anas Casarca. ***Good luck to thee* (*bhadraṃ te*): a blessing here and there interjected to fill out the verse. ***She bore*: this seems still to be *Tāmrā*, progenitrix of animals.

60. *Marsh deer*: Bos Grunniens? ***Spotted big cats* (*dvīpin*): leopards, possibly tigers.

65. *Serpents, snakes*: no clear distinction; for Kadrū, above, 1.14.

1(7.a) The Partial Incarnations

61.5. *Jarāsaṃdha*: king of Magadha. ***Śiśupāla*: king of Cedi and marshal of Jarāsaṃdha. ***Śalya*: king of the Madras = Bāhlika here? ***Dhṛṣṭadketu*: son of Śiśupāla. ***Druma*: king of Kiṃpurusa.

10. *Bhagadatta*: king of Prāgjyotiṣa = Assam. ***Ugrasena*: A Vṛṣṇi king. ***Aśoka*: further unknown, but likely to be a Vṛṣṇi.

15. *Hārdikya*: a Vṛṣṇi. ***Malla*: a tribe between the rivers Sadānīra and Gaṇḍakī.

20. *Bṛhanta*: king of Ulūka. ***Prativindhya*: a son of Draupadī.

25. *Bāhlīka*: brother of Śaṃtanu, a Kaurava ancestor.

35. *Kāśirāja*: king of the Kāśis.

40. *Pauṇḍramatsyaka*: a curious name: the Puṇḍras belong far east, the Matsyas west of the Yamunā, but Matsyaka here may mean "fish-eating tribe."

60. *Issued from no womb*: having been born from sperm dropped in a trough; below, 1.121.

65. *Aśvatthāman*: son of Droṇa: 1.121. ***The eight Vasus*: 1.91; cf. 1.93.

70. *Who puissantly battled*: details unknown; cf. below, 5.180. ***Kṛpa*: guru of the Kauravas. ***Śakuni*: uncle of the Dhārtarāṣṭras and a gambler. ***Dvāpara*: here a dice demon.

75. *Kṛtavarman*: a Vṛṣṇi warrior. ***Dhṛtarāṣṭra*: 1.100.

80. *Atri's son*: but as Dharma's son, 1.100–101. ***Kali*: dice demon. ***Yudhiṣṭhira*, etc.: 1.114 f.

85. *Dhṛṣṭadyumna*: 1.155. ***Karṇa*: 1.104.

90. *Baladeva*: Balarāma, Kṛṣṇa's brother. ***Pradyumna*: Kṛṣṇa's son.

95. *Śrī*: 1.189. ***Daughter of Subala*: Gāndhārī.

1(7.b) Śakuntalā

This episode has been made particularly famous by the dramatic adaption of it by Kālidāsa in the *Abhijñāna-Śakuntala*, which by many is judged to be the finest example of the Sanskrit play. Those who know the play, but not the epic narrative, will find a comparison instructive. Though Kālidāsa's superb poetry overshadows the epic story, the latter has a striking quality of earthy style and directness, with many samples of literary embellishment and an admixture of legal lore. Nothing in the play of Kālidāsa compares with the tongue-lashing that Śakuntalā gives Duḥṣanta in this story, and it is a relief when a divine voice interferes to set matters right. In the epic the king's justification of his refusal to recognize Śakuntalā and her son at once—the people would never have accepted him as the king's heir—has a simple logic to it; while Kālidāsa's artful weaving together of a curse—the loss of a keepsake ring, its miraculous recovery, Duḥṣanta's chance meeting with his son in heaven—and the final reunion becomes an elegant romance that is less convincing.

The story itself has nothing to do with the main events and characters of *MBh.*, which may be said to start in 1.91. Yet its inclusion is apposite: Bharata, son of Duḥṣanta and Śakuntalā, is the eponym of the Bhāratas, and his story demonstrates the divine grace that lies on the lineage. (N.B. The translation of this episode has benefited greatly from a reading by Murray B. Emeneau.)

62.1. *Dynast*: *vaṃśakara*; it implies that Duḥṣanta also was the founder of a new lineage in the Paurava succession.

5. *No one needed to plough or mine the earth*: the only senses which cr. ed. *nākṛṣyakarakṛt* produces are "not failing to plough" (*na a-kṛṣyakara-kṛt*) and "not producing taxes without ploughing" (*na a-kṛṣya-karakṛt*). Neither is very commendable. I prefer the well-supported reading *na kṛṣyākara-kṛt* (*na kṛṣy-ākara-kṛt*), as translated, which is better in

line with the idyll described. ***Lacked all selfishness*: they worshiped the Gods for no return at all, for none was needed.

10. *Rain god*: Parjanya.

63.1. *Arm-slappings*: slapping the hand on the arm was a sign of heroic challenge; cf. below, 1.125.25.

10. *Bilva*: wood apple tree (Aegle Marmelos); *arka*: Calotropis Gigantea; *khādira*: Acacia Catechu; *kapittha*: Feronia Elephaṇtum; *dhava*: Grislea Tomentosa.

15. *Circular club swing*: *gadāmaṇḍala*. ***Tiger men*: *naravyāghra* here hardly means "tiger among men"; one may think of tribals in tiger skins, perhaps even were-tigers.

64.10. *Maypoles*: *Indradhvaja*; above, 57.15.

15. *Fire halls*: for sacrifices.

20. *Nara and Nārāyaṇa* had their hermitage in Badarī on the upper Ganges.

25. *Citraratha's park*: cf. below, 1.153 f. ***Kaṇva Kāśyapa*: Kaṇva is the name of a family of seers (M-K); here he is held to be a descendant of Kaśyapa.

30. *Word-wise and step-wise* (*preryamāṇāh padakramaiḥ*): I take it that this refers to the *padapāṭha* (word-by-word) and *kramapāṭha* (step-by-step) modes of recitation. Normal connected (*saṃhitā*) récit goes as follows (*ṚV.* 3.62.10): *tatsaviturvareṇyambhargodevasya-dhīmahi, dhiyoyonahpracodayāt*; word-wise: *tat, savituḥ, vareṇyam, bhargaḥ, devasya, dhīmahi, dhiyaḥ, yaḥ, naḥ, pracodayāt*; step-wise: *tat savituḥ savitur vareṇyaṃ vareṇyam bhargo bhargo dhīmahi*, etc. ***Bahvṛca*: lit., "of many Ṛgveda verses," a school of *ṚV.* specialists. ***Who strode their strides* (*kramadbhiś ca kramān api*): I take it this refers to the measuring of a ritual area by means of a number of strides. ***Saṃhitā*: the basic collection of hymns, but also the above connected *récit*. ***Refinement of speech* (*śabdasaṃskāra*): i.e., Sanskrit.

35. *Phonetics* (*śīkṣā*): one of the six *Vedāngas*, auxiliaries or branches of the *Veda*. ***Rules of interpretation* (*nyāya*): a reference to Mīmāṁsā. ***Sentences*: i.e., to construe proper divisions and subdivisions of rites: *Mīmāṃsā*. ***Variety of rites*: *viśeṣakriyā*; it may also mean a special rite contrasted to a normal one (*sāmānya*): *Mimāṃsā*. ***Practitioners*: *lokāyatika*, which probably refers to the Nyāya.

65.20. *Viśvāmitra*: a baron who became a brahmin; below, 1.164 ff. The third book of *ṚV.* is ascribed to him.

25. *From his beloved sons*: below, 1.166.

30. *Kauśikī*: the river Kosi or Koosa in Bihar, northern tributary of the Ganges. ***Matanga*: nothing more in *MBh.*, but Harivaṃśa p. 88 ff. has this account: Prince Satyavrata Triśanku had been exiled by his father to the forest; a twelve-year famine befell, during which he (apparently as a hunter) supported Viśvāmitra's wife while her husband was abroad; gratified, Viśvāmitra gave him a boon. ***Pārā*: "safe crossing," in memory of his wife's safe crossing of the famine.

34. The verse is quite difficult. D. suggests tmesis of *atikruddha* and *pratisasarja*; but a double occurrence in the same śloka of a very rare feature is unlikely in the extreme. Hesitantly, I take *prati-* in the sense of "counter-" (e.g. *pratihastin*); and *ati* as governing *nakṣatravaṃśān* (cf. *Rāmāyaṇa* 1.59). ***Śravaṇā*: twentieth lunar mansion, α, β, and γ Aquilae.

66.5. *Abandoned*: note again the practice of abandoning an extramarital child by a river.

10. *Birds*: *śakuna, śakunta*, hence Śakuntalā.

67.1. *King*: since Viśvāmitra was originally a baron, son of King Gādhi. ***Rite of the Gandharvas*: marriage by the couple's mutual consent.

10. *Manu* gives them indeed in this order 3.21; on the various modes, cf. below, 1.96. ***The first four . . . six . . . .*, cf. *Manu* 3.23.24. ***The Rākṣasa mode*, cf. *Manu* 3.22,24, and below, 1.96, where Bhīṣma practices it. ***The Āsura mode*: *Manu* 3.24. ***Three of the five*: 67.11 cd–12 ab = *Manu* 3.25.

15. *Young King*: prince-heir. ***Took her by the hand*: by way of marriage ritual.

25. "*Done in secret . . .*": it looks like a quotation; cf. *Manu* 3.32. ***Turner of the Wheel*: *cakravartin*.

30. *His burden*: Sukthankar, *Addenda ad* 3.67.30, prefers *kāyakam* for *bhāram*; on the word cf. Edgerton, *BHS Dictionary* s.v.

68.1. *sacraments of birth, etc.*: a person underwent a number of sacraments (*saṃskāra*, "sanctification"); the most important were those ensuring conception, ensuring the birth of a son, the birth rite and naming, initiation, marriage, and death. ***The sign of the wheel*: betokening the future cakravartin.

5. *Sarvadamana*: "All-tamer."

25. *The ancient seer*: soul, or self.

30–31. *duṣkṛtam* in 30 b = acc. of *duṣkṛta*; in 31 d = acc. of *duṣkṛt*. ***Come on my own*: without having been called, as he had promised 67.15. ***baying* (*raumi*): the root *ru* is especially used of animal cries.

35. *Wifehood*: a play on the word *jāyā*, "wife," and *jāyate*, "he is born." ***Who follows the scriptures*: *āgamavataḥ*. ***Svayaṃbhū*: here for Svāyaṃbhuva's father: *Manu* has practically the same line, 3.138. The phrase provides a pseudo-etymology for *putra* as "one who saves (*trāyate*) from Put."

40. *Half the man*: cf. Bṛhadāraṇyaka Upaniṣad 1.9.3. *idam ardhabṛgalamiva svaḥ*: "The two of us are so to say each half a whole."

60. Cf. *Pāraskara Gṛhyasūtra* 1.18.1: "When he returns from a journey, he approaches the house . . . 2. When he sees his son, he murmurs 'From each limb . . . [= 68.62 only].' He then kisses his head"; cf. Oldenberg (1886, p. 298). **"*For my nourishment . . .*": line not further identified.

65. *āhavanīya*: the fire into which the offerings are made; *gārhapatya*: the fire on which the offerings are prepared; the latter is used to light the other.

70. *Menakā . . . Viśvāmitra . . .* : I take these lines as heavily sarcastic.

75. *śāla*: Vatica Robusta.

69.10. *Haṃsas*, a kind of geese, are supposed to be able to separate milk from water that dilutes it.

15. *Heretic* (*anāstika*): one who does not uphold the authority of the Vedas. ***Manu* 9.158–59 cites six kinds of sons who are heirs: (1) *aurasa* (defined, 9.166), (2) *kṣetraja* (9.167), (3) *datta* (9.168), (4) *kṛtrima* (9.169), (5) *gūḍhotpanna* (9.170), (6) *apaviddha* (3.171). Of those (1) corresponds to *begotten on one's wife*; (3) to *obtained as gift*; (4) to *adopted*; (6) probably to *reared*. Our text misses (2) the *kṣetraja*, i.e., the son begotten on one's wife by Injunction by a third party; and (5) the *gūḍhotpanna*, i.e., a son fathered by an unknown man on one's wife after or before marriage. On the other hand, it adds one, *begotten on other women* (not in *Manu*, but possibly inferrable), and one *bought*; the latter *Manu* expressedly excludes from those six sons who are heirs (9.160). Also compare n.1.111.25. Our text reads most naturally: *Manu cites five kinds of sons*; but since actually six kinds are enumerated, the present translation must be preferred.

25. *The father's water sack*: in other words, the recipient of his seed alone. D. takes it in the sense of "bellows," which agrees with the etymology. Both verses are quoted as chronicle verses in 90.30.

45. *Dakṣa*: a famous sacrificer. ***Vast-in-Cows*; *go-vitatam*. ***Lotus count* (*padma*): a very large number.

50. *I shall celebrate*: this clearly anticipates Janamejaya's question in 1.89.1.

1(7.c) Yayāti

70.1. *Pracetas*: here the first creator.

5. *Vīriṇī*: "mother of heroes." ***Sāṃkhya*: it is not clear whether the term is used technically for the Sāṃkhya system; nothing can be deduced from the context. ***His puppets*, as those of Prajāpati (= Dakṣa) above, 60.10. ***Conducting time*: since these twenty-seven are the lunar mansions that measure the lunar day and month. ***Dākṣāyaṇī*: more normally Aditi is their mother, with whom D. identifies her.

15. *Ilā*: note that the word is feminine; born a woman, she became a man. ***Vena*, etc.; ancient kings. ***Thirteen islands*: or continents. ***Non-human*: e.g., he married the Apsarā Urvaśī. ***Sanatkumāra*: a son of Brahmā, elsewhere referred to as a teacher.

20. The great seers: Purūravas's hostility to the brahmins makes little sense in view of the fact that he brought down their sacred fires. ***Three fires*: *āhavanīya* (offering fire), *gārhapatya* (householder's or kitchen fire), and *daksiṇāgni* (southern fire), charted in Caland-Henry, 1906, van Buitenen, 1968.

25. *Seers*: brahmins; again, the curious antagonism.

30. *When I was sacrificing with long Sessions*: the full story knows nothing of this; cf. 78.25 ff.

40. *Made his old age go*: the full story attributes this power to Uśanas: 78.40.

71.1. *The tenth*: Pracetas → Dakṣa → Kaśyapa → Vivasvat → Yama → Mārtaṇḍa → Manu → Ilā → Purūravas → Nahuṣa → Yayāti. ***Vṛṣaparvan* did not quite choose him: 77.5 ff.

5. *Son of Angiras* = Bṛhaspati. ***Uśanas Kāvya*: on this interesting personality cf. Dumézil (1971).

15. *For a thousand years*: for this is the Eon of the Gods (= *kṛta-yuga*), where time lasts longer.

20. *Son of Kavi*: out of Kāvya, which seems to be part of Uśanas's name. ***Began to propitiate*: *ārādhayiṣyan*. ***Sang along*: *anugāyamānā*, middle present participle; D.: *anugavad ācarantī*, taking it from a denominative *anugāyate*, which is less likely.

25. Jackals: *śālāvṛka*.

35. *Change that impends* (*upasthitāṃ vaikṛtim*): apparently just the transitoriness of things.

38. *Fellow-student*: read *sabrahmacārī* with D. (= *samānaguruḥ*).

45. *Thou hast succeeded*: clearly Śukra was never fooled about Kaca's intentions.

50. *Treasury*: holding the wisdom of the four *Vedas*. ***Killer of brahmins*: hence drinking intoxicating liquids is one of the five great sins (brahmin-murder, liquor use, theft, intercourse with a guru's wife, concourse with such sinners). ***Wine*, of course, is a guess; it may be anything from beer and mead to a hemp brew.

72.15. *No son of a seer*: no born brahmin.

73.1. *Slay the enemy*: this obviously important theme is not followed up. Indra tries to alienate Śukra from the Asuras through Devayānī and Śarmiṣṭhā, but does not in the end seem to succeed, at least it is not said. The rivalry of Gods and Asuras is further forgotten in favor of the *roman* of Yayāti.

20. *Take it*: a symbolic act of marriage. ***Ghūrṇikā*: the sudden mention of this servant girl reminds one of the usual theatrical device of presuming a servant present.

74.5. *A student*: Śarmiṣṭhā; since her father is Vṛṣaparvan's guru, she is his daughter's guru.

76.15. *All four classes*: a reference to the Puruṣasūkta *ṚV*. 10.9., where brahmin, baron, commoner, and serf are said to spring from parts of the creator's body (mouth, arms, thighs, and feet respectively).

25. *Who took my hand*: 73.20.

77.20. *Three who own no property*: practically identical with *Manu* 8.416.

78.1–5. *Seer . . . Twiceborn*: wordplay; Devayānī takes the words in their usual sense of "brahmin," Śarmiṣṭhā in the literal sense of "seer" (e.g., "royal seer" = learned king); and "member of any of the three twiceborn classes." ***The literal truth*: *tathyam*.

79.5. *Your offspring shall have no share*: although the Yādavas in the lineage of the Vṛṣṇis had dominion, their regal status appears not to have been very high.

10. *Your offspring shall face extinction*: after a last reference to them in *Śatapatha Brahmaṇa* 13.5.1.16, they disappear as a historic tribe.

15. *The title of Bhoja*: according to *Aitareya Brāhmaṇa* 8.12.4–5 the title of western kings. ***Raft and ferry*: according to *ṚV.* 7.18 the Druhyus, after their defeat by Sudās, perished in the water: = were reduced to marshy country?

20. *Anu*: name of a people who have left little trace.

80.1. *Serfs . . . Dasyus*: note the distinction being made.

25. *Yāvanas*: lit., "Greeks (Ionians)," generally for peoples of the extreme northwest.

1(7.d) The Latter Days of Yayāti

81.1. *Cast out again*: this is clearly a new theme that confirms the doctrine of transmigration.

5. *Vasumat* (*sic*): the main text has Vasumanas.

82.1. *Pūru in your body*: it has not been made clear before this that Pūru took over not just Yayāti's old age but his aged body; Yayāti thus also shows his capacity for transmigration.

5. Only verse 5 is responsive; the remainder of the chapter is extraneous.

83.1. *As you disdain*: his principal fault, cf. 5.118.16. ***You shall fall today*: there are variant versions: this verse has Indra oust Yayāti directly, as in 5.119.7; in 1.84.18 it is the Envoy of the Gods, no doubt on Indra's orders. ***Fall with the honest*: cf. 5.119.8.

5. *You fall as the sun*: the notion that falling stars are returning souls. ***The God's own roadway* (*devamārga*): the *devayāna*, or Path of the Gods, by which the deceased may travel out of transmigration to Brahman (*ChUp.* 5.10.2). As Yayāti is on his way down, he should be on the Path of the Fathers (*pitṛyāna*, ib. 5.10.3 ff.) to rebirth; this may seem anomalous, but is not: for Yayāti never actually touches earth again, but was suspended (1.18.1, though 5.119.9 places him in the Naimiṣa Forest) when he met the four kings, who themselves were on the "Gods's roadway" out of transmigration.

10. *Nor would we have dared*: justifying his discourtesy toward an elder.

84.1. *As I am older*: justifying his own silence; he expected to be recognized and once more shows his flaw of disdain, which was earlier demonstrated by his wish to transfer his senescence, and by his pride in his austerities. He will be outdone by the others' generosity. ***At leisure*: negative of *pravaṇe*, headlong," ***Follow the evil*: lit., "the evil ones' wickedness"; *asatām . . . etad* (sc. *pāpam*).

5. *I shall not retrieve it* (*nādhigantā yad asmi*): This indicates the doctrine of disattachment: nothing one owns or accomplishes makes any difference in face of what is "appointed" (*diṣṭa*) Fate.

10. *Bugs born from sweat, etc.*: there are four ways of being born, from a plant, from an egg, alive, or from sweat (insects). ***The what-to-do-what-nows do not upset me*: *kim kuryām vai kiṃ ca kṛtvā* < sc. *kuryām iti* > *na tapye*. ***Who knows the country*: *ksetrajña* "guide," which is the older meaning, but here already shading into the meaning of "[re-] embodied soul."

15. *The lengthened accent*: beyond the normal lengths of a vowel (short and long), there may, under certain circumstances, e.g., an imperative, occur an overlong vowel: it would translate as "Fa-a-all!" ***Then I fell*: this appears to mean that the measure of one's knowledge is that of one's stay in heaven. ***Compassionate*: by no means so in 5.118.18 ff.

20. *Reassured* (*pratīta*): for he knew he had fallen among his grandchildren.

85.1. *When merit is gone* (*ksīṇapuṇye*): cf. *ChUp.* 5.10.5., *yāvat-saṃpātam*. ***Hell-on-earth* (*bhaumaṃ narakam*): the hell of returning to rebirth. ***Fodder for jackals . . .* : in order to die again.

5. *When the birds of prey, etc.*: points to corpse disposal by exposure (*paropta, uddhita*), cf. M-K s.v. *agnidagdha*. ***I have never heard*: note! ***How do they fare*: *kathaṃ bhavanti*.

***Become again*: *ābhavanti*. ***Their gaping acts* (*karmaṇo jṛmbhamānād*) demanding satisfaction. ***Ogres-of-earth*: i.e., ogres of the hell-on-earth. ***How do the dead*: read *kathaṃ bhūtā*.

10. *As a raindrop*: the notion attested by *ChUp*. 5.10.6 that eventually a returning soul rains down and clings to a plant; if a man then ingests the plant, the soul passes into his sperm that may impregnate a woman. I take *asra* (lit., "tear") in the sense of "drop." *Puṣpaphala*, lit., "flower and fruit." *asraṃ puṣpaphalānupṛktam* is subject, *retas* object of *anveti*. *He*: the migrating self or soul.

11. *Herbs and trees*, cf. *ChUp*. 5.10.6. ***Wind, sky*: ib. 5.10.5 (*ākāśa*). ***Thus do the dead*: read *evaṃ bhūtā*.

12. *With his body*: read *kāyena* for the meaningless *kāmena*.

13. *Hearing and eyesight*: for all five senses.

14. *The ghost*: *vāyu* ("wind") for *prāṇa* "breath," the transmigrating "last breath", cf. Caland. (1893) ***Into the womb*: *yonim*, accusative of direction. ***He functions there*: I take *tanmātrakṛtādhikāraḥ* as a *bahuvrīhi*, qualifying *vāyuḥ*: "Whose function is effected by means of the measures-of-it"; *tanmātra* is in Sāṃkhya the object of the senses; here it seems to have the meaning of a factor in the evolution of the senses.

16. *The large Ātman*: I now prefer this rendering: it is the embodied ātman; on the whole complex cf. van Buitenen, 1964. ***A creature's body*: *prāṇabhṛtaḥ* may also be taken adjectivally to *mahātmanaḥ*.

17. *That has died*: *saṃsthita*.

18. *Gasps his last*: *suptavan niṣṭanitvā*: "having expired like a man asleep"; note form and sense of *niṣṭanitvā*. ***Ghost* (*pavana*): the last breath.

19. *To a good womb*: cf. *ChUp*. 5.10.7.

20. *Thus do the dead*: read *tathā bhūtā*.

86.1. *They hold many views*: *bahūny asmin saṃprati vedayanti*. ***Brahmacārin*: student; on his duties cf. *Manu* 2. ***Householder*: *Manu* 3. ***Doctrine*: *upaniṣad*. ***Hermit*: forest-dweller, *Manu* 6.1–30. ***Mendicant*: (*bhikṣu*): the *saṃnyāsin* or ascetic: *Manu* 6.31 ff. *That night*: D. refers to *BhG*. 2.69.

10. *Pairs of opposites*: happiness and unhappiness, etc.

87.1. *Truthless*: for one should not speak the truth if it will hurt.

5. *Kings* (*lokapāla*): or World Guardians, the four Gods who guard the four quarters; cf. below, 2.5–12. ***The country of Law*: possibly the domain of Yama, God of Death and Law. ***Mountains*: should we not read *pārvatais ca*? ***So much*: his lot hereafter is as rich as all that.

10. *Twiceborn*: here = brahmins. ***Brahmin wife*: married to a baron.

88.5. *Śibi* is the example of generosity, cf. 3.131.

20. *Grandfather*: on their mother's side. Yayāti's daughter was Mādhavī, married to Gālava; in the version of 5.118 f. she and her husband added their shares to prevent Yayāti's fall to earth. ***Gave it to brahmins*: as sacrificial fee. ***The Gods obtained*: Yayāti was known as a great sacrificer since *ṚV*. 1.31.17; cf. also below, 3.129.

1(7) The Origins (*continued*)

89–90. There is no satisfactory way of reconciling the dynastic lists of the two chapters.

89.15. *Received a son*: two traditions seem to be mixed in this extraordinary account: that Bharata obtained a worthy son only after a sacrifice, at which Bharadvāja officiated: and that Bharata adopted as heir a son of Bharadvāja, securing the legitimacy of the succession by having Bhūmanyu adopt his son Vitatha. (The account in 90.30 simply has that Bhūmanyu was Bharata's son Sunandā.) Still, the succession went to Bharata's own son.

20. *Suhotra*, etc.: all four names indicate that they were sacrificers.

25. *Sacrificial pole*: a pole erected at the east end of the sacrificial terrain, to which the animal victims were tied.

30. *A very great disaster*: twelve years of drought; below, 1.163.

35. *OṂ*: a solemn expression of consent. ***The one horn*: *viṣāṇabhūtam*: the expression is not clear. D. seems to think of a horn of plenty (? *gor iva prabhūtam*); I take it as a reference to the horn of the rhinoceros, symbol of uniqueness and solitude, since horns otherwise come in pairs.

40. *Tapatī*: for her story see below, 1.160–63.

50. *Sumanyu . . . Pratīpa*: Sukthankar recognizes a lacuna between vss. 51 and 52. ***With Bāhlika*: this indicates that Bāhlika shared the kingdom, about which nothing is known; in the main epic he remains a shadowy figure.

90.1. *From Manu Prajāpati onward*: one is reminded that according to 1.1.50 some started *Mahābhārata* from *Manu*, that is probably from 1.90–91. ***From Dakṣa*: from here until the end the chapter is in prose, with chronicle verses inserted.

5. *Yayāti had two wives*: cf. the story above, 1.70–80.

10. *Viśvajit*: name of a sacrifice that is part of the complex *Gavām ayana* ritual.

15. 15. *Hence his name Prācinvat*: play on *prācī*, "east." ***Human sacrifice*: *puruṣamedha*; a ritual is recorded, but of doubtful occurrence. ***His name Ayutanāyin*: more likely "leader of ten thousand."

20. *Karaṇḍu*: note the un-Āryan sound of the name, appropriate to tribal Kalinga.

30. *"The mother is the father's water sack"*: also quoted above, 1.69.25. ***His ṇame Bharata*: as is said *bharasva putram*, "support your son."

35. *Hāstinapura*: more often derived from *hastin*, "elephant."

45. *His name Śaṃtanu*: however fetching this explanation, the name more likely means "of sound body," in contrast to his brother Devāpi, who had a skin disease and was therefore excluded from the kingdom; cf. *Bṛhaddevatā* 7, 148; Macdonell, 1904.

50. *Gandhakālī* this is the only occurrence of the name, which is a mixture of the names Gandhavatī and Kālī; her story below, 1.94 ff; from here on still another summary of *Mahābhārata*, particularly from the genealogical point of view. The full story follows, below.

90. *Abhimanyu married Uttarā*: 4.65–67. ***Stillborn child*: 14.65. ***Having revived it*: 14.69.

95. This takes the genealogy down to Janamejaya's lifetime when he was a grandfather. ***Thus has the lineage*: the narrative reverts to the śloka.

91.1 *Mahābhiṣa*: probably out of Mahābhisaj "great healer. ***Horse Race Festival*: the Vājapeya, a variety of Soma Sacrifice during which the patron competes with sixteen rivals in a chariot race.

10. *We passed by*: *atyabhisṛtāḥ*; this version is quite different from that of 1.93.

20. *Spare you one-eighth of the sperm*: i.e., leave it in the womb while taking embryonic shape themselves.

92.11. *He was called Śaṃtanu*: yet another pseudo-etymology: "serene" being *śānta*, it presumes the spelling *śāṃtanu* ***The imperishable worlds*: for he had already won heaven.

35. *Three journeys*: in heaven, on earth, in the underworld.

45. *The eighth son*: the incarnation of Dyaus or Heaven. ***Daughter of Jahnu*: a later story has it that when the Ganges disturbed the contemplations of this sage, he drank up the river, but released it from his ear.

50. *Āpava*, a name of Vasiṣṭha's of uncertain meaning; it may be a patronymic "son of Apu," but that name is unknown; or from *ā-pū*, "purifier."

93.5. *Surabhi*: cf. 1.60.65. ***Vasiṣṭha's cow* recurs in the *Story of Vasiṣṭha*, 1.164 ff., where it is coveted by Viśvāmitra.

94.15. *As worship of Gods*: i.e., without ulterior purposes.

30. *Uśanas*: the guru of the Asuras; above, 1.70 ff. ***Angiras's son*: Bṛhaspati, guru of the Gods.

35. *Rāma the seer*: Paraśu-Rāma.

70. *The offspring of an Āryan*: that is, if we take seriously the story of Uparicara Vasu and his spilled seed: above, 1.57.35 ff. ***Asita Devala*: an ancient sage; nothing of the incident is known.

90. *Mother*: i.e., father's wife. ***Death would come at his own bidding*: justification for the accretions of books twelve and thirteen, which are put in the mouth of the dying Bhīṣma.

95.5. *The king of the Gandharvas came to him*: apparently to punish his pride.

96.1. *Choose their own husbands*: a baron's daughter had the privilege of choosing her husband herself (*svayaṃvara*).

5. *To men of virtue who have been invited*: the Brāhma mode; cf. *Manu* 3.27. ***Decked with ornaments*: the Daiva mode; *Manu* 3.28. ***A dowry is offered*: so? The text is extremely elliptic; *yathāśakti pradāya ca dhanāny api* may go with *alaṃkṛtya*, constituting the same marriage mode, but in that case the number of modes is seven instead of the required eight. If it is a separate mode, it might be associated (doubtfully) with the *Prājāpatya*; *Manu* 3.30. ***For a pair of cows*: the *Ārṣa* mode; *Manu* 3.29. *For a negotiated price*: the *Āsura* mode; *Manu* 3.31. ***Force their leave by force*: *Rākṣasa* mode; *Manu* 3.33.

10. *A girl taken off guard*: *Paiśāca* mode; *Manu* 3.34. ***Find for themselves*: the *Svayaṃvara*, not accounted for by *Manu*. The present series misses the *Gāndharva* and possibly the *Prājāpatya* modes.

20. *Cut them off*: presumably with a shield.

25. *Śālva*: who had been the choice of the eldest daughter Ambā.

35. *The vāruṇa weapon*: all manner of divine names are given to certain types of arrows, perhaps describing some peculiarity of shape, perhaps merely indicating that a spell invoking this or that God was placed on it. Miraculous powers are ascribed to such arrows.

40. *Like daughters-in-law, etc.*: in other words, he did not molest them.

50. *Gave leave to depart*: but Śālva will no longer accept her, and in consequence she curses Bhīṣma (5.170–97).

55. *Consumption*: this apparently refers to the *rāja-yakṣman*, which is usually taken for "consumption:" the ailment is clearly brought about by sexual exhaustion: in 110.1. Pāṇḍu gives as cause of his father Vicitravīrya's death that he "lived for pleasure," (*kāmātman*); in 112.15 Vyuṣitāśva succumbs to *yakṣman*, "because he lusted after his wife."

97.10. *The highest Law*: viz., of the Niyoga, "Injunction," by which a brother begets children on his deceased brother's behalf. As the context shows below, brahmins could be invoked to beget children in this fashion.

20. *You could create*: great power was attributed to total truthfulness. ***Law of Distress*: system of rules that apply in emergencies; an entire minor book is devoted to it; below, 12.129–67.

98.1. *Arjuna*: sc. Kārtavīrya; cf. below, 3.116–17.

5. *A seer called Utathya*: the story of Dīrghatamas closely resembles that of *Bṛhaddevatā* 4.11–15 and 21.25. There Utathya is called Ucathya (as he is in the Southern Recension); also, *ṚV*. 1.158 knows Dīrghatamas as Aucathya (son of Ucathya or Ucatha).

15. *A long darkness*: *dīrghaṃ tamas*; he was born blind. ***They threw him*: in *Bṛhaddevatā* 4.21 the servants do this.

25. *A serf*: according to *Brhaddevatā* 4.24 by the name of Uśij. ***Kakṣīvat*: so also *Bṛhaddevatā* 4.25.

30. *Anga*: *Bṛhaddevatā* makes no mention of Sudeṣṇā or her son Anga; but it has Dīrghatamas float to the Anga country in the first place.

99.10. *Divided the Veda*; viz., into the four *Vedas*.
20. *Lawful*: since Kṛṣṇa is a brother of Vicitravīrya.

100.30. *In the field of Vicitravīrya*: note that this is made to include the serf woman who substituted for Ambikā.

101.1. *Dasyus*: aboriginals.
15. *Their powers*: supplied by me; it may also mean "showing themselves."

102.1. *Jungle of the Kurus* (*kurujāṅgalam*): uncultivated land, contrasting with Kurukṣetra, the cultivated area.
5. *Law reigned supreme*: *dharmottaram avartata*; D.: *dharmapradhānam*.
10. *Northern Kurus*: a mythical saintly race of men north of the Himālaya. ***Temple*: *caitya*; it may be any sanctuary.
15. *Various instructions*: *nānāśikṣāsu*.

103.5. *The eyes of Bhaga*: when the Gods gave Śiva no share in the sacrifice, he assailed them furiously, taking Bhaga's eyes and breaking Savitar's arms and Pūṣan's tooth.

104.5. *Durvāsas*: an errant sage, particularly notorious for his irascible temper.
15. *Vasuṣenṇa*: lit., "armed with riches."
20. *Vaikartana*: from *vikartana*, "cutting off."

105.5. *Bought her*: a practice condemned by *Manu* 3.51–54; on some cultural implications of the bride price (*śulka*), cf. Gonda, 1954. ***Daśārṇa*: an eastern people.
10. *Rājagṛha*: "the king's house," capital of Magadha, south of the Ganges. ***Mithilā*: a city north of the Ganges, capital of Videha, opposite Magadha, between the rivers Gaṇḍakī and Kauśikī. ***Suhma*: a people in the Ganges delta in Bengal. ***Puṇḍra*: a people in Bengal, north of the Ganges, south of Assam.
10. *Tribute and corvée*: *karakarmasu*.
15. *Hāstinapura*: the text has Nāgapura, "city of the elephant."

106.1. *With Dhṛtarāṣṭra's consent*: note that though excluded from the succession Dhṛtarāṣṭra retains his seniority. ***Paulomī*: Indra's wife.
5. *Won the luxury of leisure*: the translation of *jitatandrī* is bothersome; at first sight it reads as "by whom lassitude had been overcome," which makes little sense, for after his punitive expedition Pāṇḍu does nothing more for the kingdom but goes hunting. Hesitantly I take *jita* as "won, earned"; he had earned the right to relax. It is also possible to take *jitatandrī* for *tandrījita*, "overcome by lassitude." D. glosses *tandrī* with *cetanābhraṃśa*, "lunacy," but gives no indication of how he takes the compound ("overcome by lunacy"?).
10. *Bastard daughter*: *pāraśavī kanyā*, usually a brahmin's issue by a serf woman; here a baron's issue. Devaka was a king allied with the Yādavas.

107.15. *Ghee*: clarified butter.
25. *We shall not demur*: yet attempt after attempt will be made to unseat Yudhiṣṭhira.
35. *Bastard*: *karaṇa*.

109.1. *Partial Incarnations*: above, 1.61.
10. *Agastya*; A Vedic seer, hero of many stories (e.g., 3.94–108). I have found no parallel to this curious incident; as a rule, animal victims at sacrifices were domestic. ***Dedicated to all the Gods*: *sarvadaivatya*.
15. *Not without considering*: meant to contradict Pāṇḍu's statement that deer are killed "without subterfuge and trickery"?
20. *Three pursuits*: Law (*dharma*), Profit (*artha*), and Pleasure (*kāma*).

110.5. *My father*: Kṛṣṇa Dvaipāyana. ***A shaven hermit*: *muni muṇḍa*.
15. *The Law of the Wind*: never resting.
20. *The way of the dogs* (*śvācarite mārge*): I am not sure I understand the idiom: does he

imply that, though sexual gratification is closed to him in the normal way, he will not seek it in different ways? Vs. 21, which apparently is meant as an explanation, is not helpful; it may well have been inspired by *Manu* 4.6. The translation must remain uncertain. ***Departed for the forest*: as a complete ascetic, such as described before. His wives persuade him to become just a forest dweller (*vanaprastha*).

25. *My father*: Kṛṣṇa Dvaipāyana.

30. *Kulavāsin*: a contrast is intended with "villager"; it might be rendered: "man of good family."

35. *Neck chain*: *niṣka*. ***Bracelets* (*angada*): rings with wing-shaped ornaments; they apparently were regalia, as they occur in royal names (e.g., Citrāngada, Rukmāngada, Subhāngada).

40. *Mahābhūta*: great spirit.

111.15. *Offspring in my field*: viz., by Injunction.

25. *Neither heirs nor kinsmen*: *abandhudāyāda*; the parallel passage, *Manu* 9.158 ff., has *adāyāda-bāndhava*, which Bühler, 1886, following Kulluka, translates *"not heirs, [but] kinsmen."* The present passage is cause to review this translation. ***Fathered by oneself*: *svayaṃjāta*; = *aurasa*, *Manu* ib. 159. ***Presented*: *praṇīta*, and subsequently adopted; = *datta*, *Manu* ib. ***Purchased*: *parikrīta*; puzzling and contradictory, since below the *son bartered* is excluded, as he is by *Manu* ib. 160; the same peculiarity above, 1.69.15, cf. notes. D. has the outright gloss *dhanena svīkṛta*; N. has *retomūlyadānena tasyāṃ janitaḥ*, "begotten on his wife by payment for the seed," in other words the father pays some man to beget a son for him. An application of this rule in Vetāla 19, *Kathāsaritsāgara* 93, esp. vs. 97. N. has no comment on *krītaon* at 69.10. ***Born by one's widow*: *paunarbhava*, sc. after marriage; cf. *Manu* ib. 175. ***Born before her marriage*: excluded by *Manu* ib. 160. ***A loose woman*: *svairiṇī*; not in *Manu*. ***Gifted*: *datta*, given away for adoption elsewhere. ***Bartered*: *krīta*, *Manu* ib. 160. ***By artifice*: *kṛtrima*, defined, *Manu* ib. 169, and considered an heir, ib. 159. ***Who comes by himself*: = *svayaṃdatta Manu* ib. 160. ***Come with marriage*: *sahoḍha*, = *Manu* ib. 160. ***Of unknown seed*: I can make no sense of cr. ed. 111.29 *jātaretas*; D. has *jñātiretas* (*aputrasya bhrātrādiputraḥ*); so N. The alternations *jñāti*/*jāti*/*jāta*/*jñāta* shown by the critical apparatus point to an original '*jñāta*° (f. *ajñāta*°), misunderstood as *jñāta*°, giving rise to *jñāti*° and *jāta*°. I connect this with the *gūḍhotpanna* of *Manu* ib. 159, where he is accepted as heir. ***Fathered on a lowly womb*: = *śaudra*, *Manu* ib. 160.

30. *Reckoning*: sc. the begetter. ***Manu Svlāyaṃbhuva*; not in *Manusmṛti*.

112.15. *Consumption*: cf. notes, 1.96.55.

30. *Eighth and fourteenth*: approved days, *Manu* 3.47; and being even, productive of sons; ib. 48.

113.1. *Uncloistered*: *anāvṛta*; it may also mean "nude"; perhaps both meanings are intended.

10. *Śvetaketu*: cf. *Chāndogya Upaniṣad* 6.1.

114.1. *Indra day*: the eighth day of the bright half of the month Mārgaśīrsa (November–December) and particularly auspicious; the eighth hour: midday.

5. *Yudhiṣṭhira*: lit., "steadfast in battle." ***Bhīma*: "fearful."

25. *Kārtavīrya*: also called Arjuna. ***Viṣṇu*: Aditi's lastborn son.

30. *Firmly plant the Fortune of the Kurus*: perhaps: *kurulakṣma sudhāsyati*; but *lakṣma* in the sense of *lakṣmī* is a unique occurrence, and *sudhā* is an hapax; this is too much coincidence. Perhaps we should separate thus: *kurulakṣmasu dhāsyati*, "he shall place them within the markers [boundary marks] of the Kurus," i.e., annex them. D. glosses *kurucihna*.

35. *A roar wrapped in showers of flowers*: the picturesque phrase has been rendered literally.

40. *The brood of Kadrū and Vinatā*: snakes and birds. ***Seven seers*: ancient Seers immortalized as the stars of Ursus Minor. ***And he who rises*: puzzling, since all the stars

of the asterism are visible simultaneously, at least north of the Vindhya. ***Marīci, etc.*: the seven Prajāpatis. ***Terrifier*: *bībhatsu*, lit., "he who inspires, or feels, loathing." I have adopted "Terrifier" throughout.

60. *Karkoṭaka*: a snake.

115.1. *The daughter*: Mādri.

10. *For this once*: *sakṛt*.

116.1. *palāśa*: *Butea Frondosa*. ***Tilaka*: *Clerodendrum Phlomoides*. ***campaka*: *Michelia Campaka*. ***paribhadraka*: *Erythrina Fulgens*.

20. *Bactrian woman*: obviously meant abusively; the Madras were neighbors of the Bālikas in the extreme northwest of the Panjāb. Their lower status is shown by the fact that Bhīṣma bought her and that she was a junior wife.

25. *Your children the same as mine*: particularly in conjunction with "noble lady" (*ārye*), implying that the rank of Kuntī's sons would be lowered if they were brought up by Mādrī.

117.15. *Dhṛtarāṣṭra's heirs*: note how apposite the use of "heir" is at this juncture.

118.1. *Well walled in*: *paramasaṃvṛta*: so?

10. *The fire that preceded*: being carried in a pot.

15. *tunga*: *Rottleria Tinctoria*.

20. *padmaka*: the fragrant wood of the *Cerasus Puddum*.

119.15. *Hair above the ears*: *kākanilīyane*; I take it in the sense of *kākapakṣa*, which fits well: D. takes it as a "kind of a game." ***Heads and eyeballs*: read *°śiro'kṣikān*.

30. *Tents*: *celakambalaveśmāni*.

35. *Struck his favorite charioteer*, etc.: who was supposed to watch over him? The line makes little sense.

40. *Then, seing that the boys*, etc.: This sentence, rejected by Sukthankar (1321*), must be retained or chap. 120 is uncalled for.

120.1. *Arrows*: play on *śara*, "arrow." ***Jālapadī*: lit., "web-footed," no doubt in origin an aquatic bird.

15. *Out of pity*: play on *kṛpā*, "compassion." ***The name of Kṛpa*: that is to say Kṛpa and Kṛpī.

121.1. *Havirdhāna*: an area of the sacrificial terrain where the utensils for the Soma Sacrifice were kept. ***Ghṛtācī*: one of the principal Apsarās; lit., "toward-the-ghee." ***Who had just bathed*: sc. after the menses. ***Trough*: *kalaśa* = *droṇa*, the trough in which spilled Soma juice was caught during the straining.

5. *The lordly Agniveśya*, etc.: the authenticity of this line is rather doubtful; it seems to be inspired by 1.122.20, where Droṇa declares that his teacher was Agniveśya. The word *agniveśya* means "related to [or born from] the fire hall," appropriate enough for Droṇa himself. ***Born on the Laud-of-the-Fire day*: *agniṣṭuj-jātaḥ*, if this reading is at all reliable. It is apparently an attempt to explain the name Agniveśya, which may not have been a name at all but an epithet of Droṇa. The *agniṣṭut* is the first day of the Soma Sacrifice; the words may also translate "born a praiser of the fire."

10. *Northern Pāñcālas*: and southern as well, since, according to 1.128.10 ff., Drupada will retain the southern part of the kingdom. ***A Gautamī*: her father was Śāradvata of the Gautama clan. ***Range*: *sthāman*, an artificial meaning of the word, which means "staying power." The name literally means "steadfast like a horse"; note the prākṛtism *aśvatthāman* for *aśvasthāman*.

30. *I thought I had it made*: *kṛtārtho 'smīti cintayan*.

123.1. *When it is dark*: i.e., when the lights are out. ***Started practicing at night*: Ekalavya's story, below, shows the premium that was put on blind shooting.

15. *The dog smelled*: it should be understood that it was dark in the wood.

60. *The left-handed archer* (*savyasācin*): a frequent epithet of Arjuna. It does not mean that he was left-handed, but rather ambidextrous. Being able to use both hands at pulling the string gives the archer a distinct advantage in speed and cuts down fatigue. The skill is described of Kṛṣṇa's son Pradyumna 3.18.4–5: "He changed his bow with lightning speed from palm to palm . . . as he shot and re-shafted the bow again and again, no one could spy an interruption in the continuous flow. . . ." To employ this skill effectively, two quivers were needed, one over each shoulder, the number that Arjuna will receive from the Fire (1.216.1), which are inexhaustible to boot.

70. *Returned to the five elements*: died. ***Weapon named Brahmā's-Head*: apparently a four-pronged arrow (Brahmā's heads counting four), which originally was Śiva's. This episode is a bit previous here, as Arjuna will not receive it but from Śiva in 3.41. Another application of its fourfold character is made there (ib. 15): "It can be launched with a thought, a glance, a word, or a bow."

1(8) The Fire in the Lacquer House

124.1. *Kṛpa, Somadatta*, etc.: the Kaurava elders.

20. *Sounds that blessed the day* (*puṇyāhaghoṣa*): the ritual of the Blessing of the Day (*puṇyāhavācana*), until today performed on auspicious occasions.

25. *A castle in the sky*: *gandharvanagara*, lit., "a city of Gandharvas." ***On horseback*: *aśvapṛṣṭhe*; but one hears little of horseback riding.

30. *Huge elephants*: Sukthankar reads *bṛṃhantau*, of which I am rather doubtful.

125.5. *Indra's younger brother*: Viṣṇu; D. = Upendra. ***Full quiver*: or quivers; the number cannot be made out.

10. *Commingling with milk*: *prasravamiśra*.

15. *The block of Pṛthā*: fire was drilled with a wooden awl from a *śamī* log, producing by friction sparks that were used to light straw and wood. The three fires are those of the great sacrifices. ***Āgneya*, etc.: fire, water, wind, rain, earth, and mountain weapons.

25. *Long sword*: *sumahatkhaḍga*.

30. *The moon*: because of his white garb, above, vs. 15. ***Asterism of the Hand*: the eleventh lunar sign (*nakṣatra*), identified with δ, γ, ε, α, and β Corvi. ***Slaughter of the Dānavas*: probably at the Churning of the Ocean.

126.5. *None too great courtesy*: an attitude typical of Karṇa.

10. *Like a pitcher*, etc.: *yantrotkṣipta iva*.

20. *Laughed*: in Sanskrit imagery, laughter is white. ***Indra*: Arjuna's father. ***The sun*: Karṇa's father.

25. *Kuntibhoja's daughter*: Kuntī, mother of both Karṇa and Arjuna. ***Knew the issue*: *vijñātārtha*; the pun is mine, but not misplaced.

35. *That very instant*: if one compares this instant coronation with the elaborate preparations that the Royal Consecration requires (Heesterman, 1957) and receives (below, 2.12 ff.), it is hard to believe that this consecration is more than symbolic, the more so since the Anga country was not actually under Kaurava dominion. ***Yak-tail fan*: part of the regalia; this must be one of the earlier mentions.

127.5. *The sun in the sky*: his father.

10. *Fire springs from water*: one of the names of fire is *apāṃ napāt*, "offspring of the waters"; cf. Macdonell 1897. ***Dadhīca* (also *Dadhyañc*): a mythical sage from whose bones the *vajra* was fashioned; cf. below, 3.98. ***Guha*: *Kumāra*, the God of War. The God has indeed a complex paternity: he was born from Śiva-Rudra's seed, which was cast into the fire, then received by the Ganges in a reed patch, and fostered by the Pleiades. ***Men born from baronesses*: notably Viśvāmitra; cf. below, 1.164–72. ***Our teacher*: Droṇa.

128.10. *Mākandī on the Ganges*: the region between Ganges and Yamunā toward the south, stretching down to the river Carmaṇvatī. He gave up his dominion north of the Ganges, south of the Kurus. Note that in fact the Kurus oust Drupada there and install their client Droṇa.

15. *Ahicchatra*, neuter, is the country; *Ahicchatrā*, feminine, the city.

129.15. *If you had been . . . we would have inherited*: note the conditionals *abhaviṣyaḥ* and *prāpsyāma*.

130.15. *For all that he secretly sides with the others*: *pracchannam tu yataḥ pare*: "but he secretly [stands] where the others [Pāṇḍavas] stand."

131.1. *In honor of Paśupati*: a name of Śiva, particularly for the Pāśupata sect, whose center later was Ujjayinī; the festival is unfortunately not described.

132.5. *Adjacent to the armory*: the reason for this is not made clear: was it to insure constant surveillance, as the armory no doubt housed the garrison?

133.5. *All their mothers*, sc. aunts and great-aunts.

15. *A weapon not of iron*: poison.

20. *Won't burn moles*: the Pāṇḍavas have to go literally underground from the fire. ***The blind man*: i.e., blinded by the night. ***The shelter of the porcupine*: a hole in the ground. ***Five souls*: this seems to refer to the five aborigines they leave burned in the house, though Yudhiṣṭhira himself in 25 explains it as the "five senses."

135.1. *Sapper*: whose business it was to undermine fortifications, etc.

137.10. *Urns*: in which the bones were buried, a burial practice of great antiquity; D. glosses *caityāni*, probably having *stūpas* in mind.

20. *Like the Wind*: the Wind was Bhīma's father.

138.1. *The speed of his thighs raised up a wind*: cr. ed. has *ūruvegasamīritam*, which should, but cannot, agree with *anilaḥ!* The neuter was obviously constructed to go with the *vanam* of an additional line rejected by Sukthankar as interpolation 1495*, yet was left standing after the rejection, in spite of the evidence for, and necessity of, *°samīritaḥ*. ***Āṣāḍha and Jyaiṣṭha* (text: *śuciśukra*): resp. the months of mid-June till mid-July and mid-May till mid-June. Before the monsoon breaks, which now around the relevant area is toward the end of June, there are fierce dust gales lasting until the breaking of the monsoon, which itself is accompanied by savage gusts.

5. *Banyan tree*: *Ficus Indica*, whose branches themselves strike root again; the tree often attains a wide spread.

10. *Shawl*: *uttarīya*. ***Two leagues*: *gavyūti*, which equals two *krośas*, twice the distance a voice will carry.

20. *He dark like a rain cloud*: a most unlikely description of Arjuna ("the bright one"), unless a reference to his father Indra, God of the monsoon, is understood. ***A solitary tree*: likely to be the object of worship and care.

1(9) The Slaying of Hiḍimba

139.1. *Hiḍimba*: a name with a distinct Austro-Asiatic ring.

10. *Conch-necked* (*kambugrīva*): with a neck marked by three horizontal lines, predictive of good fortune.

15. *Creeper*: *latā*: the word is feminine, and as the creeper intertwines with the tree (masculine), the word has become a symbol of loving females.

141.1. *The Bodiless God*: the God of Love, whose body was burned by Śiva when Love tempted him with the Goddess Pārvatī, a story only barely known to *Mahābhārata*; cf. 12.183.

20. *Sixty-year-old elephants*: when they are at the height of maturity; cf. Agrawala (1940).

142.20. *The grisly hour*: the power of nonhuman races increased at both twilights: here it is dawn; below, 1.158.5, it is dusk.

143.25. *Lake Mānasa*, fabled lake in the Himālaya.

35. *Maghavat*: a Vedic name of Indra, lit., "bounteous." ***So that he might destroy Karṇa*: he will catch, and be killed by, Karṇa's never-failing missile meant for Arjuna, and thus contribute to Karṇa's destruction; below, 7.154-55.

144.10. *The town Ekacakrā*: this town cannot be separated from the Pāñcāla town Paricakrā, mentioned in *Śatapatha Brāhmaṇa* 13.5.4.7; cf. Weber (1850). *Ekacakrā* means "the city of the One Wheel of Dominion," *paricakrā* "the city where the Wheel of Dominion is all around." It lay to the east of the Ganges. The Pāṇḍavas have been traveling south from Vāraṇāvata since 1.137.15, which lay fairly close to Hāstinapura, east of the Ganges. Predictably their journey to the capital of Pāñcāla (now Kāmpilyā) will take them across the Ganges (below, 1.153) to the Doāb.

1(10) The Slaying of Baka

147.5. *Putra*: because he saves from the hell called *Put*: but only if the child is a son; yet a daughter is a *putrī*.

15. *By giving the water*: presumably as a funerary oblation.

148.5. *Vetrakīyagṛha*: a proper noun, or an idiom? It translates as "house built of reed" = "house built on sand"? The only other mention (*vetrakīyavana*, below, 3.12), is derivative from this episode.

149.1. *Offering*: *bali*, supposedly a voluntary offering, but here obviously exacted tribute; even so, the brahmin's offering is voluntary now. ***A brahmin and a guest*: the Pāṇḍavas, lodged with the brahmin, had been posing as brahmins.

5. *Outside the pale of Law*: so? I read *nadharmiṣṭhāsu*, finding Sukthankar's *nādharmiṣṭhāsu* ("not among those women who are not the most Law-minded," or, in cp., "among not at all not most Law-minded women") rather peculiar. Perhaps we should simply read *na dharmiṣṭhāsu*: "neither among lowly women, nor among the most Law-minded ones." The apparatus shows that the reading is uncertain.

1(11) Citraratha

153.1. *The supreme Brahman*: ground and source of all beings, as revealed in *Vedas* and esp. *Upaniṣads*.

154.1. *Brahmā weapon*: the Brahmā-Head missile.

20. *Chattravatī*: = Ahicchattrā.

155.5. *Snātaka*: a brahmin who has gone through the formal *Veda*-training period (*brahmacarya*) and concluded it with the final bath, so that he is "bathed" (*snāta*).

15. *This uncouth act*: although a fruit by a waterfall in the forest is about as pure as anything, it is held up as an example of impurity by the still purer-minded Upayāja.

30–35. *The Time for cohabitation has come*: although *mithunaṃ tvām upasthitam* can also translate as "a pair of twins have come to you," I sense behind the exchange a ritual copulation: the queen is propositioned; she replies positively, having beautified herself for intercourse; but in the end no copulation takes place, the offering (*havya*) being sufficient; hence "stride away or stay," hence, too, the children are not really hers; cf. below, 45.

40. *The Dark Woman*: Kṛṣṇā.

45. *For his boldness*, etc.: etymology of Dhṛṣṭadyumna, *dhṛṣṭa* meaning "bold," *dyumna*, "light."

156.5. *Brahminic* (*brahmaṇya*): favorable to brahmiṇism.

10. *The city of Drupada*: the name is not mentioned, but it should be Kāmpilyā.

158.1. *That led to the north*: acc. to this direction, Kāmpilyā lies to the northwest of Ekacakrā instead of southwest.

10. *Angāraparṇa*: "of the ember-red leaves," the name first of his wood, then by transference of himself.

15. *Vaitaranī*: the river of the underworld and the dead.

25. *Agniveśya*: according to D. = Paraśu-Rāma.

35. *Citraratha*: "of the colorful chariot," *dagdharatha*, "of the burned chariot."

50. *Vaḍavā gave birth to the chariot steed*: *rathāngaṃ vaḍavā sūte*; D. *rathasyāngam aśvam*; it is a peculiar meaning for *rathānga*, which normally means "wheel." ***The name sūta*: a play on *sūte*.

159. *I celebrate my defeat*: so? The line is puzzling.

1(11.a) Tapati

163.15. *Indra failed to rain*: hence perhaps Tapatī's name, "she who brings heat." Other disasters (and Vasiṣṭha's role in ending them) are told of Saṃvaraṇa's reign, above, 1.89.30.

1(11.b) Vasiṣṭha

164.5. *The kings of Ikṣvāku*: the solar dynasty of kings.

165.1. *The feud*: this feud is recorded in Vedic literature; cf. M-K for earlier references. ***Kanyakubja*: the modern Kanauj on the river Kālīnadī, a tributary of the Ganges.

10. *Elixir*: *rasāyanam*. ***All six tastes*: sweet, sour, pungent, bitter, salty, astringent. ***Nandī*: cf. the name Nandi of Śiva's bull. ***Six measures long*: D. "long in six parts [horn, tail, dewlap, thigh, udder, head, and neck]."

35. *Pahlavas*: Persians. ***Śabaras*: central Indian mountain tribe. ***Śakas*: Scythians. ***Puṇḍras*: northeastern people. ***Kirātas*: northern Indian mountain tribe. ***Drāmilas*: Dravidians. ***Siṃhalas*: Ceylonese. ***Barbaras*: Barbarians. ***Daradas*: tribes of the extreme northwest. ***Mlecchas*: foreigners.

40. *Kauśika*: Viśvāmitra's father was also called Kuśika. ***Pressed-out*: (*suta*): D. has "purifying."

166.10. *A feud regarding their patron*: who according to the Vedic materials was Sudās (cf. M-K; also below, 1.168.5), the father of Kalmāṣapāda.

15. *Viśvāmitra ordered a Rākṣasa*: to prevent the curse from being lifted before taking effect. ***Kiṃkara*: lit., "servant."

167. *Vipāśā*: lit., "breaker of fetters," the river Beās in the Panjāb. ***Śatadru*: lit., "hundred-runner," Vedic Śutudrī, the Sutlej, the easternmost river of the Panjāb.

168.1. *hūṃ*: a powerful syllable, inserted in Vedic recitations. ***Puṣya*: identified with γ, δ, and ϑ Cancri.

20. *Amarāvatī*: capital of Indra's paradise.

25. *Aśmaka*: the word means "stone."

1(11.b.i) Aurva

170.5. *Atri*: here apparently taken as an ancestor of the Bhṛgus. ***Pulastya, Pulaha, Kratu*: Prajāpatis.

172.15. *At any cycle*: *parvaṇi parvaṇi*: are the cycles of the Eons meant here?

1(12) Draupadī's Bridegroom Choice

174.1. *Brother of Devala*: of Asita Devala? ***Utkocaka*: the only mention is in this chapter.

175.5 *Traveling in one large caravan*: *ekasārthaṃ prayātāḥ*.
15. *When you have seen the wondrous spectacle and eaten*: I prefer the reading *evaṃ kautūhalam dṛṣṭvā bhuktvā ca*; hardly anything can be done with the cr. ed. *kṛtvā dṛṣṭvā ca*: this *kṛtvā* presumes too much foreknowledge of coming events on the part of these vagrant brahmins.

176.5. *In the house of a potter*: the reason remains unexplained; in any case it must have been a clean caste. ***Diademed Arjuna*: *pāṇḍavāya kirīṭine*, which stands for Arjuna; *kirīṭin*, "diademed," is also a name of Nara, with whom Arjuna is consistently identified; for the wish, cf. below, 1.185.5 and 1.187.15: "The strong-armed Arjuna should make the occasion!"
10. *Contraption*: *yantra*, "turning mechanism."
15. *City of the Crocodile*: Agrawala (1939, p. 163) prefers the reading *śiṃśumāraśiraḥ*. ***Awning*: *vitāna*.
20. *From seats shaded by canopies*: *mahāsanaparicchadaih*; so? ***Carpets not of the rustic kind*: agrāmya°.
30. *The Champion's goblet*: *vīrakāṃsya*, which, one expects, would have held liquor; D. glosses "garland," no doubt because of 1.179.22. ***Somakas*: a patronymic of the kings of Pāñcāla, from a mythical ancestor Somaka son of Sahadeva, known to *ṚV*. 4.15.7–10; the combination shows that they were Deva-worshipers and Soma offerers. ***Through this hole in the wheel*: if it was a wheel: *yantracchidreṇa*.

177.5. *Bhoja*: not really identifiable, yet does his collocation with Aśvatthāman signify that they (and Droṇa) originally were Bhojas?
10. *Vāsudeva*: this is the other Vāsudeva, of Puṇḍra. ***Bhagadatta*: king of Assam. ***Tāmralipta*: from the coast of Bengal. ***Pattana*: seems to indicate an aboriginal settlement. ***Somadatta*: son of Bāhlīka.
15. *And Saṃkarṣaṇa . . . Vṛṣṇis all*: the Yādava contingent.
20. *Vatsas*: the country about Kausāmbī, E. of the confluence of the Ganges and Yamunā. ***Kosala*: the country about Ayodhyā.

178.1. *Himālayan elephants*: apparently an extinct species. ***For Umā*: did she hold a *svayaṃvara*? She will be Śiva's consort.
5. *Viśvāvasu, Nārada, Parvata*: here Gandharvas. ***Plough-armed Rāma*: Bala-Rāma, who wielded a plough as his emblem.
9. *Red-spotted*: *abhipadma*: "lotus-dotted." ***Covered with ashes*: pretending to be brahmins.
16. *The hardwood bow* (*dṛḍha dhanuṣ*): on the composition of the bow, cf. Emeneau (1953).
17. *Bracelets*: *angada*, cf. above, 1.110.35, notes.

180.20. *Aquiline*: cr. ed. *pralamba*, but doubtful.
21. *I heard they escaped*: he hardly could have, unless from Vidura.

181.31. *He gently constrained*: note the authority attributed to Kṛṣṇa.
35. *Ruru deerskins*: it seems these were rather lowly skins for a brahmin to have; cf.

below, 2.68.9. ***Who continued their feud*: as they well might, after the slaying of Hiḍimba and Baka.
40. *Preceded by the Brahman*: or by brahminhood; but I picture the scene with brahmins joyfully reciting Vedic blessings (*brahman*) in procession with the returning Arjuna.

182.3. *Lawless*: she could not have lied, so that the sharing had to be reality.

184.1. *You take first*: *agram ādāya*; or "the best part." ***The brahmin*: Dhaumya.
5. *Blessed by Agastya*: the South.

185.1. *Kṛṣṇa took hold*: according to *Manu* 3.44, a śūdra bride takes hold of the hem of the garment of a higher-caste husband; keep in mind that Arjuna was still posing as a brahmin.
25. *By rights*: *sādhu*, i.e., "not properly attainable by but a baron."

1(13) The Wedding

186. With some mss. I begin *The Book of the Wedding* here; cf. *vivāhahetoḥ* in vs. 1. The cr. ed. only includes chapters 1.190–91 in the *Wedding*.
5. *Catapult*: *bhuśuṇḍi*, a word of unknown derivation and meaning; it is sometimes taken for a firearm.

188.5. *The Law that is mocked*: *vipralabdha*; D. = *viruddha*, "contradictory."

1(13.a) The Five Indras

189.1. *The butcher priest*: the *śamitar* at animal sacrifices.
5. *Strengthened*: *vibhūta*.
10. *He saw a woman*: it does not become clear who she is.
15. *I am the king of the Gods*: *devarājo* is genitive of *devarāj* and goes with *mama*. ***Tree trunk*: *sthāṇu*; the word is also a name of Śiva.
20. *Pray see an escape today*: I construct *bhava* as an imperative to go with *draṣṭā*. ***Shall once more become*: *bhavitāraḥ purastāt*; it is best to take *purastāt* in the sense of "immediately"; cf. *purastātkratu*; D. awkwardly takes *bhavitāraḥ* in the sense of *babhūvuḥ* (*bhūte bhaviṣyatprayogāt*) after taking *purastāt* in the sense of "before."

190.5. *She had bathed*: sc. after the menses.

191.1. *The marriage thread*: a protective amulet cord ensuring the couple's purity until intercourse; cf. Raj Bali Pandey, *Hindu Samskaras*[2] (Delhi, Motilal, 1969).
15. I do not know what to do with *vītikṛtam* in 1.191. 18c.

1(14) The Coming of Vidura

192.25. *We shall speak in private*: we must take it that at this point Vidura leaves.

194.1. *Not grown their wings*: *ajātapakṣa*; a pun on *paksa*, "wing," but also "party of allies."

196.1. *Obligating gifts*: *mithaḥkṛtya*.
20. *If it has been ordained . . . it will stay*: *yadi vihitam bhaviṣyati . . . sthāsyate*; note the use of the first future.

197.5. *Gaya*: a famous sacrificer; cf. below, 3.93.25. *Dāśārhas*: other name of Kṛṣṇa's tribe.

1(15) The Acquisition of the Kingdom

199.20. *Khaṇḍava Tract*: *Khāṇḍavaprastha*.

25. *Made strong*: *alaṃkṛta*; or "adorned."

30. *Spiraling turrets*: *talpa abhyāsika*; on *talpa*, cf. D. Sharma, "The word *Upatalpa*," *Indian Culture 1* (Calcutta, 1934). I derive *abhyāsika* from *abhyāsa*, "repetition, multiplication," giving "many-storied, or spiraling." ***Hundred-killers*: *śataghnī*, perhaps large rocks propelled by catapults. ***Movable trellises*: *yantrajāla*; probably to afford both a shield and holes for shooting.

40. *Āmrātaka*: hog plum, Spondias Mangifera. ***Nīpa*: Nauclea Cadamba. ***Puṃnāga*: Rottleria Tinctoria. ***Nāgapuṣpa*: Mesua Roxburghii. ***Lakuca*: Artocarpus Lakucha. ***Kadamba*: = nīpa. ***Bankula*: Mimusops Elengi. ***Āmalaka*: Emblic Myrobalan. ***Lodhra*: Symplocos Racemosa. ***Ankola*: Alangium Hexapetalum. ***Pātala*: Bignonia Suaveolens. ***Kubjaka*: Rosa Moschata. ***Atimuktikā*; name of several bushes. ***Karavīra*: Oleander. ***Parijāta*: coral tree, Erythrina Indica.

45. *Cakravāka*: Anas Casarca.

50. *Dvāravatī*, *Dvārakā*: supposedly on the westernmost coast of Gujarat and now submerged.

1(16) Arjuna's Sojourn in the Forest

200.5. *Nārada*: a wandering seer god, often purveyor of messages.

10. *Properly covered*: with covered head.

1(16.2) Sunda and Upasunda

201.25. *Kaumudī festival*: held on the full-moon day of the month Kārttika (mid-October till mid-November) in honor of the war god Kārttikeya.

202.1. *Māgha*: identified with the Sickle (α, η, γ, ζ, μ, and ε Leonis) and the month mid-January till mid-February. ***Cāraṇas*: divine bards, and bards.

203.5. *Vaikhānasa*: a class of ascetics. ***Beam-Drinkers*, etc.: classes of deceased Fathers.

10. *Viśvakarman*: divine carpenter.

15. *Bit by bit*: *tilaṃ tilam*; *tila* is literally a sesame seed.

204.10. *Karṇikāra*: Pterospermum Acerifolium.

25. *Twelve months*: the oldest testimony to the duration of Arjuna's exile is found in *MBh.* 1.55.30; the Southern Recension has consistently "months," but the cr. ed. prefers "years." But it makes little sense to send Arjuna away for twelve years, a period obviously adopted from the twelve-year forest exile of all the Pāṇḍavas (*MBh.* 3). The fact that a lot does happen to Arjuna, notably the birth of a son and the abduction of Subhadrā, facilitated the change from "months" to "years." The cr. ed. consistently marks the words for "years" as open to doubt.

206.20. *A hermit's life*: i.e., a life of celibacy.

25. *In her case only*: i.e., the celibacy only applies in his relations with Draupadī.

207.5. *Anga, Vanga, and Kalinga*: the countries east of Magadha, south of the Ganges; Vanga is Bengal, Kalinga is Orissa.

208.1. Like a Horse Sacrifice: i.e., bathing there produced the same reward.

210.1. *Prabhāsa*: a ford on the coast of Gujarat, close to Kṛṣṇa's city Dvārakā.

5. *Mt. Raivataka*: a branch of the Vindhya Mountains. **Sātvata: a name of the Vṛṣṇis.

1(17) The Abduction of Subhadrā

211.1. *Candelabras*: *dīpavṛkṣa*; D.: *vṛkṣākārair dīpādhāraiḥ*.
5. *Raukmiṇeya*: Carudeṣṇa/Pradyumna, Kṛṣṇa's son by Rukmiṇī.
20. *Abduction*: the *rākṣasa* mode of marriage.

212.1. *Sainya and Sugrīva*: Kṛṣṇa's horses.

1(18) The Fetching of the Gift

213.5. *The daughter of Kuntibhoja*: i.e., Kuntī, who, be it remembered, was herself Kṛṣṇa's aunt. ***My worthy*: *māriṣa*: note this prākṛtism and stage term.
10. *The last nights of the year*: *saṃvatsaraparāḥ kṣapāḥ*. ***The twelve-month year*: *dvādaśa varṣa*; the translation is forced, as the words more naturally translate: "the twelfth year"; but the context rules out this meaning; there is no testimony here from the Southern Recension.
15. *First knot*: viz., the matrimonial knot with Draupadī. ***Cow maid's dress*: both to show her humility and her provenance.
20. *Rival*: *sapatna*; she plays on the meaning of the feminine *sapatnī*, "co-wife."
45. *Violence-loving hero*: Baladeva.
50. *Loud clapping of hands*: to accompany music and dance.
55. *Paulomī*: Indra's wife.
60. *Fearless and wrathful*: *abhī, manyumat*: pseudo-etymology.
70. *Prativindhya*: a "counter Mount Vindhya."
75. *Śrutakarman*: "of famous feats." ***Vahnidaivata*: the Pleiades, foster-mothers of Kārttikeya, the war god; hence the name *śrutasena*, "of famous armies."

1(19) The Burning of the Khāṇḍava Forest

216.5. *Drawn by silver horses*: traditionally, Arjuna's chariot had four horses.

218.15. *Vāyavya missile*: here a kind of antiwind weapon.
30. *The Aśvins held their Herbs*: since they are the divine physicians.

219.40. *Śārngaka birds*: perhaps characterized by a large horny bill, since the word derives from *śṛnga*, "horn."

1(19.a) The Śārngakas

220.5. *Mandapāla*: "the slow protector."
20. *Call them triple*: the three sacrificial fires. ***Eightfold*: according to D., resp. the fires of the wife's quarters at the sacrifice (read *patnīśālāyām* with B b), the Soma altar, the main altar, the hut of the Āgnīdhra priest, the *sadas* area, the rituals (*kratuṣu*), the *upasad* rite, and the ordinary fire.

223.15. *Thou cookest the food*: viz., the digestive "fire." ***This seat is the refuge of Varuṇa*: that is to say, make believe that this is the sea, which you cannot burn.

224.25. *Who of you*: in vs. 22 *te* in *te katamāḥ* seems to stand for *yusmākam*, the singular genitive *te* doing duty for the plural.

225.15. *The river bank*: no doubt that of the Yamunā.

Names of Important Persons of the Bhārata Line and Close Allies

Abhimanyu, son of Arjuna by Subhadrā
Adhiratha, adoptive father of Karṇa
Ajātaśatru, name of Yudhiṣṭhira
Ajamīḍha, descendant of Bharata and ancestor of the Kauravas
Ājamīḍha, patr., descendant of Ajamīḍha (= Kaurava)
Ambikā, mother of Dhṛtarāṣṭra by Kṛṣṇa Dvaipāyana, wife of Vicitravīrya
Ambālikā, mother of Pāṇḍu by Kṛṣṇa Dvaipāyana, wife of Vicitravīrya, also called Kausalyā.
Andhaka, descendants of Yadu, forming a tribe with the Vṛṣṇis
Arjuna, son of Pāṇḍu and Kuntī, fathered by Indra
Aśvatthāman, son of Droṇa

Bāhlīka, son of Pratīpa, brother of Śaṃtanu
Balarāma, also *Rāma* and *Baladeva*, son of Vasudeva and older brother of Kṛṣṇa
Bharadvāja, an ancient seer, held to be the father of Droṇa
Bhāradvāja, patronymic of Droṇa
Bharata, son of Duḥṣanta and Śakuntalā, principal dynast and eponym of the Bhāratas; plural = Bhāratas
Bhārata, any descendant of Bharata
Bhīmasena, also Bhīma, son of Pāṇḍu and Kuntī, fathered by the Wind God
Bhīṣma, son of Śaṃtanu and the Ganges, uncle of Pāṇḍu and Dhṛtarāṣṭra, "grandfather," i.e., great-uncle of the Pāṇḍavas and Dhārtarāṣtras

Devakī, mother of Kṛṣṇa by Vasudeva

Devayānī, daughter of Śukra Uśanas Kāvya, ancestress by Yayāti of the Yādavas
Dharma, the God Dharma who fathered Yudhiṣṭhira; and the *King Dharma* (= Yudhiṣṭhira)
Dhārtarāṣṭra, patr., the sons of Dhṛtarāṣṭra, esp. Duryodhana
Dauḥṣanti, patr., of Bharata, son of Duḥṣanta
Dhṛṣṭadyumna, son of Drupada, born from a sacrifice
Dhṛtarāṣṭra, son of Vicitravīrya and Ambikā, fathered by Kṛṣṇa Dvaipāyana
Drauṇi, patr. of Aśvatthāman, son of Droṇa
Draupadeya, metr., son of Draupadī by any of the Pāṇḍavas
Draupadī, patr., daughter of Drupada, Kṛṣṇā
Droṇa, teacher of the Pāṇḍavas, Dhārtarāṣṭras, and others
Drupada, king of Pāñcāla, son of Pṛṣata, father of Dhṛṣṭadyumna and Kṛṣṇā; also Yajñasena
Duḥśālā, single daughter of Dhṛtarāṣṭra and Gāndhārī
Duḥṣanta, an early descendant of Pūru; by Śakuntalā the father of Bharata
Duḥśāsana, a son of Dhṛtarāṣṭra
Duryodhana, eldest son and heir of Dhṛtarāṣṭra
Dvaipāyana, a kind of patr. of Kṛṣṇa, son of Parāśara and Satyavatī, who was abandoned on an island (*dvīpa*)

Gangā, the river Ganges, by Śaṃtanu the mother of Bhīṣma
Gāngeya, metr., Bhīṣma, son of the Ganges
Gāndhāra, name of a country and of its king Subala; also applied to Subala's son Śakuni
Gāndhārī, "princess of Gāndhāra," name of Dhṛtarāṣṭra's wife, mother of the hundred Dhārtarāṣṭras
Ghaṭotkaca, demon son of Bhīma by the demoness Hiḍimbā

Hiḍimba and *Hiḍimbā*, demons, brother and sister; the former was killed by Bhīma, the latter became his concubine and bore Ghaṭotkaca

Janamejaya, great-grandson of Arjuna, at whose Snake Sacrifice the *Mahābhārata* is narrated

Karṇa, son of Kuntī by the sun, before her marriage to Pāṇḍu; he was abandoned and adopted by the *sūta Adhiratha* and his wife Rādhā, is hence also known as Rādheya; also Vasuṣeṇa; Vaikartana
Kaunteya, son of Kuntī, metronymic of Yudhiṣṭhira, Bhīma, and Arjuna
Kaurava, descendant of Kuru, title of any of his descendants but more closely applied to the lineage of Dhṛtarāṣṭra than that of Pāṇḍu

Kauravya, = Kaurava
Kausalyā, other name of Ambālikā
Kṛpa, teacher of the Kauravas
Kṛṣṇa Dvaipāyana, premarital son of Satyavatī by the seer Parāśara, born and grown the day he was conceived and abandoned on an island; the island (*dvīpa*) functions as his patrynomic along with the rarer Pārāśarya; by levirate he became the father of Dhṛtarāṣṭra on Ambikā, of Pāṇḍu on Ambālikā, and of Vidura on a commoner woman
Kṛṣṇa Vāsudeva, son of the Vṛṣṇi king Vasudeva by Devakī and brother of Subhadrā, Arjuna's second wife; had a son Pradyumna by Rukmiṇī
Kṛṣṇā, name of the daughter of the Pāñcāla king Drupada Yajñasena (hence known as Pāñcālī, Draupadī, Yājñasenī), common wife of the Pāṇḍavas, by each of whom she had a son
Kuntibhoja, cousin of Śūra, who gave him his daughter Pṛthā as an adoptive child; she is therefore also known as Kuntī
Kuntī, second name of Śūra's daughter Pṛthā, who was adopted by Kuntibhoja. She had a premarital son Karṇa by the sun, married Pāṇḍu, and became the mother of Yudhiṣṭhira by Dharma, of Bhīma by the Wind, and of Arjuna by Indra
Kuru, ancestor of the Bhāratas, son of Saṃvaraṇa, eponym of the Kauravas; the plural may stand for his descendants

Mādrī, princess of the Madras, name of Pāṇḍu's second wife, who bore him Nakula and Sahadeva by the Aśvins; she cremated herself with Pāṇḍu, entrusting her children to Kuntī

Nahuṣa, father of Yayāti
Nāhuṣa, patr. of Yayāti, son of Nahuṣa
Nakula, son of Pāṇḍu by Mādrī, fathered with his twin brother Sahadeva by the Aśvins

Pāñcāla, name of a country and its king, esp. Drupada
Pāñcālī, princess of Pāñcāla, title of Kṛṣṇā
Pāṇḍava, Pāṇḍaveya, patr. esp. of the five sons of Pāṇḍu, Yudhiṣṭhira, Bhīmasena, Arjuna, Nakula, and Sahadeva
Pāṇḍu, son of Vicitravīrya and Ambālikā, fathered by Kṛṣṇa Dvaipāyana, and by Pṛthā-Kuntī and Mādrī the father of the five Pāṇḍava brothers
Parāśara, a seer, extramarital father (by Satyavatī) of Kṛṣṇa Dvaipāyana
Pārāśarya, patronymic of Kṛṣṇa Dvaipāyana
Parikṣit, son of Abhimanyu by Uttarā, father of Janamejaya

Pārikṣita, patr. of Janamejaya
Pārṣata, patr. of Drupada, son of Pṛṣata
Pārṣatī, patr. of Kṛṣṇā, granddaughter of Pṛṣata
Pārtha, metr. of Yudhiṣṭhira, Bhīmasena, and Arjuna, sons of Pṛthā-Kuntī
Paurava, oldest patronymic and title of the Bhārata-Kurus, descendants of Pūru
Pratīpa, son of Kuru, father of Devāpi, Śaṃtanu, and Bāhlīka
Prātīpa, patr., esp. of Śaṃtanu, son of Pratīpa, but also of the Kauravas generally
Pūru, youngest son of Yayāti by his second wife, Śarmiṣṭhā; founder of the dynasty of the Pauravas, in which the Bhāratas and Kurus descended
Purūravas, grandfather of Yayāti, father of Āyus by the nymph Urvaśī

Rādhā, foster mother of Karṇa
Rādheya, metr. of Karṇa, adoptive son of Rādhā
Rāma, abbreviation of Balarāma; or (Paraśu)-Rāma
Rauhiṇeya, metr. of Balarāma, son of Rohiṇī
Rohiṇī, first wife of Vasudeva, mother of Balarāma
Rukmiṇī, wife of Kṛṣṇa Vāsudeva, mother of Pradyumna

Sahadeva, youngest of the Pāṇḍavas, son of Pāṇḍu and Mādrī, fathered with his twin brother Nakula by the Aśvins
Śakuni, son of the Gāndhāra king Subala (hence himself also called Gāndhāra), brother of Gāndhārī, thus maternal uncle to Duryodhana and the other Dhārtarāṣṭras
Śakuntalā, daughter of the seer Viśvāmitra and the nymph Menakā, adopted by Kaṇva; wife of Duḥṣanta, to whom she bore Bharata
Śāṃtanava, patr., esp. of Bhīṣma, son of Śaṃtanu; also applied to other descendants.
Śaṃtanu, son of Pratīpa, father on the Ganges of Bhīṣma, on Satyavatī of Citrāṅgada and Vicitravīrya
Saṃvaraṇa, early ancestor of the Kauravas, father of Kuru
Śarmiṣṭhā, daughter of the demon king Vṛṣaparvan, second wife of Yayāti, mother of Druhyu, Anu, Pūru, the last being the founder of the dynasty of the Paurava-Kaurava-Bhāratas
Saubala, patr. of Śakuni, son of Subala of Gāndhāra
Saubhadra, metr. of Abhimanyu, son of Subhadrā by Arjuna
Saumadatti, patr. of Bhūriśravas, son of Somadatta
Śauri, patr. esp. of Vasudeva, son of Śūra
Śikhaṇḍin, born the daughter of Drupada, later became a man
Somadatta, son of Bāhlīka, the brother of Śaṃtanu, father of Bhūriśravas

Subala, king of Gāndhāra, father of Gāndhārī and Śakuni
Subhadrā, daughter of Vasudeva and sister of Kṛṣṇa Vāsudeva, abducted and married by Arjuna, to whom she bore Abhimanyu
Śukra, name of Uśanas Kāvya, father of Devayānī
Śūra, a Vṛṣṇi king, descendant of Andhaka, father of Vasudeva
Suyodhana, other name of Duryodhana

Tapatī, daughter of the sun, wife of Saṃvaraṇa, to whom she bore Kuru
Tāpatya, descendant of Tapatī, esp. applied to Arjuna

Uśanas, other name of Śukra Kāvya, father of Devayānī

Vaicitravīrya, patr. of Dhṛtarāṣṭra, son of Vicitravīrya
Vaikartana, another name of Karṇa
Vārṣaparvaṇī, patr. of Śarmiṣṭhā, daughter of Vṛṣaparvan
Vārṣṇeya, patr. descendant of Vṛṣṇi, eponym of a tribe, to which Kṛṣṇa Vāsudeva belonged
Vasiṣṭha, seer and grandfather of Parāśara, who was the father of Kṛṣṇa Dvaipāyana
Vasudeva, king of the Vṛṣṇis, son of Śūra, father by Rohiṇī of Balarama by Devakī of Kṛṣṇa and Subhadrā
Vāsudeva, patr., esp. of the Vṛṣṇi hero Kṛṣṇa
Vicitravīrya, son of Śaṃtanu by Satyavatī and his heir; through Kṛṣṇa Dvaipāyana father of Dhṛtarāstra, Pāṇḍu, and Vidura
Vidura, son of Kṛṣṇa Dvaipāyana, who was acting on behalf of Vicitravīrya, by a commoner's woman; uncle to both Pāṇḍavas and Dhārtarāṣṭras
Vikarṇa, a son of Dhṛtarāṣṭra
Viviṃśati, a son of Dhṛtarāṣṭra
Vṛṣaparvan, a demon king, father of Śarmiṣṭhā
Vṛṣṇi, name of a Yādava tribe, particularly that of Kṛṣṇa Vāsudeva
Vyāsa, epithet of Kṛṣṇa Dvaipāyana, the Divider of the Veda

Yādava, descendants of Yadu, esp. the Vṛṣṇi-Andhakas
Yadu, oldest son of Yayāti by Devayānī, eldest brother of Pūru of the Pauravas; founder of the Yādava line
Yajñasena, other name of the Pāñcāla king Drupada, father of Kṛṣṇā
Yājñasenī, patr. of Kṛṣṇā, daughter of Drupada-Yajñasena
Yayāti, son of Nahuṣa, father by Devayānī of Yadu and Turvaśu, by Śarmiṣṭhā of Druhyu, Anu, and Pūru
Yudhiṣṭhira, eldest son and heir of Pāṇḍu by Pṛthā-Kuntī
Yuyutsu, son of Dhṛtarāṣṭra by a commoner's woman

Concordance of Critical Edition and Bombay Edition

The concordance is of the chapters only. It is based on the marginal references marked B in the critical edition, and has been cross-checked with the *Concordanz* in Jacobi (1903). Since its purpose is principally to facilitate comparison with Sörensen, the "Roy" and Dutt translations, and other reference books that quote chapters by their number in B., the verse numbers of the Calcutta edition have not been collated: these numbers and their concordance with the verse numbers of the critical edition are only retrievable from the marginal figures marked C. in the critical edition, and, mostly, from the C. figures in my summaries.

Be it noted that the concordance, where it shows deletions [indicated by ( ), e.g., (22)], only shows deletions of chapters; it does not show the very numerous deletions of verses. For information on verse deletions the only recourse is the *apparatus* of the critical edition.

Critical Edition	Bombay
1. 1–12	1–12
13	13–15
14–19	16–21
	(22)
20	23
	(24)
21–46	25–50
47	51–52
48–52	53–57
53	58–59
54–67	60–73
68–69	74
70–91	75–96
92	97–98
93–100	99–106
101	107–8
102–4	109–17
105	112–13
106–7	114–15
	(116)
108–18	117–27
119	128 (..) (129)
120–21	130
122–23	131–32–33
124–28	134–38
	(139–40)

Critical Edition	Bombay
129–36	141–48
	(149)
137–39	150–52
140–41	153
142–57	154–69
158–59	170
160–61	171–72
162–63	173
164–66	174–76
167–68	177
169–81	178–90
182–83	191
184–214	192–222
215–16	233–25
217–25	226–34
2. 1–10	1–10
11	11–12
12–16	13–17
17	18–19
18–22	20–24
23	25–26
24–42	27–45
	(46)
43–49	47–53
50	54–55
51	56–57
52	58
53	59–60
54–61	61–68
62	69–70
63–65	71–73
66	74–75
67–72	76–81
3. 1–3	1–3
4–44	3–43
45	44 (..)
	(45–46)
45	47
46	48–49
47–65	50–68
66–67	69
68–73	70–75
74–75	76
76–79	77–80
80	81–82
81–104	83–106
105–6	107
107–8	108–9
109–10	110
111–46	111–46
147	147–48
148–49	149–50
150	151–52
151–52	153–54

Critical Edition	Bombay
153	155
	(156)
154–60	157–63
161	164–65
162–63	166–67
164–65	168
166–79	169–82
180–81	183
182–89	184–91
190	192 (..)
	(193–98)
191	199 (..)
	(200)
192–202	201–11
203	212–13
204–12	214–22
213	223–24
214–19	225–30
220–21	231
	(232)
222–37	233–48
238	249–50
239–40	251–52
241	253–55
242–47	256–61
	(262–63)
248–299	264–315
4. 1–5	1–5
	(6)
6–31	7–32
32	33 (..)–34 (..)
33–37	35–39
38	40–43
39–62	44–67
63–64	68
64	69
65–67	70–72
5. 1–44	1–44
	(45)
45–61	46–62
62	63–64
63–148	65–150
149	151–52
150–56	153–59
157	160 (..)
	160 (..)
158–64	161–67
165	168
166	168–69
167–71	170–74
172–73	175
174–75	176
177–79	178
180–97	179–96

Critical Edition	Bombay
6. 1–2	1–2
3–4	3
5–15	4–14
16	15–16
17–22	17–22
	(23)
22–44	24–46
45	47–49
46–111	50–115
112	116–17
113–17	118–22
7. 1–4	1–4
5	5–7
6	7
7–47	8–48
48	49–50
49	51
	(52–71)
50–52	72–74
53	75–76
54–56	77–79
57	80–81
58–63	82–87
64	88–89
65–88	90–113
89–90	114
91–101	115–25
102	126–27
103–63	128–88
164	188–91
165	192–93
166	194–95
167–73	196–202
8. 1	1–2
2–3	3–4
4	5–7
5	8–9
6–11	10–15
12	16–17
13–16	18–21
17	22–24
18	25–26
19	27–28
20–23	29–32
24	33–34
25	35
26	36–37
27	38–40
28–29	41–42
30	43–45
31	46
32	47–48
33–40	49–56
	(57)
41–44	58–61
	(62–63)
45	64–65
46–48	66–68
49	69–70
50	71–72
51–61	73–83
62	84–85
	(86)
63–68	87–92
	(93)
68	94
	(95)
69	96
9. 1–2	1–2
	(3)
3–64	4–65
10. 1–18	1–18
11. 1–27	1–27
12. 1–68	1–68
69–70	69
71–116	70–115
117	116–17
118–24	118–24
125	125–26
126	127–28
127–28	129–30
129–41	131–43
142	144–46
143–49	147–53
150	154–55
151	156–57
152–67	158–73
168–70	174–76
171	177–78
172–220	179–227
221–23	229(8)–31(0)*
224	232(1)–33(2)
225–68	234(3)–77(6)
	(278[7])
269–74	279(8)–84(3)
	(285[4]–86[5])
275–92	287(6)–304(3)
293	305(4)–6(5)
294–309	307(6)–22(1)
	(323[2])

*At this point an error occurs in B, chap. 228 having been skipped; the figures within parentheses are the correct ones.

Critical Edition	Bombay
310–28	324(3)–42(1)
329–30	343(2)
331–53	344(3)–66(5)
13. 1–57	1–57
	(58–99)
58–83	59–84
84–85	85
86–92	86–92
93–95	93
96–98	94–96
99	(= 58)
100–110	97–107
111	108
	(109–10)
112–25	111–24
	(125–38)
126–27	139–40
128–29	141
130–34	142–46
	(147–48)
135	149
	(150–51)
136–46	152–62
137–48	163
149–54	164–69
14. 1–47	1–47

Critical Edition	Bombay
48	48–49
49–78	50–79
79–81	80
82–85	81–84
86–87	85
88–91	86–89
92–93	90
94	91
95–96	92
15. 1	1
2–3	2
4–7	3
8	4
9–10	5
11–14	6–9
15–16	10
17–25	11–19
26–27	20
28–35	21–28
36–37	29
38–47	30–39
16. 1–2	1
3–9	2–8
17. 1–3	1–3
18. 1–5	1–5

Index of Proper Names*

*Only the proper names occurring in the text of the translation are indexed; those occurring in introductions, summaries, and notes are not.

Rāma (Dāśarathi), 29, 117–18, 139, 385
Ramaṇa, 148
Ramaṇīyaka, 79
Rāmāyaṇa, 38
Rambha (king), 174
Rambhā (Apsarā), 147, 257
Rantideva, 29, 117
Ratā, 148
Rathantari, 211, 214
Ratiguṇa, 147
Raudrakarman, 245
Raudrāśva, 210
Raukmiṇeya, 406
Rauśidaśvi, 207
Ravi, 21
Ṛca, 214
Ṛcepu, 210–11
Ṛcīka, 21, 32, 149, 211
Reṇuka, 88
Revatī, 406
Ṛgveda, 47, 159
Ṛkṣā (wife of Ajamīḍha), 214
Ṛkṣa (king), 211, 325
Rocamāna, 151, 349
Rohiṇī (star), 288, 377
Rohiṇī (deity), 150
Rohiṇī (Baladeva's mother), 359, 373
Ṛṣabha, 121
Ṛṣika, 152
Ṛśyaśṛnga, 38
Rudra, 85, 88, 97, 147–49, 153, 257, 281, 351, 370, 409, 420
Rukmāngada, 350
Rukmaratha, 350
Rukmin, 153
Rukmiṇī, 350
Rupin, 211
Ruru (a Bhārgava), 56, 60–63
Ruru (an ascetic), 60

Sadaḥsuvāk*, 245
Sādhya, 21, 85, 88, 149, 162, 251, 357, 370, 420
Sagara, 30
Saha (snake), 121
Saha (Kaurava), 245, 349
Sahacāra, 406
Sahadeva (Pāṇḍava), 28, 128, 135, 154, 215–16, 259, 298–99, 358, 360, 412
Sahadeva (son of Jarāsaṃdha), 349
Sahajanya, 168, 257
Sahasrākṣa, 79, 88, 418–19
Sahasrajyoti, 21
Saindhava, 27, 34, 350
Sainya, 407
Sama, 245, 349
Samantapañcaka, 20, 32
Sāmba, 406, 410
Saṃbhāvya, 30
Saṃhanana, 210
Saṃhitā, 160
Saṃhrāda, 146, 151
Samīcī, 403
Saṃjaya, 24–29, 34, 39, 42, 134
Saṃkarṣaṇa, 350, 354
Saṃketāngada, 121
Sāṃkhya, 174
Saṃkṛti, 30
Saṃnatepu, 211
Saṃpāti, 150
Saṃpriyā, 214
Samṛddha, 121
Samudrasena, 152, 350
Saṃvaraṇa, 159, 211–12, 214, 325–26, 328–29
Saṃvarta, 42, 148
Saṃvartaka, 91
Saṃyāti (son of Nahuṣa), 174
Saṃyāti (son of Prācinvat), 213
Sanatkumāra, 154, 174
Sanatsujāta, 34, 39
Saramā, 44
Sārameјaya, 350
Sāraṇa, 121, 350, 410
Sarasvatī, 19, 35, 40, 214, 398
Sarisṛkva, 425, 427, 429
Sārvabhauma, 213
Sarvadamana, 165
Sarvaga, 216
Sarvasāranga, 121
Sarvasena, 214
Sat, 257
Sātvata (Kṛṣṇa), 405, 415
Sātvata (people), 409–11
Satyā (Satyavatī), 236
Satyā (Satyabhāmā), 38
Satyabhāmā, 34
Satyadhṛti, 349
Satyaka, 135, 406, 410
Sātyaki, 41, 135, 153, 350, 385, 406, 410
Satyasaṃdha, 245
Satyavatī, 22, 117, 129, 133–34, 214, 226–27, 229–31, 233–36, 239, 243, 248, 261, 264, 319, 374
Satyavatī (mother of Jamadagni), 124–25
Satyavrata, 30
Satyepu, 210
Saubala, 25, 28, 135, 265, 283, 386
Saubhadra, 38, 411
Saudāsa, 254
Saumadatti, 40
Saurabheyī, 403
Sauvīrī, 210
Savitar, 146, 149, 325, 327–28, 420
Sāvitrī, 38, 325, 327–28
Savyasācin, 38, 373
Senabindu, 151, 349
Senānī, 245
Senāpati, 245
Siddha, 133, 147, 199, 218, 238, 249–50, 262, 351, 367, 395
Siddhārtha, 152
Siṃhala, 333
Siṃhī, 152
Siṃhikā, 146
Sindhu, 143, 246
Soma, 79, 82, 85, 87, 89–91, 116, 131, 148, 154, 162, 188, 211, 249, 252, 322, 333, 339, 342, 416, 425
Somadatta (son of Bāhlika), 275, 285
Somadatta (Kaurava), 261, 350
Somaka (people), 349, 361
Somaka (king), 38, 364, 377
Somakīrti, 245
Somaśravas, 45
Somaśravāyaṇa, 320
Sphandaka, 91
Sṛñjaya, 29
Stambamitra, 425, 427–29
Sthalepu, 210
Sthaṇḍilepu, 210
Sthāṇu, 21, 148, 257, 396
Sthūlakeśa, 60
Sthūṇa, 135
Subāhu (Asparā), 257
Subāhu (snake), 91

*Names beginning with palatal Ś follow the dental S.